CORPORATE CATACLYSM

Abitibi Power & Paper and the
Collapse of the Newsprint Industry, 1912–1946

THEMES IN BUSINESS AND SOCIETY

Editor: Dimitry Anastakis

Themes in Business and Society explores new issues in Canadian and international business history. The series advances Canadian business history in a global context by publishing studies that examine firms, entrepreneurs, consumers, industries, the evolution of capitalism, business-government relations, the role of the state and regulation, and the changing environment of national and international business. Supported by the L.R. Wilson/R.J. Currie Chair in Canadian Business History at the University of Toronto and the Rotman School of Management, Themes in Business and Society provides new perspectives on how business impacts ordinary people, both in Canada and around the world.

BARRY E.C. BOOTHMAN

Corporate Cataclysm

Abitibi Power & Paper and the Collapse of the Newsprint Industry, 1912–1946

UNIVERSITY OF TORONTO PRESS
Toronto Buffalo London

© University of Toronto Press 2020
Toronto Buffalo London
utorontopress.com
Printed in Canada

ISBN 978-1-4875-0556-1 (cloth)   ISBN 978-1-4875-3232-1 (ePUB)
ISBN 978-1-4875-3231-4 (PDF)

Library and Archives Canada Cataloguing in Publication
Title: Corporate cataclysm : Abitibi Power & Paper and the collapse
of the newsprint industry, 1912–1946 / Barry E.C. Boothman.
Other titles: Abitibi Power & Paper and the collapse of
the newsprint industry, 1912–1946
Names: Boothman, Barry E. C., author.
Description: Series statement: Themes in business and society |
Includes bibliographical references and index.
Identifiers: Canadiana (print) 20200210025 | Canadiana (ebook) 20200210114 |
ISBN 9781487505561 (cloth) | ISBN 9781487532321 (EPUB) |
ISBN 9781487532314 (PDF)
Subjects: LCSH: Abitibi Power & Paper Company – History – 20th century. |
LCSH: Newsprint industry – Canada – History – 20th century.
Classification: LCC HD9839.N43 C3 2020 | DDC 338.4/7676286–dc23

University of Toronto Press acknowledges the financial assistance to its
publishing program of the Canada Council for the Arts and the Ontario
Arts Council, an agency of the Government of Ontario.

Canada Council   Conseil des Arts
for the Arts   du Canada

ONTARIO ARTS COUNCIL
CONSEIL DES ARTS DE L'ONTARIO
an Ontario government agency
un organisme du gouvernement de l'Ontario

Funded by the   Financé par le
Government   gouvernement   Canada
of Canada   du Canada

There is nothing in the world that persists. Everything is in a state of flux, and comes into being as a transient appearance. Time itself flows on wide continual motion, just like a river; for neither the river nor the fleeting hour can stand still ... What was before is left behind, that which was not comes to be, and every minute gives place to another.

– Ovid, *Metamorphoses*, XV

Contents

Illustrations follow page 220

Figures and Tables

Figures

Tables

Praecipe

This book deals with an important episode of Canadian business history. A transition to continental free trade for newsprint and wood pulp facilitated a rapid growth of paper manufacturing after 1912, but within a decade and a half, well before the onset of the Great Depression, over-expansion propelled the producers into crisis. Several years later nearly half were bankrupt, the rest barely maintained solvency. Within the spectacular wave of failures, one company, Abitibi Power and Paper Ltd., stood out. It was Canada's largest manufacturing enterprise and entered a receivership that stretched from 1932 to 1946 – the longest and the most controversial bankruptcy in the country's history.

The newsprint producers were wrecked by shifts in industrial competition. Abitibi then became enmeshed by additional issues, which kept it as a headline story for years. The collapse of the company and the other producers generated disputes about three questions. For whose benefit did a corporation exist? How should the value of an enterprise be determined? When should some investors be given priority over others? Based on the answers, reorganization could confer power, influence, or fees for certain beneficiaries and might enable some claimants to recoup their investments – at the expense of others. Moreover, a settlement for Abitibi required approval from the Province of Ontario. As the claimants wrangled, the government intervened and the receivership became a question of constitutional law. Other firms encountered analogous problems but the issues were fought out bitterly in the Abitibi case. It was a fascinating saga, punctuated with episodes of devious scheming, managerial incompetence, political chicanery, misgovernment, creative accounting, fuzzy financials, legal weasels, attempted theft, and greenmail. Many of the problems that occurred are similar to those that have characterized the mega-mergers and corporate disasters of our own era. The participants comprised a veritable "Who's Who?" of Canadian business, law, and politics.

This book offers the first chronicle of how a major insolvency unfolded in Canada, from the origins to the final resolution, but the scope is broader. To explain developments, it necessarily considers how not just one firm but an entire industry collapsed, how government and corporate efforts to restore them failed until changing conditions finally allowed resuscitation. The business media like to recount tales of success but, in truth, we learn more by studying why things fail. Bankruptcy and insolvency are little understood except by specialists even though all companies, like human beings, eventually pass. Most business histories cease when a failure occurs and a person rarely gets a chance gets to ask, "Well, what happened next?" However, it may be possible to resurrect an insolvent enterprise. Since giant corporations emerged more than a century ago, their reorganization has attracted significant analysis in the United States. Few Canadian explorations have occurred save for specialized legal scholarship.[1] Within the successor company of our own era, Resolute Forest Products, the Abitibi receivership is a forgotten subject. Residents of Northern Ontario and the families of former employees, however, still recount the hardships that unfolded. They describe the period with terms like the "dark and stormy years," "the valley of darkness," "the great trough," "the black hole." Perhaps the most prosaic was offered by a retired Abitibi executive who characterized it to the author as "a long night seemingly without a dawn, a time of transition between the formative spring of the firm and an era of prosperity." This delightful, albeit apocryphal, rhetorical flight well reflected the perspective of contemporaries even though it is inaccurate. Dawn *did* come, but not until after 4,980 days.

Most cases of insolvency are resolved within two years, either with a financial restructuring, a sale to another firm, divestitures or withdrawals from business activities, or the liquidation of the remains and the distribution of any proceeds according to the priorities of the claimants. Laypersons, the media, and most legal professionals treat the terms "bankruptcy" and "insolvency" as synonyms. In a strict sense, that is not correct. In Canada, insolvency is a financial situation, whereas bankruptcy is a legal status. In both instances, an enterprise cannot meet its obligations and the liabilities typically exceed the worth of the assets. A receiver or trustee is appointed to conserve the assets until one of the standard outcomes occurs. Once a company is deemed no longer solvent, it falls under complex legal procedures but the provisions vary accordingly to how and where a case is filed. Nonetheless, for the sake of simplicity, I have chosen to use the two terms interchangeably for this book.

The surviving records from an insolvency typically consist of a petition for receivership, a judicial order, and perhaps a few affidavits or transcripts. One researcher understandably erred in claiming Abitibi's history was "extremely difficult to unravel because of the dearth of documents which survive from this period."[2] The primary action, *Montreal Trust v. Abitibi Power and Paper Co. Ltd.*, was the biggest case handled by the Supreme Court of Ontario for much of the twentieth century. The Osgoode Hall clerks dumped the documents in "the large cardboard box just to the right of the entrance to the downstairs vault" – materials too voluminous to access in the regular storage area.[3] After the case was concluded, most were filed away, lost in a Mississauga warehouse, the cartons layered with coal dust, until I located them with the help of Leon Warmski at the Archives of Ontario. The most confidential items remained in unopened envelopes fastened with the seal of the Supreme Court. When his tenure ended in 1946, Abitibi's receiver deemed old documents to be of little value and he ordered most destroyed. But a veritable industry had arisen from the case, which generated hundreds of motions or appeals and thousands upon thousands of pages of estimates, economic analyses, engineering studies, briefs, proposals, submissions, or enquiries. These documents are scattered across government archives, corporate depositories, university libraries, and public sources. Contemporaries relied upon rumours, second-hand sources, or leaks to the press because the most crucial records were sealed or unavailable. That issue also helps explain why the case seemed unending, like *Jarndyce v. Jarndyce*, the lawsuit that shaped the plot in Charles Dickens's *Bleak House*.

With small to medium-sized companies, the origins of a failure are straightforward. The main causes are weak cash flow, bad business models, poor management, insufficient marketing, or deficient product/service design. When giant enterprises become insolvent, media accounts offer brief rationales akin to "Ms. Scarlet did it in the dining room with the candlestick." The usual suspects include foolish decisions by executives, malfeasance, or a failure to adapt to a changing environment. However, the failures of big corporations originate from three dimensions, the importance and intricacies of each varying from case to case. First, there is the institutional framework: law, capital markets, and public policies. These shape managerial conduct by generating incentives and disincentives for certain types of behaviour or by leaving loopholes and deficiencies that may be exploited. Laws and capital markets can be like old generals: they are designed for fighting

earlier wars and may not be attuned to altered contexts. We have seen
this in recent decades with the dubious exploitation of junk bonds, buy-
backs of stock covered by issues of new debt, or plunging by banks into
mortgage lending. The second dimension, industrial organization, is of
key importance when professionals assess strategic difficulties. The
rivalry among a group of firms producing similar goods is driven by
entry and exit conditions, the availability of substitutes, and the bargaining power of suppliers or buyers. These factors condition how an
industry is structured and whether companies can maintain viable
positions. The third dimension entails firm-specific issues. Business
media stress this aspect because it permits a focus on the overbally-
hooed theme of "leadership," accompanied by gratuitous finger-wagging
at executive incompetence, foolishness, or greed. A professional analysis, instead, stresses an enterprise's organization, finance, and competitive strategies.

In a previous essay I noted the collapse of the Canadian newsprint
industry represented the equivalent of a toxic spill zone for historians, a
contentious subject best avoided.[4] By that, I meant it was difficult to
study because an analysis dealt with complex developments, which
required a knowledge of materials and concepts from multiple academic
fields. But during the 1930s many people believed the origins of the
debacle could be easily discerned. Several scapegoats became targets for
their ire. It originated, some claimed, from ruthless conduct by International Paper, the largest North American producer. Others believed the
provincial premiers manipulated the industry and forced excessive
growth. Investment bankers were blamed for pushing worthless securities on unwary investors, while American publishers contended everything was triggered by a producer cartel that sought dominance. There
were kernels of truth in each of these notions but they were less reasonable explanations than illustrations of the disenchantment that prevailed
during the Great Depression. Public antipathy to corporate enterprise,
significant since the turn of the century, intensified as the economic crisis
worsened. Beliefs about how executives had machinated at the expense
of the public welfare dominated press accounts, reports, and legislation
for more than a generation. There were, of course, substantive problems
associated with the rise of big companies. This study recounts many of
them, but we also should be wary of ideological biases. While conspiracy
theories or suspicions of Machiavellian plotting always make good copy,
they cannot be deemed credible unless a person can demonstrate ample
and verifiable documentary evidence.

There is a broad literature dealing with the timber trade during the
nineteenth century but historical analyses of pulp and paper remain

limited in number despite the sector's importance. The most significant work has followed the "political economy" perspective, which deals with how political institutions and economic systems influence each other. Four monographs are particularly relevant to this book. H.V. Nelles advanced a sophisticated analysis of the relationships between Ontario's government and resource companies. He stressed how weak political accountability abetted mismanagement of timber and mining ventures, and he characterized the province as subservient, a veritable handmaiden, to business. Jim Mochoruk's fine investigation about practices in Manitoba reached parallel conclusions. He illustrated how lands were alienated and how forests or minerals were depleted "by companies who did not have to make major resource-use payments to the state for prolonged periods of time." Pulp and paper manufacturers secured "a de facto monopoly over the province's best pulp lands" as the government failed to elaborate a coherent programme of resource development. Peter Gillis and Thomas Roach examined conservation efforts in Canada during the first half of the twentieth century. They highlighted the exploitive ethic that permeated forest policies and the ability of companies to "wield tremendous economic influence which provincial governments find hard to resist." They argued, "Appearing at first sight as a client of government and totally dependent upon the Crown for wood supplies, the reverse is actually true of these industries." More recently, Mark Kuhlberg has contended that the newsprint sector's problems in Ontario originated from political initiatives. His monograph provides thoughtful insights about how the province managed resources. Business people, however, would find the appraisal unsatisfactory in important ways. Scant attention is given to competitive dynamics or industrial structure and financial matters are poorly assessed. The people involved with the sector's growth and their motives are not explored well, while the wave of company failures is rationalized as an outcome of executives being "imprudent."[5] Following from the work by Nelles, researchers have appraised how the industry arose in British Columbia, New Brunswick, and Newfoundland. Ironically, Quebec, the largest paper-making province, has yet to receive a sustained analysis.[6] Histories of specific geographic areas or individual producers are available but mostly as unpublished dissertations.[7] In contrast, labour relations and mill towns have attracted good analyses. There are astute studies that consider social organization in resource-oriented communities, geography and economy in frontier areas, or the extension of hydro-electricity into those regions.[8]

Perhaps most astonishing is the sparse character of the economic or business literature. The best-known work remains two monographs by the American economist John Guthrie published during the 1940s. The studies could not meet the standards of present-day scholarship though they were reasonable for that time. Only some of his observations were derived from original data. Guthrie treated commentaries from sources like the *Financial Post* or the Federal Trade Commission as fact. More recently, Nancy Ohanian surveyed the American industry from 1900 to 1940, but she offered a statistical analysis that did not explain the logic behind changes over time. Trevor Dick wrote an oft-cited essay about the newsprint sector. His conclusion was a truism: expansion occurred in response to market forces and American demand.[9] Although numerous investigations of newsprint pricing are available, most entail economic modelling that provides only tangential insights. Two recent compendia have examined the global industry. The essays, which vary in rigour, are weighted towards European experiences and most rely unduly upon company reports.[10]

The Abitibi receivership provides a unique window not only for appraising the rise and fall of the newsprint industry during the first half of the twentieth century but also for gaining a broader understanding of the institutional framework that shaped the formation of Canadian corporate capitalism. In so doing, I have sought to move beyond the tendency to compile company chronicles that has typified business history.[11] The account seeks to convey the value that may be garnered from an interdisciplinary examination of a specific case. It differs from other published works because an emphasis is placed upon industrial evolution and the perspectives espoused by businessmen.

Researchers who have utilized a political economy orientation correctly stress how provinces tried to influence firms with the terms for resource licences, just as national authorities might impose restrictions upon trade or competitive behaviour. Nonetheless, characterizing the state as subservient to corporate enterprise is over-simplistic. Neither was it ever a dominant actor. Politicians fostered or impeded projects, especially in their pursuit of electoral support. Specific actions by governments could make business operations difficult but it is fallacious to argue they "caused" the downfall of the newsprint sector. Nor were the top executives of the paper manufacturers angels. Some are best described as "sharp dealers," who schemed, inveigled, lied, and backstabbed in their pursuit of profit. We should not be surprised that the grey in-between often characterized business-government relations, with helical-like manoeuvring as different stakeholders tried to enhance their respective interests. The limits to public sector direction became stark after 1927. Political leaders never employed authoritative dictate to stabilize the industry; that is, they refused to use direct regulation, levy fines, or suspend licences. Rather, they stressed voluntary cooperation – a course of action that failed but was retried only to fail again and again. They opposed the closure of mills and, when possible, tried to keep money-losing plants operational.

This orientation of this volume also shifts the analysis away from two topics that have preoccupied researchers. Numerous writers during the early twentieth century stressed the abuse of natural resources that unfolded in most jurisdictions. In a laudable zeal to highlight the deficiencies of government policies, various scholars have re-emphasized this theme. A few accounts have seemed a bit like Captain Renault in *Casablanca*: shocked, shocked, shocked to find corruption has existed. That issue has been present in forest products since ancient times. The malfeasance in Ontario was hardly more egregious than elsewhere. It thus is not dealt with at length, although the narrative chronicles relevant developments. Second, some authors have focused on the need for prudent resource management and socially responsible conduct. In a broader history, those issues deserve attention but they are not the central issues probed here.

To rebalance our understanding, greater consideration must be given to the roles of strategy, economics, finance, and law. The first three drove the sector's rise and then its fall, the fourth framed those developments and moulded the aftermath. Newsprint companies portrayed themselves as exemplars of a new form of capitalism – large-scale enterprise, professionally managed, that could produce mass quantities and generate significant earnings. Their shares and bonds became what later generations would call "stock market darlings." Investors' interest was piqued by the prospective returns. Most did not understand or chose to ignore several issues. Newsprint was a commodity, not a good with high value-added features or subject to product differentiation (the traits that other manufacturers utilized to generate consumer loyalty and stable sales). Customers did not perceive significant non-price differences among suppliers. The producers thus emphasized strategies geared to low-cost production but there always was a risk that competition might devolve into price-based warfare. Shipping represented a key component in the delivered price, which had a low value-to-weight ratio, and therefore regulatory policies shaped the ability to service specific markets. Like many commodities, newsprint had few substitutes but inelastic tendencies – lower prices did not increase sales. Pricing and supply were cross-related with alternative goods like pulp. Anticipating the future was difficult because sales were vulnerable to demand shifts that included seasonal variations, buying manias, and precipitous downturns. Those conditions, if they coalesced, made destructive rivalry probable.

There has been a tendency by researchers to treat pulp and paper as a "mature" industry. This is a comprehensible overestimation, especially when viewed from the present day. The inventions behind the core technology occurred during the early nineteenth century and were finalized by the mid-Victorian era but the industry remained comprised of small firms whose output depended on artisan skills.[12] However, from 1900 to 1930 numerous process innovations (incremental adjustments to manufacturing techniques) generated alterations that permitted cost reductions and efficiency gains, improved quality, and produced entirely new goods and services. Production became a science geared at achieving maximum speed and output while manufacturing knowledge became well known rather than the preserve of specialized workers. This shift propelled alterations in plant design and size, minimum efficient scale, necessary capital, and business organization. Contemporaries recognized the importance of the transformation, which became a driver behind the descent into economic failure.

Given the presumption of industrial "maturity," the sector has often been portrayed as one characterized by a stable oligopoly. Canadian researchers have reinforced this image by emphasizing data about the domestic industry even though the removal of American tariffs redefined markets to continental dimensions. The American historian Alfred Chandler used an alternative measure – the composition of the biggest firms in an economy – but he reached an analogous conclusion and argued that a small group of paper manufacturers gained ascendancy during the final decade of the nineteenth century. "After the industry stabilized, the members of the oligopoly remained much the same."[13] This perspective fit Chandler's theory of managerial capitalism, which stressed how business evolved from small owner- or partner-controlled firms to giant corporations employing hierarchies of salaried managers that coordinated activities versus a reliance upon market transactions.[14]

But it is possible to construct a more realistic portrait. Unlike other sectors where large corporations arose, newsprint did *not* evolve into an oligopoly during the first half of the twentieth century. Turnover was significant. Although firm and mill size increased over time, the entry barriers were not high, the gains from economies of scale not as great as occurred elsewhere. Numerous entrants thought they could build viable positions because American consumption of newsprint grew rapidly but, contrary to widespread expectations, older or less

economic firms departed slowly. The industrial structure became fragmented and capacity ran ahead of demand, conditions that enhanced
the potential for catastrophic warfare. A concurrent shift of newspaper
publishing towards dominance by chain organizations, enterprises that
used their buyer power to extract concessions, intensified that risk.

A set of mergers unfolded from 1924 to 1931 that were partially
intended to offset those problems. But financing the amalgamations
entailed the construction of financial structures with high fixed charges.
As long as demand grew and the newsprint price remained high, this
trend appeared reasonable, but when those conditions altered then it
added another ingredient to the recipe for disaster. This was hardly the
first or last time when myths about the benefits associated with mergers
and organizational size propelled false expectations, questionable conduct, or dubious investments. Many observers thought the corporate
groups might enhance stability but no "leader," no group of firms,
could moderate rivalry. Successful "cartelization," that is, effective collusion or implicit division of markets, did not occur. Attempts at interfirm coordination were launched but the understandings broke down
within months. Some participants chose to cheat, while many producers simply refused to join. Allegations that there was a monopoly or
that Canadian firms/governments controlled events were fantasies.
Indeed, the way the industry's descent occurred shows the falseness of
such claims.

Corporate expansion was impossible without funding and from the
beginning the manufacturers relied upon international finance. Histories have been compiled for several Canadian financial institutions,
along with the evolution of stock market regulation, but investment
banking and the role of foreign capital remain weakly explored.[15] In
contrast, there are fine studies on American developments.[16] This study
accordingly highlights how the newsprint producers became linked to
Chicago and New York financiers, along with the implications. Consideration is given to the crucial role played by life insurance companies,
who helped legitimate sales of newsprint securities. The book reviews
disclosure and accounting practices during the 1920s to show how they
influenced investor understandings. Such matters became crucial when
Abitibi failed as different groups tried to shape the legal process.

These issues explain the mode of organization employed in this book.
The rise and fall of Abitibi and its industry embraced the world with
questions of law, public policy, economics, strategy, accounting, and
finance. The geographic scope for Abitibi ranged from frontier areas to
its Toronto headquarters and the Osgoode Hall chambers of the
Supreme Court of Ontario and south to the heart of the continental

economy. The most obvious challenge for any study that deals with these types of historical dimensions is to reflect the breadth and intricacy of the subject material. The narrative takes the "top-down" perspective of strategic management, with a focus upon senior executives, financial stakeholders, investors, and politicians. Given the scale of the story, various topics cannot be fully explored. Therefore I perhaps consider issues like the impact of the receivership on workers and towns less than some readers may prefer.

This is a holistic account that proceeds chronologically but it takes the form of an episodic narrative. Each chapter is divided into several sections. Some deal with Abitibi itself, others step back and survey important issues: the evolution of provincial forest policy or of the industry, the role of capital markets, the character of bankruptcy law, and the impact of regulation. An episodic narrative can have a tendency to wander, but I have tried to arrange the book in a manner that allows the reader to grasp the logic behind developments. It also means the study unfolds not as a straight-line tale but one that sometimes diverges to look at various matters. It is hoped the account is thus enlightening not just about the origins and the dynamics of the corporate cataclysm but also about other issues that may interest readers. In this regard, I benefited from the example of Charles Royster's *The Fabulous History of the Dismal Swamp Company*, a marvellous study of property development in colonial America that encompasses crony capitalism, conniving litigants, popular delusions, marketing practices, conspicuous consumption, trans-Atlantic commerce, and the transition from an elitist society towards democracy.[17]

With the luxury of hindsight, this history can be discerned as an opera with four acts. The opening chapter serves as an overture to the drama. It sketches how Northern Ontario was discovered and opened for settlement, the efforts of the province to guide development, and the relationship between Canada's legal institutions and corporate enterprise. The next two chapters chart the rise of the pulp and paper industry and Abitibi's emergence as a successful producer. The second act, covered in chapters 4 to 6, deals with how economic success became a drift towards catastrophe. As those phenomena unfolded, Abitibi's executives conducted a set of acquisitions aimed at consolidating the firm's position but the expansion drive continued even as the price for newsprint crumpled. The chapters review the efforts to stave off disaster and the descent into economic collapse. Chapters 7 to 11 cover the third act: the creation of a receivership and the efforts to regain break-even status. The narrative reviews how Abitibi's bondholders seized control, manipulating the legal process to ensure others did not interfere with their choices. Moreover, corporate failure has consequences. Therefore consideration is given to the fates of communities located near Abitibi's mills as well as the scandals that engulfed some of the politicians and businessmen associated with the firm. Despite failed attempts to stabilize the industry, an initiative was launched in 1937 to return the firm to solvency. Under normal conditions, this would have ended the receivership but the debt holders fragmented into several groups, while other concerns manipulated the situation for their own goals. Despite a tentative approval of a plan, opponents challenged its legitimacy and the Supreme Court of Ontario rejected the scheme. Chapters 12 to 14 deal with the final act, which began with a plot by the bondholders to gain ownership for a price far below Abitibi's worth. The procedure would have left others with nothing and the province tried to block it – by delay, a royal commission, and a moratorium. With the parties unwilling to compromise, the case became a constitutional dispute. The outcome was a surprise for all, which forced negotiations and a resolution under legislation previously deemed unworkable. The last chapter, a coda, reviews the destinies of Abitibi and the principals, as well as several conclusions that may be drawn from this history.

Several stylistic points are relevant. In correspondence and media reports misspellings of locations or names occurred frequently, while American and British grammar were used interchangeably. Statements inside quotations marks have been left as written, with mistakes rarely highlighted by [sic]. In several quotes during the narrative individuals use terms that are offensive. These have been kept intact because they were the vernacular of the times and airbrushing the unpleasant is a form of misrepresentation. I have rectified obvious typographical errors, clarified abbreviations, and translated statements made in French. An analysis of a bankruptcy requires consideration of finance and law. I have sought to keep the discussion in ordinary English and to minimize professional or technical jargon. The receivership also became a universe of figures that even specialists would be hard pressed to sort out. Relevant data are presented but I have avoided the microscopic analyses that obsessed the participants. However, this is a business analysis as well as a history, and significant use of statistical information is unavoidable. Commodity-based industries can be erroneously perceived as simple. They often are quite complex.

A brief has not been carried for any interest and the narrative tries to describe the personalities fairly, along with the alternative perspectives held about the unfolding developments – warts and all. As with most human affairs, conduct before and after Abitibi's failure ranged from intelligent to foolish, from honourable to venal, from comic to tragic. The collapse of the firm and the industry, along with the ensuing tangles, hardly were "nobody's fault." I have presented these as the evidence suggests. Newspapers covered important aspects, particularly the dramatic, but many accounts were speculative, puffery, based upon selective disclosures or deliberate revelations, and occasionally just made up. Press reports are essential for tracing events and for capturing the currents of social opinion. I surveyed (and assessed) a broad range of publications. The endnotes cite the most useful sources. I also have endeavoured to highlight what was opinion versus fact. Letters to newspapers are treated as what they were – commentary – but they conveyed popular ideas. I also have made use of American investigations of the forest industries. These must be treated with circumspection because many were generated to substantiate pre-existing beliefs. This issue applies especially to studies conducted by the Federal Trade Commission, though it is evident with other probes. Witnesses during congressional hearings were often chosen or questioned in leading ways. Some had hazy memories or gave misleading testimony.

The preparation of this monograph would have been impossible without the aid provided by the staff of the Archives of Ontario. Mutual Life of Canada Limited (now part of Sun Life Assurance) allowed access to the company's files, which included the correspondence of the bondholders' representatives from 1932 to 1938. The research benefited from the resources of Library and Archives Canada; Bibliothèque et Archives Nationale du Québec; the Bank of England Archives; the New York State Library and Archives; the Ontario Hydro Archives; the Archives of Manitoba, the National Archives and Records Administration; the Library of Congress; and the libraries at Columbia University, Cornell University, Harvard University, Laurentian University, McGill University, Queen's University, the University of Chicago, the University of Michigan, the University of Toronto, and Yale University. The University of New Brunswick's library staff generously endured my habit of borrowing a wall or two. Libraries or museums in Northern Ontario hold Abitibi-related materials, but most deal with forestry rather than the issues addressed by this book. I would like to acknowledge the contributions from scholars who have investigated the development of Northern Ontario and the pulp and paper industry. I benefited from thoughtful insights by Kerry Abel, Peter Gillis and Thomas Roach, James Hiller, Richard Lambert and Paul Pross, Nicole Lang, Jean Manore, Jim Mochoruk, Bill Parenteau, Robert and Nancy Wightman, and especially H.V. Nelles. I also wish to acknowledge the aid from colleagues who referred me to relevant legal scholarship and provided good counsel as I analysed the financial materials. *Business History Review* kindly waived its copyright for an earlier essay. The research costs were covered by personal resources and support from the University of New Brunswick, not from any public agency.

Join me, then, in an exploration of this episode from the formative era of Canadian business. We will hike across the Height of Land to survey Northern Ontario as it was opened for development. We will watch the emergence of the pulp and paper industry and the rise of one successful company. But all sunny days must end. As the light edges towards the horizon, Margo Channing's caution in *All About Eve* is appropriate: "Fasten your seat belts, it's going to be a bumpy night." *Maxime si postquam audieris, possis audire deorum risu.*[18]

Abbreviations

AC   Appeal Cases, Law Reports [UK]
AO   Archives of Ontario, Toronto
AM   Archives of Manitoba, Winnipeg
AR   Annual Report
BAnQ   Bibliothèque et Archives nationales du Québec, Gatineau,
        Montreal, Quebec, Saguenay
BEA   Bank of England Archives, London
CBR   Canadian Bankruptcy Reports
CFC   *Commercial and Financial Chronicle*
ChD   Chancery Division, Law Reports [UK]
CIHM   Canadian Institute for Historical Microreproductions
CSI   *Compilation of Statements and Information Prepared by the
        Bondholders' Protective Committee, Abitibi Power and
        Paper Ltd.*, 1937
CSS   Congressional Serial Set
DLR   Dominion Law Reports
ELR   Eastern Law Reporter
FP   *Financial Post*
FT   *Financial Times*
GM   *Globe and Mail*
HUBL   Harvard University, Baker Library Historical Collections,
        Boston
JLAO   Journals of the Legislative Assembly of the Province of
        Ontario
JORR   *Board of Railway Commissioners, Judgements, Orders, Regulations
        and Rulings*
LAC   Library and Archives Canada, Ottawa
LLA   London Life Archives, London
LOSP   Legislature of Ontario, Sessional Papers

ME	*Mail and Empire*
MG	*Montreal Gazette*
MLCA	Mutual Life of Canada Archives, Waterloo
MTL	Metropolitan Toronto Library, Toronto
NARA	National Archives and Record Administration, College Park, Maryland
NBA	Province of New Brunswick Archives, Fredericton
NYSL	New York State Library, Albany
NYT	*New York Times*
OHA	Ontario Hydro Archives, Mississauga
OHQ	Minutes of the Hydro-Electric Power Commission of Ontario, Toronto
OLR	Ontario Law Reports
OR	Ontario Reports
OWN	Ontario Weekly Notes
OWR	Ontario Weekly Reporter
PC	Pamphlet Collection, Archives of Ontario
PPMC	*Pulp and Paper Magazine of Canada*
QS	Quebec Statutes
QUA	Queen's University Archives, Kingston
RR	Report of the Receiver and Manager of Abitibi Power and Paper Ltd.
SC	Statutes of Canada
SLA	Sun Life Insurance Archives, Montreal
SMPL	Sault Ste. Marie Public Library Archives
SO	Statutes of Ontario
TBHSA	Thunder Bay Historical Society (Museum) Archives
TS	*Toronto Star*
UKS	United Kingdom Statutes
WSJ	*Wall Street Journal*
WT	*Winnipeg Tribune*
YUL	Yale University Library

CORPORATE CATACLYSM

1

Empire Ontario

I hold the world but as the world, Gratiano – A stage where every man must
play a part, and mine a sad one.
                                     – William Shakespeare, *The Merchant of Venice*, I, i

The palest ink is better than the best memory.

                                                          – Chinese proverb

THE "MIDDLE WATERS" LAY BETWEEN the trading-post empires
controlled by New France and the Hudson's Bay Company. Envisaging
themselves as mariners of a great wooded ocean, French voyageurs
elaborated a commercial network along the waterways westward
around the barrier of pre-Cambrian granite that dominated the geography of central Canada. When the British established bases on the distant shores of the Northern Sea during the 1670s, the challenge at first
was not taken seriously. The governor of Quebec shared in the profits of
and reaped tax revenues from fur enterprises in the Ohio and Mississippi regions. He was reluctant to deal with the northern trade. Even
though the French government insisted upon the maintenance of diplomatic peace, demands for a counterploy soon escalated. Heresy, Jesuit
missionaries contended, might spread among the Natives and turn
potential friends into invidious enemies. Excluded from the monopoly
controlling the southwestern commerce, other Canadian merchants
sought out new areas for exploitation, operations that brought them
into competition with the British. Reports also proliferated about Hudson's Bay agents travelling into the Great Lakes to encourage a diversion of trade. Many Natives found peltry delivered to British posts
allowed better prices and an elimination of commissions paid to the
middlemen of the French system. Attempts to interdict this traffic failed

because the French could not penetrate the wilderness sufficiently, but control became essential when European fashions for beaver hats increased the demand for pelts.

The Montreal merchants secured a charter for a Compagnie du Nord, which was empowered to entrench its claims through military means. When naval raids failed to eliminate British competition, the Chevalier Pierre de Troyes was instructed to seize the English posts at the bottom of James Bay. During the spring of 1686, an expedition comprising 105 men travelled from Montreal to Lake Timiskaming and then marched overland, reaching a large lake that now straddles the Ontario-Quebec border. Earlier explorers had given this lake and the river that flowed from it, the appellation *Abitibi*, a combination of the Native terms *Abitah* (middle) and *Nipi* (water). The raiders proceeded downstream through rapids, log jams, and murky swamps towards the coastal plain. With surprise and guile, the troops seized one post and with its cannon compelled the surrender of two others. De Troyes returned to Montreal, French suzerainty apparently established, without losing a single man.[1]

This *petite guerre* presaged much of the history of Northern Ontario: an audacious venture, driven by a self-confident leader, undertaken in difficult terrain against rivals to control resources for export to metropolitan markets. Some enterprises, such as International Nickel or Hollinger Consolidated Gold Mines, succeeded beyond the most wondrous dreams of their promoters. Others, like the subject of this book, prospered, then encountered serious difficulties, but recovered to build strong positions. Most suffered the fate of the Compagnie du Nord, their claims to fortune and glory short-lived, marked by little more than the appellations for natural sites. Through military campaigns, a French presence was retained at the bottom of James Bay, although the goal of displacing the British traders never was achieved. A year after the wilderness adventure, De Troyes died of starvation while commanding Fort Niagara. In 1713, as part of a peace settlement, the French ceded sovereignty back to the Hudson's Bay Company. Its representatives administered business affairs from coastal entrepots and only moved inland if confronted by new competitors from Quebec. Although Fort Abitibi operated intermittently, the difficulty of travel from the south prevented it from being more than a collection point. As the fashion for beaver hats and the population of fur-bearing animals declined, the region became regarded as *finis terrae*.[2] Few outsiders other than missionaries penetrated this frontier, while neither the Algonquin Natives nor local agents were inclined to disturb the environment. Surrounding them was great resource wealth that could be matched with the needs of urban markets.

In order to frame the subject of this book, this chapter reviews how the territory of the middle waters was rediscovered and opened for settlement. It appraises the role of government in the development of Northern Ontario, both the image and the reality associated with public policies. Consideration then is given to interrelationships between Canadian business and law during the early twentieth century. With this background, it will be possible to examine how the newsprint industry arose and Abitibi Power and Paper emerged.

1. A young, giant land

Geography and commerce have always been interdependent and complementary. Each international economy consists of a hinterland and more remote areas oriented towards a metropolitan locus commanding financial resources, communications and marketing networks. The requirements of the cities at the centre, along with demand from peripheral territories, over time mould the intermediate zones, which collect, channel, and redistribute flows of capital, personnel, services, or goods. Exchanges of population and culture and the elaboration of institutions stimulate relationships that bind the constituent areas into a coherent structure, generating social hierarchies as locations garner alternative forms of status, income or power. Borderlands initially are quiescent territories providing a subsistence income, at best, to sparse populations. Governments and entrepreneurs typically have perceived future progress in those regions as contingent upon the elaboration of new subsystems that they can dominate. Speculative ventures can spur permanent settlements, resource exploitation, or an introduction of commercial farming. Promoters develop properties and tributary domains, which require products, services, and credit from enterprises based in intermediate zones. Governments benefit from the revenues associated with an expansion of commerce and garner fees from allocations of resource rights. Across time, a successful process of growth extends the spheres of influence for businesses and may integrate a hinterland with the heartland of the economic order. Although the conquest of peripheral lands often is expected to generate prompt benefits, it has tended to be tedious and expensive – advancing as technologies facilitate resource extraction and as durable colonies planted in hostile terrain are linked to markets. Political authorities, through legislation or assistance, try to shape the parameters of growth but rarely can ensure the outcomes of specific endeavours. In North America especially, development often has been a spontaneous process, with patterns not immediately evident due to the contradictory initiatives launched by individuals, firms, governments, or public agencies.[3]

During the nineteenth century this strategy was pursued by social leaders who coped with Ontario's status on the margins of not one, but two, economic powers. Early Upper Canada represented little more than a fringe of settlement by dispossessed or late loyalists along the shorelines of the St. Lawrence River and Lake Ontario. Defeat in the Revolutionary War, imperialist bombast by American politicians, along with armed incursions from the United States, fostered a chronic sense of insecurity among the colonial elite. A narrow transport route linked this western district to the core of the British Empire, a connection that entailed dependence upon the Montreal business community and was endangered by factors ranging from winter weather to the turbulent politics of Lower Canada. Remote from the centre, provincial leaders who feared indifference by British officials might result in an abandonment of Upper Canada insistently called for military or economic aid and railed against diplomatic concessions that matched imperial concerns but ignored colonial interests. Conservatives and Reformers, despite their many disagreements, concurred that a defensive elaboration of British institutions would make the colony distinctive from the American republic and indispensable to the empire. Some Tories envisaged an agrarian economy where yeoman farmers would defer to their betters but this vision became more sophisticated as population and business activities expanded. Provincial officials, despite their distrust of democratic practices in the republic, employed the same devices by which Americans spurred economic advancement: canal projects, land companies, railway subsidies, and a variety of research or promotional agencies. During the nineteenth century, speculation about unbridled progress led some, in moments of grandiloquent fervour, to claim the seat of the empire would pass eventually to the "western kingdom" of Ontario.[4]

Geography was the mote that troubled these visions of an Anglo-Canadian imperium. Large numbers of immigrants settled in the southern peninsula but the colony lacked access to agricultural territories such as the Ohio and Mississippi river valleys provided for coastal American states. By mid-century, when the most productive or convenient lands had been occupied, concern mounted about the likelihood of emigration southward. Surely Toronto or other towns, politicians and newspapers declared, could not be satisfied to remain as mere entrepots when, located on transport routes, cities like Buffalo and Chicago were becoming centres that handled transcontinental flows of commerce. Without new domains British North America would be geographically outflanked, kept at a low standard of living by its small size. The publication of journals by explorers of Rupert's Land popularized a solution to this dilemma: the fertile but thinly populated countries of Red River and Saskatchewan, more than 2,000 kilometres to the west, could accommodate fifty million British subjects. The prairies might support an ever-growing flood of agricultural produce, manufactured goods, and services moving through the nascent metropolis of Toronto. Imperialist myth-makers embossed the notions of a Northwest "Manifest Destiny" with claims about how settlement in a harsh climate had made Anglo-Canadians a more vigorous and pragmatic people than the effeminate citizens of the American republic.[5]

Despite the passage afforded by the Great Lakes, the frontier retreated slowly and spasmodically. The extension of colonization roads gave lumber companies access to stands of white spruce, setting a basis for an export industry near Georgian Bay. Some officials like Joseph Cauchon, the Commissioner of Crown Lands, suggested agricultural lands might be found in valleys north of Lakes Huron and Superior. But he, like most others, interpreted the appropriate course of expansion as a transect towards Manitoba.[6] The *Globe*, reflecting popular notions, dismissed the rough country that separated Toronto from the prairies. Settlement of the arable patches located between "countless rock ridges and great stretches of peat morass" was nonsense, observed Thomas Gibson of the Bureau of Mines.[7] By the early 1890s the population of the Algoma district north of Lake Huron numbered just 41,900, while the Nipissing district (which stretched from Sudbury to James Bay) contained 13,000 people. Over two-thirds of those who attempted to start farms failed, and less than a quarter made the minimum improvements stipulated by the province.[8]

The slow pace of settlement was related to the ambiguity of jurisdictional authority over the hinterland, a difficulty caused by a quintessentially Canadian phenomenon – a federal-provincial dispute. Under its charter, the Hudson's Bay Company had claimed all lands beyond the Height of Land, which separated the drainage basin of the Great Lakes from that of Hudson and James Bays. With the transfer of the territories to the Dominion of Canada, Prime Minister John A. Macdonald reasserted this claim, an initiative that threatened not only to restrict the size and revenues of Ontario but to place the ports at the head of the Great Lakes within a greatly enlarged Manitoba. Both governments would not cooperate over law enforcement, timber leases, or the allocation of mining rights in the disputed lands. In some areas, multiple courts and registry offices competed as local authorities; in others, there were none. When the federal government refused to ratify an arbitrator's award of the lands to Ontario, the provincial legislature passed an act to take possession. A stipendiary magistrate was dispatched to coordinate the northeast from the district "capital" of Moose Factory, but he deemed interference unwise since the Hudson's Bay Company provided schools, administered justice, and carried the mails. Rather, officers of the fur company were appointed as justices of the peace and local customs were maintained until the province mounted a sufficient presence. Although the Judicial Committee of the Privy Council rejected the Dominion's contention that Ontario's northern boundary was the Height of Land, federal politicians refused to accept defeat and the dispute stretched on until 1889.[9]

While the legal wrangles unfolded, expeditions charted geological features and problems for railway construction. Few areas beyond major river valleys were examined and most estimates of the resource possibilities were speculative. Some explorers reported the climate when travelling northward towards James Bay appeared to get better. It was similar to Southern Ontario, just colder in winter. Most social leaders remained sceptical about the prospects for agriculture, convinced the landscape was dominated by rock, swamp, or forest primeval.[10] In contrast, lured by the prospect of revenues from colonization, Ontario's Department of Crown Lands waxed enthusiastic. Surely, it suggested, "crops of cereals and grasses will be proved actually to exceed the yields of the most favoured sections of the United States, and even the average of our own fertile Province." The region was "a country where miasmatic exhalations are unknown, where the water is abundant, pure, free from mineral contamination and of unvarying quality the year round; where the grasses are juicy, sweet and fragrant and the forests full of aromatic leaves and herbs; where the cattle are as a rule exempt from all ailments except broken legs and such troubles as may be brought on by careless exposure, or its opposite too little ventilation; where feeding is necessary not for a longer time but for a shorter time." The construction of the Canadian Pacific Railway triggered the discovery of copper-nickel ores near Sudbury, which led the Department of Crown Lands to insist a gigantic mining industry was inevitable. Railroad and lumber firms soon provided markets for pioneering farmers. Some may have dismissed the possibility of agriculture, Thomas Gibson remarked, "And yet preposterous as it is, the thing is being done. It is being found out that the country is more forbidding in appearance than in reality." After supposed investigations by "the sharpened eyes of land-hunters," colonization companies boomed on the frontier, proclaiming how "Northern Ontario is the best field now open for settlement by persons of small capital willing to work for themselves."[11]

To bolster knowledge about conditions in the northeast, between 1898 and 1910 the province commissioned surveys that revealed diversified ecologies and "a veritable storehouse of wealth." Beneath the visible granites and gneisses, Precambrian volcanic upheavals had laid down strata of valuable minerals, while other geological changes had created large areas of fireclay and lignite. About 50,000 years ago continental glaciers pushed across the continent from Hudson's Bay, scouring and deepening basins, stripping away rock or soil, tearing against mountains. They ground the terrain down to a flat peneplain, disrupted water systems, and created myriads of small lakes. As the masses of ice melted, soils were deposited in valleys or lowlands and the coastal plain of James Bay, depressed by the weight of the glaciers, was flooded by seawater. Clays and sands settled to the bottom of an enormous meltwater, Lake Barlow-Ojibway, which formed between the retreating ice and the southern uplands of the Canadian Shield. These processes created several regions. South of the ill-defined Height of Land short turbulent rivers descended to Lakes Huron and Superior. Readily accessible to settlers, this zone contained mineral deposits, mixed hardwood or spruce forests, and pockets of agricultural land. The rocky and poorly drained uplands of the Height separated it from more northern climes. Sediments had collected in small basins within those uplands around New Liskeard, Sudbury, or Lake Nipissing, permitting vegetable or dairy production. Far to the north, the most Arctic zone was a wide plain re-emerging from James Bay with isolated stands of stunted timber. Broad, slow-moving rivers crossed this "land of little sticks," but travel was treacherous due to muskeg, swamps, or jams of driftwood, while weak soils and a harsh climate rendered the region agriculturally valueless. Between this region and the Height of Land were drift plains on a gently rolling plateau approximately 1,000 feet above sea level. Boreal forests of white and black spruce dominated the topography, with jack pine on rock ridges and white spruce, balsam fir, or white birch abundant in well-drained areas. Containing more than 288,000,000 cords of commercial pulpwood, these tracts made it possible for Ontario to take a leading position in the forest products industries, the surveyors reported. Across the landscape distorted by glacial movements powerful waters rushed through narrow meandering valleys and then plunged three hundred feet to the coastal plain. Rivers like the Abitibi, Mattagami, or Kapuskasing could generate abundant hydroelectricity for industrial production. The most prominent feature, however, was the Great Clay Belt, an area formed by the sediments that had settled to the bottom of Lake Barlow-Ojibway, which supposedly had more than sixteen million acres (amounting to three-quarters of the

size of settled areas within the province) of "excellent agricultural land
... equal in fertility to any other in older Ontario." The explorers, who
conducted their research during summer months with the long day-
light hours of northern latitudes, leaped to the conclusion that the zone
represented a wonderful opportunity for colonization.[12]

Both Quebec and Ontario conducted propaganda campaigns aimed
at enticing settlement.[13] Publication of the geological surveys triggered
a mania of speculation about the lands beyond the French River and
Lake Nipissing. These became known as "New Ontario" or "Empire
Ontario," a domain that could bring substance to the visions of a provincial Manifest Destiny. The Northeast was "a new world to conquer,"
the Department of Crown Lands asserted, a dormant region capable of
supporting an enormous populace. "In the presence of the New North,
Ontario can await all the developments of time, confident in the fact
that she will hold her place as the pioneer province of Confederation."[14]
The rugged land, "while it lessens the cultivable area, ensures fertility
to the arable soil by preserving a constant supply of moisture." Farmers
would find steady employment cutting and hauling timber. "In place of
burning off the hardwood in huge log heaps, as used to be done when
it was not a marketable article, the settler in New Ontario in clearing his
land can in most cases sell the logs at a rate that will pay him well for
his labor."[15]

Promoters described a young, giant land, four times the size of the
southern counties of the province, "where the able and willing worker
can make an independent home for himself and call no man master
upon earth."[16] For generations people had believed it was "impossible
that anything but ice and snow lay beyond the Great Divide," but, the
promoters claimed, recent developments helped "dispel this popular
delusion." Once rail lines were completed, farmers would be two days
travel from the markets of the south. Good soil, pure water, regular
rainfall, and "a climate that leaves nothing to be desired" meant they
could grow "everything that Old Ontario and the Northwest can raise
except the more delicaté fruits ... even the more tender vegetables ripen
in the open air." No country "is as free as these valleys from swamp."
Muskeg was just a form of vegetable decomposition and could be converted to prime farmland such as might be found in Illinois or Ohio.
Transport and social services were what could be expected in pioneer
districts, colonization companies admitted, but the climate offered
invigorating benefits. "A sharp, cold, winter, with plenty of snow," one
writer claimed, "is by far the most healthful as well as the most advantageous to business of every kind ... No wonder then that in our lati-
tude can be found such beautifully developed men and women."[17]

Numerous schemes were advanced for connecting Toronto with Hudson's Bay and onward to Great Slave Lake and Alaska. The growth of agriculture and industry in "the best half of the best continent that God ever made," a prominent Torontonian declared, might transform the cluster of dilapidated shacks at Moose Factory on the "noble stream" of the Moose River into a railway centre with connections in all directions, "a new Chicago of the North."[18]

Some observers were more realistic. After several years travelling across the Clay Belt, the head of the University of Toronto's forestry department questioned the quality of the timber and thought less than half could be logged on a commercial basis. He suggested forethought was appropriate for farming due to the short growing season and a need for fertilizers or drainage schemes even in the best areas. The muskeg was often so thick one could put a pole down nine feet before striking clay. But cautionary voices were hard to hear above the din of boosterism. Dismissing uncertainty about "millions and millions of acres of the very best agricultural land in the world," the minister responsible for natural resources trumped "I know a great deal more about Northern Ontario than any professor in the country."[19]

2. A grasping colonial mind-set

Only through the medium of New Ontario could the province maintain its position in the Dominion, proclaimed Premier George Ross at the turn of the century. He expected "a thickly settled country" of more than a million people by 1916.[20] Achieving this goal entailed a range of undertakings but three premises guided government policies and each impacted the development of resource businesses in positive and negative ways. First, well into the interwar era, all of Ontario's leaders emphasized the importance of farming. The Conservatives, who governed the province from 1905 to 1919 and from 1923 to 1934, insisted that agriculture was Ontario's "greatest industry" – long after it was surpassed by manufacturing and services. Provincial officials drew upon popular mythology disseminated across the preceding century about the importance of classless yeoman farmers as the foundation of democratic order. They held on to anachronistic notions that frontier areas offered opportunities for upward mobility and property acquisition, freeing citizens in the New World from the income inequalities and social dependence of the Old. Economically autonomous homesteaders had better morals, unimpaired vigour, and individual steadiness. They represented the means by which wilderness was transformed followed by iron products, leather goods, and food and beverages. Sixty years later, steel and iron products represented the biggest group, followed by food and beverages, paper, transport equipment, textiles, and then various manufactured goods.[50]

These changes were contingent upon a transformation of business organization. During the pre-industrial era, small proprietorships or partnerships characterized commercial activity. Usually servicing a small geographic area and focused upon a single activity, firms were short-lived. Management under these conditions was ad hoc, with success or failure considered a function of the owners' character – their acumen, probity, and caution. These types of administrative practices became problematic by the late nineteenth century as population growth and the construction of railway networks expanded the size of markets. New technologies and the use of petroleum and electricity for energy gener-ated economies in production or distribution that propelled a displace-ment of small firms by larger enterprises. The dominance of the "invisible hand" of market transactions was displaced by the "visible hand" of pro-fessional management. "Managerial capitalism" entailed the integration of different business functions (either through natural growth or the amalgamation of companies) and their coordination as coherent systems by hierarchies of salaried executives. Over time decision-making was commanded more by financial or market considerations than the whims of entrepreneurs. The novel manufacturing technologies had high fixed costs, which increased the need for external financing beyond the origi-nal investors. Many promoters and financiers formed corporations large enough to be recognized as "national enterprises," either to capture investor interest or to reduce competition amongst moderate-sized rivals. Between 1890 and 1915 large manufacturers emerged in Canadian sec-tors such as cement, steel, and textiles, while big enterprises were con-structed in utilities, banking, and life insurance. Between 1916 and 1930 giant firms arose in pulp and paper, foodstuffs, primary and fabricated metals, and retail activities. Great factories, networks of communications and transportation, and new goods or services: these were the physical manifestations of the organizational change. When possible, managers and financiers sought stability by rationalizing industries into oligopo-lies, coordinating market activities with other firms, and formalizing relationships with suppliers or clients.[51]

Industrialization and the formation of big enterprises were contin-gent upon international capital and trade. With small domestic capital markets, Canadian governments assiduously encouraged foreign investment. The United Kingdom accounted for more than 70 per cent of the flows of foreign capital into Canada as late as 1914, but the significance of American investment waxed. By 1930, it accounted for 61 per cent, while the British contribution declined to 36 percent. The American share of Canada's imports increased from 41 per cent to 60 per cent between 1900 and 1930, while its share of exports grew from 34 per cent to 43 per cent. American corporations concurrently built subsidiaries in sectors like chemicals, petroleum, and transport equipment.[52] Notwithstanding tariff regimes or protectionist policies on both sides of the border, across the opening decades of the twentieth century continental flows of capital and production shaped the Canadian economy.

Less obvious, but important, for the process of economic transformation were the profession and institutions of law. Commercial endeavours have always required legal services: information collection, title searches, contract preparation, enforcement of performance obligations, and management of claims. With the emergence of modern business, the scale and scope of those tasks expanded. The new forms of manufacturing required the formation of joint-stock corporations to mobilize funds and temper managerial or investor risk. Unlike proprietorships or partnerships, the enterprises required professional guidance for the preparation of documents that satisfied the terms stipulated by companies' legislation. Corporations could be formed under federal or provincial statutes, and every jurisdiction had distinctive filing requirements, disclosure obligations, and registration charges. Lawyers were needed for the creation of enterprises, the assembly of investors, and the generation of financial securities. Promoters often based their ventures upon government grants of subsidies, exemptions, resource rights, or monopoly privileges – all of which had to be negotiated and specified in contracts. Their representatives had to lobby against initiatives from other firms, defend established rights against infringement, and restrict unfavourable actions by political authorities. Some of the initial attempts to construct large enterprises failed, leading to takeovers. Where the consolidation of enterprises generated oligopolistic competitors, special problems then had to be arbitrated by lawyers who served as foreign ministers for their clients. As intermediaries between firms and financial institutions or as advisers to investors' committees, they smoothed conflicts and arranged acceptable investment packages. With the extension of corporate operations across different jurisdictions, lawyers became indispensable for exploiting variations in taxes and regulations. Some, as managers of estates and trust funds, could direct capital into specific enterprises, while others who belonged to boards of trade might press for supportive regulatory frameworks. These affairs entailed consultations with accountants, appraisers, trust companies or bankers and broadened the competencies of some beyond technical issues to the management of complex interorganizational schemes.

The legal profession became concentrated in business and judicial centres. Approximately 31 per cent of Ontario's lawyers were based in Toronto during 1900, a share that expanded to 48.5 per cent by 1940. The largest firms, most of which were located in Toronto's business district near corporate head offices, steadily grew in size. By 1932 Blake, Lash, Anglin, and Cassels was the biggest partnership, with twenty lawyers. Other prominent firms included Tilley, Johnston, Thomson, and Parmenter; Rowell, Reid, Wright, and McMillan; Osler, Hoskin, and Harcourt; McCarthy and McCarthy; and Long and Daly.[53] This pattern was not unique to law but occurred with other services, such as auditing.[54]

Despite the demand for expertise in corporate affairs, Canadian specialists remained few in number. A modest group of firms handled most affairs. The positions adopted in specific cases varied according to the parties whom they represented. Advocates contended for the enforcement of managerial prerogatives in some instances and for investor concerns in others. It was not unusual for lawyers who had helped launch an enterprise and had assured investors its securities were reliable holdings, later to shift stance and to work in conjunction with the interests of one security class versus another if that firm failed. Those involved considered such practices normal. To casual observers, as hats and arguments were switched over time, the advocacies could seem inconsistent or to be conflicts of interest. Moreover, former politicians represented a key source of competent advice about questions that arose during negotiations with government officials. Ontario did not construct an internal legal capacity for natural resource regulations until the 1920s, and it often employed private-sector lawyers to draft prospective legislation. Despite reviews by civil servants and the cabinet, there was always a potential for generous terms to slip in. The possibility of conflicts of interest was exacerbated if companies tried to facilitate their cases by employing lawyers affiliated with the party in power. When the Conservatives held office, individuals such as Strachan Johnston, Norman Tilley, or former premier Sir William Hearst might be engaged. If the Liberals or United Farmers held sway others like Ward Wright or Newton Rowell could be retained.

Webs of relationships thus linked the realms of politics, business, and law, where the significance and connections of each individual or partnership were understood by the cognoscenti. Few lawyers garnered the status of business executives since they were viewed as pleaders of other men's causes. Most did not amass huge capital or influence but some ascended to awe-inspiring heights. The latter typified several of those who became enmeshed with the Abitibi receivership. Strachan Johnston was a director of Temiskaming Mining, Blue Diamond Coal, Canadian Coalfields, Simpsons, Northern Mexico Power and Development, and McIntyre Porcupine Mines. Norman Tilley sat on the boards of the Canadian Pacific Railway; the Bank of Montreal; and the Minneapolis, St. Paul, and Sault Ste. Marie Railway. Ward Wright became a vice-president of Algoma Steel and a director of eleven companies. Glyn Osler, whose family was well connected in legal and financial services, chaired the Economic Investment Trust and served as a director of firms like National Steel Car, Bell Telephone of Canada, and Mutual Life of Canada. Leighton McCarthy was the president of Canada Life, the vice-president of the Bank of Nova Scotia and Saguenay Power, and the vice-president and director of eight companies, including Aluminium Limited and Union Carbide of Canada. Victor Mitchell, a member of the Montreal bar and widely perceived as *the* authority on Canadian corporate law, was president of the Windsor Hotel and a director for more than ten companies. Individuals who specialized in other areas of the law rarely penetrated this exalted realm but used their contacts to generate opportunities. Arthur Slaght, the most theatrical of Ontario's criminal lawyers, amassed a fortune from his dealings with mining companies.[55]

Numerous members of the profession were uncomfortable with the transition towards a corporate society. Some waxed mythologic for an earlier time when legal practices were decentralized around county courts. Justice William Riddell fantasized about how lawyers had applied their trade as a utility for the benefit of all, not necessarily for personal gain. But with the emergence of corporations, the individual who stressed service in the courtroom or the assembly hall was "largely a thing of the past. His place has been taken by the business man, the acute pulse feeler of the money market, who is ever on the look-out for investments for his clients." Contemporaries "must have a greater capacity of mastering facts. We are living in more haste – a lawyer must be prompt and ready. Time is money, and a lawyer must not make mistakes, if at all avoidable."[56] Writers to legal journals complained about how economic change stimulated the degradation of behaviour. Law supposedly provided a spiritual framework of rules, a moral plain, but many of their colleagues were no longer gentlemen or statesmen who served as models of integrity, perseverance, and social idealism. Rather, the profession now mirrored the grasping values of commerce. Sir James Aitken, in a 1919 address to the Canadian Bar Association, new company, or for a firm to transfer its business, unless express authority was granted in the charters or the general law. Even when one corporation held total ownership in another the firms were not axiomatically merged.[72] In Quebec, bonds and debentures before 1914 could be placed only against physical assets, not intangibles. Capital stock without par value was not fully sanctioned until 1924, largely due to its acceptance in the United States, and even then it remained contentious.[73]

The growing cross-border flows of production and capital, however, had practical consequences for Canadian corporate law. Bonds and mortgages traditionally were written with British terminology but by 1920 American phraseology and practices became widespread. New deeds for bonds designed in the United States failed to provide for Canadian requirements that specified investor meetings for substantive changes to capital structures. American options for debt instruments, such as convertibility of payments to gold, were written into security issues even though Canadian courts might not accept the provisions. Judicial treatment of disputed claims followed Anglo-Canadian case precedents, of course, whereas executives sometimes assumed there would be outcomes that accorded with American legal norms. Perhaps most crucially, few processes were elaborated for managing the reconstruction of failed corporations. Most Canadian judges had little experience or knowledge about business affairs, whereas in the United States specialized courts or regulatory frameworks increasingly adjudicated those matters. Canada was among the last of the industrializing nations to pass legislation dealing with bankruptcy. As will be discussed in later chapters, not only did Canadian corporate law fail to ensure accountability or disclosure, it was very weak about matters related to restructuring insolvent enterprises.

Each of the background elements discussed in this chapter was significant for the story of the "middle waters." A unique combination of geographic opportunity, government, and capital facilitated the formation of Abitibi Power and Paper. The celeritous rise of the firm and then its downfall were shaped by a knot of industrial competition, finance, law, and public policy that coupled the destiny of the factories in the northern periphery with developments in the intermediate zones and metropolitan centres of the continental economy.

2

Anson's Folly

You are dealing with forces, young man, when you speak of Wheat and the Railroads, not with men. There is the Wheat, the supply. It must be carried to feed the People. There is the demand. The Wheat is one force, the Railroad, another, and there is the law that governs them – supply and demand. Men have only little to do in the whole business.

– Frank Norris, *The Octopus*

Everybody thought I had a duster. Y'all thought ol' Spindletop Burke and Burnett was all the oil there was, didn't ya? Well, I'm here to tell you that it ain't, boy! ... I'm rich, Bick. I'm a rich 'un. I'm a rich boy. Me, I'm gonna have more money than you ever "thought" you could have – you and all the rest of you stinkin' sons of ... Benedicts!

– Edna Ferber, *Giant*

PULP AND PAPER ENTERPRISES EMERGED hesitantly in Canada, with low founding and high disbanding rates. Ventures in a new industry experience different challenges than firms that enter well-established sectors. Their managers must deal with unknown contexts, mobilize resources, and elaborate sustainable positions. Newness represents a problem because the number of companies is small, they lack role models, and stakeholders may not provide adequate support. It can take decades for an industry to establish cognitive legitimacy, that is, to become significant, familiar. Markets and governments may rhetorically endorse the new activities but garnering true support can prove difficult. With no established performance record, there is little reason to trust promoters about whether their schemes will succeed versus outcomes that will make others look like fools.[1] An American report bluntly noted: "Capital moves slowly into new regions, and this is

These conditions propelled the growth of American newsprint production from 196,053 tons in 1889 to 1.2 million tons by 1909. Demand and the modest output necessary for the economic operation of a mill created opportunities for firms to enter the industry, but the financial obligations escalated as capacity rose and as innovations allowed the manufacture of a homogeneous product. Capital investment grew from $90 million in 1889 to $409 million by 1909.[9] Most new mills were corporate-owned, with the bulk of production originating from firms with capital investments that exceeded $1 million. Intense competition drove prices down to ruinous levels and propelled the 1898 formation of International Paper, which consolidated many factories in the Eastern States. Although it played the role of a price leader, the amalgamation did not secure complete dominance and the firm's market share deteriorated.[10] By 1910 there were 777 paper-making American establishments but just 56 companies (controlling 71 mills) produced newsprint. They briefly comprised a loose oligopoly, of which the top four accounted for half of domestic capacity. However, within a decade the industry fragmented as new rivals entered (see Appendix 2.1 and 2.3).[11]

A widespread belief emerged by the 1890s that Canada might reap great benefits from the consumption of newsprint. The country, the *Globe* declared, would prove a "dangerous competitor," one destined to become "not only the foremost wood pulp making nation, but the paper manufacturer for the world, more particularly of the lower grades, such as newspaper."[12] Different interests lobbied for controls over pulpwood exports and for a manufacturing condition. Their expectations appeared valid as forest areas in the United States were depleted and less economic or more distant tracts were used. The average manufacturing cost of newsprint rose from $25 to $35 per ton, almost exclusively in response to increases in the cost of wood. South of the border analogous perspectives were raised. The *Washington Post* acknowledged Canada's "almost exhaustless source … of newspaper pulp" and suggested imports should be encouraged because firms were "rushing headlong in regular American fashion in laying waste our forests to supply American newspapers." Other publishers supported imports from Canada to prevent "extortion" by a "trust" comprised of several large producers.[13]

Small owner-controlled firms conducted paper manufacturing in Canada and serviced local markets with short production runs. A significant export trade in timber existed during the nineteenth century but few firms advanced beyond sawmill operations into higher-value manufacturing. The potential for pulp exports was explored by several companies located in Quebec. Founded in 1887 by American and

Canadian capitalists, Laurentide Paper was the first to manufacture on a large scale. The exhaustion of stands of pine lumber forced Price Brothers, a prominent lumber exporter, to reorient towards pulp production. Modest-sized companies like Belgo-Canadian, Chicoutimi, and Riordon exploited concessions near the Gulf of St. Lawrence or the St. Lawrence River that allowed shipments abroad. Significant exports to the United States, however, remained a dream delayed because American suppliers remained capable of servicing domestic consumption. The United States imported less than $1,000 worth of newsprint in 1901 and only $65,000 in 1906. Imports of wood pulp doubled during this period but still represented only 3 per cent of American consumption. The ability of Canadian firms to service the demand for newsprint and pulp also was stymied because American producers succeeded in gaining tariff protection. While allowing duty-free imports of raw wood, Washington set insurmountable tariffs for most forest products and threatened retaliation if Canadian governments taxed timber exports. Sales to the United States hence did not take off until the constraints were eased after 1907, a result of lobbying by American publishers and a congressional investigation that portrayed International Paper as a quasi-monopoly. Tariffs were eliminated provisionally on groundwood pulp, then terminated on chemical pulp, and finally on newsprint in 1913 although the commodity was not placed on the duty-free list until 1922.[14]

Within this context, there were various efforts to establish mills in Ontario but dashed hopes and lost investments proved to be the norm. One commentary by the Department of Crown Lands captured the issues that confronted entrants. An operation could be profitable only if it was conducted on an extensive scale. A plentiful supply of fibre was essential, either nearby or easily secured, and careful explorations of territories were necessary to ensure its reliability, which cost time and money. Large supplies of energy power were required because of the size and weight of factory machinery. "Few businesses require the investment of greater capital than the pulp industry," the department remarked, along with reasonable shipping facilities and freight rates to customers. "All these essentials have to be satisfactorily determined before an industry can be successfully established."[15] Even though Ontario's premiers emphasized a promising future given the availability of boundless amounts of pulpwood, efforts to build enterprises proved challenging, a situation that resulted from company difficulties and public policy ineptitude.

Government officials gave rhetorical support for the new ventures but delivered, at best, mixed messages about the appropriate pace and size. Most underestimated or did not comprehend the true scale of investment and infrastructure necessary for entrants to succeed. In fairness, it should be recognized that the same issues vexed promoters, a normal phenomenon in emergent industries. Schemes were launched with grandiose enthusiasm, only to flop soon thereafter. The Liberals, who held office in Ontario until 1905, well illustrated the misjudgment. In one annual report, the Department of Crown Lands asserted how it was spurring the "giant industry" of pulp and paper. The following year it conceded problems had occurred but insisted development was unfolding in a satisfactory fashion. A year later the department admitted producers had not met expectations. Suspended or defunct projects were rationalized away with a novel caveat: "It is better that investors should make haste slowly than there should be a collapse of even one large concern, which might shake the confidence of the people in the value of our pulpwood resources."[16] The Conservative opposition deprecated the government as incompetent but industry observers questioned whether either party would make adequate provision for paper manufacturing given their focus upon recruiting grain-growing settlers for New Ontario.[17]

The Liberal administration has been described as "remarkably willing" to assist and as comfortable in its dealings with pulp and paper entrepreneurs.[18] The reality never matched this image and most schemes went badly. The government refused to put lands up for open tender, claiming investors would not participate in a competitive process, and financial markets could not accommodate the capital obligations that might result from a bidding contest. Negotiations occurred privately with the Commissioner of Crown Lands and agreements were then rammed through the legislative assembly. Nobody except the parties interested in a tract knew that a land transfer was pending until a deal was closed and presented to the Parliament. Critics argued the province lost large amounts of money by not having a tender system. Characterizing the government as tired and corrupt, the Conservatives believed the agreements favoured those with insider access. The presence of Liberals or known supporters among the licensees appeared to corroborate this idea, even though some promotions included Tories or their adherents. The character of the negotiations left the government open to allegations of secret deals, although the claims were not later substantiated. *Pulp and Paper Magazine* went further. "One element of wrong in such privately bestowed concessions given at prices ridiculously below the market value is that a few favored people are placed in a position to manufacture at prices which are ruinous to competitors who have paid a hundred cents on the dollar for their timber limits and water power. At times when trade is depressed we know what use such favored people have made of their 'pull.'" Even when the Liberals accepted the principle of competitive bidding, the journal dismissed the change as "a matter of words rather than of substance" because the exemptions ensured "a very slight curb upon the free rein that has been allowed to the Government in the past. It can still deal in the hole and corner method" and therefore the "application of open complication [sic] is practically nil."[19]

The Liberals refused to disclose information about forest tracts or to guarantee sufficient timber for applicants. In fact, the government often did not know what was in the territories. Some agreements allocated lands insufficient for even a modest-sized mill; others designated large territories on the legitimate grounds that adequate timber was necessary for sustained operations. While the Tories acquiesced to contracts for minor tracts, they accused the government of selling out to corporations with offers of "pulp principalities" or "kingdoms of pulp."[20] Convinced small companies or farmers should receive preference, the Conservatives opposed the concessions with the same zeal that their federal counterparts had attacked the land grants the Laurier government offered for railway construction. In the overheated rhetoric of the day, the allocations were portrayed as a "phenomenal steal," a "gigantic public robbery," or "a public crime and the men who enforce it are public criminals."[21] The agreements approved by Ontario stipulated minimal commitments for licensees, which enabled them to gain possession with no down payments or for nominal amounts. There was no monitoring system and the sole options for handling non-performance were license revocation or (with a hope for the best) time extensions. The province also insisted upon a right to open concessions to settlement, a condition that might leave firms helpless.[22]

Eight agreements were negotiated for the construction of mills. All were signed before the companies secured adequate funding. The true capital requirements turned out to be three to five times those stipulated by the contracts. The government characterized the promoters as "representative men," typically lumbermen with Canadian or American business associates. It naively assumed individuals acquainted with logging or sawmills were capable of managing the concerns. Most of the licensees lacked directors with experience in paper-making, although some hired skilled personnel as plant managers. The province stipulated production to begin within three years, but none of the licensees fulfilled the condition. Six years later only two firms had operational plants.

frustrated, the government suspended further efforts. Instead, the
Tories emphasized lumbering activities, arguing that there were excessive amounts of "overmature" woods and thus exploitive logging did
not represent a problem. This stance allowed the forest trade to be used
as a collection net for campaign funds, accompanied by a manipulation
(sometimes outright rigging) of the tender process.[32]

Nonetheless, it would be simplistic just to blame the failure to launch
a viable industry upon government policy. Until railways expanded
further into Northern Ontario, most forest areas were commercially
inaccessible. The province more than doubled the annual expenditures
on colonization roads between 1905 and 1914, but these outlays
amounted to less than a tenth of the monies earned from natural
resources. Rather, public officials treated New Ontario as a proverbial
cash cow and expressed delight that the province garnered the same
amount of revenue as Quebec but from a territory that was less than a
quarter of the size.[33] Freight charges from the geographically peripheral
region, industry participants thought, appeared to make exports non-
economic, an issue compounded for pulp producers because 60 per
cent of the output was composed of water. Only integration into paper
manufacturing could reduce the costs. However, John Barber, a Liberal
and a director of Spanish River Pulp and Paper, noted that strategic
option remained non-viable as long as prices stayed low and the U.S.
had an ample supply. The average costs for manufacturing pulp by
northern firms, professional consultants noted, fluctuated just above
and other times below seasonal prices. Mills sought to contract output
a year in advance, but, given the transportation options, some could
only sell at certain periods and likely could not service American markets.[34] The Tories also stipulated the minimum threshold criteria for a
pulp and paper operation as $700,000 in capital and the employment of
200 men. These conditions put the concessions beyond the means of
most lumbermen or small businessmen, who therefore denounced the
terms as unduly harsh. In fact, the guidelines already were well below
those required for minimum efficient scale, an issue compounded by
the difficulties entrepreneurs encountered after the panic of 1907 when
they sought capital.[35]

As a result, only three mills operated in New Ontario by 1910, all dating from the Liberal era: two troubled companies and a well-designed,
modestly profitable facility owned by Spanish River. The exemplar of
the difficulties associated with constructing an enterprise was the tale
of the mill at Sturgeon Falls, a village located towards the southern
edge of New Ontario near the northwest shore of Lake Nipissing. During 1895 the municipal council offered a bonus of $7,000 to two citizens

who promised to construct a $30,000 groundwood pulp and newsprint mill employing between thirty and forty men. The speculators began work but soon ran out of money. They flipped the operation to a syndicate comprised of eight English capitalists headed by the Jenckes Machine Company, a group the press dubbed "the Occidental." The new owners pledged to build as many as six factories that could manufacture a total of 120 tons of pulp daily. The company, retitled Sturgeon Falls Pulp, had an authorized capital of $2.5 million and the investors promised an outlay of $1 million for buildings and the employment of 400 men. This announcement exceeded the terms of the timber licence covering 195 square kilometres. Issuing a revised agreement, the government declared it opposed undue exploitation and any monopoly status for the firm. Settlement within the tract, along with the cutting of trees other than spruce by other companies, might be permitted. Fanfaronades from politicians and the press then ensued – the venture demonstrated the "vast possibilities of the pulp trade" and represented "a grand source of wealth" as Canada became a "mighty competitor" in international markets.[36]

But the scheme immediately was enmeshed in legal problems as several shareholders of the original enterprise challenged the sale and forced a temporary suspension. Another speculator proposed to merge Sturgeon Falls Pulp with nine firms into a $10 million company under a federal charter. The stock had been fully subscribed in London and Berlin, he asserted, so the new enterprise would be operational within a few months. This gossamer vanished as quickly as it arose. Despite these events, the government insisted the company was "rapidly increasing its plant" and "bids fair" to make the area into an important manufacturing location. In early 1900 it was sold to Edward Lloyd Ltd., a British newspaper owner. As this new owner affirmed a willingness to fulfil the investment obligations, considerable boilerplate was re-expended about why "Canada is on the high road to become the chief producer of the world's news paper."[37] Lloyd, however, had disregarded the views of its local agents (who recommended sites in New York or the Ottawa River valley) and made the purchase without visiting the site. Within a few weeks, Lloyd claimed it had been swindled because the properties did not match the advertised descriptions. The "plant" consisted of two rusty machines located in a building that had almost collapsed because the walls were constructed with cement salvaged from a sunken ship. Lloyd sued for damages but agreed to arbitration by Sir Charles Fitzpatrick, the federal solicitor general. The managing director of the mill, who supposedly had spent $500,000 by the Occidental, pontificated during the hearings about how Sturgeon

Falls "will become the centre point on a great highway from Hudson Bay to Chicago." The province denied wrongdoing on its part and emphasized how no promises had been given about the timber, but the affair turned into a public relations disaster as Lloyd denounced the government for providing inadequate protection. The proceedings dragged out over eighteen months with extensive coverage of the shenanigans. Then the pulp mill, which had not operated for several years, burnt down, a fire that threatened to set off a store of explosives and destroy the town.[38]

Lloyd lost the case, was required to pay damages and costs, and the properties were reassigned to Sturgeon Falls Pulp. Within six months the enterprise was flipped to another syndicate of British capitalists, who retitled it the Imperial Paper Mills of Canada. Development began for a facility capable of producing 120 tons of paper per day and employing 550 men, a scheme, the managers proclaimed, that would make it the second-largest producer in Canada and trigger an influx of 2,000 settlers. This idea soon was traduced to "quite a small plant" with a maximum output of fifty tons daily, about two-thirds of the level stipulated by the lease. Imperial then encountered difficulties with the province. The company held the right to build dams for a power generating station but was not permitted to restrict river access or water flow. It proceeded without gaining consent for the construction. When flooding ensued, it ignored stop-work orders. Government inspectors arrived and blew up the dams. Despite these setbacks, the company began production and maintained a steady output for two years. It went into financial markets to secure capital for a new mill operated by a subsidiary, Northern Sulphite Mills of Canada. Imperial guaranteed the bonds but as the bills mounted the managers (trying to garner funds from the Quebec and the Sovereign Banks) hypothecated all assets, that is, they pledged them to cover the debts in case of a default. Meanwhile, press releases emphasized the company's progress and construction of a model factory. A year later Imperial ran out of money, unable even to recompense petty bills. The businesses were placed in receivership with an indebtedness of $3.5 million. One mill remained open and generated a small profit, but the other properties were closed. The bondholders insisted the company was sound despite the failure.[39]

The venture instead sloughed into a legal quagmire. The Sovereign Bank demanded the replacement of the first receiver, alleging he was incompetent. Because the firm operated under a Canadian charter with British shareholders, two receivers were appointed: one in London and one in Canada, E.R.C. Clarkson, a specialist in bankrupt firms, who assumed management of the concern. Some investors opposed his selection because it came at the behest of the Sovereign Bank, which demanded priority over the other claimants. Under court order, all earnings were devoted to paying down the obligations to the bank. Press accounts characterized this arrangement as "beneficial" because it kept the pulp mill functional. Shareholders gained approval from a British court for a suspension of interest payments and sought to replace the existing bonds with an even bigger issue. Other investors blocked that initiative in a Canadian court, alleging their holdings could be wiped out. Sturgeon Falls sued for non-payment of taxes. The Quebec Bank sued to wind up the company, then seized some assets as a means of recovering the outstanding loans – actions that triggered counter-suits. The bondholders sued for damages when the receiver proposed dismantling the defunct sulphite pulp mill. The Sovereign Bank and New York paper brokers countersued over breach of contract. Individual creditors sued for payment or the repossession of assets. One attempt to liquidate the firm was blocked as "a determined and unscrupulous attempt to wreck the company and force it into the market." A judicial sale during 1908 did not attract bidders. English bondholders sued the Sovereign Bank and sought the right to grant options on the timber limits so they could sell the properties. The unsecured creditors completed the mess when they sued for equal treatment with other claimants and claimed the original investors had forfeited all rights.[40]

Reorganization efforts were stymied by the litigation and counter-litigation. The liabilities eventually peaked at $5.2 million, well in excess of the assets. Any settlement was contingent upon approval from the province for a sale or renewal of the forest concession, but it refused and declared the monies allocated for unsecured creditors were insufficient. Stories circulated for years that while American firms were interested in buying the enterprise they were unwilling to pay more than $1.25 million, which might partly compensate the debt holders but would leave other claimants with nothing. When the properties again were put up for sale during 1911, no bids were submitted. This triggered an "indignation meeting" in Sturgeon Falls, where the citizens asked for provincial relief and charged the English bondholders with setting an exorbitant reserve price that forestalled a purchase. Finally, under court order, Clarkson was allowed to dispose of the firm. He arranged a distress liquidation for $900,000 to two Montreal investment houses, Dominion Bond and C. Meredith. The town held "a monster carnival of rejoicing." A merger promoter with grandiose plans, Garnet P. Grant, the head of Dominion Bond, reorganized Imperial as Ontario Pulp and Paper. Residents of Sturgeon Falls believed the travails were ended but, as will be discussed in a later chapter, within two years the and 20 cents for other wood, though these were subject to revision. The province further stipulated that it would control where and when wood would be cut in part because the goal remained a venture that would "create markets for natural products, and ... enable the settlers to dispose of their spruce timber removed in clearing their land, at prices which will afford them some profit."[47] Accordingly, the tender was greeted with scepticism. "While the property is an excellent one," it was doubtful whether businessmen would invest given the "cast-iron" lease conditions, one commentator remarked. The stumpage rates were considered exorbitant, but the Crown lands seemed unnecessary because settlers could provide cheaper supply. In any event, it was impossible to make the proposition pay, especially as a pulp operation, because "the freight rates between there and Toronto would just about eat up the profits." There were many better propositions closer to markets."[48] Even on the mill site, one worker reminisced, "it was a venture whose future, in some quarters, was regarded as so dubious that ... the fellows on the job would call a man an old timer if he stayed three days."[49]

Anson saw the proposal differently, and his analysis likely came down to a set of strategic issues that belied an impetuous decision. The economics for a pulp and paper operation approximated those of hydro-electric facilities (a favourite target of Canadian entrepreneurs), as well as sugar refineries with which he was well acquainted. Production required heavy fixed investment up-front, in the form of mills and machinery designed for strenuous work, high speed, and continuous operation. The output relied upon cheap electricity and wood reserves adequate for an extended period. A key problem entailed the employment of half of the workforce in forest operations, which had to be managed carefully. Once an operation was established, working capital other than raw material inventory was not a great item since a mill preferably sold to a few large customers with scheduled deliveries in carload lots. The time between production and delivery was short, minimizing credit risks. Under normal conditions, a company was not likely to have large stocks of unsold finished goods. Inventory took the form of pulpwood cut in the autumn and winter months and delivered to the mills in the spring or early summer by floating logs downstream or towing them in rafts to the mills. Settlers could supply some timber, which decreased the capital requirements. Overall success thus depended upon tight cost controls and the advance sale of output. Anson also believed lobbying with regulators might allow more advantageous freight rates to the midwestern states.[50]

Timing was crucial. American publishers between 1906 and 1909 lobbied intensively against the "paper trust" headed by International

Paper. Their spokesman, John Norris, claimed, "I have a theory I can break these people."[51] The publishers sought an end to what they perceived as arbitrary allocations of customers among American mills and unjustified price increases (which they linked to the overcapitalization of newsprint producers). Their goal was the removal of protective tariffs for pulp and newsprint, thereby dispersing the industry from its concentrated geographic orientation to more remote areas with abundant water, cheap labour, and low stumpage rates – a development they hoped could spur competition and prevent higher prices. A scathing congressional investigation of the industry, where both the publishers and producers fared badly, was followed by hearings for a new tariff bill. Norris demanded "free pulp wood, free paper, and free pulp." The initiative then broadened into a struggle about "reciprocity," the tariff-free movement of goods between Canada and the United States. Although the broader proposal failed, the drive for open borders for pulp and newsprint continued.[52] A study by the U.S. Tariff Board documented a growing inability to meet demand due to forest depletion versus the availability of inexpensive supply from Canada.[53] Woodrow Wilson's electoral victory in 1912 made tariff revision inevitable and the next year tariffs on newsprint and mechanical pulp from anywhere in the world were eliminated. Existing companies and new entrants expanded operations as this likelihood approached. Anson's initiative thus followed the examples of others, albeit with a plant in a more remote location. Moreover, despite the beliefs of publishers that free trade could keep prices low, the business press trumped the likelihood they would rise as American resources were depleted. Adding to the propitious timing, construction of the National Transcontinental Railway now approached the Abitibi limit, which also was located near the new Timiskaming and Northern Ontario Railway that serviced the region from North Bay to Moosonee.

Anson and his partner, Shirley Ogilvie of Montreal, submitted the only bid and won the tender. The final agreement vaguely assured them of a continuous supply of wood and adequate water-power privileges. The government's goals, however, varied from the entrepreneurs. Cochrane acknowledged the value of manufacturing for opening up New Ontario, but he stressed how the licence permitted settlers to earn money from the sale of timber removed during land clearing. The industry thus was an incentive for people to "take up land in that country ... until there is continuous settlement." Rather than give the company full control, he noted, the concessions were "not withdrawn from sale or settlement, so that there is no monopoly or tying up of land." The firm had to promote colonization, buy local wood and agricultural parvenu businessmen. By 1930 Chicago was the second-largest source of money in North America with about six hundred enterprises engaged in the financial security business. Only London, New York, and Berlin ranked ahead, while Paris was equal in importance. Initially known for distribution rather than underwriting, Chicago companies handled both for organizations in the midwestern states, Manitoba, and Ontario by 1914. Indeed, whereas pulp and paper companies based in Quebec relied upon British or Eastern American capital markets, Chicago became a destination of choice for Ontario producers. Based upon their experiences with firms in the Lake States, underwriters were inclined to treat securities for forest companies as akin to utilities since the firms relied upon water-power.[58]

Founded in 1865, but with activities that dated back to the 1830s, Peabody Houghteling was the second-oldest investment house in Chicago. The firm originally emphasized mortgage banking, but as modern steel-framed buildings were constructed it moved into real estate bonds, with a forte for marketing investments to small clients that earlier had been available only to institutions. By the turn of the century, the company developed industrial bonds for major enterprises, pioneering the use of serial maturities where part of the principal was paid off annually. Smith moved the house into related activities: property valuation, engineering investigations, audits or inspections, and consulting. Peabody Houghteling emphasized dealings about "industries dealing with the necessities of life": iron and steel, newsprint, agricultural implements, steamships, forest products, and water power. The company often took what the executives characterized as "finder's activities": special fees or awards of equity positions for underwriting enterprises. Peabody Houghteling already played a significant role in newsprint production in Ontario, underwriting Backus-Brooks and other companies.[59]

Smith dismissed the viability of just a groundwood pulp operation. Instead, he advanced a scheme to make Abitibi into Canada's largest forest products enterprise by constructing a four machine newsprint plant with a capacity of 220 tons daily, along with a sulphite pulp mill with sixty tons daily output, and by expanding the groundwood pulp mill to 225 tons from 150. The existing firm was deemed incapable of handling this proposal but the investors approved the formation of yet another version of the enterprise: Abitibi Power and Paper Ltd. Ten times the size of the proposed firm when the tender was granted eighteen months earlier, it had an authorized capital of $13.5 million that included issues of $2 million in preferred stock, $5 million of common equity, $5 million in bonds, and $1 million in debenture stock. Equity holders exchanged their securities on an equal proportion basis (a very generous payoff), while the company gained $3.5 million in new capital. This capitalization was intended to cover a later doubling of newsprint output, while electricity generation also was announced as a key activity.[60]

The debenture stock and $2.5 million in bonds were sold to Peabody Houghteling for retention or sale as it saw fit. The investment house received a bonus of common stock, a holding that might be liquidated later at a considerable profit. The size of the stake remains unclear but it was sufficient to give Peabody Houghteling effective control. Contemporaries had no illusions about what had happened. A few media reports suggested the investment house bought the firm but most accounts declared it had passed to Chicago control as American money "shows itself to real opportunity."[61] Anson remained president, while Smith became a second vice-president and joined the board along with another Chicago financier. McGibbon, McAndrew, and Playfair were dropped as directors. The payoff for the original investors occurred behind closed doors but was not totally harmonious. McAndrew, the corporate secretary, sued, claiming he was owed a commission on the stock and a greater share of the profits.[62]

Media reports, although praising the infusion of "new blood," questioned the financial arrangements. Montreal's leading business newspaper contended "it looks very much as if the old charge of overcapitalization can be levied with a good deal of truth against the new company. The company, as first organized, contained a good deal of water, which has not been squeezed out in the re-organization."[63] Brokers nonetheless promoted the securities with great hyperbole. One assured a client that Abitibi's financing was "absolutely completed" when the enterprise was still "in a more or less formulative state." As part of a florid sales pitch, he stressed how his brokerage just happened to have available for sale a block of preferred shares (coupled with a bonus of free common stock). It was "not what would be considered a straight high grade investment, such as a municipal bond, but on the other hand, the undoubted permanency of the demand for the production of Canadian pulp and paper mills and the fact that this company has such an almost inexhaustible supply of wood and that it is so well financed to such a strong position and fortunate enough to get off to such a splendid start, by reason of the abnormal prices it would appear it offers an excellent speculative opportunity." The properties, which were selected in an "ideal way," provided Abitibi with an eighty year supply of wood. The firm held rights to three water-power sites and licences for 9 million cords of timber, while another 10 million cords were available from nearby lands. The cost of delivered wood was expected to be $4 a cord, about a third of the going rate, and $1.5 million in profits annually could be expected at full capacity.[64]

The series of capital restructurings left a notable legacy. In the eyes of many observers, notwithstanding later accomplishments, the managers were not just concerned with building the company but with a priori creative valuation. These perceptions were reinforced by subsequent recapitalizations that used an imaginative inflation of assets. Many other companies did the same, but the actions by Abitibi's executives garnered scrutiny because they began visibly and early. "Fuzzy financials" were not a reason for the enterprise's later collapse but awareness of those practices shaped many interpretations and contributed to the later difficulties of gauging what it was actually "worth."

3. A few strokes of the pen

The Conservatives claimed credit when news about the expansion became public. Pamphlets during the 1914 election noted how "beneficial results of the far-seeing and energetic policy of the Government are to be seen on every hand" as Abitibi and similar firms provided markets for settlers and aided development. The Tories assured voters of their "wisdom and courage" for it was now accepted that "the public domain should be administered with regard to the rights of the people as a whole, as well as of the individuals who are directly interested." Timberlands would be protected from despoliation and local residents safeguarded from forest fires. At the same time the government contradictorily announced – with pride – increases in timber dues and a shift of all costs for fire-ranging to licensees from the shared arrangement they had enjoyed with the province.[65] The Tories exaggerated the Abitibi venture, proclaiming it meant the hiring of 1,500 to 1,800 workers. The company had advised the government that 170 men carried out forest operations, with an anticipated 200 to 300 men in the mill. Nonetheless, as they toured the site, politicians waxed enthusiastic about the new epoch associated with the plant, which they described as the greatest enterprise of its kind in the Dominion.[66]

The strategic orientation of Abitibi across the next five years was geared to the establishment of a viable enterprise, an initiative that was realized despite disputes with the province. From the beginning, Anson paid close attention to public relations and the dissemination of stories that could assuage stakeholders or attract personnel. Company statements emphasized how, "imbued with the firmest confidence," the executives intended to keep costs moderate with a plant of the most modern design. Exquisite paintings of the mill were sent to trade magazines while it was little more than a hole in the ground. Information was regularly distributed about equipment purchases, as well as updates about construction. After the arrangement with Peabody Houghteling was consummated, press statements emphasized the hydroelectric potential. Circulars for Abitibi securities stressed the availability of millions of cords of the "best-quality" and "well-watered" wood for economic logging. A cruise of the concessions suggested the firm had a "practically inexhaustible supply" of pulpwood, but settler timber could be cheaply floated down rivers, which ensured the mill could always operate at full capacity. Not only did Abitibi hold the right to cut wood seven inches or higher on its timber tract, one release asserted, but its power generation capabilities were assured by lakes of "enormous size" with an "unfailing supply" of water. The firm would benefit from pulp exports because other firms were converting mills to paper manufacture, thereby propelling an indefinite rise in prices.[67]

For two years the development proceeded expeditiously. An initial focus was upon the construction of a spur line to the Temiskaming and North Ontario Railway and a groundwood mill with a daily capacity of 150 tons. Veteran land grants were purchased for a town, Iroquois Falls, "the value of the wood [on the lots] exceeding the whole cost." By the autumn of 1913 Abitibi had 510 employees, with 250 engaged in taking out wood to ensure the pulp mill could operate at capacity when it was ready.[68] Work began on a regulatory dam at Couchiching Falls, but like earlier ventures, the work ran behind target and weather problems forced postponement. Press releases instead lauded how several buildings were completed despite difficulties associated with getting supplies into the remote site. Excavation for a paper mill, built of concrete and fire-proof, began during the spring of 1914.[69] Anson pre-sold the output of pulp, much of which went to firms that were short of supply. Manufacturing began during August and by October reached a rate of 160 tons daily, with an expectation of a further increase once the head of water behind the dam was raised for power generation. The initial operation relied upon wood from settlers who extracted 125,000 cords in anticipation of the production of newsprint. Anson again pre-sold the output before the first machine became operational during 1915 with a daily capacity of 120 tons, and production rose to 225 tons per day by the end of the year.[70]

Abitibi's founding benefited from propitious timing. The reduction of tariffs between Canada and the U.S. was not initially a bonanza. Within eighteen months, an influx of new manufacturers triggered overproduction and a price drop. Canadian producers later remarked

behind the new issue of bonds with this feature open was questionable and their value would be open to immediately [*sic*] criticism." After the cabinet "thoroughly and fully" discussed the matter, Ferguson advised Anson "there was no possibility of the limits being granted to you on the same basis as the original limits ... they were unanimously of the opinion that some additional charge must be made in order to justify any action which they might take in this direction." This led to an impasse: the minister was unwilling to set a price without a survey of the territory and Anson opposed a higher rate as excessive. Ferguson also made clear that any new properties must be advertised for sale and he would not consider a private deal. This constraint, Anson thought, was "quite likely to result in some outsider coming in and tendering for the limits, not with any idea of using them or developing them, but for the expectation of holding us up and making us pay a fancy price or failing which they might buy them, causing a great deal of inconvenience and trouble." Ferguson gave verbal assurances that a sale would favour Abitibi but he refused to put anything in writing. Rather "his promise was to be considered entirely a personal matter as between himself, yourself [Smith], and myself." Nonetheless, Anson convinced himself that the disagreements could be resolved. "There is no question in my mind but that the Government are going to treat us fairly. I don't think they intend to hold us up for any unreasonable price" and just sought to get a sufficient premium on the additional limits.[79]

Anson complicated matters further by applying for lands elsewhere. The geographic location of Minnesota and Ontario Paper west of the Lakehead enabled it to service the region from St. Louis to Manitoba for better net prices than Abitibi. When it operated at full capacity, the firm also sold cheaply in the central midwestern states. To deal with this competition, Abitibi needed a mill in northwest Ontario. The Nipigon concession at the Lakehead received initial consideration but was despoiled by fire and previous cutting.[80] Anson then approached the government about the English River territory, which had not attracted any interest when put up for tender earlier. Anson declared a willingness to construct a 200-ton paper mill that might be expanded to 600 tons and an investment of $10 million. In exchange, Abitibi required the advertised 7,800-square-kilometre tract, an additional 20,000 square kilometres, and rights to a water power site.[81] This second application went nowhere, however. Anson later claimed he blocked Minnesota and Ontario Paper from securing the territory and got "a charter myself with the approval of the Minister of Land, Forests and Mines on an understanding that I would turn this charter over to the Government in the event of our not making any development on the English River."

The Tories rejected all bids as unsatisfactory. Even though the province had little knowledge about the merchantable timber on the lands, Anson's request was deemed excessive. The Farmers' government, which took office in 1919, believed Ferguson was at fault and privately schemed for a deal with a lumberman rather than a paper company.[82] Anson, however, had the territory cruised. The surveyors found large areas were water or burnt over, with wood located in narrow belts along rivers or in isolated swamps. These issues, combined with the need to build transport facilities, raised the probable investment to $20 million. He decided not to proceed because the amount of available wood was small, extraordinary outlays were required for logging and driving, and a mill could not compete against better-located rivals.[83]

Anson instead pressed ahead with his original scheme but rather than alter Abitibi's capital structure the expansion was covered from earnings and short-term notes. Given wartime taxation, he questioned the willingness of American bankers to support new financing. Abitibi's lawyer feared driving Ferguson "into a corner" but also found the minister difficult to fathom. "He, however, puts me off for some reason although I have no doubt the matter will be carried out as arranged."[84] When the request was resubmitted in the spring of 1918, Anson promised a further expansion to 500 tons per day. The firm was down a maximum of twenty years of supply, which his bankers noted was "wholly inadequate." It was impossible to secure the monies for an expansion unless the firm gained territories that restored the reserves to their original capacity. Indeed, he wrote, "some of our financial people are getting a little nervous," and the problem interfered with sales of securities. When the province still failed to act, Smith advised Anson "I cannot too strongly impress upon you the necessity for following this up and I have no doubt you are doing so."[85]

Ferguson, who had claimed to have been "puzzling" about how to meet Smith's concerns, responded in April of 1919 with a crafty letter. "My ambition has been to see the largest paper industry in the world established in this Province, and my attitude toward the pulp and paper industry has been directed towards assisting bringing that about," he assured Anson. Therefore, the province was obligated to ensure ample raw material. "There can be no doubt that enterprises such as yours can be most efficiently and economically carried on the basis of large units. It must be admitted it is preferable to have a reasonable number of large mills maintained than a large number of smaller institutions. The latter involve greater overhead and operating charges, with a shorter period of life." He claimed it was impossible to outline the territory but lands south of the existing concession would be reserved, albeit subject to further discussions. In short, support again was promised but nothing was authorized.[86]

Anson forwarded this missive to his financiers, who seized upon the pledge as sufficient grounds for the sale of new bonds. "We presume that you will in due course take up with the Ontario Government the delimiting of the territory to be set aside," one responded, "and settle definitely the question of price and other details in connection therewith, so that leases or licenses in the usual form may be issued to your Company." The circulars published by the investment bankers, nonetheless, characterized the extension as part of the firm's assets and claimed it increased the collateral by 50 per cent.[87] But the Conservatives failed to implement Ferguson's promise before they lost the election during the autumn and the new government, when the letter was discovered, believed it substantiated their suspicions about Tory corruption. During a subsequent investigation by a royal commission, Anson insisted nothing clandestine had occurred. "We had nothing but Mr. Ferguson's assurance or the Government's assurance that we were going to get this wood and power." There was "no private arrangement between the Minister or any one in the department in this transaction." Abitibi "made no contribution to any campaign fund, their rule being to keep out of politics," but "the Government promised us that we should have sufficient wood and water for power to go on with at the mill. The arrangement was that the price was to be set when, and as, the wood was used." Asked whether his firm would have advanced the money without Ferguson's letter, Alexander Smith declared, "I certainly would not. I told Mr. Ferguson to his face that we would not advance any money to the firm unless we had assurance of more timber than that of the original grant." Everything was "fair and above board," he insisted.[88] Perceiving the situation as a fait accompli, the new administration eventually confirmed the rights for Twin Falls and the extension.[89]

The Conservatives never explained their treatment of Abitibi's applications, but it was derived from several issues. First, the requests exceeded 40,000 square kilometres, whereas previous grants were much smaller. For the Tories, who had campaigned against "kingdoms of pulp," notwithstanding their earlier praise of Abitibi, this must have seemed a land grab. Anson's preference for a non-competitive acquisition likely reinforced this perspective and the opposition parties would have excoriated any private deal. Second, government officials were used to handling short-term arrangements like the annual cutting licences for lumbermen. They were less able to comprehend, let alone satisfy, resource supply for mass production, a problem that bedevilled provincial forest policy until mid-century. Moreover, the department responsible for the management of natural resources was itself an administrative mess. The survey division, which assessed timberlands, lacked skilled personnel and was short-staffed during the war. The ministry, a royal commission determined, had practices, "that would not be tolerated in any business institution" and its record-keeping was "a disgrace to a country store." Members of the field staff went largely uncontrolled, while the deputy minister was rendered a cypher with documentation routed through Ferguson's personal secretary and legal materials delegated to his law firm, where they sometimes, quite conveniently, went a-wandering.[90] Third, the government probably believed that Anson's decision in 1916 to expand mill capacity validated the colonization policy and, even better, it occurred without a grant of new territories.

Then there was the logic behind the request itself: additional wood to serve as collateral for new securities. In one sense, this was based upon the need to establish values behind contractual arrangements or the future earnings from properties. However, the methods for handling these issues were quite vague. Contemporary studies of "timber bonds" concentrated on the technical processes associated with arranging the sale of securities. Debt issues obviously could mortgage assets like mills and other properties. There was little to guide the treatment of forest concessions, other than acknowledgment of a need to send out cruisers to gauge the merchantable wood. It was considered reasonable to allocate value to trees in financial statements if lands were owned freehold. Wood cut on a contractual basis could not be considered an asset. A company might claim as current assets the annual harvest from leased properties (Abitibi's situation) but the notion of capitalizing future value was dubious.[91] Moreover, whatever the government and nature gave, either might take away.

The *Globe*, normally a supporter of northern development, reflected these concerns when it characterized Abitibi's common stock as "all 'water,' undiluted by even the shadow of real money." Just "a few strokes of the pen" capitalized the resource rights to legitimate the equity stakes. Upon reorganization in 1914, $3.3 million of capitalized timber limits were treated "as one of the old firm's assets" for a company now worth $5 million and that required another $2 million. "It was no problem. Another stroke or two of the weapon that is mightier than the sword" and that sum was added as "goodwill" to the worth of the resources. The "romance of this particular timber limit" was reiterated for the debentures and gold bonds. "The most astounding feats of Indian magicians pale before the performances that have made millions

demonstrated "in the paper industry it will be plainly evident that corporations, now-a-days, have souls." Anson's management style was paternalistic. Although he lived in Montreal, he visited the northern sites frequently and was characterized by an uncritical press as handling worker complaints with the "solid rock of open and honest dealing." When mills were closed, the firm employed as many people as possible in repairs or support services. Abitibi was unionized but experienced only short-lived strikes. It thus was characterized as a case of relative peace due to an "honest and sincere and generous" management that treated labour on a personal versus contractual basis.[101] With the company poised to double the annual output, Frank Anson, with considerable pleasure, advised shareholders in early 1920 about how his company enjoyed bright prospects.[102]

3

An Industry in Transformation

I think that I understand what he is up to. He is plotting to become a Power. He has a mind of metal and wheels; and he does not care for growing things, except as far as they serve him for the moment.

— J.R.R. Tolkien, *The Two Towers*

In a very different part of the world, fortune was already planning the initial moves and motives for the creation of a new dynasty, whose varied complexion was to signify both happiness and misery for the state, and personal success or disaster for its rulers ...

— Tacitus, *The Histories*

"A POOR, SICKLY ANAEMIC STRUGGLING group of mills" had characterized their industry for the preceding twenty years, George Chahoon, the president of Laurentide Paper, reminded his colleagues in 1920. Although a burst of prosperity from the First World War allowed a "current happy position," the business experienced "violent fluctuations in market conditions and violent fluctuations in supply and demand which are most harmful." Its growth had been "purely speculative," without careful thought for the long-term welfare of either manufacturers or consumers. In contrast, J.A. Bothwell, the head of the Canadian Pulp and Paper Association, opined that despite a recent stressful period, new undertakings would increase the output of paper and years must elapse before supply overtook demand, "if it ever does."[1]

The perspectives of both executives were confirmed across the following decade. Bothwell recognized the obvious: a gap between production and American consumption. Chahoon was more prescient. Newsprint was a low-value commodity vulnerable to shifts in economic conditions. Instability and turnover had characterized the industry since its emergence. These issues intensified after 1920 and propelled the producers towards new strategic orientations, as well as tighter relationships with financial markets. But they also encountered escalating conflicts with customers. Although Bothwell's hopes were realized, the confluence of these trends set a basis for subsequent collapse.

This chapter examines those issues, which lay behind the events chronicled in the next three chapters. It focuses upon developments at the industrial and institutional levels. The first section appraises the "demand" side by looking at how newsprint production evolved after the First World War. The second section then considers the "supply" side and presents an alternative interpretation of the industrial structure and the implications for any ability to control competitor behaviour. The third part extends the analysis by appraising the links between corporate expansion and investment capital. In some cases of economic failure (such as later occurred with Eaton's or General Motors), the signs of deterioration and the potential for breakdown are recognized. In others (like Enron or the financial crisis of 2008), investors do not gauge them realistically. The section accordingly reviews why the latter occurred with the newsprint manufacturers by considering investment practices and financial reporting in the 1920s.

1. Who could lack faith with this record?

Abitibi's success was bound up with the growth of the Canadian industry but this never unfolded in a steady manner. Rather, as Chahoon remarked, it entailed bursts of capacity expansion or risky initiatives in response to market fluctuations. The requirements for manufacturing newsprint restricted the type of wood to four species: spruce, balsam, hemlock, and poplar. As a result, nearly 85 per cent of American production was situated in the Lake or Northeastern states. A large newspaper consumed about 20,000 tons annually, the product of growth on 7,500 acres of eastern forest. However, the annual wood cut exceeded natural growth by two to three times, resulting in a depletion of resources. By the early 1920s, the U.S. Forest Service believed no American firm had sufficient holdings to guarantee a continuous supply under the existing methods of timber management, and probably fewer than six firms controlled lands that could supply their mills for more than two decades. Approximately half of newsprint production was concentrated in the state of New York, but three-fifths of the firms did not possess timber concessions. Cutting was banned on most state preserves. Whereas at the turn of the century firms secured timber from nearby areas, by the early 1920s it was often transported 1,600 to 1,950 kilometres. Various reports projected the exhaustion of domestic supplies within twenty years, and for states like New York, in less than half that time.[2] Contemporary press accounts and detailed studies conducted later highlighted the possibility of exploiting forests in Alaska or the Southern states.[3] Although the pursuit of such options remained decades away, public officials were cautioned against imports. One report warned American consumers could be at the mercy of the foreign manufacturer as to prices, while another stressed the need for reforestation since Canadian forests were no more "limitless" than American.[4]

But demand in the United States had followed a geometric growth pattern for a century and this continued for most forest products. Newsprint consumption increased from 1.2 million tons in 1909 to 1.9 million tons in 1919, and 3.1 million tons by 1925. Consumption of wood pulp doubled across that period, while demand for pulpwood increased by 50 per cent.[5] Within this broad trend, there were variations from year to year, and among the different seasons within a year, which made projections of business difficult. Overproduction after 1892 kept newsprint prices low (despite complaints from publishers that manufacturers charged unreasonable rates) and they remained in the range of $40 to $45 per ton until 1915. With insufficient profitability, a decreasing number of American mills made newsprint (see Appendices 1 and 2.1), a trend that also reflected the removal of tariff barriers, which facilitated the development of new plants that exploited cheaper wood and labour costs north of the border. Canadian production doubled between 1912 and 1915 but this did not take the form of an assured wave of success as some historical accounts have claimed. Some companies experienced serious difficulties or failed when a pre-war recession triggered a drop in consumption.[6] Demand, however, then escalated due to newspaper coverage of the world crisis and wartime requirements. Neither production nor imports could satisfy the upswing, which triggered a modest shortage and a reduction of inventories. A panic characterized by hoarding and multiple orders ensued as publishers sought to guarantee supply, while the business press mythologized a "paper famine." The bulk of the shortfall, in fact, originated from International Paper's conversion of mills to alternative goods because it garnered inadequate profits from newsprint. The average delivered price (despite wartime controls) thus jumped from $41.78 per ton in 1915 to $75.05 by 1918, an advance that was not matched by a new expansion of American capacity. Once firms converted mills to higher-value products, they rarely returned to newsprint manufacturing.[7]

Imports, hitherto a modest share of the market, expanded to a third of American newsprint supply, and by 1919 Canadian daily output (which had been 540 tons in 1910) rose to 2,775 tons. "Very ambitious plans" were expected within ten years to bring this to the equivalent of American consumption during 1918.[8] Producers merrily exploited the reversal of buyer-supplier relationships. Standard contracts with customers ran for one or more years at specified rates, but some manufacturers insisted upon a conversion to six-month agreements, as well as fixed monthly purchases regardless of a customer's needs. Until 1916 prices were quoted as free on board (f.o.b.) press-room, that is, producers were responsible for freight and drayage to clients but as contracts came up for renewal they insisted upon an f.o.b. mill policy that imposed transport costs upon customers. The manufacturers, Alexander Smith declared, were "waking up" and trying to recover money they had lost in the past due to "ridiculous prices." For years, he contended, new enterprises launched by inexperienced promoters had flooded the market with cheap paper and publishers assumed sufficient supply existed to allow the sale of newspapers for a penny. Immutable natural laws had finally caught up with reality.[9]

Prices and seemingly insatiable demand spiralled with the termination of wartime regulations – a situation compounded by inflation, higher freight rates, and supply shortages triggered by labour disputes. Canadian exports of paper more than doubled between 1918 and 1920, while plants ran at excess capacity. Executives, investment bankers, and the business press universally proclaimed a new era of prosperity. The manufacturers concentrated upon contracts with big purchasers that left them less exposed to any downturn. Their executives believed corporate viability required a minimum profit of $10 to $15 per ton after operational expenses. That level of earnings covered interest, preferred dividends, and overhead costs, along with outlays for properties or equipment. At a list rate of $70 per ton, major firms reaped operating profits that varied from $18 to $42.50 per ton. But by late 1920 contract prices reached "extreme" levels as firms quoted rates at $140 per ton, although most agreements for large buyers were closer to $110. Small publishers often relied upon the spot market, where rates skyrocketed from $200 to $400 per ton. Given these conditions, operations previously deemed non-economic or geographically remote became viable, while the prices of newsprint securities soared as the manufacturers reaped windfall profits.[10] The list price thus became a crucial lure for both entrants and established firms. Although it declined across the 1920s, the average contract rate remained above the pre-1916 level. Even in 1927 it was still 50 per cent higher.

This issue intensified a wave of growth that had already staggered contemporaries as pulp and paper became the third-largest Canadian industry. Capital investment expanded from $54 million to over $365 million between 1911 and 1921, while exports increased from $8.6 million to $163.7 million. "Who could lack faith with this record?" asked the *Financial Post*. Canada's supremacy as a pulp producer was assured for many years, declared London's *Financial Times*.[11] Older companies augmented operations, while new aggressive firms were launched. From start to finish, construction of a new plant usually took a minimum of three years. Companies predicated their expansions of output upon current consumption patterns, but even if an investment decision appeared reasonable at the inception of a project, there was always the risk things might alter by the time a mill began operations. Precipitous shifts in market conditions could jeopardize a firm's cash flow. Because newsprint was a low-grade commodity, the trade press regularly acknowledged this phenomenon could be triggered even by short or seasonal turndowns. Managers also experienced difficulties judging whether output was likely to remain balanced with, or exceed, demand. There were few sources of coherent data despite newspaper reports of monthly production or exports. In 1920 several companies announced their plans for enlarged operations, which represented a 25 per cent increase in total capacity. It inaugurated a pattern that unfolded across the decade: an upsurge in demand triggered a groundswell of investment, followed by a lull or by postponements as market conditions eased, and then another surge as entrepreneurs believed higher consumption allowed room for new or bigger operations.

The risks became evident in late 1920 when a recession collapsed demand. The manufacturers were forced to curtail their plans and suspend dividends, but the reversal of fortune proved disastrous for companies focused upon pulp production. A wave of bankruptcies unfolded: Nipigon Fire, Nashwaak Pulp, Kaministiquia Pulp, Mattagami Pulp and Paper, and Dryden Paper. The recession proved especially unforgiving for firms with questionable capital structures. Western Canada Pulp and Paper, financed for five to six times its actual operations, not only failed but dragged down the Home Bank with it. Western's shareholders, who lost everything, learned from a subsequent investigation how the assets had been presented at inflated figures to legitimate sales of financial securities. The *Financial Review of New York* suggested it was "hardly likely that investors who experienced losses as a result of too careless buying in those days will soon forget what they have learned." The journal told readers to invest only in "seasoned" companies and fundamentally sound industries with

1920 and 43 per cent by 1930. Mills in the Southern states, respectively, increased from 4 per cent to 8 per cent and 17 per cent of aggregate capacity. Sulphate pulping, invented during the early twentieth century, was particularly useful for southern pine, a fast-growing softwood. Difficult to bleach, it was first employed for kraft wrapping but by the mid-1920s experiments demonstrated a potential for newsprint. Changes in transportation and productive technology also enabled the Pacific Northwest to become a supply source, raising its portion of continental capacity from 3 per cent during 1900 to 8 per cent by 1920, and to 18 per cent by 1930. Producers based in the Northwest states and British Columbia did not merely supply coastal regions but became an alternative for mid-continental customers.[22]

Pulpwood costs rose as timber was depleted in the Northeast and Lake states but American firms continued to add capacity in those locations because their executives favoured the familiar, situating mills in areas where there were clusters of producers. Only four firms relocated to Canada. When firms shifted toward higher grades of paper, this occurred mainly through the rehabilitation of mills rather than the construction of new facilities.[23] Smaller mills logically should have been closed or converted but many continued to produce newsprint. The physical size and costs of the equipment made transfers away from antiquated sites difficult. Often built inland on logging rivers, many did not have easy access to transport networks. However, the original costs of their machines had been written off and the owners thus milked the investments. They legitimated the operations because fixed costs and all or most variable costs could be covered. Indeed, the higher the proportion of fixed costs in company operations, the less likely firms were willing to relocate or to close inefficient factories. Some focused upon specialty goods or client niches, which others were reluctant to service, and in so doing realized returns that justified continued operation. By the late 1920s, the capital in American newsprint production exceeded $1 billion. The staying power of the mills became a crucial factor that led to excess capacity.[24]

Exports of pulpwood from Canada abetted their survival. Imports from Quebec and New Brunswick declined as mills were constructed in those provinces, leaving Ontario as the most significant Canadian source. Exports expanded between 1920 and 1928, peaking at 34 per cent of all pulpwood cut in Ontario and 40 per cent of American imports. Mills in locations like New York and Pennsylvania imported more than half of the pulpwood used in production. Nonetheless, although Ontario was a valuable source it was never indispensable. Even at the height of the trade, it supplied less than 8 per cent of

American consumption.[25] The imports from Canada went to mills producing a variety of paper goods (not just newsprint), and government officials later noted American firms tended to diversify purchases to avoid dependence on specific sources. Some executives, like Abitibi's L.R. Wilson, linked the decline in the list rate for newsprint with purchases of Canadian wood by American mills. The firms could then convert it and remain low-cost producers because they were not burdened by the debt financing that was necessary for the construction of new factories.[26]

Intense lobbying by various interests pushed Canadian governments to embargo pulpwood and pulp exports. A royal commission in 1924 contended the domestic manufacture of all pulpwood would have enhanced capital investment by $150 million and supported 33 additional mills, each producing 100 tons daily and employing another 8,000 men (expanding the workforce by a third).[27] But there never was a realistic likelihood of controls being instituted. The Canadian Pulp and Paper Association and the provincial premiers, fearing retaliation, opposed any restrictions. American producers had continued to lobby for an end to the free trade regime and nearly succeeded during 1922 in gaining duties that would have undermined the viability of chemical pulp mills in Canada. Not only was Congress likely to retaliate against any export controls, but the American government also had numerous ways of imposing penalties. Canada imported twice as much from the United States as she exported. Most of the sulphur used to produce chemical pulp originated from Louisiana or Texas, and few efforts had been made to develop alternative supplies. In addition, although the population of Northern Ontario never achieved the million-person goal Premier Ross had set in 1900, it represented an important voting bloc. Newspapers and local boards of trade argued against export controls, convinced that reliance upon the domestic market might leave settlers subject to the whims of local mills. The rate offered to farmers "scarcely pays the cost of getting the pulpwood cut," but if exports "could be created, the settlers will receive a better price."[28] Ontario's premier admitted "we cannot put an embargo on pulpwood," although he followed up with standard boilerplate about how the province would ensure the industry received the fullest advantage.[29] It is likely the government never grasped the catch-22 dimensions of the situation. Excess capacity had begun to emerge by 1924 but the exports Ontario would not restrict compounded the issue by allowing the survival of American producers.

A further shift entailed vertical integration: the internalization of successive stages of production or distribution within the same firm. This strategy allowed the avoidance of uncertainty and transaction costs with independent buyers and sellers, the elimination of duplicate sources of overhead, and the ability to reap increased returns to scale. But it was undertaken with a risk of lower flexibility and an expansion of administrative and other costs. Vertical integration has usually entailed much higher capital requirements for the amalgamated operations.[30] Early American anti-trust law portrayed the strategy as a form of market coercion: making the entry of new rivals difficult, foreclosing markets to non-integrated firms, and facilitating price discrimination.[31] Only limited empirical evidence to support such notions has ever been uncovered in the massive amount of research about this issue. Efforts to raise market power, in practice, tended to fail, a development that occurred due to numerous issues, like the further evolution of industrial structure or shifts in the relationships between buyers and sellers. Vertical integration as a coercive tactic proved unsuccessful, especially when markets were competitive.[32]

Most Canadian mills were pulp operations before 1920 and companies that integrated into newsprint production (like Abitibi, Spanish River, or Laurentide) remained distinctive. Pulp often was sold in spot or daily markets like general merchandise rather than on long-term contracts and was therefore subject to severe price fluctuations. Alexander Smith later observed that sulphite pulp, in particular, was "a devil," "a hunger or a burst ... a very undependable product."[33] Specialized plants had to dry pulp before shipment, and it was converted back to slush form at a paper mill. Vertical integration represented a logical step because the generation of pulp represented about two-thirds of the cost in paper manufacturing. Companies that integrated into the manufacture of newsprint could realize significant cost savings. In contrast, finer paper grades still were made in small batches and required a range of pulps.[34] The risks of a strategy focused upon pulp often surfaced across the preceding half-century. As noted earlier, the recession of the early 1920s triggered a wave of bankruptcies, of which one was important and had serious consequences for the industry.

Founded in 1857 as a wrapping paper factory in Merritton, Ontario, Riordon Pulp and Paper developed a sulphite mill at Port Hawkesbury, Quebec. As one of the oldest enterprises, it received laudatory media coverage, which suggested the firm went "from strength to strength" with a "consistency that has known no deviation." In recognition of this status, Carl Riordon was chosen as the first president of the Canadian Pulp and Paper Association. An aggressive strategy during the 1910s (that included the construction of a huge mill in Abitibi-Témiscamingue) extended its operations in Eastern Canada. Financier I.W. Killam and his firm, Royal Securities, facilitated a merger in 1919 of Riordon, its subsidiaries, and other firms into a new enterprise: Riordon Company. Capitalized at $60 million, with assets valued at $81 million, it ranked among the top ten Canadian manufacturers. Riordon controlled 10,590 square miles, with 25 million cords of pulpwood, extensive stands of lumber, and numerous water-powers – one of the biggest holdings worldwide. A commentator noted how "it is a safe guess [this] will be copied or attempted by other Canadian pulp and paper companies who are selling bond or stock issues in the United States market."[35]

Riordon was a pulp and timber company that, despite the expansion, still produced only a modest amount of paper. Carl Riordon exited the firm shortly after the merger. The firm continued to issue bonds, but with too many commitments and too little working capital, Riordon crumpled into receivership. The common share price fell from $224 to $4, while the value of the equity plummeted to $1.04 million versus a declared worth of $43 million. Perceived as a disaster that badly damaged Canadian industry, the failure became a subject of intense speculation. The business press and many executives blamed Killam as the "conductor" behind the expansion, not the Riordons, even though they had benefited handsomely. Anger over the failure triggered demands for an investigation by someone the investors could trust. However, since his firm owned large amounts of Riordon securities, Killam was able to shape the reorganization process. He demanded shares be placed in a voting trust and threatened other investors with liquidation if they did not acquiesce to his rearrangement proposals. However, even though the capitalization was slashed in half, multiple efforts by Killam and others to resuscitate Riordon came to nought and the properties languished for four years.[36]

Numerous executives concluded from the experiences of Riordon and similar companies that long-term survival required integration into newsprint or other secondary products. Firms pursuing this orientation soon led the industry, but a significant number remained focused upon pulp. In 1920 there were thirty-eight non-integrated Canadian mills producing 2,707 tons daily. A decade later, forty-three independent mills generated a total of 3,157 tons per day, while another 182 operated in the United States, three-quarters of which were also not integrated. Canadian and American firms making alternative types of paper relied upon these enterprises for supply. Although most were individually small in size, they contributed to the stock available and thereby influenced pricing during periods of oversupply or weak demand.[37]

2. Struggles for dominance

Even as demand waxed, a transformation of publishing in the United
States generated long-term problems. Between 1860 and 1909 the number of American newspapers grew from 3,725 to 17,211. However, metropolitan markets then experienced a process of consolidation as
smaller or weaker journals succumbed to competitive rivalry. The number of papers decreased to 9,008 by 1925. For urban areas with more
than 8,000 residents, daily publications declined from 2,441 to 2,116, but
the termination of weekly organs was dramatic – from 12,145 to 6,435.
During this period the average daily circulation also increased by
nearly 25 per cent. Put simply, fewer but much bigger papers characterized publishing. The victors bought out the losers, thereby maintaining
entry barriers. With improvements in transportation, large publishers
were able to extend their reach, competing in hitherto inaccessible areas
against small local papers.[38]

As part of this change, multi-unit or "chain" publishers became dominant enterprises. In 1910, 13 firms operated 62 papers but by 1923, 31
firms controlled 153 dailies. The trend peaked in 1929 when 59 chains
controlled 325 journals, which accounted for 40 per cent of total daily
newspaper circulation. Scripps-Howard, the first major chain, had
secured control over twenty-five newspapers. William Randolph
Hearst owned six papers in 1904 but twenty-five years later owned
twenty-eight dailies, more than a dozen Sunday publications, a portfolio of magazines, and a newsreel company. By using the same copy
across multiple markets, the cost of news production could be lowered.
Multi-newspaper companies shared marketing, human resource management, and distribution costs. Their central offices negotiated advertising with clients hoping to reach mass audiences who demanded
significant rate concessions. Because chains tended to be regional rather
than national, they constituted oligopolies or monopolies within geographic markets. By the late 1920s, mass-circulation papers accounted
for nearly two-thirds of American consumption of newsprint. The two
biggest enterprises, Hearst and Scripps-Howard, were the largest consumers in the world. The Hearst group alone accounted for more than
a third of chain purchases.[39] Hearst and the other large publishers initially built their positions by selling penny (one-cent) papers. Over time
the firms sought any form of advantage that kept costs down or displaced competitors. Newsprint normally represented a fifth of production costs for newspapers but this rose to a third or more for those with
a daily circulation over 200,000. The big publishers bought up supply
from individual mills, which were pleased to have reliable business,

but the practice sometimes made newsprint unavailable or costly for smaller papers, triggering complaints about how the chains received discriminatory preference.[40] Although several publishers, like the *Chicago Tribune* via Ontario Paper, integrated backward to secure resources, most firms relied upon independent sales arrangements.

Publishers editorialized about the sanctity of market forces but they disingenuously characterized *any and all* attempts to stabilize (let alone raise) prices as anti-competitive conspiracies, as noxious threats to freedom of the press. It was a smear they endlessly disseminated from the 1880s to the 1960s. Producers had "virtually a monopoly over [the] present supply of newsprint manufacturing in the North American continent," they claimed during one congressional hearing. "Each time the price has soared to undreamed of heights, each time higher than the past." The "present operatives" controlled all economically viable sites and potential entrants would not risk the construction of new facilities without making careful estimates of consumption.[41] This perspective intensified as chain organizations displaced smaller newspapers within the American Newspaper Publishers' Association. It demanded retaliation against Canadian governments or producers whenever actions were perceived as inimical to American (that is, their own) interests. American politicians, fearful of offending the publishers, sycophantically catered to their concerns and ignored the reality that the chains (usually ruthless oligopolists within their own sector) were the main beneficiaries. Instead, they stressed a need for cheap newsprint to ensure a "free press," or the survival of small journals. Most historical accounts understate those activities and the siege mentality producers assumed against what they perceived as a politicization of their trade.[42]

The spike in prices after 1915 triggered disputes across the following six years that left publishers and manufacturers highly antagonistic towards each other. Wartime inflation propelled an initial confrontation. Strong demand, as we have seen, generated upward pressure on newsprint prices, but the labour cost of making paper also doubled between 1915 and 1918. Pulpwood became nearly 50 per cent more expensive, while other costs rose, such as freight shipments or commodities used during processing.[43] Some publishers responded by adopting a tabloid format that appealed to commuters but used less newsprint. Although each had alternative goals, small publishers, chains, and industry association representatives demanded investigations and the prosecution of papermakers for supposed anti-trust violations. Under intense pressure from American legislators in 1917, the Federal Trade Commission (FTC) was asked to substantiate the concerns. Its report was hardly an objective analysis. Indeed, the entire matter appears to have been pre-judged. The bulk of the evidence took the form of submissions from publishers or materials printed in their trade journal, *Editor and Publisher*. Although the commission claimed to have sought data about manufacturers, it sidestepped a proper review by arguing insufficient time, accounting variations, and problems with data collection made an assessment difficult. The report evaded a material analysis of manufacturing costs and instead proclaimed financial statements "as a rule, threw little light on this question because of inflations growing out of amalgamations, reorganizations, etc." Instead, the FTC advanced a fawning endorsement of the publishers' perspective. Higher prices and the shift to f.o.b. mill freight costs had cut newspaper profitability and "constitute an economic loss to the country as a whole, which will be found to be very considerable in amount."[44] The agency presented a complete fiction to legitimate its recommendations. A "paper famine" (which it accepted as fact rather than acknowledge how hoarding by publishers had driven events) originated from a diversion of one-third of Canadian production away from the United States, "artificially starving the domestic market." Therefore, for the public's welfare, all paper goods should be pooled and distributed by a government agency. The FTC had no authority to enforce any proposals and even before the report was released it sought "cooperation" from the Department of Justice, which filed indictments against various Canadian and American manufacturers, claiming they had engaged in illegal sales cooperation. Both governmental agencies had more important cases to deal with. Therefore, they accepted a plea deal, *nolo contendere*, where the defendants did not admit guilt but agreed not to contest the matter. The single firm that refused the deal was acquitted. In fact, the Canadian firms named in the suit accounted for less than a fifth of continental output and could not have directed competitive rivalry even if they wanted to. The settlement was reached with three understandings. The sales agencies of the producers agreed not to coordinate future marketing efforts. In exchange, only token fines were to be imposed and the FTC agreed to arbitrate a list rate acceptable to all parties. But public officials then welched. The Department of Justice, after renewed lobbying from the publishers, demanded another investigation. The FTC, staffed with personnel sympathetic to the publishers, imposed a list price that discriminated in their favour. The producers responded with a court appeal that triggered yet another set of adjudications. Eventually, they gained a victory that overturned the publishers' efforts to have the government dictate prices. Nonetheless, the FTC for decades thereafter ignored the understandings behind the plea deal and portrayed it as proof that the Canadian manufacturers had pursued anti-competitive behaviour. While all of this went on, American politicians launched their own "investigations" and passed resolutions demanding retaliation against Canadian firms or possible restrictions on pulpwood exports.[45]

Learning from these experiences, most Canadian firms thereafter declined to cooperate with enquiries by Congress or government agencies. The manufacturers, while espousing the need for harmonious seller-customer relations, never forgot the publishers' willingness to employ political intervention. George Chahoon believed the conflicts showed how American officials paid "political homage to the best organized Trust on earth." The "market for our products is in the hands of men who have been willing to use their great political influence in any direction in order to obtain their immediate requirement. In the past these men have made and remade tariffs in order to satisfy their selfish aims ... they are capable of making and remaking governments for the same purpose." A vice-president of International Paper went further. "Congress had gradually yielded to the clamors of the paid agents of the publishers." An "invidious treatment" of the producers ensued, who were "deprived of all protection and bedevilled by inspired Federal regulation and interference."[46] Over the next forty years newsprint served as a political football as American authorities tried to document inimical conduct. The investigations included multiple studies by the FTC, the Tariff Commission, and the US Forest Service, as well as forty-four sets of hearings by congressional committees.

But, despite allegations advanced by the publishers, was it ever possible for a giant firm or a cohesive group of producers to control competitive conditions? Was newsprint ever subject to "cartelization?" With the rise of managerial capitalism, mass manufacturing entailed the construction of giant enterprises that exploited economies of scale or scope. Studies later conducted by the American Paper and Pulp Association mapped significant economies of scale that propelled increases in mill and company size over time. Labour productivity also improved with plant size.[47] Some executives thus fantasized that price leadership or collusive behaviour was possible.[48] However, an analyst in 1927 observed that every effort to control competition failed. "The vitality and efficiency of independent producers ... have prevented large unwieldy consolidations or loose secret understandings from dominating the market for any time to the advantage of insiders and the corresponding disadvantage of the public."[49]

Many historians and economists have inferred that a tight oligopoly characterized the sector during the first half of the twentieth century.

the twentieth century and by 1910 they accounted for half of North American capacity. Another twenty-seven entered during the following decade and by 1920 that group accounted for half of total capacity. Twenty-nine mills started up during the 1920s and by 1930 they accounted for nearly 45 per cent of continental capacity. The operations of new producers, of course, were predicated upon future demand growth. The influx of entrants did not signal a displacement of the older manufacturers, but it diminished their potential to act as market leaders.

The newsprint sector was not just fragmented, it became more turbulent with each decade because recent arrivistes were unlikely to accede to any understandings amongst established firms about perceived market shares or their relationships with customers. New entrants as follower firms ran the risk of higher expenses (reflecting the need to build markets and acquire intangible knowledge) and therefore could incur lower profits versus existing firms. However, the ratio of capital to output was high, and by the late 1920s, the proportion of fixed to total costs in newsprint production became twice the norm for manufacturing industries. Profits hence were earned primarily on the final increments of capacity, which meant all firms tried to operate mills at high rates. Assertive entrants and existing firms that expanded operations sought to pre-sell output before new facilities began production, even if this meant offering rate concessions to garner business. The need to achieve scale economies propelled firms to sustain operations rather than reduce or close mills if they could cover variable costs and at least part of the fixed costs. As we will see in the next two chapters, this pattern characterized most entrants, who rejected proposals for cutbacks that put their investments at risk. The issue was first highlighted during the recession of the early 1920s, which Philip Dodge of International Paper, decried as "the most critical, the most difficult period" in the industry's history. In terms later applied to his own company, Dodge blamed the entrants who showed "we have in our ranks a large number of cowardly and selfish men!" Some mills ran near 60 per cent of capacity, while others ran their normal maximum. It was due to "the selfishness of the people in our own ranks, that we are in this trouble. Gentlemen with a mistaken shortsighted view, not looking to the future, not considering the ultimate effect of what they are doing, rushed into the market and were willing to accept almost any price that would fill their mills to capacity."[55]

The sustained entry of new firms eviscerated the ability of any single company or group of producers to exercise leadership. A common indicator in economics used to gauge the likelihood of collusive behaviour or above-average profits is the concentration ratio – the combined market share of the top four firms (CR4). If this rate is below 50 per cent, an industrial structure is deemed "unconcentrated" and usually cannot even be characterized as a "loose" oligopoly. Under those conditions, even if firms try to cooperate, there are just too many players and some find it worthwhile to "cheat," wrecking any efforts to maintain price-setting or competitive understandings.[56] Appendix 2.6 illustrates the patterns of concentration from 1890 to 1940. The data indicate that a case can be made that the threshold for a concentrated structure within the United States was exceeded before the introduction of free trade, but not after. Historians who have perceived the Canadian producers as an oligopolistic group have based their interpretation upon the shares of domestic output. It is true that the top four companies by that gauge might be considered a concentrated group. But this is bogus if appraised at the continental level. Appendix 2.6 shows that even as the significance of the Canadian sector waxed the four largest firms remained below the relevant threshold. Especially if appraised from a cross-border perspective, the largest firms operating from Canada fell short of any accepted gauge of oligopolistic confederacy.

Appendices 2.7 and 2.8 take the analysis to a final stage by mapping the patterns of market shares for individual factories. In many ways, this was a crucial measure because companies, including those with multiple plants, had to operate each near full capacity to achieve scale economies. From 1890 to 1910 the market shares for individual mills were extremely fragmented. Across the following three decades, though factory size did increase, the influx of new firms meant the market shares of individual plants remained low. No Canadian mill exceeded a 5 per cent share of North American capacity, and the tendency to rise even to this level only occurred when mill size exceeded 400 tons of daily output. If production was pre-sold, a moderate-sized mill (in the 200- to 250-ton range) could be quite efficient and hold a secure position. Not only are high barriers to entry necessary for an oligopoly to emerge, but there must be relative stability in the composition of firms and their market shares for collusive behaviour to succeed. The tables in Appendix 2 demonstrate how the claims that a "monopoly" existed were silly. The industry structure did evolve towards greater concentration but by the late 1920s this still hovered well below the level where collusive behaviour might succeed.[57]

A grand legend has been International Paper's alleged status as a "dominant" firm. The company was organized in 1898 through a combination of companies from New England and New York. The amalgamation, like others during the first merger wave in the United States, was intended to bring stability and end price competition. Although International was the largest producer and therefore for two decades served as the key price-pacer, the strategy never worked because it did not hold a serious cost advantage. Within two years experts realized the firm could not achieve the promised post-merger economies. The cost of manufacturing actually rose after consolidation. Many of the mills, located on exhausted watercourses near denuded forests, were practically worthless.[58] Moreover, entrants (some, like the Great Northern Paper Company of Maine, which constructed gigantic facilities) soon eroded the company's position and intensified price rivalry. International accounted for about 60 per cent of American newsprint production in 1901, but this decreased to 30 per cent by 1911 and to 18 per cent during 1922. More significant was its deteriorating share of newsprint sold in the United States, which dropped to 11 per cent. With only low profits earned from the commodity, International diversified into alternative paper goods. By 1922, more than half of the company's earnings were derived from products other than newsprint. International produced less newsprint than its two largest American rivals, Great Northern and Crown-Williamette Pulp and Paper. By spreading itself over alternative types of goods during the 1910s, International forfeited any realistic possibility of governing newsprint supply. The company tried to regain its status by improving mill productivity, increasing exports, and organizing an informal cartel – none of which worked. By the early 1920s it held a portfolio of old inefficient mills.[59] The average cost of newsprint production, approximately $75 per ton, was significantly higher than many of International's rivals. With the depletion of its American timber reserves, the company had to buy pulpwood in the open market. A researcher during the 1920s described International as "a good example of those numerous trusts which have failed signally to triumph from the alleged economies of combination." Based upon an analysis of its earnings, another described the firm as marginal or "limping," with brief periods of sustained results offset by lengthy passages of weak profits or significant losses.[60] Still, International remained the largest American paper-maker. This led publishers, politicians, and the FTC to stereotype the enterprise as a "paper trust." Although the firm was repetitiously targeted during investigations of alleged anti-competitive conduct, none uncovered sufficient evidence for legal action.

International inherited timber plants in Quebec from its predecessor firms and press accounts assumed it would construct a paper mill, ideas the corporate managers quickly dismissed. The firm also secured more than 4 million acres of pulpwood either as speculative holdings or to exclude them from competitors. Across the first two decades of the twentieth century, it bought pulpwood cut by settlers for export but refused to establish local mills. Following the removal of tariff barriers, International claimed the danger from Canadian rivals was "overestimated" and once transport costs were considered "the Canadians will be hardly in a position to undersell us." But this position was soon reversed and for more than a decade International tried to overturn free trade. The loss of tariff protection, President Philip Dodge insisted, was "oppressive and unfair."[61] Compounding the situation, Quebec instituted constraints on pulpwood shipments to International's American mills. The firm attempted to mitigate the threat by promising to construct a plant at Trois-Rivières but stalled until 1920 when it received additional tax concessions.[62] The producer, nonetheless, was a hobbled giant plagued by labour disruptions, declining newsprint output, and serious losses. International was to play a key role in the cataclysm that engulfed the sector but did so as a firm trying to rebuild competitive position, *not* as a dominant enterprise.

A further layer of complexity was added as manufacturing activities were reconfigured in ways that altered the economics of the industry. During 1910, although thirty-eight mills operated in Canada, only twelve made newsprint with a total output of 540 tons per day. Most were unspecialized operations, newsprint was just one of several types of paper manufactured. Plants typically turned out eighty tons or less daily by using one or two machines with widths that ranged from 86 to 120 inches.[63] Though located close to timber stands the factories still incurred significant costs for the arrangement of wood stocks. The siting and size of the mills also were conditional upon the availability of local means for the generation of electricity. Steam plants were quite small, ranging from 10 to 5,000 horsepower, and alternative sources sometimes powered the different operations within a mill. With little information available about various processes or the requirements for achieving consistent pulp mixes, output was prone to many defects: slime spots, crush marks, dandy blisters, bubble or blow marks, blemishes, lumps, pinholes, and thin streaks. A lack of objective testing techniques and problems with paper machines themselves meant that even a standardized pulp mix could not guarantee a satisfactory end product. Quality control, therefore, was dependent upon mill superintendents and workers who worked by rule of thumb or experience, with jealously guarded knowledge derived from years of apprenticeship and employment. Self-contained units or separate buildings often housed different operations to isolate problems during production, minimize disputes among personnel, and protect the expertise of never made money on the transactions but this was nonsense. The profit opportunities were enormous. Investment bankers reaped commissions from purchases of securities, gained from the spread between offer prices vis-à-vis the minimum levels specified by firms, and often received securities for later sale if the companies prospered. To reassure clients underwriters adopted the same tactic as Peabody Houghteling with Abitibi. They characterized newsprint companies as analogous to hydroelectric enterprises, an assertion that resonated with investors because some firms had electric-power subsidiaries. Many were listed in newspapers and Moody's *Survey of Industrials* as "utilities" with stable earnings.

Then there were the buyers. The investing public, the *Financial Post* noted during 1921, looked at newsprint through "rose-colored glasses" but it believed there was legitimate need for the "heavy financing." Royal Securities argued the market worth of new securities was not generated by investor enthusiasm but from popular appreciation of the companies' greater worth. Quotations on stock exchanges, it contended, did not discount the ultimate values, although they supposedly would be much higher in the future. Others perceived troubling hazards. Investors, *Pulp and Paper Magazine* contended in one of its jeremiads, did not care for the use of pulp and paper securities as "mere gambling counters," where prices were put up without regard to intrinsic value. Most funds were raised for legitimate purposes, it acknowledged, but speculation triggered "periodic and violent see-sawing of values." Long-term prosperity meant investors should not become "the football of Stock Exchange gamblers, whose only aim is to make money out of the rise or fall of shares."[69] "The trade welcomes the constructive investor; it resents the destructive gambler." When a periodic slump occurred, it argued, investors were inclined to attribute the ensuing collapse of security prices to manipulation by the companies' managers or directors.[70] The Investment Bankers' Association of America acknowledged the industry had risks like periods of excess capacity and price-cutting that might lead to "in the end, a survival of the fittest." However, it argued, there were plenty of executives capable of meeting adverse conditions and their past successes assured investors about the safety of their stakes.[71]

Large Canadian-controlled life assurance companies represented the key market for newsprint securities, which legitimated them to other investors. The amount of life insurance issued grew from $267.2 million in 1900 to $3.98 billion by 1930, while the total annual income of the issuers increased from $13.5 million to $177.2 million. The revenues of additional business initially added little to the surplus of an insurance company, which provided returns for policyholders or shareholders. New business also generated liabilities in the form of policy claims and regulatory obligations for additional reserves. Life insurance firms traditionally had placed their capital in real estate, municipal bonds, or loans, investments that appreciated slowly. Because the portfolios comprised a host of small or short-term transactions with significant administrative costs, the managers sought larger and more reliable sources of income. As regulatory policies eased after 1910, they shifted towards investments among railway, public utility, and government securities. Public officials then allowed the purchase of industrial bonds, along with preferred shares if dividends were paid for at least five years. Common shares could be added if a 4 per cent dividend rate or outlays of $500,000 were maintained for seven years.[72]

By the close of the First World War, it was apparent that interest rates would decline, a trend that also would generate an appreciation in the values of bond holdings, permitting the reinvestment of enormous profits and a diversification into corporate offerings.[73] Sun Life Assurance took the most aggressive stance. "We have enlisted many large groups of the brainiest, [the] most experienced men on the continent to work for us to maintain our interest earnings," President Thomas Macaulay declared. "We get their co-operation by becoming stockholders in the outstanding basic corporations they direct, so that we share in all the profits they make." A firm's securities were acquired if the earnings "make it almost a foregone conclusion" that the securities would significantly increase in value. Though Macaulay claimed the firm was cautious, he noted the policy also assumed a long-term retention of securities, "regardless of market fluctuations; looking for our profit not on the stock exchange but in the steady growth and gradually increasing prosperity of the corporation."[74] Representatives of Sun Life claimed large firms had to offer new stock regularly. Established investors could purchase the securities at prices well under the anticipated market values. In addition to annual financial statements, one officer noted in defence of the policy, "there are other important avenues through which desired information can be elicited" such as "the confidences extended to the Company by virtue of its position and reputation in the investment field." By 1928 public utility, railroad, and industrial securities accounted for 55 per cent of Sun Life's assets, and nearly half of that portfolio was placed in common stocks.[75]

Other insurance companies did not immediately replicate this strategy due to the recession of the early 1920s and because several of Sun Life's holdings (like Riordon) went bust. But the approach seemed to be legitimated as returns and dividends increased. Mutual Life of obligations grew by 79 per cent.[81] These fixed charges exacerbated the susceptibility of the companies but it would be baloney to suggest the rates charged were excessive. The cost of capital always is industry specific. Notwithstanding marketing promotions that forest firms were akin to public utilities, neither investment bankers nor rating agencies were ever fooled. Sales of power constituted a minute portion of company revenues. The average cost of capital for pulp and paper producers was 6 per cent before the First World War and it remained in that vicinity across the 1920s. Interest and preferred dividend charges ranged from 5 to 8 per cent per annum, depending on the priority and riskiness associated with specific securities. In contrast, electrical power companies consistently incurred lower rates.

Observers later suggested a greater reliance should have been placed upon common stock, but the Canadian market would not absorb huge equity issues. Although directors and underwriters recognized that leverage (in an upward financial market) could enhance price–earnings ratios, there is no evidence that the potential for the reverse was appreciated.[82] Recent scholarly investigations have also documented several behavioural issues that likely shaped managerial conduct. Finance specialists tend to presume the policy choices by corporations are made independently of other companies, that is, that managers focus upon the implications for their own firms when defining capital structures. However, executives lack knowledge about what constitutes an "optimal" scheme of capitalization. They consequently consider the financial structures or apparent health of "peer" firms as information. Both practices can generate a replication effect.[83] Individuals also tend to overestimate their ability to control outcomes, which can lead to unrealistic assessments.[84] Overconfident managers, for example, who believe that their firms are undervalued in markets, view external financing as overpriced, especially when equity capital is involved. They therefore pursue a pecking order of internal financing over debt and debt over equity.[85]

In Canada, to a greater degree than in the United States, bonds and preferred stock remained the *sine qua non* for prudent investors because they were secured by mortgage deeds. Common stocks were considered speculative securities, *caveat emptor*. Nor were investors well served by reports in business publications, which comprised verbatim summaries of financial statements. Press analyses rarely went beyond simple gauges like the current ratio, earnings per common share, or whether a nominal profit had (or had not) been earned. Given the levels of debt and the newsprint prices that prevailed before 1925, many observers believed the producers could meet their obligations based upon ratios like return on assets or times-interest earned. Moreover, they assumed company statements reasonably reflected earnings or the value of assets. In fact, all firms had reporting policies that were dubious, even if judged by the weak standards of the times, which delayed the dissemination of information about the potential for trouble.

This issue can be traced to deficiencies in Canadian law. Following British practice, a firm's directors served as guardians of shareholder interests, but they were legally defined as servants of a company. Canadian statutes mandated them to maintain true accounts, establish policies for the inspection of records, and release annually a balance sheet and a statement of profit and loss. Shareholders had no rights to inspect books or records. The "privilege" of inspection was confined to cases where an individual had a definite object in view and the documents could be expected to substantiate the concern. Neither Canadian law nor the courts took account of the conflicts of interest that might arise when company directors were *de facto* managers, promoters, or financiers. Whereas investors were inclined to emphasize the stability or growth of earnings from their holdings, the manager-directors often were more concerned with opportunistic objectives like empire-building or gains from sales of securities.

Statutory law emphasized the maintenance of records about ownership stakes, not the accuracy of financial statements or the protection of investors. Before 1917 the Dominion Companies Act did not even order a firm to hold an annual meeting. Ontario's company law stipulated an annual meeting, as well as the submission of an abstract of a firm's financial status. The balance sheet merely had to disclose several categories: cash, debts owing to a firm, stock in trade, capital expenditures, short-term and long-term debt, amounts owing on equity issues, and indirect or contingent liabilities. Neither the federal nor Quebec statutes stipulated regular audits, whereas Ontario's bill mandated the appointment of auditors either at an annual meeting or upon an application to the provincial secretary. The legislation thus facilitated lax reporting. As a manual for the Bank of Nova Scotia observed, "character, capacity and capital and it would appear precisely in that order" were expected to guide financial affairs.[86]

An auditor symbolically acted as the shareholders' representative during an audit.[87] But even if knowledge of potential misconduct was garnered, the officer was not obligated to notify the shareholders.[88] As the judge in a widely cited case remarked,

> An auditor is not bound to be a detective, or ... to approach his work with suspicion or with a foregone conclusion that there is something wrong.

He is a watch-dog but not a bloodhound. He is justified in believing tried
servants in whom confidence is placed by the company. He is entitled to
assume that they are honest and to rely upon their representations, provided he takes reasonable care. It is not the duty of an auditor to take
stock; he is not a stock expert; there are many matters in respect of which
he must rely on the honesty and accuracy of others. He does not guarantee
the honesty of all fraud.[89]

In another oft-cited case, it was claimed the auditor "has nothing to
do with the prudence or imprudence of making loans with or without
security. It is nothing to him whether the business of the company is conducted prudently or imprudently, profitably or unprofitably. It is nothing to him whether dividends are properly or improperly declared."[90]

Neither federal nor provincial legislation required the officer to warrant the declared value of properties, securities, or book debts. An auditor's responsibility was defined as an arithmetic verification of whether
financial statements *appeared* to reflect a true state of affairs. The individual was not responsible for matters of judgment, which were
deemed in the provenance of the directors. If entries were clearly
absurd, then the figures could be questioned, but the courts circum-
scribed an auditor from speculating to investors. It was not enough to
report that the documents might not exhibit a correct view; the examiner had to show where entries were manifestly wrong. In one prominent case, the judge noted: "an auditor who gives the shareholders
means of information instead of information respecting a company's
financial position does so at his peril and runs a very serious risk of
being held judicially to have failed to discharge his duty."[91] Lower
courts in Canada began to shift away from this perspective in the interwar era, but the enforcement of review protocols was anemic at best.[92]
Audits were not subject to regulatory oversight but rested upon a presumption that the examiners would be guided by the norms of their
self-governing profession or a concern for their personal reputations.
Prosecutions for malfeasance were rare, in part because directors were
designated as responsible under statutory law when patently false
information was circulated. If arguable values were attached, an auditor was not expected to protest too much. This, of course, left great
room for parboiling the books.

The institutional barriers to information disclosure were compounded by the acceptance of the "proprietary theory" of accounting.
Supporters of this perspective drew upon economic theory and argued
the function of a firm was to maximize shareholder wealth. They minimized the importance of retained earnings and stressed the supply of

data that enabled investors to calculate the dividends available for distribution. Proprietary theory thus emphasized balance-sheet presentations (with the measurement of assets, liabilities, and equities) as overviews of liquidity and solvency. Although the "entity theory" of accounting (which stressed income statements and data about ongoing flows of revenues and costs) emerged as a competing school, it was rarely employed in Canada before the 1940s. Standard references like the *Annual Financial Review* replicated corporate balance sheets, and the coverage of operating results was selective and inconsistent. Many Canadian firms refused to report even summary data about sales (let alone breakouts of costs) on grounds of confidentiality.[93]

Large manufacturers published consolidated statements. The documents typically comprised four or five pages, without notes or explanations, along with a terse narrative about the ability to meet liabilities or dividends. The concept of consolidated accounting gained acceptance in North America during the early twentieth century but it was devoid of accepted criteria. Neither the American Institute of Accountants nor its Canadian counterpart drew up principles to guide company actions.[94] In Britain during the 1920s, consolidated statements were not viewed as the primary reports of a company, nor were they considered to reflect a single economic unit. If viewed critically from a legal perspective, the records supplied data about a fictitious structure, a corporate group comprising a parent firm and subsidiaries or controlled affiliates.[95] In Canada, as in the United States, there was a tendency to assume that the property of a large enterprise did not exist in a traditional sense but, rather, took the form of an integrated unit of facilities, equipment, and personnel. A merger or amalgamation was considered the formation of a new and legally distinct company.[96] Concurrently, executives claimed consolidated statements were more representative portraits of the true scope of modern business.

Consolidated accounting enhanced the potential for illusory presentations or outright chicanery by obscuring debt-to-asset coverage or the performance of particular operations. The technique mattered because it allowed the camouflage of discrepancies between the probable value of assets and the prices paid during acquisitions. Bonds and preferred stock supposedly were secured by tangible assets. Inflated prices not only could generate excessive leverage but might also mean that a firm had insufficient earnings capacity relative to its obligations. In addition, big enterprises often retained a portfolio of business activities: paper mills with different productivity rates or operating ratios, pulp mills, hydroelectric systems, railways, and property improvement enterprises or retail outlets. Indeed, when the companies later were activities like retailing. Nearly half took the form of horizontal integration, that is, they occurred between firms making similar goods. In some cases, the competitive framework was altered towards oligopolistic structures.[2] Contemporaries perceived this phenomenon as understandable, given the rise of mass production, but many found it troubling. "It is inevitable that one or two big corporations should control an industry," an article in Collier's declared. "The place for the small fellow is not in the production of staples but in the specialties which demand craftsmanship and in which prices do not so much count."[3] Newsprint represented a lesser element within the merger wave but the changes wrought after 1924 were significant. The Eastern Canadian component was transformed from a structure characterized by small or medium-sized companies with single mills to a more concentrated setting that included four corporate groups with multiple factories.

Experts advanced numerous rationales: the need to achieve economies of scale and scope, the ability to capture synergistic gains and lower costs, needs for augmented resources to meet changing strategic demands, the desire to "rationalize" competition, and the pursuit of greater size or market share for its own sake.[4] Each of these justifications surfaced among the newsprint mergers but when examined historically the amalgamations grew from tangled roots and were predicated upon arguable logic. This chapter examines those developments. The first section considers how Abitibi responded during the postwar spike in newsprint prices and the recession that followed. It appraises the transition to a new presidency, along with a shift in strategic orientation. The chapter then reviews the evolution of several enterprises that became components of the Abitibi empire. The fourth section appraises the culmination of those initiatives: the 1927 merger with Spanish River Pulp and Paper. The final section examines the refinancing that followed and its implications. Throughout this chapter an emphasis is given to financial and accounting issues because everything always, *always*, **always** came down to the money. That is true whenever mergers and acquisitions occur.

1. A romance of Canadian industrialization

A Maclean's article, "Everybody's Doing It," highlighted how Canadians gained experience buying wartime bonds and, therefore, it was "a logical step" to seek larger returns than fixed-income investments could provide. The reporter described how a Toronto broker owned forty-three shares of Abitibi common stock, which he unloaded in January 1919 for $50 per share or $2,150 "and considered himself lucky." Two days later the stock price began to soar. By Christmas, it reached a level that would have netted him an additional $12,350 (more than six times an average person's annual income). One Canadian and one American, "each of whom has an international reputation in the financial world," were believed to possess 60 per cent of Abitibi's common equity and had not traded their shares during the year, providing them with a theoretical gain of $6.6 million.[5] A "runaway action," Abitibi stock rose to $355 per common share by the spring of 1920. The company paid a 30 per cent dividend, a return previously deemed impossible. With the high profits, investors thought the stock might split two for one but the directors chose a five to one division, raising the nominal value of the firm's equity from $5 million to $25 million. This move also involved a conversion from a par value of $100 per share to no par value. One paper acknowledged how the change appealed to investors precisely because it enhanced "the speculative element." Other press outlets rationalized the split by describing Abitibi's capitalization as low relative to other firms. Companies like Price Brothers and Laurentide soon followed and gave investors huge windfall returns. *Pulp and Paper Magazine* rationalized those actions, noting the firms earlier had struggled to prevent the seizure of assets and did so "solely by the unwillingness of the creditors to take them over and incur the risks and responsibilities of management."[6]

Anson decided to take advantage of the restructuring and double the capacity at Iroquois Falls to 500 tons per day. The company, he announced, would buy the widest machines available so it became the biggest producer in the world.[7] However, the onset of recession delayed the initiative and cash flow problems forced a suspension of common dividends within eighteen months. The common stock that traded at $87 after the split collapsed to $21.50 per share. Reversing its perspective, the *Financial Post* accused the managers of "rosy prognostications" and "bright colorings." "The average investor doesn't like to be fooled; and he feels the spokesmen for Abitibi have fooled him." The *Globe* portrayed the development as one of the "fruits of enthusiasm" because investors had disregarded "intrinsic values." Other observers described the split as excessive but claimed satisfactory earnings would later occur. "It is the invariable experience that whenever a setback occurs ... that group or those individual stocks that have most lately had a rise are the first to slump, and usually show the most serious effect of the downward movement." Profit margins had never been high but problems were unlikely because newsprint did not experience the price declines of other commodities.[8] *Pulp and Paper Magazine*, engaging in its own sophistries, claimed any problems originated from how the *Globe* while he also served as a manager for the Artificial Silk Company of Philadelphia. In 1905 Mead, in conjunction with his father-in-law, Henry E. Talbott, secured funding for a reorganization of the business into the Mead Pulp and Paper Company. From the beginning he emphasized a strategy geared to volume production with consistent quality. Mead took control of marketing, eliminated jobber operations, and created one of the foremost agencies for paper sales. He served as vice-president and treasurer until 1912 when he was appointed president. Across the next decade Mead continued to direct the firm, but he was drawn into a web of Canadian relationships.[16]

During a voyage to Britain during 1898, Mead's aunt, Katharine Houk Talbott, sang at several concerts aboard the ship. Impressed by her voice, Francis H. Clergue, the mercurial entrepreneur who was establishing industrial facilities at Sault Ste. Marie, met her acquaintance and learned her husband operated an engineering firm. The following year Clergue contracted with the H.E. Talbott Company to build a railroad to iron mines north of the Sault, along with new steel mills.[17] As part of his empire-building, forest concessions were secured for the supply of a pulp factory, the first in New Ontario. Clergue, whose pomposity always was greater than his competence, told visitors it was "the largest in the world, managed with wonderful skill for an enormously wealthy syndicate of American capitalists" with sufficient orders to operate indefinitely. Never a shining beacon about the potential for forest industries, the mill encountered serious difficulties garnering sales, an issue not disclosed even though Clergue expanded the facility.[18] It represented the first of his speculative ventures, which devolved into an obsessive effort to build a steel factory at Algoma. The stone buildings of the paper mill served as attractive props as he tried to garner support for the grander enterprise.

The firm was required to invest only $400,000 for the mill and give work to 400 employees, much smaller commitments than other ventures approved by the Liberal government. The cost of production was projected at $25 per ton versus an expected market price of $30, but pulp prices collapsed from $100 to $8 per ton between 1895 and 1899. Clergue's larger "Soo Bubble" inevitably burst in 1903, ending, as one newspaper smirked, "the most extraordinary example of mushroom financing the country has seen in recent years." Beginning with the pulp operation, "millions of dollars have been wasted in an attempt to create an industrial universe in little more than the Almighty, according to Moses, spent in creating the world." It came as no surprise that the Sault Ste. Marie Pulp and Paper Company also had heavy losses.[19] It was put up for sale and was bought by

Figure 2 Predecessor Companies of Abitibi Power and Paper

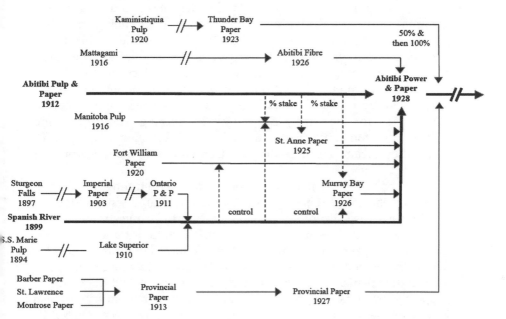

American businessmen who claimed profits from the mill were assured once it returned to "well-tried methods," but the woods operations remained closed for two years. The downfall of Clergue's conglomerate triggered riots by unpaid workers, forced the imposition of martial law, and compelled the province to intervene and ensure the creditors received payment. Desperate to resuscitate the larger Algoma project, Ontario guaranteed $2 million of bonds floated by the reorganized company, a bailout portrayed by supporters as a commitment to the progress of New Ontario and denounced by critics as a "payment out of public funds of the princely salaries of Soo officials" by a party trying to avoid electoral defeat. Once reopened, the pulp mill struggled, was reoriented towards making tarpaper and then damaged by two fires.[20]

In a *coup de main*, a syndicate of English financiers gained control over the paper enterprise during 1909. When reciprocity negotiations raised the prospect of free trade between Canada and the United States, they approached Talbott about his American connections through which the output of a new factory might be sold. A $1 million scheme to rebuild the plant was traduced in favour of an $8 million up-to-date facility. The promoters wangled a land concession and a twenty-year exemption from municipal taxes in exchange for doubling the mill's size.[21] Talbott's company took a larger stake in the venture when tentative understandings with American publishers unravelled. The enterprise was separated from the Algoma project and incorporated as the Lake Superior Paper Corporation with Talbott as president and George Mead as vice-president.[22] Mead later admitted he became involved to raise capital for the family company.[23] Everything was progressing well, the investors could operate the mill or reap a profit by selling it off – except they became ensnarled in the machinations of merger promoter Garnet P. Grant.

The financier had gained prominence by orchestrating amalgamations such as Tuckett Tobacco, Canadian Canners, and Canada Machinery. In each case, Dominion Bond, his Montreal investment house, floated new securities in British markets, with Grant and associates then collecting substantial profits.[24] As the removal of tariff barriers for newsprint loomed, the promoter decided to construct a large enterprise around the Spanish River Pulp and Paper Company.[25] Of the ventures supported by Ontario's government at the turn of the century, Spanish River was the only one that could be considered a true success, but its founding was controversial. The head of the company, W.J. Sheppard, was considered "a man of eminent standing in the business world": a director of the Trusts & Guarantee Company, a director (and later vice-president) of the Traders' Bank of Canada, and the president of Georgian Bay Lumber. However, the investors included a coterie of lumbermen and well-known Liberals. They gained rights to a 15,540-square-kilometre tract near Espanola north of Georgian Bay in exchange for minimal obligations – a mill with a twenty-ton daily capacity. One promoter flipped his stake, amounting to a thirtieth of the tract (which had cost him nothing) for $10,000, and the Tories, who considered the scheme just the latest "principality of pulp," declared $300,000 in public wealth was lost by a wasteful government. The investors expected to have the factory operational within fifteen months but only raised $400,000 through a preferred share issue that offered a bonus of three common shares "fully paid" for every two preferred. A cooperative government extended the licence until they garnered sufficient funds for completion.[26] By 1906 the firm operated an efficient, well-designed pulp mill with a 120-ton daily capacity, which led the pro-Liberal *Globe* to praise the "great industry" at Espanola as one whose success was assured "by reason of the foresight and sagacity of its promoters."[27] Sheppard and his associates, however, considered it secondary to their lumbering activities. They negotiated a sale to a Wisconsin syndicate, which walked away from the deal alleging the properties were falsely represented. The mill generated modest earnings and in 1910 they arranged a purchase by the Montreal promoter.[28]

Though most of the original directors remained after the takeover, Grant and his associates took over the board in stages. He insisted Spanish River's annual profit could be decupled by expanding operations. The authorized capitalization was tripled and by 1913 the declared worth of the assets grew from $2.5 million to $13.6 million. While this included outlays on plants and equipment, it was accomplished largely by revaluing the timber limits, which generated an image that the properties were sufficient to finance bonds and maintain a worth of $107.50 for each $100 preference share.[29] Grant then acquired the defunct Sturgeon Falls mill in a distress sale. Retitled Ontario Pulp and Paper, its assets were boosted to $1.4 million and then $2.5 million. New capacity was promised upon a sale of bonds that offered a 25 per cent bonus of common stock and interest. Grant noted how further debt could be issued only up to three-quarters of the worth of any new assets, but he assured clients the financing was prudent because the issues of debt and equity were well below the grandiose levels authorized by a compliant board.[30]

Grant, with others, became the centre of the first Canadian boom in pulp and paper securities. "Up to a year or two ago there was only one paper company listed [Laurentide, on the Montreal exchange] and its securities were quoted at long intervals," a reporter noted. Investors traditionally would not touch the stocks of most producers, but this perspective changed as new mills were completed to benefit from continental free trade.[31] A sudden spike in the stock prices for Spanish River during June 1913 portended the climax of Grant's manoeuvres: a merger with Lake Superior Paper. The deal entailed expanding the equity from $8 million to more than $20 million, thereby making Spanish River the biggest paper manufacturer and the third largest company in Canada. Lake Superior shareholders were to receive instalment payments and a stock bonus that added 25 per cent to the value of their holdings, while the amalgamated firm guaranteed Lake Superior's bonds. Men loyal to Grant would assume all top management positions.[32]

Grant confused prior luck with wisdom. This time his appetite for profit choked him. The proposals to raise Spanish River's capitalization and distribute a stock bonus were greeted sceptically. The business press, especially the *Monetary Times*, questioned the affairs of the "merger genius" and other speculators. "The results of many of the

leaving little for new plant and equipment, a policy that also ensured Mead recouped his stake.

Mead contended the opportunity was open to the Canadian industry "very largely to control the markets of the world," but he never overcame a crucial weakness: the firm's resource rights.[41] Each autumn, at the shareholders' meeting, he insisted there was an adequate supply of timber for thirty years, an assertion that fell far short of the truth. The Conservatives believed Spanish River's original concession was an example of fraudulent craftiness by their predecessors. Premier Whitney always characterized the grant as excessive. Like Anson, Mead approached Howard Ferguson for gaining additional properties but his enquiry turned into a calamity. If the minister's letter to Anson during 1919 appeared supportive, his response to Mead, written less than a month before the provincial election, was gushing. The government, Ferguson, wrote, recognized that Spanish River had made large investments and it was desirable therefore to provide "stability by insuring it as nearly as possible an ample supply of raw material. That is the general policy of the Government with respect to such industries ... there would seem to be no doubt but that your present supply of wood is sufficient to meet your requirements only for a very few years." He appreciated the reluctance to make further expenditures without additional lands. "There can be no doubt that industries such as yours can be more economically and efficiently conducted on the basis of large units, and it is in the best interests of the Province as a whole that a reasonable number of large mills should be maintained, rather than a large number of small mills, which mean an increase of overhead and operating expenses, and shorter life to the industry." Ferguson promised to reserve a 13,000-square-kilometre tract. Even when the Tories lost power, he declared that "the proposition is such a sound business one." No doubt his successor would take the "same interest, and pride, as I have done in encouraging the growth of such an excellent and beneficial enterprise as yours."[42]

The correspondence, Ferguson's secretary later claimed, disappeared "inadvertently" after the minister left office but when a royal commission began an investigation it mysteriously surfaced in a basket on a clerk's desk. During the hearings ministry officials testified about how Spanish River was a "nuisance" that made endless complaints about its shortage of wood, but perceptions of corrupt dealings mounted as some witnesses proved conveniently forgetful or replied to questions about campaign contributions from the firm with circuitous answers like "Not to my knowledge" and "None that I have any idea of." Others argued Spanish River had more than sufficient timber for all time. The commission decided a land grant had not occurred and the new government should deal with the matter as it saw fit.[43] The revelations nearly destroyed Ferguson's career, but he reversed the situation by portraying himself as a victim of the investigation and a wily George Mead. Ferguson crowed, while campaigning in 1923, about how an unsophisticated Farmer's government eventually "gave away" to Spanish River the lands it had sought four years earlier. In fact, Drury's administration believed Ferguson had created a legal fait accompli, but waited until the end of its term to approve the concession. Even then it imposed tough restrictions. The agreement stressed how the lease originated from Ferguson's pledge but the government cut the territory, split the lands into sections that made exploitation difficult, left all fees subject to change, and limited the deal to twenty-one years without a renewal. Having attacked Spanish River's dealings publicly, it was never realistic that Ferguson might flip-flop back into support. Throughout the balance of his career he opposed most of Mead's requests. Even when grants were allocated he introduced conditions that weakened their value.[44]

A generation later, Ferguson insisted acceptable terms would have been worked out. "How are you going to get people to have faith in the Province and invest their money if after a little you are going to allow them to be wiped out without any consideration at all." There was an unwritten law that a timber licence would be renewed, "it has been the practice for years." This was utter nonsense as he repeatedly favoured small politically connected lumbermen over Spanish River. By 1928, although several of its concessions neared expiration and were logged out, the province declined to deal with the issue.[45] Mead's efforts to gain adjustments went nowhere. The concessions for Espanola and Sturgeon Falls had clauses that allowed the government to allocate wood for other enterprises, thereby limiting the resources available for his mills. Ferguson's government not only refused to remove the constraints, but falsely asserted (despite its loss of the original documentation) the lands were much smaller in size than indicated by the agreements (which could enhance the province's ability to divert timber).[46] The spruce for the Sault Ste. Marie mill was spread over a large territory and could only meet half of its requirements. Lake Superior Paper had successfully negotiated cutting rights with the Algoma Central and Hudson Bay Railway, which had reserves along its route that could solve this difficulty, but Ferguson blocked this option.[47] The proposal was revived during the 1920s and attracted support from ministry officials but once again the government rejected it, without explanation.[48] Mead twice proposed to create a mill near Sault Ste.

Marie, which could manufacture bleached sulphite pulp. Canadian companies had not made the commodity and the production process used wood previously deemed worthless. A new electrical complex also would supply Espanola and Sturgeon Falls. The government failed to proceed with the requests, again without official explanation. However, while ministry staff did not perceive problems, Ontario Hydro likely challenged the second enquiry. It had started to focus upon the north and planned an integration of valuable water sites into a scheme controlled by the province.[49]

Meanwhile Spanish River was drawn into a growing nexus with Abitibi and Alexander Smith. In 1916 the firm authorized Mead's agency to handle its American sales, while Anson retained control over Canadian marketing activities. The arrangement meant that by 1920 nearly 30 per cent of Canadian newsprint exports passed through Mead's firm.[50] Meanwhile, wartime conditions accelerated the reorientation of American and Canadian resource companies from British markets and towards American capital. Royal Securities and Peabody Houghteling became major financiers for the paper manufacturers. Both firms were enlisted between 1919 and 1921 to sell securities that allowed an expansion of Spanish River's capacity to 670 tons daily.[51] On the basis of Ferguson's letter discussed above, Peabody Houghteling agreed to underwrite $3.5 million of bonds. It conceded to investors that in 1915 Spanish River's "saleable output was entirely too small to support its capitalization on the basis of earnings" but legitimated the securities because the firm had "'natural advantages," which included "a practically inexhaustible supply of pulpwood immediately available at reasonable cost." However, unlike Abitibi, the investment bankers never joined Spanish River's board. Mead ensured all directors were individuals loyal to him. He used the refinancing to remove Stavert, the last representative from the Lake Superior investors.[52] Nonetheless, the geographic vicinity of Abitibi and Spanish River, along with expectations that manufacturers should coalesce into larger units, stimulated beliefs that an amalgamation was a logical, if not inevitable, destiny.

Within weeks of Smith's appointment as Abitibi's president, rumours about a merger proliferated. Heavy share turnover ensued as some press reports claimed "nothing tangible" to the speculation and others suggested "fairly definite intimations." During the spring of 1924 a deal based upon an exchange of stock was reached, at least in outline. Spanish River carried a higher debt load but had more working capital. The terms appeared to favour Abitibi but gave Spanish River majority ownership. Despite press claims an agreement would occur within days, Alexander Smith rejected the proposal as one that gave insufficient recognition to Abitibi's properties and lower production costs.[53] The discussions were suspended when weak sales triggered selling of newsprint securities and a cutback in output by both firms. Mead continued to seek consolidation but the preferred shareholders of Spanish River blocked subsequent proposals as overly generous to Abitibi. Given the size of a combined firm, market analysts also questioned a syndicate's ability to sell the securities within Canada and declared they "would not go into investment hands immediately." During early 1925 another push occurred, this time from George Mead who claimed to have garnered support from those who had opposed an amalgamation. Under the scheme, Abitibi's common equity was scheduled to expand from 200,000 shares to at least 882,874. The redemption of other bonds and preferred stock was anticipated as part of any settlement, along with permanent increases in the annual dividends. Brokerage houses dismissed the arrangement as "amazing," since the combined earnings barely exceeded the likely dividend and interest charges. If the newsprint price dropped, the firm was likely to default. A deal involving "vastly higher dividends" was "not sound business, and there seems little defence for it," one journal decreed. The difficulties of financing the scheme soon became insurmountable. Press reports during succeeding months claimed other options were explored, including an amalgamation of all Northern Ontario companies, rumours fostered by concurrent speculation about takeovers amongst Quebec producers.[54] The repetitious circulation of merger tales left most media outlets dubious that anything would ever happen. The *Financial Post* could not resist sneering about the "speculative fancy." International Paper had never paid a common dividend, whereas Abitibi paid $4 per share and was a regular target for gossip, "but never to the extent of bringing out official admission that such plans were under consideration." There was "no fire behind all this smoke." Abitibi might be "one of the best holds for a long pull" but a merger had to overcome the profit-sharing rights of some Spanish River investors that, "while not interfering in the slightest with the operations of the company," were quite valuable.[55]

2. Businesslike politics

Sometimes "strange developments" unfolded with pulp and paper enterprises, a newspaper commented. If the information was disclosed, the public "should read it again and having made quite sure that their eyes are not deceiving them they might profitably surrender their minds to some pertinent meditations."[56] This issue was fully

Abitibi and a revision of Hollinger's contract with Northern Canada Power. A series of discussions, miscommunications and bargaining ploys unfolded across nine months as each attempted to garner a superior outcome. Alexander Smith needed the facility but refused to pay cash and stonewalled for the lowest price rather than the actual cost. Noah Timmins of Hollinger, in vain, tried to recoup the investment and threatened a start-up of the plant to force concessions from Northern Canada. A.J. Nesbitt, with the weakest negotiating position, blustered about how his London lawyers were ready to begin proceedings but he feared losing Northern Canada's main customer.[63] The final settlement, which was accepted by all three parties and not imposed by the province, slashed Hollinger's rates in half through a new contract with Northern Canada. Abitibi purchased the Island Falls complex and incorporated it as a subsidiary, Abitibi Electrical Development (AED). Historian Mark Kuhlberg claimed the company paid an "exorbitant price" that was "roughly four times" what the mining company had expended. In reality, Smith cleaned Timmins's clock. The nominal price was at or just below Hollinger's actual outlays.[64] But Smith refused to pay cash. Instead, Hollinger received AED serial bonds that were secured by a power contract from Abitibi. Hollinger had to wait years to recoup its expenditures, which severely decreased the deal's net present value. Though the provisions were kept secret, all three firms claimed victory. The business press, nonetheless, realized the takeover was a heavy loss for Hollinger. Abitibi gained control over all power sites on the upper river. AED generated modest earnings and a decade later ironically provided one of the firm's few reliable streams of revenue.[65]

Smith also joined with George Mead in several ventures, which extended Spanish River's operations westward to the Prairie provinces and eastward into Quebec. The relationship was predicated upon Peabody Houghteling's coordination of the financing. Two schemes were small and slated for future development. Murray Bay Paper gained cutting rights north of the St. Lawrence River near La Malbaie. It planned to construct a 125-ton mill using turn-of-the-century machines cannibalized from Tidewater Paper Mills, a small Brooklyn company. With an expectation that operations would begin during 1929, the venture employed modest capital and appeared viable because it had a reliable source of groundwood pulp and a power plant.[66] Ste. Anne Paper, located in Beaupré, relied upon timberlands that Mead secured after a struggle with the American owners. Scheduled to start up during 1927, it was to be twice the size of Murray Bay, have an up-to-date mill, and benefit from easy access to the mid-Atlantic market.[67]

Just as Anson had considered a development at English River during 1919, George Mead chose to expand into Northwestern Ontario, but this initiative proved to be very convoluted. Following the nationalization of the Grand Trunk Pacific Railroad, the Mead Investment Company gained ownership of a lease that two contractors had finagled from the system, which granted privileges for harvesting pulp along the route. But under terms of the original land grant, the province, not the railroad or the federal government, retained all timber and mineral rights. Upon disclosure, Ontario refused to see the transaction as valid and deemed the territory forfeit, but the province was essentially confronted by a fait accompli.[68] Premier Drury made his anger clear about what he deemed surreptitious tactics by Mead. Even if the province refused to accept the arrangement, the lease remained unaffected and the pulpwood could be extracted until the courts overturned it. To resolve the problem, the government chose to proceed as if Ontario had made the deal by sanctioning the lease predicated upon the construction of a 120-ton pulp mill (with a later commitment for a newsprint factory) and by arranging for federal authorities to issue a new contract. Mead then wangled a lengthy set of concessions from town officials, along with arrangements for electricity from a local utility.[69] Fort William Paper was set up with an outlay of just $3 million versus an authorized capitalization of $15 million but the market collapsed just as the mill went into operation. Then Mead's associates discovered the merchantable timber on the lands was less than half of the estimates. They accordingly sought tracts that could feed the plant for sixty years or more.[70]

The lobbying efforts went nowhere, a situation that turned into a muddled mess. Two other companies made enquiries. Beniah Bowman, the responsible minister, conceded the government had a responsibility to take care of existing industries. It could "not very well consider applications from parties who have not spent any money in the creation of an industry ... but who have merely a prospective enterprise in view." But since Mead wanted new territories without competitive bidding (in violation of government policy), Drury deferred the entire matter. Not just the earlier dealings related to Fort William had antagonized his government, the disclosure of Mead's correspondence with Howard Ferguson made an arrangement politically difficult, if not impossible. Still believing his firm would gain the concession, in the summer of 1922 Mead proceeded with the construction of an eighty-ton newsprint mill. The capacity was doubled based upon a financial package arranged by Peabody Houghteling. Spanish River took a direct stake in Fort William, although technically the mill

remained quasi-independent.[71] Intensive lobbying by municipal officials attempted to spur the province towards a grant of additional territory. Lawyers for the province generated a prospective agreement,
albeit but for a different geographic area and for a mill double the size
the one under construction. When this news was leaked to trade
papers, the representatives of another firm, Thunder Bay Paper,
launched a counterlobby. They claimed to have received "great encouragement" about how the province would take care of their enterprise
but, like Mead, they opposed competitive bidding "because bonding
houses would be very chary in advancing money to mills whose timber supply, which is the heart of their business, must be obtained in
such an uncertain manner."[72] Three weeks later, the government again
reversed course and advertised the tracts for sale but nothing was
done before the United Farmers lost the summer election. Howard
Ferguson as the new premier then announced a freeze on new leases.
Ostensibly instituted to foster conservation, the action coincided with
the appointment of a federal royal commission to investigate whether
pulpwood exports should be banned. But the true thrust of the policy
soon became obvious. James Lyons, the minister of lands and forests,
publicly chastised the paper manufacturers for meeting supply needs
from their proprietary concessions and paying colonists little more
than it cost to remove logs. Instead, he declared they should treat the
tracts as reserves and buy more from settlers. New projects hence
would be approved with respect to the province's need for investment capital *and* a linkage of mills with colonization areas, with each
local industry serving as a nucleus for agricultural development.
Though he asked for voluntary cooperation, the implicit threat was
obvious. A report later stressed how the Lakehead companies were
"all practically directly dependent upon the wood secured from settlers and private owners of timber lands, no Provincial Crown areas
having been acquired by them." Major J.L. Hartt, a sawmill operator,
was chosen to oversee the new arrangement, which cognoscenti
believed would enhance the government's ability to exploit natural
resources for political gain.[73]

As if things were not difficult enough, Ontario Hydro in early 1924
advised Fort William Paper it could not provide additional power but
opposed any grant of water rights that facilitated an expansion of private sector supply. The company's lawyer denounced the move as
"manifestly unfair" for "we had hoped to continue along sound,
straightforward, business lines." He expressed surprise that a branch
of the government "now proposed to place obstacles in the way of our
sincere efforts." The utility previously had carried out a development

at the Lakehead, with massive cost overruns that were enfolded into the power rates. Hydro, one adviser told the premier, was "asking such an exorbitant amount it was out of [the] question" for an industrial concern.[74] Fort William Paper received electricity from Kaministiquia Power, an enterprise controlled by Sir Herbert Holt, but the situation during 1924 was exacerbated by a water shortage. Mead hence bought out Kaministiquia as a means of controlling part of the electricity supply, even though this solution allowed Holt to gain a stake in the larger enterprise. The firm pressed Ferguson for additional energy and after six months received assurances about how the government wished to "facilitate the Fort William Paper Company in its endeavour to keep the wheels of industry running for a temporary period." Tedious negotiations resolved the immediate difficulties but a permanent solution required an expansion of supply. "We have no desire to control power as a competitor of Hydro," company representatives stated. "We want power; we want it quickly; we are prepared to develop or see it developed ... for at present our whole development movement is halted until this practical proposition is adjusted." The Hydro Commission, however, was only prepared to undertake a project that covered the entire Lakehead region – one not scheduled for completion before 1931.[75]

This mess went on for several years and ended poorly. Local sawmills complained about how their mills had run idle for several years due to the lack of timber sales. In response, Ferguson allowed lumbermen to extract the jack pine from a tract Fort William wanted, a decision that undermined its value. Mead's firm could only get at the pulpwood through a narrow corridor, which made the forest operations inordinately expensive.[76] Conservative lobbyists conspired with the premier and the minister of lands and forest about the allocation of another block of land that was integral to the concession. Provincial Paper Mills, a small company and the main supplier of paper for school textbooks, needed poplar, not spruce, for manufacturing. By pre-arrangement the pulpwood in the territory was tendered during 1925, supposedly after "a careful cruise and estimate of the entire Nipigon region contiguous to these and the other established plants such as the Provincial Paper mills, whose concession was limited as to cordage." The estimates instead were deliberately misrepresented as one-tenth of the actual amount, which lowered the net cost for the winner of the tender. Fort William bid higher but the lands were arbitrarily awarded to Provincial Paper. It had to spend just $1 million for a doubling of capacity and was vaguely obligated to construct a soda mill, "when and so soon as market conditions warrant." In what amounted to an invitation to

schedule. Seaman wanted a licence for 3 million cords of pulpwood but with onerous terms: no competitive bidding, the timber at a base rate without any bonus, and the right to select from a broad array of lands. The last condition could prevent a rival from assembling the contiguous properties necessary for an economic operation. In exchange, he promised a 200-ton mill located near Winnipeg, generous purchases of pulpwood from settlers, and additional traffic for the railways.[84] This move set in motion a Byzantine struggle among several firms, the provincial and federal governments, Winnipeg business interests, and settlers. When Seaman's advance was rejected, he exercised an option to gain a stake in Manitoba Pulp. The plans for a mill at Pine Falls then stalled after a bill authorizing the construction of a railway link failed to gain approval. The partners switched their plans to a Winnipeg location but, despite multiple requests for additional tracts, federal officials refused to jettison competitive bidding or to authorize a grant that created a *de facto* monopoly. Relations between McArthur and Seaman turned acrimonious as they separately or in combination tried to secure lands. Increasingly, they conspired against one another and, unbeknownst to Seaman, during the autumn of 1924 McArthur persuaded the department to put up a 104,000-square-kilometre concession for auction.[85]

Advertisement of the sale set off a political firestorm. The auction contained restrictions that blocked settlers and sawmill operators from securing permits to cut wood for five years while the winner chose its lands. The province questioned the terms of the sale and feared it might prevent the establishment of a second mill. In the face of vociferous opposition, federal officials declared no action would be taken unless it received provincial approval, a move that just intensified the controversy. McArthur, in an effort to win support from Winnipeg interests, exacerbated the hullabaloo by inflating the employment estimates for his mill 300 per cent. Tales also circulated about how the head of Minnesota and Ontario Paper, Edward Wellington Backus, offered him $1 million for the lease in order to gain possession of the tracts and stop any construction. Frustrated by what he considered monkey business, Manitoba Premier John Bracken rejected proposals that entailed allocations of timberlands without competition and he dismissed a rate of $0.80 per cord as unreasonably low.[86] After several months of discussions, federal and provincial officials agreed upon an auction for the 103,000 square kilometres of timberlands but with regulations that ensured sawmill companies and others might gain access to some wood. Seaman and Chisholm thereupon withdrew the financing for Manitoba Pulp (nominally over the political controversy but actually due to the revised terms), although they indicated Spanish River might offer support. According to McArthur, he then met with representatives of that firm and Backus at a conference in Minneapolis where a sizeable bribe was offered if he did not bid at the auction, which could allow them to gain the pulpwood without competition. McArthur offered Spanish River a stake in Manitoba Pulp greater than the one Seaman had held – but only if a mill was constructed. When they could not reach an agreement, he divulged these latest twists to the press. McArthur claimed the other firms had no interest in a local mill and just "were trying to use us to tie up the proposition for an indefinite period of time."[87]

McArthur elected to bid, despite the lack of a financial backer, with the hope that he might then use the properties as collateral. He won the auction but counterbidding by Spanish River raised the price to $2.80 per cord, a rate, McArthur admitted, that made it impossible to finance the venture. "Obstructionists Pull Hatchets in Public Sale," headlined the *Winnipeg Tribune* and it declared the mill was "lost to Manitoba – at least for a long time." McArthur secured an extension, then asked federal officials to overturn the sale price, this time with Bracken's support. Opponents could not help gloating about how the province had come full circle to endorse the terms Seaman had sought. McArthur insisted the project would advance "this year because it is this year or never ... The royalty matter is not as important as some people imagine."[88] He sought out investors for a traduced mill that could be constructed for just $1 million, claiming it could draw upon wood from settlers rather than the timber berth. With two weeks to spare before the sale was declared forfeit, McArthur found his white knight. In a stunning reversal of fortune, Spanish River and Manitoba Pulp announced a joint alliance for the $6 million construction of a 200-ton mill that could function on a "sound perpetual basis." "I have not sold out my pulpwood interests in Manitoba to the Spanish River Company and I don't intend to," McArthur proclaimed in high dudgeon. The new allies told the press the project would advance if they received guarantees about sufficient wood and timber fees comparable to those charged in Northwestern Ontario. Within days it became apparent they already had wangled a private deal with federal officials that just required provincial sanction. The companies were offered everything they had sought for a mill "somewhere in Manitoba": a selection from the lands proffered during earlier negotiations, no auction, and the original rate of $0.80 per cord extended to the chosen tracts. Bracken acquiesced because the lands were to be allocated in a way that fostered new settlements, while providing adequate timber for the mill. To deflect criticism, he insisted his government did not have any responsibility for the deal because natural resources were under federal jurisdiction.[89]

This latest twist generated howls of outrage because Pine Falls re-emerged as the probable mill site. "Somebody is manufacturing a smokescreen," decried the *Winnipeg Tribune*. "The hidden hand that knifed the first Seaman deal is forcing the Spanish River company to locate the mill up in the backwoods." "Certain concealed interests made it their business" to ensure the mill was not near the provincial capital and required "acceptance of their ideas part of the price for their silence" when the new terms were developed. "There are occasions when logic and economic advantage and all other ordinary considerations go by the board. The question of location is, after all, the question of how to cook the hare. The man who has or can catch the hare has the position of real authority." Seaman, now allied with Backus, exploited the backlash by renewing the bid for a mill near Winnipeg, contingent, of course, upon an adequate supply of pulpwood. Because the understandings with Manitoba Pulp specified an award of 1 million cords for a 100-ton mill, opponents who wanted another factory considered this grant unreasonably generous but they deemed the contract even more offensive when it was published. The agreement specified just a $2.5 million investment for a 50-ton plant that employed 120 men, did not define the mill location, and placed no limits on the pulp it could grind and export. The detailed appendices made all of the territories discussed across the preceding four years available to the promoters. While the original berth retained the bonus price McArthur had offered in 1921, the remaining areas were without extra fees. Manitoba Pulp could widen its acquisition of properties if the capacity was expanded to 200 tons per day.[90] The deal represented for McArthur the last chance to have a mill constructed in the province, which had always been his prime concern. Bracken's acquiescence to the scheme reflected several issues. There were guarantees of prompt construction, while both the promised employment and supplies necessary for the mill's operations benefited several areas that supported his party. The Seaman-Backus alternative was simply unpalatable. Seaman's reputation was damaged by the revelations about interfirm skulduggery and back-stabbing, an issue he compounded by publishing more of the incriminating correspondence. Backus had disregarded both federal and provincial officials the previous year when his operations triggered serious flooding. Several days after the McArthur-Spanish River alliance was revealed, Backus announced an expansion of his pulp mill at Kenora. Bracken probably suspected the fresh effort to gain timber concessions was intended to supply that plant. It certainly was. Kenora was predicated upon the exploitation of timber near the English River but (as Frank Anson had previously discovered) Backus now understood the wood was at the wrong end of the concession, which meant very high costs for its extraction.[91]

With an agreement in hand and public relations no longer a concern, Spanish River executives altered the venture, starting with a confirmation of Pine Falls as the mill site. A Spanish River executive took command. McArthur was promoted to the symbolic role of chairman but resigned the following year when he sought treatment for terminal cancer. Mead replaced him and Abitibi took an equity stake when the enterprise was reorganized into the Manitoba Paper Company. Peabody Houghteling retailed the bonds for the venture and told investors about how the factory (upgraded to 250 tons daily or twice the size of McArthur's proposal) epitomized "the last word in paper mill practice." The entire production, a promotional statement emphasized, "will be marketed under contract of sale by The G.H. Mead Company of Dayton, Ohio, the largest distributors of newsprint paper in the world."[92]

Manitoba Paper not only had the right to request additional timber but federal authorities were obligated to guarantee that no concessions were granted for competing mills until detailed estimates proved there was sufficient wood for their continuous operation. Opponents insisted the available pulpwood was capable of supporting three other firms and therefore Manitoba had been sold out. The promoters behind Manitoba Paper had "a 25 percent desire to get into the papermaking industry and 75 percent determination to keep other people out." It was "a monopoly double ringed with safeguards against competition," reinforced by a "fine agreement truly measured in terms of the private interests who are to benefit from it."[93] With much sound and fury, Backus and Seaman tried to mobilize support but their lobbying came too little, too late. Federal authorities would only sanction a mill in the remote north. Additional agreements in early 1927 guaranteed Manitoba Paper 6 million cords of pulpwood and the company exploited the provisions to widen its holdings. Pine Falls not only gained a capability for underselling the Backus group, the facility compensated for the timber problems at Fort William Paper and neutered Backus's planned expansion at Kenora. Spanish River, as critics had predicted, selected lands in a way that blocked a rival in the province's southern areas and left them "undisputed masters of the Manitoba field."[94]

Alexander Smith meanwhile sought to reinforce Abitibi's strategic profile and his first large-scale acquisition, Mattagami Pulp and Paper, presaged things to come. Mattagami represented the second attempt to exploit the Clay Belt's forest wealth, an endeavour launched by Duncan Chisholm and other Toronto businessmen in 1914 for the construction of an unbleached sulphite pulp mill at Smooth Rock Falls. Although the prospectus described the venture as having splendid limits, excellent power facilities, and capable management, from the beginning some observers speculated about whether this "particular bit of financing may be allright" since the underwriter, I.W. Killam's Royal Securities, seemed to be "taking altogether too keen an interest in the stock market end of the Pulp and Paper industry."[95] With claims that the properties were worth $9 million, the firm issued $2 million of first mortgage bonds, $1.5 million of preferred stock, and another $2 million of common equity. The securities were sold privately. The only public notice declared the firm well capitalized.[96] Although press releases across the next four years asserted things proceeded splendidly, significant turnover among the operating management occurred. The capital proved insufficient and a plan to build a newsprint mill was never fulfilled. Royal Securities in 1919 floated another $2.5 million as debenture stock secured by a second mortgage on the assets. Killam agreed to retain half of the issue in exchange for a seat on the board of directors and a move of the company headquarters to Montreal, where he could more easily monitor things.[97]

Mattagami never reported a profit, never paid dividends, and was overleveraged. The company's plans were derailed when the Ontario Tories signed a contract with the New Ontario Colonization Company, which ostensibly was concerned with settlement but sought to strip and export timber from the areas closest to the mill. The company blackmailed Mattagami by refusing permission for the use of local water rights and by claiming the properties where it illegally operated might be flooded. The difficulties were further compounded by a decision to have Mattagami manufacture sulphite pulp. This process required twice the amount of pulpwood and a higher output for achieving breakeven status. The company failed to pay the fees for its timber concessions and water leases from 1919 to 1921, and in the midst of a recession defaulted on the bond interest, leading to the appointment of a receiver.

Geoffrey Teignmouth Clarkson had gained a prominent reputation as a liquidator and assignee for failed enterprises. Born in Toronto in 1878, at the age of fifteen he started work for his father's firm, which specialized in trusteeship and bankruptcy. A separate company, founded by Clarkson and several partners, provided an array of accounting services and served as one of the leading auditors. Clarkson himself was an acknowledged expert on banking and during his career acted as the auditor for five different banks. Although a shy retiring man in private, he became a public figure from his investigatory role during numerous controversial enquiries. Meticulously professional, he was known for concise, often blunt, appraisals of questionable conduct. His analysis of the Home Bank failure was typically unforgiving. He castigated the lack of experienced managers, their failure to fulfil the functions for which the bank was chartered, and the "disregard of the safeguards by which the business of all efficiently managed banks are protected."[98] Well connected with the Tories, Clarkson investigated sensitive subjects like the Hydro-Electric Power Commission, racetracks, oil and gas pricing, and Consumers Gas. His companies provided auditing and financial services for the Supreme Court and various government agencies. Clarkson by the 1920s had become an authority on the pulp and paper industry. Through him Drury, Ferguson and other officials would have learned about everything related to Mattagami.

The receiver took over a schmozzle. He advised the court that the company lacked clear accounting practices and could not gauge production costs accurately. Customers deemed the quality of the pulp unacceptable. There was no internal marketing department. Mattagami instead relied upon commission agents who charged more than twice the normal rate. In an attempt to avoid bankruptcy, the executives hypothecated all of the trading assets to Molson's Bank even though this action violated the bond mortgage. Clarkson doubted whether a sale of Mattagami could raise more than $2.3 million. Upon the disclosure of these findings the value of the debenture stock plummeted to the equivalent of 40 cents on the dollar. Rather than close the mill and sell it as defunct, the operation was continued at the risk and cost of Molson's Bank. This arrangement allowed the bank to recoup more than would have occurred under liquidation. The obligations to Molson's Bank were paid off two years later and, as the firm's value rebounded to $5 million, it then functioned for the benefit of the bondholders. By 1925 the plant operated at full capacity, earning a modest increase in the surplus.[99]

As the company recovered, the principals fell out. Killam and W.D. Ross (a director of the Bank of Nova Scotia), as the largest owners of debenture stock and as bondholders, pressed for a judicial sale that could pay off the debt and allow a new financial structure. Given the firm's low market value, this was likely to occur at rates where the creditors and common shareholders got nothing. Killam's reputation, damaged by the Riordon collapse, just compounded the opprobrium with which other investors now viewed him. Chisholm and his colleagues tried to block the "wash-out" by claiming Killam's fiduciary relationship with Mattagami placed him in a conflict of interest. They believed he should be blocked from purchases of bonds or debenture stock, whether held by him directly or via Royal Securities. An extended receivership, they contended, would allow a recovery and restoration of shareholder control.[100] The creditors and equity holders also appealed for the province to prevent a sale. Even though he had contributed to the situation by failing to control the New Ontario Colonization Company, Ferguson had little sympathy. The premier advised an appellant that the investors had been misled by the appearance of a substantial enterprise and there was nothing left. The situation was analogous to giving credit to a private individual who turned out to be worthless. There was, he scathingly added, an "old maxim that says 'the seller should beware of the purchaser.' In other words when a man gives credit he must take responsibility."[101]

Solicitors for the former owners of Mattagami pressed the government for additional resources that might abet a resuscitation of the enterprise. Since the applicants had no legal standing after Mattagami went into receivership, these efforts were rebuffed. Drury refused to meet the lobbyists and told his staff they must see Clarkson. Two years later they tried the same manoeuvre with Ferguson, with identical results.[102] Killam and his associates similarly tried to gain new lands during 1925. They submitted three bids for concessions the province put up for tender. The final one exceeded a competing offer from Kimberly-Clarke. From the beginning, the government favoured the latter and it made self-serving justifications when Killam's bid was rejected. The real reasons were never stated but were obvious. Kimberly-Clarke had a long-standing obligation to construct a paper mill at Kapuskasing. It announced a decision to proceed just before a provincial election, which allowed the Tories to tout the new jobs. Stable long-term output was anticipated through a contract with the *New York Times*. Both companies had extensive resources, assuring prompt completion, whereas Mattagami had an abysmal record of non-performance. Despite his posturing, Killam still did not have legal control, indeed would not have until a judicial sale occurred. Opposition from other investors and problems with improving the mill delayed that development for another eighteen months. Killam's proposal also was never politically viable. He refused to pay more than 30 cents on the dollar for Mattagami's unsecured creditors, comprised mostly of settlers who had cut timber. Rejecting the bid allowed Ferguson to grandstand about how he stood up for them even though it changed nothing. The premier likely anticipated, given press rumours, Killam's true goal was an addition of assets to inflate the firm's value that would allow a subsequent sale for a handsome profit. In any event, Killam's reputation was mud.[103]

Legal proceedings did not advance until the spring of 1926. The conflicts of interest were sufficient for the judge to demand that Killam post a $1 million bond. When a sale was held in October, he submitted the only bid at $7.25 million, just above the reserve bid but below the value estimated by the receiver. Although some parties later implied Clarkson and Killam colluded, the financier had access to all records and knew how much to offer.[104] The properties were flipped to Abitibi during December, even before the sale closed, in a deal with terms that lowered Abitibi's net cost to $5.25 million. The firm floated a $2 million bond issue for the new subsidiary, Abitibi Fibre, and arbitrarily revalued the properties to $9.25 million. How much Killam received cannot be ascertained but he recouped the original investment, earned a commission on the sale, and received a bonus in the form of part of a new bond issue. Killam also flipped his debenture stock for bonds of the new subsidiary. Having received the securities at a rate of 90 cents on the dollar, he refused to sell for less than ninety-nine.

Abitibi only made a cursory acknowledgment of the acquisition. Since Mattagami was a marginal enterprise, why did the company make the purchase? First, Killam made considerable noise about how production might be expanded once he gained control. Whether the threat was real or a bluff, the takeover eliminated a competitor that could cut into markets in the midwestern states. It removed any risk of Mattagami being sold to International Paper, which was expanding pulp operations just across the provincial border. Abitibi's executives believed they could secure additional concessions or draw upon other properties to supply the mill. The acquisition enhanced Abitibi's status as a Northern Ontario producer and modestly diversified its product mix. With the restoration of Mattagami towards breakeven status, the mill appeared viable given the prevailing commodity rates. However, the sulphite operation became unprofitable after 1927 when prices declined.[105] The acquisition also had long-term consequences. A private agreement confirmed Royal Securities as a prime agent for future sales of Abitibi securities. Second, and crucially, the financial house in 1928 exchanged its Abitibi Fibre holdings for bonds of the parent company and became the second-largest debt holder. Ten years later this status enabled it to make or break any deal affecting Abitibi's future. The firm's vice-president later showed he was quite prepared to use tactics like those employed in the Mattagami case, no matter who was hurt.

finance, Mead marketing newsprint. The real competitive advantage among Mead's enterprises always was the sales agency, which out-performed other companies, including International Paper. It con-trolled Abitibi's American sales and received an above average commission rate. His earnings from the merger are not known but Mead acknowledged losing at least $8 million on Abitibi's common stock by 1932. If true, it is probable he held at least a seventh of the equity of the merged firm, though Alexander Smith was the largest shareholder.

Mead never criticized Smith's management or the financial state-ments until the firm entered receivership. He only spoke once about the insolvency and claimed he had known the 1928 assets amounted to $94 million versus the declared valuation of $178 million. The fail-ure did not occur for a lack of funds "but because the president of the Abitibi company, without consultation with his directors, had purchased a competing company for $12,000,000 and also built a power plant on which he had guaranteed payment on the bonds, again without knowledge of his directors, in conjunction with the Ontario Government. Therefore the Abitibi company found itself with an obligation of some $15,000,000 which it did not have."[123] This was twaddle, a deliberate attempt to leave himself out of responsibility for the debacle. The board Mead chaired reviewed and approved all of Smith's actions. They were discussed at annual meetings and received heavy press coverage. In fact, the merger was not consummated until Mead got it on his terms: payment based upon the *full and unquestioned acceptance* of the book values of his companies. The appreciation of Abitibi's shares during 1927 was determinative since it augured well for the likelihood of selling out at a significant profit. A legend later circulated that the merger was "engineered" by National City Bank but there is no evidence of any substantive participation in the amalgamation, which had resulted from five years of negotiations among Smith, Mead, and their subor-dinates.[124] National City had never financed the firms. Peabody Houghteling, Royal Securities, and Nesbitt Thomson handled the share exchange. Abitibi, nonetheless, soon entered a fateful relation-ship with the American bank.

4. Capitalists of all degrees

Once the amalgamation was finalized, Abitibi had twenty-one bond issues, various notes and money obligations, and seven preferred stocks. Given the perceived riskiness of the newer ventures, several had dividend or interest obligations well above the norm for forest compa-nies. Table 2 outlines the post-merger financial structure and illustrates

Table 2 Abitibi's Capital Structure, 1927–1928

	Pre-Merger	Post-Merger*	After Refinancing
Funded Debt			
Abitibi Power & Paper	$12,251,700	$12,183,000	- - - - -
Subsidiary companies	9,635,000	44,312,832	- - - - -
Purchase money obligations	- - - - -	- - - - -	$ 416,976
First mortgage 5% gold bonds	- - - - -	- - - - -	50,000,000
Total Funded Debt	*$21,886,700*	*$56,495,832*	*$50,416976*
Preferred Stocks			
Abitibi 7% cumulative	$1,000,000	$1,000,000	$1,000,000
Preferred of subsidiary companies	4,000,000	12,498,500	- - - - -
Abitibi 6% cumulative	- - - - -	9,643,300	34,881,800
Total Preferred Stock	*$5,000,000*	*$23,141,500*	*$35,881,800*
Total Debt and Preferred Stock	*$26,886,700*	*$79,637,332*	*$85,298,776*
Common Stock & Declared Surplus	$13,339,976	$58,162,558	$59,145,391
Total Capitalization	**$41,226,676**	**$137,799,890**	**$145,444,167**
Total Declared Assets	$43,985,025	$177,042,409	$177,919,211
Annual Fixed Charges	$1,397,542	$7,721,814	$4,643,108
$ per ton at:			
100 per cent capacity	$7.51	$11.59	$6.97
80 per cent capacity	$9.39	$14.48	$8.71
60 per cent capacity	$12.42	$19.31	$11.61
40 per cent capacity	$18.78	$28.96	$17.42
Promised Common Dividends	$1,250,000	$2,000,000	$3,952,468
$ per ton at:			
100 per cent capacity	$6.72	$3.00	$5.93
80 per cent capacity	$8.40	$3.75	$7.41

Sources: SMPL, B-2, Box 1, File 6, 16825–9, Spanish River Pulp and Paper Company in Liquidation, 1928; *Annual Financial Review* (1927); *Moody's Survey of Industrials* (1927, 1928); Abitibi Power and Paper, *AR* (1927, 1928), 2–4; Spanish River Pulp and Paper, *AR* (1926, 1927), 3–5; *WSJ*, 13 April 1928.

* Press reports about the financial structure after the merger were incorrect because numerous obligations were disregarded. Abitibi's releases stressed the parent companies' debt and ignored the affiliates or subsidiaries. Press accounts gauged the debt at $42 million to $49 million and totally misestimated the preferred stock.

how the fixed charges were unsustainable. Three months after the amalgamation was finalized, Smith therefore moved to create a less expensive package but the capital was well beyond the resources of Canadian brokerage houses to assemble.[125] Abitibi undertook the just waiting for someone to come and tell them what to do with their savings. Take a good look, eat a good lunch, and then go down there and tell them."[133] Mitchell contended the firm was not just a purveyor of stocks and bonds. His "Bank for All," beyond the hucksterism, offered a form of utopian capitalism. It would advise and teach invest-ing to "person[s] of limited resources, all of whose capital and income are necessary to insure life's future comforts."[134] There were "capitalists of all degrees," including the person "who owns a single bond, or who has a hundred dollars in the savings bank." They participated in the supply of "active capital," investments that propelled upward move-ment of the economy and personal income. The money funded new and improved equipment for factories and thus increases in production levels, as well as "a continual readjustment of wages as will enable the people to buy them."[135] As the world's largest commercial bank, National City operated a network that could guarantee the circulation of new securities but to maintain revenues it needed ever-growing flows to "merchandize," which by 1928 included legitimate enterprises, risky mining ventures, and highly questionable Latin American offerings.[136]

While the staff at Abitibi's headquarters finalized the official estimate of the company's assets, the board authorized a new issue of 6 per cent preferred stock. Approximately $9 million were designated for the redemption of the Spanish River preferred shares. A syndicate headed by National City (which included both of Smith's companies, Wood Gundy, and Royal Securities) was enlisted to sell another $16 million. A further tranche of $10 million completed the distribution. Approxi-mately three-quarters of this equity were used to replace the preferred equity of Abitibi's other subsidiaries and the balance was applied against various debt issues. Sales brochures stressed how Abitibi gained full control over the remaining stock and might reap savings.[137] Other than the preferred shares of Spanish River, little was ever learned about who had owned the securities and reaped the benefits. With the former affiliates, the shares were held either by Spanish River and Abitibi, by Mead-controlled investment vehicles, or by "individuals immediately associated" with the companies. Press accounts later assumed the senior executives and other insiders were the true winners.[138]

The second stage entailed a retirement of the existing bonds and debt instruments, followed by a syndicate sale of $50 million in 5 per cent gold mortgage bonds.[139] Headed by National City and Royal Securities, this distribution required the services of thirteen investment banks based in locations like Boston, New York, Chicago, and London, but it was oversubscribed within days. Sales promotions stressed how the elimination of high interest or dividend securities allowed Abitibi to reap substantial savings, which *was* true. The new debt and preferred equity increased the amount of fixed income securities but the package slashed the annual charges to more manageable dimensions. The reduction gave substance to the later claim that the financing was prudent. But this ignored a simple reality. Smith had paid far too much for the acquisitions and Abitibi ended up heavily leveraged.[140] Table 2 illustrates the implications according to different levels of rated capacity. During 1928 Abitibi realized $55.62 per ton of newsprint from its sales. The production costs averaged $43.13 per ton but the pre-tax costs totalled $55.51. These included interest and preferred dividend charges of $9 per ton. Thus, even with the refinancing, the firm barely achieved break-even, with little room for capital expenditures, taxes, depreciation, or maintenance. It remained at the same level during 1929 when Abitibi secured greater sales but less earned per ton.[141] The union with Spanish River thus mattered. If it had not occurred, the firm probably would have avoided receivership.

Even under propitious circumstances, economic gains from mergers take years to accomplish and can prove illusory.[142] In the best of all possible worlds, after a company is refinanced, the market value of new securities remains stable – proof that both the offered prices and assessments of corporate capabilities are accurate. Neither occurred with Abitibi. Within twelve months the company began cut-backs, not from a rationalization of business activities but from industrial destabilization. Despite short periods of recovery, the price of Abitibi common shares declined from $80.75 during April of 1928 to $54.73 by July the following year. The new preferred stock decreased by a fifth. Only the bonds, mortgaged against the assets, held their value. The plan to raise the common dividends became a misadventure as the cash flow weakened. The board was forced to suspend them in December 1928 when earnings crumpled to $1.33 per share versus the scheduled distribution of $5.[143] For George Mead there must have been a sense of déjà vu. Everything started to fall apart more than a year before the Wall Street crash as the newsprint industry slipped into its own private depression.[144]

5

From Prosperity to Crisis

As a vast fire will fill the air to a great distance with its roar, so the sacred flame which the mighty Barnacles had fanned caused the air to resound more and more with the name of Merdle. It was deposited on every lip, and carried into every ear. There never was, there never had been, there never again should be, such a man as Mr. Merdle. Nobody, as foresaid, knew what he had done; but everybody knew him to be the greatest that had appeared.

– Charles Dickens, *Little Dorrit*

There are very few men – and they are the exceptions – who are able to think and feel beyond the present moment.

– Carl von Clausewitz, *On War*

THE ROARING TWENTIES WERE A euphoric period for Alexander Smith. Vacationing in South Carolina during the winter or early spring, he could enjoy his yacht *Cutty Sark*, a 122-ton vessel with a crew of twelve. George Mead handled most of Abitibi's sales. Day-to-day matters were delegated to operational officers who, with the exception of L.R. Wilson, rarely met Smith. Free to concentrate on financial issues, he established a permanent residence in New York City, travelling north for meetings of Abitibi's board or visits to company sites. Smith kept an apartment at 999 North LaSalle Street in Chicago, one of the city's most prestigious addresses.[1] He launched several ventures intended to enhance his wealth further. Arriving in Galveston on his yacht with two partners, he announced the construction of a sugar refinery proposed by Anson. However, his affairs now came under enhanced scrutiny. Disgruntled investors increasingly filed lawsuits against what they perceived as more than questionable dealings. Smith and several associates, for example, lost a Massachusetts case where they were accused of wrongdoing in a corporate reorganization that let them gain control over a regional oil market.[2]

Peabody Houghteling split into two firms with different owners and managers during 1927. The original enterprise still handled accounts for the Midwest. A new firm entitled Peabody, Smith and Company handled Canadian and Eastern American affairs. Alexander Smith's status was confirmed during May 1929 when the company occupied the twelfth floor of a new skyscraper at 63 Wall Street, across the street from the National City Bank and two blocks from the New York Stock Exchange. The move attracted press attention because the architects designed the facilities in a modernistic style rather than the conservative mode investment bankers tended to favour. The financier now was at the centre, a businessman sought out by reporters for his views.[3]

Smith's career appeared to be reaching a culminating triumph but a maxim of Michel de Montaigne loomed. "Fortune, seeing that she could not make fools wise, made them lucky ... but success was wholly in the power of Fortune; these may answer the same, but with a contrary turn."[4] One cannot buy fate. Problems of space, time, and mass were soon to overwhelm Abitibi. This chapter covers the beginning of the disaster. The first section considers how and why newsprint supply grew across the 1920s. The second looks at several issues that altered the dimensions of strategic rivalry and moved the producers into intense competition. The third part reviews the first crisis and the efforts to stem deterioration. Throughout the chapter, the analysis questions the ability of any firm or government to temper what became a drift towards catastrophe.

1. Johnny Canuck's material assets

Modern investment theory presumes economic behaviour reflects the sum of rational choices by people and groups who reach decisions in evaluative ways that help them realize certain goals or preferences. But rational actors do not necessarily drive business developments. Investor psychology can generate manias or panics, while corporate behaviour may be tempered by obsessions, phobias, or escalations of commitment to failing courses of action in the hope of ultimate success. Poor regulatory regimes or disparities in access to information can facilitate deviations from "logical" conduct. Moreover, individual actors may pursue goals where each step taken makes sense to them but the result is a collective cataclysm. When difficulties arise, they presume *others* will step back or show restraint, while they still pursue their strategies. Because newsprint profitability was vulnerable even to

"nowhere near the saturation point," though it was unclear how long the growth might continue. Moreover, while the sector benefited from American capital, Canadians owned three-quarters of the equity of the publicly listed producers and their profits enhanced the national wealth. The commitments financiers placed in the industry were "for more than a ten-day hold and a ten-point rise ... the investor can not go wrong in following the lead of men such as these." Advertising drove American demand but even if it eased further increases in newspaper circulation ensured prosperity. Doubters, it was claimed, did not comprehend how the reading public still grew in size or how publications like the tabloid press created new market segments. It was ridiculous to expect any decrease. Moreover, the inventories of paper held by producers and publishers declined to record low levels. This proved "consumption to-day is following closer on the heels of production than for many moons past."[15]

The rosy optimism ignored several inconvenient matters. First, newsprint alone was profitable for the manufacturers. Pulp mills already were burdened by overproduction. Although imports of pulp by the United States grew, Scandinavian rivalry decreased the Canadian share. Short periods of enhanced sales were followed by longer times of slackened demand and price weakness.[16] Second, because profitability required operating near full capacity, even a marginal departure from that status risked deleterious consequences. Notwithstanding the perceptions about steady growth, any "balance" between supply and demand proved short-lived. It only occurred twice, from late 1922 to early 1924 and from early 1925 to mid-1926, and even then surplus capacity was reported at different times. Newsprint supply was elastic because mill construction soon closed any gaps between output and consumption. Of course, individual factory experiences varied: some achieved full capacity lengthy periods, others less so.

Third, the price of newsprint continued to decline from the postwar spike. The list rate of $80 per ton at the close of 1922 dropped to $70 within a year, held at that level until late 1925, and then was cut to $65. Executives dismissed the trend because the biggest firms usually announced the prior sale of their output. Canada's share of continental production still grew, some rationalized, so where was the problem? Price weakness, instead, reflected seasonal "dullness" that would recover within months or "topheaviness" (surplus capacity that firms might offset by cost reductions, new efficiencies, or manufacturing at high levels to achieve scale effects).[17] The ability to handle slack demand seemed to be confirmed during a 1924 mini-recession when firms curtailed output to 85 per cent of capacity and made sufficient money to pay dividends. Some observers conceded that weak companies might be forced to close, but usually it was argued that lower prices just kept mills busy.[18] Even at those rates, various producers secured averages of $20 to $25 per ton in net profit. What mattered, executives stressed, was the failure to realize *higher* prices because American mills had not yet moved away from newsprint, though the lower rates were expected to force their conversion. But even if this did not occur, they suggested, the survival of American firms was irrelevant because newsprint was sold globally, so opportunities abounded.[19]

Such arguments were misleading at best and delusional at the worst. The price decline impacted the vitality of existing and new manufacturers alike but several issues complicated the trend. Producers and the trade press emphasized changes in the "list" or posted price, that is, the average rate specified by sales contracts. As legal scholars later noted, this amounted to "a fiction," "a base, an approximation, a hypothesis, or an unreality."[20] As with other commodities, the list price was not a uniform offering. There were recognized grades with accepted differentials between them. Varying the pulp mixture or the speed of machines could alter grades. The homogeneous character of newsprint and the standardization of manufacturing further abetted the ability of buyers to substitute suppliers. Hence, an economist characterized the sector as "almost self-regulatory in regard to monopolistic attempts ... When a monopoly is attempted by a group of mills and the price is unduly advanced, it encourages 'grade-shifting' and soon the would-be monopolists find themselves in an oversupplied market."[21]

Collusion was effectively impossible because contracts occurred on a point-to-point basis. Sales were made f.o.b. mill (that is, loaded at the factory and ownership immediately consigned to the purchaser). Sellers never quoted a price other than that for a client's location, and a purchaser was not allowed to buy except at a price equal to what would have been charged at the ultimate destination.[22] Muddling the situation further were the jobbers upon whom small newspapers depended. These companies handled a tenth of all sales with shipments spread over many customers. They charged higher prices but offered credit (which amounted to a discount on sales), whereas large manufacturers demanded payment within sixty days. Jobber prices did not always change at the same time as those offered by large companies and they fluctuated widely during temporary surpluses or shortages. This could add significant pressure for an overall adjustment.[23]

A detailed week-by-week analysis of news and business media from 1921 to 1927 reveals little evidence of price leadership. Companies signalled their inclinations through informal discussions or press stories, which were followed by announcements of contract prices after the waters were tested. The enterprise initiating an explicit change in the list price varied and it usually originated from sales agencies like the Canadian Export Company and G.H. Mead or from smaller firms like Donnacona and Belgo-Canadian. A shift never became final until International Paper announced its rate because the firm might try to undersell rivals. International occasionally signalled that a rate increase was not pending, but it often matched cuts slowly and only on three occasions did the firm initiate a list price change.[24]

Moreover, newspaper chains began using their buyer power to reshape supply and price. William Randolph Hearst *always* believed the cost of newsprint was excessive and he expected special conditions for his firm's volume purchases. It was an attitude the magnate, quite hypocritically, maintained even during the 1930s when producers were forced into bankruptcy and his own enterprise (also hovering on the edge of insolvency) could not pay for supplies. The Hearst group used two subsidiaries, the American Paper Company and the Newspaper and Magazine Paper Corporation, to spread its requirements amongst manufacturers. These agents tried to play firms off against one another or targeted small firms that sold their output to a single customer. Once a price concession was garnered, other producers were asked to match it or risk losing business. The chains moderated anticipated price increases in this way during 1922 and 1923 and then began forcing reductions, either in official rates or via hidden concessions. Philip Dodge of International Paper condemned the practice, arguing the publishers "sandpapered the manufacturers" so the list rate was "forced down and down and down."[25]

A crucial dynamic unfolded as the big publishers had interlocking conditions inserted into contracts. These "protective clauses" stipulated that, regardless of the rates specified in the agreements, if a major sales agency or one of a designated group of firms (typically Abitibi, Great Northern, and International Paper) offered a lower price, the supplier was obligated to match it. The earliest instance occurred during 1920 when Backus-Brooks accepted a clause in order to secure a contract. These protective clauses became standard practice by the middle of the decade. Hence, if a chain compelled a key producer to lower its price, then others, industry-wide, had little choice but to do likewise. The same result occurred if one or more small firms were pressured into offering lower rates, because competitors then felt it necessary to meet the new level. Since it only took one contract to force all others to similar terms, the interlocking clauses became *the* key force behind a downward price spiral.[26]

Although official prices were published, the true rates were kept confidential. To ensure the highest level of capacity use, it was standard practice to offer terms that discounted the delivered cost. Some contracts were made explicitly below a list rate but prices also could be adjusted by grade modifications. Most companies charged differentials for rolls of newsprint versus sheets or less-than-carload shipments. The techniques for manipulation included rebates, special freight allowances, and sliding point systems (prices related to volume purchases). In some instances a commission was paid to a publisher's purchasing agency. Because agreements were negotiated privately and the business press was reluctant to acknowledge circumventions of the official rate, it is impossible to map the practices fully. Nonetheless, reports about the deals circulated, such as the Beaverbrook newspaper chain in Britain receiving a price $5 below the list price during 1925.[27] The pressure from such arrangements eventually triggered an across-the-board slash to a new base in accord with the protective clauses.

Pulp and Paper Magazine railed against each cut. Producers, it argued, responded with panic whenever the prospect of surplus output arose. Their executives behaved like "fond relatives [who] were preparing themselves to sit mournfully at the bedside" of an expiring patient because "it looked as if Mr. Newsprint was about to suffer a serious decline, if not a complete collapse. Those who are about to mourn, however, do not reckon sufficiently with the vitality of the patient; for we find ... a liveliness on the part of Mr. Newsprint that must astonish those looked for feebleness, and delight those who depend upon his activities and for their daily bread."[28] In business, "strategic windows" are brief periods when an enterprise can launch an initiative that reshapes how a product is perceived and thereby achieves a leading position. The journal failed to recognize the reverse possibility – an interval in which investment choices stimulate weakness and then catastrophe.

This unfolded, the *Financial Post* correctly predicted, as a "race," an increase in Canadian production without precedent or an equivalent growth in demand that the journal, like most others, accepted without question. "Taken by and large there is no reason to forecast gloom and decimation." Expansion could not have a permanent effect unless the race became "too fast and furious." After all, an executive like the head of International Paper would not authorize new capacity while "believing that the industry is about to enter the worst period in its history."[29] But that was precisely what happened. As shown in Table 3, manufacturers installed plants and equipment during the early part of the decade at a rate that paralleled but exceeded demand. Canadian

Table 3 Average Annual Change (%) in Newsprint Demand and Supply

	1918–1920	1921–1923	1924–1926	1927–1929	1930–1932
U.S. Newsprint Consumption	6.7	8.8	6.5	4.6	−9.1
North American Production	5.1	6.4	9.8	5.4	−9.7
Canadian Production	9.1	13.8	16.2	13.0	−9.8
North American Capacity	3.8	7.5	7.6	10.3	3.8
Canadian Capacity	10.1	12.6	11.6	19.0	6.1

Source: Extrapolated from Appendix 1.

production began to outstrip American output during 1924 and two years later accounted for nearly a majority of the continental trade. Producers augmented the number and size of mills at a staggering pace. Expansion occurred south of the border but not on a similar scale and American mills only began to convert away from newsprint after 1928. However, the growth of demand slacked from 1926 to 1930 to a quarter of the average annual increase in Canadian capacity. By the summer of 1928 the available resources surpassed consumption by 15 per cent at the continental level; the Canadian industry had a surplus of at least 20 per cent. Even then, more facilities were built, a process that ultimately brought the level of excess to about 50 per cent. Everyone knew what was happening. Most ventures were publicized with considerable fanfare, while newspapers listed mill capacities and the dates for new operations. Several undertakings were delayed for a year or two but almost all announced projects were completed, including those launched after early 1928 when the excess capacity was obvious. Once committed to a new plant, companies continued, hopeful that things would work out, fearful of the risks of withdrawal like default and the loss of resource rights or market share.

Before 1924 Ontario and Quebec each accounted for two-fifths of Canadian capacity but the greatest expansion occurred in the latter province. It had lower labour costs and stumpage fees, was closest by rail to eastern markets, and benefited from access to capital markets in Montreal and New York. Nearly a quarter of the additional resources were spread amongst new mills in Atlantic Canada, British Columbia, Manitoba, or Newfoundland. Approximately a quarter of the expansion originated from companies that were not engaged in papermaking operations before 1925. Thirteen producers had no substantive affiliations with the biggest enterprises or with corporate groups. These so-called independents, located predominantly in Quebec, included Price

Brothers, Brompton, St. Lawrence, and Lake St. John. Fraser, a New Brunswick company, and Nova Scotia's Mersey Paper emerged as independents at the close of the decade. The augmented number of rivals, along with the widening excess of supply versus demand, meant companies with new or expanded facilities could only earn sufficient revenues by finding new customers or (and much more likely) stealing those of rivals.

Executives for the largest companies later insisted the capacity expansion originated from new entrants or moderate-sized rivals. Their own firms were not significant contributors. This was fiction. Between 1924 and 1930 the daily capacity of the companies that became components of Abitibi grew from 1,309 to 2,013 tons; the total for the firms merged into Canada Power and Paper jumped from 875 to 1,944 tons; the Backus-Brooks group from 350 to 825 tons; and Price Brothers from 440 to 1,120 tons. In a farrago of obfuscation, investment bankers subsequently absolved themselves of responsibility. Harry Gundy later told a parliamentary committee that the earnings, even after 1927, were "so satisfactory as to command ready supply of capital by investors" and the new capacity "was not brought about by any uncontrolled extension of credit." The head of the Canadian Bankers' Association declared "men of standing, experience and good repute" analysed the producers carefully. They financed them with legitimate offerings that exposed investors "to no greater risks than those normal hazards to which all commercial undertakings are of necessity subject." Perhaps there were some "for which too rosy a picture was painted in order to capitalize the popular speculative fever but these were few and far between." Instead, he attributed the industry's difficulties not to unwise choices but to the weather, that is, environmental circumstances beyond anyone's influence such as decreased exports or "the reluctance of our own people who have money to spend it as they used to do."[30]

If firms were lured by the profit opportunities, provincial administrations hoped to capitalize on the gains associated with economic development, but their success varied. In Quebec symbiotic relationships between government and business enabled companies to secure relatively unfettered access to resources. Like Ontario, the province encouraged agricultural settlement in the north. The policy proved unsuccessful and by the 1920s rural depopulation, francophone emigration to the United States, and high unemployment represented serious threats. Whereas nationalists believed the nurturing of Quebecois firms and the diversification of local economies were appropriate goals, the government of Louis-Alexandre Taschereau perceived industrialization via hydro-electric projects and one-company towns as the only strategy

stumpage fees were raised to levels exceeding other Eastern Canadian locations, the government crowed with each passing year about how it had collected the largest revenue ever. Allocations of timber concessions were suspended for two years and when resumed were subject to blatant manipulation. Thus, while Ontario contributed to the industry's growth, it was never the key source. It garnered just a fifth of the capacity installed in Canada from 1924 to 1930. Not only did the province's share decrease, numerous anticipated ventures proved illusory. Lyons promised the development of 1,000 tons of new daily capacity at the Lakehead. Slightly over half of that sum was ever realized. Another mirage surfaced during the autumn of 1926, in the midst of an election, when Howard Ferguson announced how Alexander Smith would establish at Cochrane a 200-ton newsprint mill employing 500 men. Noting the lack of water in the area, opponents dismissed the statement as just "political propaganda." Ferguson insisted his government had persuaded Smith about "the great stimulus it would be to the whole district to place a large permanent industry where it will not only assist in industrial expansion, but will provide a pay-roll that will make an excellent local market for the farm produce of the district." But the premier left a back door wide open, as his secretary noted to a local official. "The question of water supply is one for the company to deal with and not for the Government." Historians disagree about whether the pronouncement was just an electioneering stunt, but the question is moot – three months later Cochrane ratepayers refused to pass the bylaws needed to make the scheme viable.[44]

If Abitibi's executives retained any illusions about the attitudes of provincial officials, they had vanished by this point. The Farmers' administration, just before its electoral defeat, approved the timberlands Anson had sought. Although the Tories did not alter the terms, they took another year before issuing the order-in-council that activated the agreement. Unlike other contracts, it did not specify the appropriate fees. Instead, the firm was instructed to pay rates the cabinet set every five years, subject only to a provision that the charges could not exceed "the price at which the general public shall be permitted to cut on other portions of the Crown domain." Drury's government moved the bulk of the Abitibi Extension westward away from the "reserve" along the Quebec border Ferguson had promised in 1919. The territory was nearly twice the size of Abitibi's original grant but its design meant the available rivers flowed north away from the mill site. Not only did this make extraction costs excessive, the company had to spend $1.8 million for a 42-kilometre railroad to move timber out of the Extension. Even then, only 10,000 cords of pulpwood were accessible, although the executives thought another 600,000 cords might be reached with additional construction. Several attempts to secure small nearby tracts were rebuffed by Ferguson without explanation.[45] The firm also sought properties that permitted a conversion of Abitibi Fibre from pulp to newsprint production. Clarkson disclosed during the Mattagami receivership that additional wood was required just to keep operations going. Two months after Abitibi completed the acquisition it requested lands north of the mill, which Mattagami had sought for years. Staff within the Department of Lands and Forests supported the application but wanted to stipulate the timber must be used for making paper, not pulp. The department's official statement promised a positive response. "The Government, realizing the necessity of keeping intact going concerns, is now considering all these inquiries." The reality was less edifying. The lands were put up for auction but the province rescinded the sale after Abitibi and two other firms had submitted bids, again without explanation.[46]

Ontario claimed to be helpful with established firms but the experiences of the largest enterprises (Abitibi, Backus-Brooks, and Spanish River) never conformed to that image. The writer in *Saturday Night* legitimately observed that most of the existing mills "contrary to general belief, are now without timber supplies sufficient to ensure permanency." He wanted changes that guaranteed each operation adequate resources for at least sixty years. But the issues went further. After 1923 just two entrants to New Ontario succeeded in acquiring extensive properties. Only one undertook the construction of productive operations and it took a long time before fruition. After the enquiry into the failed colony at Kapuskasing, Premier Drury, hoping for a local industry, turned over 25,000 acres of pulpwood to Spruce Falls Pulp and Paper. Wisconsin-based Kimberly-Clarke then bought the firm but would commit only to a sulphite pulp operation and demanded up to eight years before building a 75-ton newsprint mill. Construction began but was suspended when the postwar recession intensified. The firm's executives claimed the pulp factory would cost four times the original estimates and they demanded contractual extensions that the government had little choice but to accept. The problems continued: large stores of pulpwood were washed away by flooding, a fire destroyed the construction camp and power project, the mill's start-up difficulties became so extensive they were falsely attributed to sabotage. Premier Drury later recalled how the "place became a disreputable huddle of disreputable shacks, mostly tenanted by disreputable people. I was in one way relieved when we got word that a fire had wiped the whole thing out."[47] The company met its supply requirements by purchasing

wood from settlers but continual losses convinced the executives a
large expansion represented the only solution. This move was accompanied by efforts to secure additional rights that culminated during the
bidding contest with Mattagami. Whereas other producers preferred to
operate outside of the apparatus of the state (and deal with political
officials intermittently as issues arose), the representatives for Spruce
Falls mounted the equivalent of a "full court press." The sustained lobbying included the creation of ongoing relationships with key personnel, particularly Howard Ferguson. The *New York Times* took a
half-ownership position, which slashed financial requirements and
guaranteed a market for the output. Spruce Falls finally proceeded with
the construction of a 550-ton newsprint mill, which opened in the
autumn of 1928 with enormous publicity or, as the company's vice-
president commented, just "about the time the seriousness of the situation of the industry was fully realized."[48]

2. One of the greatest industrial coups

During September 1925 the *Financial Post* suggested that the newsprint
manufacturers were "getting themselves into excellent financial shape"
and "setting their house in order against any possibility of too keen
competition. They are ready to meet it."[49] In fact, from 1924 to 1928,
head-to-head rivalry intensified and this phenomenon, not just the
expansion of capacity, created severe price-based competition. The shift
began with a reorientation of International Paper. Philip Dodge, the
president since 1913, had concentrated upon converting mills to alternative paper goods and had launched several hydro-electric projects.
These manoeuvres, along with the construction of the Trois-Rivières
plant, stabilized International's performance but Dodge approached
expansion north of the border reluctantly.[50] In May 1924 he denied
reports of discord within the company. Two days later the board of
directors forced his resignation. It unanimously affirmed a commitment to low-cost plants in Canada and appointed Archibald R. Graustein, who was just thirty-nine years old, as the new president. The son
of a Prussian-born Boston milkman, Graustein, who quickly emerged
as a prodigy, carried out undergraduate and then law studies at Harvard. He joined the Boston firm of Ropes, Gray, and Gorham, and participated in several large corporate reconstructions where he gained
expertise in what were then termed "broad-gauge financial policies,"
that is, the extensive use of capital for major undertakings. During 1922
Graustein was appointed to the bondholders' committee in the Riordon
bankruptcy as a representative for Boston interests. Across the next two

years, the committee supervised all decisions to preserve the resources.[51] Observers characterized "Archie" Graustein as incredibly smart but austere, a work-obsessed person who took few breaks. He had a gift for mastering details, organizing complex ventures, and (unlike Alexander Smith) learning everything about a business. Although Graustein was moderate in physical height, those traits later led many to portray him as "a veritable giant," the "most feared man" in the paper industry, one who manipulated both competitors and governments.[52]

With extensive connections and insider knowledge, Graustein was expected to secure the Riordan properties. Three weeks after his appointment as president, the bondholders applied for a judicial auction and leaked stories about how International would gain possession. They paid a price that recompensed Killam and other senior investors but left nothing for the creditors and equity holders. An agreement for a takeover was reached by the end of the year but it took until the following summer to finalize the sale.[53] The transaction, a "stupendous bargain" at less than a third of the market value, overnight altered International's status by providing it with two huge pulp mills, water rights, and nearly 26,000 square kilometres of timberlands – about the combined size of Connecticut, Massachusetts, and Rhode Island. The acquisition, the firm declared, marked an "official recognition" that Canada would secure all future growth in the supply of newsprint due to its cheap wood and electricity. International desired "to avail itself of these economic factors and to work with them instead of against them." The Riordon properties would steady earnings to a degree not previously realized. "Paper, lumber, and power are three commodities for which there will be an increasing demand as our civilization becomes more closely coordinated."[54] Analysts believed the takeover guaranteed International had an unlimited pulpwood supply.[55]

The firm announced a doubling of the Trois-Rivières mill's capacity and the construction of a massive factory at Gatineau near Ottawa. The new facilities were equal to the combined capacity of its American newsprint mills. Incorporated with the latest innovations, each was capable of manufacturing eight times more newsprint per day than the best of their American counterparts. Moreover, the new machines were much wider than comparable equipment in older mills, an attribute favoured by chain newspapers.[56] Within two years an additional $105 million was invested with the Canadian subsidiaries. International, Graustein asserted, was "advancing its commanding position by following a definite and carefully worked out program," but it was predicated upon several doubtful assumptions. Any gaps between consumption and supply were deemed temporary because "steadily increasing demand" offset any risk with greater capacity, a perspective Graustein maintained until 1930. Net earnings would improve as the new mills came on line and International's American factories were reoriented towards other forms of paper. Because manufacturing those products required less electricity than newsprint, enhanced revenues might be secured from power sales. But the strategy also contained a peril: until the conversion process was well advanced, International's capacity devoted to newsprint was double the pre-1925 level. The new operations slashed its average costs by $10 per ton within a year, thereby enabling the firm to pursue a volume strategy (with price-cutting if necessary) to maintain operations at full capacity.[57]

Geographic expansion into other regions, particularly Atlantic Canada, constituted another element of the strategic reorientation. International had long held properties in New Brunswick and circumvented export regulations by cutting pulpwood on private, not public, lands. Dodge, when pressed about local production, contended "bankers simply laugh in the face of promoters" for endeavours "situated in a wild country with a sparse population." Threats of retaliatory action by the province were pathetic; it repeatedly extended the leases on promised guarantees of eventual action.[58] In 1925, elected to encourage economic growth and halt outward migration, a new government privatized a planned hydro-electric facility on the St. John River to an International Paper subsidiary. The company promised to undertake an investment of $40 million if it secured "necessary rights." Despite difficult negotiations, International acquired not only additional timberlands but control of all possible power project sites located downriver. This ensured the company would not have future rivals in the Saint John and Miramichi valleys. In 1928 it finally agreed to construct a 550-ton mill at Dalhousie, which did not start operations until the worst of the Depression three years later.[59]

The firm concurrently bought lands in Labrador and investigated a newsprint mill at Corner Brook. Graustein agreed to buy the plant (which had not been profitable since it opened and was on the edge of default) but only if the colonial and British governments accepted a contentious agreement. International Paper spent $2.5 million for an operation with assets written down to $335,000 and it committed to double the capacity from 400 to 800 tons. In exchange, the Bank of England was obligated to buy $10 million of preference stock, while the governments guaranteed $20 million of bonds. With the debt load reduced, observers perceived the Newfoundland facility as a low-cost operation that had easy access to European and east-coast markets.[60]

Both deals were controversial because Graustein exploited his bargaining leverage to extract concessions from small provinces desperate for economic development. His tactics rekindled perceptions of International Paper as a ruthless behemoth – one, as the leader of the opposition in New Brunswick decried, that took advantage of politicians willing to violate the public trust and engage in "an exhibition of servile subserviency to the Big Interests."[61] International further garnered an array of options or properties in Manitoba and Ontario either directly or through intermediary companies. Similar to the company's earlier undertakings, the holdings had several functions: speculative investments for exploitation at some future point, lands that could be withheld from use by competitors, or manoeuvres intended to alarm or distract rivals. None developed significant operations. All were later abandoned or repossessed for non-compliance with licence terms.

Those endeavours, nonetheless, paled in comparison to others launched by the firm. International's declared assets doubled to $231 million between 1924 and 1926 and then mushroomed to $767 million by 1929. A forceful acquisition and construction strategy in the Southern states placed an emphasis upon the manufacture of kraft paper, which could be used for a wide range of purposes, including wrapping materials, corrugated cartons, and containers. Demand cycles for kraft products were short and unstable but offered significant profit potential. By 1930, with five mills, the Southern Kraft Corporation was International's most successful subsidiary.[62] The centrepiece of Graustein's program, nonetheless, was an expansion of hydro-electrical activities. Given the capital-intensive requirements associated with the development at Trois-Rivières, Dodge sold off the water rights in exchange for guarantees about inexpensive energy supply. Graustein, in contrast, saw power sales as a means of smoothing financial performance. Several older American mills were converted to electrical generation and International established linkages with larger generation and distribution systems. In several stages the firm gained control over the New England Power Association, one of the largest utility groups. The manoeuvres entailed multiple rounds of recapitalization and organizational restructuring, but New England was so gargantuan that International never gained more than a minority stake and the investment was never consolidated with its other activities.[63]

Nearly half of the hydro-electric investments were focused on one venture. Constructed over four years, Gatineau Power entailed a massive construction of infrastructure, as well as the acquisition of local utilities and related services. The project fit well with Taschereau's development policy and gained support from the Ontario government.

Confronted by a looming energy shortage and heavy Hydro debts, Ferguson was unwilling to shoulder the costs associated with new operations. His administration never enforced the licences for timber concessions that International Paper or its intermediaries secured in Northern Ontario, a practice that was always easily explained. They were chickenfeed in comparison to the vote-getting benefits provided by a deal that assured cheap energy from Quebec. Negotiations between Graustein and the Hydro Commission led to a thirty-year supply agreement that appeared to cover anticipated demand and allowed purchases at advantageous rates.[64] International built smaller projects in New Brunswick but that province insisted the facilities must also be used for paper manufacturing.

The scale of these endeavours prompted a paean of acclaim about Graustein's "constructive imagination." *Barron's* suggested "a sleeping giant has awakened to seize revolutionary economic changes in the industry." The investments placed International "head and shoulders above any newsprint competitor" with "an impregnable position." One writer claimed the industry "had never laid the foundations for permanent prosperity" because it was still characterized by old inefficient mills. "No Moses had appeared" to lead it out of the wilderness even though the day of the small plant "with its patch of woodland yielding a cheap, though limited, supply of raw material is gone. The era of large-scale production with ample capital investment … has arrived." The *Financial Post* argued International's future was assured. "Ten years hence the company should be coining money."[65] As the scale, pace, and multi-industry character of the initiatives escalated, some were shocked and appalled. Even the *Financial Post* by 1928 wondered whether Graustein "is perhaps planning one of the greatest industrial coups ever conceived in the mind of man" and "intends to acquire what amounts to the complete control of the forest assets and newsprint making equipment on this continent. The achievement of such an end would be without parallel in the annals of industry and finance."[66]

Market gossip periodically circulated that International might acquire rivals like Abitibi but little evidence ever surfaced to corroborate such tales. Indeed, the notion was contrary to Graustein's *modus operandi* – making acquisitions on the cheap, not at their market worth. Moreover, his company was less stable than appearances suggested. Press accounts, while lauding the new ventures, also kept postponing forecasts about when investors might expect an improvement of International's earnings. After 1926 the hydro projects were perceived as the ultimate means for achieving a turnaround. Professional analysts deemed the returns on International's equity unattractive and some stressed how its profits from newsprint declined after 1925. When International's shares rose in value during 1927, investors were cautioned about how the stock "undoubtedly attracted a speculative following that would perhaps scarcely maintain its holdings through a period of generally declining prices."[67] Though substantial, International's expansion amounted to just a fifth of the increase in newsprint supply from 1924 to 1930. It merely kept the firm's share of North American capacity stable (see Appendix 2.6). The new capacity in Quebec was scheduled to come on line from 1926 to late 1927, the mills in New Brunswick and Newfoundland not until after 1929. The firm sold equity for funding the Riordon acquisition and the initial expansion program. Thereafter new issues of debt or preferred stock were used, which weighted the capital structure towards financing with heavy fixed charges (see Appendix 3). If International operated at less than full capacity, the risk of default was quite significant.

International's growth accelerated the combination of rival mills into corporate groups, although there is only fragmentary evidence that it propelled specific amalgamations. Rumours about mergers of Quebec firms, started circulating during 1922 with tales that suggested international financiers were masterminds of the prospective schemes but the stories actually originated from local promoters. One entailed the consolidation of four companies, thereby creating a $75 million enterprise, "a strong combination [that] will tend to strengthen the hands of Canadian manufacturers" and ensure the "removal of [the] dangers of competition." That tale proved to be a mirage, but Sir Herbert Holt and James Henry "Harry" Gundy later brought together the firms and several others. Holt, with a reputation as a veritable "captain of industry," sat on more than a hundred corporate boards, and was the titular head of the Royal Bank of Canada. Gundy was a wheeler-dealer, a respected capitalist who coordinated numerous mergers or reorganizations across the 1920s.[68] He helped float capital for the Bay Sulphite Company, a concern formed to supply pulp to British newspapers, during 1923 but the main investor went bankrupt. After trying to get other producers to buy the mill, the financiers conducted a friendly takeover, retitling it Port Alfred Pulp and Paper. An aggressive promotion of equity and bond sales quadrupled the capitalization over the next two years but the firm never expanded the level of pulp output, while a new paper mill managed to operate at only half of its rated capacity. Port Alfred acquired partial stakes in Anticosti Corporation and Quebec Pulp and Paper.[69] Holt and Gundy then purchased the St. Maurice Valley Corporation, as well as 85 per cent of the common stock of Belgo-Canadian Paper. Holt became president (and Gundy, vice-president) of a reorganized St. Maurice but the assets of Belgo-Canadian were not consolidated with the enterprise. This manoeuvre was followed by acquisitions of Canada Paper (a fine-paper producer) and Laurentide Paper.[70]

Early in 1928 the companies were reorganized as subsidiaries of a new enterprise, Canada Power and Paper. The process was replicated two years later with a takeover of Wayagamack, a kraft paper manufacturer, and an intended merger with Anglo-Canadian Pulp and Paper. Gundy later claimed the underlying reason was to create "harmonious groups" and "eliminate causes of friction in the industry which were destructive." In fact, Canada Power and Paper was a holding company. The managers of the former enterprises were kept in place and operated their firms as before. Few efforts were made to redistribute output according to plant efficiency. Canada Power acquired most of the common stock of the subsidiaries but, unlike Abitibi, never converted the financial structure to something more orderly. The mergers did create a multi-site enterprise that was larger than International Paper's Canadian subsidiary, one that might compete against it on a comparable basis. "Rationalization," instead, revolved around the hydro-electric facilities. Shawinigan Water and Power, a Holt-controlled enterprise, sold electricity to International's Trois-Rivières mill. Laurentide's hydroelectric subsidiary was sold to Shawinigan, which strengthened its position vis-à-vis Gatineau Power. Gundy never admitted that apprehension about International had any influence, although he conceded it was "a very active, progressive concern" that "would, no doubt, have been in the minds of their competitors."[71]

The group with the most troubled formation, was Backus-Brooks, which arose from the empire-building escapades of an American lumber baron who was introduced in the preceding chapter. The son of a New York stone mason and farmer, Edward Wellington Backus acquired a Minnesota sawmill in 1883 and across the following two decades organized a syndicate to exploit timberlands in the state and launched an array of enterprises that included railways, mining companies, telephone utilities, and a bank. William F. Brooks gained a working interest in exchange for capital that permitted the acquisition of water sites on both sides of the border. Their activities were reorganized into Minnesota and Ontario Paper, a holding vehicle that remained under Backus's control. It eventually comprised a network of companies that ranged from North America to Scandinavia, which only Backus fully comprehended. He was notoriously secretive, often working through intermediaries or shell companies to obscure business manoeuvres.[72] Where his firms provided much-needed employment, Backus was considered a "modern Napoleon," "a man of splendid physique ... the head of a statesman and shoulders of a gladiator." Politicians, businessmen, and the Toronto press considered the industrialist a buccaneer, calculating at best, deceitful at worst, "a slippery old man" Sir Joseph Flavelle sneered.[73] Across his career innumerable disputes unfolded with state, provincial, and federal governments, as well as the International Joint Commission, which included violations of licence agreements, failures to honour contracts, ecological damage, attempts to create local monopolies, fraud, and tax evasion.

A cosy affiliation with the Liberal government helped Backus to secure resource rights in Northwestern Ontario but after the 1905 election the permits were cancelled, which the Conservatives then flipped to their supporters. Thereafter, the Tories never trusted Backus, convinced that he had twisted their political opponents to get the rights. One Backus-controlled mill was built in Fort Frances. A contractually stipulated extension of the plant and the construction of another factory at Kenora were delayed for a decade as the businessman claimed sufficient pulpwood was unavailable. The Tories, who thought the delays illustrated how Backus was a devious operator, denied all requests. It took him fifteen years to secure additional properties, this time from the United Farmers, in the form of the English River concession that Frank Anson had rejected. Intense controversy ensued because Backus exploited his relations with a local MLA, Peter Heenan, and other known supporters of the government. The publication of a licence that specified a nominal expense for a large territory had a predictable outcome. The Tories responded with merciless attacks on what they portrayed as a surreptitious deal that originated from political ineptitude, hypocritical venality, and outright chicanery.[74]

Across the early 1920s Backus extended his American business activities but different attempts to acquire properties or develop mills in Manitoba and Ontario were stymied. His opportunity came with a Lakehead project, Great Lakes Paper, that had failed to progress due to multiple disputes among the promoters, Ontario's Hydro Commission, the municipalities of Fort William and Port Arthur, and the province. Backus quietly gained a position as a minority partner. Great Lakes in 1923 agreed to build a pulp mill that would supply his Ontario factories but the promoters declined to construct a newsprint plant even though it was a licence condition. After further disputes amongst themselves and with the province, the other partners sold out to International Paper. Backus had little choice but to gain full ownership by repurchasing their stakes at a premium from International. After negotiations with Hydro guaranteed an acceptable quantity and price for electricity, in 1928 he announced the construction of a mill with the widest paper

machine in the world. Backus now believed he was on the way to consolidating a forest products regime that encompassed Ontario and several Lake states.[75]

Within three years the Canadian industry thus was transformed from
one of moderate-sized to small mills into four corporate groups and
numerous independent firms. Smaller-scale unofficial relations, joint
ventures, or resource-sharing arrangements tied various independents
together. The corporate groups theoretically constituted an oligopoly
within Canada but *only* if they were prepared to coordinate operations.
Such initiatives were to prove short-lived and only included a few of
the groups, never all four. The independent mills accounted for nearly
half of Canadian capacity and had little incentive to support collective
efforts. But the transition towards multi-site enterprises also reconfig-
ured strategic rivalry. The corporate groups overlapped geographically
and could more easily service the requirements of chain newspapers
than single mills. Ontario and Quebec producers had been somewhat
distinctive. The former concentrated upon the midwestern region, from
Buffalo to Chicago and St. Louis; the latter sold to the north-east and
mid-Atlantic states. Those areas provided sufficient demand for each
but this altered as the size and number of mills grew. Full capacity operations were needed to cover the financial obligations. After 1925 the
logic for invading markets became irresistible and escalated the degree
of head-to-head competition.

The structure of railway rates was crucial to this amalgamation of
geographic markets. Transport costs historically have borne little relationship to sale prices. Other things being equal, shipping as a component of total expenses for customers is more significant for bulky
commodities than for goods with high value added. The transport
share tends to be less important when prices are high or climbing, but
it can become a critical matter if they are low or declining. For example, during the Great Depression freight charges reached nearly a
quarter of the delivered value of newsprint.[76] Until the early 1930s
most shipments were by railroad. Thereafter water transport took a
greater share given the access of Quebec and Atlantic Canadian mills
to coastal markets and the construction of new infrastructure for Great
Lakes travel.[77] Freight rates were fixed by law or regulation and were
out of the control of either producers or customers. They consisted of
multiple classes, groups, and subgroups of prices. Although the tariff
structure rested upon basic principles, the rules and procedures were
vague or self-contradictory. Regulators took into account topography,
percentages of idle capacity, or seasonal variations that influenced car-
rier costs. Distances of haul were not treated as homogeneous factors,

that is, rates for longer distances were not just multiples of shorter ones. Intense lobbying could turn hearings into long sessions. Canadian and American regulators therefore were loath to amend the rate structure. Historical precedent prevailed, which often was derived from practices adopted before the creation of the regulatory agencies. In addition, under Canadian and American policy, previously published schedules by carriers, not actual charges on shipments, were used to compute new rate levels.[78]

The result was a framework that favoured older centres of production like New England and New York but also southern Quebec. The rates for newsprint shipments were *never* according to distance from markets. As shown in Figure 3, the United States was segmented into several zones east to west. The largest was termed "official territory" and contained half of the American population and the bulk of industrial activity. Newsprint manufacturers based in the northeast enjoyed low rates for haulage 2,600 to 3,400 kilometres to cities like Chicago because railways had sought to build up business in the late nineteenth century. Thus, the firms retained a competitive advantage versus manufacturers located nearer.[79] The policy was contentious but midwestern producers failed to have it overturned as unreasonable.[80] Papermakers in southern Quebec, often termed the "Grand-Mère group,"[81] were located relatively close to mid-Atlantic urban centres but they also retained advantageous rates. Canadian regulators chose to reinforce the preferential status of the Quebec producers further. North and west of Grand-Mère an arbitrary line was used to segment mills and designate shipping costs.[82] This mattered because a variation of $1 per ton on the delivered price was enough for customers to reject contract proposals. The implications are illustrated in Table 4, which summarizes shipping costs from different mills. Iroquois Falls, Espanola, and Sturgeon Falls were classified as "eastern" mills with rates similar to the Grand-Mère group.[83] "Western" points, especially the Lakehead and beyond, had cheap rates for locations like St. Louis and Kansas City but operated at a disadvantage for the Midwestern states. This regime prevented most Ontario companies from supplying the north-eastern and mid-Atlantic markets handled by Québec companies. The deputy minister for Ontario's Department of Lands and Forests argued the midwestern states were "naturally tributary" to northern mills because they had "a freight advantage to their logical market of from $2.00 to $5.00 over Quebec and eastern Canada."[84] Table 4 demonstrates this was false. An advantage for locations like St. Louis, Kansas City, or Omaha only existed for mills located at the Lakehead or further west. Locations designated by regulators as "Eastern," which included most

Figure 3 Railway Freight Territories

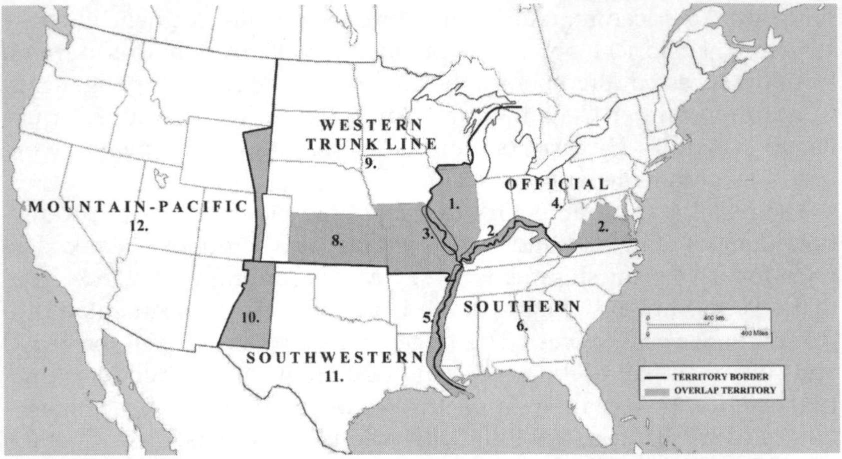

Source: Interstate Commerce Commission, Bureau of Transport
Economics and Statistics, Freight Rate Territory Classification.

of Abitibi's operations, had rates for midwestern markets similar to
Quebec producers. There was nothing to block Grand-Mère enterprises
from going after business in the Pittsburgh to Milwaukee area where
the sales of Ontario's firms were concentrated, especially if Quebec
manufacturers were prepared to accept low profit for high volume.

By the early autumn of 1925, the *Financial Post* began to speculate
about the future. The following spring it suggested executives were
aware of the risk of overproduction "and they ought to know."[85] Few,
including the *Post* in other articles, conceded this was true. The head of
Price Brothers acknowledged the industry's expansion generated uncertainty because it lacked precedent, but he made the statement as part of
an announcement about how his own firm was making another capacity
increase. A proposal by Alexander Smith to double Abitibi's output generated widespread concern about the potential risk unless the capacity
was timed to match market trends. Senior managers at International
Paper, in contrast, insisted there was greater threat of undersupply. The
North American market was "far from saturation." Viscount Rothermere, a British press baron, went further and claimed a shortage loomed.
New York's *Journal of Commerce* insisted the doubters were not as numerous as they had been a year earlier and dismissed any concerns because
excess capacity occurred periodically.[86] Across 1926 the ability of
demand to match supply still appeared true. At year's end, Archibald

Table 4 Newsprint Railway Freight Rates, per ton, 1928–1930

From/To	Boston	New York	Philadelphia	Buffalo	Pittsburgh	Cleveland	Detroit	Chicago	St. Louis
Trois Rivières	$6.80	$6.80	$7.60	$5.70	$6.10	$6.40	$6.40	$7.70	$9.10
Grand-Mère	6.80	6.80	7.60	5.70	6.10	6.40	6.40	7.7	9.10
Ottawa-Hull	6.80	6.80	7.50	5.70	6.10	6.40	6.40	7.70	9.10
Iroquois Falls	8.80	8.80	8.80	5.70	6.10	6.40	6.40	7.70	9.30
Espanola	8.30	8.20	8.20	5.70	6.10	6.40	6.40	7.70	6.90
Sturgeon Falls	7.60	8.10	8.20	5.70	6.10	6.40	6.40	7.70	9.10
Sault Ste. Marie	9.10	9.50	11.40	6.90	6.90	5.90	5.80	6.60	5.80
Fort William	15.60	15.20	14.80	10.70	10.70	9.70	7.80	9.00	7.40
Pine Falls	16.40	16.00	15.70	11.00	12.50	9.60	9.60	9.60	7.40

Source: Adjusted from cwt. rates quoted by Guy Tombs Ltd., in J.N. Stephenson, *National Directory of the Canadian Pulp and Paper Mills and Allied Trades, 1929* (Gardenvale, PQ: 1930), 180; *CSI*, A8.

Graustein proclaimed the situation fundamentally sound. One analyst even suggested competition would decline because there were few timberlands left unclaimed. In fact, firms already had begun to alter their marketing practices in anticipation of intensified rivalry.[87]

The Canadian producers tended to sell their output through sales agencies: G.H. Mead for Abitibi and Spanish River, and the Canadian Export Company, St. Maurice Sales, or other firms for Quebec producers. An initial consolidation occurred during 1926 as part of the Holt-Gundy efforts. St. Maurice combined its marketing operations with Belgo-Canadian into a new corporation, which also handled contracts for several other mills. Then the Hearst group enticed Brompton Pulp and Paper to withdraw from the Canadian Export Company and bought all of its output.[88] Press stories suggested cooperative selling might be adopted as a method for handling any excess capacity but intercompany negotiations were triggered by lower demand during early 1927. A "gigantic conception" of joint marketing by the producers was advanced as a collective effort to counter International Paper, which had begun to seek out clients in anticipation of the completion of its new mills. The official goal of this agency, the Canadian Newsprint Company, was characterized as an "energetic broadening of the market for Canadian newsprint through the development of overseas business."[89] With a single sales force and less direct competition, press commentators suggested an immediate cut of the list price below $65 per ton was less likely. It might prevent competitive "turbulence" as the lower rate propelled the closing of inefficient mills, which supposedly then would trigger a short-lived price spike followed by another drop. Whether there was any realism in those speculations was a separate matter because 1,540 daily tons of new capacity were scheduled to come on line by the end of the year.[90]

The marketing organization was capitalized at $5 million of preferred shares, with another 10,000 no par value common shares distributed pro rata among the members according to their output. The initial participants included Abitibi, Spanish River, Manitoba Paper, Fort William, Ste. Anne, Laurentide, Port Alfred, St. Maurice, Price Brothers, and Anglo-Canadian. The company apportioned orders among the mills and purchased their output, which then was resold to publishers. Executives from the firms comprised the board of directors but two former Spanish River managers held the positions of president and treasurer, which led to subsequent claims that Canadian Newsprint was a device controlled by George Mead and geared towards creating a sales monopoly. Numerous mills never joined, while the participants retained the right to withdraw on short notice. International declined to participate but claimed it would cooperate. Canadian Newsprint announced a pricing arrangement that offered a uniform rate for customers by their location regardless of where newsprint was produced. It anticipated the policy introduced by International Paper six months later, which will be discussed below.[91]

The organization handled sales for a quarter of North American output and it was well known that this share would drop to less than a third of Canadian (and a fifth of continental) capacity by the end of 1927. Chain publishers suggested the agency constituted a gigantic trust, a price-fixing cartel. The *Financial Post*, more accurately, noted too many producers did not join to allow it to hike rates.[92] In theory, savings might be realized from shared marketing and lower transport costs as shipments were made from mills close to customers, but the real gains entailed a restriction of spot market pressure and a squeeze out of jobbers. The *Post* legitimately stressed how with many firms refusing to participate "there will naturally always remain the possibility of price cutting by some of the producers." Few therefore doubted the venture amounted to an interim measure, "a prelude to an ultimate newsprint concerto which will end in a loud crescendo of mergers between the various interests involved."[93]

3. Cat out of the paper bag

The marketing association unravelled within six months and collapsed just as Abitibi began the process of refinancing. The reasons were never mysterious. The initiative was launched while most executives perceived "a remarkable and almost uninterrupted growth year by year." Even "the cleverest man in the industry," Archie Graustein, misread how fast things were changing. Excess capacity, he reiterated just before Christmas in 1927, made it difficult "to maintain prices at levels justified by capital investments and costs of manufacturing," but a worldwide increase in consumption would soon restore a balance.[94] Some analysts suggested the association enabled the industry to pass through a critical period. This was wishful thinking. Within two months of its formation, North American production eased back to the level that prevailed a year earlier when mills operated near full capacity. The addition of new mills meant the average production rate lagged about 10 per cent behind 1926 and, by the autumn, capacity use was between 80 and 85 per cent. The groundwood pulp market collapsed and advertising lineage in newspapers decreased across the summer of 1927, making it clear that production had reached a point where surplus capabilities undermined competitive stability.[95] The corporate mergers also brought into question the logic behind the marketing association. Abitibi's amalgamation and the creation of Canada Power gave the two groups a majority on the board and an ability to control the allocation of sales contracts.

The incentive to undercut the list rate proved seductive as market conditions weakened, a situation compounded by the start-up of International's Gatineau plant. With a large proportion of Canadian producers outside the cooperative association, one analyst observed, "the inevitable happened. Certain mills resolved that they were not going to have their machines idle, even if the Heavens fell, or the bottom fell out of the market." It was an open secret that independent mills made freight concessions that kept their prices below the official level of $65 per ton, a "way of finer shading yet of announced reduced prices."[96] Several, based upon their proximity to eastern urban areas, offered reductions (when combined with low freight charges) that brought the cost for customers down to the $58 to $60 range. The trigger for an explicit shift of the list price was a contract St. Lawrence Paper signed with Scripps-Howard, which was well under the rate and entailed a loss of sales for several members of the marketing association. The Hearst chain, engaged in negotiations with Canadian Newsprint, then demanded a rate around $57, while blustering about how it might buy from Scandinavia. Through an affiliate, Canadian Paper Sales, the association reached an agreement-in-principle for a ten-year contract with Hearst that entailed annual sales of 300,000 tons. The chain was promised most favoured treatment and conditions that matched the best offered to other customers. If Hearst gained control over other newspapers east of a line from Montana to western Texas, the association was granted first options on supply. Hearst operations, in turn, could draw for extra newsprint from the allocations designated for later years. The chain paid a basic freight cost and specified charges to certain cities but the association absorbed further expenses and gave credit for charges below the designated rates. These measures ensured pricing was segmented regionally, with nominal rates that ranged between $63 and $71 per ton according to a newspaper's location. However, William Randolph Hearst personally received a special commission and his firm gained a remission of any costs over $50 per ton, conditions which brought the real price to $59 per ton.[97]

Abitibi and Spanish River transferred to the association control over their existing sales with Hearst for 125,000 tons annually. The executives of the companies assumed that the sales arrangements would continue undisturbed. Brompton and Anglo-Canadian, both completing the construction of mills, also expected to benefit. However, most of the business allocated by the marketing association apparently went to

Holt-Gundy companies. Even though the new Hearst contract was not finalized, the deliveries began during January, disguised as "spot tonnage." Inevitably, information about the scheme leaked, was published in American papers, and turned into a gigantic blunder. The organization officially established to abet a stabilization of the list price was revealed to have emasculated it and discriminated in favour of Hearst. Upon disclosure, customers attacked the deal as inequitable, a violation of the understanding that all buyers received similar treatment. They demanded equal terms based upon the interlocking clauses in their contracts. Alexander Smith conceded the outrage represented "a serious indictment of our relationships with our customers." An implicit signal also had been sent about the future. As one newspaper noted, if a customer shifted business for a reduced price "is there any guarantee that this customer having broken the square – shall we call it the hollow square? – will not shift his connection for a further concession from somewhere else?" An "unprofitable industry is an unstable one" and once the price was cut other mills would slash prices further.[98]

Attempting to salvage the situation, the president of Canadian Newsprint was made a scapegoat, forced to resign, and the scheme was cancelled with the euphemistic declaration about how it was "unsound in principle." Anglo-Canadian and Brompton withdrew and promptly concluded separate deals with Hearst for the promised business at $59 per ton.[99] Price Brothers then announced its withdrawal. Hearst sued for breach of trust, demanding $24.7 million in costs and damages against Canadian Paper Sales and the association's members. They filed a countersuit, claiming Hearst had not paid for delivered newsprint. Hearst had the Canadian Newsprint Company's bank accounts in New York seized and attempted to grab possession of newsprint on loading docks. The suits later were settled out of court for unnamed amounts. "The cat is out of the paper bag," the *Financial Post* smirked. Montreal's *Journal of Commerce* jeered about how "the paper companies simply can't start to make secret arrangements without 'spilling the beans.' Secrets of this kind are bound to leak out." As buyer power regained ascendancy, the publishers had "a chance to play one mill off against the other and run away with the bacon while they are scrapping over the empty paper."[100] Newsprint executives blamed the collapse upon the producers that still added capacity or upon Brompton and Anglo-Canadian for putting their own interests first.[101] International Paper was not blamed, then or later, for the fiasco. Not a shred of documentary evidence has ever been produced demonstrating either its involvement or how things unfolded as part of Machiavellian plotting by Graustein.[102] Fred Ker, the editor of the Hamilton *Spectator*, was

Figure 4 International Paper's Delivered Price Policy, 1928

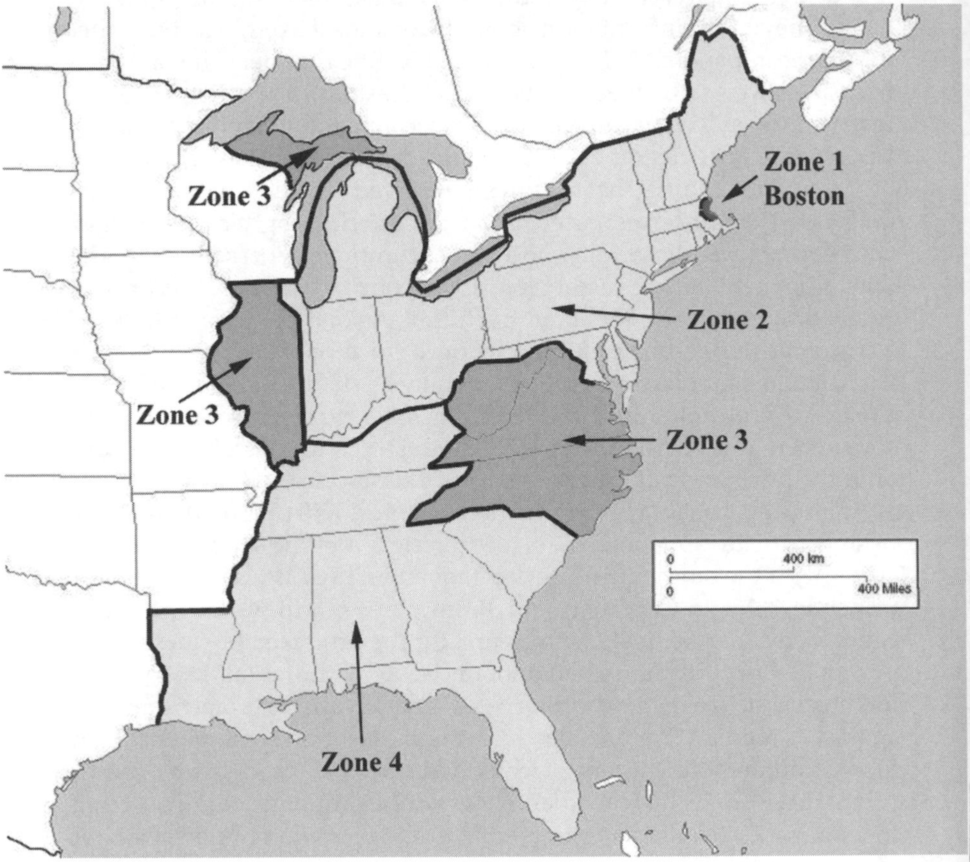

Source: NARA, RG112.4, Federal Trade Commission, Economic
Investigations, 1929 Newsprint Paper Investigation files; CSS 9320,
Newsprint Paper Industry (Washington: GPO, 1930), 37.

quite biased but from confidential sources he became convinced the
Holt-Gundy group arranged the deal with Hearst and "did their best to
get away with it." After the business was lost, the group was "beaten all
along the line by the I.P. and the independent manufacturers."[103]

The situation became more muddled by an alteration of International
Paper's pricing practices. In November 1927 the firm announced the
sale of newsprint at $65 per ton but it equalized freight charges to keep
the delivered price between $68 and $71 per ton depending upon location. As shown in Figure 4, International segmented the United States

east of the Mississippi River into four zones, with uniform prices designated to locations within a zone and fixed differentials applied between
zones. The zones approximated railway regions, although there were
notable variations. Zone 1 comprised the city of Boston and Zone 2 covered most of the "official territory." Zone 3 consisted of several separate
areas located where freight rate territories overlapped, while Zone 4
covered most of the Southern states. This crude policy was refined the
following year with a segmentation of the zones into eight districts and
in 1932 special classifications were given for coastal ports. The scheme
bore limited resemblance to the complicated framework formalized
amongst paper manufacturers during the 1930s. Customers in the
southeastern states, which were not serviced by Canadian firms,
received the highest equalization payments (up to $8.20 per ton), a pol-
icy that let International match the rates from overseas suppliers. Those
offered for sites in "official territory" ranged from $0.60 to $4.10 per ton.
This scheme did not amount to a price cut but, rather, brought International's rates into line with the concessions or discounts already available from rivals.

International altered the policy more because it made economic sense
rather than from any belief that a dominant position might be constructed. The company already incurred a substantial deficit on newsprint but the scheme abetted a high-volume/low-profits strategy where
mills operated at full capacity. Customer relations were improved by
eliminating minor price variations, which originated from regulatory
rules for specific routes. Standardization also decreased the likelihood
of complaints about discrimination between large versus small buyers.
Moreover, the industry amalgamations now positioned International
against competitors with multiple mills and the ability to supply from
alternative sites. Within a year most adopted analogous systems, again
because it benefited them.[104] The new policy therefore, unlike International's subsequent actions, did not attract criticism in the business
press nor does significant evidence exist that most rivals deemed it
unfair. Indeed, marketing techniques like freight equalization or delivered pricing could not of themselves achieve quasi-monopolistic conduct without an explicit agreement amongst producers. Product
differentiation for commodities is negligible, which allows significant
interfirm uniformity in pricing without overt collusion. International's
executives ironically thought the policy made it easier to detect the
moves of rivals. This was false. Even if competitors adopted similar
schemes, there was nothing to prevent secret exemptions or undercutting rates for specific locations. The latter occurred either by direct price
reductions or ignoring zone boundaries – common tactics after 1929.

Over the following decade producers sought to shape newsprint prices but it had little to do with selling technique. Nonetheless, there were real losers from the reorientation. Smaller, older American mills found it difficult to match the prices offered by large producers. Paper jobbers were squeezed out, while firms already disadvantaged by regulatory freight rates faced stronger competition in their "normal" territories.[105]

The U.S. Federal Trade Commission in two investigations later critiqued the geographic policy and some writers therefore have characterized it as predatory. However, the Commission's stance was as much ideological as fact-based. Across the interwar period it contended anything other than f.o.b. mill pricing represented unfair competition because rigidity and uniformity were introduced into selling practices, which it alleged were akin to those conducted by a monopoly. This perspective later hardened into what became known as the "doctrine of implied conspiracy." Based upon a radical extension in the use of circumstantial evidence, the FTC contended that a scheme to control prices existed if separate enterprises pursued analogous conduct because the result was the same as if similar rates were achieved through overt collusion. Zone-delivered prices were average prices, which meant some buyers paid more than real costs while others paid less. From the Commission's perspective, if *a group of firms* pursued this orientation, it ran contrary to court rulings that characterized a non-discriminatory system as one where purchasers proximate to a seller's plant held a natural price advantage over those that bought at a distance. The FTC, however, could not forbid interfirm discussion of terms, discounts or rates unless there was direct evidence of collusion. American courts also were reluctant to interfere with new marketing techniques if they seemed to boost efficiency. For nearly thirty years the Commission unsuccessfully sought to get its perspective endorsed by Congress or the judiciary.[106]

International Paper's policy change, nonetheless, introduced confusion in the wake of the Canadian Newsprint failure. During May the company matched rivals by altering its official rate to $62 per ton for the balance of 1928 but the move failed because other firms then undercut this level.[107] Although Canadian Newsprint nominally operated for another year, the members repossessed control over their marketing activities. The association, the *Financial Post* argued, had been "holding the umbrella" for firms that had never joined it. Those companies, quite ironically, still retained their customers' goodwill. The members who had not withdrawn were "more or less wrecked on the Hearst contract rock" as their operations dropped to 60 per cent of capacity.[108] Spokespeople for the association downplayed the withdrawals but "decided murmurings" about a price war were leaked to reporters. The independents were described as outlaws determined to sell all of their output. Press commentaries noted the prevailing price barely covered total costs even if mills operated at full capacity. A few recognized Canadian Newsprint tended to comprise mills with high costs.[109] With the industry overequipped and consumption stationary, various commentators pronounced "super-bearish" conditions would last at least two years.[110] Producers, a corporate officer stated, knew there must be some "bloodletting," adding grimly "the patient will not be on the way to recovery until he has first been thoroughly exhausted." Some observers expected the list price to drop to $50 by the end of 1929 no matter what was done. Then "the cry will be: 'the greatest good to the greatest number and the greatest number is number one.' It may be a case of every man for himself, and devil take the hindmost."[111]

Various executives and much of the Canadian press suggested the provinces might right the situation. The *Financial Post* insisted American publishers would do anything possible to thwart moves that benefited the industry even though at the current price "the Dominion of Canada is practically giving away her valuable forest resources." The journal promoted the creation of an authority to govern output, a campaign launched with lines from Thomas Babington Macaulay:

> "Now hearken, Conscript fathers
> To that which I advise.
> In seasons of great peril
> 'Tis good that one bear sway;
> Then choose we a Dictator
> Whom all men shall obey."[112]

Montreal's *Journal of Commerce* acknowledged support for such action "in the Street" but found the idea appalling. The industry was "as sound as a bell" despite the "prevailing hysteria." The situation could only be rectified over time as firms rejected money-losing contracts. Natural market adjustments inevitably did more "than all the attempted price-regulations and suggested Dictatorships put together." The real problem, the *Journal* contended, lay in the willingness to grant secret conditions or change policies as firms sought business. A "rock bottom price" of $55 without rebates would force restabilization. Newsprint was no more sacred than other sectors and must go through periodic crises. Although some commentators perceived further mergers as a panacea, others did not expect the amalgamated companies to cut output because an advantage accrued to those that maximized production.

The industry journal noted there was nothing to stop new mills for starting up and demanding a share of business. "A Dictator would need a battle-axe to adjust a situation like that … But, even so, has anyone a better plan to suggest, other than to let nature take its course!"[113]

Most historical accounts suggest Ontario and Quebec were the driving forces behind the efforts to avoid a price war but these have misconstrued what occurred. The producers met during early June with the goal of forming a new marketing organization. Independent firms were promised one that would operate differently from Canadian Newsprint but the negotiations did not progress. A reduction of output was proposed but again, with the new Hearst contracts about to begin, several independents refused to cooperate.[114] Discussions continued with a growing consensus about the need for "pro-rating," a shared distribution of output, as well as some means for price maintenance. However, by September there was little optimism due to the problems associated with implementing those options, along with petty jealousies or feuds amongst the firms.[115]

Provincial officials insisted timber should not be depleted at a financial loss but Ontario and Quebec were averse to taking overt action, hoping the industry would do something on its own.[116] Alexander Smith seized upon the *Financial Post*'s campaign and asked for a bill authorizing the appointment of an Ontario production controller, whose decisions would be backed up by penalties for non-compliance, a proposal the lands and forests minister, William Finlayson, decried as "absurd" and "extremely dangerous legislation." When it was suggested a conference of producers with the provinces might be an option, the minister concurred but stipulated the inclusion of Quebec and preferably "all the Banks and Bond and Security Houses." The firms, Finlayson argued, "should appoint a Committee who would canvas the situation at once and try and find some remedy for the over-production, so that all the mills would be kept running to the greatest possible extent" and "there is the large amount of wood that is purchased from the Settlers." Finlayson characterized informal discussions with Quebec as "very friendly," but the minister "told them frankly that we would be opposed to attempting to control the industry in any way. I also pointed out … that it would be very dangerous to do anything that might antagonize the newspapers and look like an attempt to put up the price." At best, a meeting might be held that included the manufacturers, the banks, and securities dealers. The provinces then would "tell these parties that they have created the present situation themselves, and that the two Governments expect them to work out some satisfactory solution." This "might bring a little pressure to bear on them and get the outlaws to come in, and would at the same time not be a party to the arrangement." Ferguson was unwilling even to go that far. "I do not think we should allow some of these people to make use of the provincial authority to pull their chestnuts out of the fire"' Still, if the firms would not cooperate, the penalty clauses in company licences might be invoked to prevent long-term harm. "They have had some months now to settle their differences, and I do not think we should allow internal dissension in industry to work to the injury of the Province." Taschereau concurred but liked the idea of a conference that sanctioned a producers' committee to coordinate activities. Such action could "make more reasonable some of the '*independents.*' Of course, it is not our intention to take drastic measures, but there is a very strong feeling in the paper industry that if Ontario and Quebec will join hands, a firm attitude will be useful."[117] Ferguson was out of the country during the summer and therefore arrangements proceeded slowly, with the expectation of a conference during November.

The stance taken by the provinces and the unwillingness to adopt direct regulation reflected popular notions about industrial self-government or "associationalism." The rise of managerial capitalism triggered debates about how to establish greater forms of order, in particular how to prevent ruinous competition that threatened large and small business alike. "Competition was the life of trade only when trade was piratic, merciless," declared Jerome Eddy in a best-selling book. "Competition, good old-fashioned 'cutthroat' competition, belongs to trade's buccaneering days when every industry flew the black flag and the appearance of a competitor meant war to the knife." Justice Oliver Wendell Holmes similarly argued that the value and importance of competition was greatly exaggerated.[118] The spread of trade organizations and chambers of commerce generated widespread beliefs that industrial cooperation, instead, could enhance social welfare. During the 1910s business leaders promoted "open-price systems" where individual firms set their prices but trade associations then disclosed the data. Supposedly geared towards the establishment of "frankness" about terms, prices, and bids, the real goals were price maintenance and higher profits. Although the American Supreme Court in 1922 outlawed open-pricing as anti-competitive, the compilation and dissemination of information about markets became a key function of trade associations.[119]

Many writers believed those organizations could help ameliorate problems like labour disputes and unstable wages. Herbert Hoover in a best-selling booklet noted the risks to society if an elite through their control of property determined the welfare of others. The corporate

feudalism of the "robber barons" who dominated early industrialization, he wrote, "contemplates one human animal dealing to other
human animals his just share of earth, of glory, and of immortality."
However, the dispersal of ownership in business enterprises now
restricted the ability of executives to act unilaterally. Hoover suggested
that the combination of their efforts via industrial associations would
generate a "sense of mutuality with the prosperity of the community"
and a stronger sense of their social responsibilities. Economic or social
groups thus would be oriented away from warring interests and
towards cooperation.[120] Hoover, as Secretary of Commerce and then as
President, sought to relax American anti-trust policy and entrench
industrial self-government as a key feature of economic policy. He
believed quasi-official public agreements could bring order to business
practices, standardize production, and reform labour conditions. The
FTC followed a parallel course through its Trade Practice Conferences,
which fostered the elaboration of fair-trade codes. In theory, each code
was a statement of how the notion of fair competition and concepts of
corporate ethics applied to an industry. In practice, the codes included
rules intended to suppress rivalry (such as the prohibition of price discrimination or selling below cost) without referencing them against
statutory requirements that banned malicious conduct. The American
government and the FTC opposed blatant price-fixing but, when
deemed in the public interest, were prepared to tolerate cooperation
that reduced competition and price warfare.[121] These contradictory
notions shaped the efforts to stabilize newsprint from 1928 to 1942.

For six months after the collapse of Canadian Newsprint the nominal
rate remained at $65 per ton f.o.b. mills, plus freight. Despite protesta-
tions about the dangers of price warfare, firms engaged in cut-throat
marketing with freight rebates, concessions of several dollars per ton.
By the autumn of 1928 some offered newsprint below $50 per ton. It
was well known the list rate would drop further and a break occurred
during October when Price Bros concluded a deal with Britain's *Daily
Mail* newspaper group for $48.50. Price Brothers then offered North
American customers alternative sales plans: annual contracts but with
revisions after six months to match price cuts by the largest producers;
or five-year contracts with a rebate of 25 per cent on any gap between
production costs and contract rates, subject to a provision that Price
would cover up to 75 per cent of losses. It guaranteed the costs would
not exceed $56 per ton.[122]

Several days later International Paper announced the sale of a large
amount of tonnage to the Hearst chain. A memo sent to all customers
promised similar treatment but the terms were not released, which

triggered a mania of speculation. Press reports claimed the deal offered Hearst $50 to $52 per ton and covered 40 per cent of its requirements for five to ten years. Abitibi actually had submitted the lowest bid but lost the sale when Smith refused to offer a low rate on a multi-year basis.[123] Premier Taschereau denounced what he called a cut of $20 from three years earlier but few observers expressed surprise. With the list rate "so badly shot to pieces for some weeks past that no one knew definitely what the price actually was," one noted. The Hearst contract became "the snag on which the trade craft struck." Some reporters thought the biggest producers might try to crush new or smaller rivals. Others realized the entrants operated mills with low (sometimes *much* lower) costs. It now was, the *Globe* remarked, "a free-for-all price battle, the object of which is pushing the weakest to the wall, 'the survival of the fittest.'"[124]

As part of the deal, International transferred a contract for the *Chicago Daily News* to Abitibi, an action characterized as a "dicker" but one that restored the Hearst business lost earlier that year. International and Abitibi "have taken the bull by the horns," one newspaper suggested, and intended to force a showdown that damaged firms without stable markets or strong finances. Various reports, more cautiously, suggested International sought to retain its customers and keep the official price at a level that could be maintained.[125] A few executives blamed "the Quebec crowd" (including Abitibi) for the rate cut even though Lake St. John, Anglo-Canadian, and Brompton held contracts with Hearst and had to match the price. Several newspapers, particularly the *Globe*, denounced International as "the prime mover in this price-slashing warfare which may result in a complete over-turning of the newsprint world."[126] The *Financial Post* countered that the situation was unlikely to get out of hand because prices had not descended to the 1913 level and the producers were "not in a tight corner for virtually all occupy a strong financial position." They might scale back depreciation or depletion but were at risk only if the lower rate lasted for several years or dropped further.[127]

During the first week of November the producers began meeting in Montreal with Backus-Brooks, the publisher mills, and most of the independents in attendance, but not International Paper. A consensus to organize along the lines of the Canadian Newsprint Company soon emerged but there was disagreement about how to handle ownership. There was a concurrence about sharing production at a rate of 80 per cent of capacity.[128] Near the end of the talks, the day before sessions were scheduled to include provincial officials, Howard Ferguson sent a letter to the Ontario manufacturers, which was released to the press for maximum sensation. He deplored their "very unfortunate condition" and stressed how the province expected emigrants to northern districts to have work opportunities and markets for their timber or other goods. The government had decided, he asserted, "the industry would be on a sounder basis and would insure continuous employments and market if large, financially-strong units were built up." Small firms during depressed periods were likely to reduce, perhaps suspend, operations, thereby hurting local communities and retarding the general progress of the north. Financially strong enterprises were capable of continuing operations, maintaining payrolls and markets, as well as protecting the stakes of investors. However, the producers had failed to take appropriate action. "Methods have been pursued that have created what appears to be a condition of chaos." The government "does not intend to stand quietly by and see settlers and wage-earners suffer, and small investors all over the Province have their savings jeopardized while those responsible for the efficient operation of the business spend their efforts in a keen competition for who can get the largest share of the market for his own particular mill, regardless of what becomes of the rest of the industry, or how the public interest generally may suffer." Their contracts contained conditions and obligations that were often in arrears. If the firms did not take immediate steps to put the industry on a satisfactory basis, the province would consider what action it might take to protect other stakeholders.[129]

Described by the *Globe* as a "wrathful ultimatum" and by his biographer as a "blunt warning," Ferguson's missive amounted to political theatre aimed at assuring northern voters about the government's concern for their welfare.[130] The *New York Times* accurately described the letter as an "appeal." The *Financial Post* thought it, at best, "a well-timed prod." None of the companies issued responses and no correspondence survives that confirms his bluster was taken seriously. Instead, it came as a surprise to the executives. Ferguson's complaint about how colonists might not be able to sell wood to mills seemed "somewhat of a mystery" because additional purchases entailed more overproduction. The producers unanimously declared government intervention unacceptable and worse than a continuation of the existing situation. The premiers and relevant officials then joined them, "sitting in" for part of two sessions during the conclave.[131] Just three days after the release of his letter, Ferguson flip-flopped, an action all historians have ignored. The manufacturers, he trumped, were showing "a remarkable spirit of co-operation and this proves that personal contact solves all difficulties." The governments suddenly declared a willingness to assist the producers, not restrict them, because the executives were reasonable people who appreciated the need to examine things from a national perspective, rather than from the selfish interests of their own mills. Repeating his earlier letter almost point by point, he now insisted they would ensure the "stabilization of the industry, continuation and increase of employment, local markets for the farmers or their pulpwood, and security to the investors." It was his last public remark or action for a year, thereafter the Quebec premier did the talking.[132] Taschereau emphasized about how paper pricing constituted "a matter of private contracts, which the publishers should make with the manufacturers." The producers had to "agree among themselves and adjust their own difficulties without interference from us."[133]

Despite the announcement of a concord that included most producers, the terms were kept secret, subject to working out technical issues. The negotiations stretched across the winter with numerous false reports of agreements, along with multiple declarations from provincial officials about how they did not know what was going on. The slow progress originated from the difficulties of sharing production, which entailed transfers and price adjustments. Some firms operated at capacity and it was not clear whether others could take over portions of the output either on an operational or legal basis. Any arrangement required the concurrence of publishers who had contracts that defined rates, delivery points, and features like sliding scales that adjusted price with order size. The manufacturers found these quite troublesome and when publisher representatives joined the discussions the negotiations became even more convoluted. In addition, 1,100 tons of new daily capacity were scheduled to start during 1929. Some observers therefore expected the official rate to crumple to $52, no matter what was done. "What the ultimate future holds for prices lies in the laps of the gods," one remarked. "Watching a hockey game in a snow storm and trying to keep one's eye on the puck is just about as easy as finding out the true situation," declared another.[134]

The market had become "decidedly mushy," noted *Pulp and Paper Magazine*. One of its commentators described how economic laws now functioned in a pitiless fashion. Although the producers had the bear by the tail, they could get not a firm grip and were desperately afraid to release the hold. The price decline prevented even new efficient mills from covering operating costs, let alone their interest burdens. Many would soon be in "very hot financial water." Though prices were already non-economic, the companies could not limit price slashing. Rather, "in the mad competition for orders that will keep mills running next year, the low rates and special favors will be given to every publisher shrewd enough to drive a stiff bargain," thereby leading to "the

suspicion that there is no price bottom." Inevitably, if publishers realized cost savings, they would just intensify circulation rivalry and
demand more concessions. "With it will be swept away much of the net
profits and the sound goodwill that the past years have built, for price
competition will be met with similar weapons and net gains to the field
as a whole will be few and small."[135]

American publishers, along with the FTC and members of Congress,
alleged the premiers commanded the negotiations. Such assertions
were far afield. Some of the perceptions were derived from overblown
rhetoric from the premiers themselves such as a declaration by
Taschereau that with cooperation it was possible to control the situation
and the governments would ensure the producers stuck by their agreements. "We have the raw material, the labor, and the power; therefore
we believe we should be masters of the market." Taschereau denied
claims from American critics about political direction of the association
responsible for pro-rating. It was composed solely of manufacturing
representatives, he insisted. The governments had "absolutely no control over that board, nor anything to say regarding the appointments to
such board," and "we never contemplated enacting legislation to fix the
price of paper." However, he also declared publishers should pay a fair
price and described the Hearst rate as too low. If buyers and sellers did
not reach an understanding, the provinces might take measures to protect Canada's forest wealth.[136]

International Paper did not attend the November sessions and Graustein complained the Hearst contract was misrepresented even though
Alexander Smith in advance approved the message the firm had sent to
customers. Ferguson encouraged Graustein to renounce the deal, stating "upon full investigation you found it would be disastrous to the
whole industry and you felt sure they would relieve you under these
circumstances from carrying out such an impossible suggestions." "I
cannot help feeling that if [the] Hearst people [are] fully informed of
situation they are sufficiently public-spirited and interested in [the]
paper industry and all that depends upon it to make reasonable changes
in contract to overcome disaster. This should apply even more strongly
to other customers with whom you can deal more effectively." The suggestions, of course, were silly and would have exposed International to
massive damages. Ferguson made no threats. He merely expressed
regret if International stayed outside the group of firms trying to stabilize the situation.[137] Taschereau held well-publicized meetings with
International's executives where he asked for a revision of the Hearst
deal. Whether a *quid pro quo* was reached is speculative but the parties
likely concurred that International did not have to join the cooperative

scheme and could maintain high capacity operations in Quebec *if* it reduced those south of the border, a strategy the firm already had started. For those who distrusted big business, the circumstances looked like outright manipulation. A writer for *The Nation*, a progressive American magazine, popularized a myth: the situation was conspiracy-driven by International. The premiers were "summoned to New York" where they received their marching orders to bluster and threaten. Graustein then, it was claimed, visited Canada where an agreement was worked out "after several days of conferences behind carefully locked doors."[138]

The producers, in fact, held numerous meetings with International and the publishers across several months as they sought an outcome acceptable to all. International insisted prices must be set according to supply and demand, not by collective regulation or government control. It withheld an announcement of its 1929 price schedule, although buyers were assured any terms would be retroactive to the start of the year and not entail a departure from the geographic policy. The publishers opposed price controls and expected a scheme that did not discriminate in favour of Hearst. The efforts to achieve an accord were subjected to multiple re-debates because some producers argued that after allowing for average overhead costs their mills could not break even[139] Concurrence around a realized price of $55.20 after deduction for freight rates was reached by late January. It took another five weeks to get all of the parties to endorse the proposal. Production was to be smoothed voluntarily through a new association, the Newsprint Institute of Canada (also called the Newsprint Association of Canada). A fee per ton of output was charged to compensate factories that coped with high transport costs. In theory, advantageously positioned mills would subsidize geographically remote producers. The armistice also was predicated upon an understanding that firms would not raid others' customers. The Institute adopted a geographic pricing scheme like International's, along with a subsidization of transport costs. It was a solution generated and developed by the producers. No evidence exists that proves the rules originated from the premiers.[140]

Taschereau thereupon declared the crisis resolved. The governments never went down on their knees to placate the big American firms, he asserted. Rather, "during the negotiations, we found goodwill in the directors of International Paper, good will which our Canadian manufacturers have not always given us. If an arrangement has been concluded it is due, in large part, to the goodwill and intervention of the International Paper Company and the interests of the Hearst company in the United States." The industry hence was "at the dawn of still finer days than it has ever known."[141] Fred Ker advised his colleagues in the publishing industry not to negotiate long-term deals. He believed the pooling agreement could not last and "the fat will be in the fire again by the end of the year." Even this, he hinted, was a generous estimate because some mills were already trying to circumvent the pact. Like other publishers, he did his part to undermine it by treating tonnage transfers as contraventions of contracts or by refusing deliveries sanctioned by the cooperative arrangements.[142]

American consumption increased marginally during the spring of 1929, creating an illusion of success but the producers failed to work out a scheme for pro rata distribution until the summer and considerable disagreement remained about how capacity and machines should be assessed. Despite occasional rhetoric from government officials about how they might discipline non-cooperative firms, neither Ontario nor Quebec proved willing to use more than persuasion or bluster. Legislation to give pro-rating authoritative force was never passed. Resource rights were not withdrawn, nor were fines or additional charges imposed. Voluntary choice remained the hallmark of corporate conduct and no producer was put in a hammerlock to enforce compliance. The governments promised a harmonization of timber regulations as part of the stabilization efforts. Neither did so. By the end of 1929 even the option of altering licences was "impossible," Ferguson conceded. "I doubt the wisdom of drastic action that might tie up the mills for the present time."[143] Press accounts suggested the premiers might arbitrate disputes. They never did. Ontario introduced legislation that obligated companies to move towards sustainable yield practices in land management, develop forest plans, and submit data about their licences, logging, purchases, and financial status.[144] There was no connection between the bill and the newsprint crisis, however. Its introduction had been promised a year earlier. The opposition Liberals legitimately dismissed the statute as "pure advertising and pure propaganda" designed to make people believe the government was committed to conservation. On most matters, the Liberals denounced Ferguson as a dictator or the head of a government that put Mussolini to shame. Their leader, William Sinclair, declared the same applied to this act but the real objective, he pronounced, was a continued alienation of natural resources to giant companies, "the same old situation in a new dress." The public would remember how the government "sold the timber wealth of Ontario to citizens south of the line." Members of the Department of Lands and Forests later admitted the bill was just political theatre, "window-dressing."[145] The real goal was not regulation but, again, more purchases of settler timber.[146]

A successful initiative in business self-government required consensus about goals and then uniformity in response. It was on these rocks that pro-rating soon floundered. Every publisher-related mill refused to participate, arguing the output was consigned through internalized relationships and thus did not entail competitive sales. The head of Spruce Falls Pulp and Paper, for example, offered only a charade of support. Under the terms of the agreement with Ontario, the firm had spent $30 million to construct a mill, a model company town, and infrastructure. It "went through with that bargain I believe you will agree 100%," the president noted to Ferguson. "Not one drop of water was added. Each security was taken down at par. We did all this expecting to run full, even at [the] reduced price of paper." Rival companies operated successfully for years, met their obligations, and paid "quite handsome dividends on common stock, besides piling up surpluses. "They should have considerable fat on their bones." Nonetheless, the premier complained. "The rumour comes to me that you are not playing the game." He had heard stories about how Spruce Falls would be responsible if the Institute failed. "I do not like these disturbing rumours and it will be rather awkward if this arrangement should collapse and it be charged against one of our own Ontario producers."[147] The executives of the publisher mills were convinced the other producers sought not price stability but a rate increase. That development would antagonize customers, trigger new construction, and transfer production to locations with lower transportation costs. It thus was unreasonable to subject their operations to the will of those "who, if they meant what they repeatedly said, rested their price policy on the slogan 'might is right.'" The situation resulted from "the indescretion [sic] of others, and in spite of our strong protest, we can not see our way clear to submit further to suffer from the consequences of their acts." Previous failures to control production for copper, rubber, and wheat were "noble illustrations of the disaster" likely to occur.[148]

The uncooperative stance of the publisher mills was a fatal flaw. As we shall see, it was a weakness that surfaced repeatedly across the next decade. With this precedent, other producers demanded exemptions, especially those for whom newsprint was not the primary product. Graustein refused to join by claiming International could be prosecuted under the Sherman Anti-Trust Act, an assertion that other executives like Alexander Smith might have used. This was spurious because all producers long before had worked out how to circumvent the American statute. Even if negotiations were conducted in the United States, sales contracts were always signed in Canadian offices and title was assigned to customers when shipments left the mills, not on delivery and regardless of the methods used to allocate freight charges. International Paper initially kept production levels in Quebec near Institute norms but it ramped up production in Atlantic Canada and Newfoundland (a tactic matched by other firms). Graustein kept peace with Taschereau by closing several American plants and transferring the output, manoeuvres carefully publicized. The FTC later claimed the Newsprint Institute amounted to an anti-competitive conspiracy because it controlled 70 per cent of Canadian output. This was a grand embellishment that failed to acknowledge the non-participating firms and American rivals. Even the FTC's data showed the Institute, at best, represented about 42 per cent of 1928 output and capacity in eastern North America, a share that dropped sharply as new mills became operational across the following year.[149]

Indeed, the situation had been papered over rather than resolved. An observer in *Saturday Night* mocked: "Now that price fixation has become an accomplished fact, the investing public will, no doubt, be told that 'all is well.' Already there are signs of a well-concerted movement to 'whoop her up.' But in vain in the sight of the bird should the net of the fowler be displayed. The whine cannot become a whoop over night – not unless we are ready to say good-bye to logic and reason."[150] Feuds and bickering progressed in private. Backus-Brooks executives complained to Ferguson, hoping he might intercede. The Institute was unsatisfactory and the industry had to "go through a real housecleaning process ... which means real grief for everybody in it. This will mean a free for all fight for business." Various Institute members quietly sold for a real price of $35 per ton versus the official rate, and therefore if "the International Paper Company, Price Brothers and some of the others had been allowed to stand on their own bottoms during 1929, the result to all of these Companies would have been most disastrous." Only an amalgamation of the major firms could stabilize the industry. Backus executives bemoaned about how the Hearst chain declined to accept paper from their mills, how International and Abitibi cornered business, and then "refused to turn over to us any Hearst tonnage for shipment." Graustein was "cheating at every turn of the road." Nothing could be accomplished as long as International ran its mills at full capacity and used the alibi about cutting American production in recompense. Backus executives believed the midwestern states should be reserved for their own operations but the Quebec mills "probably fear that if they begin to turn this business over to us they will never be able to get it back again." Moreover, the Backus companies charged higher prices than the Institute norm and thus were required to remit monies for distribution to other firms, an arrangement they deemed unfair. When Consolidated Water and Power of Wisconsin announced an increase in plant capacity, its president advised them he would not cooperate with the Institute in any way, shape or form. "That being the case it behooves us to compete with him and protect our customers against any price he may make them."[151]

The amelioration of market conditions during the summer of 1929 convinced many the tribulations were over. The *Globe* insisted "utter demoralization" was averted. Industrial rationalization "sometimes used to disguise monopolistic designs" this time entailed "a subordination of individual or sectional interest to the general welfare" and met "all the requirements of a movements sound in principle and beneficial in practice." An analysis in *Maclean's* acknowledged "the immediate future is not so clear, for it is obvious that the industry cannot adjust problems of major dimensions such as it has been facing, in a day or a year." Despite the problems "the newsprint stocks are not doing so badly" and readers were assured the future "seems bright enough." While there was little chance of firms soon building profit margins, if consumption rose the market would catch up with capacity and the producers could again dictate prices. Canada remained a "dominating factor" with almost unlimited resources. "Already in a position of outstanding supremacy, there seems little cause for apprehension regarding the long-term outlook for the industry as a whole, once the present disconcerting difficulties are effectively ironed out."[152]

6

From Crisis to Catastrophe

The process of Lapham's financial disintegration was like the course of some chronic disorder, which has fastened itself upon the constitution, but advances with continual reliefs, with apparent amelioration, and at times seems not to advance at all, when it gives hope of recovery not only to the sufferer, but to the eye of science itself.

– William Dean Howells, *The Rise of Silas Lapham*

War is cruelty. There is no use trying to reform it, the crueller it is, the sooner it will be over.

– William Tecumseh Sherman

"LIFE IS JUST A BOWL of cherries, don't make it serious, life's too mysterious," a well-liked song suggested. Popular history has attributed the onset of the Great Depression to the Wall Street crash but serious difficulties had already emerged in various sectors, not just newsprint. During the 1920s, financier Sir Joseph Flavelle acknowledged, Canadians experienced an enlargement of wealth and "an almost revolutionary change as compared to my boyhood days, in the general standard of living." But he cautioned "there is no boom in Canada," with agricultural areas hard hit and "a good many industrial plants that are either shut down or going along in a crippled way."[1] The status of the newsprint producers evolved from distress to cataclysm between 1929 and 1932. Many at first believed their problems, like those of other firms, were temporary. Unemployment levels rose but some industries did not experience serious difficulties until the spring of 1930 as bullish trading pushed security prices back up on stock exchanges. The worst would soon be over, executives reassured an uneasy public, and a recovery was inevitable because the market "correction" had disciplined sharp operators. Even by early 1931 the head of the Canadian Pulp and Paper Association insisted Canadian business had not deteriorated as far as elsewhere and "the lessons learned during the past twelve months" would soon prove valuable as more prosperous conditions re-emerged."[2]

Instead, the competitive situation assumed the traits of a quantum singularity, a black hole that collapsed matter and energy into its well. Few observers grasped the complex developments and the tendency to seek simple answers or scapegoats became epidemic. An American senator during early 1929 contended all difficulties within the newsprint sector originated from Canadian efforts to impose "monopolistic control" and throttle newspaper publishers.[3] In Canada's Parliament one member derided the federal administration headed by W.L.M. King for not calling in the producers "and reading the Riot Act to them." "We find Mr. Graustein, President of the International Paper Company, comes over from New York, and, with some others gets a strangle hold on our resources; they create overproduction and the next thing we know is that instead of Canada getting $80 per ton for her newsprint, a contact is made with Mr. William Randolph Hearst, whose publications have always been hostile to British traditions, for $50 a ton." Historian Mark Kuhlberg recently repeated this perspective, attributing the collapse to a war between International Paper and the rest of the industry. Publishers and American officials advanced analogous suppositions, claiming the provincial premiers were the architects of the disaster.[4]

If only it had been so straightforward. As we have already seen, many players and forces propelled events. No dominant firm, groups of enterprises, or politicians exerted control. Rather, the breakdown resulted from choices by the leaders of numerous enterprises. When Canadian politicians intervened, their efforts were half-hearted, rarely enforced and, if anything, compounded the difficulties. In the end, it came down to economics, competitive forces, and finance. This chapter examines the descent into the economic singularity. The first section reviews how, even as the crisis worsened, Alexander Smith sought to ensure his company's future but the net consequence was an overextension, which weakened Abitibi's viability. The chapter then appraises the movement towards ruinous competition that rendered half of the producers bankrupt, the rest nearly so. The concluding section discusses how Abitibi then dropped towards receivership and the unsuccessful attempts to stave off disaster.

1. Your market had run away

Even as the industry's downward spiral accelerated, Alexander Smith continued with his "expand or die" philosophy. Abitibi made three acquisitions, which were intended to stabilize competitive conditions or protect the future. The first originated as a small 1920 entrant, Kaministiquia Pulp and Paper. Business interests from New York and Toronto constructed a thirty-ton pulp mill at Port Arthur, with claims it would later expand to a newsprint facility, but the firm entered receivership after less after than six months of production.[5] Consolidated Water Power and Paper of Wisconsin, headed by George W. Mead (no relation to Spanish River's president), had long imported pulpwood from Ontario and seized the opportunity, buying the assets in 1922 at auction for 29 cents on the dollar. Retitled Thunder Bay Paper, the mill was doubled in capacity as a supplier for Consolidated's American mills. The facility owned minor lands but was dependent upon wood from settlers.[6] The Farmers' government promised additional concessions but did not deliver before it lost the 1923 election. Mead and his representatives became embroiled in tortuous negotiations as pulpwood exporters, timber contractors, and other papermakers competed for resource rights and the Tories sought political benefits. Thunder Bay in 1926 finally gained territories that contained less than half of what it sought – but on onerous terms. The lease specified the construction, in stages, of a 125-ton sulphite pulp mill, a 400-ton newsprint plant, and an expansion of the pulp mill to 400 tons. The province set employment quotas for each stage of productive operations and, adding insult to injury, required the firm to take settler wood in amounts and at rates it stipulated.[7]

In December 1928, just as machinery for the mill was installed, Alexander Smith negotiated a takeover. Neither party declared a rationale for the action. Consolidated had stretched its resources to handle an expansion that now faced a dubious future. Mead was frustrated by Ferguson's handling of timber negotiations and probably welcomed the chance to exit but he blackmailed Smith in the process. For Abitibi's president, acquisition amounted to a strategic imperative – remove an unwanted competitor but ensure Mead did not sell to a rival. The acquisition cost was $14.1 million, whereas Consolidated had spent only $6 million. Newsprint contracts for the mill remained with the Wisconsin company, requiring Abitibi either to divert business from other operations or drum up new sales, while the lease with the province obligated a doubling of the newsprint output by 1931. The takeover gave Abitibi control over eight of the thirteen mills in Northern

Ontario but entailed the addition of an unnecessary plant. Reinforcing the questionable logic of the move and the poor timing, the same week as the acquisition was completed Abitibi passed on payment of its common dividend and two weeks later partially closed the mills at Espanola and Sturgeon Falls.[8]

A new subsidiary, General Power and Paper, technically financed the purchase and then a deal was worked out to manage it as a joint venture with Canada Power and Paper. The final arrangements entailed compensation of $9 million in cash and $5 million in bonds, but covenants for the remaining debt allowed Consolidated to repossess the plant if any default on payments occurred. Thunder Bay, moreover, went into default on the provincial lease less than a year after the takeover. Abitibi refused to expand the mill, the managers arguing that even if the government reacquired the forest properties the operation could survive on settler wood. The mill operated at 80 per cent of capacity during 1929, dropped to 28 per cent in 1930, and thereafter was idled. The subsidiary was a steady cash loss, even though Abitibi failed to make payments to creditors, designating them as "deferred liabilities." Abitibi's bondholders later, incredulously but accurately, noted "it is difficult to imagine Abitibi having realized advantages of sufficient moment to offset the cost" for Thunder Bay.[9]

The second effort involved the Bathurst Company, the first paper manufacturer in New Brunswick. Distant from markets and lacking sufficient pulp operations to allow a reasonable return on investment, the sixty-five-ton mill struggled, especially as the size of rival enterprises increased. In 1928 a Montreal brokerage firm bought the properties. Reorganized as the Bathurst Power and Paper, the venture was controlled by a holding company, Newsprint Bond and Share, which in turn was owned by seven producers. Approximately a quarter of the purchase price was paid at the time of acquisition and the balance was financed by bank loans with the stock as collateral, the owners then making monthly payments that were modest for each. Abitibi held the second largest stake but International Paper, which owned a third and retained effective control, was the real beneficiary because the takeover strengthened its position in dealing with the province. Though the consortium claimed the venture would stabilize the industry, it expanded the electrical supply and doubled the newsprint output. Not until 1931 were the operations reconfigured towards the manufacture of kraft paper. Bathurst ran at a deficit after 1928. As the owners ran into financial difficulties during the Depression, most bailed out and Nesbitt Thomson bought out the company. Abitibi ceased paying in 1931, the investment eventually written off as worthless.[10]

Unlike the prior two acquisitions, the third was a successful enterprise. An American, I.H. "Ike" Weldon, founded the St. Lawrence Paper Mills in 1909 and in 1913 acquired Barber Paper, the consolidated enterprise then retitled as Provincial Paper Mills. Operating three plants in Quebec and Ontario, within several years it became the largest Canadian manufacturer of fine paper. Weldon and his American associates, although holding a minority of the equity, retained control. Provincial acquired a stake in the Port Arthur Pulp and Paper Company, which in 1916 planned to develop a sulphite pulp mill on the mistaken belief that the province would tender adequate timber concessions. Although the firm failed in its lobbying efforts, it proceeded with construction, assuming settlers could supply wood.[11] Provincial continued to increase the stake in the enterprise and secured full ownership during 1920. Because Provincial, as the largest producer of book paper, was indispensable for educational materials and periodical publishing, the executives sought to enhance timber supplies for the Port Arthur mill. In 1921 the Farmers' administration set up an auction for a Lakehead territory but conveniently restricted the tender to fine paper companies. Submitting the only bid, Provincial gained not only the territory, but a twenty-one-year contract for all book paper required by Ontario's Department of Education. The forest concession was supposed to contain 320,000 cords of wood but actually had five times that amount.[12] Another sweetheart deal in 1926, timed for the provincial election, brought lands that supposedly contained 2.5 million cords. Provincial was required to double the small mill's capacity, which entailed a modest investment, and could be required to build another plant "when and so soon as market conditions ... will justify such expenditure." Enhancing the arrangement further, the first license was extended to run coterminous with the new tract.[13]

Under these conditions, the price of Provincial stock soared and in 1927 Toronto financiers via Dominion Securities bought the company for $8 million. The takeover entailed a "huge payout" to the shareholders but was costless for the acquirees because the company, upon reorganization, issued new preferred stock and more bonds, while the common equity remained privately held. Weldon stayed as president until his death a year later and his management team never altered. Although the largest book paper company in Canada, Provincial was modest in size relative to the newsprint producers and Abitibi secured ownership in 1930 by exchanging common stock on a share for share basis. The deal revalued the company at $11.8 million, 50 per cent higher than prior to Dominion's takeover, although no capital outlays or property additions had occurred. For the owners, the buyout was worth nearly $3 million, "all profit after a hold of three years."[14] Provincial was not consolidated with the new parent. It remained legally separate, the management team again unchanged, its office next door to a new headquarters that Abitibi was building on Toronto's University Avenue. Because Provincial required poplar for its operations, the real gain for Abitibi entailed the stands of pulpwood in the timber limits, which Howard Ferguson had denied to Fort William Paper. Alexander Smith logically would have presumed Abitibi's other mills could exploit the tracts once a more understanding government was in place. The acquisition also began a diversification from the dependence upon a single product. Unlike the newsprint firms, fine paper manufacturers still enjoyed prosperity. Protected by tariffs from American competition, they had stable markets reinforced by loyalty agreements with dealers. Provincial remained profitable. The preferred stock provided modest but stable dividends for its parent.[15]

Alexander Smith's bane was Abitibi Canyon. Prior acquisitions of water rights were aimed at ensuring electrical supply for the mills but Smith, like Archibald Graustein at International Paper, believed large power developments might stabilize cash flow. Consequently, although the company seemed to have no further needs, it applied for the Canyon, 300 kilometres north of Sudbury, even before the purchase of Island Falls from Hollinger was closed. The application for a site previously characterized as remote and unreasonably expensive also represented a pre-emptive strike to ensure it did not fall under the sway of competitive interests.[16] Abitibi received a twenty-year lease and additional forest properties with an understanding that the site would be developed to a capacity of 275,000 horsepower. Since the application related to a venture occurring well in advance of a market for the power, a completion deadline was not specified and nominal rent was charged for the first three years. Abitibi had to file plans within eighteen months and the government could order construction if a legitimate demand emerged.[17] The firm thus gained control over all exploitable powers on the Abitibi River just as a conflict arose over the roles of private versus public sector utilities in frontier areas.

Business concerns had long perceived the supply of electricity as an obstacle to growth in New Ontario. "The North is fed up with power famine prices in a land of power plenty," declared the Cobalt *Northern Miner*.[18] Having established a quasi-monopolistic position in some areas, Canada Northern Power dictated supply terms and often dismissed grievances about service conditions. During 1927 the heads of several mining enterprises met with Hydro officials and unsuccessfully argued that demand growth legitimated lower rates. In a coordinated

promoters, and, as a result, "this basic industry has been hopelessly loaded almost to the crack of doom."[47]

Ferguson engaged in his own form of finger-pointing and later placed much of the responsibility on the publisher mills, including Spruce Falls even though it had assiduously paid court to him. He insisted he supported the Newsprint Institute and encouraged "in every way within my power" manufacturers to cooperate with it. "I am firmly convinced that if the paper industry is to be preserved from a serious breakdown, if, indeed, not a total crash, it can only be done through the industry as a whole sharing the burden on an equitable basis." When Frank Sensenbrenner, the head of Spruce Falls, repudiated a charade of conformity with the voluntary association, Ferguson claimed the move came as "a shock" since he had "always regarded you as the sheet anchor upon which I could rely for stabilizing conditions in these try-ing times." If Spruce Falls broke away and slashed its price, "it will be a signal for a campaign of piracy which will ultimately destroy the whole investment, as well as the commercial importance, of this huge enterprise." He thought they had reached the bottom of the depression and a tide of improved conditions would appear with a reasonable period. "I must tell you that it hurts me very deeply to think that Spruce Falls Mills, whose birth I attended, whose baptism I performed, and whose progress I have endeavoured to encourage, should be the one institution to initiate a course that inevitably, to my mind, means destruction." Sensenbrenner dismissed these assertions for the twaddle they were. He told the other producers their failure to recognize eco-nomic conditions had stopped them from gaining additional business. Not one of his suggestions about marketing policies was adopted. Instead, the existing firms still sought higher prices as an ultimate goal, which just aggravated "an already bad situation." They enabled new firms to take enough business away from the Ontario and Quebec mills and "produce cheaper paper, even at the cut price, than the mills of the two provinces which were bearing the entire burden of curtailment." Due to "the gravity of the situation confronting the industry" and "in self protection" his company was prepared to cut its rate.[48]

As discussions began about the 1930 rates, most firms sought a com-promise. The bellwether, however, was Mersey Paper, which offered $3 below the list price for new business. This time the premiers issued "paradoxical statements," a mix of double-speak and bafflegab. On one hand, they insisted the provincial role entailed assistance for the indus-try but not intervention for price-fixing. On the other, they declared a need for "moral pressure" and for "fair and equitable returns" via a higher rate of $60 per ton. When a government sought to fix the price of merchandise, Taschereau in quixotic contradiction remarked, "it generally fails to attain the desired end," but a price war would trigger ruinous competition as firms were pushed out of business. The inevitable result would be a "big trust or combine in the near future."[49] However, once again, the provinces failed to enact legislation that could ensure compliance. Once again, they did not punish firms that refused to cooperate or chose to undercut stabilization.

An increase to $60 per ton amounted to an added cost of $20 million per year for American publishers. In the wake of the stock market collapse, they dismissed the notion and described the premiers as hypocrites who, having fostered excess capacity, now demanded quotas to minimize the distress inflicted upon mill towns. Ferguson and Taschereau were derided as modern Canutes who sought to hold back economic forces and preserve higher cost mills at the expense of more efficient operations. "This means nothing more than a flourishing of the big stick over the heads of both manufacturers and publishers," declared the *New York Times*, an attempt to force "uneconomic control of production and price in place of the law of supply and demand." The *Globe* suggested it entailed clumsy efforts "to impose artificial and arbitrary price-fixing."[50] Fred Ker, now the Canadian representative on the ANPA's price committee, was blunter. The premiers had "run amuck on the subject of price regulation" and were playing local politics. With all the new mills starting up, they were "going to find themselves holding a very poor hand in this grand game of poker into which the newsprint situation has developed."[51] He suspected they knew little about the "practical aspects" and had succumbed to "some political urge which will land them both in trouble and embarrass the whole country if they don't watch their steps." Ker and other publishers, who denied responsibility for the debacle, propagated an alternative dogma. At the root of all problems was how production "during the past ten years passed from the practical paper men who had a knowledge of market conditions to the giddy stock promoters who in order that they might issue lots of stock, promoted new companies, merged and enlarged old ones, and inflated the industry." Ker accused the Holt-Gundy group of "inexcusable expansion and price cutting."[52]

A simple issue complicated the prospects for stabilization. The Hearst agreement, negotiated with International Paper, gave the buyer a right to cancel on short notice if pricing was not kept acceptable. The provinces had lobbied the firms into renegotiating the contract to a rate of $55 per ton versus the original price of $50. Nine months later the companies were asked to accept another price jump. The premiers sought an abrogation of the very deal they had previously demanded, a ridiculous idea.[53] Despite an implied threat of government "discipline" by Taschereau, the practical options were few. International's properties were mostly freehold and those in Ontario were speculative. Neither government was willing to use the one tool that could force compliance: a tax imposed on a sliding scale against a minimum fixed price. Graustein hinted International might accept a rate advance to satisfy "Canadian sentiment" even though he "did not think that this was a good time." "We are Canadian in our sympathies and our outlook." Privately he warned Taschereau that if the list price was raised the publishers just would cut consumption and give their business to non-Institute mills. A hike might put such pressure on the Institute "that will make it blow up exactly as the Canadian Newsprint Company blew up eight months ago. In other words, if one tries to hold the umbrella too high the umbrella may be ruined."[54]

With International wavering, Abitibi, St. Maurice, and Price Brothers announced a $60 rate but also offered a discount to $55 per ton for six months if customers accepted contracts lasting three years. No other firms followed, while American buyers denounced the move as "a hold-up." "To cure over-production by raising the price of the article produced seems a fantastic way to go about it," editorialized the *New York Times*. "Canada's Mailed Fist Strikes," the *St. Louis Star* proclaimed, with a "high-handed" attempt to cure overproduction with "an artificially created exorbitant price" that was "an economic monstrosity." Buyers, the *Washington Post* declared, should not be expected to pay tribute to mills that were obsolete, based on watered stock, or that were geographically remote. The Canadian industry had been "in a constant state of economic turmoil" since the war. An increased price was bound to stimulate greater production, thereby intensifying the downward cycle. The publishers' association demanded American authorities retaliate against what they deemed the hand of provincial dictate.[55] But other interests reached alternative interpretations that matched their own biases. For some, the premiers had demonstrated their subservience to large corporations, which included Taschereau's "pèlerinage" (pilgrimage) to International Paper. "There were many persons who regarded it as undignified for the Premier of this province to have to go hat in hand to a foreign capitalist who had already made millions by exploiting our forest wealth."[56]

Most producers remained quiet as the politicians blustered against the opposition from south of the border. The price of newsprint, Ferguson insisted, was a domestic matter beyond American government control. "We never have had any thought of attempting to fix any price, or suggest a price for newsprint," but "price is the underlying factor in the success of any business" and at the existing rate settlers in Northern Ontario earned less than $5 per cord on delivery. Taschereau was less diplomatic as he demanded a $60 level. He would not meet with publishers or manufacturers as a beggar, he stated. "I threatened. Like the boy who wants the piece of soap I will not be happy until I get what I want." The premier denied claims the provinces conspired to force an artificial price. "Nobody will contest the right of Canadian manufacturers to raise the price of their products when they think they ought to do so, and least of all should our neighbors of the South while they are endeavouring to obtain a general raise of the customs tariff against Canadian goods."[57] But it was for naught. Despite a statement by the Newsprint Institute that a $60 rate would remain unless market conditions altered, the undeclared members were not willing to proceed without industry unanimity. A week later International announced its rate would be unaltered for the first half of 1930. The move came as "no great surprise" and matched the "discount" offered by the three companies that had declared their rates. It killed the possibility of an advance as competitors rolled back their plans and declared the prices after June were "undetermined."[58]

As recriminations swirled, the members of the Institute put the publishers at fault. The producers, Fred Ker advised his colleagues, "are counting the days until the shoe is on the other foot and they are able to give us what they consider a dose of our own medicine." But he was convinced "the days of high-hat and high-hand are over." William Chandler, the head of the ANPA price committee, thought it was unlikely the manufacturers could get together, "with or without the premiers." Considerable bitterness had developed amongst the Institute's participants due to "their recent adventure in price-fixing" and the publishers accordingly lobbied to get independent manufacturers to withdraw. Each "should pick out a price policy for the future that would be sponsored by the company itself, and not by the Institute or by the Government."[59] Others blamed International and ignored the refusal of most producers to hike rates, as well as the price-cutting initiatives of other firms. The opposition in the Quebec legislature, argued the premier, "begged Mr. Graustein not to start a crisis in this Province" and had merely threatened to prevent "him from cutting down trees in some concessions." The Liberals allowed "the creation of a state within the state," an enterprise "so powerful that it did not care for the Prime Minister or his Government," "a company the aim of which, it is notorious, is to bring ruin to the other companies in the province." Taschereau, they argued, was "helpless," whereas Graustein acted as an "independent in a country which is not his own," even though everything his buy the output for fifteen years, an arrangement guaranteed by Hearst's American sales agency, but it was contingent upon the colony guaranteeing a large proportion of the bonds and granting 26,000 square kilometres that contained 20 million cords of timber. However, no assurances were provided about the likelihood of the venture or the sale of output. In response to widespread opposition and pressure from International, the government delayed enabling legislation and then cancelled writs for the timber licences so it had sufficient time for a review.[74] Scepticism about the project was confirmed when Hearst worked another deal whereby it acquired an ownership position in Canada Power and Paper and that producer took a stake in Dominion. The swap entailed a "union of interests" similar to those between the *New York Times* and Spruce Falls: Hearst agreed to pay market rates for paper but garnered a discount through dividends, effectively cutting the rate. Canada Power was required to wait for the existing Hearst contracts with International to conclude in 1937, but its production then could meet half of the chain's needs.[75]

Difficulties previously occurred when demand slowed or stalled for brief periods, but this time excess capacity combined with the implosion of the North American economy, which made the status of the industry and specific firms a straightforward matter of numbers. American consumption of newsprint dropped from 3.8 million tons to 2.8 million between 1929 and 1932. The surplus capacity relative to demand rose from 27 to 46 per cent. Press reports obscured the trends by focusing upon monthly exports and by stressing any improvement no matter how small or temporary. Consumption was dictated by newspaper circulation and the number of pages printed, with the latter dependent upon advertising lineage. Both were correlated with personal income. Circulation revenue dropped marginally but tended to hold up across the worst of the Depression. The real shift was advertising lineage, which peaked in 1929 and crumpled to two-thirds of that level by 1932. Advertising revenue, which constituted three-quarters of the monies earned by American newspapers revenue, dropped from $797 million in 1929, to $624 million in 1931 (the lowest since 1924) and to $500 million in 1933 (less than 1920).[76]

These trends hobbled the Newsprint Institute. Firms belonging to the association operated at 81 per cent of capacity during 1929 and at 59 per cent during 1930, whereas Canadian firms that had not joined operated at 98 per cent and at 93 per cent, respectively and American mills at 80 per cent and 76 per cent. With no legislative penalties instituted by Ontario or Quebec, there was nothing to enforce production transfers among the Institute's participants and, after January 1930, most firms also ceased making equalization payments.[77] In September the Institute chair, John Price, resigned in protest over the unwillingness of the members to adhere to the association agreement, a situation capped by the "aggressive action" between Canada Power and Hearst that constituted "a direct and flagrant violation" of the Institute's rules. Price Brothers, he announced, would act independently, a move followed by St. Lawrence Paper.[78] Price's successor admitted there was so much "bickering and horse-trading that it [the Institute] has not been carried out properly." The head of St. Maurice Paper noted this had been long expected. "All these cooperatives sooner or later blow up." Fred Ker, citing the deal with Hearst, characterized "the Canada Paper crowd as 'out-Grausteining' Graustein in their defiance of premiers." Price, he claimed, "caught some of the crew, as it were, making off with the only lifeboat" and did the only thing possible, disclose the facts. Others saw dark humour in the collapse. "The newsprint pool indubitably ended in a scrap of paper," the *Globe* wisecracked.[79]

Price Brothers subsequently sued, alleging twelve companies including Abitibi owed the Institute $2 million for differentials in tonnage that were to be equalized by cash payments if firms exceeded their allotted output. The claim for damages was based upon an inventive use of production data. Along with Anglo-Canadian and Canada Power, the firm argued it had served as a "creditor" for the Institute and received $487,210 during 1929 for curtailing production and the monies owed for 1930 amounted to $787,000 for 1930, plus interest. In rebuttal, the defendants stated payments were voluntary and there was no contractual basis for the claim because the provinces had never passed legislation authorizing the Institute. When the suit came to trial, testimony revealed Price Brothers did not occupy the moral high ground but had used the same tactics as IPP and Canada Power: the payment of cash and stock to newspapers, either in exchange for sales or to escape contract provisions. Quebec's Superior Court dismissed the case with costs, noting the firm offered and concluded deals with terms that contravened the Institute agreement.[80] Abitibi later demanded $150,000 from the Institute for equalization payments but never collected the monies.[81]

An illusion of stability was retained as what was left of the Newsprint Institute limped along for another eight months. Abitibi and CPP declared they would sell at the list rate to "protect" clients from price fluctuations. IPP concurred, stating that while it had opposed higher charges "any decrease in price is unjustified." Official news about pricing tactics was rare but press accounts acknowledged sales at lower rates and undercutting especially by American mills. Desperate for business, Minnesota and Ontario Paper sold "at any price." One journal elimination of excessive freight costs now caused by an illogical geographic distribution of tonnage," along with other "losses and leaks." His company would only join a combine based on efficiency ratings. "Unless these fundamentals are used as a cornerstone and unless the other policies in which International believes, and to which it has adhered in recent years, are written into the code of the proposed consolidation, we shall continue to paddle our own canoe."[88] This time, media reports insisted, the "one big merger" appeared closer to realization than ever. "Consolidation should speed the adoption of a unified general policy designed for the progressive and profitable development of the industry," stated *Pulp and Paper Magazine*, if it was "based on drastic economic reorganization." A merger needed to be "sound and clean and straight. The other kind has been tried and found wanting." Any "water" in the equity of the constituent companies had to be squeezed out and overvalued assets written down. But even before the publication of these stories the merger efforts were abandoned as yet additional price cuts triggered desperate battles for tonnage and more firms spiralled towards insolvency.[89]

3. An almost impossible condition

For Abitibi, an inexorable deterioration unfolded between the summers of 1930 and 1932. It was a fate shared by Alexander Smith's other ventures. The Texas sugar refinery went bankrupt just as the Great Depression began. His investment company's sojourn on Wall Street lasted less than two years and was wound up during 1931, leaving Smith with just his holdings in Abitibi bonds and stock. The value of the securities plummeted as conditions worsened and as other producers reported losses or filed for receivership (see Figure 5). But few people had accurate knowledge about the company's finances. The Canadian press, honouring a code of silence about information that could worsen morale, was cautious about discussing specific firms. Investors learned little when the 1930 results were reported. A two-sentence narrative acknowledged operations were curtailed by the severity of the depression that resulted in "higher inventories, the liquidation of which is receiving the continuous attention of your management." Whereas in 1929 Alexander Smith told shareholders there was no reason to doubt firms would again achieve prosperity, he now just noted how the industry might benefit from any improvement in general business conditions.[90] The company reported significant earnings but the statements obscured the worsening reality. The balance sheet presented consolidated results, with nearly two-thirds of the assets lumped into a

Figure 5 Market Value of Abitibi Power and Paper Ltd., 1928–1946 (C$ Millions)

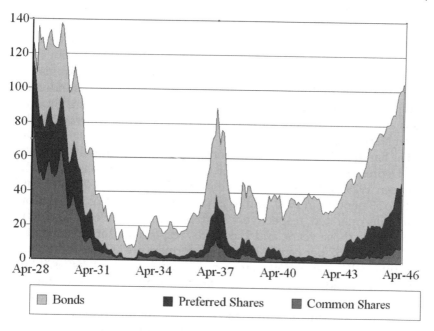

Sources: Extrapolated from monthly data published in
Annual Financial Review, Financial Post.

category of properties, plants, and equipment. The inclusion of Provincial Paper made the performance look better than it was. Smith noted the current assets had increased and exceeded current liabilities by a ratio of more than three to one. He did not point out that most inventories (which constituted three-quarters of the current assets) comprised mountains of rotting wood at different mills. In addition, stories were planted to reassure investors all was well. One even declared the managers' intention to undertake more power projects as soon as the Canyon venture was completed.[91]

The weakening of the company became a matter of mathematics driven by two variables: price and capacity level. If newsprint sold at a rate of $80 per ton, Abitibi prospered. The breakeven level (including payment of the bond interest) when the company operated at full capacity was just above a price of $50 per ton. At a price of $40 or lower the company could not handle variable costs for production, let alone the fixed costs of mills. The rate of production mattered. If the mills action against layoffs, Howard Ferguson noted there was "certainly already too much unemployment, and many of our industries are in none too flourishing a state." He conceded "it will be a little time before we can look for a very great improvement in industrial conditions generally. The paper business is no exception to this." None of the companies were making money but the government, he claimed, was pressing them to operate at least part-time. "It would be a very serious situation if we had a further shut-down and shrinkage in employment."[97]

By 1931 many towns were desperate. Local politicians and union leaders, for example, denounced the handling of Thunder Bay Paper as disgraceful because the mill had been semi-idle since 1928. The premier did not have, one petitioner complained, "any idea of the extreme resentment existing here against the Abitibi Co." Workers were "reduced to a pitiable condition," but then read in the press how the firm still paid preferred dividends and, during 1929, earned 47 cents per share on common stock, "which is nothing but water." The government should "straighten up these financial manipulators that are today in control of the paper industry ... By endeavouring to hold up the price by artificial means, they have lost their markets, resulting in wide spread un-employment and great suffering for their unfortunate employees."[98] If companies failed to maintain the output stipulated in licenses, petitioners insisted, forest and water rights should be cancelled. Other demands varied from efforts to force production sharing or a shift to a laissez-faire system with each firm able to gain business where it could.[99]

Responsibility for handling the crisis, however, had passed to a new premier. Ferguson resigned during the autumn of 1930 to take up the position of High Commissioner in Britain. Thereafter, he exercised no real influence, although he sent missives to his successor, George Henry, rationalizing about decisions made when he was office and offering advice that almost always was ignored. Whereas Ferguson was an autocratic, wily showman, Henry was reserved, a person, his biographer observed, more akin to a public servant than a politician. Originally a farmer, he had significant relationships within the corporate world and had become wealthy with a personal motto to "plough the straight furrow": act honestly and prudently. "To hold public confidence and get things done a man must be moderate in opinions and in methods." Party members considered him a safe, solid but not inspiring choice as leader, an experienced administrator who oversaw the development of much of the provincial highway system. 'You can't make a Bonnie Prince Charlie out of George Stewart Henry," one

columnist sneered. "You might as well grow rambler roses on a gaso-
line tank." There was as much romance in the new premier "as there is
about a first mortgage or a milk bottle."[100]

Henry, unlike Ferguson, had no pretensions about understanding the
forest products industries. He was realistic about the government's
ability to influence companies. Even if it interceded, excess capacity
and low demand made success dubious. He feared "notifying the mills
that they are in default and must listen to our dictation" might create
"an almost impossible condition" such as a movement of production to
Quebec or American mills. Intervention could open a Pandora's box
where the government had to do the same thing with other manufacturers. The province then would face litigation while investors viewed
Ontario negatively, a situation that could intensify the Depression. Several members of the Tory caucus wanted assertive action. Major-Gen-
eral Donald Hogarth of Port Arthur demanded an investigation of the
Newsprint Institute. Ontario could regain more than $25 million of
business, he claimed, if its restrictions were removed. Ignoring basic
economics, he then demanded production be distributed across northern mills so they received fair and equitable shares.[101]

Henry conceded the situation was grave. The intensification of price
warfare during the spring of 1931 triggered three weeks of conferences
amongst executives, bankers, and government representatives. William
Finlayson, the minister of lands and forests, emphasized the need for a
solution to the "awful mess," but "an impenetrable veil of mystery"
surrounded the discussions. The producers rejected any interference on
price matters and the discussions about pooling tonnage went nowhere.
"I told one official," Finlayson stated later, "you can't expect us to carry
all the load up there. You took the profit out of the country when times
were good, and when you start operating again you've got to do your
share to relieve this situation." The government sought something
"that will have your jobless people employed again, before the situation is so far advanced that they cannot lay something aside for next
Winter and any depression that may be then existing."[102] Public pro-
tests mounted in the wake of the failed conferences. Finlayson attended
a mass meeting at Fort William and, in vain, stressed the difficulties
associated with punitive action. Cancellation or confiscation of resource
rights was a breach of faith, "killing the goose that laid the golden egg."
Calamity would result if the province, as critics suggested, "put all the
newsprint companies on the toboggan slide and let them all go because
they are no good, anyway." Such action "would mean ruin to thousands of widows and other investors. It would mean a situation of
chaos and disorder. It is unspeakable! What good would it do?"

this undertaking, and the methods adopted, are perfectly sound if presented to the public in a way that they can understand."[108]

Economic difficulty can turn into disaster as firms make escalating commitments to failing courses of action. Trying to cut its liability for Thunder Bay Paper during 1931, Abitibi paid off the balance of the ownership stake. Unbeknownst to outsiders, this was covered by a new loan from the Royal Bank. The bank insisted upon minimizing its exposure by securing the debt with a lien against Abitibi's inventories, an assignment of receivables, and a pledge of Provincial Paper's common stock. This arrangement breached the terms of Abitibi's bond mortgage because it gave any claim by the Royal Bank priority over the debt holders. After Canada Power entered receivership later that year, that company's protective committee decided to abandon its stake in Thunder Bay. Two notes due at the beginning of 1932 were not paid, whereupon Consolidated Water and Power repossessed Canada Power's half of the Thunder Bay equity. Smith agreed to purchase the stock for a small amount of cash and a contract that allowed monthly instalments until 1941 but with a set of onerous conditions. If Thunder Bay's current liabilities exceeded the current assets, if any tax liens were filed against the property, or if Abitibi failed to make either principal or interest payments, the entire firm reverted to Consolidated. Having sunk $6.4 million into the affiliate, Abitibi gained full ownership supposedly for another $3.1 million, but it incurred costs of $1 million annually while the mill remained idle. Thunder Bay could only operate by transfers from other Abitibi operations. It had not kept up with payments to the local power utility and the provincial timber fees were in default. In all, the acquisition imposed heavy penalties but Smith thought losing the affiliate entailed worse options: a major write-off and the likelihood that Consolidated would then sell output from the mill at $8 to $10 below the list price.[109]

The acquisition was not disclosed for more than a year. When the financial statements were released they indicated an unspecified $4.3 million "obligation" associated with Thunder Bay, while a vague phrase referred to further "contingent and contractual liabilities" of $2.2 million. Meanwhile, to sustain Abitibi's operations, Smith manipulated the use of short-term bank loans. The amount of loans increased during 1930, were cut back just before the 1931 fiscal year ended, and then reexpanded over the following eight months. Their true role was not disclosed in the annual reports: coverage of shortages in working capital. Loans from the Royal Bank and Banque Canadienne Nationale were "secured," again undisclosed, by the assignment of accounts receivable and bank account deposits from subsidiary companies. Abitibi also coped with rising costs associated with the idle mills such as caretaking, insurance, and taxes. The expenses reached $1 million during 1931, equivalent to more than half of the net profits reported for that year.[110] In June the directors took the next ominous step – suspension of the dividends for the preferred stock. Rather than admit the actual reason, insufficient earnings, they claimed the goal was preservation of working capital due to the Depression. The move was widely expected. The business press accepted the firm's rationale by stressing how the 1930 earnings had covered the dividends and how the firm was "one of the more efficient" producers.[111] Through these manoeuvres Alexander Smith forestalled a sudden collapse but in the process he wrung out Abitibi's credit. There were few provisions under British or Canadian law for a firm to be placed in receivership prior to a default on the bond interest. Debt holders might seek court intervention if they could demonstrate the "doctrine of jeopardy" applied: attempts by shareholders or unsecured interests to seize assets, unauthorized disposal of assets covered by the bond mortgage, dereliction of management, or seizure of property for non-payment of taxes. But there was no method of recourse without proof of jeopardy and the executives covered up the deteriorating situation until almost the end.[112]

The statements released in March 1932 presented the rosiest possible image, with a declaration about how the operating income was sufficient to cover bond interest one and half times. Inventories were lower, while bank loans supposedly had been cut by nearly a quarter. There was no prospect of an upturn, Smith acknowledged, but newsprint consumption was "well maintained, while industrial capacity would decrease as obsolete plants closed."[113] The *Globe* thus believed Abitibi held a relatively satisfactory position and noted the working capital status was "a trifle lower" but "relatively as strong as before." The *Wall Street Journal* recognized a write-down accounted for half of the reduction of inventories but it assumed that as they were exhausted at one mill operations then shifted to another – thus the future boded well. The *Financial Post* shared these perceptions, albeit with a remark that a reduction of excess capacity would take more than a decade.[114]

But the data released by Abitibi were fictional, abetted by a set of accounting tricks. The statement of profit and loss stressed changes in the accumulated surplus, which indicated a drop in net worth but camouflaged the imminence of disaster. The contingent liabilities for OPS were not declared, which included the additional capital still needed for the project's completion. Stakes in the capital stock of other companies and advances comprised nearly a third of the current assets but their liquidity was unclear. A write-down of wood to reduce inventories to current values was designated as "profit from operations," along with supposed earnings derived from required purchases of bonds for the sinking fund. Deferred liabilities were used to cover current items. Idle mill costs were not specified. On the basis of the 1931 report, an analyst might anticipate $2.8 million in operating profits during 1932. However, Abitibi's pending obligations for that year were almost four times greater, even if dividends and the Canyon venture were excluded.[115] Despite the limited disclosure of information, it should have been obvious that receivership was inevitable.

The shortage of funds triggered discussions among the legal officers of the firm and Hydro about the ramifications for OPS. Smith then approached the premier. Capital markets would not accept new securities unless they had governmental support. When Smith asked for $5 million to guarantee another bond issue, Henry delegated the matter to the utility and Geoffrey Clarkson's company was hired for an assessment.[116] The resulting audit revealed OPS required at least $8.6 million for completion but the parent firm no longer had liquid assets of its own. Abitibi's unpledged assets nominally totalled $16.1 million but this figure dropped to just $3 million after allowing for advances and inventory write-offs. The trading credit was a pitiful $2 million because legal covenants restricted the availability of alternative instruments or the use of most assets as security. Montreal Trust held $3.6 million for OPS in a reserve account but the bond deed required $2 million to be retained until after the project's completion for the settlement of contractor accounts. Once the dam became operational, revenues could meet all costs and leave a modest surplus for Abitibi in the form of stock dividends. However, the company would not use all of the power it was obliged to buy due to the production cutbacks. If Abitibi fell into receivership, it could disavow the Hydro contract. The firm might walk away or buy from alternative sources. Hydro, nonetheless, was liable for yearly purchases of 100,000 horsepower and would lose annual sales of 40,000 horsepower to Abitibi and its subsidiaries. The province might sue OPS but collection was doubtful even if a lawsuit was successful. Hydro would incur an annual loss of $1.1 million until it obtained new customers and the province had to reindemnify the utility if that happened. No other firm had sufficient resources to meet the capital obligations. If Abitibi failed, its bondholders might avoid liability simply by getting court-approved relief from the contracts. On this issue Clarkson was blunt. "No evidence has been provided to definitely indicate that the Bankers of the Company are or will be willing to provide special assistance to enable the Company to avoid bankruptcy."[117]

Government aid seemed the only solution. After reviewing the possible options, Clarkson advanced a proposal that was not discussed with Abitibi's officers. If payments were spread out over sixty months or took the form of securities with extended terms, the completion costs might be cut to $6.7 million. A bailout of $4 million was suggested: half as cash to cover equipment or installation expenditures and the remainder as compensation to Hydro for lost sales. The province might guarantee an infusion of $500,000 from Canadian banks and, in exchange, receive $2.6 million of unissued Abitibi bonds, a reconfirmation of the "put-back clause," and $4 million in second mortgage OPS bonds.[118] Henry was ill but insisted upon controlling any decisions, which delayed the review into late April. The premier, Clarkson, and Hydro representatives agreed Ontario "would come out of a bad mess better by giving the necessary financial assistance and taking such securities as Abitibi had," along with an undertaking to indemnify the commission against losses. Without consulting the company, the government's contribution was slashed to $2.5 million. It was made contingent upon an equal contribution from the firm and a pledge of $2.6 million unissued Abitibi bonds. The bailout required cabinet approval, as well as a recall of the legislature to pass authorizing legislation. Sir William Hearst drafted a bill, but by mid-May events caught up with everyone. Despite prior assurances it had given about funding Abitibi's share, the Royal Bank refused to "pay another gale day of interest" given the company's status. Smith claimed Abitibi could stay afloat but, Henry later recalled, they "became more definitely seized with the serious situation in which the parent company was. Up till that time [they] were not just as sure." Clarkson learned the firm was draining the last reserves much faster than expected, indeed at a pace that meant Abitibi could not meet the pending interest payment on its bonds. On his recommendation the plan was jettisoned. All securities were worthless with a bankruptcy, Henry commented, so the government was "not disposed to be of very much assistance" to executives who would be "definitely out of the picture."[119]

Abitibi's directors later attributed the final slide into receivership to the inability to raise money for OPS, a story that became folklore. In fact, as Clarkson had learned, the liquidity was exhausted by late 1931 and every asset was pledged to creditors. The firm could not meet day-to-day cash needs. Even if the Canyon venture had never been undertaken, Abitibi would have gone bankrupt no later than September 1932. Ironically, an earlier start to construction would have allowed a completion of the complex and an activation of the Hydro contract before Abitibi entered receivership. If that had taken place, some of the events chronicled in later chapters would not have happened.

A cone of silence descended around the company's affairs, with no discussions by the press, but many investors guessed what was coming. Market trades of Abitibi's senior securities essentially ceased after January 1932 and the common share price collapsed from $3 to $1 during the spring. Few records have survived from the final days of the firm's solvency, leaving the tenor of events a matter of conjecture. A mix of futile attempts to raise cash likely preoccupied the executives, with continued discussions about "one big merger" and the countdown to default. On the afternoon of 29 May, three days before the bond interest payment was due, the collapse took another casualty. While preparing to leave Montreal for an emergency meeting of the board of directors in Toronto, Victor Mitchell, the firm's lead counsel and the president's closest colleague, succumbed to a heart attack. Alexander Smith's management group had reached the end of the string. There was nothing more they could do.[120]

Plate 1. Stationmen hauling "muck," Abitibi district, 1909. The reality early settlers faced. LAC, R3584-1-2-E, PA-061812.

Plate 2. Spanish River's Espanola mill, c.1910s. Giant machines and bare-footed workers. Author's collection, postcard, unknown photographer.

Plate 3. Frank H. Anson, c.1916, Abitibi's entrepreneurial founder.
Author's collection, unknown photographer.

Plate 4. The Abitibi mill, c.1922. Author's collection,
postcard, unknown photographer.

Plate 5. The mill, modern but still labour-intensive, 1923. UCR/California Museum of Photography, Keystone-Mast Collection, KU44847.

Plate 6. Abitibi's No. 1 machine, 1923, "the biggest in the world." UCR/California Museum of Photography, Keystone-Mast Collection, KU44829.

Millions Spent on Texas Sugar Refining Plant; More Industries Are Promised Texas City by Smith; Diamond Star Brand Sugars Gaining in Popularity

THE MEN AND THE REFINERY

Plate 7. Alexander Smith sails into Galveston, 1924.
Galveston Newspapers Inc.

Plate 8. George H. Mead at a polo club with his wife, c.1934.
Mead Corporation.

Men seek the deciding "yes" or "no" of the analytical chemist because his conclusions are based on facts—facts which he is best equipped to gather—best qualified to weigh and judge.

"Yes" or "No" to a Bond?

When you come to The National City Company for bonds you come to an organization with resources enabling it to gather and weigh carefully the essential facts back of every bond it recommends.

At any one of our offices in more than 50 leading cities you will find a cordial welcome by men who are constantly studying investment problems—and who will gladly help you select high-grade bonds.

These experienced men are well qualified to analyze your present holdings, and may be able to suggest advantageous changes.

Regardless of the size of your investment account, we invite you to come and see us, or to write for our Current List of Bonds of liberal yield.

The National City Company

National City Bank Building, New York

Offices in more than 50 leading cities throughout the World

BONDS
SHORT TERM NOTES
ACCEPTANCES

Plate 9. National City's mass marketing was aimed at the middle class.
National Geographic Magazine, December 1922.

Plate 10. Abitibi's 1928 gold bond issue. Author's collection.

Plate 11. Premiers G. Howard Ferguson (left) and Louis-Alexandre Taschereau (right), with Prime Minister King, 1927. LAC, Canadian Government Motion Picture Bureau, PA-125133.

Plate 12. Archibald Graustein (left) with New Brunswick Premier
John Baxter, 1930. Restigouche Regional Museum.

Plate 13. Geoffrey Clarkson (second from right) leaving Osgoode Hall, June 1932, with his partner H.E. Guilfoyle (centre). The other two persons unidentified. City of Toronto Archives, Fonds 1266, 27075.

Plate 14. Joseph Pierce Ripley testifying before Congress.
Author's collection, photograph likely by Harris & Ewing.

Plate 15. Abitibi Canyon, January 1931, already six months
behind schedule. Ontario Hydro Archives, 267.

Plate 16. Abitibi Canyon, Winter 1932, nine months from completion
and needing a bailout. Ontario Hydro Archives, 269.

Plate 17. Premier George S. Henry did not disclose
his OPS bonds. LAC, L. Lyonde, PA-053852.

Plate 18. Senator Arthur Meighen, self-righteous and thin-skinned.
City of Toronto Archives, Fonds 1257, 1057.

Plate 19. Premier Mitch Hepburn, mercurial Depression populist.
Toronto Star Archives, 054699f.

Plate 20. Attorney-General Arthur Roebuck denounced
the "Abitibi swindle." City of Toronto Archives, Fonds 1266, 36008.

Plate 21. Liquidator Roy S. McPherson, "the worm in the bud."
Archives of Ontario, C306-0-0-2182.

Plate 22. Herbert J. Symington was on "a salvage job."
From a photograph by Karsh, courtesy Estate of Yousuf Karsh.

Plate 23. Premier George A. Drew, "clean up the Abitibi mess."
LAC, L. Lyonde, PA-053853.

Plate 24. The Supreme Court of Ontario, c. 1935. Sitting, (left to right): Chief Justice Hugh E. Rose, Chief Justice William Mulock, Chief Justice F.R. Latchford, Justice Hugh T. Kelly. Standing (left to right): Justice J.A. Hope, Justice Nicol Jeffrey, Justice W.E. Middleton, Justice A.C. Kingstone, Justice R.G. Fisher, Justice C.P. McTague, Justice William T. Henderson, Justice C.A. Masten, Justice J.A. McEvoy. Law Society of Ontario Archives, P797.

7

The Vale of Receivership

"Look young man, here is my breast, if you want to strike here, then strike; if you would prefer the neck, then here is my throat, ready." And he, Neoptolemus, both wishing and out of pity for the girl not wishing to, cut her windpipe with his knife. The life-springs gushed out. Yet, even as she died, she was most careful to fall in proper fashion, hiding what must be hidden from the eyes of men.

– Hecuba

As flies to wanton boys are we to the gods – They kill us for their sport.
– William Shakespeare, King Lear, IV, ii

UNTIL BIG CORPORATIONS FELL INTO the maul, many observers advised firms to undertake actions that might sustain the value of shareholders' equity – cut costs, prune labour, or delay outlays on plants or equipment. Faith in the private sector could weaken further if companies reduced dividends to preserve working capital, the *Financial Times* warned. The payments should be maintained because "people throughout the country are dependent quite as largely upon the income from their investments as is the average worker upon the return from his labour."[1] Some writers linked the economic crisis to policies such as splits of common stock when corresponding increases in assets or profits had not occurred. Firms thus should repurchase shares to bring them in line with the actual scale of operations. Others proposed the formation of a holding company to buy securities and reflate prices back towards 1929 levels. Few offered ideas about where such funds might be found.

But most people considered the Depression a time of chastisement. "We have had our fling and are now called on to pay the price," Sir amongst public officials, different technical processes in alternative jurisdictions, or the application of varying criteria for appraising the settlements offered to claimants.

The modern law of bankruptcy is rooted in statutes adopted during the late medieval period, which limited declarations to specific situations and social groups. As trading networks were extended with improvements in transportation and communications across Europe, failing debtors occasionally fled – either with the expectation of circumventing payment or with the hope of starting anew. Early statutes sought to ensure creditors received satisfaction or some form of composition. English common law imposed a cumbersome procedure as creditors filed writs to attach some assets against the outstanding obligations. A debtor's property was seized by the order of their attachments – first come, first served – triggering a stampede to collect. This phenomenon, in one of the curious twists of legal jargon, became known as "constructive possession." Stressing the rights of creditors, various statutes tried to clarify matters by requiring a full surrender of assets and a distribution of the proceeds pro rata by the size of claims. Until the late twentieth century, all legislation rested upon the assumption that bankruptcy emerged from intentional acts. Individuals were not rendered bankrupt but became so through conscious behaviour such as fleeing from creditors, fraudulently blocking an attachment of property, overextending their obligations, or precipitously withdrawing from the marketplace. Offenders, a Tudor statute declared, were persons "who craftily obtaining into their hands great substance of other men's goods, do suddenly flee to parts unknown, or keep their houses, not minding to pay or restore to any of their creditors, their debts and liabilities." This notion was later broadened to include individuals who had not committed positive acts, by defining the very failure to meet financial obligations as criminal conduct. The legal fiction was extended to the point that a debtor was viewed as responsible even if the person filed a voluntary petition for assignment. After all, legislators reasoned, prudent citizens never needed the protection afforded by bankruptcy law.[11]

With the extension of mercantile capitalism abroad, distinctions were made between traders and individuals whose income came from agriculture or industry. Merchandise traders dealt with flows of capital and credit across long distances. They minimized risk by spreading funds amongst ventures, creating partnerships, or avoiding specialization. Since even the most reputable of traders might fail due to unreliable transportation or communications, a two-part framework in English law was articulated. "Bankruptcy" statutes dealt with traders and defined conditions that permitted their discharge from past debts, whereas "insolvency" laws applied to failures by non-traders and authorized creditors to have them imprisoned. Individuals who fell under the latter type of statute, if they were able to raise sufficient funds, could gain a release but remained accountable for squaring the liabilities. The terminology was reversed in North America, with insolvency laws covering situations where traders had been rendered bankrupt.[12]

The treatment of commercial failure varied within the British Empire. Although statutes in the United Kingdom stressed the need for equitable settlements, creditors retained the right to take unilateral action if a borrower's condition threatened their investments and many continued to exact claims on a first-come, first-served basis. Few of the thirteen American colonies permitted a discharge through bankruptcy proceedings. Some restricted relief to traders; others relieved all traders, dealers, buyers, and sellers. Colonial statutes, seeking to discourage fraud, encouraged honest debtors to make disclosures of failing circumstances. But the insolvent received the right of action, that is, a preference was given to voluntary assignment on the assumption that debtors (not creditors) required assistance. First claimants usually did not receive preferential liens and losses were spread among creditors pro rata to preserve a fair distribution of the costs.[13] In British North America the subject was handled with similar ambivalence. All matters relating to property and civil rights were modelled after English law, but statutes dealing with bankrupts or the maintenance of the poor were excluded. Legislation for the relief of insolvent debtors who had been imprisoned or for the winding-up of companies was enacted in Upper Canada, New Brunswick, and Prince Edward Island. Emulating American practices, the Nova Scotia assembly would not accept a bankruptcy act but did pass a bill that encouraged an insolvent debtor to disclose assets in exchange for a judicial discharge. In Lower Canada, the civil code provided the most substantive treatment by permitting *cessions de biens*, voluntary or judicial assignments of property for the benefit of creditors. After the rebellion of 1837, importers in Montreal secured passage of a bankruptcy ordinance that enabled a narrow class of traders to seek a judicial discharge. This initiative provoked demands for legislation aimed at preventing imprisonment for debt. The Parliament of the United Canadas passed a bankruptcy act, which operated in Quebec and Ontario for different periods. When the statute expired, it was replaced by a statute that authorized voluntary assignments and compulsory liquidation for bankrupt traders in Canada East and all bankrupt persons in Canada West.[14]

Considerable opposition to the regulation of bankruptcy was voiced during the pre-industrial era and even proponents were uncertain about its veracity. A bankruptcy law, while a fine idea in principle, the *Canadian Journal of Commerce* remarked, "holds out a positive rascality" if it enabled individuals to assign "on such each terms as any calculating rogue can generally succeed in wrestling from his reluctant creditors." Given a lack of capital and lengthy periods for the trans-Atlantic movement of goods, merchants depended on a system of long credit. "Still there is no help for this state of things but patience. In the long run sound trading will tell. Wholesale firms who trade cautiously, as men who have much to lose, are able to stand by and assist their customers when the speculative and pushing man breaks down and drags his customers with him."[15] Allegations of fraudulent defaults or discriminatory settlements by wholesalers were widespread, especially in rural Ontario near the terminus of the international credit chain. Insolvencies triggered by economic downturns frequently were attributed to the liberal treatment of debtors. One town council seeking a repeal of any protection for traders characterized the 1864 bill as "a legalized inducement held out to parties to cheat, and a great means of demolishing numerous people who, otherwise, might be tolerably honest."[16]

Under the terms of the British North America Act, authority over bankruptcy and insolvency was ceded to the Dominion. Pressured by commercial interests, the federal government replaced the colonial statutes with a measure that gave traders the right of voluntary assignment. Quebec representatives resisted attempts to extend the provisions to non-traders, while members from rural Ontario perceived the legislation as an illegitimate windfall for irresponsible merchants. When economic conditions deteriorated, some opponents linked the ensuing wave of insolvencies to reckless import practices by wholesalers. The bill, one legislator claimed, was "a shield, behind which knaves sheltered themselves, for the purposes of cheating honest men." All efforts to regulate bankruptcy had been unsuccessful and Upper Canada had prospered even without a law, Ontario's first premier, John Sandfield Macdonald, asserted. "There were men constantly failing, and were constantly appearing none the worse of it, their failure had hardly been announced until they were in the full tide of business again."[17]

This opposition to protection for traders strengthened across the latter half of the nineteenth century. Opponents questioned the ability of the state to regulate commercial failure. Lacking a professional civil service, the government delegated the appointment of official assignees to local judges or boards of trade, a process rife with conflicts of interest. Few obstacles blocked insolvent firms from securing legal discharge since actions moved through the district courts with limited supervision. Critics claimed individuals abused the process by threatening to let claims drag out through legal proceedings if they were not offered time extensions or devaluations of liabilities. Debtors had no incentive to stop trading before their difficulties became insurmountable, while creditors could not take remedial measures prior to failures. Amendments to the law in 1875 tried to strike a compromise. On one hand, protection was extended to incorporated trading companies and all occupations matching a description of traders. On the other, regulations were tightened with the conversion of assignment to an involuntary process initiated by a creditor's demand. To prevent surprise actions by debtors, special meetings of creditors and local judges had to review proposed settlements. The federal government took over the appointment of official assignees to ensure qualified individuals filled the positions. District courts were authorized to suspend or refuse discharges if the debtors' assets did not realize 33 cents on the dollar. None of these measures satisfied those who perceived insolvency protection as a special entitlement. Commercial groups who saw possible value in regulation were disenchanted by the ill-considered tinkering with the law. Opponents consequently were able to force a repeal of the legislation in 1880, along with a declaration that none of the earlier statutes should be revived.[18]

Boards of trade in urban centres, importers, and periodicals like the *Monetary Times* perceived this as a disaster. E.R.C. Clarkson, one of Ontario's first specialists in company receivership, attributed the regulatory problems to "a loose and irregular administration," which did not control trustees but allowed district courts to excuse debtors after cursory enquiries. Thus, "palpable frauds were condoned and the true intent of the measure prostituted." On behalf of the Toronto Board of Trade, he suggested the superior courts take responsibility with careful investigations, the submission of accounting records, and tight control over relief to debtors.[19] Similarly, the Canadian Manufacturers' Association was advised that as the law descended into "a state of incompleteness," parties necessarily fought for their rights "under the diverse and necessarily defective laws." The result was "confusion, injurious to our credit abroad, oppressive to unfortunates at home and out of harmony with an awakening national life."[20]

Farmers, mechanics, and merchants in towns or rural areas opposed the reintroduction of legislation on symbolic grounds. Among those groups, the topic crystallized perceptions of growing social inequality or an erosion of values associated with the transition towards an industrial economy. In a representative pamphlet, Thomas Ritchie, chair of the Belleville Board of Trade, claimed the urban dispensers of credit were operating in a "silent crafty manner" to reinstitute bankruptcy regulation. This constituted a "special class enactment," or "a patent State insurance system." If protected against losses, unscrupulous traders might speculate recklessly. Any benefits would accrue to "the big calico dealers in Montreal and Toronto" who could charge "just what they pleased, without any limit whatever other than what they might choose to dictate among themselves." But there were laws "pertaining to trade and commerce which cannot be ignored any more than we can ignore the law of gravitation by lifting ourselves to the sky by our bootstraps or the property of inertia in matter by dashing our heads against a stone wall with impunity." Creditors should remember, "if need be by painful experience, that they must have regard to the laws of supply and demand or suffer the penalty attached not by men but by God."[21]

Despite lobbying by mercantile interests, entrenched opposition blocked federal legislation for nearly forty years, forcing creditors to seek redress under provincial law. Ontario enacted a measure, under its civil and property rights powers, in accord with earlier practices. Similar statutes were passed by all of the territories and provinces except Quebec, which reverted to the terms of the civil code. Although phrased "creditors' relief," the legislation stipulated a requirement for voluntary assignment by debtors. An assignment for the benefit of creditors took precedence over any judgments against an estate, but a creditor could not force a debtor to act and there were no provisions for regulating the composition of settlements. Most provinces introduced Fraudulent Conveyances or Fraudulent Preferences Acts, which permitted discriminatory settlements, independent of bankruptcy, to be set aside. Creditors could also file civil suits under Chattel Mortgages or Bills of Sale Acts to foreclose on pledged assets. When Ontario went further and sanctioned pro rata distributions among claimants, the federal government challenged the legislation as ultra vires. On appeal, the Judicial Committee of the Privy Council acknowledged measures about bankruptcy passed by the Dominion superseded provincial protocols, but if it failed to act the provinces could define procedures for voluntary assignments under their civil rights powers.[22]

The repeal of the federal legislation created a further problem because all mechanisms for the termination of failed companies were eliminated. Municipal boards of trade gained a partial remedy in the form of a federal Winding-Up Act. This statute authorized the compulsory or voluntary liquidation of federally incorporated companies that became insolvent. Subsequent amendments extended the terms to insolvent provincial enterprises, but judges refused to accept applications against those firms if insolvency could not be proved.[23] The statute brought matters related to the liquidation of companies under the control of provincial supreme courts. Judges retained the discretion to grant or refuse petitions; and a winding-up order, once issued, stayed further proceedings without court approval. A liquidator and inspectors would then be appointed to manage the estate and arrange asset distributions. Meetings of creditors, shareholders, or other claimants could only be called if sanctioned by a court. However, because the act did not cover "acts of bankruptcy" and was employed as an administrative tool when companies failed, debtors never received a discharge. In addition, conflicting rulings rendered procedures under the act highly ambiguous. Different cases left unclear whether a liquidator served as the representative who enforced the rights of the unsecured creditors or whether those claimants could take independent action. Ontario and New Brunswick courts would not accept a liquidator as equivalent to an assignee or a trustee in insolvency and the officer could not question unregistered mortgages or conveyances. Where a receiver was appointed by bondholders or a court for an insolvent firm, a liquidator could not displace the officer.[24] Further measures for handling railroads, telegraph companies, or banks were spread through a range of statutes rather than included in the Winding-Up Act.

Importers and British investors pushed for a new federal law after 1900, garnering support from business associations and lawyers. As the volume of trade expanded with industrialization, many business interests perceived the depersonalized handling of economic affairs as a necessary concomitant for long-term growth and a mark of professional conduct. The shift also mirrored a spread of legal formalism amongst Canadian and British courts. This reorientation placed greater emphases upon procedural rules and on the objective enforcement of contracts – depersonalizing the adjudication of legal disputes. When the Canadian Bar Association established a committee to prepare a law for regulating the management of bad debts, the Canadian Credit Men's Trust Association wrote its own proposal with a mixture of provisions from the 1875 statute, the British Bankruptcy Act of 1883, and the Winding-Up and Creditors' Relief Acts. A bill based upon this draft was introduced by the Borden administration as a war measure and a modified statute was proclaimed during 1919. The cursory debates repeated those that occurred with earlier legislation and focused upon the machinery of bankruptcy proceedings or the qualifications of different officers. All discussions centred upon the handling of general creditors, small proprietors, or partnerships – not secured creditors or big corporations.[25]

The Bankruptcy Act specified three modes of procedure. A debtor could propose a voluntary composition of the outstanding liabilities. When accepted by a majority of the general creditors, a court then confirmed the plan and discharged the debtor. Alternatively, the debtor might make an authorized assignment for the creditors' benefit and the court would issue a receiving order to take possession of the assets. If an apparent act of bankruptcy occurred, a creditor could petition for an assignment with a receiving order. A court would then appoint a trustee and inspectors to make discovery, administer the estate, and distribute the assets. The fundamental principle embodied in the Act was the right of general or unsecured creditors to shape bankruptcy proceedings. They nominated the trustee and inspectors, and those officers had to follow their directions so long as the statute's terms were not contravened.[26]

Expected to simplify matters, the new regime was confusing and failed to achieve some of the intended goals. The Bankruptcy Act was superimposed on the existing body of provincial law. Established protocols had to be consulted since it did not give definitions for numerous technical issues, such as what constituted the property of a debtor, or who were general creditors versus secured creditors.[27] A complex document, it dealt with topics covered superficially or clumsily by the Winding-Up Act: examinations of the origins of insolvency, administration of assets, protection of unsecured creditors, and mechanisms for the impeachment of prejudicial transactions. Federal legislators expected most actions to proceed under the new measure but they failed to give it precedence over the Winding-Up Act. Instead, the statutes worked somewhat in competition even though they differed in substance and process. Federal legislators expected the Winding-Up Act to be used only in exceptional cases and, given variations in terminology between the two statutes, case law required a court not to apply it unless thorough documentation showed the interests of the general creditors would be served since the Winding-Up Act altered the rights and remedies of all parties concerned in a liquidation.[28] The bankruptcy statute more carefully defined the rights of unsecured versus secured creditors, provided superior facilities for investigations of insolvencies, and provided better protection against prejudicial transactions. Under its terms, bankruptcy and a meeting of the general creditors had to occur before a receiving order might be issued. Under the Winding-Up Act, any party able to demonstrate insolvency could request an order. Banks, insurance companies and railways might be wound up under the latter bill but could not be liquidated under the former. In bankruptcy, the assets were vested with a trustee and administration resided with the unsecured creditors. With the Winding-Up Act, title to the assets remained with the firm but control was taken from the directors and later placed with a liquidator.[29]

Serious difficulties were encountered almost immediately. The new statute authorized the creation of federal bankruptcy courts staffed by provincial judges, but the Ontario Court of Appeal questioned its constitutionality. The federal government was forced to pass amendments that vested jurisdiction with the chief justices of provincial supreme courts but the original schema was not deleted from the act.[30] In cases of voluntary assignments, insolvent companies often nominated their own trustees or cooperated with the appointment of unqualified individuals, not the professional officers licensed under provincial law. With the Act's confusing terminology and weak enforcement provisions, many individuals found voluntary assignment a convenient mechanism for avoiding obligations. Indeed, more cases were filed during the recession of 1921 to 1924 than during the worst of the Great Depression.[31] Further amendments tried to curb these abuses by creating an office of custodian and by designating official receivers who would take possession of assets until the creditors appointed trustees. However, complaints proliferated about unnecessary delays, high costs, illegitimate failures, or collusion between debtors and trustees. An investigation, initiated by the Council of the Bar of Montreal, was expanded by the Canadian Bar Association and a committee of the House of Commons. After documenting numerous problems, additional amendments stipulated the licensing of trustees, cost controls, and the creation of a Superintendent of Bankruptcy.[32]

As if this regime was not confusing enough, under pressure from institutional investors, the federal government passed a Companies' Creditors Arrangement Act (CCAA) during 1933 with a provision copied from the British Companies Act of 1872, which enabled an insolvent company or a creditor to apply for a restructuring of the firm's secured and/or unsecured debts. Large domestic enterprises tended to be financed by British capital before the First World War with corporate bonds backed up with trust deeds that authorized a majority of debenture holders to vary the terms of the deeds. The clauses were deleted as firms increasingly raised capital in the United States, but this created a new problem. Financial structures could not be easily modified without explicit provisions for reorganization by agreement. This issue became acute during the Great Depression when it was almost impossible to sell new securities. Under the CCAA, several options could be offered to debt holders: new securities which ranked ahead of the existing debentures, sales of assets of a new firm, or mortgaged assets to cover

the outstanding obligations. However, few organizations had sufficient resources to "buy" the assets of a giant enterprise. Sometimes only the firm in jeopardy could amass the capital. The property of a corporation did not exist in a traditional sense since its value was as an integrated unit of facilities, resources, and personnel coordinated by salaried executives. The organization itself was the only "property" which a big firm "owned" and only the managers had the knowledge necessary for handling day-to-day operations. Indeed, the gap between the nominal worth of the assets and the company's real value constituted the "going-concern" value or "goodwill" derived from the intangible worth of managerial expertise.

Debt holders were the key interests when a big enterprise failed.[35] Following British precedents, most industrial bonds were secured with a charge against the property, present and future, of companies. This condition remained dormant unless a firm defaulted, but it had to be publicized through registration, usually by the issue of a mortgage with a filing under a statute like the Ontario Bills of Sale and Chattel Mortgages Act. Accordingly, federal jurisdiction did not axiomatically apply after a default, even if companies were incorporated under Dominion legislation. Because most assets were covered by the charge, even with a filing under the Bankruptcy or Winding-Up Acts there was little or no property other interests could touch before the bondholders were recompensed.[36] A trustee appointed before the sale of a debt issue was responsible for the enforcement of bondholder rights. Courts used this agent to personify the investors since the security class could then be handled as a single character rather than as a rabble. Trust deeds for the bonds required consent to the reconstruction or amalgamation of debts. Most stipulated a majority of the holders could bind the group to a solution. However, although the trustee initiated action after a default, it was relieved of liability so long as it undertook no direct action. The lawyer engaged by the trustee, therefore, was separate from those who served the bondholders but the person was usually cooperative. Actions would be challenged only if a consensus was missing or if the return on the mortgage was threatened.[37]

If the bondholders could act cohesively several options were available. When a large portion of a debt issue had been retired the balance might be recouped by selective sales of assets, thereby avoiding any obligation to manage the business. In cases where a company no longer operated or revival was out of the question, they might accept the appointment of officers who would prepare the surviving assets for liquidation. The trust deeds also could be enforced by foreclosing upon a firm like a piece of real estate and then selling it by public auction, but this represented a course of the last resort unless another company was prepared to buy the enterprise for most of its nominal value – an unlikely prospect in troubled times. The fourth and normal option was an application for receivership. The trustee or a friendly creditor sued the corporate individual for default, but instead of asking for an execution on the property, the court was advised a public sale might hurt the claimants by destroying the enterprise's going-concern value. Instead, it was asked to appoint a receiver who would preserve the assets until favourable conditions emerged or the secured creditors found a purchaser, otherwise they would be saddled with deteriorating facilities. Most applications were accepted on grounds of jeopardy, that is, to avoid an interruption or cessation of business as subordinate claimants sought repayment. Moreover, even if factories were closed, maintenance had to be carried out, as well as taxes and insurance paid. Additional outlays were normally needed to revive a company. The receiver would be authorized to cauterize the wounds or amputate the dead and expiring components. To fulfil those obligations, certificates ranking ahead of the bonds could be issued as new money. An officer of the court, the receiver, nominally worked for the benefit of all claimants, but the bondholders, the initiators of the process, could sponsor a person likely to follow their suggestions. Eventually, a purchaser (sometimes a financier or another corporation, perhaps an agent for the bondholders themselves) would "buy" the property at a judicial sale or auction and the assets would be reconstituted as a new firm – the shell of the insolvent enterprise cast off into the nether-world appropriate for malicious spirits.

Because every type of asset could be mortgaged, receivership became the standard mode of handling corporate insolvencies. Throwing a large enterprise into bankruptcy risked intervention by judges, a court-appointed trustee, or others who might try to impose their own notions of what constituted a "fair" settlement. Receivership was guided by common law and narrow procedural rules. Once appointed, a receiver could not be displaced by a liquidator under the Winding-up Act or a trustee under the Bankruptcy Act. If a liquidator was initially appointed, court approval had to be secured before a receiver could take possession of corporate assets, but this was granted as a normal matter of course. Secured creditors and the receivers, along with agents appointed on their behalf, could then carry on outside of the scope of the Bankruptcy Act.[38]

Canadian practices were analogous but varied procedurally from those in the United States, where the favoured technique was an "equity receivership" – a process that was lengthy, costly, and vulnerable to abuse. Developed for the insolvency of railroads, which could not be allowed to cease operations despite their troubles, it was then employed to reconstruct industrial corporations. Receivership in equity differed from receivership in bankruptcy (where a neutral officer was appointed to administer a bankrupt's assets). The initiative to undertake the process was typically taken by a distressed company with the aid of an approachable creditor who gained court approval for the appointment of a receiver favoured by the firm. There was no provision for an independent, objective review of financial situations. Reorganization plans often were drawn up by biased committees or "friendly" receivers. Ratification required majority creditor support and some firms, therefore, offered inducements to dissenters to gain their agreement. Courts exercised little control, and the safeguard of investors often fell to insiders or stakeholders who used the process to further their own goals.[39] During a congressional investigation chronicling numerous manipulations, equity receiverships were characterized as "the most odious and flagrant of all the 'rackets' in America" applied against "some helpless corporation that has plenty of property and even sometimes plenty of money" by special interests or carefully composed committees.[40]

Regardless of the type of process, launching a receivership was the first mystery in a rite where many aspects were masked. Behind the symbols of credits and debits, it was a forum for disputes about influence, power, and control. Prompt manoeuvring dictated who shaped the legal process. A company's board of directors was suspended and the shareholders dropped in status beneath the alternative types of creditors. No longer able to review managerial decisions, they could rarely block those groups gaining recompense from the corporate remains. Officers from large institutions usually represented the bondholders and established "protective committees." They portrayed themselves as solid citizens and all others as reckless "strikers," that is, as obstructionists or less significant groups who were out for personal profit or who sought to block appropriate actions. The senior executives of a failed company were labelled as foolish or wasteful miscreants and were then dismissed. Lower-level officers stayed since they were needed for day-to-day operations. Regardless of which group gained ascendancy, the "outs" invariably charged the "ins" with corruption, dominance by greedy interests, or a failure to protect investors. The "ins" characterized the "outs" as unrealistic, not prepared to take necessary actions, or proponents of unsound options.[41] With this initiation, the process of rehabilitation began.

2. In an entirely friendly way

Occurring as the Depression approached its nadir, Abitibi's insolvency coincided with several other failures, along with an array of battles over corporate restructuring, which triggered numerous complaints in the business press. Defaults had become alarmingly "fashionable," one columnist declared. Bondholders could not intervene before a failure, often did not know how to organize, and "in disgust and hopelessness" did nothing. All too frequently equity investors remained in control, while those who owned debt securities were "robbed of their fair rights" as others rode "rough shod over their supposed privileges." The resulting compensation, another writer remarked, often amounted to a sop.[42]

Few protocols existed for safeguarding bondholder rights when a company failed other than unilateral organization by those with the largest stakes. Although institutions often held major blocks, most securities were widely distributed. Lists of the owners could only be secured from senior executives or from the brokers who had sold the securities. Many organizational meetings thus did not attract sufficient participants to authorize action or broke up in confusion after disagreements over goals and procedures. With unclear rules, key investors and financiers could manipulate the process to secure the appointment of representatives on protective committees who would safeguard *their* interests. Some of the rigged committees asked for postponements of scheduled payments without offsetting remuneration, while others proposed new securities, which lowered interest rates or restricted payments to whenever operations finally generated sufficient funds. Exchanges of common stock were offered for bonds, providing the holders with ownership stakes of questionable value – *if* the right of foreclosure was surrendered and write-downs of corporate assets were accepted.[43]

By 1932 many institutional investors, also with troubled finances, perceived such manoeuvres as illegitimate attempts to impose the costs of failure upon them. "In ancient days the word bond carried some meaning ... Now it is a joke," the president of the Montreal Life Insurance Company argued. One firm after another had defaulted without apologies, the executives believing that market conditions would be blamed rather than the actual causes like mismanagement, the failure to build up reserves, or the payment of unwarranted dividends on watered stock. As companies deteriorated, "bondholders sit helplessly on the side lines, utterly powerless to interfere. They may fret and fume, get hot under the collar ... at this needless and apparently purposeful destruction of their capital" but could not stop it. Promoters and "the unrighteously indignant wreckers" directed events after a failure by conspiring with the trustee for a debt issue, which knew "on which side its bread is buttered."[44] Learning from those experiences, the representatives of the Abitibi bondholders demonstrated *they* were not going to yield to pleadings for softness: *they* would have their bond. Their protective committee would gain control and prevent, by fair means or foul, interference by others.

The announcement of Abitibi's default surprised casual observers because the annual report released three months earlier indicated a viable, albeit weakened, company. Many observers still thought Abitibi was simply too big to fail. The firm reinforced these notions by claiming the omission of interest was temporary until additional capital was secured for Ontario Power Service (OPS). The default was just technical, the *Wall Street Journal* intoned, the firm's plans delayed by Victor Mitchell's death. Putting the best spin on the situation, newspaper accounts suggested the earnings still met the firm's obligations and payment might occur belatedly. In any event, the company had shown "financial strength" by using up its inventories of raw pulpwood wood and avoiding new timber purchases. The managers had sixty days to raise funds to cover the debt interest before lenders could launch legal proceedings. Consequently, the press did not acknowledge the firm had failed until mid-summer. Even the *Financial Post* insisted the "present embarrassment" occurred despite a strong position, except for some contingent liabilities that Abitibi had due to the collapse of the investment market. Operations like OPS and Thunder Bay Paper "would be a source of future strength" if they secured adequate funding.[45] While Abitibi was delisted from Canadian exchanges, its securities continued to be traded in the United States. But the key investors quickly moved to protect their stakes. A week after the announcement, National City invited the major bondholders to Montreal for a conference. Most participants signed an agreement depositing their securities with Montreal Trust and the group then elected a protective committee comprised of representatives from financial institutions.[46]

The most prominent Canadian member, Edward E. Reid, the managing director of London Life, had been involved with reorganizations of municipalities rendered insolvent by the Depression. His colleague Charles M. Bowman, the chair of Mutual Life Assurance of Canada, was well connected politically and the only representative familiar with resource firms. Bowman's sudden death in October of 1932 led to the appointment of Walter Harold Somerville, Mutual Life's general manager. A skilled actuary and former president of the Canadian Life

Insurance Association, Somerville, like Reid, was familiar with municipalities, not industrial companies. Sun Life Assurance, the largest
holder of Abitibi bonds, did not put an officer on the committee because
the company had extensive holdings of preferred stock. Sun Life was
represented indirectly – first by John Leslie, a vice-president of the
Canadian Pacific Railway, and later by Andrew Fleming, the president
of the Hartt and Adair Coal Company of West Virginia. This arrangement allowed Sun Life executives to claim that they did not participate
in the decision-making. In fact, they were always consulted, and there
is no evidence that they ever disagreed with the committee's choices.
Three other positions were allocated to financiers associated with the
1928 bond sale: Stanton Griffis of Hemphill Noyes & Co. of New York;
Harold P. Janisch, a vice-president of the National Bank of Boston; and
George W. Pearson, a vice-president of the Continental Illinois Company of Chicago.

Joseph Pierce Ripley, vice-president of the National City Company of
New York and the organizer of the meeting, was chosen as the chair.
Born in Illinois during 1889, Ripley had graduated from Cornell University and then worked for ten years as an engineer before turning to
investment banking. Well over six feet tall, dark-haired, square-jawed
and huskily built, he seemed the physical embodiment of a financier.
After joining National City in 1925, Ripley specialized in the syndica-
tion of industrial securities, loans to European governments, and venture capital for aeronautical enterprises. More traditional than other
officers in his company, he was cautious and known for meticulous
preparation. Although executive practices at National City later became
controversial, Ripley remained loyal and described the firm as the finest investment bank of its day.[47] His role was predicated upon his experience with troubled firms. He had played no part in Abitibi's 1928
refinancing. Ripley headed the protective committee for Cuban Domin-
ican Sugar, helped reorganize West Virginia Coal and Coke, and guided
a management turnover at Remington Rand. National City had financed
all of those failed companies.[48]

The committee was formed in a standard manner but the arrangement had serious implications. Since the default occurred just four
years after the bond issue, National City's involvement might be interpreted as part of its fiduciary responsibility, a perspective that Ripley
promoted. "Our purpose is to cooperate with you and other holders of
Abitibi securities towards working out the situation as best we can
strictly to their advantage ... Our path of action is as yet not clear, but
our desire in respect to your good selves is only one of cooperation and
mutual help."[49] However, the financier was guided by practical

editing by Ripley. The first among innumerable analyses, his was the most crucial because it advanced an interpretation later adopted as gospel and used to legitimate all actions undertaken by the bondholders. A review of the 1928 refinancing sought to prove the funds retired securities of the predecessor companies and never entailed a "buy out" of proprietary interests. The issues of bonds and preferred equity were legitimated as reasonable given the earnings record. Indeed, Ripley claimed that after the financing Abitibi was one of the soundest newsprint companies, with a capitalization "conservative in proportion to production capacity and earning power." The merger with Spanish River and the terms of the share exchange were never questioned.[55]

The collapse was attributed to two issues. Although the expansion of the pulp and paper industry was portrayed as natural and logical, the pattern had been "unsound" and represented "a serious obstacle to the restoration of profitable operations." The unsuccessful attempts to achieve stabilization had replicated previous initiatives for rubber, sugar, and coffee. "Perhaps such efforts deserve to fail ... Anyway, we now find the law of supply of demand asserting itself powerfully." In essence, Ripley's analysis blamed the industry's problems on the weather. A combination of economic forces, beyond the control of individual firms, had devastated the reasonable plans of corporate leaders. Second, Abitibi supposedly would have escaped financial jeopardy if Alexander Smith had not continued the expansion program. Only the purchase of Provincial Paper was considered reasonable. Participation in the stabilization efforts was derided as expensive and foolish. OPS appeared "to have been improvident from the start," with unrealistic estimates of electrical power demand, insufficient monies for construction, and non-disclosure of the put-back arrangement. No advantage was gained by the acquisition of Thunder Bay Paper that offset the costs. In a feat of legerdemain, Ripley suggested that the bondholders and National City had not known about the acquisitions of Thunder Bay Paper or OPS and would not have sanctioned them.[56]

Exclusive of the obligations related to Provincial, Thunder Bay, or OPS, an audit by Price Waterhouse guesstimated that Abitibi earned about 80 per cent of the bond interest during the first five months of 1932 but this figure dropped to 40 per cent if amortization costs were included. The scale of the disaster had few parallels in Canadian business. At the peak of its operations during 1929 Abitibi's sales amounted to $31.5 million and it earned a net profit of $4.1 million. The probable revenues for 1932 were just $12.5 million; the forecast for 1933 was even worse.[57] Ripley argued the bondholders, therefore, could not expect payments for years and must control all decision-making. "This should be considered the corner stone upon which the formation of the Bond-holders' Protective Committee rests … So far as the active operating management of Abitibi is concerned, such facts as we have been able to obtain indicate that it is recently efficient. As regards the general administration of the Company's affairs, the record speaks for itself."[58] An analysis of data later submitted to the Supreme Court of Ontario indicates that even these projections understated the disaster. If *all* of Abitibi's obligations were included, the firm would have posted an operating loss of $10 million for 1932 – regardless of whether it functioned at 1 or 100 per cent of capacity. At the prevailing price levels, each increment in production, if spread among the plants, just offset the marginal costs associated with additional output.[59] Only closing or liquidating the least efficient operations could alter the breakeven level. Longer-term actions required major reductions in production costs and a reorientation of marketing efforts.

An August meeting in Toronto brought together the senior executives and the bondholders' council. Alexander Smith indicated he had no valid argument to block action, but he claimed sales would drop once the firm entered receivership. He refused to answer questions about Abitibi Canyon, particularly on the "put-back" clause in the OPS contract. Contradicting Smith, George Mead and L.R. Wilson claimed neither sales nor corporate morale would be affected since further price declines were inevitable. Both thought a reorganization of Abitibi was unlikely within eight months. The committee unanimously concurred and, on Ripley's recommendation, selected for the office of receiver the one person who had already demonstrated his value to the vested interests associated with Abitibi: Geoffrey Teignmouth Clarkson.[60]

The decision to proceed to receivership revolved around what lay-persons might perceive as abstruse technicalities but were, in fact, crucial matters. In a default, the mortgage deed authorized Montreal Trust, the trustee, to carry on the business or to sell the assets. The trustee had the option of not going via the courts, but that was the usual practice because a receiver was a judicially sanctioned officer and the legal persona of a firm remained intact. In theory, a receiver was expected to manage a firm's affairs in a way that conserved its value for *all* investors. In reality, the officer was a delegate of the bondholders. Most receivers were experienced administrators who belonged to the Canadian Insolvency Association and were licensed by the federal or provincial governments. They were public accountants by training and usually belonged to major partnerships. The combination of professional norms and concerns for their firms' reputations supposedly ensured they handled the function in a reasonable manner.[61] A receiver was given wide discretion provided his acts appeared to be bona fide. The officer did not need to keep the bondholders waiting for the best price but could seek a fair value through a private sale, a liquidation of assets, an adjustment of productive operations, or an auction. However, the receiver could not draw out fees or make expenditures without court approval, a condition that meant that the trustee and the bondholders' council had to approve them in advance.[62] Justice Riddell promptly approved Clarkson's appointment and Abitibi was ordered to surrender all assets and records to his control. After posting a bond for due and proper performance, Clarkson was empowered to carry out any actions he deemed necessary, subject to ratification by a Supreme Court justice. He had to submit statements from time to time but there is no evidence that these were ever challenged. In accord with standard procedures, Clarkson was authorized to borrow monies for cash flow and capital expenditures and could issue certificates for the new debt, which had priority over the existing securities.[63]

Several days after the receiving order was issued, the game rules were altered by a seemingly innocuous manoeuvre. Because his firm had not been paid for $11,323 in trade goods, Charles Wadge, the secretary of Canada Packers, filed a petition asking for Abitibi to be placed in bankruptcy and for the appointment of a custodial trustee. Since the insolvent firm had unsecured obligations exceeding $850,000 and another $6.75 million in deferred liabilities or bank debts, Harold Shapley, Wadge's solicitor, claimed the creditors would never be repaid unless Abitibi was reorganized. In the midst of the proceeding, he modified the petition and contended their interests might be better served under the Winding-Up Act. This new motion conveniently received immediate consent from the lawyers for the trustee and the bondholders. Since it seemed to be pro forma, Justice Sedgewick ordered the firm wound up and (on the recommendation of Shapley) named as a provisional liquidator the brother of the receiver, Frederick Curzon Clarkson. The court then directed him to notify the general creditors that all claims must be filed within two months or be excluded from consideration.[64]

Business reporters found this action mystifying since the timing seemed illogical and did not match other insolvencies. The protective committee "had nothing to do" with the motion, although it should view "the step in an entirely friendly way," Ripley assured his colleagues. The receiver and their counsel had feared that "some undesirable law firm" might file the application and then participate "with an unconstructive attitude." If the company was not placed in bankruptcy "by parties friendly to us, somebody else would in all probability do it any way."

Canada Packers "retained a law firm in Toronto with which we know our lawyers can work in harmony ... So, all boiled down, the placing of Abitibi in bankruptcy was something which probably had to come anyway and, as it all turned out, it has come about in such a way as to have a law firm with which we all know we can deal with and with a so-called Liquidator, a partner of G.T. Clarkson, in whom we have confidence." If asked, they were instructed to say the initiative was launched without their knowledge but was necessary for a reorganization.[65]

Ripley did not reveal the true facts to his less knowledgeable associates, probably to ensure deniability. Shapley was an associate in Osler, Hoskin, and Harcourt, the counsel for the bondholders' committee. Glyn Osler, Shapley, and the solicitors for the preferred shareholders had met during early September to ensure that the legal regime was structured to favour their clients. The general creditors and common shareholders eventually would have to be brought into a settlement. However, it was in the interests of the senior classes to have those claims reduced as low as possible and to have other groups excluded from the supervision of executive decisions. Shapley was instructed to have the appropriate motions filed by a sympathetic interest even though he knew none of the unsecured creditors. Wadge, he later claimed, just happened to enter his office one or two days after the meeting with a request for a petition. The law firms representing the preferred shareholders covered all of the expenses incurred by Shapley and Frederick Clarkson.[66] This *coup de main* was legal since anyone could seek an application of the Winding-Up Act but it clearly suborned the process. The unsecured creditors would have filed for the appointment of independent inspectors, who might have served as a check upon Geoffrey Clarkson. A subsequent court order followed established precedents and authorized Montreal Trust to proceed with its action at the provincial level notwithstanding the winding-up order, a decision that blocked the liquidator from interfering.[67] With one deft trick, the avenues of redress were restricted and a compliant officer, with an obvious conflict of interest, was put in place. But no one anticipated the filing under the Winding-Up Act would become the fulcrum for battles that unfolded a decade later about whether the province of Ontario had the right to shape the terms of a corporate reorganization.

3. Too many chickens

Despite gaining control, the bondholders' council was reluctant to interfere with the management. The situation was dire. Clarkson later noted, "Abitibi not only had not one dollar in its till but it was

$1,000,000.00 short."[68] His first goal was a standard gambit: reduce administrative expenses. Salaries and allowances for the top executives were halved within four months as Alexander Smith and his closest associates were fired. Clarkson wanted to slash the outlays further but found that reductions had to be timed to avoid disruption or demoralization. Abitibi, like many large organizations, "is somewhat like a large family," with many employees having been friends for a long time. There were "certain political relationships between the old Abitibi crowd and the Ontario government," Glyn Osler advised Reid, "which it was wise not to disturb. On this account there have been probably some retentions on the staff which are justified only on account of the old-time relationships."[69]

Somerville was satisfied with this performance but Reid was critical. He believed a subordinate of the receiver carried out most of the early initiatives. If Clarkson was giving full attention to the firm, "he is evidently doing at long range because it is reported to me that he is not at the Abitibi offices more than perhaps once in a week or two. He may be a super-man and able to handle things satisfactorily in that way but I certainly could not do it myself."[70] Reid's private adviser cautioned that the receiver might not be up to the challenge. "In the present Abitibi organization are most of the men (except Alexander Smith) who are still Alexander Smith men. Between you and them is only Mr. Clarkson. He is not a practical paper man and they know it. Thus it is only natural that they will advise him as best suits them ... I do not know Mr. Clarkson but reports to me from Toronto are that he is really a Banker's Man. I do know that he is not a paper man." Despite assurances from his colleagues, for nearly a year Reid remained uncertain about Clarkson's ability to understand Abitibi's problems. Conservative and a penny-pincher, he was never satisfied, particularly with the expenses for audits or project assessments, and he viewed the fees submitted by Clarkson's company as "entirely excessive."[71]

The scale of the difficulties was not understood for several months. Clarkson's first obligation was a statement of affairs about Abitibi's worth. Standardized data about operational costs were available but the financial records were mud. Across the summer of 1932 Price Waterhouse was unable to appraise the capital assets or locate many documents. What they found was disturbing and kept secret, even from the court. The valuation of the timber concessions, for example, was a major question because an arbitrary value had been inserted for cutting rights based upon a rate of $1 per cord. Nearly half of that assessment then was declared "excess" and transferred to the firm's capital surplus. But by 1932, unable to make the payments on its licences and timber fees, the firm was in default for almost all of the concessions in Ontario and Manitoba. Since these contained 30 million cords of pulpwood, technically assets worth $30 million worth of assets had disappeared. The same problem existed for Ste. Anne and Murray Bay and lowered the real value of those properties from $15 million to $7 million.[72] However, in his confidential report Ripley had reiterated earlier data that placed Abitibi's worth at $181 million. Regardless of how they analysed the statements, neither Clarkson nor the auditors could come up with estimates anywhere near this figure. Any evaluation entailed a string of qualitative assumptions, each of which could be critiqued, but the task was essential before tackling more substantive decisions. That Smith's management had parboiled the books was obvious but, Clarkson reasoned, any new estimates would be as subjective as the original. Trading and current assets hence were reevaluated in terms of their imagined "market" or "replacement value" to show how much might be recovered. The receiver never explained how these notions were determined. Given the replacement costs and Abitibi's earning capacity, the assets inevitably were worth substantially less than the official accounting values.[73] The securities of the subsidiaries were written down, sometimes by as much as 93 per cent. This process devalued Abitibi's assets to $116.8 million. A later write-off of OPS discounted them to $87.3 million. Clarkson developed a statement of affairs that presented the balance sheet not as assets and liabilities but as entries that showed the ability to make payments. Liabilities, for example, were designated as preferred claims, cash advances from banks, or obligations to the bondholders. This technique further depressed Abitibi's apparent status and helped to lower expectations when a summary was published in 1933.[74]

Short-term, there was little that could be done. Like most insolvencies, Abitibi's downward spiral accelerated after the default. The costs for idle properties quintupled from 1929 to 1933 and peaked at the equivalent of half of the annual interest obligations. Sales of newsprint collapsed below 40 per cent of the 1929 level and pulp sales to a third. Although other firms posted their rates, the prices Abitibi actually realized were kept confidential. Those for newsprint dropped from $52.24 to $30.35 per ton. Put another way, if Abitibi had been capable of covering depreciation, preferred share dividends, and the bond interest, it would have lost $22.02 per ton during 1932 and $23.15 in 1933. Operating costs were slashed but these entailed mill closings, layoffs, and three savage wage reductions. Clarkson thought the firm might sell, at the best, 300,000 tons (about 44 per cent of capacity) during 1933. The situation was dire because all cash resources had

8

A Time for Investigations

In times of great opportunity and contest for privilege, life always sinks to its lowest depths of materialism and rises at the same time to its highest reaches of the ideal. When the waves of the sea are most towering its hollows are most awesome.

– Theodore Dreiser, *The Titan*

People who don't expect justice don't have to suffer disappointment.

– Isaac Asimov

THE GREAT DEPRESSION, OBSERVED business writer Peter Drucker, showed man "as a senseless cog in a senselessly whirling machine which is beyond human understanding and has ceased to serve any purpose beyond its own." With the threat of "being thrown on the industrial scrap heap in one's prime or even before one has started to work," a person felt "helpless, isolated, and atomized as against the forces of machine war. He cannot determine when unemployment is going to hit and why; he cannot fight it; he cannot even dodge it."[1] The sense of individual self-worth was ripped apart by the struggles for subsistence – the fear of losing whatever one still had, along with petty indignities that reinforced feelings of inferiority or shame. Although many citizens sought constructive solutions to the economic crisis, it also fostered a sense of meanness, a desire to blame something, some-one, for the misery. Class divisions were reinforced, along with the desire to attack the status, privilege, or wealth of those who seemingly prospered at the expense of the many. Populist politicians seized upon these beliefs, attacking "parasites" and "spongers" who did not share the travails of average people. This social atmosphere fed into several controversies that unfolded after Abitibi's collapse. Although the company itself was not involved directly, the investigations and hulla-baloo had relevance for later developments. This chapter examines three scandals that unfolded between 1932 and 1934. The first section examines the consequences of plant closings by reviewing the experi-ences at one mill town: Sturgeon Falls. Financial practices also came under intense scrutiny during the Great Depression. The second section contrasts how this unfolded in Canada and the United States. The chap-ter's other sections review the biggest controversy: the fate of the Abitibi Canyon project.

1. A pretty good business

The workers and towns dependent upon Abitibi's operations were the first to pay the costs associated with the failure. In receivership, finan-cial expenses and depreciation no longer applied, but a harsh reality confronted the company. By the summer of 1933 the nominal list rate dropped to $33. Abitibi only secured sales by offering much lower prices. Even without accounting for woods operations, ongoing expenses, or overhead, most of the mills were non-economic for the indefinite future.[2] Clarkson might have boarded up factories not in use. Trying to forestall such actions, local politicians and labour leaders called for the province to impose penalties since Abitibi's concessions were granted in exchange for certain levels of output. The petitions ignored the loss of business as the Depression worsened. Most alleged output from one facility would be unjustly consolidated at another. For example, since Thunder Bay Paper had benefited from property tax relief, the councillors for Port Arthur demanded production be kept at two-thirds of capacity and not moved to Fort William or Sault Ste. Marie. Delegations from those towns, in like fashion, asked for the withdrawal of resource rights if their mills were not sustained.[3] Premier Henry told Clarkson only the most non-economic operations could be shuttered and manufacturing should spread around if possible. The premier was reluctant to intervene because a cancellation of timber concessions might trigger litigation and make the province appear unattractive for investors. In addition, the Tories feared harsh action would just precipitate a broader shutdown and a transfer of production elsewhere.[4] Abitibi's operations thus were never curtailed as far as con-ditions warranted or the bondholders desired, but the province's demands for keeping mills open (rather than allowing a consolidation of operations) kept the firm weak for years. Clarkson walked a fine line and was not heartless. He ensured Anson's widow and sister received pensions to prevent their being reduced to penury. While the company failed to pay provincial fees for forest and water rights, it sometimes provided monies that sustained local schools or part-time work for laid-off employees.[5]

The receiver's plans now and then were deflected, as one case will highlight. The Pine Falls mill in Manitoba was the second most efficient operation but it closed in 1931. A contract with Manitoba Power accounted for two-thirds of the carrying costs and obligated Abitibi to pay a minimum amount for electricity. When Clarkson refused, the utility threatened to sue for recovery. Bluffing, the receiver declared he would place the subsidiary in bankruptcy and then buy elsewhere. Unwilling to lose its major client, Manitoba Power compromised for half of the past due amount and agreed to defer the contract during the shutdown.[6] Handling the province proved more difficult. The minister of Crown lands pressed for a start-up of the mill and logging operations. With its revenues stretched thin by the Depression, the Bracken administration could ill afford the relief expenses for Pine Falls. Dissatisfied with Clarkson's response, a bill was introduced that authorized nationalization of the mill and a resumption of production. Losses incurred by the government would be charged against the properties ahead of the bondholders' claims. The receiver lobbied federal authorities and mobilized sufficient pressure to force a withdrawal of the legislation. The province countered by imposing a tax surcharge on Manitoba Paper that covered the relief costs. It then suggested the tax would not be imposed if the firm provided temporary work by purchasing 20,000 cords of pulpwood. Clarkson capitulated since this option imposed lower costs, even though the useless timber was dumped near railway sidings. Government pressure continued for another two years until Clarkson was forced to restart the mill or face new taxes and a loss of resource rights.[7]

For many towns in Northern Ontario the initial concern associated with the economic downturn was with transients, "drifters" who had to be moved on lest they become a relief burden. But chronic unemployment soon became a way of life, a condition that lasted from several years to nearly two decades. The unskilled workers who earned low wages and had little, if any, savings suffered the most. Cutbacks hit those engaged in forest operations early as 1928 as the pulpwood piles at mills accumulated. With lost wages and further reductions, waves of unemployment rippled through local economies. No one was prepared because of the lack of a social security net. The federal and provincial governments deemed unemployment relief to be a municipal responsibility. Agrarian representatives, who had held significant influence in the national Parliament, refused to fund social programs for urban centres because the policy might accelerate rural depopulation. Public officials instead dodged responsibility, either by suggesting excess labour could be siphoned off through emigration to agricultural areas, or by scapegoating immigrants as a factor that led to job losses for other people.[8]

Ontario had a small welfare department for care of the elderly, the insane, and children, but it was not capable of handling a massive displacement of able-bodied people. Although some municipalities had departments that doled out aid, the province had not enacted legislation that authorized assistance to those who were capable of working, or to their families. In some communities charitable agencies or voluntary societies handled relief efforts, emergency committees in others. Relief distribution was inconsistent and withheld from any deemed "unworthy" like transients or unmarried individuals. Between 1930 and 1932 most officials considered the problem temporary, one that could be handled by public works. Provincial and federal authorities each agreed to assume one-quarter of the costs, with the balance covered by municipalities, but the outlays were a pittance relative to the magnitude of the crisis.[9]

By 1932, nearly a third of all male wage-earners were unemployed and more than 400,000 Ontarians needed direct relief for survival. The misery was well illustrated at Sturgeon Falls, now a town of 4,300. Abitibi's mill, the only large enterprise in the area, employed 200 men who earned a monthly payroll of $20,000 to $25,000. The town also bought electricity from the company and earned a significant proportion of its revenues from resales of power and water.[10] When the mill was closed in November 1930, some workers moved elsewhere but most stayed, convinced the situation would be short-lived. Direct relief provided $7.20 for work during three days per week. By May of 1931 about a quarter of the town was rendered destitute. Many households sufficed off a mix of voluntary cooperation, carloads of charity shipped from elsewhere, or clothing contributed by sewing groups. Two hundred and fifty families had water and light arrears totalling $27,000, along with another $12,000 owed for rent. The town itself owed $50,000 to Banque Canadienne Nationale but less than 40 per cent of local taxes could be collected. The school boards ran out of funds. The town launched public works like sewer construction, which were financed by bonds that the province guaranteed, but as tax arrears accumulated the municipality was unable to cover the interest.[11]

Local representatives declared that Queen's Park must force the mill to reopen or that it had to secure an agreement with Quebec that allocated some production for the plant. Granting timber concessions to

Abitibi, they argued, implied a moral obligation for the use of natural resources in ways that benefited the whole population. If production did not resume, the company should sell the facility or lose the resource rights. A "good share of what must be considered as the property of our Canadian citizens is being monopolized by a certain group of financiers and may remain idle and unproductive indefinitely." Government officials expressed sympathy but pointed to the practical difficulties. Abitibi had inventories of unprocessed pulpwood sufficient for several years, the minister of lands and forests noted. He rejected the demands as naive. Even if the rights were terminated, two years were needed to transfer the mill to another owner and no rational firm would do so during the Depression. The government also believed that abrogating the contract could trigger a hostile business reaction and lead to a drop in the provincial credit rating.[12] The town council then attempted to get monies creatively. It earned $102,945 in taxes on local properties assessed at $2.1 million. Those held by Abitibi were valued at $800,000, which generated $38,000 in taxes and $13,000 for separate schools. Closing the plant ended all understandings, the mayor claimed, and the council inflated the worth of Abitibi's properties to $4.6 million, hoping to quadruple the payments. The firm refused to pay and on appeal, without evidence being heard, an arbitrator slashed the assessment to $700,000.[13]

By the winter of 1932, Sturgeon Falls was reduced to a barter economy with eggs or timber for currency. Wood was stripped from city lots and piled up in sheds behind homes. Potatoes from gardens received a value of 40 cents per bag or five bags for one bag of flour. People without regular income could not procure food and other necessities as storekeepers closed credit accounts. Children and expectant mothers lacked proper clothing or nutrition, one petition observed, while idle young men "are on the streets continually meeting undesirable companions ... Children even beg food at our doors. Leftovers, anything to satisfy their hunger."[14] Desperate, civic officials constructed a new industry as the basis of the economy: welfare fraud. The mayor and a committee took over all decision-making. They superficially scrutinized invoices and gave whatever they thought was fair. A relief officer signed orders for food, clothing, and rent vouchers but he never asked for proper records. School children were invited to the town hall for informal distributions of clothing vouchers. Most of the town's maintenance expenses were charged to the relief account in order to collect federal or provincial funding. Regular and temporary municipal workers received vouchers as compensation. The script was used like cash although it had no monetary value. Civic employees endorsed the vouchers back to the municipality or used them as income supplements for purchases of supplies. Voucher recipients never knew what prices were charged since the local merchants decided how much the script was worth. In practice, they provided clothing and supplies only after using it to liquidate outstanding debts. Some swapped or bought vouchers, then inflated the bills before "selling" them back to the town, which then sought recompense from the province. Most destroyed their records to cover up what occurred. Civic officials reached an agreement whereby landlords accepted two-thirds of overdue rent but provided altered documentation so the town might demand the full amount from the province.[15]

Appalled by press stories about widespread deception and a sudden influx of bills from the town, the province appointed a royal commission to investigate. Headed by Justice James McNairn Hall, its mandate was not to find criminal fault but to ascertain the extent of the fraud. The hearings produced front-page stories for newspapers across the winter of 1933. Reporters revelled in the testimony, which varied from tales of swindles to foolish cheating that could be held up to ridicule. Even horses had been put on relief. "Owners couldn't buy feed for their horses, so the horses were given jobs by the town. Nothing is supposed to be given for horses, but they got it here," one witness jeered. Another told how people flocked to Sturgeon Falls because it was the only town that gave direct relief. More than 700 new residents arrived between the Octobers of 1931 and 1932. "There were not enough houses for all, so they lived in sheds and stables and old tumble-down shacks that no one had lived in for years." Three families comprising nineteen people lived in one shack. "That is what I call a wonderful investment in real estate," remarked Judge Hall, who wondered how they all fit into the hut. "They hang themselves on hooks on the wall at night," an investigator said "gravely."[16]

The town paid $1,000 for a wood lot even though lumber was freely available from Crown lands. The mayor and councillors then had the timber stripped for delivery to their homes. Several contributed their share to relief recipients "as a gift." The commission's counsel could not resist the dark humour in the situation. "I see. So they all had a drag for wood." Local charities cooperated with a scheme where municipal relief funds were recycled as "donations" to secure matching federal and provincial monies. Town officials juggled and padded rents to cover the one-third of the relief bill they were supposed to pay. As the monies received fluctuated from month to month, rents went up, dropped, and went up again. Most landlords recovered rent arrears by simultaneously collecting from tenants and the town. With the

were placed under the stewardship of the Department of Municipal Affairs. Supervision of relief activities was transferred to the Ontario Municipal Board. An entire generation was lost for Sturgeon Falls. The factory did not reopen for sixteen years. As its properties deteriorated, Abitibi's tax assessments were reduced and squatters occupied company houses. Most men sufficed off the dole, those who went elsewhere were treated as transients. As the years passed, many forgot how to work or lost even the will to do so. By 1940, 2,655 people still received relief, a pattern that was eroded only by wartime demands and new regulations that slashed welfare rolls regardless of need. Successive efforts to find a purchaser for the mill failed. Only Espanola suffered more among Abitibi's operations. That plant was boarded up a week after the release of the Hall report and the town of Espanola was rendered derelict.[23] Other mills and operations suffered variably. Pine Falls remained closed until 1935; Sault Ste. Marie and Fort William Paper did not resume normal activities until 1936; and Iroquois Falls operated on half of capacity through most of the receivership.

2. A public accounting

As the gap between daily misery and an oft-promised recovery widened, the credibility of corporate leaders deteriorated. Not understanding the economic collapse, many people blamed foolish judgment or greed. The situation had resulted from a "want of confidence between man and his fellow man" derived from wildcat speculation in stocks and a desire to get rich quick, Justice William Raney told jurors during a case. "How can you expect men to invest their money in legitimate building and other enterprises when such things are going on?" Others blamed managers for a lack of prudence. Herbert J. Symington, the counsel for Maple Leaf Milling, admitted to the shareholders that commodity gambling by the senior executives exacerbated the firm's losses. Once the company was reorganized, given the reputation of its products, they could "look forward with confidence to an early revival and restoration of our export trade, which already shows sign of improvement."[24]

Such optimism rapidly disappeared. A tripartite creed had been promoted to legitimate the rise of corporate enterprise: economic progress tended to enhance the standard of living; financiers and managers were reliable agents of development; difficult environments could be overcome by thoughtful business leaders. The Great Depression seemed to put the lie to such notions. Beliefs that things might turn around were undermined as meetings between executives and politicians generated a haboob of murk and hot air but little substance. Business columnists, seeking scapegoats, linked the earlier wave of mergers and expansion (which they had acclaimed) to the Depression. Companies had financed such initiatives via multiple issues of common stock, preferred stock, bonds, and debentures, a writer in the *Financial Times* asserted, creating capital structures where even experienced investors found it difficult to estimate true values. If the issues were simplified to just common stock and debt, the stakes could be clarified.[25] The integration of banks with trust companies and underwriters, along with unrecorded connections to other institutions, created too many conflicts of interest, the *Financial Post* decreed. Small investors were "certain to be the butt of their saw-off agreements" because they would have great difficulty getting independent advice when bankers (who wished to offset weak returns on loans or other operations) dumped securities upon the unwary. Despite the "conservatism and high tradition" of Canadian practices, "the entering wedge for such evils has been driven into the banking structure." The public welfare was "jeopardized by the attempt of different individuals to serve more than one interest." It would be preaching "a gospel of perfection and a policy of impracticality" to ban interlocking activities but investors needed a new deal with reviews of financial conduct that received too little analysis or criticism.[26]

Best-selling books offered poison pen caricatures of financiers who "were as stupid as they were ruthless and greedy," determined to take other people's money and never give it back. One withering sketch portrayed Charles Mitchell of National City as an actor who had all the elements of his art but could not create the necessary illusion because he was too perfect at each of the separate tricks. Another commentator described bankers as an obscene life form. "Enormous and with no necks they look like hooked and helpless frogs or like fat bass or logy groupers hauled suddenly out of the water ... They pant, they twitch in their seat, they make gestures finlike and feeble – one can imagine great gills behind their jowls straining to breathe the alien air."[27] But other writers generated valuable analyses. Frederick Lewis Allen, best remembered for a memoir of the 1920s called *Only Yesterday*, produced a thoughtful book, *The Lords of Creation*, which traced business finance from the turn of the century. Max Rosenthal, later a lawyer for the Securities and Exchange Commission, provided a polemical but well-researched study of a reorganization, appropriately entitled *The Investor Pays*.[28]

Canadian politicians and the media were reluctant to investigate questionable behaviour, fearful the publicity associated with airing business's dirty laundry would worsen things. An attempt to force an

investigation of life insurance companies by a young Ontario representative, Mitchell F. Hepburn, was suppressed as contrary to the national
interest. Prime Minister R.B. Bennett claimed it might trigger complete
demoralization in the business community.[29] Strong pressure from
groups who had lost their investments compelled the banking committee of the House of Commons to investigate the formation of Canada
Power and Paper. The committee collected copies of annual reports,
along with statistical information, but the ill-prepared members never
examined the data carefully, accepted statements on faith, and even
apologized for having the temerity to seek testimony from financiers
like Harry Gundy and Sir Herbert Holt. The witnesses denied wrongdoing, were evasive about their dealings, and instead blamed provincial governments or "supersalesmen" like Charles Mitchell. They
wrapped themselves in indignant hauteur that anyone could think they
had contributed to the debacle. The committee's report amounted to a
truism: the producers had overbuilt their facilities.[30] *Pulp and Paper
Magazine* responded with a scathing critique: "[W]e frankly do not see
that it has got anywhere." The committee did not determine responsibility for the corporate failures or how to discourage unwise projects.
After reading the evidence, the editor heckled, an ordinary person
might be excused for reaching the impression that nobody made anything out of the mergers during the previous decade. Investors might
"ask whether the financiers gave their services for the fun of it, or with
the Boy Scout idea of doing the industry a good turn. There are some
who would delete a few words from that sentence, namely to omit 'Boy
Scout,' and 'a good turn'!" The journal believed the origins of the collapse lay in the illusions that senior executives had held about how
firms could always operate at full capacity, along with investors' willingness to finance dubious operations. Some were "unwisely undertaken and unwisely located" because provinces insisted upon new
mills even as consumption declined."[31]

In marked contrast, American enquiries into business activities were
plentiful and lengthy. Some took the form of systemic appraisals, others
were viperous castigations of managerial or legal practices. The subjects for congressional investigations included bankruptcy procedures,[32] bankruptcy and receivership proceedings,[33] real estate
bondholders' reorganizations,[34] municipal bankruptcies,[35] and railroad
financing and reorganizations.[36] A large amount of reform legislation
emerged from these efforts. Although the enquiries have attracted significant scholarly interest, at the time most received modest press attention because the hearings consisted of rambling or inconsistent evidence
that seemed poorly connected except to the lawmakers. Public

attention could be captured when prominent executives gave testimony or a juicy anecdote was recounted but often businessmen stonewalled or circumvented questioning. Several investigations, such as those conducted by the Senate Anti-trust and Monopoly Subcommittee, were well covered. Those hearings were chaired by politicians hostile to big business, who sought to document their pre-conceived notions and literally went a-hunting. But one investigation attracted spectacular headlines by targeting Wall Street financiers. It had serious ramifications for the Abitibi receivership.

The Senate Committee on Banking and Currency was charged with investigating the 1929 stock market crash, but short of money and qualified lawyers the subcommittee responsible for the enquiry initially floundered. Richard Whitney, head of the New York Stock Exchange, and other executives denied questionable practices, deflected questions, or patronizingly lectured the senators.[37] Late in January 1933, the position of counsel for the subcommittee was offered to Ferdinand Pecora. Fifty years old, the eldest son of Sicilian immigrants, Pecora worked as a law clerk while attending New York University Law School and later became chief assistant district attorney for New York County. He gained prominence through well-publicized investigations of the sinking fund for the State of New York, abuses of bail bond businesses, bucket-shop operators who victimized small investors, and milk-graft scandals in New York City's health department. His 1929 investigation of the failure of the City Trust Company resulted in a bribery conviction of the former State Superintendent of Banks.[38] Critics accused him of political theatre, grandstanding, and manipulative inquisition, but Pecora captured the public mood when he later recalled that before the Senate committee appeared "the demigods of Wall Street, men whose names were household words, but whose personalities and affairs were frequently shrouded in deep aristocratic mystery ... Never before in the history of the United States had so much wealth and power been required to render a public accounting." Timing also mattered – the hearings occurred during February of 1933 at the height of a disastrous banking crisis.[39]

Pecora shifted the investigation towards stock exchange practices and had Charles Mitchell subpoenaed for a recall. The financier, the previous spring, had treated with the committee with contempt, denying allegations about his firm's involvement in a sordid manipulation of Anaconda Copper stock, which he characterized as a great American investment.[40] His bank wanted the hearings delayed and it disclosed evidence very slowly. Although Pecora gained access to the firm's minute books, he could not assimilate the information due to a shortage of

a loss.[53] Northern newspapers expressed concerns about how the premature termination of construction impacted local relief expenses. "The
Hydro should come North," declared the Cochrane *Northland Post*,
since the situation permitted a "clean sweep" of private power interests. If the government truly believed in public ownership, then it must
be for the whole province, not just for privileged areas. Most press commentators, nonetheless, urged caution. The OPS bonds went to persons
who "got the wink" for making easy profits, charged the Kapuskasing
Northern Tribune. "Now that things have gone awry" and the bond price
had crumpled "these insiders" were demanding protection. Equitable
terms, the *Globe* surmised, could mean a return to the "old days of private exploitation of the public" if the government was forced to "hold
the bag" by fully compensating the OPS investors. Mismanagement or
carelessness might leave it with an expensive asset, but, the paper conceded, legitimate claims had to be satisfied. Most press editorials recommended acquisition at a "rock-bottom" price and with considerable
sacrifice from the security holders. A scheme advanced by the *Globe*
called for $5 million from the government to cover completion costs in
exchange for a first mortgage on OPS assets. The investors would
receive income bonds that did not pay interest until the venture became
profitable. Revenues from power sales would be applied to their
redemption, leaving "the property debt-free as a perpetual public
asset." Abitibi should also release Hydro from its contracts and surrender all relevant leases or privileges[54]

This proposal, like many others, ignored the bondholders' legal
rights. Once the subsidiary defaulted, the enterprise could be placed in
receivership after sixty days. They might request court approval to
defer payments and raise funds to complete the project. In real terms,
only $400,000 was required, just enough for the installation of the first
generator and start-up. They then could move for a judicial sale, take
full ownership, and hold Hydro to the original contract, which stipulated sufficient purchases of power to cover all interest obligations once
the facility became operational. Moreover, any outside party might bid
during the sale and force the same result. At least two firms expressed
interest, but the government was disconcerted by an enquiry from A.J.
Nesbitt's Northern Canada Power. The result if it gained control was
politically untenable – a private monopoly in the north versus a public
monopoly in the south. One minister remarked that even an infusion of
public funds that let private interests finish the work was going too far.
The premier told Nesbitt that the province would acquire OPS. Just
before the official default, the decision was leaked to forestall unwanted
action.[55]

The government planned the takeover as a two-stage process: secure overwhelming ownership of OPS bonds and then take possession. Financial issues were delegated to Geoffrey Clarkson, while legal matters were delegated to Strachan Johnston, the counsel for the bondholders' trustee, a situation (once again) rife with conflicts of interests. The advisers advanced several proposals but the government defined the terms of acquisition. In Henry's view, the Hydro Commission was just an agent taking possession on behalf of the province – it had no decision-making role. The utility's engineers assessed the facility but the commissioners were excluded from the negotiations and were never asked about the propriety of the transaction. When the cabinet reviewed the final proposal, John Cooke, the utility's chair, was concerned only with ensuring the province would cover any losses.[56]

Various options were appraised but the largest debt holders were not prepared to make sacrifices. Few, if any, OPS bonds could be bought cheaply and any gains would have been eliminated as speculators pushed up the price of the remainder. Following an appraisal by several auditors, Clarkson recommended a new issue of Hydro bonds exchangeable at $70 per $100 OPS bond, the going rate on the Toronto exchange and the minimum return acceptable to the major holders. Wishing to minimize its short-term expenses, the government adjusted the interest rate to a sequence with increases in the payable interest over the life of the bonds. The province also insisted upon a right for redemption at any time. The purchase was contingent upon agreement from 90 per cent of the bondholders, but the investors were asked to accept nine months of lost interest. Because the terms altered the net worth of the securities, the purchase price then had to be reset at $90 per $100, which returned them to the level of compensation recommended by Clarkson. Through the manoeuvre, the province also gained legal control over funds held by Montreal Trust for the project's completion, which decreased the actual commitment of funds.[57]

The deal was controversial even before the terms were announced. As the price of OPS bonds rose in response to gossip about the takeover, Liberal critics inferred sinister influences were at work. Traders and the business press understood the exchange was worth about 70 per cent of the existing securities. They believed the government was securing the Canyon on reasonable terms. Northern newspapers argued that "Henry protects [the] North." Not only had the premier ensured the availability of power, a government contract that safeguarded purchases of electricity was "an ace in the hole." Still, even the Sudbury *Star* could not avoid remarking about how the bondholders stood to lose only ten cents on the dollar even though "the financing of this project has gone 'blooey.'"[58]

Keying on the $90 figure, political opponents denounced the package as a capitulation to moneyed interests. The *Toronto Star* insisted the project was unnecessary and occurred because Premier Ferguson needed to take care of his "friends." The *Globe* falsely alleged a "high pressure lobby" shaped the negotiations. The province was saddled with an unnecessary debt for a white elephant, a confiscation of taxpayers' money for which there was no moral obligation to pay. "There will be a nice melon cut by Montreal and New York speculators who took a chance on the Abitibi development," claimed Harry Nixon of the Progressive Party. The head of the Ontario Liberals suggested the bondholders had "every reason to hold a service of thanksgiving."[59]

As with the unsuccessful bailout earlier that year, the takeover took longer than anyone expected. Although the terms were announced in July, the bondholders did not receive an offer until September, but even the $90 rate proved insufficient to get investors to exchange securities. Only when the government sanctioned an increase to $94.44 was the target achieved. The time limit was extended to December as the province garnered $19.5 million of the $20 million issue. Concurrently, nuisance suits encumbered Hydro's litigators as creditors tried to seize OPS assets.[60] Moving the firm into receivership further slowed the acquisition. After filings and title searches, the order for a judicial sale was not issued until March 1933. Not until the following month did the government finally introduce legislation authorizing the acquisition of OPS.[61]

These delays and the terms of the takeover would have been unimportant had not Henry's private affairs triggered a political firestorm. Even his opponents conceded the premier was a well-meaning and likeable individual, but he lacked Ferguson's ability to gauge the public temper. One colleague snickered that if Henry had to cross a pasture containing one "cow flap" he would step on it.[62] Only as the purchase deadline approached (and the completion of the buyout was certain) did the premier disclose to the cabinet that in 1930 he had bought $25,000 of OPS bonds. A day after the takeover he revealed the situation to a tense caucus. The premier also spoke at length in the legislature but the published version never mentioned his ownership stake. Instead, off the cuff, he insisted "These bonds mean less to me than a scrap paper. I am not a politician. Were I one, I would not have got into this situation." One party member quipped that when "Premier Henry told his followers that he was no politician, he can rest assured that they implicitly believe[d] him."[63] The disclosure got worse when information was tabled in the house. The premier was a director of North American Life, which held $200,000 of the bonds, and he sat on its investment committee. Hydro commissioner Arthur Meighen owned $3,000 of the securities but directed investment trusts that had increased their OPS holdings from $55,000 in 1931 to $322,500 by the summer of 1932.

Henry rationalized away his behaviour, declaring that he never believed the OPS dealings "would ever be up for review by the Government, and almost before I knew it I found myself in the possession of private information that would have made it very unfair for me to sell the bonds and get some innocent purchaser involved in a situation in which the future was very doubtful." He told Ferguson that they were "a gilt-edged proposition and a matter of straight investment." He had not disclosed the matter to the cabinet because "I desired them to have free and open mind with regard to the purchase." Henry might have given the bonds to a charity and thus avoided criticism. He failed to recuse himself from the cabinet deliberations because "I had to carry along some who were not very enthusiastic in agreeing to what was ultimately decided upon." The premier defensively told Ferguson how the editor of a newspaper had told him, "If you had been a political crook, you would not have been caught, but because you are honest you find yourself in difficulty."[64] Henry contended to Sir Joseph Flavelle:

> I had no intimation whatever of the way things were riding until Mr. Alexander Smith, President of the Companies, came into my office asking Government assistance towards the completion of the Canyon development. No one seriously criticizes the purchase or the price, and all openly, at any rate, believe in my integrity. It is hard for one to feel that criticism should follow under such circumstances, but, as I say, this is political life – a hard and exacting one – and we all have to take our batterings and disappointments when they come.

In early 1934, far too late, he gave the bonds away to a charity.[65]

Henry's ownership of the securities represented a blatant conflict of interest and permanently left his reputation darkened. His directorship of North American Life was not unusual for the times but participation by public officials in corporate affairs was on the decline. Certainly, by the standards of later generations, it was unacceptable. Henry claimed he did not discuss the issue with Thomas Bradshaw, the president of the firm, or with the investment manager, but even Strachan Johnston, acting as the lawyer for the trustee of OPS, characterized the premier as a "bad boy." It remains uncertain from Henry's appointment books whether he attended the meeting that authorized North American

Life's purchase of OPS bonds.[66] Meighen disclosed the holdings of his trust companies during the meeting with Attorney General Price in June of 1932. Despite subsequent allegations, there is no evidence that he was involved with the takeover, but ethically, if not legally, his attendance at the meeting with Price was inappropriate. He never recused himself and his firms continued to trade OPS bonds across the summer of 1932. Meighen claimed he had not done anything wrong, but external perceptions were soon different. Even before the names of the OPS bondholders were disclosed, he expressed concerns that people might believe that he had attempted to benefit either his personal finances or those of his companies. Meighen asked for the appointment of an investigatory commission with authority to determine whether he had done anything "dishonourable or discreditable or not in conformity with the best traditions of public service." He recommended the selection of a judge whose appointment originated from a different political party. Henry, however, failed to act on the request and cited the legal proceedings for the OPS acquisition as a rationale.[67]

The premier believed he weathered the crisis when the Tory caucus reaffirmed support for his leadership. Even Liberal-oriented newspapers, at first, conceded the acquisition was necessary. The *Toronto Star* acknowledged the premier had never pursued a dishonest motive in the past. It doubted whether Henry would lead his party into the next election but thought this was due to the desire of some Tories to run on a "beer and wine" platform. The *Globe* thought Henry had driven "a hard bargain," although it could not resist commenting that "it was evident that he came into possession of considerable loose funds and being pestered by bond salesmen, acquired $25,000 worth the Ontario Power Service securities." But the most accurate assessment came from the *Toronto Telegram*. "Posterity will probably agree with Mr. Henry that he did well in securing the Abitibi undertaking on these terms, and that the price paid was by no means excessive. In justice to Mr. Henry it may conclude that he acted entirely in the interests of the Province and without thought of the effect of the transaction upon his own fortunes. The unfortunate feature of the situation is that posterity will not vote at the next election."[68]

4. The royal inquisition

"Hard times are the historic foe of governments," the *Mail and Empire* observed. By 1934 the Conservatives were riven by infighting, resignations, along with the loss of campaign volunteers and financial support. Numerous party members wanted Henry to resign but the probable successors appeared even less capable of generating electoral support. Ontarians were disillusioned by what many perceived as the government's inability to control taxation, along with its policies that promised only retrenchment and limited social assistance. In contrast, the New Deal policies south of the border suggested how a government might try to abet the Depression.[69] The provincial Liberals had struggled for nearly thirty years, but in 1931 they chose a new leader, Mitchell F. Hepburn, who was still in his first term as a federal member of Parliament. Hepburn was a skilled orator, mercurial, and provocative. Liberals and friendly newspapers portrayed "the Chief" as a vigorous young campaigner seeking to overturn an old tired regime. Opponents considered him a man without shame, a purveyor of untruths, and a reckless demagogue. Hepburn gave substance to those perceptions by making exaggerated promises, which included his ability to cut provincial expenses in half and provide shorter working days for employees without weakening their income. Ontario, he trumped, was "over-governed by commissions and boards." If elected, he would force lower interest rates, repudiate contracts, and have a "big parade out" of expensive civil servants and Tory appointees. Even sympathizers were appalled by "the graceless boisterousness with which he slings mud. In this pastime, his aim is good, but his mud is unnecessarily dirty and indiscriminately applied."[70] Like other Depression populists, his first campaign had a virulent anti-corporate orientation that was encouraged by two associates: Arthur W. Roebuck and Arthur Slaght. "In my humble opinion," Hepburn declared, "the financial racketeers of this country have so disregarded the laws covering bribery and the manipulation of watered stocks and promotion schemes that there is an actual danger of our whole monitory [sic] system being destroyed." The Liberals would not be neutral "and for my part I do not wish to be a puppet of St. James Street." The Tories were "on the side of the big interests," whereas his government would have a "social organization interested in the people as a whole."[71]

The Liberal campaign stressed the growth of provincial debt under the Tories. The party's leaders attributed much of it to an overexpansion of the Hydro system, which they believed was driven by patronage and insider arrangements. They promised to tear up power agreements made by Ferguson and to investigate contracts for "questionable" deals. Developments such as Abitibi Canyon, Hepburn insisted, provided "evidences of graft and corruption everywhere; the Administration reeks with it." Liberal partisans considered OPS to be "a losing proposition" that entailed the construction of unnecessary capacity, while the takeover seemed to be an attempt by the idle chatter."[89] Henry hired his own lawyer. Meighen foolishly represented himself. Latchford blocked other lawyers from asking questions even though the government's counsel defamed several during the hearings. Henry's counsel declared he had never witnessed a proceeding characterized by a "conduct of matters with such bias and such evident animus as has been exemplified." The government's counsel was headed by "two political traducers of my client coming hot and flushed from the hustings before your Commission to endeavour to justify the very statements, the very charges, that they have made up and down this Province ... the whole setting offends against one's innate sense of justice and against the law of natural justice." Hydro employees gave testimony with threats of dismissal looming. The officer who signed the OPS contract appeared "with the sword of Damocles hanging over his head, his walking ticket in his pocket."[90]

Other than John Cooke, no effort was made to subpoena those who had made decisions and much of the "evidence" took the form of inferences and innuendos, not direct proof. When it became clear that Alexander Smith had conducted all negotiations for Abitibi, Latchford first dismissed the testimony as too costly to secure, then rejected the notion of a private hearing (remarking he would sooner be in Iceland than New York during August), and finally proclaimed it would have little value. One lawyer quipped in response that there was nothing like making up your mind before any evidence was submitted. Latchford became notorious for his musings in open court about supposed impropriety by lawyers like Strachan Johnston, the "master hand that had acted for the power crown," and Norman Tilley in past (but totally irrelevant) cases. The justice portrayed Clarkson in dark conspiratorial terms because the receiver had earned fees from Hydro. He characterized stock market dealings as little more than gambling. Acknowledging he once had toured the Canyon, Latchford ruminated about how there must have been "an intimate relationship" between the contractors, OPS, and Abitibi.[91]

The hearings were conducted as a prosecution from the start. The two justices blocked any cross-examination of witnesses other than by the commission's counsel. During the mornings Slaght made accusations so they could appear as headlines before any rebuttal. He posed loaded questions that reporters recounted as fact. The commission then ruled the questions out of order. Tilley became so outraged by the tactic that he accused Latchford and Slaght of "team play" that facilitated "a tirade of abuse." Tilley spent the afternoons disproving the claims but these received little press coverage and were ignored by pro-Liberal dailies. Slaght ranged far from the commission's mandate with his slurs. He portrayed an investment trust as a venture intended to lure "the public to hand over money ... when the president and trader can sit week after week and deal in stocks on margin, which means they had not enough to pay, they had to put up margin, borrow money even, to play the ups and downs of the New York Stock Market." He claimed the OPS acquisition required "Meighen's brains, judgment and decision." Meighen denounced him as a coward, "worse than false." When Slaght claimed he was not attacking the trust companies the former prime minister managed, Meighen futilely complained about the damage. "I can produce papers here to show the results of this performance; they are terrible!"[92]

Normal rules of evidence and most forms of court procedure were disregarded. Exculpatory evidence was deliberately withheld from Meighen and Henry. McRuer, for example, removed relevant Hydro files and secretly kept them in the briefcase next to him, a practice that was revealed just before the end of the hearings.[93] But, ironically, the investigation discovered little new. No incriminating documents that substantiated the claims of corruption or payoffs were ever found among the premiers' papers, records at Lands and Forests, or at Hydro. Only a half-hearted effort was made to secure files from Abitibi. Indeed, a full enquiry was never conducted. The hearings stressed Henry's and Meighen's ownership or relationship with OPS bonds but not one of the exhibits or documents actually dealt with that subject. The commission failed to subpoena Henry's correspondence or hear testimony from Clarkson (although the 1932 bailout was a key part of the evidence). Instead, it relied upon press accounts, public statements, and an informal auditor hired by the Liberals (who never secured access to relevant materials). The hearings were brought to a sudden close once Henry, Meighen, and Cooke testified.

Despite the sound and fury of the investigation, the commission's report was brief. It argued the Canyon venture was improvident by emphasizing the original desire of Hydro engineers to use small sites for servicing electricity demand. Smith's negotiations with the government brought about the abandonment of an economical scheme in favour of the expensive Canyon project. The commissioners avoided discussing why other options were rejected. Although it was a private (not a government) venture, they alleged a holding vehicle "with virtually no assets" gained a provincial lease. Without any evidence, Latchford and Smith argued the report that had recommended approval "was manifestly submitted to provide a basis for the contract dates." The performance requirements were inadequate and any protection for investors "was from the first illusory because [it was] dependent on the handle Abitibi. Full competitive advantage required management to be "a solvent, well-financed, and intelligent operation." Moreover, legislation was needed to adjust the resource rights on a "mutually advantageous" basis, to enforce his proposals for the settlement of claims, and to circumvent federal legal constraints. A property as big as Abitibi involved "so many points of Government relationship that it would not be possible for us to proceed with any reorganization without the goodwill and co-operation of your Department."[2]

Sweezey's group hoped to grab some of the assets but he was quite unrealistic about Abitibi's problems or the pace at which they might be resolved. It made little sense to bring the company out of insolvency if it was likely to slide back again. The construction of winning conditions required developments at several levels and this chapter explores the initial efforts. First, the receiver had to staunch the worst of the financial hemorrhage and divest unsustainable activities. Second, it was necessary to establish the legal venue for a return to solvency but, with its own goals, the province increasingly attempted to shape corporate reorganizations. Third, and most problematic, competitive conditions had to stabilize. Direct regulation represented the most logical solution, but it remained a form of intermediation that neither politicians nor executives accepted. Their preferred option was another iteration of associationalism. Consequently, not until 1936 did things improve to the point where the odds for successful reorganization seemed practical.

1. Now nearly useless

The ability to turn a troubled firm around is a function of its condition and the urgency of time. Some operational actions can be launched quickly but strategic changes entail lengthy periods before positive returns are garnered. If an enterprise functions near the breakeven level, profitability may be regained by cost-cutting tactics or marketing initiatives aimed at enhanced sales. However, when operations drop well below breakeven status, painful choices are necessary.[3] From 1932 to 1935 Abitibi's earnings after operations averaged less than two-fifths of what was necessary to meet the bond interest. The earnings from the three active plants just offset the carrying costs associated with the closed factories. Most of the operating income came from minor parts of Abitibi's portfolio: Abitibi Electrical Development (AED), Kaministiquia Power, and Mattagami Railroad. Between 1932 and 1934 a small stream of earnings allowed Clarkson to pay off the Royal Bank. Once that debt was liquidated, the shares of Provincial Paper were released and the fine paper company supplied modest profits through the balance of the receivership. Given these conditions, the receiver postponed most renovations or improvements indefinitely.

Stabilization encompassed a set of Hobson's choices. The pact whereby the G.H. Mead Company handled American sales was recognized as the most dangerous liability even though the use of a marketing organization was standard practice. Legally, those contracts were in the hands of the agency, which Mead treated as *its own properties*. It did not disclose financial data and took months to answer requests for information. Contrary to the claims of Abitibi's senior executives, Clarkson realized the relationship was not exclusive.[4] Concerned with his own firm that hung precariously near insolvency, George Mead was slow to respond. Although he had been Abitibi's chair and dominated the marketing activities, Mead refused to take any responsibility for the collapse. Sales, he declared, "continuously declined because of the Abitibi Company's refusal to meet competitive conditions." Other firms took tonnage away "because of our price maintenance and their price cutting." The agency, in fact, had been unwilling even to suggest rate reductions for cities like Cleveland, Akron, and Cincinnati until other manufacturers matched the low rates available from smaller firms. Mead rationalized this disastrous course by claiming that Abitibi was "the least destructive of all the major producers." He then hypocritically recommended the bondholders should ensure Abitibi regained its rightful market share. The executive council had considerable difficulty figuring out what had been done and by whom. "Abitibi seems to have sat by for years living up to its strict obligations," Ripley observed, while other firms made subversive concessions. "Why not make open effective discounts for quantities and be done with the monkey business?"[5] Mead's letter, one adviser remarked, was a defence of a ruinous policy. Sales had been cut in half and the firm retained massive inventories of useless timber. "You have wood, power, management, mills and *nothing else* to put in them." Several members of the bondholders' council could not understand why Mead still received generous compensation.[6]

Moreover, the industry continued to race helter-skelter toward the bottom. Price Brothers slashed its list rate to $48.50 per ton in June 1932. Mead matched the action but refused to cut further. The result was the loss of substantial tonnage to International Paper after it secretly offered an even lower price. A new round of destructive competition began early in 1933 when Hearst reneged on its promise of future business to Consolidated Paper (the former Canada Power and Paper). The trustee in bankruptcy for Price Brothers set a rate of $40 in an effort to grab the prospective sales. Meanwhile, Great Lakes Paper, which was also in receivership, covertly offered a rate of $38 (plus $1 only for freight charges) to virtually every Mead customer. Abitibi continued selling at the $45 level until Eddy Paper grabbed its *Cleveland News* contract by offering a contract rate of less than $40. Mead's clients then invoked the interlocking price clauses to secure similar reductions. By the spring, the industry was thoroughly disorganized as secret rebates and other dealings brought average rates below $33, an unprofitable range for any producer.[7]

The contracts of G.H. Mead were its only real assets and the "receivables" (comprised of advances from Abitibi) were less than the liabilities. No significant capital had been put in the agency and it operated off of a line of credit from Abitibi. But the small equity of the enterprise, Clarkson discovered, had been surreptitiously pledged by George Mead to two American banks as collateral on a loan for one of his other companies. In addition, he was offered $1 million for Abitibi's contracts. Although Mead turned it down, he communicated the proposal to the banks that financed Mead Corporation, the new parent enterprise for his businesses. Fearful he later might accept a similar proposal, the receiver asked for an assignment of the contracts to Abitibi but Mead refused either to transfer the agreements or to deposit them with a trustee. When the American government imposed a banking moratorium during March 1933, the agency fell further into arrears as cheques from customers were returned unpaid. The receiver had little choice but to advance funds. As if the situation was not messy enough, the agency sold Abitibi pulp without disclosing the source, thereby enhancing the likelihood it might substitute supplies from other firms.[8]

Getting control became imperative, but Mead refused to negotiate and demanded $750,000 for the capital stock. Suing Mead was an obvious course of action but out of the question. The litigation could destroy the relationships the agency had established with customers. Placing it in bankruptcy might cancel the sales agreements and block the recovery of the funds Abitibi had supplied. With the legal bills likely to exceed $1 million, the only option was to submit to Mead's greenmail. In essence, Abitibi had to buy back its own contracts. Clarkson then set up a revolving credit scheme that gave the firm authority over all financial issues. Because Abitibi did not have knowledgeable staff, the agency's personnel had to be retained until a marketing department was constructed. They accepted personal service contracts in exchange for half of the annual profits. George Mead not only got a share of those profits but personally pocketed a further $36,000 per annum, after he signed a covenant that enjoined him from unauthorized sales for other firms.[9] Since a disclosure of this solution could damage Abitibi's competitive position, it was kept secret. A report by the receiver noted the acquisition but never discussed the issues. Investors and some commentators therefore believed too much was paid for a subsidiary comprised of "intangibles." Clarkson seemed to legitimate those charges by writing the agency down. It failed to earn profits until 1940 and Abitibi phased out the pact when wartime demand expanded sales.[10]

Divestiture of several questionable subsidiaries similarly proved difficult. Given the depth of the Depression, few firms were willing to acquire marginal businesses. There was a possibility that buyers might use the assets to attack Abitibi's markets, an outcome worse than the costs of retaining the properties. Murray Bay Paper in Quebec had never started up and Abitibi's executives doubted it could operate at a profit. Production costs alone put the cost of output several dollars above the going price for newsprint and made sales even in Montreal impossible. Nominally worth $5.8 million, its forest concessions represented the subsidiary's real value. Donohue Paper, a small producer, leased the reserves, but the fees amounted to less than half of the annual shutdown costs. Murray Bay also purchased electricity from Quebec Power. By early 1933, Donohue Paper was in arrears and the utility threatened action because Murray Bay had defaulted on its contract. Clarkson then discovered another unpleasant surprise – Alexander Smith had clandestinely pledged all of the pulpwood for an advance from Banque Canadienne Nationale. Determined to recover the money, the bank placed a lien on the inventory and seized the firm's deposits at a local branch.[11]

Building the mill was a mistake in the first place, one adviser observed, and Abitibi had two options: board it up or sell. The real question, another commented, was whether it might be acquired "for a song" by a publisher.[12] But only Donohue Paper wanted the facility. If the investment was written down, it could operate the mill profitably. Donahue offered a release of Abitibi from most claims and promised small payments spread over five years in the form of credit for timber purchases from the deteriorating woodpile at Ste. Anne Paper. The value of the proposal was $89,600, minus a liquidation of $50,000 in secured or preferred claims. The bondholders' council perceived this as little more than theft, but the deal freed Abitibi of the carrying costs.[13] The compensation, Glyn Osler noted, was trifling in comparison with the original investment but it seemed advantageous to liquidate. The firm had a small output, he rationalized, so market conditions would not be disturbed and the deal ensured local employment that would appease the province.[14]

Any logic for retaining the other Quebec subsidiary was under-mined by the divestiture. Ste. Anne Paper had a modern mill but its massive woodpile would be worthless within a few years. Once again Alexander Smith had pledged the logs and other assets as collateral for a bank advance. Getting rid of the operation was further con-strained when the Ontario Supreme Court issued new guidelines that stipulated tender bids and judicial sale for all divestitures. Every pro-posal Clarkson received lacked substance. Donohue offered to take Ste. Anne but he learned that the company actually served as a stalk-ing horse for the Hearst chain, which wanted another supply source but was unwilling to expend any capital.[15] A representative of a "first class outstanding company with unquestioned credit," Ripley later stated, then approached him. The firm was willing to buy the mill for cash but not for anything like the $15 million figure at which it was valued on the Abitibi books. However, the offer was so low as to be simply out of the question.[16] The matter dragged on into 1936 when Ripley revealed the applicant was Arthur Schmon, the head of Ontario Paper, a Chicago *Tribune* subsidiary. The company had operated a newsprint mill at Thorold, Ontario, since 1912 but for two decades the province refused to grant forest concessions. Instead, the firm built up a portfolio of leased properties in Quebec. It now planned to construct a large mill at Baie Comeau. An acquisition of Ste. Anne made more sense to Premier Taschereau. When the proposal was disclosed Hep-burn and Heenan, fearing a loss of the Thorold mill, characterized the transaction as unfriendly and threatened to fight a sale unless Quebec agreed to a reallocation of production between the two provinces. Ripley dropped the matter because an acquisition could not occur "without stirring up a lot of trouble," but the obstruction by Hep-burn's government was pyrrhic. Schmon kept the Thorold facility and completed the new mill, which became the main supply source for the Chicago newspaper.[17]

Abitibi also was stuck with Thunder Bay Paper. Having invested a sizeable stake, the key issue was whether to spend more on an unneces-sary mill. Smith had not maintained the payments and Clarkson was notified in late 1932 that the original owner, Consolidated Water Power and Paper (CWPP), intended to repossess. With a reversion to CWPP (or if it then sold Thunder Bay to another company), the output could be sold at $8 to $10 below market price. Abitibi, Clarkson concluded, was better off if the payments and the shutdown costs continued. To forestall a default, he made an emergency loan to catch up on the back payments. Clarkson met with CWPP's president, George W. Mead, and tried to wangle concessions but was told the Wisconsin company could handle all costs should Thunder Bay revert to its control. Both firms, however, wanted a deal. Mead agreed to defer the capital payments if the interest charges were met. This arrangement cut Abitibi's bill and allowed the mill to operate at 50 per cent capacity, thereby providing local employment. The earnings were used to pay down yet another undiscovered advance to the Royal Bank that Smith had used with Thunder Bay's assets.[18]

Thunder Bay, however, had no contracts of its own and if the mill was to resume operation then production had to be moved from other sites. Moreover, the timber concessions remained in default. Abitibi was allowed to extract lumber but the government would not alter the legal status of the woodlands so it could later influence a reorganization.[19] Ripley described the situation as a muddle that was resolved by having Thunder Bay supply the clients of Manitoba Paper for two years after the pulpwood reserves at Pine Falls were exhausted.

Mead, despite the deal, remained unhappy because he had only Clarkson's word about the arrangement and he still held a portion of Thunder Bay's equity as security. Consolidated would rank low with other general creditors when Abitibi was reorganized, although it still retained the right to foreclose and dispose of the property elsewhere. Mead argued that Abitibi was living up to the letter of the agreement but not the moral spirit. After lengthy negotiations, he offered a close-out settlement in return for $2 million, along with the accrued interest owing for the remaining equity. Clarkson determined the true value of Thunder Bay was about $3.8 million. If Mead's remaining stake was acquired, then another $1.7 million in claims, for which Abitibi was potentially liable, became irrelevant. In 1936, despite opposition from Abitibi's junior investors, he finally secured court approval for a loan and completed the buyout.[20]

Some problems would not go away. In Manitoba, the Bracken administration was attacked almost continuously over the shutdown of the Pine Falls mill. By 1935 the government's caucus wanted something done and Clarkson advised Ripley that unless a new arrangement was reached the premier might take radical steps ranging from higher taxation to the cancellation of resource rights. However, reopening the plant entailed a transfer of production that could trigger retaliation from other provinces. Bracken was bluffing because punitive action would damage Manitoba's ability to attract investment and there were no reputable buyers available. Both sides wanted a deal. Clarkson agreed to restart the mill at a quarter of capacity, hoping the output could be sold in Western provinces. In exchange, the government amended the contract with Manitoba Power to lower the cost of electricity.[21]

Apparent solutions sometimes metamorphosed into difficulties. During his first nine months, Clarkson not only laid off personnel but ordered cuts in the wages and shift hours for mill workers three times, with corresponding reductions in the timber operations. Bush work, as historian Ian Radforth has well documented, was dangerous, a task conducted seasonally by individuals who worked in isolation, lived in scattered ill-equipped camps, were subject to callous supervisors, and paid poorly due to a piece-rate system.[22] Many cutters were Eastern European immigrants and some drew upon social-democratic concepts from Eastern Europe, which led Abitibi executives to blame a "red element" or "red unions" for any unrest. Due to the severity of the Depression and an abundance of surplus labour, employers in Northern Ontario managed to block worker demands for better conditions. Then, as the worst of the downturn eased during 1933, a series of strikes spread across the region. An initial dispute at Pigeon River Timber descended into a bitter confrontation with strikebreakers and the arrest of fifty "offenders against the peace."[23]

During the autumn Spruce Falls ran short of wood and sent out representatives who offered higher prices. Settlers diverted some deliveries to Spruce Falls, which interrupted Abitibi's supply and created pressure for it to raise purchase rates. The workers for Spruce Falls then seized the opportunity and walked out, forcing the company to increase wages and reduce their eating costs. Abitibi's managers at Smooth Rock Falls were cautioned to watch the developments but not trigger problems, which they foolishly told the Toronto headquarters was unlikely because their bush workers earned more than those at the rival mill. They failed to mention that labour peace was kept during the early receivership only because the Mattagami plant had eighteen months of pulpwood. To the surprise of the managers, the cutters walked out just as that reserve was used up. Clarkson's response was one-sided:

> The reds and the bushmen were aware of this and pulling the strike as they did they expected to land us in a position where we would either have to grant their demands or shut down the mill; ... we made up our minds to fight until we could get to a proper footing, and in doing so we were seriously handicapped by lack of protection, the Government taking the attitude that the rates paid to the settlers and the men for wood were too low and that the whole matter should be compromised by granting them concessions. Our attitude was that the adjustments which we had made did grant concessions which enabled competent men to earn very satisfactory returns.

When supervisors near Iroquois Falls also ignored warnings, activists persuaded a majority of the workers to strike. Clarkson claimed steps were taken to prevent the strikers from entering camps or enlisting additional support. He first refused to negotiate or sign an agreement with the "red union," then flip-flopped and granted concessions that ended the strike. This occurred, he told the press, after the arrests of provocateurs had "a salutary effect." In secret, Clarkson confessed the truth to Joseph Ripley. "Beyond that, also, computations made indicated that the rates formerly being paid to settlers and to labour were inadequate."[24]

The bush problems soon spread to the factories, where Abitibi had some of the strongest union locals in the industry. Abitibi paid rates lower than were offered in American mills but higher than non-unionized Quebec plants. The workers at Iroquois Falls had suffered from the reduced operations and lower wages. During the spring of 1934, their representatives called for a restoration of the pay to pre-1932 levels, an increase in the minimum wage, longer shifts at mills, and additional improvements if the price of newsprint rose. American union officials intervened because they wanted wage comparability with factories in the United States. They threatened to lobby for quotas on imports from Canada if this was denied. Clarkson agreed to match the American rates, an offer that was rejected by the Canadian locals who wanted higher levels. The receiver thought they were trying to get "forty hours' pay for thirty-six hours' work" so the American unions could then demand comparable action south of the border. He was prepared to accept a strike rather than a deal that might act as "a stepping-stone for getting higher American wages at American mills." Sustained negotiations led to a settlement that placed Abitibi on a par with American rates and stipulated it would match future increases that occurred in the United States.[25]

Another wave of unrest broke out during the autumn, but this time internecine fights occurred among the workers themselves. Half of the pulp cutters in three camps walked out and temporarily occupied Iroquois Falls. They raided other sites, literally dragged men out, stole foodstuffs, and set up pickets to blockade the camps, shutting down most operations in the Abitibi and Algoma districts. The Liberal minister responsible for forests and mines, Peter Heenan, twice attempted to gain a reconciliation by offering government guarantees about better management of the accounts used to determine their pay and controls over basic amenities like drying rooms for clothes, bathhouses, and reading rooms. He was not prepared to deal with wage-related matters, though Heenan suggested a board of enquiry might review worker complaints. These efforts failed because the strike leaders wanted the wage increase Abitibi had granted at Iroquois Falls to be extended to more than a dozen other operations.[26] This time the dispute stretched on for six weeks. The firm, which had a five-month supply of pulp-wood on hand, refused to negotiate and claimed the strikers were not a recognized union. Seven hundred workers at the Sault walked out, but another five hundred refused to join. Municipal officials denied relief to the strikers, which left them dependent upon local organizations, particularly Finnish community centres. Incidents between different worker groups punctuated the dispute with attacks on camps by individuals "wielding knives" and rumours of wounded men who failed to secure prompt medical treatment or disappeared. Workers opposed to the strike blamed "agitators" and radicals engaged in "class war," while the press stressed how some wore "red ribbons" or were arrested with red flags. But support for the walkout remained limited to the Finnish workers, and it petered out after several clashes with police that led to arrests and the destruction of picket shacks. An uneasy stability in labour relations settled in as Abitibi and other firms refused to grant higher wages until the newsprint price rose to a level that made operations more economic.[27]

2. Snugging up

By 1935 the bondholders' council assumed Abitibi would be among the last of the producers to regain solvency. Espanola and Sturgeon Falls were written off as non-viable, while the other sites needed operations at 70 per cent of capacity to achieve break-even. The council also believed much of the "water" in the financial structures of other firms still had to be wrung out. A list price of $47 per ton would allow Abitibi to meet the bond interest, but even that rate did not cover minimal capital expenditures, let alone the growing arrears of interest and preferred dividends. In addition, negotiations with the province were necessary to recoup resource rights and resolve claims against Abitibi or OPS.[28]

Despite those reservations, Ripley and his colleagues began to put a framework in place for an eventual reorganization. With court approval, the first official meeting of the bondholders was convened in June 1935. It adjusted the membership of the protective committee and sanctioned a registration of bonds for recognition by the judiciary. For technical reasons, two titles were given to designate the bondholders' agents: the Bondholders' Representative Committee and the Bondholders' Protective Committee. The first term normally was employed until 1939, and thereafter the second was used, in part to reflect changes in the committee's membership, but also (as we will see) a shift in its mission. Reflecting their status as envoys for the debt holders, the members of the committee were made co-defendants in the main legal action, *Montreal Trust v. Abitibi Power and Paper*.[29] Now with untrammelled control, they assumed Abitibi would be restored through a traditional process: a foreclosure upon the bond mortgage, followed by a judicial sale via public auction. The focus, Strachan Johnston asserted, should be upon, "snugging up" the company and removing any problems so they could act when it seemed propitious.[30] But from this point things began to go astray, owing to initiatives by the Liberal government.

Like many Depression populists, Mitch Hepburn espoused virulent anti-corporate rhetoric during the 1934 election, but he was never known for consistency. Within a few months of taking office, the premier modulated between being an opponent of big business and its quiet facilitator, while always claiming he looked out for "the little guy." One American publication could not resist lampooning his behaviour. "The time Premier Hepburn contrives to spend in the laps of the financial men – particularly while on vacation – has convinced many that the 'Hepburn bark is worse than the bite.' His loudly-proclaimed aversion for the 'monied interests' has come to be viewed as Huey Long theatrics ... platform stuff."[31] The shift, of course, also reflected practical politics. The Liberals needed to build support, especially in Northern Ontario, a task best accomplished by greater employment. Their handling of another insolvency generated a statute that created an alternative method for restructuring firms. It was to become the fulcrum of the Abitibi reorganization efforts.

Algoma Steel was controlled by a holding company, Lake Superior Corporation, which had a complicated capital structure. Philadelphian financiers controlled a majority of the common stock. English investors retained much of the debt and a syndicate run by financier Sir James Dunn held the largest block. When the enterprise collapsed in 1932, Dunn, unwilling to cooperate with other investors, first secured the appointment of a sympathetic receiver and then sought government assistance. Following the 1934 election, Hepburn indicated his willingness to pass legislation that might help revive the company. Dunn engaged Liberal lawyers Newton Rowell and Ward Wright as agents. His actions, veiled in secrecy, sought to transfer the assets to a new enterprise that had none of Lake Superior's obligations. The scheme rested upon two principles: the right of bondholders to recoup their money fully from an insolvent firm and the concept of majority rule. Less clear were the rights of minority investors, which the financier and his lawyers dismissed.[32]

The mortgage or trust deed for bonds normally required payment in cash after a judicial sale and courts considered the terms of a sale binding if investors representing three-quarters of the principal amount approved. There were well-established precedents in British and American case law for settlements that entailed an exchange of securities, particularly when sanctioned by legislation that characterized the arrangements as "fair and equitable."[33] Dunn controlled two-thirds of the bonds but was determined to forestall what he deemed nuisance lawsuits from dissenters. Given his promise to resuscitate Algoma, the Hepburn administration introduced a bill that sanctioned Dunn's proposal for reorganization and lowered the bar for approval to half of the principal. The financier's associates concurrently compelled a meeting of debt holders to approve the terms. The bondholders were offered common stock that was worth less than their holdings. The common and preferred shareholders would receive nothing. A week later Ward Wright sought judicial sanction of this arrangement. He moved so quickly that dissenting investors never had a chance to mobilize. Seeing no opposition, the Ontario court did not appraise the equitability of the package and granted approval. Even though it was no longer necessary, the Algoma bill was passed two months later, which closed off any avenue for appeal.[34]

Almost completely unnoticed, a short bill was passed on the final day of the spring session of 1935 and received royal assent at the same time as the Algoma statute. The Ontario Judicature Amendment Act (OJAA) seemed an innocuous piece of bureaucratic housekeeping, just another law about the administration of insolvency. The sole press commentary characterized it as a statute that would "facilitate straightening out the affairs of several currently embarrassed corporations."[35] The declared intent was to bring Ontario mortgage law in line with British practice. The government argued that under existing laws whenever property was sold under a mortgage it must be for cash unless stipulated otherwise in the trust deed. Many corporate documents were silent about this issue. In accord with the Algoma Steel case, the OJAA authorized judges to sanction a sale of assets for something other than cash and legitimated a similar option for insolvent companies. Approval required a meeting of the bondholders and acceptance by a simple majority of the principal. The courts then could validate the settlement. Government members also believed this option forestalled any possibility that Canadian companies traded on American exchanges might be reorganized in states like Minnesota or New York.[36]

The Hepburn administration had two companies in mind for the OJAA: Abitibi and Great Lakes Paper. But the logic drew upon behind-the-scenes plotting. Peter Heenan hoped to ease Northern Ontario unemployment by the conversion of existing mills towards goods for "assured" markets. In January 1935 he predicted a $10 million program would retool factories for the manufacture of artificial silk. This promise was based upon the feelers between the government, Robert Sweezey, and several venture capitalists, which were outlined at the beginning of this chapter. The plan centred upon the creation of sulphide pulp facilities using timberlands and other assets stripped from insolvent or defunct companies. The modifications to the Judicature Act had obvious relevance for the scheme.[37]

Concurrently, Sweezey advanced another proposal for Abitibi's reorganization, one that amounted to a variation of what had occurred with Algoma. It entailed an infusion of $10 million, the conversion of the debt into new preferred stock, and an exchange of the old preferred into no par value common stock. The bondholders would receive a lower interest rate and investors were expected to waive arrears of accrued interest or dividends "so that if the future earnings of the Company are greatly expanded they will be able to participate in this future prosperity as compensation." When Ripley's committee rebuffed this scheme, Sweezey tried to mobilize support by circulating phoney rumours about a merger of Abitibi with Great Lakes Paper. He then declared action was needed to keep the company from falling under American hegemon because 47 per cent of the bonds were "held in New York" by "a self-appointed bondholders' committee." The acquisition of the Mead sales agency supposedly proved George Mead "is now anxious to repossess Abitibi." Moreover, because investors would decline offers that might be subject to U.S. securities regulations, they would prefer, Sweezey claimed, to turn their holdings over to a group that proceeded under Ontario legislation. "I hold a large number of Abitibi bonds, and it seems to me that the bondholders have been fooled too often ... I would like to see a Canadian committee formed. I don't want to be on it, because I expect to make a proposal, and I don't want to be in the position of both buyer and seller."[38]

The noise from the promoter forced Ripley to break from his usual stance of not talking publicly. There were no immediate plans to reorganize, he declared to reporters, despite the "many stories" circulating. Realistic proposals had not been received and, he noted "smilingly," his committee was composed of four Canadians and three Americans. Sweezey's ploy, in fact, was dead on arrival. Ripley and Clarkson met him several times as a matter of respect since the promoter claimed he represented a group of bondholders. Sweezey's knowledge was vague, his estimates of production costs far off the mark, and the capital infusion obviously inadequate. The bondholders expected full repayment, not a conversion of their money to new securities with dubious value. Ripley's committee dismissed the proposal as rank speculation from a striker and refused to let it be considered by a meeting of the security class.[39]

Press commentators later suggested Ripley's committee crafted the OJAA for the government, but the truth was more indirect. The lawyers involved with the receiver and the committee lacked connections to the Liberal government and were distrusted by Hepburn's associates as Tories. But Strachan Johnston, the lawyer for the bondholders' trustee, was enlisted by the Liberals to prepare a first draft of what became the OJAA. Johnston had provided similar services for other governments. There is no surviving evidence to prove the representative committee was aware of his involvement. In any event, the minutes of the bondholders' council indicate the members still assumed reorganization required foreclosure and a judicial auction. The possibility of utilizing the OJAA was not raised until a year later, after their lawyer, Glyn Osler, noted the ownership pattern for the bonds made securing approval for a plan difficult. Indeed, "anything might happen to Abitibi" if a "certain majority" of bondholders became active. As the committee moved forward, the desire for a speedy result and for minimizing the need to compromise with the junior security classes were to make the OJAA an attractive lure, fatally so.[40]

3. The liquidation of the liquidator

The Liberals remained convinced the Conservatives facilitated an "Abitibi swindle," even though the royal commission did not substantiate this. Arthur Roebuck launched secret investigations into the contracts for Abitibi Canyon and Quebec power companies, hoping to find materials that could substantiate the government's perspective, regardless of the actual facts. In a speech during March 1935, without prior cabinet approval, he claimed the Hydro Commission had incurred more than $22 million in excess expenses. Unless a massive increase in consumption occurred, the existing contracts would take up more than half of the utility's revenues and bankrupt the system. Over two days of invective demagoguery, he likened the Tories to English buccaneers who engaged in a "slaughter of Hydro" and alienated into private hands the most valuable water power in Northern Ontario," thus committing a "great betrayal" of the concept of public ownership. "Pizzaro's Spanish freebooters found nothing as fabulous as this in the temples of the Incas." The agreements amounted to "burglar's raids," as well as "bloody treason" that was "illegal, unenforceable, and *void ab initio*."[41] Hydro's staff knew these assertions were false and the province faced a power shortage within several years.[42] Caught unawares, the premier had little choice but to affirm the need "to save Hydro from the coupon clippers" and he introduced legislation to annul some agreements and deny judicial redress.[43]

Roebuck hired Lewis Duncan, one of the foremost experts on bankruptcy law, to determine if further action might be taken. Knowing the outcome sought by the attorney-general, Duncan suggested that Hydro was a contingent creditor with claims that exceeded $192 million. This sum comprised lost revenues from the power contracts, bills from the contractors, Abitibi's failure to provide sufficient capital for the project's completion, along with imaginary liabilities *to Montreal Trust and the bondholders* for the Canyon venture. In contrast, the utility sought $1.4 million in 1932 when the liquidator asked creditors to submit their claims. By considerable legerdemain, Duncan argued the OPS acquisition gave the utility all rights held by the original bondholders and it was owed an additional $6 million (the gap between the purchase price and the project's bond issue), plus interest. Based upon the official value of Abitibi's assets "a substantial dividend should be paid to [the] Hydro-Electric Power Commission of Ontario." There was, of course, no discussion of the realism of such claims. Duncan and Roebuck hoped the province might secure at least partial compensation, even if it meant extortion by withholding resource rights from Abitibi.[44]

Duncan was engaged as a counsel for the Hydro Commission and was asked to secure the appointment of new trustees for Abitibi, AED, and OPS that were accountable to the unsecured creditors. Roebuck wanted the firms placed under the Bankruptcy Act even though OPS no longer existed and AED had never been adjudged insolvent. The utility then might force a generous settlement.[45] Duncan applied for the removal of Frederick Clarkson as Abitibi's liquidator by arguing Justice Sedgewick had erred in two ways: the interests of the bondholders versus those of other claimants were not acknowledged; and the selection of Clarkson was improper since the general creditors had never met. Duncan claimed Hydro had not learned about the orders that created the receivership or required unsecured creditors to file their claims by November 1932. The utility supposedly did not know this until the Hydro commissioners met on 14 May 1935.[46]

The court received the application with scepticism but the utility's lawyers were stunned by the admissions made during discovery. Frederick Clarkson had not carried out the normal tasks of his office. He had never conducted an independent review of creditor claims, except for a

brief reconciliation of bills with Abitibi's accounts. Not only had Clarkson failed to assess the profitability and losses of the firm, but he also
confessed to not knowing the amount of accrued bond interest or depreciation. He denied any knowledge about how much the receiver, his
brother, was paid for services. The liquidator received copies of court
documents but "[m]y instructions to my solicitor were not to consent or
to object to any orders" since a judge "would not make an order authorizing their own officer to do something which might be to the disadvantage of some creditor." The hapless officer was not consulted about
the purchase of the Mead agency, the sale of Murray Bay, or Thunder
Bay. Nor was he aware that the firm that represented the preferred
shareholders was paying his own lawyer. "I thought that if the company
was re-organized eventually we would receive a bill."[47] The examination of Shapley revealed how the lawyers filed to put Abitibi into bankruptcy, how they switched the application and placed it under the
Winding-Up Act, and then how the receiver's brother was appointed.
With convoluted logic, Shapley insisted the creditors would be looked
after and his sole role was to advise the liquidator about what was going
on. "I took the position that Fred. C. Clarkson could not consent to any
of these orders, and they said, well we are not going to the expense of
serving you with a notice of motion every time we want to invest a certain sum of money, and I said I don't ask you to do that, but I am not
going to consent to any orders."[48] In a bizarre round of questioning,
Shapley unsuccessfully denied there were blatant conflicts of interest,
particularly with respect to the compensation he and Clarkson received
from the lawyers for the preferred shareholders. Once they realized how
damaging their testimony had become, Clarkson and Shapley refused to
answer further questions, citing grounds of privilege.[49]

Before the examinations could be recapitulated in court, Hydro's
application was dismissed on a technicality – a formal notice already
had been filed in bankruptcy proceedings. Duncan, in high dungeon,
claimed he had never heard of a similar decision. The ruling, he proclaimed to the press, made the Bankruptcy Act "a dead letter" since a
claimant might force a dismissal just by filing a dispute notice. Creditors would then have a higher court overturn the decision before bankruptcy proceedings could proceed. The decision came "very close to an
abuse of the process." It was something that most judges would con-
demn in small cases where "struggling lawyers and accountants were
actors." Despite this harangue, an appeal was never filed. Roebuck
fired Duncan, owing to his lack of success and the high cost of his services. The utility planned to launch a new suit but the lawyer chosen
then declined due to a conflict of interest.[50]

The depositions had revealed Frederick Clarkson to be incompetent but it was not in anyone's interests to let the machinations become public. By mutual consent, the testimony was suppressed in exchange for Clarkson's voluntary resignation. The government suspended further action after receiving assurances that Hydro's claims would not be prejudiced and a new liquidator would be appointed who was acceptable to the province. Hepburn suggested the appointment of Ernest Jay Howson from the accounting firm of Thorne, Mulholland, Howson, and McPherson. A respected fellow of several accounting societies, Howson had conducted numerous audits when the Liberals controlled the federal government. The other parties opposed this high-profile appointment but accepted the selection of Howson's colleague, Roy Sharvell McPherson. Forty-five, a resident of Forest Hill, professionally respected, and a director of Loblaw Groceterias, he had carried out receivership duties for modest-sized firms but nothing of the scale associated with Abitibi. From the government's perspective, McPherson had one valued trait: he was a staunch Liberal. The bondholders' representatives perceived the appointment as an empty gesture since they and the receiver handled all management decisions. A liquidator, they felt, became significant only when a settlement was reached, and even then he had to follow court orders about the distribution of assets. In fact, McPherson was the proverbial worm in the bud. Based upon Roebuck's guidelines, he believed his role should be proactive for the general creditors and common shareholders. McPherson hired Dunn's lawyers, Rowell and Wright, both prominent Liberals. The liquidator should not be satisfied without cause, he later observed, and McPherson soon became convinced that the bondholders would not proceed justly.

Duncan's failure did not end the efforts to recoup monies from Abitibi. Stewart Lyon, the new chair of Hydro, was a fierce partisan who deemed the Canyon venture a boondoggle. Lyon dismissed Tory claims about its benefits as "a good deal of effrontery" about a "development by a private company for its own profit." He believed "a great many politicians were in on the deal," even though that was "relatively legitimate, as the bonds were those of a private corporation and not guaranteed in any public way." The insolvency of "this beacon asset" prevented the local population from being exploited by a firm like the Canada Northern Power Company, which had "charged the gold mines and everybody else in the north all the traffic would stand."[51] With Lyon convinced that dubious cost overruns had occurred, Hydro delayed paying the bills constructors submitted for their work at the Canyon. The disputes continued for several years until Hepburn finally demanded settlements, at least for the largest suppliers like Canadian General Electric.

Despite Lyon's insinuations, the total cost of the project was $22.2 million versus the original 1930 estimate of $22.5 million, all covered by bond capital. Further expenditures on related infrastructure raised Hydro's investment to $30.5 million, a significant outlay but one that paled in comparison to the debt of $577 million incurred from system development across the preceding generation. Lyon reminded Mitch Hepburn that the province was liable for Hydro's debts. With most of Abitibi's mills closed, the Commission received only $10,000 per month for power to Iroquois Falls and Smooth Rock Falls, whereas it was supposed to earn $300,000. Abitibi "got itself and the Government into the vast expenditure," Lyon declared. "Is the Company to go free, and are the taxpayers of Ontario to pay the whole shot?"[52] Hydro's engineers knew electricity from the Canyon was necessary to ameliorate a pending shortage. Lyon instead trumped about how the utility had 100,000 horsepower "for which we are unable to find profitable use" and must pursue everything Lewis Duncan had claimed the province was owed.[53]

4. I never met a group of men so disloyal

Abitibi's rebirth depended upon a stabilization of competitive conditions, a development that receded whenever expectations rose that it might occur. As the Depression approached its nadir, bankrupt and near-bankrupt enterprises desperately fought for business, a situation exploited by the newspaper chains. In June 1933 the Powell River Company of British Columbia negotiated a supply deal with Scripps-Howard for newsprint delivered at $30 per ton in Philadelphia. Frustrated by the previous flops as the sector imploded, provincial authorities declined to support further intervention. Corporate executives lobbied federal officials for restrictions upon newsprint exports if sales were below production costs. H.H. Stevens, the minister of industry and commerce, was unsympathetic. The manufacturers had created their own problems, he declared. The chief fault lay with financiers "only interested in selling bonds and clipping coupons" or promoters who perceived newsprint "as magic a word as the discovery of a gold field." The executives did not oppose the speculative binge even when the dangers became obvious. The companies, Stevens admonished, should concentrate upon rebuilding and assign a greater role to engineers or scientific personnel. The federal government would not be a "fairy godmother."[54]

With Canadian politicians unwilling to act, for several years any improvement was contingent upon initiatives south of the border. Within the Roosevelt administration, a few officials who hoped to revive the American economy proposed an agency modelled after the War Industry Board, with the authority to control production and prices. That option, one adviser argued, represented the sole means by which unrestricted competition and "insensate greed" might be ended "before too large a percentage of the people have been starved into either hopeless resignation or desperate revolt." Most business executives still perceived industrial self-government as a more desirable tool. Some were prepared to tolerate a "partnership in planning," but only as a stopgap tactic for easing the crisis.[55] Secretary of Labour Frances Perkins and several officers devised a compromise via another iteration of associationalism. An implementing agency, the National Recovery Administration (NRA), would bring "order and security into the anarchy of modern business operations." The enabling legislation was vague and left open several courses of action: the introduction of genuine planning, the enforcement of vigorous competition, or the legitimation of efforts by firms to coordinate markets. A network of committees was created under the NRA authority, mostly comprised of members from trade associations, along with nominal representation from labour. Each would develop an acceptable code of "fair competition" with guidelines about trade practices, wages, and working conditions. The government anticipated social gains because the codes had to sanction wage increases, specify acceptable hours of employment, help eliminate problems like child labour, and acknowledge the right of workers to organize and bargain collectively. In exchange, business was offered relief from anti-trust laws, a concession that might let the committees sanction quasi-cartels, albeit under "public supervision."[56]

The head of the NRA, General Hugh Johnson, was less concerned with the details of the codes than with gaining acceptance of the program's legitimacy. The NRA was whatever the committees made it, he declared. It was not appropriate for the agency to control a sector but an industry could "come to this table and offer its ideas as to what it thinks should be done." He characterized traditional trade associations as ineffective as an old ladies' knitting society, whereas the NRA offered these "formerly emasculated" organizations a cloak of legitimacy. Johnson concentrated upon a quick adoption of codes for the largest industries. A publicity campaign promoted consumption as a patriotic duty and encouraged consumers to buy from companies that "did their part" by subscribing to the NRA codes.[57] Despite a burst of enthusiasm, which created a short-lived mirage of a country marching back to prosperity, the NRA never generated a recovery. An increase in factory production, due to enhanced government expenditures and a build-up of inventories by manufacturers before the codes took effect, soon faded. Popular support for the NRA waned within a year, while many businessmen rejected the initiative from the beginning. Preparation of the codes took longer than expected, not only due to difficulties in achieving consensus but because the Roosevelt administration insisted upon public hearings. Many executives arrived in Washington ill-prepared for the lobbying and external scrutiny. Dominated by corporate interests, the industrial committees stressed the enhancement of profit margins via codes that included production quotas and price guidelines. Once several sectors gained those terms, others rushed in for the same. By the middle of 1935 more than 700 codes were published under the NRA's aegis, 568 with forms of minimum price policies and over 120 with manufacturing constraints.[58]

The realities of the experiment were highlighted by the experiences of the newsprint sector. An industrial committee was organized during July 1933, and it proposed raising the list rate from $40 to $46 per ton. The protection offered by the NRA did not include newsprint consumers, who suddenly were confronted by the prospect of higher costs while their own goods still sold at depressed rates. The American Newspaper Publishers' Association denounced the recommendation, arguing that the producers did whatever they thought they might get away with. The publishers' counsel went further: "no more striking monopolistic effort could be cited than this attempt of a small group of manufacturers, who admittedly cannot supply half of the country's requirements, to set up a control, through this code, of the price structure of newsprint paper."[59] In October General Johnson assembled representatives from the United States, Canada, and Europe for negotiations about a minimum rate. The participants agreed to a pricing armistice, which was renewed through the spring of 1934. The ceasefire rested upon several conditions. Prices for 1933 and 1934 could not be set below $41 per ton, participating firms would not propose delivery rates beyond 1934, and those for 1934 had to be adjusted quarterly to ensure consistency amongst the manufacturers. Johnson gratuitously threatened a tariff increase against Canadian firms that did not follow those rules. A parallel group, the Newsprint Export Manufacturers' Association of Canada (NEMA) was organized to work with American firms.[60]

With these understandings in place, President Roosevelt signed an initial code, although it did not include price-fixing terms. A supplemental code recommended the Canadian and American suppliers not exceed the $41 rate, file information about their price schedules, and create a joint committee for the review of measures that facilitated "the elimination of unfair practices and destructive competitive prices." A Newsprint Code Authority could adjust prices in accord with costs, currency fluctuations, or alterations in the sector's economic health. The American government also announced a ban on dumping, which Canadian producers interpreted as a sign of resolve for ending the pricing chaos.[61] Small publishers were prepared to accept the supplemental code. Even though it created a potential for higher rates, they were promised uniform rates and equality of treatment. Many believed the chains, especially the Hearst group, wanted special concessions. In some cases, the largest publishers had received a differential of $8 per ton from Canadian suppliers versus American producers. However, the Publishers' Association, which was dominated by the chains, rejected the supplemental code and claimed again that it was really the manufacturers who sought a monopoly. "Their God-parent, they hope, will be the NRA." The code was "violative of sound business economics," "repugnant" to anti-trust laws, and contravened numerous statutes, including the NRA's enabling legislation. Because it required cooperation from Canadian exporters, they claimed, for every dollar American producers gained from compensation for higher costs under the NRA, two dollars were put into the pockets of Canadian firms. In response, the NRA's Canadian adviser suggested the publishers were willing to destroy American producers if it kept supply cheap. The firms would be "squeezed to death." by new costs that originated from government initiatives aimed at economic recovery and "cutthroat price cutting by a few, perhaps desperate, foreign mills."[62]

Lobbying by the publishers blocked an intended swap of controls over working hours and higher minimum wages in exchange for protection from sales below costs. They managed to delay most of the initiatives for rate management but failed in one crucial area. A committee of American producers, with input from Canadian firms, revised geographic pricing in a way that started to bring consistency to marketing practices. The United States was classified into ten zones with the midwestern region designated with a base price. Differentials were allocated among the zones (see Figure 6). Special provisions were instituted for ports that received European imports. The FTC later claimed the scheme did not reflect transport costs, which the producers dismissed as false because the agency failed to consider recent decisions by

Figure 6 Newsprint Industry Price Zones, 1934

Area Legend: 4. Base Price; 1. –1.50; 2. –1.00; 3. –0.50; 5. +1.00; 6. +2.00; 7. +3.00; 8. +4.00; 9. +5.00; 10. –1.00 but variation by location and whether transport by rail or port. Major coastal ports received separate rate designations.

Source: NARA: RG9, NRA, Hearings on Proposed Recommendations in Respect of the Stabilization of the Newsprint Industry, 1934.

railroad regulators. The geographic system under the new framework was again weighted towards eastern manufacturers. It did not end destructive rivalry; companies still offered concessions or rebates regardless of zone prices. But publication of the framework helped to legitimate the drift towards uniform pricing by geography. The system became entrenched for more than a generation after wartime regulators sanctioned its use. However, the chain publishers denounced zone pricing as an attempt to "obtain absolute power" over consumers. Any and all forms of rate management, they proclaimed, contravened the anti-trust laws and the NRA Act.[63]

Members of the Newsprint Code Authority proposed a Newsprint Planning and Adjustment Board. Johnson was prepared to accept this but he stipulated a minimum price could not become effective until set by the board. The nine members were to include three from the producers, three from the publishers, two from labour organizations, and one impartial chair appointed by the head of the NRA. Proposed decisions were subject to Johnson's veto and his consent was required if votes were not unanimous. The producers accepted the scheme, the Publishers' Association rejected it. Nonetheless, implementation efforts proceeded, on the basis of alleged "scores" of supportive letters from smaller newspapers. The Publishers' Association demanded new hearings, which became a forum for more criticism. No government authority, its spokesmen argued, should be "placed in a position to tell [the] newspaper publishers of this country how much paper they may use in the production of their newspapers, from whom they must buy it and how much they shall pay it."[64]

The incessant opposition derailed the efforts to find an American solution for stabilizing newsprint. Other interests within the federal bureaucracy believed Johnson contravened his agency's mandate by accepting codes that contained market-fixing provisions. Through several rounds of political games, they undermined the administrator until he resigned in a pique of frustration. Moreover, the NRA had a two-year life span; the codes were then expected to wither away. Despite its problems, in 1935 President Roosevelt called for an extension, describing the goals and principles as sound. Before Congress could act upon the request, the Supreme Court ruled the NRA unconstitutional.[65] Regardless, by late 1934, the newsprint producers had given up on a "do-nothing policy." Every proposal, the NRA's deputy administrator commented, was derailed by the large publishers "who took the attitude that the domestic industry was not fit to survive." Their objective appeared to be "holding down Newsprint prices to a level ruinous both to the domestic and Canadian producers." A government-commissioned review later advanced a quixotic interpretation. The industry "probably emerged from the code period in no better condition than it entered it" because of the failure to alter the price situation and because the sector was "still at the mercy of its customers." The opponents "created a situation of a delicate and inflammable nature." The refusal of the Roosevelt administration to force a price advance thus was rationalized as "the safest and wisest course."[66]

Price levels were uncertain throughout the period of the NRA experiment, as producers anticipated rate-setting by the industrial committee. Mills announced rates month by month and the official level remained fixed at $40 per ton. In late 1934 most American and Canadian producers announced an increase of $2.50 for the following year but St. Lawrence Paper bolted, contracting with Scripps-Howard and Hearst for sales at the $40 rate. Outraged, Quebec Premier

Taschereau denounced the action. The publishers, however, refused his demands for renegotiation and the best the premier could do was to raise St. Lawrence's stumpage fees and cancel some cutting rights. Anglo-Canadian Paper then claimed it had to match the rate, setting in motion an industry-wide imitation. When American publishers claimed that they would use alternative sources if the government persisted in demanding higher prices, Taschereau dismissed the assertion as "pure bluff." At a December conference with the manufacturers, he reiterated his demands for an end to cutthroat competition. If they could not control themselves, the rules would be changed. All contracts would have to be registered with a disclosure of all terms. Punitive legislation would empower harsh action against companies guilty of undercutting their competitors.[67] In counterpoise, the Publishers' Association threatened that if the premier "and certain Canadian banks by unusual restrictions" vitiated contracts, it would *"advise its members to turn their attention immediately to other available and potential sources of supply."*[68] Taschereau considered the situation "almost desperate. We cannot depend on the industry to get over its troubles and I never met a group of men so disloyal to each other; the agreements between them are mere scraps of paper."[69] The producers could not be brought to heel, however, without the cooperation of Ontario.

Hepburn initially tried to avoid taking a stance and remarked that he would support federal initiatives to help the industry *if they received his prior approval*. Prime Minister Richard Bennett presumed the premier sought "blank cheque legislation," refused, and then denounced the move.[70] Hepburn told Taschereau they should "obviate the self-destructive activities of the newsprint producers" but nothing substantive followed. Instead, he released a fog of rhetorical gas. Ontario was

> intimately interested in the welfare and happiness of the workers responsible for the maintenance of manufacturing concerns and cannot and will not detach itself from any well and directed timely move towards frustrating attempts at price fixing or reductions that may be ruinous to the trade and disastrous to the workers. The question of dependability of contracts in no way enters into a sane determination to eliminate unfair price disturbances that would operate to the disadvantage of all classes immediately interested. If prices are reasonably and consistently controlled, having regard to cost levels, the services of the worker must surely be reckoned with and the relationship he holds to society and the duty society owes to him given constant consideration.

The "fair-minded newsprint consuming public" recognized "a standard wage for the worker cannot be paid if slashing of prices is condoned." Hepburn deplored the lack of reasonable prices and complained about how American publishers sought the destruction of a great Canadian industry. But his only assurance to Taschereau was that Ontario would not take advantage of Quebec's situation.[71]

Peter Heenan wanted to go further. Although timber licences stipulated minimum levels of output, "cut throat competition and the violation of agreements" prevented Ontario's mills from improving their competitive positions. Heenan misinterpreted the initiatives undertaken during 1928. He believed they entailed regulation of machine installations as a means of ensuring that each province got a fair share. The subsequent expansion of capacity meant Quebec mills received a disproportionate amount of business.[72] Despite the minister's requests, Hepburn rejected taking stronger action, either in the form of new legislation or regulation. More could be accomplished, he told Taschereau, through conciliation. His party had pledged to reduce bureaucracy, not increase it.[73]

Ontario instead focused upon easing unemployment by any means, which entailed attempts to increase output, not decrease it. After meeting delegations of lumbermen, Heenan cut stumpage fees, reduced export fees, terminated the manufacturing condition for pulpwood from Crown lands, and redistributed unused timber limits to exporters. Approximately 10,000 men supposedly received jobs and firms promised that the wood would not be sold to American mills. But the arrangements were never policed. With Canadian firms in no condition to buy, American companies benefited as rafts of unprocessed logs floated across the Great Lakes. Heenan's deputy minister later accused him of making surreptitious deals despite the earlier promises of constructive reform. The gains went to "a select coterie of operators and concessionaires," while the province did not even get the benefit of additional revenues. As noted earlier, Heenan also wanted the paper companies to manufacture new goods. Stories were leaked about how American investors might acquire three of Abitibi's plants for the production of artificial silk, even though Clarkson never received any queries. Knowledgeable press observers were underwhelmed. "Calling Mr. Aladdin!" one editorial mocked. Behind the "smoke of many rumours," political expediency was at work. "The pressure of unemployment is great in the riding of Nipissing, especially in the town of Sturgeon Falls, and a by-election there has just returned another Liberal by a large sustained majority. The hope of resumption of operations by the Abitibi mills was no doubt well played up."[74]

Peter Heenan later portrayed the government's policy as one of assertive direction where it held "the whip hand over the fellows that won't play ball." He sought

> to coax these fellows to play square with each other, and not to go out and try to take tonnage away from each other, by cutting prices and secret commissions. And they said, Sure, we will promise to be good boys. It seemed to me that they went out of the door determined that this was all poppycock, and that they would do as they liked; and they continued to do it. So we got these companies together and talked the matter over; and they admitted that there was no salvation for them unless the Government use[d] strong-arm methods to make them behave themselves.[75]

This account was silly bunkum, both with respect to how the government's policy emerged and how it was implemented. Hepburn repeatedly declined to take punitive action. The head of one trade association complained about how efficient mills needed a fair return. Instead, well-connected interests pursuing "selfish considerations" blocked the "courageous stand" they made to stabilize economic conditions. The counsel for Great Lakes Paper stressed how the government could help Ontario gain a better share of annual tonnage without threatening publishers with "the bogey of possible exorbitant prices."[76]

The premier's reluctance to act more forcefully reflected his personal inclination, as well as the suggestions from advisers he trusted. Banking interests insisted new legislation could scare off investors.[77] Sweezey derided the "aggressiveness" of companies who kept mills running to capacity so they could pay debt interest. The promoter suggested the threat of action might prove sufficient but he expected, with an easing of the Depression, consumption would overtake supply within eighteen months and the "question of price will then right itself." Several months later he argued American publishers could not object to the provinces trying to improve living conditions for average workers. The premiers should regulate the paper companies "so that they may not exceed the percentage of business available to all." Insolvent firms could then be refinanced, "all of which require not less than a total of twenty million dollars to put them in good operating condition" though "you will understand of course that each company should be taken separately and refinanced on its own merits." Being supported by "the most successful industrialists," his security house and others were, of course, "looking forward towards the rehabilitation of the industry."[78]

Hepburn increasingly relied upon Charles Vining, the new head of the trade association for the Canadian industry. Quotas and production controls, Vining cautioned, were uneconomic and easily overturned by customers who held contractual rights. The earlier initiatives, "prolific sources of dissension," were ineffective. Indeed, they could never have worked until the producers rationalized their capital structures. The government might purchase or lease certain mills and keep them inoperative but this option had obvious drawbacks. Vining, instead, suggested the government support a now-discredited will-of-the-wisp: further mergers. Amalgamation of the producers was "the only ultimate solution" for eliminating excess capacity, competitive rivalry across different geographic regions, or reconfiguring corporate finance. "The question regarding consolidation is not as to its desirability but as to the method of accomplishing it."[79]

Although the premier believed provincial authority over forests legitimated intervention, for a year he stalled. During this period the producers reached a consensus about the need for cooperative action, albeit as a temporary expedient. A meeting in June 1935 attracted widespread participation that included executives from International Paper. A voluntary agreement proposed a reallocation of tonnage amongst Canadian manufacturers, with the hope that decreased rivalry might stabilize prices. Over the following months, the producers inventoried machines, disseminated copies of contracts, and negotiated a scheme that could shift up to 170,000 tons to firms that operated at very low capacity. The consultations were shrouded in secrecy for fear that the scheme might be derailed if even one firm bolted. In addition, "publicity or indiscretion by which the buyers of newsprint learned of our plan might create such serious difficulty as to destroy the chance of success."[80] Concurrently, American producers created a new organization, the Newsprint Manufacturers' Association, which called for cross-border "constructive government action" because half of their industry remained bankrupt. With reserves exhausted and costs rising, the remainder would eventually follow. Stabilization of the relationships with publishers must occur on "a mutually fair basis which will endure from decade to decade." A temporary fix only delayed "the evil day of complete collapse." As the producers aligned with the notion of public sector support, Hepburn's reluctance to act eased.[81]

The solution was a small step beyond associationalism: industry self-regulation but this time with a tangible possibility of enforcement. Negotiations between Heenan and Taschereau during early

1936 reached an understanding about the need for an even-handed distribution of tonnage between the provinces and between "long" and "short" mills. Companies were advised not to make new commitments pending the efforts to find a solution. Mutual concurrence between the governments and the trade association's executives about a framework took until June.[82] The preceding year Quebec passed a statute raising stumpage fees $1.35 to $6 per cord, with a promise that if firms conformed to the province's expectations they would receive the lower rate. A similar bill in the spring of 1936 authorized Ontario to raise stumpage fees by as much as 500 per cent and remove timber concessions when a company was deemed to have operated detrimentally to the public interest. These provisions avoided direct involvement in price-fixing, circumventing both American anti-trust law and federal jurisdiction over international trade.[83] But the scheme reiterated the problems from the 1929 Newsprint Institute. The producers were advised "the newsprint industry must proceed itself to remedy its weaknesses" and "the industry must find a way to eliminate unfair disparities in the operating positions of various manufacturers." The goals of the governments remained a distribution of employment across mills and an avoidance of any concentration of production with several firms or one geographic region. Output was to be prorated by each company's share of total capacity. Workers and Crown revenues then might benefit from "fair and stable conditions." The trade association would collect and disseminate data about consumption and supply patterns, while most disputes would be settled by intercompany negotiations. If the "principle of equitable operations" could be maintained, Vining told Hepburn, then each firm might function near 80 per cent of capacity "an operating ratio which few industries enjoy. This would automatically provide the equitable distribution of production, employment and public revenue which presumably are the objectives of your conferences with the Government of Quebec."[84]

This time provincial authorities indicated a willingness to serve as final arbiters or exact penalties against cheaters. Hepburn proclaimed that his government would oppose destabilization by those "who may try to obtain a selfish advantage by destructive methods" and would apply the laws against any situation that adversely affected wages or the "proper" use of forest resources.[85] The provinces, Taschereau commented, had "nothing to do with fixing the price; we are concerned in fair and stable conditions of production for proper protection of wages and Crown revenues," showing how the premiers still did not grasp how interlocking price clauses had sustained the cycle of "destructive competition." Taschereau remarked that prices would be set by negotiations between producers and their customers in accord with their business judgment. Public policy was aimed at a "maintenance of this natural market price by insisting that all manufacturers adhere to it without deviation so far as permitted by bona fide contracts or conditions already existing." Once a majority of manufacturers and their customers agreed on a rate, provincial authority would be employed only to ensure it was "strictly uniform." Taschereau resigned several days after this concord but his successors reconfirmed a willingness to achieve stable conditions.[86]

If some executives hoped these grand-sounding ideas might decrease competitive turbulence, the dreams soon evaporated. Once again, the scheme only applied to firms in the two provinces, which never constituted sufficient capacity to shape pricing or supply tendencies. Once again, publisher-related operations like Spruce Falls and Ontario Paper operated on their own terms. These weaknesses became obvious within a month. Most of the manufacturers had drawn down their stocks of pulpwood by the spring of 1936, and production levels rose as the continental economy improved. Widespread speculation thus circulated about a price advance to $45 per ton, a rate that could allow Canadian firms to cover interest obligations (or more accurately, those with deflated capital structures and the ability to operate near full capacity).[87] Continental supply still exceeded demand by a million tons annually but a balanced relationship appeared possible by 1938. Lord Rothermere, the publisher of the *Daily Mail* group in Britain, suggested an advance to a mill rate of $50 (or $57 when delivered in New York City) was within the foreseeable future. Canadian producers, he declared, should end their "ridiculously" pessimistic attitude and throw off the yoke of intimidation by big American customers. But even before price discussions got underway amongst the manufacturers, Maine's Great Northern announced an increase to only $42.50 per ton. Since interlocking price clauses always cited the company as a reference point, the move stymied the possibility of higher rates.[88] Vining reflected the ensuring consternation when he exploded in frustration about how it was "even more disappointing and outrageous to find our own companies involved in such weaknesses of contract system that they again appear compelled to follow Great Northern unless they adopt a policy of repudiating all contracts, which I think nobody would wish to see." Not only had it become obvious that firms had to phase out the interlocking clauses, Vining declared, but also the secret concessions that "honey-combed" pricing practices. The producers were "victims of weaknesses" brought about by a buyer's market that had prevailed for a decade. As production levels rose, "I would begin to reproach them as a group only if they fail to show enough pluck to start the remedial process."[89]

Any return towards a sellers' market was contingent upon the ability of firms to withstand individually and collectively the bargaining power of the largest publishers. "Across the brighter horizon," one journal commented, "rises the shadow of Hearst. By subtle propaganda his agents are accused of keeping the industry in a whirl for the newsprint industry." The chain, unbeknownst to many observers, hovered near bankruptcy but still accounted for a fifth of American consumption. Its contracts with five producers were scheduled to expire in 1938, which opened the largest amount of demand to competitive bidding in a decade.[90] Hearst's purchasing organization selected Abitibi as a new target and offered 100,000 tons per annum if the firm offered a concession below the list rate for several years. Given the company's precarious status, various stakeholders wanted the deal, in part because they doubted prorating could work. Strachan Johnston discussed the offer with Hepburn and Heenan. The premier stated the new policy represented the last opportunity for stabilization and with Quebec's promise of cooperation the government would not allow anything to jeopardize it. Accordingly, they rejected the Hearst proposal and forced the termination of negotiations. Heenan reiterated to Clarkson that Ontario expected prorating in proportion to average shipments and would not interfere with price-setting unless something jeopardized that scheme. After extensive lobbying and meetings with other producers, approximately 63,000 tons were transferred to Abitibi but even with this contribution the company still operated well below the industry average.[91]

Mitch Hepburn and Quebec's newly elected premier, Maurice Duplessis, announced an intention to coordinate provincial policies in October. They concurred about the need for an "orderly handling" of capacity, including a ban on the construction of new mills while existing factories remained idle. Sympathetic newspapers like the *Globe* bloviated about how "the two young Premiers" had allied for "a united effort to drive back the frontiers of the Northland, to develop the rich empires of timber and mineral resources, and to transform into real wealth the vast potential values which lie in the North country." Both politicians immediately circumvented the "pact": Quebec by sanctioning the Ontario Paper plant at Baie Comeau and Ontario by authorizing new pulp facilities. Hepburn, trying to extract lower hydro rates from Quebec utilities, then charged that it had instituted a sales policy intended to undersell and destroy Ontario paper mills.[92]

Even though the list rate still hovered at an unprofitable level, the governments proclaimed success because another collapse of newsprint prices did not occur. In fact, little effort was made to enforce prorating for eighteen months because mixed signs of recovery appeared even before the scheme took hold. American production was cut in half during the Depression as companies converted plants to the manufacture of fine papers, while imports from Canada increased to almost three-quarters of American consumption. Approximately 3.6 million tons of newsprint were shipped during 1936, whereas in 1929 shipments amounted to less than 3 million tons. Though most companies remained weak, some observers believed the corner had been turned. Robert Sweezey told his clients that carefully chosen newsprint investments "will prove to be both safe and profitable." Insolvent companies would be restructured if investors "no longer delude themselves with the idea that securities must be worth the price they paid for them in 1929." Most investors had accepted their losses and "support can now be found for any equitable plan of reorganization which will put the security holders' property back into solvency."[93]

10

Reorganization Plots

Justice belongs to those who claim it, but let the claimant beware lest he create new injustice by his claim and thus set the bloody pendulum of revenge into its inexorable motion.

– Gowachin aphorism

It's gettin' so a businessman can't expect no return from a fixed fight. Now, if you can't trust a fix, what can you trust? For a good return, you gotta go bettin' on chance – and then you're back with anarchy, right back in the jungle.

– *Miller's Crossing*

CORPORATE REORGANIZATION HAS NEVER REPRESENTED a legal issue in the sense of litigation to settle disputes. Rather, as an American ruling noted, it entails "the exercise of administrative jurisdiction." Receivers and judges must make decisions on many business matters. Briefs or motions are presented to courts but they often entail choices about policies or courses of action for which alternative views may legitimately be taken.[1] General factors like competitive conditions, demand trends, and pricing can influence how those options are assessed. For example, thoughtful consideration of earning patterns is necessary for creating a viable financial structure, but expectations may shift as investors focus upon current versus future profits, or as they employ different time frames and measures to determine those figures. Resuscitation entails an assessment of a firm's worth, but value is an attribute of mind, not something concrete. Numerous measures are available: the book value of properties, their appraised value, their replacement value less depreciation, their value as a "going concern," the perceived "fair market" value, and the purchase price received at the time of a sale. A firm's operational worth, as estimated by engineers, rarely matches investors' perceptions as reflected in the prices they pay for securities. Inevitably, people utilize the modes of valuation that best advance their own cases, while disparaging others. As we have seen, markets are also not rational. Prices and notions of worth fluctuate in response to speculation or issues that have limited, if any, relationship to a specific enterprise. Finally, there is the matter of power and influence. Participants may focus upon gaining an outcome that fits their own objectives, where a sound financial structure may be a desirable matter but not the key one.

Those issues now came to the fore. Controversies had unfolded in numerous reorganizations, with several major precedents within the newsprint sector. Ripley's committee was familiar with those cases, which demonstrated that, despite the best intentions, anything could happen. The first section of this chapter examines how restructuring sometimes unfolded "efficiently" or became a proverbial battle of numbers. Then, consideration is given to the Great Lakes Paper, which had a different outcome but one that was perceived as destabilizing. The third section of the chapter reviews how Ripley's committee prepared the groundwork for restoring Abitibi and the problems it encountered.

1. We, the insolvent

Every effort to create a new corporate structure during the Great Depression was different. Despite the severity of the economic crisis, investors holding bonds or preferred stock had a reasonable chance of recouping their principal and perhaps the accrued obligations. In contrast, common shareholders normally were the losers since courts considered their holdings worthless, mere water, once assets were reappraised. General creditors often got little or nothing. However, these were tendencies. Numerous twists and alternative results occurred as stakeholders tried to influence the legal process. Two cases, which received extensive press coverage, illustrated how the struggles might unfold.

Canada Power and Paper was the first of the major producers to fail. A holding company, it did not control many assets directly and did not have full ownership of some subsidiaries. Most of the original executives were retained following the merger of their firms into the larger enterprise. Many already held significant investments or received liberal amounts of common stock for the new corporation. The preferred equity or debt issues typically were left unchanged, not refinanced. Additional securities were then issued to raise more capital. The new company announced the historical pattern of dividends would continue, which it did – for less than three years. None of the constituent firms built new facilities after 1926. Though economies were anticipated from a rationalization of operations, few efforts were undertaken because the mills were geographically proximate. Canada Power reported a profit during its first year and then continuous losses. Dividends were suspended in February 1931. Under pressure from the Montreal Stock Exchange, Harry Gundy was forced to admit the operations had dropped to 43 per cent of capacity and could no longer meet the fixed charges.[2]

As the first producer to collapse, Canada Power experienced the least difficulty in securing reformation. Before the insolvency became public, former minister of finance Charles Dunning was appointed the chairman of a securities protective committee. His selection was alleged to have been at the behest of Edward Beatty, the chair of the Bankers' Committee. Recapitalization was expected to presage the "one big merger" Beatty and his colleagues planned. The protective committee included executives from British and American financial interests, officials from life insurance companies, a member of Clarkson's company, and Strachan Johnston for the trustee. The Bank of Montreal and the Royal Bank, which had issued loans worth $14.5 million to Canada Power, had indirect representation. Although the committee said it served all investors, no public meeting was ever held to sanction the representatives. Instead, it worked under a cloak of secrecy.[3]

Within two months Dunning declared the financial structure required radical revision because the company lacked working capital. It had assets "potentially valuable but at present non-productive." He proposed slashing the capitalization from $103.6 million to $52.6 million, which could reduce the annual fixed charges from $6.6 million to $2.8 million. These estimates excluded the common equity, secured bank loans, and the firm's stakes in Anglo-Canadian Paper and Anticosti Island. The assets would be written down to $84.2 million from $213 million for a new company, Consolidated Paper, with Canada Power and Paper then cast off into the netherworld of the deceased. International capital markets still had significant liquidity in 1931, a condition that allowed the issue of new securities. In return for common stock for the new firm, the debt holders were expected to pass up accrued interest and to accept new bonds that operated on an income basis for five years, that is, until 1936 any interest payments were contingent upon the company achieving sufficient earnings. The securities also had a sinking fund arrangement, which guaranteed their liquidation. Preferred shareholders were offered common stock without par value and of dubious worth. The common shareholders and general creditors might receive the equivalent of 10 cents on the dollar. The committee reserved the right to select a majority of the new directors but refused to disclose the plans. Responses to the scheme were mixed but many observers described the terms as reasonable and efficient, conveniently ignoring the "wash-out" of the junior classes.[4]

The speed of Dunning's committee overwhelmed opponents. Early in the Great Depression many investors were not aware of their legal rights and the ways to slow or derail proposals. Alteration of the capital structure of an insolvent company could not take effect unless it was sanctioned by a court. In theory, a petition from at least 15 per cent of shareholders might delay approval. Judges were supposed to consider whether proposed changes were equitable, but following British precedents they mostly acted as rubber-stamps, sanctioning proposals that garnered majority approval without considering any unfairness. They invariably approved schemes that originated from persons who seemed honest or that appeared to match what normal businessmen might do. Provided most interests made some sacrifices, courts would not carefully compare relative costs, that is, whether some claimants gave up more than others. There also was no accepted rule, as in the United States, that the senior classes of investors must receive full compensation before the others got anything.[5]

Because the securities were fragmented among the component firms and different investor classes, no single group was able to garner special treatment. Dunning asserted "liquidation and litigation would demoralize the whole situation and might spell disaster to one of Canada's greatest industries." Former executives of the Belgo-Canadian Paper Company objected the loudest. They deemed the stock swap insufficient and told the shareholders to demand better terms. A protective committee for the preferred shareholders was mobilized in opposition but the Dunning committee would not make concessions and sufficient bonds were deposited within two months that it was able to compel settlement meetings. The opponents stretched the process out by several months but eventually capitulated. Despite widespread complaints about the write-off, public officials insisted nothing could be done.[6]

Some media commentators expected the new firm to reflect a removal of "old influences." In fact, since the bondholders chose a majority of the directors, financial institutions still dominated the board. Gundy and Sir Herbert Holt were excised, along with their immediate associates, but most other executives remained. LaMonte J. Belnap, an American engineer, was named president. However, the reduction of assets

and capital proved insufficient. Continuing problems forced a renegotiation in 1936 that slashed the purported worth of the assets to $68
million. Common shares were issued to bondholders in exchange for a
deferral of interest payments, while strengthened terms for the sinking
fund sought to speed a liquidation of the debt. Not until the 1940s
did Consolidated Paper achieve earnings sufficient to cover all
obligations.[7]

Price Brothers, in contrast, became an example of how tenacious
investors could upset plans and trigger a war of numbers. The company held timberlands equivalent to the size of Massachusetts, predominantly in Quebec's Saguenay River valley. By the spring of 1932,
having helped spur the race to the bottom, the working capital was
exhausted and the firm could not meet interest or sinking fund payments. Unauthorized loans had been made to an investment trust the
Price family controlled, and the firm was saddled with the debt of a
subsidiary, Price Realty, which owned a new office tower in Quebec
City. The papermaker's main client, British press baron Max Aitken
(Lord Beaverbrook), in a *coup de main* during the annual meeting displaced the Price family that had managed the firm since 1820. Professing "sympathy for the young Price boys," he denied seeking control,
but then established a committee tasked with developing a new financial arrangement and had his brother appointed president.[8] Bondholders were requested to accept a new debt issue that paid interest only if
there were sufficient earnings. Preferred stockholders were expected to
waive their dividends for five years, in exchange for an eventual distribution of new common stock.[9]

Beaverbrook's intervention attracted immediate resistance, although
Price Brothers was moribund. Press rumours suggested the press baron's goal entailed a merger of much of the industry "under his banner."
Alternatively, he might start a newsprint war that could make the previous troubles "look like a pink tea party." Critics denounced his
scheme because it offered no concessions and asked for a unilateral surrender that reduced everyone else to just one-seventh of the voting
rights. Various investors and creditors forced the withdrawal of the
proposal and the company then officially defaulted.[10] Protective committees were mobilized for the different securities. The one for the
bondholders comprised Ross McMaster (president, Steel Company of
Canada), Thomas Bradshaw (president, North American Life Assurance), and financial executives from three countries. The preferred
shareholders' committee included an Aitken representative and Herbert J. Symington for I.W. Killam's firm, Royal Securities.[11] Because
investors slowly registered under the deposit agreements, a temporary

receiver was not appointed until April 1933. However, the largest creditor and the supplier of electricity to Price Brothers, Duke-Price Power,
intervened to have the firm declared bankrupt. Gordon Scott, a well-
known accountant, was chosen as the trustee. Operating under federal
law, Scott as a trustee could act as a more proactive agent than Clarkson
because he retained the authority to manage proceedings, adjudge proposals, and seek the best settlement. He was independent, not simply
an agent, even though day-to-day management was shared with bondholder representatives. Despite several interruptions during the insolvency, Price securities continued to be traded "on the curb" in Montreal
and New York.[12]

Once Beaverbrook claimed he was no longer involved and professed
his companies would buy newsprint in the open market when their
contracts with Price expired, two syndicates fought for control. As Price
went into bankruptcy, the contract with Duke-Price Power was voided.
The utility (controlled by Alcoa), in cooperation with Mellon financial
interests from Pittsburgh, considered intervention as a means of restoring that arrangement. Another syndicate, comprised of twenty-five
Canadians and headed by J.M. McConnell and R.O. Sweezey, wanted
the newsprint operations.[13] Despite several months of negotiations
with the bondholders' committee, those initiatives went nowhere.
However, by the early autumn, with Sweezey willing to facilitate the
refinancing, Bowater's advanced a proposal. The British company had
one of the biggest newsprint distribution networks. Enhanced control
over resource supply was necessary if its factories were to operate at
capacity. Eric Bowater promised a majority of the directors would be
"representative Canadians." He agreed to market Price's output and
pledged a continuation of sales to Beaverbrook's chain. With a package
that included full payment on the bonds and an infusion of new money,
the bondholders' committee recommended approval.[14] Scott and his
inspectors deemed the scheme unacceptable, but the key opposition
came from the preferred shareholders. The Bowater's proposal officially promised investors subscription rights for new securities, but the
rumoured terms suggested all equity holders might be wiped out.
Unsecured creditors were offered just 25 cents on the dollar. There was
also considerable ambiguity about the timing of a formal offer and
whether some creditors might get preferential treatment. Perceptions of
unfairness then mounted when it was disclosed the bondholders had
tried to wangle a surreptitious deal with Quebec about Price's timber
limits.[15]

Beaverbrook and Lord Rothermere of the *Daily Mail* group (with
Duke-Price Power as their underwriter) then advanced an alternative

proposal, which provided new capital, but indicated the equity holders might regain control if they put up sufficient money. Their package offered one-third of the voting stock to each of three interests: the common shareholders, preferred shareholders, and the underwriter. Creditors would receive certificates of indebtedness paying interest. This scheme soon gained common shareholder approval. In response, the Bowater's proposal was modified heavily. A new bond issue was intended to cover the interest arrears, while equity holders were offered a chance to purchase a majority of the securities. A quarter of all earnings were pledged for a sinking fund, which could ensure the prompt liquidation of the debt. Creditors were promised 75 per cent in the form of cash and securities, while the British firm promised a new contract for Duke-Price. When the terms were disclosed, preferred shareholders learned the package would cut the value of their stakes in half.[16] Herbert Symington, on their behalf, proclaimed this too high a sacrifice and demanded a better package because Price's financial status had begun to improve. After subsequent amendments, with near-unanimity, the creditors and common shareholders approved the Bowater's proposal. Four-fifths of the preferred then voted against, killing it.[17]

These manoeuvres triggered an alternative initiative by Scott, which was based upon a proposal from the Hearst Corporation and Royal Securities. Hearst offered a contract guaranteeing production at full capacity, while its partner ensured $12 million for the purchase of the plant, thereby freeing Price from debt. Because of his firm's involvement, Symington temporarily resigned as the chair of the preferred stockholders' committee. The bondholders' committee approved this new proposal and cautioned that rejection of it or the Bowater's scheme could result in a judicial sale that wiped out all equity. Nonetheless, seeking better terms, the preferred shareholders refused to give approval.[18]

Over the following eighteen months, a variety of ideas circulated but nothing moved forward. The severity of the Great Depression limited the ability of underwriters to float securities, and by the mid-1930s institutional investors, no longer willing to accept losses on their portfolios, insisted upon repayment of the debt and accrued preferred dividends. A new effort to break the impasse was launched during February 1936 by Pacona Ltd., a holding enterprise formed by a syndicate of Lehman Brothers, Saguenay Power (formerly Duke-Price), and other unsecured creditors. It proposed a payoff for the bondholders in full: $13.7 million for the principal and accrued interest. The company then would force a judicial sale and buy all assets for $20 million, whereas Price Brothers was nominally worth $68 million. Although a settlement for unsecured creditors was promised, nothing was offered to the equity investors. Pacona bought up securities and by April secured all but $877,200 million of the $11 million bonds in circulation.[19] Even as Pacona consolidated the holdings, a group of shareholders and Canadian banks advanced yet another scheme. It proposed an infusion of capital through an issue of new securities, the payment of accrued bond interest, and then a restoration of the old securities. Preferred shareholders were asked to waive their accrued dividends in exchange for common stock, while common equity holders were offered a 75 per cent exchange rate for new stock. Both equity groups unanimously approved this alternative. Saguenay Power rejected it. The creditors voted 358 to 4 in favour but with Saguenay Power opposed, the approval only amounted to 62 per cent of creditor claims, well short of the threshold required under the CCAA. Pacona declared the proposal unsound and claimed Price could never meet the interest charges. Symington tried to negotiate a compromise but Pacona refused. Symington, in turn, alleged the enterprise was just a front for Alcoa. The struggles went into court where, after numerous motions and delays, the proposal was rejected on technical grounds – it had not secured approval from three-quarters of each investor class.[20]

Holding almost all of the bonds, Pacona demanded Scott put the assets up for judicial sale late in 1936, but Pacona concurrently advanced yet another proposal. If it was not approved within a reasonable period, the firm threatened to force a sale. Pacona announced an agreement with eight banks for a financial advance that covered the purchase and it was capable of borrowing additional funds. By arrangement, an issue of $14 million in first mortgage bonds would be deposited with the banks as collateral. Pacona would then convert the existing equity into 63,000 new preferred shares and a million common shares. The current preferred shareholders were offered one share of new preferred, one share of new common, and warrants for other common stock. The common shareholders would gain only warrant rights and a quarter share for each common share. The owners of Pacona were promised two-thirds of the new common stock. Through a set of technical manoeuvres, Price Brothers was later expected to assume Pacona's debt and pay off the unsecured creditors. The majority shareholders of Pacona deemed this scheme the only way out of the impasse. Pacona, despite its holdings of Price bonds, legally was an unsecured creditor. Its main asset was the power contract for Price, an agreement that required a solvent producer.[21]

As if things were not murky enough, rumours circulated about how Price Brothers had developed its own reorganization plan. Supposedly the firm gained underwriting for $15 million in new bonds and another $4.2 million of convertible debentures. Preferred shareholders, so the tales went, would get new shares, while the common holders retained their securities unaltered, though some additional shares might be issued.[22] Whether there was substance behind this yarn was never clear. Nonetheless, although the reorganization expenses already exceeded $1 million (a staggering amount to Canadian observers), press commentators anticipated an end to the trusteeship because Price's operating status had improved since 1934. Therefore, although the market value for a preferred share had dropped to $1 in 1932, by early 1937 it exceeded $115. As even more rumours circulated about how British or Canadian interests opposed an American takeover, Royal Securities advanced a counterproposal whereby it would buy out the bonds and infuse sufficient working capital. The preferred holders were asked to accept a lower interest rate and several common shares for each $1,000 in principal, along with some common equity as compensation for the dividend arrears. The existing common shares were to be exchanged on a one-to-one basis.[23]

This plan quickly ran into difficulties because Price bonds contained a clause authorizing payment in gold. During the Depression, the price of gold rose from $20.67 to $35 per pound. Pacona demanded payment in gold or the equivalent, which meant a premium of $180 for every $100 in par value. However, Canada and the United States had disallowed gold payments for international transactions and most investors deemed those types of clauses defunct. Scott declared compensation in gold impossible but agreed the bondholders could receive Canadian funds, as well as a premium for the cancellation of the securities. Pacona countered by demanding an even higher premium, a condition rejected by everyone else. Concurrently, Saguenay Power threatened the termination of the electrical contract unless it received higher rates. Unable to get its way, the American syndicate attempted to force a judicial sale but the application was rejected.[24] The court, instead, authorized the trustee and shareholders to buy off the bondholders. After sustained negotiations, a deal sanctioned the payback of $141 for every $100 bond, consisting of the principal, accrued interest, and a premium. Quick approval by all shareholders followed as Royal Securities put together a package that cut the capitalization of Price Brothers in half to $30 million, along with new bonds to replace the existing issues. Ironically, given the need to mollify the claimants, the reverse of a normal restructuring occurred: the annual charges were *increased*. Until wartime conditions stimulated demand, the firm barely met the obligations and was "profitable" only because unusual depreciation rates were employed.[25]

Having worked behind the backdrop, the winners finally appeared on the public stage. Symington headed the new board and the majority of the directors were chosen by Killam (who assured everyone they were friendly to Lord Beaverbrook). Aitken's brother became vice-president, while members of the Price family received managerial positions. Col. Charles Jones of Nova Scotia, the managing director of Killam's Mersey Paper, was appointed president.[26] Heavily publicized in the business media, the Price Brothers case demonstrated how determined investors could upset plans if other parties got too much and they too little. With a twist of irony, Herbert Symington soon became a central player in the Abitibi case, but this time he was on the side of dissident bondholders.

2. A spider web of intrigue

Even as the Price Brothers battles unfolded, the Hepburn administration learned that restructuring a firm was neither simple nor did it represent a panacea for industrial stabilization. Problems could arise as investors or companies pursued profit-seeking objectives and engaged in behaviour not necessarily consonant with the public interest, issues that became manifest with Great Lakes Paper. During the early 1920s, the network of companies controlled by Backus-Brooks was conservatively managed. Through his holdings, Edward Wellington Backus retained tight control and kept debt obligations limited. This altered precipitously as the firm undertook an aggressive expansion in the Lake States and Northwestern Ontario, along with new dealings in Scandinavia. By 1928 the common stock comprised less than a quarter of the capital structure of Minnesota and Ontario Paper. Under the terms of its 1919 charter, Great Lakes was obligated to build a newsprint mill at the Lakehead but the promoters postponed the scheme for nearly a decade. Backus emerged as a minority investor in 1923 and the Ontario government incorrectly believed he had full authority over Great Lakes. Frustrated by the continuing delays, the province issued an ultimatum in early 1927 and threatened to revoke the resource rights if construction did not proceed. The three men who controlled Great Lakes had failed with several efforts to develop properties elsewhere and had grown discordant. With the provincial ultimatum as an excuse, the majority investors, Lewis Aldrich and George Seaman, sold out to International Paper, which was exploring timberlands in the Nipigon district. Backus had little choice but to buy back the stakes for an undisclosed premium. Two of his mills were dependent upon pulp shipments from Great Lakes. Direct competition with International represented an unreasonable risk. It took him a year to finalize the transfer of resource rights of Great Lakes (the collateral for financing) and an acceptable contract from the Hydro Commission. The original plans for the factory stipulated two 264-inch machines, but Backus chose to install four 304-inch machines, the widest in the world. The development was funded by a bond issue, which gained approval from his investment bankers a month after the collapse of the Canadian Newsprint Company. However, with Minnesota and Ontario Paper already heavily leveraged, they insisted upon the separate incorporation of Great Lakes. The mortgage deed was pledged against the assets, a theme stressed in advertisements for the bonds that were slow to sell. Backus also was instructed by the bankers to complete the construction with no further debt. The timing could not have been worse. The first machine became operational during the spring of 1929 but it took another year to finish the equipment's installation.[27]

Business for the Backus-controlled mills collapsed due to the worsening economic crisis and disputes between the industrialist versus several American publishers. Minnesota and Ontario Paper defaulted in January of 1931, but a classic instance of collusive receivership unfolded. Exploiting weaknesses in American law, the businessman wangled a management role along with two friendly receivers. The difficulties related only to the parent company, he insisted. Because the value of the properties exceeded the outstanding debts by "tens of millions," a deal for refinancing could end the receivership "in a comparatively short time." He argued that the corporate group was still profitable, but by the summer the bondholders documented the scale of the losses and the auditors questioned the reliability of the financial statements. When press rumours circulated about a possible reorganization of the Backus empire, Premier George Henry cautioned he would demand a "showdown" to safeguard provincial interests.[28] In a vain effort to stave off bankruptcy, Backus complicated the situation by making a duplicitous transaction. He withdrew $2 million in cash from Great Lakes in December 1930 and, as collateral, transferred to its treasury shares from two of his personally-controlled companies that were allegedly worth $10 million. Backus then authorized the issue of $8 million in preferred shares. When the shares were received, he converted $5 million of them into Minnesota and Ontario par value common stock, thereby wiping out their value. He used the infusion from Great Lakes to claim the parent firm had improved under his management. Supposedly the funds would be repaid and the securities redeemed later. The shares remained on the books at their official value despite demands for rescission, that is, for the transactions to be set aside because they amounted to a swindle. Bankers and security holders in the United States forced the ouster of the president and the two receivers. He was then prosecuted on both sides of the border for fraud. In addition, sixteen separate lawsuits were filed by individuals seeking $2.4 million for fifty promissory notes that Backus had signed before the collapse.[29]

Backus initiated a publicity campaign and lawsuits against the new receivers, portraying himself as a wronged entrepreneur who was trying to foil a plot by corrupt financial interests who "conspired to consummate a $70,000,000 steal." Although he received a sympathetic hearing from a congressional committee in 1934, American courts later dismissed his statements as pure fiction.[30] *Pulp and Paper Magazine* was equally dismissive. Backus, it commented, made an embroidered tale about how "his magic wand" was waved to create firms but the situation instead turned into "one of the biggest legal fights in the industry." The receivers countersued, alleging Backus had not filed the suit in good faith and plotted to interfere with the receivership. They claimed Backus had stolen $7 million for his private use, most of it lost in stock speculations.[31] Some perceived as a tragic end the sudden death alone in New York of "the last of the great lumber barons," three weeks after the courts dismissed Backus's final appeal, but the circumstances provided considerable fodder for salacious gossip. Police found in his hotel room three wills, over 200,000 shares of stock in various companies, and $37,000 in undeposited cheques. His estate turned out to be worthless relative to the claims, and the ensuing legal cases delayed Minnesota and Ontario Paper's reorganization until 1941. The settlement allocated to the debt holders a mix of bonds and equity, while the general creditors received nominal cash amounts and common shares. Deemed to have no stake in the assets, the shareholders got nothing.[32]

After Great Lakes Paper also defaulted, specific problems followed from the terminology in the deed for the bonds. Short of someone coming along with a cash offer, the only way the properties could be bought was by an American method where the debt holders developed a reorganization plan. American bankruptcy courts often accepted nominal bids from protective committees, dispensed with the device of a judicial sale, and authorized reorganization by injunction. These practices were unacceptable in Canada. The courts would not accept a bid in cash unless a receiver recommended it as a fair value. If the bid went too high, the amount payable to each non-depositing bondholder could reach a point where people then chose to withdraw their securities from deposit. This, in turn, could topple the bidder's ability to mobilize the capital necessary to complete the deal. A judicial sale thus was the only option.[33]

The case again highlighted the small world of Canadian business and law. The two investment banks in the United States responsible for the bonds fell into receivership before the Backus group collapsed. National Trust was engaged as trustee and an officer from the firm was appointed as the receiver. The lawyers who later guided Algoma Steel out of bankruptcy represented Great Lakes. Strachan Johnston was the counsel for the trustee and provided advice to the bondholders about the constitutionality of different options. Frederick Clarkson temporarily served as the liquidator, until he resigned to accept the post at Abitibi. Harry Gundy, although not on the bondholders' committee, attended the sessions as a substitute representative. The largest holders of the bonds were life insurance companies and investment trusts. But Senator Arthur Meighen held the pivotal role of committee chair. Media rumours suggested the former prime minister, following his resignation in 1926, might be appointed as the legal counsel for National Trust. Instead, as we have seen, he became vice-president and general counsel of Canadian General Investment. The financial house handled funds for estates or institutions but was not a brokerage. Operating as a closed trust, the firm was not required to publish its holdings or interests. The receiver occasionally attended meetings of the bondholders' committee for Great Lakes, which "nearly always took place at Senator Meighen's office."[34]

Geoffrey Clarkson served as a consultant when the receivership began. The costs of closing the mill were higher than operating it at a loss, he observed. A shutdown risked a loss of personnel and deterioration of the mill. Like Abitibi, the company had no sales agent or independent marketing arrangements. Great Lakes shared contracts with Minnesota and Ontario and other Backus companies. The former parent could abrogate them at any time by claiming Great Lakes had wrongfully managed tonnage. Minnesota and Ontario Paper maintained higher output rates than other firms, whereas the Canadian firm was far short. In exchange for a promise not to compete against its former parent, Great Lakes was allocated a third of one contract. The receiver then engaged an American firm, Parsons & Whittemore, to handle sales. Clarkson later claimed he knew little about the marketing agent, John Gefaell, but the dealer seemed "to be a man of very substantial means."[35]

Little could be done for several years but by late 1934 Great Lakes achieved a small operating profit. Quite ironically, just after the Liberals had vilified him over the Abitibi Canyon scandal, Meighen and his associates began discussions with the province about how to return the firm to solvency. Proceeding under federal legislation, with the requirement to secure three-quarters approval from every security class, was dubious. They agreed to wait for the passage of the OJAA. Meanwhile, the bondholders considered three options: sell the assets to another manufacturer, take over and manage the firm on their own, or accept cash and an investment stake in the firm. After they decided upon a judicial sale, bids were received from R.O. Sweezey, Canadian International Paper, a cross-border banking syndicate, and Lynn Aldrich and John Gefaell.[36]

The bondholders insisted upon full repayment but were divided about which offer was acceptable. The first two were dismissed as unreasonable. Slightly less than a majority favoured the Aldrich-Gefaell proposal, but Mutual Life and several institutional investors opposed the scheme. Arthur Meighen, however, lobbied in favour. He believed there was a fiduciary duty to maximize the recovery of funds for the accounts managed by his firm. By mid-October, he persuaded three-quarters of the bond principal that the proposal offered the highest and most dependable payback. Lynn Aldrich represented the *Chicago Daily News*, which sought greater control over its newsprint supply. The key to the proposal was an arrangement whereby twenty-five American publishers agreed to take tonnage annually for a decade, thereby ensuring the profitability of Great Lakes. In exchange, they received a second class of preferred shares deposited in a voting trust. Dividends on the shares provided the publishers with a rebate, which was tantamount to cutting the newsprint price. This plan allowed the debt holders to retain control, cut the fixed charges, but left the original equity investors nothing. The scheme was not a reorganization but an exchange of securities contingent upon the negotiation of sales contracts.[37]

Rumours also circulated about renewed plans by publishers to gain control over newsprint companies. The Hearst group, Sweezey claimed to Premier Hepburn, was willing to take all output from Great Lakes in exchange for an equity stake. "Such a procedure would encourage other publishers to deal with presently defunct companies on a similar basis, and the industry in a short time would pass into the hands of the United States publishers, with Canadians, in the truest sense, being only 'hewers of wood and drawers of water.'" Most of the Canadian producers opposed the proposed deal for Great Lakes. They contended it rekindled cut-throat tactics since the manufacturers either had to offer similar concessions or raid the clients of other firms as a means of offsetting the loss of business. The "dangerous" scheme was one that made market stability impossible, Charles Vining claimed, because "the hypodermic of price concessions and marketing methods" utilized for resuscitating Great Lakes would generate new bankruptcies. "In this plan the public interest is clearly involved and the matter cannot be treated as merely a private transaction."[38]

Great Lakes, one newspaper commented, became a "spider web of intrigue, politics, finance and law." Members of the industry utilized every mechanism to derail the Aldrich-Gefaell proposal, from lobbying with the province to a media-whispering campaign about how the deal was baneful to Canada. Archibald Graustein was described by the press as "the Napoleon" of their efforts. Graustein conceded he was "a believer in competition and the law of supply and demand free from government control," but told Hepburn that "the Gefaell offer had in it the germs of a price war," which could see wages reduced and timber fees lost. "I do not think you want any of these things even though I do feel you may get them unless you and we can cooperate to avoid them."[39] Nine producers offered to buy out the output of Great Lakes Paper through a syndicate, Black Sturgeon Newsprint. However, the option did not match the payoff for the bondholders, and under its terms, one or more of the investing producers could tie up the affairs of Great Lakes to the detriment of the debt holders.[40] Members of the Hepburn administration were of mixed views. They could hardly challenge the Aldrich-Gefaell proposal on legal grounds since Great Lakes was the first case to proceed under their own legislation, the OJAA. The scheme ensured employment for many workers in the Thunder Bay area. It might transfer some American production north, but resuscitation of the mill also would divert business from Abitibi. All of the publishers participating in the proposal were customers of Great Lakes and therefore it was suggested to the premier the deal would cause "only a trifling disturbance." Great Lakes intimated that it was prepared to return some timberlands, which could be redistributed just before the next election. Finally, Col. Frank Knox, the owner of the *Chicago Daily News*, was a candidate for the Republican nomination in the 1936 presidential election.[41]

Under intense pressure from the lobbyists, the province came out in opposition. The bondholders and other creditors responded that it had no right to impede a business transaction. The government, Meighen contemptuously declared, "undermines the title to every timber limit in Ontario" and sought "to control the disposition of private property." Many newspapers questioned the "interference." The *Financial Post* decried the sensationalism with which other producers had attacked the deal. It showed that "'big business' is less concerned over the public than its own interests." The real goal was to raise newsprint prices versus "putting in order its own notoriously overcapitalized household. Make the consumer pay fictitious prices? Is this the idea?" The bondholders, the *Globe* editorialized, were acting within their own authority.[42] However, despite rhetoric about a need to defend the public interest, the opposition was declawed almost immediately. The government declared that it was not prepared to cancel any timber rights. The industry association then acknowledged its own unwillingness to have a precedent where the sanctity of leases was challenged. Repudiation was "a policy of self-destruction."[43] The bondholders then offered, and the province accepted, a deal whereby the publishers did not receive dividends until newsprint reached a higher price. A planned $2 per ton reduction from the market rate was delayed for three months. Heenan sanctimoniously proclaimed a resolution had occurred "on terms which protect the public interest and which are therefore satisfactory."[44]

Institutional bondholders tried to block the action, but with the government's sanction, it gained court approval. Despite the reorganization and the sales contracts, Great Lakes still lost money. Major improvements were required to lower costs and, within a few months, the board chose to defer payment of the bond interest for several years. C.H. Carlisle, the new president, had headed the Canadian subsidiary of Goodyear Tire and Rubber. As a stranger to the industry, he found many of the established practices difficult to accept. "Timber limits were granted without any apparent system or reason. The industry has been used as the means of profiteering instead of carrying on an organized and legitimate business." While acknowledging a need for government control, he dismissed the notion that the producers could ever achieve a unified direction.[45] Carlisle soon demonstrated his only goal was stabilization of the company, regardless of the impact on others. Vining inferred that "the Great Lakes crowd" would cooperate with the efforts to prorate output (even though that was never in the deal with the province) because a letter from the firm had acknowledged the importance of working in harmony. The trade association, therefore, insisted some of the business for Great Lakes should be reallocated to other producers.

Carlisle refused to consider the matter. The Supreme Court had sanctioned the sales contracts and the province had "consented to" those arrangements, he countered. Any deviation left the firm legally exposed. Quasi-rationing schemes contravened the Anti-Combines Act and would just "create a great deal of dissension and ill will" with American publishers. When pressed, he labelled demands from the industry association "wholly pettish and non-constructive." Carlisle claimed to he had "no jurisdiction" over contract management.

> It would be just as consistent to ask a farmer who had his investment in land, who had cultivated it intelligently and through fertilization and otherwise had produced more than the average, who had gone out and secured a market for his product and done it legally without breaking prices and being unfair, to ask that farmer to divide his product or sales contract with the less imprudent farmer. That is just contrary to human nature and especially to the Scotch.

His refusal to make concessions also was a function of simple economics: with the list price still low, even at full capacity Great Lakes was unable to cover the debt interest. To the frustration of Vining, he refused to join the trade association, pay any of its costs, and skipped meetings. At the same time, Carlisle lobbied to reconfigure the company's forest concessions towards geographically contiguous areas and block punitive actions such as higher timber fees.[46]

Although the other producers were prepared to allow "for a natural period of confusion," their demands escalated during the year after the reorganization. "Great Lakes is not playing the game with us or with the industry," Vining complained. Carlisle maintained that his firm must pursue an independent course, given the premier's statements about the need to ease unemployment. Peter Heenan warned Carlisle that the firm was not conducting itself in accordance with the government's goals "nor in the direction of harmony and co-operation with other manufacturers." Carlisle dismissed this.[47] Great Lakes, he remarked, "was an awful mess when I took it over, but it is now quite well straightened out. The Company is making good money, and we are a contented organization." As the months passed Carlisle became more obdurate. The firm would support "any constructive plan" that focussed upon ensuring an equitable selling price or an economical zone system. Any distribution or equalization of contracts represented an illegal restraint of trade. His discretion was limited by the voting trust controlled by the American publishers but as the worst of the Depression eased he also contended that prorating was just unnecessary. "To agree to a policy where an emergency does not exist, a policy that may lead you into endless trouble, is not a wise procedure." Great Lakes carried out every agreement to the letter of the law and did not give secret rebates, so the province need not fear it might resort to "sharp or underhand operations."[48] Despite repeated prodding from the industry association, the premier gave up trying to bring the firm into line. Though Carlisle remained unrepentant, Hepburn assured Vining, "his attitude toward the industry is constructive" and would "show no lack of cooperation when and if specific circumstances require it." Then, in rationalizing double-think, the premier asserted, "when need arises the Government will require The Great Lakes Paper Company and every other Ontario newsprint manufacturer to do its part in execution of this policy, on the same basis and to the same degree."[49]

3. I am bewildered

Frustrated by the lack of change in Abitibi's status, Peter Heenan told Joseph Ripley during early 1936 that his council should get on with reorganization. Ripley indicated a willingness to start the groundwork, with his now constant refrain "always, of course, bearing in mind its primary obligation to serve the best interests of the Bondholders." However, they had to secure money on reasonable terms and could proceed only with "an attitude of cooperation on the part of the Provincial Government."[50] The bondholders' claim had accumulated to $63.5 million in principal and accrued interest. Ripley's official stance to investors stressed how unsettled conditions and an inability to mobilize capital represented serious problems.[51] Quietly Ripley, Milton Cross, and Clarkson prepared a tentative scheme, but before any proposal could be taken public the status of the resource rights had to be resolved. The chair was blunt about how they should proceed: "Abitibi is one thing if a settlement is reached and it is another thing if it is not reached. And it is still a third thing if a settlement comes in between nothing and the desired goal we have in mind. The result of our negotiations with the government will have a profound effect upon the market value of any new securities issues for the purpose of raising new money."[52]

Ripley believed the firm should be reorganized on its own, though the bondholders' council thought a merger with a bigger enterprise might work. He did not want the problems encountered by other firms. The result was one of the most comprehensive reviews undertaken during the interwar generation. The first action entailed a revaluation of the assets that served as the collateral for a new financial structure. This assessment would allow an objective appraisal of potential options. Three consulting firms were engaged to look at the mills, the electrical power facilities, and the timber operations. They were instructed to determine the worth and earning capacity of the properties, which had undergone minimal, if any, maintenance. The consultants were also to specify the improvements required for lower manufacturing costs and whether factories might be converted to make other goods.[53]

This initiative raised several conflicts of interest that were to bedevil the participants. Strachan Johnston, as the lawyer for the trustee, insisted that the reports must first go to Montreal Trust, with nothing disclosed to others, not even to Clarkson. Under normal conditions, the valuations that appraisers furnished set the basis for a reserve price when a firm was put up for sale. The engineers needed to consult with the receiver during their investigations, but the proceedings, Johnston stated, "might be severely and plausibly criticized" if the data were given to some parties and not to others. Glyn Osler, the bondholders' primary lawyer, concurred because a simple reconstruction of the capital was not possible. He admitted the information might be exploited because bondholders' committees "have sometimes had private axes to grind." Ripley, however, demanded access to the reports. "Certainly I have no 'private ax[e] to grind' but I cannot imagine anything more upsetting to the general run of bondholders than to see our properties advertised for sale before the committee has a plan." It also was necessary to have them available for any talks with underwriters and investors. After sustained negotiations, with court approval, access was granted to Clarkson, McPherson, and the bondholders' committee – with the proviso that the contents could only be divulged to solicitors and professional advisors. As in the Canada Power and Paper case, the participants expected this restriction to lessen the chance that other interests might raise demands.[54]

Given the scale of Abitibi's activities, the preparation of the studies stretched out for fifteen months, but a report was released during the autumn of 1936. All calculations ignored Provincial Paper, Espanola, and Sturgeon Falls. On a reproductive value basis, the engineers believed the gross worth of the mills, hydroelectric plants, woods equipment, and other properties amounted to just $71 million. If allowance was made for depreciation and deferred maintenance, the "net sound physical value" dropped to $48.7 million, about one-quarter of the pre-receivership figure and only 40 per cent of Clarkson's 1933 analysis. The cost of constructing equivalent facilities was guesstimated at $78 million. Several analyses estimated income levels at different levels of output and prices. If Abitibi produced 500,000 tons of newsprint and 55,000 tons of sulphite pulp, then its annual net income was conservatively set at $2.5 million before income tax or interest. Other calculations, taking into account price or demand increases, rejigged this figure to $4.1 million. To achieve even the lower figure, a large infusion of money was required for capital expenditures, maintenance, and working capital. Although the engineers advanced an estimate, the sum subsequently used by the bondholders' committee was derived from

Abitibi's mills manager. He predicted the minimum improvements required $8.3 million. These could raise the output to over 650,000 tons per year and allow significant cost savings. A separate assessment by Clarkson indicated a need for at least $3 million more to establish sufficient working capital. Yet another supplemental report reappraised the company's operations based upon the impact of those adjustments and an increase in the price for newsprint. The earning capacity estimation was raised to $5.9 million. The worth of the properties was rejigged to $73.8 million. But since this sum was predicated upon the infusion of capital for plant improvements, the calculation actually amounted to $65.5 million.[55]

Ripley's second major action was an assembly of *The Compilation of Statements and Information*. This document disclosed an unprecedented amount of information about a Canadian business. It contained a breakout of the financial statements since 1928, engineering reviews of the properties, analyses of the industry, copies of relevant legislation, resource agreements, and licences. The *Compilation* became known as "the Bible" and was a key source of information after its publication. Ripley had insisted upon its preparation in case the bondholders proceeded for reorganization via American courts. The document met the standards required by the Securities and Exchange Commission.

The third initiative entailed resolving the outstanding issues with Ontario, an issue deemed pressing since most of the resource concessions had expired. A quiet lobbying campaign sought to establish the bondholders' legitimacy with the premier and temper the hostility Hepburn expressed during the Abitibi Canyon scandal. The representative committee, he was advised, represented the one group capable of accomplishing a reorganization and forcing compliance from other investors. With an initiative from anyone else delays were likely to multiply and "go along endlessly unless the Bondholders get their cash." The premier was assured a plan the bondholders advanced would be fair and not finalized without the government's informal consent. They had "more invested in the Company than all the other classes of securities put together," whereas the values "for the Common Stock in the old Company Balance Sheet were established by using fictitious values on timber rights and water power rights." The bondholders would put the plants "in finest shape," provide employment, and thereby reinvigorate public revenues.[56] When Clarkson, Ripley, and Colin Kemp first met Hepburn in late November 1936, the premier declared he would only deal with Ripley "as the logical party" for settling license and related matters. The premier declared a repetition of Price Brothers must be avoided. Quebec had let the firm pass "into the hands of interests who might pursue an independent course and upset the proceedings for stabilization of the Industry which the two Provinces were insisting upon." Heenan participated in the negotiations about timber concessions but the premier insisted upon having final approval for most things. Ripley handled all discussions related to the hydro contracts, timberlands, and bad debts. Although Clarkson and Ward Wright were present at several meetings, one observer later noted that "no one but Ripley could begin to describe the endless mass of detail that he had to weigh through because he did it single handed."[57]

Disentangling Abitibi's relationship with the province proved thorny. Hydro officials wanted to reopen earlier claims: arrears on the power contract for the Espanola mill, contracted purchases by Ontario Power Service, expenditures for the Canyon project, and even a fantasy that 30 per cent of the OPS bonds somehow remained unpaid and owing. In compensation, they demanded two power plants on the Sturgeon River, the generating station at Espanola, Kaministiquia Power, and a distribution system for Fort William.[58] Clarkson and Ripley rejected the attempted grab because the facilities were essential for mill operations, but they agreed some transfers might occur after the firm was solvent. The bickering ended when the provincial secretary reprimanded Hydro officials: "You appreciate how anxious the Government is to have this organization completed and I certainly do not want any objections raised of a purely technical nature but it is our desire to facilitate matters in every way possible."[59] With the Hepburn administration committed to consolidating the utility's expansion into New Ontario, the parties decided upon a modest property exchange. The key issue became an acquisition of the Crystal Falls generating station near Sturgeon Falls. For Abitibi it would be a small loss for good riddance, whereas Hydro needed the station to meet anticipated demand. The province offered a release of all claims, including those related to OPS, *quid pro quo* with the transfer of the facility and its transmission lines.[60] Both parties perceived this arrangement to be fair and kept the terms confidential. The government hardly wanted to publicize that after Roebuck's earlier demands the settlement amounted to less than one-twentieth of what he had sought. Ripley's committee had its own concerns. As reorganization came closer, some investors wanted a high payback. The chair of Hydro therefore advised that

> no figures as to the amount of the Corporation's debt to the Government or the value of the property transferred to the Government in settlement of that debt shall, at the present time, be made public. It will be difficult enough ... to secure the consent of the bondholders to the transfer of the

Crystal Falls plant to the Government without increasing the difficulty by placing what many might regard as an exaggerated value upon the property.[61]

The natural resource rights were tediously negotiated one-by-one, but a settlement was reached contingent upon a $14.3 million investment pledge from the bondholders. The government agreed to reinstate and rearrange the pulpwood and water rights if Abitibi was reorganized on a basis later approved by the Supreme Court. This understanding could be extended for an additional year but became void if a reorganization did not occur within the specified time. The terms, save for marginal variations, matched those that prevailed before 1932, and the concessions were scheduled for renewal with common periods of twenty-one years. Abitibi would be released from all liabilities, and the province agreed to assist various river improvements. The areas for the Sturgeon Falls mill reverted to the Crown after three years if it did not reopen. Heenan demanded the bondholders sell Espanola and Sturgeon Falls. Hepburn and Ripley rejected the suggestion. In exchange, the company agreed to restart the Fort William mill at the earliest possible date.[62]

Arthur Roebuck was frozen out of the negotiations. He privately demanded further reviews and still insisted Abitibi owed the province at least $28 million.[63] Roebuck not only was told to accept the settlement but was instructed to introduce the authorizing statute in the legislature, which was written by the bondholders' lawyers. Most of his speech was another diatribe against the Canyon project, including how OPS "had no legal right to generate power on the Abitibi River," held "an outlawed lease," and saddled the province with the obligations when "the bubble burst." Suddenly and without elaboration, at the close he announced the acquisition of Crystal Falls to "settle for all time so far as the Commission is concerned, the unfortunate Abitibi tangle." Press reports ignored most of the speech (only mentioning the final statement) and declared matters were now "amicably arranged."[64] It was one of Roebuck's last assignments. Two weeks later the premier forced his removal from office for opposing the government's handling of labour unrest. The legislation was passed but the government delayed proclamation until June 1937, when the firm's reorganization appeared imminent.[65]

Hepburn tried to shape issues that lay outside the province's jurisdiction. He felt Dominion Securities was a reasonable underwriter and opposed the use of Royal Securities. He was sensitive about the latter, not only because it was controlled by Killam but also due to the firm's role in the struggle over Price Brothers. Although the concerns were rarely stated overtly, all parties understood its involvement might extend Montreal's or Britain's influence over the Ontario industry. No discussions had been held about the new management for Abitibi. When pressed by the premier, Ripley speculated about the possibility of Clarkson as the new chair and George Cottrelle, the head of the Commerce Bank and a known Liberal supporter, as the president: "The Premier approved this slate 100% and commended it ... He could not think of a better arrangement." The bondholders' executive counsel soon squelched this idea. Somerville warned the selection of Clarkson and Cottrelle "would not be popular" and would be perceived as top-heavy with financial, not industrial, ability.[66]

The periodic circulation of unsolicited reformation schemes in the press by brokers and underwriters frustrated Ripley. Most were never submitted to the committee but were published as speculative ideas to gain attention. Some news stories were outright fiction, such as a tale about American investors "with good financial backing in the far west" who had approached McPherson and the common shareholders. Ripley did not understand how anyone could develop a plan before an understanding was achieved with the province.[67] One proposal, however, which was submitted in secrecy, received careful analysis, and it well illustrates the problems associated with the unsolicited schemes. E.A. Charlton, a former manager of International Paper's Newfoundland subsidiary, and Field Glore, a New York investment house, recommended an amalgamation like the "one big merger" pushed by the Bankers' Committee several years earlier. They divided the Canadian industry into three groups: "longs" operating at high capacity, "shorts" operating below the industry average, and small producers. A single company, they suggested, could be formed by merging eight members from the second group, which represented 42 per cent of capacity: Abitibi, Brompton, Consolidated Paper, Great Lakes, Lake St. John, Minnesota and Ontario, Price Brothers, and St. Lawrence. The combined firms produced 1.3 million tons of newsprint during 1935 and had a capacity of 2.2 million tons, which theoretically could be expanded to 2.6 million tons with $25 million in new money. "Complete proration," if ever carried out, would award an additional 300,000 tons to the amalgamated firm and "it is clear that this group is in a position to obtain the lion's share of increased tonnage which should come to Canada if present consumption trends persist." Reorganizations of the companies individually were not viable because the investors had to accept "a terrific write-down of their position or must hope against hope that the future will bail them out."

A pro forma balance sheet suggested a new enterprise, Confederation Paper, would have assets of $332 million. Only a merger, the promoters argued, could guarantee price stability and the pursuit of greater economies. Power contracts could be reset, unnecessary lands abandoned, and "real savings should result from an allocation of tonnage to mills closest to the consumer. Insofar as it is politically possible, important savings should be effected from shutting down some of the mills now operating at part time, and concentrating tonnage in the lower cost units, which could be run to capacity." The presentation tried to demonstrate that Confederation could succeed at a depressed price of $40 per ton. If the rate went higher "the profit possibilities become very considerable."[68] The promoters assumed the debt of the combined companies could be reduced from $175 million to $58 million and they advanced a complicated set of deals. The allocation of securities was according to a formula predicated upon the theoretical earnings of each enterprise across the next decade. These projections then were penalized to the degree each firm had bank loans or preferred creditors (which had to be paid off in cash). Finally, a "bonus" or demerit was added to reflect working capital and prorating status. Abitibi was offered 30.5 per cent of the distribution in the form of bonds, debentures, and common stock.[69]

An analysis by Milton Cross attempted to figure out the logic for all of this but found only a brief description of the formula and no data that documented the anticipated earnings. The submission contained little information about the properties or financial positions of the component companies. The plan, Cross realized, offered insufficient working capital for day-to-day operations and ignored any factory improvements. Financing, he thought, "will require practically all of the present cash and marketable securities of the constituent companies," which reduced the net monies available to a paltry $250,000. Charlton's backers claimed high earnings would replenish the cash. Cross could not verify any of their calculations.[70] Initially hesitant, Ripley came out in opposition because the scheme entailed an amalgamation of enterprises, "four of which are in the Courts, all in one grand re-organization and merger step." There were at least thirty different groups that had to agree versus five for Abitibi alone. "I am bewildered to see how you could keep everyone put at one simultaneous time." Charlton asked for a large allocation of capital stock to the underwriters but it made more sense to pay them "a moderate and fair cash spread." While conceding that negotiations might change things, the distribution for Abitibi was "out of line." Ripley thought it was more logical to get the individual companies out of receivership and let the owners later decide about a merger. "All boiled down ... the thing is impractical ... When I think of the many problems we have to deal with in trying to get Abitibi reorganized, I am simply stumped at the thought of multiplying that by six." Colin Kemp of the preferred shareholders' committee agreed but suggested that "it would be good politics to let some one of the other companies take the responsibility of upsetting it."[71]

Although this proposal and others were rejected, by late 1936 the pressure for action became irresistible. The investment manager for Sun Life insisted that further delays were unrealistic "for the longer it is let go the more difficult it is going to be, due to the excessive speculation now taking place in securities."[72] One prescient observer also noted:

> ... in the Abitibi reorganization picture, not only is there the usual competition between powerful banking groups for handling of the new financing, but in addition, behind the scenes, there are other factors at play ... On the one side are British interests with Canadian associates, who have large holdings of junior securities of other Canadian newsprint companies including some with relatively top-heavy [sic] capital structures. On the other hand is American and Canadian institutional capital which hold most of the Canadian newsprint bonds. The British-Canadian group has sought to delay reorganizations indefinitely.[73]

The British interests were an oblique reference to Harold Sidney Harnsworth, Viscount Rothermere. In 1924 he founded Anglo-Canadian Pulp and Paper, which operated a large mill near Quebec City. As we saw in previous chapters, Rothermere sought but failed via Robert Oliver Sweezey to grab some of Abitibi's assets. His newspaper chain, along with Lord Beaverbrook's, benefited from the Price Brothers reorganization. In 1936 his agents spent more than $5 million to acquire a quarter of Abitibi's devalued common shares and over $2 million in bonds. It was in Rothermere's interest for the company to remain weak – open to external influence or takeover. In confidential letters to Clarkson, he insisted its debts were "singularly small" and the business could remain under a receivership for several years more when higher prices might allow an emergence free of all liabilities. Recapitalization was "incomprehensible" because the industry was "now through all its troubles." The uses of wood fibre were increasing each year. "This is the cellulose age ... the German and Japanese Governments are going to stimulate production of all kinds of substitute fibres to clothe their people [which] will have a profound influence in a short time on the price of logs and of timber limits." The stakes of the equity holders, he insisted, should not be jeopardized by raising new securities, especially from financiers inclined to "rush to the rescue of an industry which is on the threshold of unexampled profits." With prophetic words, Rothermere cautioned, "I hope you can reassure me that no such scheme is being considered for it is certain to be opposed in the courts."[74]

11

The Battle of the Plans

So now I see it was folly to be consoled by the Ides of March: for though our courage was that of men, believe me we had no more sense than children. We have only cut down the tree not rooted it up.

– Cicero

A corporate reorganization is a combination of a municipal election, a historical pageant, an antivice crusade, a graduate-school seminar, a judicial proceeding, and a series of horse trades, all rolled into one – thoroughly buttered with learning and frosted with distinguished names ... Men work all night preparing endless documents in answer to other endless documents, which other men read in order to make solemn arguments. At the same time practical politicians utilize every resource of patronage, demagoguery, and coercion beneath the solemn smoke screen.[1]

– Thurman Arnold

IN ALL TRUST THERE IS the possibility of betrayal. Capitalism as an economic system assumes social trust will prevail for several issues: the sanctity of contracts, the legitimacy of purported worth in exchange relationships, and mutual acknowledgement of the status of different participants. Insolvency, by its very nature, brings each of these into question. Most crucially, it challenges social understandings about the relative dignity of different groups.[2] Equity holders, "the owners," are removed from control, drop to the bottom of the claimants, and may lose all they have title to. Debt holders, who had little influence over company practices, rise to the top and may seize everything. Thus a corporate reorganization can entail some form of "betrayal," especially if shareholders are stripped of their property and esteem or if the rights of lenders to enforce collection are blocked.

Abitibi's dire straits had compelled the different investor groups to withhold demands, but as a renascence became tangible in 1937 each sought to influence how the distribution of the corporate remains occurred. All became preoccupied with estimates, appraisals, computations, and seemingly endless recalculations of figures, ratios, proportions, and statistical reckonings. A trickle of ideas became a river of suggestions, modified proposals, and renegotiated amended plans. Each rested upon certain expectations about future earnings, as well as the prerogatives of specific interests. Each had complex terms that provided varying allocations. "With plans and more plans appearing from day to day, it has been difficult to follow them all," moaned one participant.[3] However, the company's status remained insufficient to guarantee a full return to all and they disagreed about what was available. The common shareholders opposed any reorganization. The bondholders, who differed over how they should be paid and how much others should receive, shattered into several factions. As if caught in a ritual dance, moves triggered responses with greater gyrations and higher emotions until everything whirled around and around, only to collapse. Legitimate disagreements, misperceptions, plots, and petty games poisoned relations among the participants. The year began with widespread expectations for a definitive resolution. It ended with a debacle that set the basis for a confrontation between the bondholders and the province as the case began to broaden from a matter of commercial insolvency into one of constitutional authority.

1. Hopes, squabbles, and plagiarism

With an understanding with the province apparently reached, Montreal Trust requested the Supreme Court of Ontario to recognize the terms of the bond mortgage and its rights as the trustee to enforce repayment. Lawyers for Abitibi and the bondholders filed a pro forma defence, which recounted the background of the receivership.[4] Trouble nonetheless unfolded as the agendas of the various interests diverged. Ripley and his colleagues moved forward with their own plans. They struggled to define a package that might garner approval from a majority of the debt holders. Two routes were available: a rearrangement of the finances of the existing firm and the appointment of acceptable executives, or a foreclosure via a judicial sale and the creation of a new company. Strachan Johnston had gone along with previous decisions, but as reorganization became imminent the lawyer distanced himself from the committee. As a solicitor for Montreal Trust, which was responsible for the bondholders as a class, from his perspective the simplest course of action was the traditional mechanism, a judicial sale, because it likely ensured a maximum return to the investors. He disagreed with Glyn Osler's growing desire to pursue the first option under OJAA, albeit via the guise of a judicial sale, a manoeuvre Johnston suspected was unconstitutional. Ward Wright, the attorney for the liquidator, was frozen out of the discussions but sought something for the common shareholders and general creditors. There was little chance with a judicial sale, but if it was blocked, a better settlement might be reached under the Corporate Creditors Adjustment Act.

Johnston and Wright wanted acknowledgement of Ripley and Osler (even though they had done all of the work), along with the bondholders' committee itself, excluded from any recognition in the tentative deal with the government. Only their own law firms should be given credit, Johnston asserted. A reference to the committee was an "unwarranted intrusion." In fact, although Montreal Trust held a legal right to Abitibi's assets under the bond deed, the Supreme Court of Ontario would never approve any deal the bondholders' committee and the receiver did also not sanction.[5] McPherson wanted a superior settlement for the shareholders even though a liquidator had little status in the legal proceedings. Under the Winding-Up Act, McPherson's role was defined narrowly: responsibility for the distribution of assets as part of a company's liquidation and even that duty unfolded under court order. Unlike a trustee in bankruptcy, he could not arbitrate or impose an outcome. He might propose a compromise. Neither the courts nor the secured creditors had to consider it. "He was only a party because he wanted to be, and succeeded in getting himself made a party, that he is not a necessary party and that his approval or signature can make no difference whatsoever to the reorganization of Abitibi," noted one attorney.[6]

Wright tried to block Clarkson from disclosing the consultants' reports, arguing that he and the liquidator had not participated in the appraisals. McPherson thought the assessments were stale-dated because they had been made a year earlier. Fearing their use might lead to a settlement that left the shareholders and general creditors with nothing, he wanted to ban the release of anything that estimated the company as worth less than $70 million. Muddying the waters further, Wright characterized the statement of defence by the bondholders as prejudicial for a fair trial. He moved to strike the committee and its members as parties to the case and asked that McPherson be named as Abitibi's defender in all further proceedings. This suggestion seemed reasonable to the Master of the Supreme Court, who had only dealt with minor cases. Without consulting precedents or reviewing the usual protocols, he granted the request, thereby forcing the committee and Montreal Trust into an appeal that took a month to overturn. The bickering sickened Ripley as a "perfectly foolish squabble."[7] Despite the tussle, several members of the bondholders' council did not realize that the liquidator opposed their plans. Walter Somerville still thought McPherson seemed friendly and indicated a willingness to meet with him.[8]

Expectations about the need for (and the terms of) a reorganization were conditioned by shifts of the competitive situation. The list price had hovered near $40 per ton since 1933, although fierce rivalry and secret concessions kept the true rates much lower. An upturn in demand began towards the end of 1935 due to growth in newspaper circulation and the conversion of magazines from book paper to less expensive newsprint. A year later Canadian mills operated on average at 80 per cent of capacity, achieving record levels of output, though most firms still had unprofitable operations.[9] Walter Somerville thought the marketing of newsprint remained "perfectly absurd" because the companies had not rejected the use of inter-locking price clauses.[10] Industry executives expected consumption to exceed supply within two years and the list rate to rise by $5 or more. The American Newspaper Publishers Association dismissed such forecasts as propaganda aimed at forcing premature sales. Lord Rothermere, in contrast, argued that even current demand could not be covered if prices remained below $50 rate. He characterized a rate of $57 in 1937 or $65 by 1939 as "not unusual or excessive" and insisted that without a major international disturbance a shortage was likely within five years. He thought a price jump might increase publishing costs by half, but then claimed this would trigger an "unavoidable" reduction in newspaper size so publishers could pay "the vastly increased cost."[11]

Charles Vining argued higher expenses absorbed any gains from the 1936 price advance. The interlocking clauses made it possible "for a single manufacturer by timidity, vanity or faulty judgment to be bullied, cajoled or bamboozled into a decision sealing the fate of the whole industry and for a whole year." A rate of $47.50, he contended, represented the real minimum level for an efficient producer. The sound course was to exercise moderation until conditions shifted to a seller's market. Producers, he cautioned, should not forget that prosperity carried the seeds of its own destruction.[12] Nonetheless, prices escalated in Europe and on the American Pacific coast, where a shortage of capacity already existed. Production in Canada mounted across the winter with new monthly records. Rates for the following year were usually set in the autumn, but in late March, no longer willing to put up with Great

Northern's obstruction and needing an adequate rate to end its losses, International Paper announced a $7.50 hike to $50 per ton for 1938. Within two weeks most American and Canadian producers adopted a similar stance, and almost all refused to accept interlocking clauses in their new contracts.[13] This development by itself could not affect 1937 earnings and, as the *Financial Post* acknowledged, there was "an element of doubt" about the ability to sustain the new level. Nonetheless, for the first time in seven years, the producers were able to garner significant new financing and the values of their securities escalated on stock exchanges. Clarkson could not resist claiming partial credit. It seemed obvious, he remarked, that the bondholders would get all of their money and accrued interest. The preferred shares had risen to three-quarters of their nominal market price. "This all means that the security holders of the Abitibi Company have, as a result of the receivership, recovered an enormous amount of money which looked as though it was lost, in 1932."[14]

Ripley advised the bondholders in late March about the consulting reports and negotiations with the government. With the company operating at higher capacity levels and a pending advance in the list price, a return to solvency appeared feasible, along with a full return of their principal and the arrears of interest.[15] The letter triggered the publication of numerous schemes for reorganization from enterprises not involved with the receivership. The business and popular press gave especial attention to pitches that originated from Wood Gundy, an underwriter for one of the 1928 preferred stock issues and a firm that held significant amounts of Abitibi securities in trust for clients.[16] Harry Gundy was convinced the bondholders would not deal fairly, and his company advanced proposals in three iterations, each intended to mobilize support by offering favourable terms for the other securities.

The initial version provided meagre information. It suggested the debt might be paid off by new bonds and a cash offer. To liquidate the accrued interest and the claims of creditors, Wood Gundy proposed a supplemental sale of debentures with an option that permitted their conversion into common stock. All securities were to be sold to Wood Gundy as a block, which would then place them on the market. The company expected an option on 200,000 common shares as part of any sales arrangement. Almost everyone dismissed this scheme because the new bonds were not going to be worth anything near the old. A second and more detailed proposal offered for $1,000 of bond principal a package comprised of new first mortgage bonds, convertible debentures, and some common stock. The three equity classes would be allowed to purchase part of a new issue of 1.3 million common shares, but Wood

Gundy suggested additional capital might have to be raised via another stock sale. Most parties also rejected this proposal as obviously insufficient.

A final proposal upped the ante by allowing for each $1,000 of principal a more substantive package: $600 in first mortgage bonds, $740 in "cumulative income" bonds, and convertibility for some securities based upon a complicated scale at different prices. New money would be secured through another debt issue in which the interest rates varied by maturity date and alternative rankings were given for liquidation of the securities. The share exchange in this third package favoured the preferred stockholders. Their shares were valued at a rate of forty-three times that of a common share, whereas they traded at seven times the value on the American exchanges. Abitibi's assets and revenues, Gundy proclaimed, could handle all claimants and leave something for the common shareholders. It was impossible to take a dim view of "prospective earning power" in a country like Canada.[17]

Through the winter and spring of 1937, Ripley provided the liquidator with copies of drafts as the bondholders and preferred shareholders talked about a possible plan. But McPherson advised Hepburn that any proposal should be deferred at least six months because "radical" and "astounding" market changes meant large-scale financing was unnecessary. Only $5 million in short-term money was required, he argued. Anything else should be done after Abitibi was taken out of receivership and a new board of directors became familiar with market conditions. The "present undoubted upward trend" meant a plan by the bondholders would discriminate against the equity investors. McPherson claimed the true value of the company exceeded $75 million. The shareholders therefore not only had a substantial stake but, with industrial improvement, "a constantly growing equity in the undertaking." They were entitled to majority ownership, whereas the bondholders would likely give them less than a quarter.[18] The government asked Ripley to work with the liquidator, but McPherson went into court demanding action on the Wood Gundy plan. He insisted that a reorganization must proceed under the CCAA. Then, without consulting anyone else, McPherson secured judicial authorization for formulating his own scheme. His proposal, released in mid-May, copied the final Wood Gundy iteration with a mix of first and second mortgage bonds for the debt holders, while preferred stockholders were offered common shares for their holdings and the accrued dividends. The common equity holders would receive 10 per cent of the new common shares. McPherson's plagiarism went beyond the Wood Gundy circular and was obvious to all. Ripley scathingly remarked how he had taken "one of our proofs" and inserted "many paragraphs deliberately copied, word for word" into his scheme. The stances hardened a week later when McPherson's lawyers submitted a motion challenging the validity of the bond mortgage. Thereafter Ripley refused to deal with McPherson "because I see every evidence that he is not trying to cooperate."[19]

Although technical matters often dominated the discussions, the bondholders' council rejected the Wood Gundy and McPherson schemes on several grounds. First, they ignored the findings of the engineering surveys and, as discussed later in this chapter, were predicated upon highly imaginative estimates of future earnings. The requirements for new money or working capital were downplayed. Second, the proponents provided minimal, if any, documentation either about the fixed charges or about Abitibi's ability to handle them. The proposals required new issues of serial bonds. A specified proportion of this type of debt had to be liquidated annually, a provision that increased the annual payments and required a system to determine which certificates got paid off first. Investors usually perceived this type of scheme to be less attractive. Third, the ability of investment bankers to sell the securities or of purchasers to implement sophisticated features (such as convertibility into common stock) was, at best, dubious. Given previous unpleasant experiences with newsprint securities, bonds and stocks now had to be near the true value of assets, not pie-in-the-sky notions. For example, under McPherson's plan, the second mortgage bonds had an option that allowed their conversion to common stock. If the securities were sold at par Abitibi needed assets worth $111 million to make a $25 subscription price for common shares operative; $117 million at $30; and $129 million at $35. Fourth, the theoretical worth of the existing securities became a concern once detailed calculations were done. For instance, under the terms of McPherson's plan, each old share of 7 per cent preferred stock had a market value of $39. Under the scheme later advanced by Ripley's committee, it was $64.85. Wood Gundy's desire to reserve sales to itself and extract a cut as the underwriter was dismissed as a snatch.[20]

Ripley expected the major stakeholders to agree that the central issues were the need to bring the company out of receivership and to do it soon. The *Financial Post* thought both were unlikely. "The Abitibi scramble has just started" because negotiations and legal disputes could prove lengthy, it concluded.[21] The government's imposition of a twelve-month limit for the approval of a proposal might entice other interests to slow the process, either to force concessions or gain a return to solvency without changing the financial structure. The original owners of Mattagami Pulp and Paper pursued this option in 1925 but failed. Abitibi's common shareholders now declared a willingness to fight to the highest courts. The architect of their efforts was Collin Brooks, who supposedly had just arrived in Toronto to write about Canadian society. An author of poetry and over two dozen books in fiction, finance, and economics, Brooks was the editor of the *Sunday Dispatch*, the weekend newspaper of the *Daily Mail* chain. His real mission was to safeguard the interests of Viscount Rothermere. He was "Lord Rothermere in Canada in the sense that Lord Tweedsmuir is the King of Canada," one pundit smirked. Some observations were scathing because it was impossible to separate the press baron's business interests from his hard-right politics. In the 1920s his editorials in the *Daily Mail* lauded Benito Mussolini. As the Depression worsened, this orientation broadened into endorsements for Oswald Mosely's Union of Fascists, the promotion of appeasement, and personal friendships with Nazi leaders. Brooks, one writer sneered, was really an agent for "Britain's Public Hitlerite No. 1."[22]

He acted, nonetheless, as an eloquent spokesman for those who believed in "the sanctity of equities" and whatever value survived in Abitibi shares. Real and moral ownership always resided with the equity investors, Brooks remarked. Those who owned bonds had legitimate claims to interest arrears "and in due course when the time is ripe to their principal if they want it. Beyond that, they have no right." He dismissed as "nominal and certainly debateable" any claims that Abitibi's worth must reflect balance sheet values. Brooks claimed the company's failure originated from "outside interests": American publishers who forced prices "down to a grossly uneconomic figure." However, with the industry in apparent recovery, he now advanced his own alternative fantasy. Abitibi had entered "a phase of such prosperity" that reorganization was unnecessary and might lead to foreign control. With newsprint at $50 and a "roaring price" for pulp, the firm might earn up to $14 million in 1938, sufficient to pay the bond interest, preferred dividends, and a small common dividend. "If you have a company making profits at that rate it can buy itself out of the present mess." Abitibi should emerge from receivership "in a business-like way" with the equity holders in control. Only minor actions were required such as new second mortgage bonds to cover the interest arrears and allow "a quicker chance of dividends." The debt might even be liquidated by selling more securities. Press commentators familiar with Abitibi treated these assertions as make-believe. A solution similar to Price Brothers (where new bonds paid off the debt holders) required $63 million, well beyond anyone's capabilities. The projections of future earnings were based upon "intangible factors." Even if they proved true, the chance of any dividends was remote.[23]

Brooks cultivated a relationship with Mitch Hepburn, began organizing a common shareholders protective committee, and enlisted Arthur Roebuck (no longer in the provincial assembly) as his solicitor. Stories planted in newspapers foretold a pulp mill boom akin to the 1920s as "the cellulose age" fostered an "industrial revolution" with new types of plastics and textiles.[24] Brooks offered his backing to any scheme that provided a positive outcome for the shareholders or deflected reorganization. The third version of the Wood Gundy proposals was likely written to gain his support. With heavy publicity, a Toronto investment company offered to raise new money for ending the receivership but unknown to most observers Brooks sponsored the scheme. The bizarre proposal revolved around distributing warrants for convertible debentures and doubling the common stock. The former would pay off the interest arrears and once solvent Abitibi could issue more debt. Despite a claim that the bondholders would be fully compensated the new securities offered far less than the worth of their holdings. Indeed, the scheme required raising the debt from $48.3 million to $75.9 million, though it was argued that the new debentures offered "elasticity to the capital structure," since they might be converted into common stock. A table projected hypothetical earnings if Abitibi achieved a price-to-earnings ratio of twelve times, but the investment firm suggested the ratio "might rise to 15 or 20 times," a silly notion even in the 1920s.[25]

Roebuck defined his role as a vigorous defender of small investors. Convinced the bondholders were the epitome of soulless financial interests, he never perceived any dissonance that the payments for his services, "refreshers," came from Rothermere, another corporate behemoth. The former attorney general worked with McPherson and had Brooks and Gundy appointed as inspectors who would assist in an asset distribution.[26] Roebuck was a marginal player in the legal proceedings, but he sharpened the growing acrimony with petty games and his snide comments. During court sessions he besmirched Ripley by stressing how National City had been the subject of a Senate investigation. Roebuck opposed the participation of the preferred shareholders' committee by arguing it held "trifling" amounts of stock and therefore the representation had a "frail character." The four largest shareholders retained less than a third of the preferred equity, whereas Wood Gundy had more in its own right. It was a popular, but totally false, belief. The securities were held in trust. Wood Gundy had few voting rights of its own. The firm's real importance lay in Harry Gundy's extensive connections. Roebuck also threw out ideas about how the rights of the bondholders' committee under the deposit agreement somehow had expired. These efforts went nowhere but they indicated the shape of things to come. A tour de force in negotiation and financial statesmanship was necessary for a successful compromise, the *Globe and Mail* observed. With wide differences among the investors, it divined a portentous future of "tedious and protracted court struggles which will prevent any group getting either interest or dividends until they are concluded in one, two or three years."[27]

2. All interests asunder

Meanwhile, behind closed doors, "the real moves on the chess-board" occurred as Ripley's group constructed its own proposal.[28] The issue, in his view, was "clear cut as between right and wrong." The committee planned to give "Abitibi to the people who own it" – the bondholders. The other schemes took "a slice out of it for somebody else."[29] Negotiating an arrangement, however, proved difficult. All debt holders expected the recovery of the principal and accrued interest, but Ripley wanted a deal that the preferred shareholders' committee, chaired by Herbert Molson, could co-sponsor. He therefore advised the bondholders' council to make concessions that recognized their interests. The negotiators, however, could not risk releasing information beyond a narrow range of confidants, which precipitated intense speculation about what might emerge. They also worked with a serious disadvantage: a detailed knowledge of the complexities of Abitibi's operations. One participant characterized the engineering report as "bigger than a family Bible and weighing several pounds."[30] Moreover, although the province said it was willing to finalize resource rights, Hepburn would not act until he reviewed the bondholders' plan and received assurances about new capital for rehabilitating the properties. The premier refused to announce "a tentative basis of agreement" until mid-May, five months after the original understandings. Even then, he suggested, there were "reservations." As the documents went through successive drafts, other officials tried to alter accepted matters or to rephrase clauses. Ripley hence kept counselling those who made enquiries about how it was impossible to finalize asset values or issue a valid plan. A deal might be a deal, but *only* when it was signed and sealed.[31] Confidential copies of the arrangement with the province were submitted for judicial review early in June even though the government still stalled. Hepburn's carousing buddy, Arthur Slaght, who represented dissident preferred shareholders, tried to persuade him against signing. The premier did not approve the documents until the end of the month, and

only after ministry officials advised Heenan how the delay was coun-
terproductive. Approval of any reorganization proposal rested with the
courts, they noted, so the government's view was irrelevant.[32]

The committee's plan went through more than seventeen iterations.
Each version floundered once they got down to specific terms: the
amount of new capital, types of bonds, interest rates, the convertibility
of securities, the timing of subscription rights if warrants were issued,
and the prices or profit levels necessary for certain provisions to become
active. Ripley's committee decided by the spring of 1937 that a judicial
sale under the OJAA was the only means of preventing others from
overturning a proposal. The Molson committee was ambivalent and
wanted greater thought about how the CCAA might be employed. But
it would not pursue the one course of action that could render the need
for a judicial sale moot: raise sufficient money for paying the bondholders off in cash. When a judicial sale occurred, it was possible to void the
claims from unsecured creditors, but the representative committee
agreed upon a maximum of $750,000 for recompense, a more than ade-
quate sum. Ripley, however, would not issue a "blank cheque" to
McPherson since, two years after his appointment, the liquidator had
still not provided estimates of the creditor claims. Ripley and his colleagues were uninterested in how new common stock might be distributed; "all we care about is the total," he insisted, which should not be
excessive. To satisfy Molson's committee, they accepted the idea that
more new equity could be issued but stressed this did not guarantee
any compensation for the old shareholders.[33]

By late April the negotiators reached a consensus about a "Midway
Plan" that originated from Molson's committee. Given Clarkson's estimates, approximately $14 million in new money was required, but with
markets still recovering from the Depression, the debt could not be sold
unless it was secured by a lien against Abitibi's assets. Under normal
circumstances, the bondholders would have had their original holdings
replaced by new securities backed by a first mortgage. Instead, the
Midway Plan proposed the use of alternative types of debt instruments:
income bonds and debentures. The bondholders were also to receive
common shares as part of the compensation package. Seven-eighths of
the new equity was scheduled for allocation among the current shareholders, but only if they exercised subscription rights for the new stock.
The preferred committee felt that they should get something even
though it doubted whether the shares had "any value other than that of
a nuisance value." Ripley acknowledged that the Midway Plan was not
"entirely fair" because they could not sell new securities anywhere near
the nominal value of the old. Whether this might occur in the future

was just speculation. The real issue, therefore, was how much they had to yield, "which cannot possibly be defined by figures. It gets down to a question of broad judgment."[34]

The release of the Gundy and McPherson plans upset the negotiations, which had reached a delicate stage as the bondholders and preferred shareholders tried to settle their differences. Ripley issued a statement that characterized the proposals as unacceptable, but their publication forced the premature finalization of a plan, even though there were questions about whether it could garner sufficient support. Walter Somerville warned that it might be necessary to "sweeten the packet" because the terms looked as if they were shaving the bondholders closely.[35] Wood Gundy was certain to enlist dissidents against anything endorsed by the Molson committee. Some preferred shareholders opposed a judicial sale because the option did not guarantee a high payback. Rush meetings ensued, accompanied by a round-robin aimed at collecting signatures of concurrence. Numerous items were postponed so the proposal could be released. The missing items included the composition of the board of directors and a designation of the underwriters. The negotiators accepted most requests from Molson's group, including a longer time for the preferred shareholders to exercise warrants, a higher number of new shares for each old share, and (fatefully) a last-minute change of the official title to a "Plan of Sale of Assets and Reorganization" since it entailed a share exchange.[36]

Ripley and his colleagues would not grant approval until the preferred committee signed off. Just as its members were about to ratify McPherson contacted them about "a wonderful Plan which he was about to submit." Although the liquidator's earlier proposal was widely derided, the committee recommended a postponement to see what this contained, but contrary to expectations McPherson did not submit it quickly. An exasperated Ripley wondered "whether they want to support our Plan or do something else." After several days of delay, McPherson arrived for a conference but refused to submit his proposal (even though the members of Molson's committee were among the investors he represented), whereupon they approved the bondholders' plan subject to their rights to offer amendments or later recommend another proposal.[37] McPherson then met with Ripley and claimed he would supply a copy of his plan in exchange for that of the bondholders. A discussion about the Judicature Act, subscription warrants, and the amount of new money necessary for Abitibi highlighted their irreconcilable disagreements. McPherson then declared there was little value in an exchange given their perspectives. A subsequent understanding for a swap fell through when McPherson unilaterally released his version to the media.[38]

A short document couched in legalese, McPherson's latest scheme, a "compromise or arrangement" to be conducted under the CCAA, was convoluted. Once again, it was not supported by an explanation of how the components were determined, the reasons for investors to accept the terms, or the company's ability to manage the new structure. Nor in succeeding months did the liquidator explain any of those topics, although the scheme favoured the common shareholders. Each $1,000 of bond principal and the accumulated arrears was to be exchanged for $600 of new first mortgage bonds, $700 of new second mortgage bonds, fractional bond warrants that might buy additional second mortgage bonds, and $1.25 in cash. The 7 per cent preferred shareholders were offered five new common shares for each existing share, the 6 per cent holders were given 4.5 shares for each one, and the common equity holders were to receive one-fifth of a share and common stock purchase warrants for each one. This meant a capital structure with $73.7 million of debt and up to 3.5 million common shares (see Appendix 7). McPherson claimed it ensured $9 million of new capital, but how it would do so was as clear as mud. A quarter of the first mortgage securities paid a lower interest rate and took the form of serial bonds.[39]

While he had a right to advance a proposal, the liquidator did not understand that he could not force its consideration. Only Montreal Trust, as their trustee, could compel a meeting of bondholders. McPherson's lawyer told Hepburn the compromise protected all parties. The premier, however, dismissed the liquidator's request for a talk.[40] When copies were sent to Abitibi's investors, the *Globe and Mail* wondered whether they might "fall in line." Ripley countered with a withering denunciation. The proposal, he argued, did not provide sufficient capital, imposed excessive fixed charges, did not specify mechanisms that prevented a dilution of security values, and charged excessive prices for warrants. Serial bonds made sense for a utility with steady earnings, he legitimately noted, but not a resource company exposed to market fluctuations. A default on bond interest could put the firm back into receivership. McPherson's plan compounded that risk with heavy sinking fund obligations. It also made the liquidator the sole person who could select new directors, a demand that ignored a simple issue: only one group held legal sway over Abitibi and it did *not* share power.[41]

The public critique, however, paled against a private analysis prepared by Milton Cross, which mapped how the preferred shareholders were certain to have a worse outcome under McPherson's latest scheme versus the one he had published in May. The owners of common stock appeared to benefit, albeit very, very slightly. In any event, the latest proposal was contingent upon the willingness of investors to exercise proffered warrants at the conversion prices. For it to work, the total worth of the assets *had* to range from $111 million to $137 million.[42] Put simply, to give his scheme legitimacy McPherson needed a radically higher value for the assets. He secured court approval to commission yet another analysis. Based on theoretical tonnages and delivered prices, but without any explanation of how the estimates were reached, a consultant projected an annual income of $6.7 million and, via creative inflation, a company worth $86 million. This still was insufficient, so McPherson requested a follow-up from another specialist. This time, the liquidator's forecasts were dismissed as unreasonable and the consultant refused permission to publish his report about the value of Abitibi's assets, owing to "the difficulty of properly interpreting such a hypothetical figure."[43]

Strachan Johnston submitted "the Ripley plan of reorganization" to Justice Charles McTague in mid-July and requested authorization for a bondholder meeting in October under the terms of the OJAA. McPherson's attorneys, in opposition, derided the Judicature Act as an intrusion into federal jurisdiction over bankruptcy and they countered with demands for meetings of all security classes under the CCAA. But after four hours of arguments McTague granted Johnston's motion, subject to the caveat that the liquidator could renew his application five days after the bondholders met.[44] The last iteration of the Ripley plan, when published a week later, marginally adjusted the Midway drafts. It sanctioned an issue of $14 million in first mortgage bonds to cover capital expenditures and provide working capital. The settlement for the debt holders comprised three elements that were well understood by financial experts but would have seemed mysterious to an average citizen. A $24.1 million issue of "general and refunding" mortgage bonds covered $500 of the principal for each $1,000 bond. Another $33.8 million in income debentures was deemed equivalent to $700 for the principal and accrued interest. Those securities contained a feature that permitted their conversion into common stock. The balance of the compensation took the form of common shares allocated at the rate of five per $1,000 bond or 241,335 in total. The committee again indicated it had no interest in how the balance of 1.4 million common shares might be distributed, but the plan suggested five new shares for each 7 per cent share, 3.5 for one for the 6 per cent shares, and one-tenth for the commons. The equity groups had fifteen months to buy two million more shares via subscription warrants.[45]

Control of the management was essential for success and Ripley's committee was never going to let McPherson determine the selection of directors. During the winter of 1937, the members discussed possible appointments, including the receiver and the chair himself, although much of this unfolded less as serious appraisals than as inter-mutual commendations about the work conducted in the preceding five years. The plan designated the bondholders with the right to elect eight "Class A" directors (versus seven "Class B" directors by the shareholders) annually for seven years or until the debenture issue decreased to $3 million. The negotiators hit an impasse in May about how and when this should be done. Ripley thus ordered the deletion of any references to individuals when the plan was published, though they needed "some platform in respect to management." They chose to keep most of the operating managers in place but decided financiers must dominate the board to prevent another default. As we have seen, this was a normal practice. The early discussions considered the retention of George Mead but that notion was soon dropped. The "Class A" slate ultimately comprised Clarkson; the committee's attorney, Glyn Osler; Andrew Fleming from the Molson committee; William Smith, the assistant managing director; most of the bondholders' council (Reid, Ripley, and Somerville); and a new president and Hepburn friend, George Cottrelle, from the Bank of Commerce.[46]

Members of the representative committee were assigned investors to lobby and they received detailed memoranda that cross-compared plans and provided answers to the questions that might be raised. All bondholders received a discussion paper by Ripley. It sought to show how reorganization under the plan allowed the management to adopt "progressive policies" and rebuild morale "from a condition of uncertainty." Approval also was legitimated as the sole means by which a renewal of resource rights could be ensured. Ripley cunningly added a remark about how Hydro had substantial claims related to OPS, a dangling inference that a rejection might reactivate them. The bulk of the discussion mapped the new financial structure, which was characterized as conservative. Professional advisors insisted that the securities bearing fixed interest charges should not exceed $40 million and therefore, after allowance for the first mortgage bonds, the general refunding bonds were capped at $24 million. The income debentures were not secured against the assets. They only paid interest if the company's profits were sufficient and had no provisions for the payment of arrears – constraints that minimized the risk of a new default. The convertibility of the securities supposedly offset the risk of long-term losses since Abitibi's equity would appreciate as its performance strengthened. The plan had obvious strengths: reduction of the fixed charges; a simplified structure; adequate working capital; a provision for legal judgments; and full payment to the general creditors.[47] The *Compilation of Statements and Information* mapped how the engineering studies assessed properties and determined physical value or production levels, which indicated the anticipated capital requirements and earnings. Those who later came out in opposition often ignored this data and based their arguments upon broad principles or mere speculation. For while Ripley and his associates couched their presentations in dispassionate terms about what was sensible, the approach had a basic flaw – it ignored context.

In the spring output by Canadian mills achieved higher levels. Journalists confidently predicted a seller's market unless economic recovery was somehow halted. Some executives expected higher costs would absorb at least a third of the price advance scheduled for 1938 but demand growth proffered short-tonnage companies like Abitibi significant gains.[48] But the signs of a recession emerged by the early summer and a few analysts cautioned that the existing production levels were not sustainable. Most, however, believed that pent-up demand ensured further growth. A circular by R.O. Sweezey & Co. was typical. It forecast a "progressive increase" in consumption and higher prices.[49] The inventories of Canadian mills dropped to record lows as firms diverted to the American market tonnage previously shipped overseas. Publishers still purchased contracted monthly quotas even though advertising lineage declined. By late summer, despite the forecasts published by firms like Sweezey's, it was well understood that advance buying was propping up demand. As American newspapers tried to soften the impact of the 1938 price increase, their stocks of newsprint, which usually amounted to 28 days of supply, rose from the equivalent of 36 days in May to 59 days in August, the highest level since 1924. But many producers dismissed the risk posed by this trend. They believed shortages and price escalations in foreign markets, along with announcements about the construction of mills in the southern American states, indicated a boom era had returned.[50]

Abitibi earned $1.2 million in 1936 and Clarkson thought the annual earnings might reach $5 million (the first strong performance since 1927) but others began disseminating rosier projections. The press repeated but never fact-checked those claims. The bondholders' council believed the trumping was misleading at best, fabulist at worst. Anticipating a higher price for 1938, a "responsible group" declared that Abitibi could make $14 per ton or $8.4 million in profits. Wood Gundy claimed that the 1938 earnings under its proposals ranged from $8.1

million before depreciation to $9.9 million *after* interest and deprecia-
tion. McPherson accepted these conjectures as truth. Investment dealer
Ward Pitfield declared that Abitibi's performance during the summer
augured well. The securities offered "speculative and investment
merit" and if the list price rose to $55 per ton even the Espanola mill
became viable. Pitfield's analysis, the most detailed, covered a range of
output levels and generated earnings forecasts that varied from $9.7
million to $14.7 million in 1938, with even the lowest level allowing
profits that averaged $17.63 per ton.[51] Most of those who opposed the
bondholders' plan accepted such estimates, which soon became
mirages.

Viewed retrospectively, all of the forecasts began with a basic error –
the authors assumed Abitibi reaped the list rate based upon sales in
New York, whereas actual revenues were garnered *after* the deduction
of transport costs, which were $8 per ton or higher depending upon a
mill's location. Though the official list rate in 1936 was $41.50, Abitibi's
realized sales on newsprint averaged $32.96. Thus, even at a $50 rate,
the net profits were insufficient to cover the bond interest, let alone the
preferred dividends or any arrears. The estimates similarly presumed
that a spike in sulphide pulp prices during the winter was permanent,
even though anyone familiar with the industry knew the commodity
experienced sharp fluctuations. Every one of the forecasts assumed that
Abitibi operated *throughout the year with every mill at full capacity*, something it had *never* achieved. The "responsible group" based its estimates
upon a capacity rate of 600,000 tons annually, Gundy, upon a range
from 550,000 to 750,000 tons. Abitibi's mill managers appraised the theoretical maximum output at 535,000 per year but believed 440,000 tons
was the best the firm could actually achieve. Greater output could only
be secured if $6.6 million in capital expenditures resolved the problems
that resulted from obsolescence and deferred maintenance. To make
600,000 tons or more required the restoration of the Espanola and Sturgeon Falls mills. Espanola required $1.1 million just to become opera-
tional and another $2.7 million for proper modernization.[52] The
improvements would take several years to complete. McPherson and
the dissidents ignored another inconvenient fact: provincial acquiescence was contingent upon $14.3 million in new capital. In short, the
authors of the estimates had visions of sugar plums, whereas economics served cold gruel.

Moreover, with the North American economy convalescing from the
Depression, a wave of restructuring efforts unfolded in 1937. Many
entailed acrimonious disputes such as had occurred with Canada
Steamships, Nova Scotia Steel, and Gypsum, Lime, and Alabastine

north of the border, or with Brown Company, Missouri Pacific, and Standard Gas to the south. Congressional investigations into corporate activities, a feature of American public life since 1932, continued to unearth questionable behaviour, chicanery, and outright fraud. For instance, a Senate enquiry documented how Kuhn Loeb surreptitiously liquidated shares just before a railroad filed for reorganization. Assertions that no wrongdoing had occurred fell upon unsympathetic ears. "It looks as if insider knowledge paid. Kuhn Loeb certainly knew what it was doing," snapped the committee chair, Missouri Senator Harry Truman.[53] An investigation of protective committees by the Securities and Exchange Commission generated a massive report that chronicled a seemingly infinite number of abuses.[54] A government sensitive to reasonable expectations from investors, a lawyer for the agency told the American Bar Association, could no longer tolerate the prevailing attitudes towards corporate restructuring. Business had endorsed an "entrepreneurial philosophy which has caused the virtual disappearance of the ancient standards for trustees." Commissioner William O. Douglas went further, declaring a need for sweeping changes that included the elimination of conflicts of interest and devious techniques. Despite dogged opposition from the financial sector, new legislation was passed that the *Wall Street Journal* derided as "meddlesome lawmaking" and "a gratuitous invitation to tax collectors to cause futile complications and delays."[55] The Chandler Act and the Trust Indenture Act overhauled the process of corporate reorganization. The statutes eliminated the equity receivership technique, imposed significant constraints on financiers and other vested interests, expanded court control, mandated the selection of neutral trustees, and outlined new procedures for how restructuring was proposed, confirmed, and consummated. Though most participants in the Abitibi battle were not familiar with the details of those revisions, as subjects of regular press coverage they constituted an important backdrop and were sometimes cited to legitimate arguments.[56]

Many press reports acknowledged Ripley's committee held a tactical advantage by going under the OJAA even though a wave of litigation might result. Most newspapers maintained a neutral stance, with reviews of the different plans along with the arguments of proponents and opponents. Several journals made sharp observations. The *Wall Street Journal* deemed a "revamping" of Abitibi of "vital import." The *Globe and Mail* emphasized the areas of agreement. While everyone agreed the bondholders were owed full compensation, the major issue was widely perceived as the treatment of the equity holders. Disputes over the amount of new money, one paper contended, were a matter of "deciding whether the company should owe the bank or owe the bond-holders." The volume of new shares if the subscription warrants were fully exercised troubled the *Globe and Mail*'s financial editor. The *London Financial News* characterized the "very full capitalization" envisaged by the Ripley plan as regrettable, but inevitable. It doubted how the new common shares ever could be worth more than $17.50, the asking price. Even the existing shares, which sold in the market for $5.37, seemed "grossly overvalued."[57]

To no one's surprise, McPherson and Brooks declared opposition but other dissident investors emerged within days. The plan, some bondholders argued, expected them to take a subordinate position versus the securities that provided new working capital. This left them with two options: accept a diminished status indefinitely or convert their holdings into common stock. A Winnipeg group formed a protest committee and argued, instead, the terms were too gener-ous by allowing a fifteen-month "option" period in which the equity holders could exercise warrants. Convinced this would create uncer-tainty about the company's ownership, they wanted the time reduced to three months. The bondholders should also have purchase rights for stock at the same rate as equity investors. Many dissidents believed newsprint demand ensured Abitibi's 1937 earnings before depreciation and taxes would almost cover the interest on the exist-ing bonds. Further advances in the following two years might allow preferred dividend payments. Some became convinced Abitibi was nearly at a stage where it could return to normal operations, except for an agreement on how to cover arrears and creditor claims. Under this scenario, an infusion of new money appeared excessive. One English investor insisted the firm could be left alone for a year to "work out its salvation" and repay everyone without the costs and injustice associated with reorganization. With the industry on the verge of great profits, it seemed unreasonable "to have a long-awaited redemption torn away." Under the Ripley plan, the "eventuality of receiving dividends may be almost relegated to eternity." Dissident preferred holders doubted whether small investors could raise the capital needed for exercising warrants. A failure to pay the total of $33 million might diminish their group's ultimate stake from three-fifths to less than a third of the equity. Fifteen months was too short a period for exercising the warrants, they insisted, because there was little chance the firm could achieve its full earnings within that time frame. The common stockholders argued they were denied a "fair share" because the promised equity position was negligible. Others disliked specific provisions such as the right of the bondholders to hold directorships for eight years, which some characterized as a breach of company law.[58]

With an election scheduled for October, the province tried to stay out of the disputes but the premier was lobbied to assume a stronger role. He should remember, a Liberal importuned:

> When a company like Abitibi goes into receivership it has been custom for years for the receiver to keep everything about that company a deep dark secret. We get to think this is quite all right because it has always been done. Actually there is no dirtier trick played by the capitalist on the little security holder … He gets nothing while the big fellow tires him out of his holdings. From time to time the receiver frightens him with some non committal or discouraging remarks. And finally when the receiver's companions and insiders have all they want the company is shown to have been making a lot of money for a long time. This has developed into such a racket in the states that one of the [corporate] secretaries said the other day he could see no reason why a receivership should last an ordinary lifetime.[59]

Another writer asked the premier to see that justice was done "and not all for the party with money." He hoped "Messrs. Wood Gundy or others who have purchased the stock for a few dollars, will not be allowed to get away with high way robbery, having already made money on the original investment, and wish to make another killing in the reorganization, at the expense of the unfortunate." Others pressed for local gains while the province still had leverage, such as a Sturgeon Falls clerk who wanted the mill reopened, saying that "we should hit the iron while it is hot." When he responded, Hepburn typically noted the "remarkable progress" that had occurred but then stated that the matter was a subject for the courts and that correspondents should "understand how helpless we are at the moment." He avoided public references to the reorganization but continued to excoriate George Henry over the Abitibi Canyon scandal.[60]

Ripley feared what might happen if they did not gain adequate support but assumed there was every reason for confidence. The Molson committee represented a third of the preferred shares. Most of the balance was deposited in trust with the liquidator. The co-sponsorship by the Molson committee was highlighted during the plan's release even though the preferred shareholders could not vote. At the end of August, it declared the proposal sounder than any other option and dismissed projections of high earnings as unrealistic. The committee rejected the idea that Abitibi might perform its way back to solvency as ridiculous.

Future earnings could not repay the $28 million of accrued interest and dividends. Wood Gundy, which proclaimed itself as the *true* guardian for the preferred holders, immediately denounced the statement.[61]

Approximately $16.4 million, a third of the bond principal, was deposited with Montreal Trust and a vote representing $24.1 million constituted a clear majority. Most of the deposited bonds were represented on Ripley's committee and it requested proxies from other owners. The largest holders were consulted during the preparation of the plan and could be counted on for support: Sun Life, the single biggest, held $5 million; the Dominion Mortgage and Investments Association (which represented major investors and other life insurance companies) influenced $7.2 million; the British Association of Investment Trusts, finally, could shape the proxies for another $4 million. These groups placed the favourable vote near $20 million. The holdings of loan and trust companies were never disclosed but amounted to at least $1.8 million, of which three-quarters were owned by the firms themselves, and the balance was kept in trust. Many of the biggest investors had already written down their holdings. On average, the Canadian life insurance companies appraised their bonds at three-fifths of the declared par value. The settlement terms would let them recoup that book value and maybe more.[62] Large British investors confirmed their acceptance and indicated an unwillingness to make further concessions. The Dominion Mortgage and Investment Association endorsed the proposal after Somerville gave an impassioned plea about the repercussions that could happen with a rejection. Reid similarly contacted major investors. "So far I have heard of no company intimating reluctance to approve the Ripley Plan."[63]

Resistance, nonetheless, mounted from several directions. During the spring Ripley met with Herbert Symington and I.W. Killam of Royal Securities, which owned at least $3 million that originated from the Mattagami purchase. The initial sessions were friendly but Royal Securities had never participated in the negotiations with the preferred shareholders and the meetings took place just as the conferees reached a basic agreement. Symington believed success required support from the other investor groups. Unlike Ripley, the lawyer thought in political terms, "a question of a shift here and a shift there to try and satisfy people." He conceded everything was contingent upon the estimates of earnings but thought the engineering reports were too low. Those from Wood Gundy and others were excessive "although a great many people think anything is possible in newsprint these days." Symington relied upon information submitted to the Banker's Committee earlier in the decade, which Ripley deemed "general and indefinite." The discussions that followed descended into abstruse disagreements over the types, terms, and sale prices of debt instruments. Ripley was irritated by suggestions that they could be sold at higher prices or that only simple interest-bearing bonds should be utilized. He insisted that convertible securities were required even though they were somewhat speculative because the conversion option had to be "within reasonable distance from the market." To his frustration, Symington still sought amendments when the final proofs for the plan were reviewed. Symington even suggested that the committee should let the liquidator take credit and publish it as his own. "All of which ... I found a little difficult to agree with," Ripley snarled. Symington and Killam thus remained dissatisfied, convinced superior terms should be offered. When the plan was published Royal Securities, quite conspicuously, declined to endorse it.[64]

The cautions from Lord Rothermere never were taken seriously. Ripley thought the press magnate would change his mind once he understood the entire situation. The financier reminded Rothermere about the government's demand for a prompt reorganization and insisted that his committee was not advancing a "promoting scheme." Symington, during his discussions with Ripley, had noted the lack of an obvious leader for the common shareholders. He suggested that when the process reached a stage where a full agreement with other investors was necessary Rothermere might be approached. "It is only under such a circumstance that he will give a final decision." The views of Collin Brooks were little more than a camouflage for his boss.[65] This was a complete misread. The press lord continued acquiring Abitibi stock. He descended upon Toronto in September, ostensibly to study the paper industry, while proclaiming in speeches how the "cellulose age" could spur demand.[66]

Rothermere intervened by privately refusing to consent to anything not sanctioned by the liquidator. He derided the Ripley proposal as unjust and misleading because it ignored "tremendous strides" towards prosperity. Just as a new era of high profits beckoned, the bondholders would displace the equity holders. Abitibi may have been valued at $150 million in 1928, he blustered, but it was now was worth considerably more. Only the capacity for generating future profits should be considered and these would amount to $5.7 million for 1937 and $11.5 million for 1938. Abitibi owed just $16.5 million in arrears, but Ripley and his associates proposed to seize a company with strong earning power "to satisfy so relatively small a claim." The plan was hard on small investors who deserved "especial consideration." Accordingly "the only thing to do – and this will be done – is the contest, if it be necessary, through every Court in the Empire the legality of the Ripley Plan."[67] When his opposition was leaked to the press, the representative committee treated it as a declaration of war. Rothermere may have acquired a quarter of the common equity, Ripley answered, but this ranked junior to the debt and preferred shares on which $112 million were owed. The common shareholders were not entitled to dictate the terms. If the press baron was so sanguine about the future, he and his allies could discharge the bondholders' "relatively small claim" by paying it off in cash.[68]

During September the dissident bondholders coalesced into a "defensive committee" chaired by Sir Henry Drayton, a former finance minister and the president of Ward Pitfield's brokerage company. The members disagreed with two issues: the designation of first mortgage status for the securities that provided $14 million in working capital, and the conversion of the existing bonds into second mortgage or unsecured instruments. Instead, they argued, a "spectacular improvement" during recent months had so changed things that there was no reason why the bondholders should make "sacrifices."[69] They questioned the urgency for action since the firm was in recovery. Further government review was not necessary so long as Abitibi regained solvency within a year. The Ripley plan, they contended, was predicated upon a balance sheet more than ten months old and showed a "lack of foresight and imagination." Abitibi "may be technically bankrupt but in effect is not." It was always possible to postpone capital expenditures if the earnings did not meet projections.[70] Nonetheless, viewed with the luxury of hindsight, such arguments were patently unrealistic. The prices for Abitibi securities peaked in April and declined across the summer, which shrank the firm's market value from $89 million to $62 million. The onset of a recession precipitated a stock market collapse in late August and within two weeks newsprint manufacturers cut output, while publisher inventories skyrocketed.

A week before the scheduled meeting of bondholders the defensive committee published its own scheme (see Appendix 7). The key difference was an elimination of the prior lien bonds, which placed the debt after reorganization at $59.1 million versus $71.9 million in the Ripley plan. The capital was to comprise an issue of first mortgage bonds, a secondary class of income bonds that were convertible into common stock, and 2.1 million common shares of which approximately 15 per cent would go to the bondholders. Both plans offered analogous terms for the preferred and common shareholders, although Drayton's was slightly more generous, an aspect lauded by the press. Ripley publicly rejected what he considered a proposal that was submitted on short notice and relied upon "overly optimistic" notions. The dissidents presumed the improvements to mills and equipment could be carried out eventually, whereas his committee recognized the need for immediate action. Drayton responded with personal invective. Ripley "must shoulder a large proportion of the responsibility for any over over-optimistic estimates" since he was a vice-president at National City during the 1928 sale.[71] But the problems with this latest proposal went well beyond what contemporaries recognized. Drayton insisted Abitibi needed only $2 million for repairs and deferred maintenance. He ignored what was required just to sustain the mills due to the lack of capital investments for over six years. The defensive committee assumed additional funds could be raised through the sale of Provincial Paper and Ste. Anne. A list price for newsprint well above $50 per ton was essential for success but Drayton wishfully talked about a $62 rate similar to the mid-1920s. The proponents also ignored how pulp prices by August entered a free fall. The hasty preparation of the Drayton plan would have been evident to a careful reader. The published description of the proposed capital structure contained numerous errors. If its terms for warrants and conversion of securities were fully met, then another 400,000 common shares had to be issued. Nonetheless, since the proposal had a chance of derailing the Ripley plan, Wood Gundy and the stakeholders aligned with the liquidator chose to back the dissidents. Newspaper reporters eagerly anticipated a "battle of the ballots."[72]

3. Paying for the show

"One of the most imposing arrays of legal talent ever to attend a Canadian corporation meeting" assembled at the Royal York Hotel on the fifteenth of October. The same day the business sections of newspapers headlined cutbacks in newsprint production and forecasts of poor business for the next six months. Not only did the senior lawyers from each of the firms engaged by different groups of bondholders attend, but also others like those for Molson's committee, Harry Gundy, and the three Arthurs (Meighen, Roebuck, and Slaght). Approximately two-thirds of the bonds were represented.[73] Ripley introduced several amendments, which he hoped might assuage those who thought an infusion of capital was unnecessary. These sanctioned an accelerated debt reduction if excess earnings occurred. The new capital was also secured by a deed with a floating charge against the assets but, he claimed, did not modify the rights of the other bonds. Ripley unsuccessfully tried to mollify the critics by emphasizing how the amendments enhanced their "lien" and "security."[74]

The ensuing debate devolved into a split between those who held or represented large amounts of bonds versus those with small or moderate holdings. The opposition came predominantly from the latter and was voiced by representatives of the Drayton committee along with several prominent investors. Press accounts characterized their statements as "eloquent, vigorous, and substantial," although "angry, snappish, and nasty" constituted more apt adjectives. Drayton questioned the validity of the meeting and tried to force an adjournment, a proposal that was rejected, "although those voting for adjournment appeared to be almost as numerous as those voting against it." Drayton and his associates then denounced the proxies held by Ripley's committee, many of which dated to 1932, as "grave-yard" or "moth-eaten" votes and, reporters diplomatically noted, "other picturesque expressions of a somewhat similar nature." All of the opponents targeted the debentures intended to provide working capital. James Ralston, attorney for the defensive committee, argued the prior lien for the securities was unnecessary and excessive. The income bonds that formed the other major component were "neither fish, flesh, nor good herring." Ward Pitfield suggested Abitibi's improved earnings should torpedo the plan (which he derided as more a chemical formula rather than a reorganization) since the bondholders would be "sunk" by the rights associated with the debentures if hard times re-emerged. Dalton McCarthy promised lengthy litigation as the only guaranteed outcome and expressed little sympathy for bondholders who supported the plan but had written down the book value of their investments. Arthur Meighen did not possess bonds but clients of his investment trust had kept their securities. He denounced the "immediate concessions" the plan granted to the shareholders. The convertible debentures represented a $6 million "sacrifice" though the bondholders' money had carried the properties for five years and preserved any equity value. In his view, only the shareholders stood to benefit. Meighen contended that a favourable vote allowed Ripley to select the board. With investors scattered across North America, the firm was at the mercy of the directors he chose.

Herbert Symington blamed Abitibi's problems on the weather, this time international economic conditions. He questioned the OJAA's legality but stressed how the Ripley plan wiped out much of the equity. Instead, the shareholders should have a longer time to see if the company recovered or if they could raise sufficient capital to permit a return to solvency. His firm did not accept the Ripley and Drayton schemes as viable. Therefore he suggested a postponement that could allow negotiations with other investor groups. Ripley resisted this and similar proposals for delay, noting how more than forty-eight schemes had come under consideration in the preceding five years. He dismissed claims that he was autocratic and could not resist sarcastically remarking about how many present had not attended the 1935 meeting or were ever known to own bonds. Supportive statements about the Ripley plan received little coverage in news reports but were voiced by all of the major institutions, especially the life insurance companies. They described the convertible debentures as inexpensive and preferable to bank loans. Their arguments focused upon the need for sufficient funds to ensure that Abitibi did not default again. The plan, the treasurer of Sun Life declared, placed it on a solid foundation. Firms did not get into trouble if they had large amounts of working capital. A representative for Canada Life noted that the dissidents had never contributed to Abitibi's reconstruction, whereas the committee undertook a "noble effort."[75]

The outstanding bond principal amounted to $48.3 million. The meeting approved the Ripley plan by a vote of $23.9 million to $7.7 million. Royal Securities, the second-largest holder, abstained. Symington stated it wished to remain free of entanglements. The meeting closed with the election of the directors recommended by Ripley's committee. Some participants still hoped for a truce among the contending interests but there seemed little likelihood. "Legal costs on all sides will run high, noted the *Financial Post*, "and most of these are expected to be met out of the resources of Abitibi. Some shareholders feel they will be paying for the show."[76]

During the weeks leading up to the meeting, McPherson's lawyers filed a flurry of motions aimed at invalidating the bond mortgage. They unsuccessfully challenged the March ruling that overturned the Master of the Supreme Court's order appointing him as the defendant for Abitibi. They also failed to have the other interests removed as parties to the case. The key motion reiterated McPherson's previous claims and alleged Montreal Trust could not recover any funds because National City was a "dominant trustee." The true intent of the mortgage deed, they argued, subverted Canadian law by enabling National City to do business in Ontario. The bondholders, therefore, had no right to enforce the mortgage because it was invalid. If that was true, then they were not owed *any* money.[77] The attorneys for the bondholders countered by portraying McPherson as an ordinary litigant with no standing. Strachan Johnston, who noted the liquidator had never questioned the mortgage, was incredulous at the statement about whether the bondholders should collect. "That is an extraordinary defence for an office of

the court who has made affidavits admitting that $65,000,000 are due."
When Johnston, with court approval, sought to depose McPherson for
discovery, he refused to be sworn and argued that any statements might
prejudice the rights of the creditors and shareholders. Johnston and the
bondholders' attorneys then filed to commit McPherson "to the common gaol of the County of York for contempt," strike his motions, and
require that he pay his own legal bills. For further measure, they
demanded the production of all documents he had received, including
the correspondence with his lawyers.[78] McPherson's counsel resisted
disclosure, but under court order, a significant amount was submitted.
Abitibi's lawyers were hardly models of professionalism either. They
postponed the submission of a statement of defence until just before
the bondholder's meeting. When probed about the delay, one
remarked that it was "too big a matter to be made a public football."
Justice Kingstone snorted, "You are successfully making a football of
it now."[79]

The trial in late October was a one-day hearing with most of the facts
admitted by all. Strachan Johnston asked for a confirmation of the
mortgage's validity, while McPherson's barrister focused upon the
claim about National City. Kingston reserved judgment, but his ruling
the following month rejected the liquidator's assertions and characterized the assertion that National City was a trustee in Canada as stupid.
Diverging from the usual dry phrasing of judicial statements, Kingstone castigated McPherson's action as a farrago. Although the liquidator could submit matters to the court, he remarked,

> It is questionable, however, whether in such a case as this there is any
> real justification for the attack made on the validity of this mortgage on
> the grounds advanced by him. What good purpose is served by raising
> and pressing specious, narrow and technical objections to the legality of
> a document that, broadly speaking, has served the purpose of protecting
> millions of dollars of investors' money, and in which there is no sugges-
> tion of fraud or improper conduct on the part of anyone, is difficult to
> understand or appreciate.[80]

Three days before Kingstone's ruling, Strachan Johnston filed a
motion in Charles McTague's court for a sale under the Judicature Act.
It soon became apparent that everyone wanted to participate. On the
opening day of the hearing, more than a score of nationally known lawyers packed the room. With so many counsel present, McTague insisted
they designate only one to present each line of argument. Johnston
indicated he acted for Montreal Trust, the trustee, not as an agent of

Ripley's committee. On that basis, he outlined the bondholders' agreement, then moved a public sale in accord with the Ripley plan. McTague invited the opposition to present first. Dalton McCarthy argued the central questions revolved around how much money was needed and how it should be raised. Everyone agreed about the need for additional funds but the proposal was "extravagant." The OJAA, in any event, was not applicable because Abitibi, as an insolvent enterprise, was subject to federal law. The statute also applied only to an actual judicial sale, not a rearrangement or reorganization. Since things would be "a hopeless muddle" if they followed the process dictated by the Bankruptcy Act, McCarthy portrayed action under the CCAA as the logical solution.[81]

Clarkson, the sole witness called during the hearings, declared that Abitibi required a minimum of $11 million for plant improvements. The firm should come out of receivership even if economic conditions did not improve, he argued, because insolvency hampered even a basic ability to make strategic decisions. Clarkson insisted on remaining neutral, stating that he had not estimated whether the Ripley plan was fair but he doubted the bondholders ever were going to get 100 cents on the dollar. When pressed, the receiver refused to estimate future earnings or specify how they might be affected by provincial demands for manufacturing in specific locations regardless of the financial implications.[82]

Most of the lawyers followed McCarthy's lead. Gordon McMillan, McPherson's counsel, declared that the OJAA could not be used to alter a firm's capital structure. James Ralston, McCarthy's colleague, then harangued the court about how "the right of action cannot be destroyed by an act of the province of Ontario" and prophesied a stream of lawsuits if the convertible debentures were approved. The liquidator only got surplus monies once the bondholders were satisfied according to their own consciences. There was nothing to limit how much they might take. Arthur Meighen's statement was pure bombast. The plan was "the most indefensible proposal" ever brought before a court. It failed to reward the bondholders for their long wait and did not constitute full payment. The convertible feature of the debentures represented the "joker" in the deal. "Conversion is a delusion," he jibed. Since firms had good and bad years, the bondholders would not always be paid. If there was money in the treasury the company could meet its obligations, but in difficult times the debenture interest was forever lost. Indeed, "bookkeeper management" could allow the manipulation of the financial statements to accelerate the conversion of the securities.[83]

Arthur Roebuck was in the most curious position: expected to attack a piece of legislation he had sponsored two years earlier. He rationalized the act as a means for enforcing a mortgage and falsely claimed it facilitated discussions among investors and encouraged them to reach a moderate settlement by majority vote. Roebuck agreed sacrifices were appropriate when Abitibi first entered receivership, but no longer. The common shareholders were "being very badly used." Dropped to the bottom of the claimants, they had lost "nearly everything we ever possessed" and would "get only the crumbs that fall from the rich men's table." With a judicial sale the shareholders might receive little, whereas market demand and higher prices might soon allow the liquidation of all indebtedness. He said, "We would rather take our chances on that rather than accept this plan."[84]

Norman Tilley closed the hearing with a defence of the bondholders as the group with the most at stake and the ones who should have "the say." An expert in constitutional law, Tilley argued that federal and provincial legislation stood "side by side," not in contradiction. The Judicature Act never specified how a sale had to occur and left the method to those in charge. There was no requirement for a cash purchase. The plan was "a pretty fair arrangement." The equity investors were "lucky to get a fraction of a share. It is difficult to get the common stockholder in the picture at all." E.R. Long for the preferred shareholders concurred and likened the situation to a person buying for $8,000 a home once mortgaged for $10,000. "There is a feeling the $8,000 is not enough for the purchaser to pay."[85]

Among the members of the Supreme Court, Charles McTague had the most experience with corporate law. Although it was not his function to arbitrate or impose a settlement, he believed a reorganization should be undertaken only if the litigants agreed upon a package that satisfied everyone. "It may not be perfect, but it is better to have a living company than receivership," because any court ruling was likely to be appealed. When Glyn Osler countered that negotiations just delayed things further and that the case should be "pushed," McTague cautioned how it would move forward on the merits. The Ripley proposal was not flawless, Strachan Johnston noted. "There is nothing perfect on earth." Contradicting Roebuck, he acknowledged being the first author of the OJAA and insisted the suggestions about whether there had to be a sale for cash were irrelevant. Descending into an esoteric discourse, he contended the terms "reorganization" and "'reconstruction'" had neither commercial nor legal meaning and the CCAA was not designed for the situation. However, if Glyn Osler's "uncompromising attitude" continued he was prepared to withdraw the motion for approval of the

Ripley plan. "Common sense should be introduced in this matter." After sustained arguments, McTague adjourned the hearing, hoping for the best.[86]

Under the justice's direction, the lawyers signed a covenant pledging their discussions to strict confidentiality. Except when the McTague received reports in open court, press stories across the following month were just speculation that ranged from "settlement near" to "little progress." The central problem for the attorneys remained the matter of new capital. Osler insisted they should stick with estimates of future earnings from Clarkson rather than the claims from individuals who did not have actual knowledge about company operations. McCarthy deemed it inappropriate to sanction additional debt since no other producer was so burdened. If further loans proved necessary, the new securities would rank so low that they would "really not [be] in the picture at all." As the negotiations proceeded he backtracked and suggested they might delay until it was clear whether the optimistic forecasts had substance. As a result, the lawyers inched towards a solution that hinged upon providing a reorganized firm the right to issue between $8 million and $12 million of new bonds in an emergency. A side agreement promised to double the compensation for the common shareholders. McPherson professed a willingness to alter his plan for an agreement. With the expectation of a concord by January, Strachan Johnson told McTague: "The parties are very close; they are almost embracing." In fact, petty sniping continued in public and private. Arthur Slaght still pushed for a dismissal. Ralston repetitiously complained about how the bondholders' meeting was tainted by "stale proxies" or the "dual interests" of individuals who held both bonds and preferred stock.[87]

The method of reorganization became the fulcrum upon which the talks failed. While Gordon McMillan deemed the OJAA unconstitutional, he also believed McPherson was liable to lawsuits from disgruntled investors. When he tried to persuade the others that sufficient votes could be garnered for a solution under the CCAA, they pointed to Rothermere's tactics during the preceding year. Even if there was an agreement to step back from the provincial statute, "Lord Rothermere might change his mind and revert to his policy of postponing any reorganization, leaving the bondholders to carry the property for a further long period." Glyn Osler vetoed the use of federal legislation, and then McPherson rejected any deal that involved the Judicature Act. Mutual recriminations and back-biting intensified with the stalemate. "I must be perfectly frank in saying that although Senator Meighen's oratory is very impressive, I very doubt that he has any real point," complained

Ripley. Johnston accused Osler of botching the hopes for a settlement by undercutting his efforts to broker a compromise. He was frustrated by his counterpart's unwillingness to trust a verbal agreement. "I do not need to enumerate here the many ways in which, for the past five years, I have endeavoured to meet your wishes for the Bondholders' Committee. I have given you advice, gratuitous as it may be, during the conduct of this action. You have sometimes failed to take it, and whenever you failed to take it, you have made a mistake. I am not writing this letter without prejudice. I am angry and properly angry." Osler dismissed the comments but Johnston could not resist a final swat. Osler had disregarded his warnings about the OJAA. "If you have any resentment regarding my remarks I can assure you I am perfectly indifferent. At a later date, when I am not so angry, I will perhaps enumerate. for your benefit the many particulars in respect of which I think you are under great obligation to me in connection with this action." Reluctantly, just before Christmas, Ripley told the lawyers to advise McTague that all settlement attempts had failed and he should render a decision.[88]

In what was becoming a standard element of the judicial decisions related to Abitibi, the bulk of McTague's ruling recapitulated the lengthy saga. He then noted how the OJAA granted a court the right to authorize a sale if those holding at least 50 per cent of the outstanding bonds voted in favour and, under certain circumstances, to do so with a smaller favourable vote. Abitibi should be taken out of receivership as soon as possible, but the judge believed a fairer deal seemed possible. Because the terms for the new debentures meant interest payments would not be made if the firm experienced uneven earnings, the opposition of the dissidents was justified and proper. McTague expressed his appreciation for Strachan Johnston, who had acted as a trustee for all bondholders, not just the plan's proponents, which "indicated a proper appreciation of its duties under the trust deed."

The central question entailed whether a provincial act applied to an insolvent company. The Ripley plan might have been brought under the CCAA, McTague commented, because it was "essentially a scheme of compromise and arrangement to be brought about through the medium of a sale to a new company." While the OJAA might be *intra vires* for solvent firms, it could not be applied to failed companies because only Dominion statutes applied to the bankrupt. But, he noted, the Ripley plan failed to satisfy even the terms of the Judicature Act. It received a majority of votes at the October meeting, but these amounted to not quite half of the outstanding bond principal. A court consequently "should be very slow and cautious about sanctioning a scheme which results in confiscation of contractual rights at the will of the majority unless the majority is at least what the Legislature has fixed." McTague thereupon dismissed the motion for a sale.[89]

Arthur Roebuck cackled with glee as the case foundered. "The good ship Abitibi is like a craft I once sailed in. It was originally named the 'Merry' but after some unfortunate incidents became known as the 'Merry Turnover.' We passed over a sunken sand bar once just as a squall hit us. The gravel in the sand through which the keel was passing prevented her response to the tiller, and she did her stuff ... So with the Abitibi. The legal sand bar has gripped her keel and the men at the tiller are futile. In a squall she'd turn over." Once the bondholders accepted the need to proceed under federal legislation, "the past delay will be justified by greater further progress and more universal satisfaction."[90]

12

Darkest Hours

Equity sends question to Law, Law sends questions back to Equity; Law finds it can't do that; neither can say so much as say it can't do anything … And thus, through years and years, and lives and lives, everything goes on, constantly beginning over and over again, and nothing ever ends. And we can't get out of the suit on any terms, for we are made parties to it, and must be parties to it, whether we like it or not.

— Charles Dickens, *Bleak House*

We have known each other many years, but this is the first time you've come to me for counsel or for help. I can't remember the last time you invited me to your house for a cup of coffee, even though my wife is godmother to your only child. But let's be frank here. You never wanted my friendship. And you feared to be in my debt.

— Mario Puzo, *The Godfather*

OF WHAT VALUE IS A bond that cannot be enforced? This was the problem engendered by McTague's ruling and it led to five years of conflict. The key requirement for any debt instrument is certainty about its terms and reliability. Corporate bonds during the late nineteenth century were simple records comprised of a few pages. Nearly all were what are now called bearer bonds, unregistered documents with no records of ownership. Any important terms were written within. By the interwar period, the securities were negotiable instruments supported by a detailed mortgage or trust deed that specified rights and enforcement provisions.[1] Most legal discussions thus focused upon the role of a trustee during a default and the grounds for any exemption from liability, not the propriety of reimbursement or how collection might be pursued.[2]

With the failure of the Ripley plan, the receivership plunged into what most considered its grimmest period, one during which a resolution seemed either impossible or likely to have an unjust outcome. The investors remained divided, with the Drayton group and the equity holders still advancing ideas. However, the representative committee fell under the control of those who wanted full recompense. Any willingness to compromise vanished as the disagreements became a protracted fight to the finish. Ontario's government was drawn into the dispute, first over the question of whether the bondholders were high-handed, and then over the potential consequences. The Abitibi case became a matter of constitutional law, one that asked whether the province could block preferred creditors from exercising their contractual rights. That development was not inevitable, and this chapter examines how the insolvency was altered into an obdurate war between business and political interests. The opening section deals with the committee's attempt to reverse Justice McTague's decision. This is followed by an analysis of how shifting environmental conditions impacted the newsprint producers and undermined Abitibi's position. The final section reviews how the bondholders foreclosed on the mortgage and the firestorm that ensued as they did so.

1. The anomalous position

In the aftermath of Justice McTague's decision, no one could figure out what was going on because further conferences were not scheduled. The bondholders had three options: an appeal aimed at reinstating the use of the OJAA; a scheme that might be pursued under federal legislation; or an indefinite continuation of the receivership. Arthur Roebuck wondered whether Ripley might accept further concessions. If that occurred he believed Clarkson and McPherson should sponsor a new initiative, "for they have the colour of impartiality. It may be a very light shade of impartiality, but it is evidently not the deep pigments in which Ripley is painted." The chair represented the bondholders only as "modified by his own interests," Roebuck believed. "Ripley and his Rough-Riders" were sparing for bargaining position, hoping to find a way around McTague's ruling. "Funny things happen in court but that would be the funniest to date."[3] Sir Henry Drayton assured his supporters the defensive committee was willing to cooperate with others. Press commentators expected something from McPherson because his action theoretically remained active. Others stressed how even McTague deemed the liquidator's scheme dead on arrival. Only the *Financial Post* recognized a fourth option: a cash sale of the assets. The court might order an auction where the highest bidder gained control. The paper questioned whether anyone could raise sufficient capital, but it also thought an auction could not provide a sufficient return for the bond-holders. The journal did not realize there was a fifth possibility. They could make a low winning bid that left nothing for other investors and then resell for a deal that guaranteed them full compensation.[4]

Ripley's committee still considered the OJAA *intra vires*. It was pre-pared to act under federal or provincial law but principally wanted a positive outcome. Convinced that no plan the bondholders deemed fair could be achieved under Dominion legislation, it chose to appeal McTague's ruling. An appeal also might determine whether consent from the other investors was required if a sale did not occur for cash.[5] The motion, filed a week after McTague's decision, argued that he had erred in saying the OJAA could not be applied to insolvent companies. Rather, the justice improperly considered the matter as a compromise of bondholders' rights and failed to accept a fair plan that a majority approved.[6] Over the next two months the submission was backed up with massive documentation comprising four volumes, of which vol-ume one (which focused upon the notice of motion) alone contained 575 pages. Strachan Johnston and Montreal Trust disagreed and chose to oppose the appeal. Not only did they believe the OJAA was uncon-stitutional, they thought a superior result could be achieved by another plan or a judicial sale.[7]

Thus they went, Roebuck smirked, for "another canter around the Abitibi track," where the issues had been "mulled over so thoroughly" that every point was made with "full elaboration." McPherson's coun-sel unsuccessfully tried to block the appeal and then responded with a submission that covered every possible aspect. The Ripley plan was characterized not as a sale but a reorganization. No purchaser existed and no new money would be secured, while directors appointed by the bondholders would control the management. Even though the argu-ment had been dismissed before, McPherson's lawyers again chal-lenged the legitimacy of the representative committee. They emphasized the disagreements among the debt holders and characterized the prof-fered terms as unfair. Only at the end of the submission, and almost as an aside, the lawyers noted nothing might be done under provincial law because there were properties and investors outside Ontario. Dal-ton McCarthy for the defensive committee repeated these arguments. He dismissed the need for an "early" reorganization and claimed an extension from the province was easy to get. McCarthy reiterated the committee's objections to the Ripley plan, stressing how it required too much money.[8]

Although not an original party to the dispute, Wood Gundy was allowed to appear with respect to the OJAA. The provincial Parliament, its lawyers contended, had no right to enact legislation that altered a bankrupt company. Allowing the case to go forward gave the legislature a weapon to oust the federal laws for that issue."[9] Arthur Roebuck suggested that the common shares still had a market value above that assumed by the Ripley plan and thus Abitibi was not bankrupt in fact, only in law. He concluded by stressing an issue noted by McTague: the plan had not mustered a majority of the bond principal, as the OJAA stipulated.[10]

Norman Tilley, the bondholders' counsel, noted that the province had set a deadline of one year. According to previous court orders the committee was the sole representative of all bondholders, he argued. A majority favoured the plan, whether present in person or by proxy. It was not necessary to also have a majority vote of the outstanding principal. Moreover, the court could adjust a settlement and direct how the liquidator distributed assets – once the bondholders received full compensation. He challenged McTague's criticism of the new securities. The non-cumulative feature for the debentures was essential for the set-up, and Tilley rejected the possibility of ever gaining approval under the CCAA. His submission meandered as the hearing continued. He portrayed the Drayton plan as fatally flawed because more could not be done for the bondholders without taking away from the equity holders. McPherson's scheme was dismissed as non-viable.[11]

"Not a soul has said a word in support of Tilley and Osler and his client Ripley," Roebuck puffed. "The fact is that the more one talks about Ripley, his plan and methods, the worse it gets for Ripley." In fact, the lawyers for the preferred shareholders supported Tilley, along with the counsel for Royal Securities, who indicated that the firm now supported the plan. Still, the hearing was difficult for Tilley given the combined opposition of the trustee, the liquidator, the common shareholders, and dissident investors. Comments from the bench indicated a hostile perspective towards his presentation. When Tilley insisted the plan was a sale, Justice Latchford snarled, "If this is not a reorganization of the company then I cannot read the English language. I have been reading English for some time and I think I know something about it." Justice Henderson agreed but commented that all parties wanted to fight the matter out. When the hearing concluded, it was unclear where things would go, regardless of the outcome. The *Financial Post* had editorialized that the investors would be "paying for the show." This was quite accurate. Unlike most service expenditures during the receivership, records survived for the appeal. By the standards of the time they were staggering: $225,000, all covered by Abitibi.[12]

The decision in June 1938 was a narrow three to two ruling. A member of the minority, Justice Henderson, provided a careful summary and described how bizarre the tangles had become in terms analogous to those employed by *Yes Minister*'s Sir Humphrey Appleby:

> We have the anomalous position that the plaintiff, the trustee set up by the trust deed, represents all the bondholders and is contending here that there is no appeal. We have five defendants, the members of a bondholders' committee declared by the Court to represent all the bondholders who are the appellants. We have counsel on behalf of a further committee representing a large body of bondholders contesting this application. We have a further anomaly of counsel for the trustee, the plaintiff, moving the adoption of the resolutions passed at the bondholders' meeting, and launching a motion for approval of the sale, and now opposing the appeal from an order refusing approval. However, the order was made and has never been appealed from and therefore stands as between the parties to the action ...[13]

For the court's majority, the central question was whether the Ripley plan could proceed under the Ontario statute. They insisted it amounted to a reorganization, despite the image of a sale, because the assets were not offered for purchase. At the same time, they acknowledged that a true auction could be a disaster. The bondholders would be better off if they secured a partial payment of the overdue interest, but the Ripley plan was deficient because it proposed compensation in the form of second or third mortgage securities (on properties for which they already held a first charge) and shares that were not backed by assets (since they were collateral for the bonds). All of this, in any event, was moot. The OJAA could not be applied because the federal government held exclusive authority over bankruptcy. Even that was moot. The plan did not gain approval from owners comprising a majority of the bond principal. Although Tilley argued that the OJAA allowed approval by a majority of those present at the meeting, it was "only a suspicion."' The clause was not clear and "the less said at this stage of this case, the better."[14]

The minority believed the province had the right to enact the OJAA and that it applied to solvent and insolvent firms. The plan amounted to an action to enforce rights under the trust deed. Not only were the bondholders entitled to full payment before anything might be distributed to others, but it was also "quite apparent that nothing like the amount of money necessary to discharge this debt could be obtained by a cash sale." A majority of those present at the October meeting was satisfactory for approval and, they noted, even the CCAA used the term "present and voting." The vote was a fraction of 1 per cent short of the legislative requirement. Justice McTague erred by questioning the convertible debentures. Abitibi's status may have improved, but millions of dollars remained in interest arrears. The court had no role in any distribution to equity investors, but it was difficult to understand their opposition, given the bondholders' rights. The plan was, if anything, "generous to shareholders." The Drayton group's disagreements might be logical if a "too liberal" distribution was offered, but their own scheme stipulated analogous terms for the unsecured creditors and a bit more compensation for the shareholders. Accordingly, the minority declared that they would have allowed the sale.

The press understandably portrayed the outcome as a complete defeat for the bondholders but never recognized two other consequences. First, the court (despite the reservations expressed in the ruling) indicated that an exit from receivership should occur via a judicial sale, thereby setting in motion the struggles that dominated the next five years. Second, McPherson was delegitimized. Even the majority on the court dismissed the significance he and others placed on the Winding-Up Act. While the liquidator continued to participate in the proceedings, the bondholders thereafter ignored him except when the office was required for mundane matters. McPherson was rarely advised about developments until after the fact.

In the immediate aftermath of McTague's decision, Ripley felt he could not carry on as the chair of the representative committee. The members deferred action during the appeal but even after the final ruling they hesitated to make changes. For most of the year Ripley still handled negotiations with the province. Poor economic conditions, which are discussed in the next section, slowed the need for action, but the committee's funding was potentially threatened by a change of its chair.[15] From June 1932 to the end of 1937 it spent $159,331. The preparation of the Ripley plan cost another $307,649.[16] The City Company of New York covered most of the outlays. The firm had exited security-related activities by 1938 and was not willing to provide monies.[17] During the autumn, on Ripley's recommendation, the committee elected Herbert Symington as the new chair, with an understanding that Royal Securities would cover its expenses. Born in Sarnia, Ontario, after his legal training in Toronto he was appointed assistant solicitor for the Grand Trunk Pacific Railway. Symington appeared in most of the major

railway rate cases and at different points represented each of the western provinces, along with major companies like Winnipeg Hydro. He
moved to Montreal and quickly moved up within the corporate realm.
Along with his roles with Royal Securities and Price Brothers, he served
as a director of the Canadian National Railway, Trans-Canada Airlines,
Bawlf Grain, Calgary Power, International Power, Federal Grain, and
Ottawa Valley Power. Symington also was well-connected politically, a
close confidant of C.D. Howe, who later enlisted him for prominent
wartime roles. A biographical sketch contended he had a "considerable
understanding of handling men," subject to several caveats the author
tried to massage. "Hard-headed, direct, forceful, sometimes on first
acquaintance men think him irascible. But that isn't so. Rather he is
clear-cut in thinking and expression. He never leaves you with any misconception on what he has on his mind."[18] Ripley stayed on the committee but thereafter played a marginal role, especially after he assumed
managerial responsibilities related to American wartime production.
Arthur Meighen also was appointed, thereby ensuring that those who
wanted full compensation shaped all decisions. The changes were not
disclosed until March 1939 – well after the next initiative triggered controversy. Many observers thus did not comprehend the turnover, and
for years opponents still portrayed Ripley as a sinister guiding hand.

In December 1938 the preferred shareholders' committee disbanded.
Herbert Molson, who underwrote its activities, died earlier during the
year and the members served without remuneration.[19] During the year
several life insurance companies sold off nearly 90 per cent of their
holdings of preferred shares. The largest liquidation was by Sun Life,
which dumped securities worth $70 per share during the summer of
1937 for less than $20. Most of the insurance companies now held only
Abitibi bonds and they had no reason to care about the equity investors. A new committee for the 6 per cent holders was formed but the
membership was not disclosed for months. Headed by David Gibson, a
director of London and Western Trusts and National Life Insurance, it
comprised Arthur Slaght and a mix of speculative interests who hoped
to benefit from a settlement. This new committee, unlike its predecessor, was thus unlikely to cooperate with the bondholders.[20]

2. Abolish the whole thing

Despite the forecasts of Ripley's opponents, newsprint manufacturing
entered an accelerating decline in the autumn of 1937. The output by
Canadian firms did not regain the 1937 level once more until 1946. Several forces pushed the American economy into recession: substantial

cuts in federal spending (on the mistaken notion that economic recovery was well advanced), a tightening of the money supply, and the introduction of social security taxes that reduced disposable income. Stock exchange values collapsed with heavy selling that started a week after the bondholders' meeting. By the following spring total manufacturing decreased by a third and unemployment again exceeded 20 per cent of the male workforce, making it the third-worst turndown in North America during the twentieth century.[21] The newsprint producers, however, intensified the impact upon their sector because they had set a 1938 list price of $50 per ton, a $7.50 increase. American publishers, trying to buffer the cost impact, accumulated inventories, which, despite the carrying costs, provided them with lower costs for a sustained period. The manufacturers did not expect the sales to represent a problem because some mills could ship to Britain, where the list rate had reached $62.25. Spot prices abroad were even higher. Publisher inventories in August 1937 attained a level not seen since 1924 and by early 1938 they constituted a six-month supply.[22] Great Northern offered a rate at $48 but even that represented a cost increase. The rest of the producers stuck with the $50 price. Output consequently was slashed. By the spring of 1938, the average Canadian mill operated at two-thirds of capacity and many at less than half. The impact was worse for firms that emphasized commodities like sulphite pulp, where earlier price advances were reversed.[23]

The dynamics of the recession differed from the crisis a decade earlier. First, American production of newsprint had been cut in half since 1931 and the country was more dependent upon imports (see Appendix 1). Research proved the viability of southern pine as a substitute fibre. Nonetheless, the first newsprint mill in the Southern states was not scheduled to become operational until 1941. Publishers in coastal areas sought out less expensive supplies from Europe. That option vanished with the imminence of the Second World War, but as American consumption decreased in 1938, the producers knew demand would not improve if they slashed the list rate.[24] Second, International Paper lacked any incentive to participate in another war. The directors, led by the Boston financial interests who gave Archibald Graustein the presidency, forced his resignation in February 1936. International's performance since 1930 had been abysmal, the aggregate losses almost double those of its nine largest rivals combined. The Canadian subsidiaries accounted for most of the hemorrhage and remained unprofitable into the 1940s. Lower capacity rates raised production costs but even a modest price cut jeopardized International's solvency. When Great Northern chose in late 1937 to undercut the list rate International refused to

match the move. Graustein's replacement, Richard Cullen, had commanded the development of kraft paper operations in the Southern
states, which now accounted for most of the firm's profits. His management team instituted an autarchic strategy, beginning with the divestiture of the Newfoundland operation. International also had never
received significant payments on large components of its electrical utilities and arrears had accumulated for others. The investments were
written off, divested for $1. Instead, the firm continued its strategic
reorientation. By 1940 the production of kraft paper was twice the level
of newsprint.[25] Third, the other disruptor of a decade earlier, the Hearst
chain, could no longer flex its market power. Vastly overextended, it
failed in a last-ditch effort to raise debt during 1937. As a condition for
funding, bankers insisted William Randolph Hearst guarantee half personally. Under a court-ordered reorganization, a trustee assumed control of his companies, while parts of Hearst's private estate (which, to
the fascination of the press, included his art collection) were liquidated.[26] Canadian manufacturers were asked to defer the unpaid
accounts in exchange for collateral nominally worth $25 million. Few
firms thought the value was that high. Instead, the producers organized
a syndicate that apportioned monthly purchases to Hearst newspapers.
Sales occurred for cash or credit guaranteed by pledged assets, a practice that continued for more than five years. Meanwhile, other creditors
pursued monies from what was left of Hearst's empire.[27]

For the Hepburn administration, the recession not only threatened
economic recovery, but it also precipitated an ugly scandal. All of the
pulp ventures the government had promoted failed. The largest,
Sweezey's Lake Sulphite Pulp, collapsed in headline-grabbing fashion
with bitter recriminations about malfeasance and fraud, charges some
investors linked to Peter Heenan and by association the premier. The
minister denied responsibility and insisted everything had been done
properly. Only an influx of new capital was needed, he declared. "To
me it is unthinkable that any good citizen would for political manoeuvring or propaganda try to embarrass this Company from getting on its
feet or advertising to the world that an Ontario industrial endeavour is
financially embarrassed." Sweezey and other promoters denied blame,
but businessmen and much of the press considered the government's
support to be "deeply disturbing."[28] The scandal became a spur for yet
another effort to institute production controls.

The role of "policeman to the industry's proration policy" was where
"the state exercised its most profound influence," H.V. Nelles has
argued. The government acted as a "political arm" of the trade association, which "requisitioned intimidating letters," and if non-compliance

persisted, then "appropriate orders-in-council would be forthcoming to raise pulpwood dues to prohibitive levels."[29] In fact, as we saw earlier, the provinces handled prorating fitfully from 1935 to 1937. Across the next four years they at best proceeded half-heartedly and at worst generated a muddled mess. On some occasions, Peter Heenan portrayed Ontario as an initiator of the policy and on others, he declared "the industry is the spearhead of all this, the Government has just kind of gone along with them." But the minister later conceded prorating was never carefully worked out. He had believed that once the central provinces decided to cooperate all of the others would fall in line.[30] The underlying problem was the accord negotiated with Taschereau. It was only a verbal understanding about three principles: ensure a "fair division" of tonnage and revenue; spread employment and wages among mill towns to minimize social relief problems; and promote recovery and stability. Charles Vining later testified about how little thought was ever given to implementation.[31]

At a January 1938 conference, industry representatives were told that they could rely upon a sympathetic interest from the two provinces, but neither was prepared to enter into any agreement about, nor act in a policing capacity for, stabilization efforts. The premiers declared that while severe price-cutting must not occur (because it endangered worker wages), Canadian or American laws that banned price-fixing must not be violated. Hepburn went further than Duplessis and "indicated my desire to be completely disassociated from the industry's general activities, except as their actions directly affect employment and revenues."[32] Oversight was entrusted to a committee nominated by the manufacturers and approved by the provinces. Its role entailed the collection of data about capacity and output patterns and the dissemination of statistical reports. The committee had no authority or means for ensuring compliance. When output levels risked exceeding guidelines, firms would be cautioned and expected, on their own, to enter negotiations with other producers to rectify the situation. Neither the committee members nor the trade association coordinated those discussions. There also were no provisions for joint or uniform enforcement by the provinces. Each acted as it saw fit.

Since the committee acted as a liaison, Vining later noted, it ran into the problem of serving two masters.

The manufacturers have looked upon the committee as representing the governments, and the governments have regarded it as representing the industry[,] thereby a personification of trouble and dispute. The committee has been blamed on one hand for harshness or laxity of governmental action, depending on the point of view, and, on the other hand, has been held at least partly responsible for deficiencies in breaches of policy over which it has had no semblance of control.

Vining thought stability was maintained during 1938 because the producers took the premiers' threats "at face value, with fear in some cases and with relief in others." On at least one occasion Duplessis called executives to his office and cautioned them against disruptive behaviour.[33]

The severity of the recession, nonetheless, accounts for the initial willingness to tolerate prorating. Most producers deemed it irksome but, as the average output of mills declined, the need for restraint was obvious. By the winter of 1938 the manufacturers slashed output by a third. With a list price of $50 per ton, most could handle the lower capacity. Excess stocks, they believed, would return to normal by the summer, but it took more than a year because American consumption remained weak. Government pressure to minimize employment reductions extended the period of surplus inventories. Maurice Duplessis demanded that the manufacturers avoid layoffs, and he opposed price-cutting because it threatened wages. In any event, most producers now deemed price warfare to be self-defeating. A reallocation of shipments towards overseas markets became the key means for carrying out any transfers of output, thereby minimizing the disturbance of competitive positions. Prorating also conferred a gain: an ability to reject contracts with inter-locking price clauses, since a producer's share of output was somewhat protected.[34] The result was a dual list price system for two years: most Canadian firms charged $50 per ton, while several American producers posted a slightly lower rate.[35]

But the provinces weakened prorating by shrouding it in mystery. No public statements or guidelines were issued. Duplessis and Hepburn refused to answer questions from reporters after well-publicized meetings with the committee. Critics inferred the premiers were up to "some kind of backstage improprieties" they were "evidently ashamed to talk about."[36] Support in the Canadian media was much less robust than for previous stabilization attempts. This reflected not only scepticism about the policy but also anxieties that had accumulated from the controversial handling of other issues by "Hepler and Duplessini" (as one pundit characterized them). The financial editor of the *Globe and Mail* conducted a jeremiad against prorating because he believed it penalized efficiency, damaged international relations, and forced an uneconomic situation to persist. American politicians renewed their prior accusations about how the provinces and Canadian firms restricted competition. The American Newspaper Publishers' Association denounced the policy as yet another effort to maintain a cartel that would "collect many millions of dollars from United States publishers in order to put substance back on phantom securities."[37] The Federal Trade Commission launched a third investigation but it failed to substantiate violations of the law and found only "rumors." The final report, which mostly updated the 1917 enquiry, emphasized actions by American firms during the NRA experiment. But a lack of corroborating evidence did not block the FTC from concluding with an insinuation. It was "general knowledge" that the provinces abetted efforts to maintain or increase price. They also used licenses for timber concessions "to whip manufacturers into line."[38] American officials never let facts get in the way of prior beliefs. The Department of Justice declared it would investigate further, and across the following generation, congressional hearings castigated prorating as an intrigue to abet a cartel, thereby converting innuendos into accepted legend. After all, the chair of a Senate committee later declared that everyone knew the newsprint producers had chosen to "escape to Canada," a "device" to avoid American law that let them trade "without hindrance to their reprehensible practices of monopoly pricing."[39]

But prorating was fatally flawed. Publisher-controlled mills again received exemptions, which amounted to a sixth of total output from the two provinces and a quarter of Ontario's. Those plants operated near full capacity, whereas prorated mills remained at lower levels. The exemptions imbalanced the efforts to achieve a "fair division" of production. The volume of affected business did not force the collapse of the policy. Rather the exemptions first generated perceptions of favouritism and then became excuses for non-compliance.[40] Provincial officials described Ontario's legislation, which authorized higher timber fees or fines, as "a gun at the head of the operators," but it was as effective as a cap pistol. For example, two subsidiaries of Minnesota and Ontario Paper initially conformed to the policy but soon began to overship. They cut back under a threat of government action but then resumed the excess production. Plans to bring the mills under control through an order-in-council were shelved when ministry officials realized the parent firm might transfer production south of the border. Mills in Atlantic Canada and Maine operated at full capacity and undersold other producers. By early 1939, faced with a choice between losing contracts or giving rate concessions, firms in central Canada quietly adopted the latter.[41] A private analysis submitted to Hepburn was blunt. "Certain companies have been allowed to ignore prorating with impunity." Others that relied upon the statements by provincial officials lost contracts and remained short of tonnage because "the promised protection was not forthcoming ... There has been no semblance of the strict enforcement which the Governments declared would be applied." Prorating, Charles Vining conceded, was "a stabilizer, a preventative," but it was "deficient as a cure" since industrial prosperity was contingent upon "positive, aggressive and enterprising effort." He thought of asking the governments to "abolish the whole thing, that we keep our hands off" and let the producers "go at it again in any way they think best. But in my sober moments I reflect ... the whole bottom would shoot out of the works ... if they were allowed to go free."[42]

Great Lakes Paper again illustrated the policy's failure. Its president, C.H. Carlisle, in response to Hepburn, attended trade association meetings but this was his sole concession.[43] Another year and a half of repetitious negotiations failed to secure transfers of production from the company. Finally, Peter Heenan issued an ultimatum demanding all Ontario producers indicate their willingness to comply. Carlisle resigned in protest on the deadline date. Based upon press stories that the firm would adhere to the market price, Heenan trumped that it had accepted prorating. Newspaper reports, buying this balderdash, claimed the "threat" from Great Lakes had ended in response to a government "ukase."[44] Earl Rowe, a former leader of the Conservative opposition, was appointed as the new president. After several conferences, government officials proclaimed peace had come in the form of an amicable agreement. A small amount was transferred to a Quebec producer to "render justice to claims," but the company's contracts and sales were not disturbed. Vining publicly denied an agreement was reached. Rowe insisted that Great Lakes never joined the prorating scheme. Indeed, he was a more tenacious opponent than Carlisle. The firm would cooperate but only as far as its "unique position with reference to contractual arrangements" permitted. The firm's contracts stipulated that newsprint must be manufactured at the Fort William mill. Proration thus "would violate every principle which made the reorganization of the company possible," and prejudice the recovery efforts of other firms.[45] Great Lakes advised the province it could not carry out any transfer proposals asked by the industrial association.[46]

Notwithstanding the government's belief in a supposed understanding, Great Lakes negotiated deals with two Cleveland papers below the market price. Provincial officials denounced the action as another instance of "the old cutthroat scheme which damned the whole industry" and risked placing it back in an "unbalanced state." But briefings for the premiers had already mapped a blatant disregard of prorating by other companies. If rival firms chose to bid for the same contracts, Heenan argued, the list rate might be forced down to $35 per ton and Great Lakes returned to bankruptcy. He told Hepburn that "we will have to either keep hands off and let the industry wreck itself or make the companies who are disregarding the regulations toe the scratch."[47] For two years the minister had portrayed Great Lakes in compliance with prorating. He now admitted to the press this had never been true.[48] Rowe, unsympathetic, once again reiterated how proration threatened the reorganized Great Lakes.[49]

The need to seem to be doing something was thrust to the fore when Duplessis openly criticized Donahue Brothers, perhaps the most egregious offender. The Hepburn administration then passed an order-in-council to fine Great Lakes $500,000 for non-compliance. It was never proclaimed. Rowe later characterized the move as little more than blackmail. The order was rescinded, without explanation, shortly after the outbreak of the Second World War, and the tonnage transferred to a Quebec producer in 1938 was restored.[50] The production levels at Great Lakes continued unimpeded. Heenan, in sanctimonious dungeon, deplored the reversal:

> I got these people to agree that they were going to do the right thing. Then after this was repealed they went out and again got off the deep end. So that I am in this position now that I don't propose without further consultation with the two premiers and a fair understanding with the two governments how far they propose to go, I don't propose to make a fool of myself and ask my colleagues to make fools of themselves by passing Orders-in-Council every week or so and then repealing them without them having some effect.[51]

The minister still sought a redistribution of output, but no formula was acceptable to all parties, and opposition mounted with complaints about the policy's inconsistency and exemptions.[52] By the autumn of 1940, despite investigative press articles touting a future for prorating, it was a dead letter. Stability, as discussed in the next chapter, did emerge, but it resulted from new shortages and wartime regulation on both sides of the border.

Many observers believed prorating was necessary for Abitibi's recovery. With the company dependent upon provincial toleration of its now-expired resource rights, Clarkson's official statements did not challenge government policy overtly. His annual reports and confidential briefs to the court, however, recounted an alternative narrative.[53] Several contracts held by the Mead agency expired at the end of 1938.

Discussions with customers revealed that if a base rate of $48 per ton was offered, Abitibi would keep most of the business, but the province opposed any concessions. As a result, the firm lost 75,000 tons of output, of which half was snapped up by Great Lakes and the balance by a mix of U.S. and Scandinavian mills, all of whom offered a lower price. Moreover, Abitibi and other "short" companies were supposed to receive monthly contributions for their respective shares. Over the following three years, the company experienced below-average levels of output due to the failure to enforce prorating. Concurrently, the trade association decided producers that had not shipped beyond the average of mills in Ontario and Quebec and that complied fully with provincial policies were not obligated to transfer output, a stance that left Abitibi perpetually below the norm.[54] Even when transfers occurred, the company experienced few gains. The contracts imposed additional costs that limited Abitibi to either breakeven operations or small profitability.

Clarkson thus deemed Abitibi's share of output "unreasonable." Moreover, Ontario insisted the firm allocate production across six mills rather than rationalize production. Manitoba Paper and Ste. Anne ran well at rates below the company average, Sault Ste. Marie and Thunder Bay somewhat above. Even when Fort William operated at 28 per cent of capacity, Heenan refused permission to close the mill. Clarkson only managed to reduce output marginally at several plants. This pattern increased costs and backfired on the government's desire for greater employment. With higher expenses from the spread of production, Clarkson responded by slashing forest operations, a choice that was kept confidential to prevent public outrage.[55] Not until 1941 did he fully disclose how Abitibi had lost business.

Abitibi remained exposed to other aspects of the Liberals' exploitation of timber concessions for political gain. Under the Forest Resources Regulation Act the governor-in-council could deprive limits, although the firm's lawyers believed this was "an unthinkable contingency." Fort William Paper received a concession on which it had cutting rights for twenty-six years, but the Tories had required the mill to buy settler wood even though that practice imposed higher costs. When the Hepburn administration pressured Abitibi for the reopening of Fort William Paper, the managers realized that three-quarters of the wood had to come from the concessions. Their plans were subverted by Eddie Johnson, a Lakehead lumberman closely connected with the Liberal Party. His firm had previously attempted to access the concession and he now claimed Abitibi had enough in storage to supply its operations for more than a year. Johnson's real objective was to take advantage of a spurt in prices and strip the timber. His firm secured an order-in-council authorizing the cut. Clarkson, in futility, argued that the decision was not just "unfair and unjust" but a destructive waste that violated the lumbering practices the province itself had stipulated.[56] Hepburn's government engaged in self-serving justifications to portray anything else as unsound. "This deal is no steal," Heenan maintained. The province should avoid "this picayune stuff and get down to hard-boiled economics ... If we don't the timber will rot in the bush and hundreds of men will be on relief." Despite his claims, the decision was almost universally condemned.[57]

The recession and continued instability raise an important question. If the plan proposed by Ripley's committee had been approved, could Abitibi have weathered the following two years? The firm would have returned to receivership if the Wood Gundy, McPherson, or Drayton proposals were adopted because they provided insufficient working capital and imposed substantial fixed charges. An analysis of the likely outcome under the Ripley plan is more complicated. By late 1937 all of the inoperable mills, except Espanola and Sturgeon Falls, resumed operations. The year's earnings doubled from 1936 and approached those estimated by the Drayton group. Approximately two-fifths of the profits originated from Manitoba Paper and the electrical and railway subsidiaries, lower than experienced during the early years of the receivership but still significant. Ste. Anne operated at a loss and a technical "profit" for Thunder Bay was accomplished by decreasing depreciation. At this level of performance, the earnings covered the obligations for the senior securities under the Ripley plan but not capital expenditures or payments on the income debentures. Abitibi's revenues and earnings during 1938 dropped below the levels achieved the preceding year but remained above those for 1936. They improved marginally during 1939. If the Ripley plan had been adopted, Abitibi's status would have been a closely run matter. The firm would have had to suspend interest payments for the income debentures and postpone outlays on the mills or equipment, but the new working capital should have provided a sufficient buffer until conditions improved.[58] Moreover, the managers of a solvent enterprise would have prioritized marketing initiatives and possibly (like Great Lakes Paper) resisted governmental direction.

Nonetheless, an alternative perspective gained sway within the representative committee. Herbert Symington previously had been willing to accommodate other investors. Prices for the firm's securities deteriorated during the struggle over the Ripley plan. Their worth fell to $27 million during April 1938 from a peak of $89 million a year earlier. The market value further crumpled to $25 million by the spring of 1939, but the amount of bond principal and the accrued interest grew to $68 million. Symington decided shareholder equity no longer existed and his committee had waited far too long to collect.

3. Abitibi fat in the frying pan

The bondholders always had several legitimate reasons for not using the CCAA. Firms with closely held or simple financial structures were reorganized under the statute, but thus far the process had been applied to only a half-dozen big enterprises. The act failed to specify a means for assessing properties or earning power and therefore left the probable stakes of different investors unclear, a serious problem for an enterprise like Abitibi. Similarly, courts lacked the authority to review whether a corporation could handle financial charges once returned to solvency. Nor were they allowed to block payments to junior securities if true equity disappeared. The act provided no rules for controlling protective committees or deposit agreements. Finally, the requirement for approval by three-quarters of each security class created an insurmountable barrier, particularly if a bloc of investors chose to "muscle in" for the extraction of payoffs or concessions.[59]

The Drayton group still pressed for action under the CCAA, convinced a fair value could not be realized via a judicial sale. It proposed a scheme whereby the debt holders received three-quarters of their claim in new first mortgage bonds and the balance through a mix of debentures, preferred stock, and common stock. Most of the common equity after recapitalization would be allocated to the preferred shareholders, with slightly less than 10 per cent to the owners of old common stock. Various interests lobbied the government to organize a meeting so the contending groups could find common ground. They suggested Premier Hepburn or Peter Heenan might serve as facilitators. Although several initiatives required an extension of the order-in-council that authorized a renewal of Abitibi's resource rights, the government refused while the appeals process continued. The bondholders' committee meanwhile delayed and debated about submitting the case to a higher court. Ripley conferred with Heenan and Hepburn, but was told the timber limits would be allocated only upon a reorganization, not before. He requested a new statute that might facilitate a foreclosure on the bond mortgage. The province quashed this idea and insisted a termination of the insolvency must occur under existing legislation. "Eminent counsel" then assured the press that the notion that Abitibi's assets might be put "under the hammer" was impracticable. A foreclosure amounted to a last resort that the equity holders would oppose and a court was unlikely to authorize. With the outstanding bondholder claims versus assets worth less than $80 million, they argued, financing a purchase constituted a prohibitive barrier.[60]

Nonetheless, by the winter of 1939 Hepburn and Heenan agreed an end to the receivership was essential for lessening the unemployment in Northern Ontario. The bondholders' committee communicated its views through several briefings. The premier was told that "the ticker always told the truth." The consolidated net earnings since 1933 averaged substantially less than the interest charges. Even if a person assumed security exchanges were "a hundred per cent wrong" and the market valuation was doubled it would barely equal the claims they were entitled to enforce in the courts.[61] Substantive input was not solicited from others although Hepburn received several independent assessments. These also supported unilateral action. One noted a "natural recovery" by Abitibi might be impeded by "European unsettlement." It could take more than three years before the earnings reached a level that permitted the shareholders "to bale themselves out."[62]

Symington's committee, now referring to itself as the "bondholders' protective committee," during February floated a trial balloon in the press about a foreclosure. The story triggered predictions of protracted litigation. Arthur Slaght told Hepburn that a new pitch from the Drayton group was reasonable but if putting the firm "through the wringer" was a goal of "the Ripley interests," the province should not cooperate.[63] Peter Heenan announced the resource rights would not be confirmed prior to the government's acceptance of a reorganization scheme. The press interpreted this as a signal that the province expected a mutual agreement among the contending interests, a "death knell" to foreclosure. Two days later Hepburn forced the minister to backtrack and Heenan publicly acknowledged Ontario would accept whatever course a court approved. An order-in-council was proclaimed that afternoon, which allowed the 1937 order to go into effect if a reorganization occurred within a year. The government reserved the right either to extend the time frame or cancel the order. Put simply, the way now was open for *any* solution, provided it received judicial approval. Hepburn during a speech in the legislature noted that six schemes remained in circulation. He insisted his administration was neutral, not concerned with the rights of different stakeholders or with the merits of any plan. That prerogative belonged to the courts and therefore "this Government will not interfere in any shape or form in the matter ... This Government is taking no sides in the matter." But the premier then quoted liberally from an unpublished plan by the bondholders, characterized it as "eminently fair," and declared there was nothing left for others. The statement precipitated an immediate slump of Abitibi stock values, a jump for the bond prices, and howls of outrage from the press and the financial sector.[64]

Hepburn's declaration politicized Abitibi's reorganization. For five years the Tories had muddled along with ineffective leaders who were little match for the premier's oratory or bullying, but in early 1939 Col. George Drew became the head of the party. The first chair of the Ontario Securities Commission, Drew was familiar with business affairs but, more critically, he was a focused opponent. The Conservatives now portrayed themselves as guardians of small investors and they seized the opportunity to excoriate Hepburn as a puppet of greedy financiers. Abitibi, they insisted, was not an ordinary company: it was under the control of the cabinet, which had already created a fiasco with the OJAA. Like the Liberals five years before, the Conservatives advanced an array of alternative facts couched in fiery rhetoric. The junior security holders were being "frozen out" for the benefit of Joseph Ripley, "the same man who had taken $25,000,000 from the people by means of an original prospectus that had not been lived up to." Someone had to speak for the people on whom the securities were unloaded because the investment house had "scuttled away" after the sale. The premier was "in the confidence of Ripley, who is a cold-blooded and shrewd New York business man, not in the paper business at all." Hepburn had put one of the largest firms "into the stock brokers' hands," was "loading the dice" for "Ripley the Ripper," who destroyed the rights of Canadian stockholders so he could be "the new paper king in this country." Symington was "cheek by jowl" with Heenan, while the lawyers acted like "crows gathered around a carcass" as the province acted as judge and jury for a closed doors agreement that not even the bondholders had seen. When Hepburn claimed he only learned about the plan the day before the order-in-council was approved, Drew with relish noted it was well known that discussions had circulated within the government for weeks. "Any one who knew about that could without having to spend a cent go into the market and make a killing." He successfully demanded the production of correspondence related to Abitibi, a move that later triggered an investigation of Heenan's department.[65]

The Tories rewrote history as they demanded action by claiming the Liberals did not recognize how a heavy debt load was "an important safety factor" for ensuring prudent management. A bondholders' purchase of Abitibi, they contended, was akin to International Paper's acquisition of Riordon in 1925. The resulting formation of a company without funded debt could generate problems likely to bedevil the industry for years, with Ripley as a new Graustein. The flip of positions was completed as Liberals stressed the priority of bondholder rights versus those with equity stakes. This all made great theatre. Despite the statements emphasizing the treatment of small investors, what mattered for the Tories was gaining an acceptable outcome for the preferred shareholders, not the common. In addition, everyone ignored a simple reality: Abitibi's shares had remained on the markets. The trades amounted to four times the number of common shares and three times those of the 6 per cent preferred equity since June 1932, or five times and four times, respectively, since 1928. A large proportion (probably the bulk) of equity holders were not original investors, but people or firms who acquired stakes post-receivership. Though less active, the bonds and 7 per cent preferred stock also had experienced significant transactions.[66]

The premier came under savage attack from Arthur Roebuck, who argued it was unjust to contend Abitibi's assets were inadequate for paying off the debt. Nor was the unfairness cured by assertions that the junior investors might pay off the bond principal and interest. Instead, Hepburn, the "mouthpiece" of the Ripley committee, had given the debt holders the idea they might "put the screws on and obtain this valuable property for themselves," while he threatened other investors with a big stick to do as they were ordered. Hepburn dismissed Roebuck's right to talk about Abitibi since he had represented the common shareholders. No longer involved with the case, Roebuck rejoined, "That investment may be largely lost, but for the government to join with the senior security holders in ruining what remains of its value will be keenly resented across the sea and elsewhere."[67]

The worst fears of other claimants were realized when Symington's committee released a "Plan of Procedure." The CCAA was deemed impractical because it seemed unlikely that the unsecured creditors and shareholders would ever accept a settlement that left them with nothing. A judicial sale was defended as the standard procedure for enforcing a bond mortgage. After foreclosure, the committee proposed to distribute common shares for a new firm amongst the debt holders on the basis of 40 shares for every $1,000 of principal. These securities would be placed in escrow because the unsecured creditors and shareholders then were allowed several years to acquire up to 1.9 million shares via warrants. The warrant issue was voluntary and "generous," the committee cautioned, "it is not required, nor is any method of division prescribed, by law." Sixteen per cent of the shares were available to the 7 per cent preferred holders, 72 per cent to the 6 per cent preferred, and 6 per cent to the common shareholders. The new company might issue additional shares and borrow as needed but further loans exceeding $10 million required approval from the bondholders, who also held first rights for any public offerings.

A careful analysis of the document was necessary to find a crucial set of restrictions. The debt holders chose the board and it could not be restructured before the expiration of the escrow arrangement. Sales of common shares were banned below the $36 rate at which warrants were exercisable. Moreover, the protective committee reserved the right to alter the division or to terminate this "opportunity" if anything impeded reorganization. Assenting bondholders became pro rata owners of the new firm. While the time frame for depositing bonds was not specified, at least half of the outstanding principal was required for implementation of the plan. But there were two important conditions. Dissenting bondholders were entitled just to a distributive share of the *purchase price* after expenses and charges, not the monies earned if it was then recapitalized or resold. They also only had until the end of April to remove securities from deposit, a provision that was not understood for several weeks. Thereafter, bonds might be deposited but not withdrawn, locking the investors into the group that backed the Plan of Procedure. Moreover, the deposited securities could be used as counters for payment in a sale, which gave the protective committee an absolute advantage. Anyone else had to raise nearly $75 million in cash. Knowledgeable observers grasped the implications. Non-depositors would incur heavy losses and the committee intended to submit the lowest possible bid, perhaps $25 million. Put simply, it intended to steal the company.[68]

The reorganization of Canada Power in 1931 was considered "efficient" and realistic but social attitudes had altered since. Even among newspapers that favoured the Liberals, the reaction was one of shock and appal. Bold headlines mirrored those for stories about impending war in Europe: "Abitibi Fat is Now in Frying Pan," "Abitibi Power Pot Is Boiling Furiously," "Battle for Abitibi," "Winner Take All?" The *Globe and Mail* failed to understand how "a level-headed man" like Hepburn could consider the warrant offer realistic. *Pulp and Paper Magazine* decried how Abitibi was being "sold down the river" at a fraction of its value, which amounted to a "ruinous blow" for the country's prestige. The plan dismissed the equity investors who helped "build the house." The *Financial Post* labelled the scheme "unduly harsh" and proclaimed it was a sad day when the future of Canadian industries warranted "the stripping of capital structures to the very bone."[69]

"Seldom has any proposal brought forth the amount of comment that has greeted the latest moves to remove Abitibi Power and Paper Co.

from receivership," one editorial commented. All groups claimed wide-spread support but most letters to newspapers treated the Plan of Procedure as over-reaching, unconscionable, akin to the "policies of the late Captain Kidd." Some correspondents emphasized what they deemed conflicts of interest. "It seems inconceivable that those men who so enthusiastically put together a profit making machine in 1928 should now ruthlessly desire to tear it apart." A female investor in Philadelphia decried how she had bought preferred stock as a safe investment when it was first offered but the market value dropped within two days. One writer, who owned bonds and preferred shares, suggested the conduct of the bondholders "savors just a little bit too much of dictatorship." Most complainants still believed things would work out because: Abitibi was a major enterprise in a great industry, the government would protect their rights, or the presence of conspicuously able men on the other committees suggested a compromise was possible. At the same time, concern was expressed about the withdrawal of the institutional investors, which probably meant small fry were left "out on the limb." A few emphasized the need to keep Abitibi as a Canadian company. Consequently, many writers advanced alternative schemes or endorsed one of the previously published versions.[70]

Missives sent to Hepburn and Heenan were less diplomatic. "If the Company is not worth the Bond issue as the Prime Minister said, is the Government investigating who was responsible for unloading all these securities on the public, and taking steps to hold them responsible?" A lifelong Liberal declared that "it looks as though the Common Holder is to get Naught and the Gov't is not helping the situation at all." Others complained about how the company seemed to be rich enough to afford a stream of receiver's fees, consulting charges, lawyers' expenses, capital account payments, and acquisitions. The Liberal Party was supposed to defend the underdog, commented one writer, not "a group of International Bankers who will walk away with a baby and let the little fellow stand naked." "The vicious practice of unscrupulous financiers should be well known to you," another scolded the premier.[71]

A cottage industry of brochures and circulars sprang up. Many entailed considerable time and thought, the authors hoping to indicate a route forward. A pamphlet by Stanley Stanger, the president of Montreal's Guardian Trust and a member of the preferred shareholders' committee, was insightful. He assured readers if "the Abitibi differences are settled around a conference table the result will win far more popular acclaim than if a settlement is attempted through the courts." Capitalization was naturally contentious. "Market values are as likely to reflect a state of mind as a state of intrinsic value. The present securities, rather than serving as a measure of inherent values, have now become mere evidences of rights to acquire securities in the reorganized company." It was not just the income generated from assets but the uses of income that made disagreements inevitable. Bondholders were concerned with sound management and the safety of their stakes. They emphasized the ability to meet fixed charges and the appraisal of physical assets or original costs less depreciation. Equity holders were concerned with earning power and deemed asset valuation irrelevant except for the impact upon future profits or share prices. However, concepts like fair market value or going concern value never had been intended to imply the price the assets might receive through a forced sale. American judges, Stranger contended, were inclined to dismiss asset valuation in favour of the earnings derived from business operations as the true gauge of corporate worth. Everyone during a corporate failure professed to deserve a superior position, even though legal tradition gave bondholders the right of foreclosure. However, American rulings by the 1930s stressed relative priority among claimants versus absolute priority and the need for concessions or compromise.[72] "By virtue of their relative position," Stranger noted, bondholder committees "become skilled in the niceties of dictating what is best for themselves and at the same time in prescribing for others." Foreclosure could result in such a low capitalization that the firm could undersell competitors. The directors of a reorganized Abitibi would hold "a position of virtual dictatorship in the pulp and paper industry." But Stranger insisted "keen sighted men of conciliatory disposition" could achieve an equitable outcome that avoided this scenario.[73]

Arthur Roebuck, less optimistically, held a perspective shared by many. "If the junior security holders remain idle, they are going to lose their hide." A new common stock committee promised to work with the preferred committee, "since we are all in the same boat, all in danger of being dispossessed." Letters sent by another committee, this one for the general creditors, stressed the need for cooperation against the "unconscionable" sale."[74] The preferred committee denounced the plan as proof of an "obvious intention to deal with this entire situation without consulting the shareholders." The warrants were illegitimate at the proposed rate. Not only did the 6 per cent preferred holders had to raise $50 million to liquidate their portion of the debt, but this meant $144 were required to gain a share with a market value of $8. The 7 per cent stockholders had an even worse position and would have to offer $417 for each share nominally worth $100 but selling for less than $14.[75]

It advanced a counterproposal for the bondholders: first mortgage securities for an amount slightly less than the accrued interest, and secondary general mortgage bonds equal to the principal on the old issue. Most of the new common equity was allocated to the 6 per cent preferred, with the other equity investors receiving small portions. The committee's chair argued the Plan of Procedure would encounter colossal legal costs, delay and "friction," whereas their scheme could proceed without a war.[76] It, however, repeated basic flaws from earlier ideas, particularly the supposed willingness of the bondholders to roll nearly two-thirds of their claim into secondary securities. The package proposed large annual charges but only in one year since the merger had Abitibi earned enough to cover the expenses. It once again included income bonds that paid interest only when sufficient earnings were achieved. The scheme also included bonds that might later be converted into common shares. This option only made sense if the firm earned high profits and paid large dividends. Finally, it assumed a divestiture of Provincial Paper and other subsidiaries to raise capital, leaving just a core group of mills. Thus, although many newspapers treated the scheme as viable, the *Financial Post* dismissed it by noting a responsible board of directors was not going to pay out substantial dividends since the industry had "such amazing capacity for ups and downs."[77]

The defensive committee had to fend off rumours about its dissolution. Drayton decried how they had opposed a Ripley scheme two years earlier and now were confronted by a new one. If bondholders did not deposit their securities, their payments from the judicial sale would be a pittance. But acquiescence with the Plan of Procedure meant they received only common stock. Once converted to an equity position, the bondholders no longer held an enforceable first charge upon the properties and their stakes had an unknown marketability. Since the protective committee had banned withdrawals after the end of April, they would not know the purchase price or the likely remuneration. To retain complete freedom of action, the defensive committee told investors they should withdraw any securities from deposit. The plan from the preferred shareholders represented an alternative but needed modifications that included bondholder control of Abitibi until the interest and arrears claims were satisfied and a sufficient reserve was developed. Drayton's group also emphasized how prolonged litigation loomed because most reorganizations purportedly offered "some degree of fairness" to all stakeholders.

The defensive committee ignored the possibility that once out of receivership, the bondholders might reap large gains if Abitibi was resold. But Drayton did grasp the significance of Herbert Symington. "I do not know whether those that seek control are looking to Abitibi as

Abitibi or to a much broader field in connection with the newsprint industry. If they are looking to the larger field, where Abitibi would only be considered part of the whole," Symington could put "the whole future" of the company in his hands or those of his agents.[78] Drayton identified a key point that knowledgeable participants would not talk about publicly. Royal Securities was the only Canadian firm with the resources and connections necessary: first, to mount a successful bid at the sale; second, to ensure the purchase of Abitibi by another company; and third, to carry out the refinancing. As the chair of Price Brothers and connected to Mersey Paper, Symington was positioned to amalgamate Abitibi with those companies, thereby transferring control to Montreal interests and giving I.W. Killam a major position within the industry.

Press accounts emphasized the need for compromise but the reality was more muted. "I am very confident that, without too much delay, we shall be able to take Abitibi out of receivership," Symington advised Hepburn. After seven years of effort, he insisted "there are no available means of removing Abitibi from receivership and placing it effectively capitalized on a competitive basis" other than by foreclosure and sale. Even before its publication, most institutional investors and the British Association of Investment Trusts endorsed the plan. The committee registered with the U.S. Securities and Exchange Commission so transferable certificates of deposit were available for bonds placed with American depositories and a filing request was sent to bondholders a month later.[79] While letters of protest against the "harsh" and "confiscating" sale appeared in newspapers, the bondholders' council remained silent, convinced the plan went further than the law required. Following several weeks of pleas from the other committees, the bondholders' council agreed to a conference on 11 May. The meeting adjourned without result after two and a half hours. His committee was prepared to examine any workable scheme, Symington declared, but the opponents offered nothing new. The investor groups talked about forming a joint committee to continue negotiations but it never met.[80] By June slightly more than half of the bonds were pledged to the plan. The option for deposit, but not withdrawal, remained open for constructing a larger majority and thereby minimizing any resistance from a court.[81]

With the groups unable to find a consensus, some newspapers suggested a mediator or arbitrator might help. During the summer Thomas Bradshaw (the head of North American Life Assurance), Howard Ferguson, and Gordon Scott (the former trustee for Price Brothers) offered to serve as an independent committee. After seeking input from the various interests, an initial proposal was leaked during August and a more detailed presentation was released in October. The "committee of compromise," as it was dubbed, did not offer a full scheme but a framework from which a solution might be achieved under the CCAA. The proposal followed the distribution outlined in the Ripley plan but offered a more generous payoff for the preferred shareholders. Each $1,000 bond would be converted to 40 shares of "cumulative dividend preferred stock" that had voting rights, a par value of $25 each, and possible redemption at $35. The equity holders and secured creditors were to receive a junior class of new common shares. A cash payoff was available for unsecured creditors that accepted discounts of their claims. The scheme rested upon the assumption that Abitibi's assets were worth at least $120 million. After deducting the bond principal and accrued interest, a net surplus of $50 million of "theoretical equity" hypothetically existed for the shareholders and creditors.[82]

The press greeted this idea with fulsome praise, one that avoided "ruthless action." With a deteriorating international situation, most commentators felt it was important to get business matters in order. Foreclosure was "fast disappearing down the river" because wartime demand was likely to enhance sales and Abitibi's value. Therefore, harsh measures would not be approved by larger bondholders, whereas the conversion feature gave them an opportunity to participate in the company's future.[83] The compromise garnered support from the Drayton group, the equity investors, and general creditors. But there was a universe between media reports and what unfolded behind the scenes. Well before the compromise framework was released, Symington told Bradshaw there was no equity left. If anything, a deficiency existed. The bondholders were not willing to go through another round of meetings aimed at taking "large sums of money out of their own pockets." If the effort again failed, "then the bonds amount to absolutely nothing in this country." Bradshaw, indeed, was misleading the public about a "forlorn hope." Symington doubted the other investors could agree among themselves "as to how the carcass should be divided." He dismissed the $120 million valuation as something that was "so out of line with actual facts" that it meant the proposal entailed flooding the market with worthless pieces of paper. "You should realize the true position which seems to us to be that this is a salvage job."[84]

4. From sitzkrieg to blitzkrieg

The bondholders intended to file for a sale during the first week of September but their affairs were subsumed by the outbreak of war. Newspaper editorialists thought that the province would assume the role of a trustee to ensure common cause during the hostilities. No investor therefore would be sold out. Because firms like Abitibi bore the costs of the proration policy, Ontario was obliged "to show fair play to equity securities."[85] The Hepburn administration accordingly declared a sale of the Abitibi properties inadvisable. It indicated an intention to rescind the March order-in-council, but this move was rejected after negotiations with Abitibi's lawyer. Instead, legal proceedings were held in abeyance while the government conducted a "review" of forest enterprises. The bondholders agreed not to proceed with the sale while this occurred.[86] Hepburn pressed Clarkson for a report on Abitibi's status during the war but the receiver replied that no one could predict the future. Although the outbreak of hostilities reduced British demand, this was offset by the loss of Scandinavian competition. Clarkson suggested the 1940 profits might be just below the 1937 level, still insufficient to cover the bond interest. There also were new costs (like guarding properties) for which Abitibi was ill-prepared, "where this will go no one knows."[87]

A phony war set in as the committee of compromise tried to mediate a solution. Its credibility rested upon Thomas Bradshaw's reputation from a lifetime in insurance and finance. Ferguson and Scott were useful but lacked his business stature or connections. Bradshaw died suddenly during November. He was replaced by James Murdoch, the president of Noranda Mines and a known supporter of the Drayton group. A meeting brought the committee together with members of the government, the bondholders' representatives, and their lawyers. Ferguson later commented, "[W]e did not get very far." Symington treated the matter as "a cold business proposition, they held the securities and they were entitled to foreclose, the same as any other transaction. Of course, there was not any use arguing that legal feature, and nobody attempted." When pressed, Symington declared, "There is no sentiment in this. I do not feel the slightest moral obligation to anybody. We have our rights, and we propose to exercise them." Meetings with different groups followed during the winter of 1940 and the committee tried to enlist support from Sun Life. However, they "ran into a cold north wind." Murdoch, incensed by the situation, denounced foreclosure as "grabbing the property at a time when there was no possibility of selling it."[88]

A committee of the Ontario legislature began an investigation of Heenan's ministry during January 1940. The *Globe and Mail*'s financial editor thought the probe might help achieve an Abitibi compromise, but the hearings instead focused upon the government: its tolerance of timber exports, the controversy over Lake Sulphite and other mills, and allegations of gross managerial ineptitude.[89] False reports led Heenan again to indicate a friendly reorganization might occur, while new rumours spread about the probability of a foreclosure effort. In early March a deputation from all groups save the bondholders bemoaned how Symington's committee "declines to co-operate to terminate receivership." They advanced yet another scheme, analogous to that from the committee of compromise. The scheme was so ill-prepared, a special provision later had to be inserted "to compensate for any possible future loss."[90] Drayton complained how despite government promises nothing occurred due to the "unwillingness of a certain group to effect a settlement." The province held the key to the situation, he declared, and it had to compel a reorganization that ensured an immediate cash return to the bondholders.[91]

The "Abitibi 'Sitzkrieg Front' Stays Unbroken" declared the *Financial Post* early in May 1940, but like the military situation in Europe, Abitibi's phony war came to a sudden end. Spokesmen for the equity investors claimed to have unanimous support although proxies or deposits had never been solicited. They characterized the bondholders as pursuing a "Hitler attitude," with plans to merge the firm's mills with other companies into a giant combine "for their own personal gain." Press rumours again suggested other initiatives were pending but Symington's patience over "the waiting game" was exhausted.[92] He reminded Hepburn that the legal proceedings were suspended because the government claimed it needed a short time for a "review." Approximately 60 per cent of the bonds had been deposited with the protective committee. It no longer was prepared to stay the action given "a much longer delay than you originally contemplated has taken place." The premier declared his opposition to the move. Lawyers for the province, however, perceived little likelihood of other interests bidding since wartime restrictions blocked large transfers of American or British capital. With unanimous cabinet support, the government characterized the committee's decision as a breach of faith. The average citizen, Peter Heenan asserted, would criticize it if the bondholders were able "to seize this opportunity when investors all through the Commonwealth, including England, are at war in an attempt to save the Empire." He called for a repeal of the order-in-council that allowed a reorganization if it gained judicial approval. The premier instead told the government's lawyers only to advise the court the province was against a sale.[93]

The renewed application shocked the press and most investors. One editorial claimed it was a move that had "All Financial Canada Watching." A wave of denunciations arose from different interests, who deemed the action "obnoxious," ill-timed, and "arbitrary injustice." David Gibson, the chair of the preferred shareholders' committee, asked how any group of Canadian businessmen could and approve in these tragic hours such an act? ... Its injustice is unworthy of Canadian business standards." Symington's group had selected "the darkest days in Canadian and British history in centuries" to force a sale "at a time which will shatter the confidence of our Canadian investing public."[94] McPherson joined with dissident bondholders, equity holders, and unsecured creditors in opposition. This time, Montreal Trust characterized the timing of a foreclosure as "opportune" and it realigned with the bondholders' committee. Because the legal preliminaries were completed the year before, the process moved quickly. Less than a week after the notice of motion was filed, Justice Middleton set a hearing date. As a contingency, Symington's committee filed a proposal with the U.S. Securities and Exchange Commission. During the short hearing, opponents argued it was not appropriate to have a judicial sale during a world war, Norman Tilley counterargued that because Abitibi's mills were running at 90 per cent of capacity, it was an ideal time. A lawyer for the province noted the government might refuse to renew licenses (leaving the firm with only two of its seven forest concessions) or rescind any rights to cut timber. However, his instructions were "not to make any threat or promise" but merely suggest an adjournment.[95]

Middleton's ruling three days later drew heavily upon Justice Kingstone's 1937 judgment. The bonds, he remarked, now were in default for over eight years and no one claimed a redemption was practicable. The bondholders had remained quiescent for two years. Those who were against a sale pointed to improvements in Abitibi's position but the changes did not enhance the firm's ability to pay the bond interest or earn a profit. Despite Clarkson's management, recent success did not ensure the same for the future. "Surely eight years delay in realization ought to satisfy even the most optimistic of those concerned of the impossibility of this," Middleton remarked. He did not deem the province's caution about a forfeit of timber limits a matter for the court. Accordingly, the assets could be auctioned and the bondholders were at liberty to buy them.[96]

The opponents hoped to stop the action by suggesting a conflict of interest between Montreal Trust and the protective committee, but an attempt by McPherson's lawyers to stay the ruling was squashed. Petitions to Ontario, Quebec, and the federal government against the "obnoxious and unjust" proceedings went nowhere. The process moved inexorably forward as newspaper advertisements were placed and the Master of the Supreme Court fixed a minimum reserve bid, while the protective committee called again for deposits. Opponents reacted with bitterness. Numerous commentators suggested alternative schemes or variations upon previous plans. These invariably entailed walks down a well-trodden cow path: packages of securities that already had been rejected or that rested upon discredited assumptions. The preferred shareholders denounced the sacrifice of more than $35 million in equity as something without parallel in Canadian financial history. The firm's working capital had improved during the first year of the war. Therefore payments could meet the current interest and part of the arrears. "Certainly, this is not a 'bankrupt' company in the usually accepted sense of the word."[97] It appeared the bondholders would get a property that not only satisfied their claims but allowed them to reap generous profits. Consequently, the arguments of opponents were coloured with a sense of despair. Most saw foreclosure as unnecessary. At no prior time was the differential between the real value of the properties and the amount of a cash offer so great. "No wonder the average man is bewildered," one declared.[98]

The protective committee avoided public comments but in private the members were blunt. With the collapse of security prices since 1937, Symington told one broker, financial markets now valued the firm at $30 million and this seemed "to be a complete answer to any contention that people are, in your terms, 'being sold down the river.'" It was "a very courageous man" who would consciously profess an outcome near the full bondholder claim. He scathingly rejected the demands of other investors.

> You speak of compassion for the shareholders. The original shareholders lost their money long ago. A speculative group, who bought largely in 1937 and from whom most of the present agitation comes, guessed unwisely and, therefore, wrongly, the same as other unsuccessful speculators. The issue of pieces of paper, representing an equity where there is no equity, only means a chance for those who have lost to get out at the expense of somebody else getting in to take the loss, as there is no real value. On the other hand, I might suggest compassion for the bondholders ... who now surely have a right to salvage what they can of their investment.

It was an auction, not a foreclosure, he contended. Despite claims about how foreign interests might advance competing bids, there was no likelihood from either British or American interests, war or no war. Therefore, "ask yourself ... if questions of law and equity are taken from the judgment of the Court and it be left to agitators and speculators, who have lost, to say whether bondholders rights are to be confiscated or not."[99]

Lawyers dominated the debates about the Ripley plan in 1937. This time, with few avenues of redress, letters or telegrams flooded into newspapers and the premier's office. One declared he was "among the thousands of lambs going to be sheared … on the Abitibi block by Mr. 1940 Shylock of Toronto." Another, in a letter entitled "On the Eve of the Abitibi Blitzkrieg," also derided the "cold-blooded Shylock proce-dure." After condemning how Abitibi's finances were conducted after the merger, he insisted "the ugly picture should also make it quite clear to all those who directed the company into the ditch, that they have a heavy moral responsibility to the common and preferred shareholders … to salvage something from the wreck."[100] Others complained about how the letter of law was being used to seize property from the weak. They hoped "some agency of beneficial government" might block "the immoral aspects" of a foreclosure. Most submissions asked for support of one of the earlier proposals. Some advanced conspiracy theories. "There is no question but that the Insurance Companies are being used a front by Messrs. Ripley and Symington in order that these gentlemen, and those back of them can get control of this vast Ontario enterprise." Symington was "really acting for the Ripley committee to hide the fact that Americans are seeking to obtain control." The province thus should intervene because it was against the nation's welfare to pay off Ameri-can interests.[101] A paper manufacturer came much closer to the proba-ble outcome by noting the authority Royal Securities and Lord Beaverbrook retained over Price Brothers. Now, he suggested, with Symington's aid, they schemed to control Abitibi.[102]

Overarching the situation was one issue: did the province mean busi-ness when it claimed timber rights might be withdrawn after foreclo-sure? Most reporters thought Hepburn's request for a postponement was never serious and the failure to rescind the order-in-council about Abitibi's resource rights was cited as proof. A financial editor noted, Symington and Ripley "are not silly. They are shrewd men who have shown through their careers that they always know exactly what they are doing and where they are going." If they disregarded the statements by Hepburn and Heenan, "it must be because they are sure the Prov-ince will take no action which would throw men out of work." The assets were worthless without the Abitibi plants and the government likely had decided what mattered were experienced hands and capital. Edward Reid gave substance to this perspective with several state-ments that indicated the government's stance dictated the committee's action. A female investor denounced Hepburn's "effrontery" for telling people to buy war bonds while his "disgraceful turn-about-face" administration hypocritically did not act. What was at stake was "a test for capitalism" and the province had failed as a social trustee.[103] The government remained conspicuously silent. Letters to the premier went unanswered. Hepburn's few statements dodged responsibility and consisted of muddled suggestions about how little could be done or how affected investors might try to seek redress from federal authorities. While acknowledging the province could withdraw the firm's timber limits, he stated more closed mills and ghost towns would result.[104] George Drew, in contrast, denounced the sale as "a mortgage upon public assets" where the "ultimate ownership of this property by the people of Ontario has already been asserted." While acknowledging the "sanctity of contracts," he noted "there is an old legal maxim that 'He who seeks equity must do equity.'" The foreclosure was dangerous because "if the opinion becomes general that the small investor is completely at the mercy of those who are able to obtain control of any company the very lifeblood of new industry will cease to flow."[105]

Those still associated with the defensive committee were at their wit's end about what to do. Richard Hanson, the interim leader of the federal Conservative Party, decried the timing of the sale as inopportune. Symington told him the government would not oppose it, notwithstanding any perceptions to the contrary.[106] Dalton McCarthy falsely claimed to Hepburn that major financial institutions no longer sanctioned a judicial sale. Three options, he argued, were available: impose a moratorium over corporate indebtedness; require resource companies to incorporate under provincially; or rescind the 1939 order-in-council. The province could impose equitable terms for a restructuring of Abitibi. While considerable criticism would result, it must block "the catastrophe looming before the junior security holders."[107] Few bondholders were willing to lose their stakes. The last resistance from dissidents crumbled as four-fifths of the securities were deposited and the Drayton committee withered away.

On the eve of the sale, Noranda Mines applied to the Supreme Court for an indefinite adjournment. It asked that Clarkson be instructed to distribute $7 million from the current assets as payment on the bond principal and accrued interest. The receiver then should continue the payments semi-annually. Middleton refused to entertain the request but Justice Urquhart granted a hearing. Abitibi's status was improving with $12 million in current assets and a monthly profit of $800,000, Noranda's litigator argued. This meant the current assets might be used for partial reimbursement. Urquhart noted how this was long known. A company could not stay indefinitely in receivership, he conceded.

The appointment of a receiver should result in "ultimate and speedy sales." There were no guarantees about the future and he would not pre-judge whether a judicial sale was competitive. Because the bond-holders had a right to a remedy after eight years, he ruled the motion was premature but agreed Noranda could reapply if the sale failed.[108]

When the sale was held the court accepted only one bid. An invest-ment dealer left an "intriguing envelope" on the desk of the Master of the Supreme Court but he refused to read it because the regular submis-sion process was not followed. The bondholders offered $30 million. The low valuation was based upon Symington's belief there was noth-ing left for the junior securities. Ironically, as discussed in the next chap-ter, with an upsurge in wartime demand and prices by late 1940 that had become absurd. Most of the proceeds from a higher bid, however, would have gone to the non-depositors. Regardless, the tender was below the secret reserve price set by the Master. The judicial sale thus was declared closed and abortive, making the route to a solution uncer-tain. "When there are so many ideas as to what may occur," the *Globe and Mail*'s financial editor commented, "the investor feels it is any-body's guess."[109]

13

A Constitutional War

I have, since I came into prison, been several times in such a case that I thought to die within the hour, and I thank our Lord I was never sorry for it, but rather sorry when it passed. And therefore, my poor body is at the King's pleasure. Would God my death might do him some good ... Nevertheless, it is not for the Supremacy that you have sought my blood – but because I would not bend to the marriage.

– Robert Bolt, *A Man for All Seasons*

Funny, when I was a little boy I wanted to be good. But I could never seem to manage it somehow. And if you're not good, the good people will throw you to the wolves. So you might as well just be bad.

– C.J. Sansom, *Winter in Madrid*

NO ONE SINCE 1932 HAD heard from Alexander Smith, who still held bonds and over 100,000 common shares, but he agreed to testify before a royal commission eight years later. While acknowledging the complicated issues behind Abitibi's failure, he now linked "excessive and unjustified prices for newsprint" to the wave of over-production and destructive competition. A recurrence "in anything like the same catastrophic degree" was unlikely, he assured the commission, because executives and governments "had lessons enough, to keep some sort of harness on it." Smith conceded he had a moral obligation to Abitibi's investors. "After all, I built this company – perhaps mismanaged this company." A successful resuscitation, he believed, was possible only with sacrifices from each security class. These included reductions of the debt and preferred stock charges, as well as a write-off of the common shareholders since they had to "take the brunt." Smith said, "The last thing I would want to see would be this patient taken off the operating table and put back on again. You might as well put a zipper in it."[1]

Smith, like many others, recognized what was needed for a resolution but with their entrenched positions the investor groups refused to compromise. This difficulty was overlaid by another stalemate. Given public outrage over the plan of procedure, the Hepburn administration opposed a repetition of the judicial sale. Symington's committee, however, insisted upon the sanctity of contractual rights. Each sought an outcome on its own terms but neither could escape the situation without the cooperation of the other. The deadlock metamorphosed the receivership from a matter of insolvency into a constitutional question about the province's right to control business affairs. This chapter examines how that occurred. The first section considers the renewed efforts to find a solution and how Ontario's intervention against another sale precipitated a prolonged legal struggle. The next part examines how wartime regulation altered the newsprint sector. The third reviews Abitibi's wartime problems, along with the end of the constitutional fight by an unexpected decision by the highest court, the Judicial Committee of the Privy Council, which set a basis from which the receivership might be concluded.

1. The unfortunate, extravagant, and futile course

The failure of the auction triggered yet another drop in the market value of Abitibi bonds, while the prices for the equity again escalated. More schemes surfaced, each portrayed as a wise solution that reasonable people should accept. The two options in the wake of the abortive sale were obvious: Noranda Mines could resubmit its application for payments on the bond interest, or the bondholders and Montreal Trust could retain the right to ask for another auction. Both courses attracted immediate opposition. Sir Robert Borden, who reflected popular opinion well, denounced a wartime sale without competitive bidding as farcical.[2] There were two points of agreement among most commentators: it was not an appropriate time and the matter was now on the doorstep of Mitch Hepburn – it was *his* responsibility. The cabinet consequently rescinded the order-in-council that had sanctioned any plan approved by the Supreme Court but this did not arrest the matter. Symington's committee could reapply after a month for another sale that used the same reserve price. However, after six months it had the right to seek a sale either with a lower reserve bid or possibly without one.[3] George Drew demanded immediate action to prevent further confusion, which he defined as blocking a transfer of any assets unless the arrangement was satisfactory to the province. Investor rights were important, he argued, but far more crucial were the welfare of the employees and the communities that were dependent upon Abitibi. The bid of $30 million for a firm earning $8 million in 1940 was "conclusive proof" of how it was improper to allow such proceedings with money markets frozen by the war.[4]

Seeking to delay things, the premier resorted to a time-honoured tactic: an enquiry by a royal commission comprised "of three outstanding men" who might recommend an equitable solution. Justice Charles McTague was appointed as the chair. Not only had he been involved with several rounds of the Abitibi litigation, but he was also the most knowledgeable member of Ontario's Supreme Court about corporate law. Albert E. Dyment had started out in the family lumbering business in Algoma, served as a Liberal MPP from 1894 to 1908, and then went on to the elite of Canadian big business. He was chair of Canadian General Electric and a director or manager for numerous enterprises including the Royal Bank of Canada, Dominion Sugar, and Maritime Coal, Railway, & Power. The third was Sir James Dunn, the president of Algoma Steel. Hepburn portrayed it as a strong team that "will command the respect of the people of Ontario." Most observers endorsed the commission but the selection of Dunn represented a dubious choice since he was known to be sympathetic to the Liberals and had orchestrated Algoma's brutal reorganization. The *Globe and Mail*'s financial editor declared the province held "life and death powers" over the firm and "it now proposes to exercise its powers in the direction of life."[5] Despite this initiative, the protective committee applied for another sale. Justice Middleton acceded to a request from the province for a stay until the commission completed its work. Action was adjourned *sine die* but the committee could resume the action on a week's notice.[6]

McTague invited Clarkson to develop a reorganization plan (which he declined) and announced anyone could bring a scheme before the commission. The phrasing of the statement led press reports to imply that a proposal the commission recommended and the government approved would then be imposed by Ontario's legislature. The six weeks of hearings brought testimony from most of those ensnarled by the receivership, with submissions that ranged from precise thoughtful analyses to hazy unreliable reminiscences of past events, from misleading presentations to unbending restatements of entrenched biases. About two-fifths of the proceedings entailed tedious recapitulations of Abitibi's properties and their values, the terms associated with the resource concessions, industry trends, and the drawn-out court cases. Another fifth dealt with the 1928 refinancing and the composition of the different investor groups. The balance reviewed many reorganization schemes, including some that had never garnered real consideration.

Dry accounts characterized most of the testimony, but occasionally a moment of levity brightened a session. Charles Keys, a New York investment banker, and several associates had submitted a proposal in late 1936, which was discussed at length with the protective committees. The effort proved futile, he recalled. "I think that most of these gentlemen had opinions or convictions being that we were more or less busybodies and that they wish we would go home and jump in the lake. As soon as we were convinced that a sufficient number of these interests felt that way to make it impossible to do anything at that time, we withdrew and dropped the matter."[7] With relations among the contending interests poisoned, some witnesses let their animus fly. The bondholders, Arthur Slaght declared, had a "throat grasp" to seize all future profits "unto their own bosom." Their spokesman, as they sought this bonanza, might be "the voice of Mr. Symington but the hand is the hand of Ripley and the Committee." Norman Tilley, in turn, derided opponents for raising specious and technical objections.[8] Several sessions entailed the interrogation of old participants. Called to discuss the Bradshaw committee, Howard Ferguson spent much of his testimony rationalizing the province's treatment of the industry while he was in office. Zotique Mageau appeared for Sturgeon Falls and reminded the commission that over half of the town remained unemployed. Most had done nothing for seven to eight years but lived on "the dole." Many now lacked the willingness or capacity to work although the welfare department insisted the abled-bodied might be exempted only with medical certification.[9]

The centrepiece of the hearings was the testimony of Herbert Symington, the sole time he spoke in a public venue. Once again, the 1928 financing was defended as reasonable, while the descent towards receivership supposedly resulted from two "very unfortunate commitments" – OPS and Thunder Bay. The bondholders had exercised the rights of anyone who held a defaulted contract, he argued. Symington could not resist sniping about how in other cases "it was not considered a crime for the government to exercise its legal rights and foreclose the mortgage." Following the dismissal of the Ripley plan, Abitibi's fortunes "developed distinctly in an adverse direction. All the bright outlook and fanciful figures vanished overnight." It might be argued that market values were not final, he remarked, but experience over time demonstrated that those assessments were relatively correct.[10] Symington censured the efforts to stop a judicial sale. It left "Wall Street wondering especially whether investments in Canada are apt to fare better in that Dominion than they do in various Latin-American countries." Much of the opposition he castigated as a "racket" put up by would-be dealers who sought "a method of allowing them to unload their worthless interest on a new set of unfortunate speculators." Moreover, stock exchange records mapped how shares had turned over multiple times yet "people have come here and in the papers and talked about protecting original purchases."[11]

Symington denied that the commission held jurisdiction over the case. His committee rejected any scheme based upon "the unfettered discretion of a department administrator." Any statute the province passed to force reorganization was unconstitutional. Rather, contractual disputes had to be settled through the established procedures and standards of the judicial system. "Discretion is the engineer of chance, rule the guarantor of stability. Legal rights and duties should not be created, impaired, or destroyed by administrative discretion posing as an agency of justice." Most of the alternatives were based upon speculation about future earnings. If the commission and the province imposed an arbitrary scheme the bondholders would "wait, not nine years, but an indefinite number of years in the hope that something will turn up while worthless paper is scattered through the market." In contrast, his committee comprised outstanding citizens who did not act from impure motives.

> These men are the keepers of their own conscience, and nobody can make them act in conflict with that conscience ... After all, a bond debt is only a promise to pay with a provision for realization, if payment is not made. Take away that contracted right of realization and you take away the whole value of the security, and nothing but an unsecured debt is left; you repudiate contracts; you ruin the financial standing of the community and you destroy the system of justice and the administration of justice under which we have grown, and which we endeavour to preserve.[12]

The commission's report was not submitted until April. It recapitulated history to demonstrate the inadequacy of Canadian laws and stressed how there were no provisions to ensure an objective appraisal of whether there was surviving equity. The protective committee deemed itself "the sole judge" and sought the "pure fiction" of a sale. With insider information and the lack of competitive bids, it could buy the company for less than its real value. In the United States, courts were authorized to investigate and ensure a plan was fair, equitable, and feasible. The Securities and Exchange Commission also could intervene. Similar provisions in Canada required modifications of federal and provincial legislation, changes that the commissioners hoped public pressure might generate because "the old mortgage procedure of foreclosure through the fiction of a sale seems to us to have no place in corporate reorganizations today." In addition, the commissioners argued that deposit agreements for security classes should be the exception, rather than the rule, and that the powers of protective committees should be limited. Judges needed the authority to disregard such agreements and stipulate independent votes.[13]

Both the province and the public had a huge stake in the industry. The government's role as a trustee for society originated not just from its ownership of natural resources but from law. It had "a vested interest based on the sanctity of contractual relationship[s]" to ensure "equitable obligations to the investing public" that provided monies "on the strength of the Government's given word." A general feeling of insecurity prevailed that could be dissipated only by the removal of any suspicion that political considerations, not ordinary justice, shaped those dealings. Therefore, "the day of dispensing favours in the form of timber concessions to new political friends has long gone by."[14] The need to prevent a sale when no likelihood existed of independent purchasers making an offer seemed obvious. A sale was also subject to wartime taxes that could prevent Abitibi from regaining solvency.

Their recommendations constituted "obviously far from a definite and complete solution." Indeed, they dodged the central question, deeming it unwise "to define what should be done about that in the future ... no plan heretofore proposed is now practical."[15] Given the unpredictability of future earnings, the best option entailed a preservation of the status quo and it was thought that perhaps the financial situation might work itself out. Their "plan" therefore amounted to modest tinkering: an extension of the time limit for the existing bonds from 1952 to 1965, as well as a restriction of past-due interest and any interest on unpaid interest for 1932 to 1940. The company should maintain a specified level of working capital, with any excess used to pay down the bond principal. Once the receiver and the liquidator were able to resign, for five years or until the bond principal decreased to $35 million, a board selected by the bondholders and preferred shareholders should manage Abitibi. But the commissioners acknowledged that even this scheme required consent from the participants, along with an agreement to discontinue legal actions.[16]

With the royal commission unwilling to submit concrete proposals, no one was clear about what, if anything, could be done. Press accounts described the report as constructive, but each stakeholder saw what it wished to see. The equity investors thought their position had been vindicated and the commission had offered a workable basis for reaching an agreement, despite the lack of details. McTague later commented in an interview that he felt all through the case that there was something for the shareholders. But without an agreed method about how to assess the company there was no way to it give measure. The bondholders, in contrast, felt little good had resulted and thought the report just proved there was nothing for the equity investors.[17] McTague suggested Hepburn call a meeting to see if the various parties might agree about a request for federal legislation to bring the recommendations into effect. "This is much the shortest route to getting the matter finally wound up," he said. The premier, who intensely distrusted the King administration, refused to consider this even though a provincial law was obviously unconstitutional. With nothing to stop another judicial sale, Hepburn asked about alternatives and McTague noted that a moratorium appeared to be one of the few available.[18] Two protective committees had suggested the same, but more as a contingency than a specific course of action.[19]

A law imposing a moratorium on financial obligations was not novel. Governments have employed the tool since ancient times as a means of controlling payments for sovereign debt, especially during wartime or emergencies. Moratoria have rested upon two assumptions: property or values are temporarily depreciated, and therefore it is appropriate to postpone payments to a future date when business conditions are more "normal." Nonetheless, they always have been controversial because, while some debtors may benefit, creditors are penalized, the availability of loan capital can decrease, and future costs for borrowers tend to be raised. They also vitiate contractual rights, the essential prop of the economic and social order.[20] Despite those problems, moratoria were considered short-term solutions for defaults on rural or household property loans during the Great Depression. Farm mortgage foreclosures had been a significant problem since the First World War, and non-farm residential foreclosures then became a concern as disposable income fell and unemployment soared. Similar to the American housing crisis of 2007–12, real estate prices declined, with the consequence that owners who could not make payments were unable to sell their property for the outstanding principal of the loans. Home mortgages in the 1930s tended to be short-term, non-amortizing loans that were refinanced on maturity, a condition difficult to secure as domestic economies shrank. Demands for action against seizures by banks compelled twenty-seven American states to pass legislation to halt or limit foreclosures. A few imposed blanket moratoria on properties with mortgages contracted before specific dates, but most granted relief for mortgagors who were current in payments of interest and taxes despite being delinquent on the loan principal. Some restricted lenders from securing deficiency judgments or allowed a redemption period in which a mortgagor could regain ownership.[21] In 1934 Canada's Parliament passed similar debt relief legislation, purportedly "to keep the farmer on the farm,"[22]

In Ontario, Premier George Henry had difficulty with the notion of suspending payments on contracts. The average individual, he observed, thought only of that person's situation when financial difficulties were encountered, not "the vicious chain of circumstances" that might result from their deferral. Banks or loan companies had largely ceased to authorize property loans, but he was cautioned about how restrictions might eliminate the ability to secure mortgage credit in the future. Insurance companies feared funds invested for mortgage loans would be withdrawn and placed elsewhere.[23] Nonetheless, in 1932 the government passed legislation that imposed a limited moratorium to block foreclosures or sales for the non-payment of loan principal. Foreclosures required judicial approval and court officers were instructed to serve as intermediaries between parties to gain acceptable solutions.[24] As the Depression worsened, the cabinet debated whether to expand the legislation. At the same time, individuals (usually characterized in the press as widows or similar dependents) who relied upon interest from mortgage investments demanded the government not take "punitive action." Henry feared their situation might be rendered as deplorable as those who could not meet payments. Backbenchers within the party's caucus were outraged that a Conservative premier would dare violate the sanctity of contractual rights. They compelled the government to limit the statute to mortgages that predated March 1932 and to stipulate rules that narrowed its applicability to cases where individuals could document an absolute inability to pay.[25] Due to continued economic difficulties and lobbying by local officials, the legislation was renewed across the 1930s. It intruded into federal jurisdiction over insolvency, but the law's constitutionality was never challenged. There were also debates about defaults on municipal loans, but tighter regulation by provincial agencies was adopted rather than a moratorium.

Although there were few precedents dealing with the proscription of foreclosure for corporate securities, with both political parties in concurrence, a statute was passed that stayed a sale of Abitibi's assets. The move officially was temporary, legitimated by a claim that stakeholders needed an opportunity to appraise the plan submitted by the McTague commission. Further proceedings were prohibited and the attorney general's approval was required for a new action. The act was back-dated to 1939, thereby abrogating the order-in-council that sanctioned a transfer of Abitibi's assets after a sale. The moratorium was to end in late 1942 but renewals eventually extended it to 1945. Despite the passage of the legislation, the government again prevaricated and did not proclaim the act for six months, hoping the threat alone would stop the bondholders.[26]

Hepburn never explained the reversal of position and why the government now was concerned about protecting the equity holders and others when it had not done so earlier. It certainly fit his self-professed support for aiding the "little guy." However, the government was well aware that speculators now held much of the equity. Several ministers cited wartime restrictions on capital flows and the losses imposed by a foreclosure as rationales. But a major concern entailed the risk that a moratorium posed to Ontario's reputation as a safe locale for international investment, especially because the province was still recovering from Hepburn's repudiation of hydro contracts several years earlier. The premier always distrusted Abitibi's lawyers, who had extensive connections with the Tories, but it is likely the government's revised stance was conditioned by the new composition of the protective committee. Herbert Symington was a close associate of Prime Minister King and C.D. Howe, whom Hepburn detested. The premier forced the removal of the deputy counsel on the Abitibi Royal Commission because the individual praised the Rowell-Sirois report on dominion-provincial relations.[27] Once the bondholders gained control after a sale, the key question remained: what did they plan to do with the firm? Symington proverbially was in the catbird seat. With 85 per cent of the bonds deposited, if a new sale occurred just $6 million less expenses was required to pay off non-assenting bondholders.[28] He could replicate Killam's manoeuvres with Mattagami and Riordon by merging Abitibi with Price Brothers. Ontario's largest newsprint company thus could end up with an executive the premier likely could not influence.

The government pressed the bondholders to meet with other groups but frustration mounted as the impasse continued. Symington's counsel argued that the commission report did not respect the legitimate interests of the debt holders. Suddenly legal stances flipped. Now the protective committee claimed provincial intervention was ultra vires, an intrusion into federal jurisdiction over bankruptcy. It planned to proceed with a sale once several questions were resolved, especially the tax status of payments.[29] In October, the bondholders accordingly restarted the process adjourned the previous November. On the same day, the government proclaimed the Abitibi Moratorium Act. After several procedural delays, the parties again appeared before Justice Middleton. The counsel for the committee noted that no efforts had been made to implement the commission's recommendations, the bondholders had not sought special legislation to realize goals, nor had an application been filed for court approval of the liquidator's scheme. Therefore, the committee applied for a judicial sale and asked the moratorium statute be ruled unconstitutional.[30]

When Middleton ruled two days later, most of his decision was a recitation of prior developments. He noted about how the statute ignored the case facts and did not specify any date other than its expected termination. But even that provision could be extended indefinitely. Moreover, not only did Abitibi have operations in several provinces, but a winding-up order had also been filed in 1932. Middleton insisted that a firm operating under a Dominion statute did not require permission from a provincial legislature. The moratorium law could not restrict the leave granted under the Winding-Up Act and was ultra vires "in so far as it seeks to control or limit the powers of the court." Middleton ordered a sale but specified it was subject to a reserve bid.[31]

McPherson sought leave to appeal. Following a brief hearing, Justice William Roach questioned Middleton's decision. The original 1932 filing, he argued, gave Montreal Trust leave to invoke the jurisdiction of the provincial court. Therefore, any regulations passed by the legislature must be accepted. Because provincial authority covered civil and property rights, along with the ability to adjust judicial procedures, Ontario could also pass legislation to postpone a proceeding. Roach emphasized the recommendations of the royal commission, noting how government assistance was necessary for Abitibi's success and for the protection of the "legitimate interests" of other investors. He granted the request and stayed any sale until the full court reviewed the case.[32]

In many ways, the three days of hearings that ensued before the Ontario Court of Appeal were visions of proceedings past, as lawyers for the contending parties drew upon decisions or selectively cited facts that buttressed their arguments. Counsel for the provincial attorney general declared the moratorium act did not destroy rights but just postponed their enforcement. Splitting hairs, one even claimed the act did not interfere with Abitibi but just with the mortgagee. Dalton McCarthy, on behalf of the liquidator, stressed the constitutionality of the statute. He noted how Abitibi's earnings had improved and therefore a settlement under court supervision represented the logical course. Arthur Slaght, with his usual theatricality, expostulated about how a sale was scandalous. A price of $30 million was "ridiculous" for a company worth more than $100 million. For the bondholders, Norman Tilley focused on the core issue and questioned the province's right to pass any legislation under the heading of "administrative justice" that restricted access to the courts.[33]

On 21 March 1942, in a four-to-one ruling the court dismissed the appeal and ruled the Moratorium Act unconstitutional. It was not a unified judgment. The members of the majority got to their decisions by alternative routes. Justice Riddell observed how all counsel "argued at great – but not too great – length, with quotation of many authorities," most of which had only an indirect bearing on the case. He complained "the Legislature is – no doubt with the best intentions – interfering in matters beyond its control." Justice Fisher rejected the very notion that the province was dealing with a matter of civil and property rights. "The whole aim and object" he said, was "to prohibit a particular action already commended under a valid power conferred by Dominion statute." Moreover, the Moratorium Act vested jurisdiction with the provincial attorney general, not the courts. Justice Henderson, using alternative citations, stressed how laws about property and civil rights "must not be legislation aimed at a particular person or corporation, but must be general in character." The provincial legislature was not competent to deny access to the courts for a specific case. Justice Hogg concentrated upon reviewing the situations subject to appeal to a higher court and then insisted that the province was invading a field of legislation allocated to the Dominion. Only Justice Gillanders accepted the argument about the province's authority to deal with insolvent corporations under its property and civil rights powers. In his view, the legislation did not mandate a distribution of the company's assets among the creditors. It just postponed proceedings and therefore, in pith and substance, did not contravene federal law. Nonetheless, while the act fell within the province's authority, Abitibi's creditors might gain some benefit from the delay solely as a "charitable hope."[34]

With the full support of the Tories, the government responded the next day with two bills: one extending the moratorium to June 1943, another referring the matter to the court of last resort, the Judicial Committee of the Privy Council in the United Kingdom. Although the province was not a direct party to the case, Hepburn and the attorney general wanted the decision reviewed. The second statute had the province grant itself a right of further appeal notwithstanding the existing rules or procedures. "Not a member of this House wants to see this great company sacrificed on the auction block at this time," the premier stated, "particularly when British investors are powerless to protect their interests." The firm was "in good shape" and "making more than is needed to pay the bond indebtedness." Leopold Macaulay, speaking for the Conservatives, could not understand why the bondholders felt their mortgage should not be subject to the moratorium act "while the little fellow is." Abitibi was "in the hands of men who do not seem to realize that there are equitable considerations which should be advanced in times like these."[35] Hepburn hemmed and hawed about how he had "exhausted all my other resources" and lacked authority in the matter but then stated the government did not intend to use "the big club" of its control over natural resources to bring finality. The consequences of cancelling the timber and water licences were dire: higher unemployment and loss of revenue to the province. Macaulay responded with a withering critique of the premier's shilly-shally. "We are trying to prevent a gigantic steal being put over on the helpless shareholders," he said. If the protective committee was prepared to extract the last ounce of blood, "then those who live by the sword must perish by the sword, if you get your sword there first." He wanted to know "what clique will be in control when this business is unravelled."[36]

The bondholders inevitably sought to block the initiative, and when the parties appeared before a panel of Justices Robertson, McTague, and Madsen, this time the arguments had little do with the original dispute but centred upon whether the province could force another appeal. The Proclamation of 1763 and the Privy Council Appeals Act, the provincial attorney general and the preferred shareholders' counsel argued, sanctioned a resort to the British court. The latest statute, they declared, was just enabling legislation that removed some restrictions contained in previous laws. Arthur Slaght attacked the decision on the previous appeal as an outrage, one that "tied his clients hand and foot." Norman Tilley contended the latest statute was beyond the legislature's powers. In any event, he added, the Judicial Committee of the Privy Council was out of touch with Canadian business and could not appreciate the issues associated with the newsprint industry.[37]

The central question for the court revolved around the legitimacy of the appeal request. Since the British North America Act did not grant permission for provincial parliaments to alter the right of appeal to the Privy Council, some lawyers contended the province was engaging in "creative power." Much of the hearing was taken up with references to colonial statutes and cases that defined the legal process. Middleton's order also was interlocutory in character, an intermediate step. Only final decisions, not interlocutory judgments, could be appealed to the court of last resort, although the province contended that the order for a sale was final in form, given its effect on the rights of the different parties. The main judgment delivered by Chief Justice Robertson sidestepped the controversy. It was not necessary, he stated, to determine whether it was possible for the legislature to extend the right of appeal. In his opinion, the act did not fall within the power of a provincial parliament. Specifically, the statute was not related to the administration of justice under the terms of the British North America Act "and no attempt was made to support it under any head." However, rather than strike the law down, the court treated it as irrelevant and focused upon whether the appeal request conformed to the usual requirements. While appreciating provincial concern over the disposition of the Abitibi properties, the court refused to declare whether the legislature had the right to impose a moratorium, but because this represented a new issue the application was granted. The Chief Justice could not resist taking a swipe at the appellants in his closing remarks. "It may well be that even if the statute is found to be valid, it will at best do no more than postpone the inevitable," he said, and a sale for cash would then be carried to completion.[38]

Justice Arthur Masten, in a separate opinion, accepted these rationales but his analysis was blunter: "Not only has the whole situation become most confused and difficult, but also a situation has arisen where wide-spread public interests are involved, and where, if allowable in law, the disentangling assistance of the Judicial Committee should be invoked." The province owed a duty to protect the public domain and the junior investors, but it also had "the obligation to see that the contractual obligations held by the bondholders are not lightly disregarded." Based upon his past experience in company law, he said, "I have been strongly impressed by the unfortunate, extravagant, and futile course of the present litigation." He stressed how the McTague Commission had documented the inadequacies of existing legislation but insisted that "the difficulty could easily be met" if the parties agreed to present their positions before a court and accept an adjudicated settlement under the CCAA. Since the passage of the Chandler Act, he noted, American law contained valuable provisions for a solution.[39]

With the appeal process expected to take at least another year, the Abitibi case had outlasted many of the individuals assigned to handle it. Norman Tilley never saw the outcome: he died two months after the appeal hearing. Among the participants in the legal aspects of the receivership, in death, he alone was praised as an outstanding, fair, and internationally famed counsellor, with "accomplishments [that] have acquired the aura of the legendary." Most others simply had their passing acknowledged, with polite references to their careers and their hobbies or interests. Justice James Hall, who headed the Sturgeon Falls Royal Commission, died in 1935. Justices Latchford, Kingstone, and Sedgewick also passed between 1938 and 1940, while Justices Masden and Riddell did not live to the end of the case. Albert Dyment, Abitibi Royal Commissioner, succumbed after a long illness in 1944. Tilley's partner, Strachan Johnston, died in September 1941. His son handled things until the trustee chose a new lawyer. *Montreal Trust v. Abitibi Power and Paper* was assumed by a new generation of litigants, most of whom just wanted the matter done and over with.[40]

2. Wartime paper

While those struggles continued, Abitibi's recovery, along with the state of the industry, was altered yet again – this time by the international situation. As newsprint sales increased from 1939 to 1941, media commentators claimed this originated from "abnormal" circumstances: the loss of European supply to a "mere dribble," higher consumption as the public focused upon foreign affairs, and the construction of inventories by customers. Though prices remained stable, North American supply still exceeded annual demand by more than a million tons. Within the new context, the paper manufacturers now portrayed their key roles as earners of foreign exchange (to fund the war effort) and the preservation of output so a free press could "function without fear of shortage or high cost."[41] Some mistakenly expected demand to shrink with the conversion of business operations to military functions. Charles Vining thought the war might provide a period of grace for stabilizing the sector, but he expected the postwar situation to be more difficult than anything that had previously occurred.[42]

Although the Canadian government, and then the American, began instituting controls in 1939, it took three years before pulp and paper came under full regulation. In Canada, some interests still stressed the need for prorating but support for the policy disintegrated. It had never been popular among the manufacturers. Many deemed the policy irksome, at best, but they especially disliked the inconsistent implementation. By 1940, nine companies had received exemptions. Despite denials by government officials, suspicions were widespread that the cases originated from political favouritism. Exempt firms, petitioners to the Ontario legislature declared, should not obtain the advantages of the policy without the obligations.[43] Opposition mounted because the policy addressed the symptoms, not the causes, of the malaise. "As a cure-all, prorating is no more effective than sedatives which are used to compose the patient and relieve his worst pains," noted one executive.

It could "never secure a ton of business" and created disincentives to obtain new business. Only the dynamics of world competition could trigger improvement – whenever demand exceeded supply. Conservative leader George Drew was more caustic: "The patient is sick and we are trying to find out how best to operate. But we run into this situation where we are stopped for fear of hurting somebody. This history of pro-rating has not proved too satisfactory."[44] Ontario tried to keep two-thirds of output under the framework but Quebec granted exemptions that reduced the coverage to half of production in that province.

Most companies just ignored prorating. With nearly a third of capacity still idle, Vining warned Mitch Hepburn:

> Various and devious forms of price-cutting or concessions by Canadian mills and their agents are now being practised on an extensive scale ... Price stability has become undermined to such an extent that an open collapse of the market price is merely a matter of time unless strong corrective action intervenes. Once a general price collapse occurs its correction may prove impossible for a considerable period. Practices already existing involve an unnecessary loss of United States exchange which we estimate at $2,000,000 to $3,000,000 a year. This loss, in wartime, is a public crime.[45]

Communities located near mills that had not benefited from prorating, in contrast, perceived it as discriminatory. They sought either to end the policy or terminate the exemptions. Within this context, provincial forest policy remained thoroughly muddled. Ontario had banned new newsprint mills but still supported the construction of sulphite pulp factories, even though none of the projects authorized by the Hepburn administration progressed. The government also refused to restrict exports of logs, despite widespread beliefs that they allowed American mills to make newsprint. Peter Heenan acknowledged the government kept few records and relied upon assurances from exporters that newsprint was not an end use. Under pressure from the Conservative opposition, a committee of the Ontario legislature investigated and the testimony about malfeasance, questionable contracts, and lack of control proved highly embarrassing. A report by the Liberal majority whitewashed the findings. The minority report provided an unrelenting critique of stupidity and sheer incompetence. Mitch Hepburn was compelled to replace Peter Heenan. Officially, the action was portrayed as a transfer to another position, but the opposition parties and most observers considered it removal for gross ineptitude. His replacement quietly began a reform program aimed at professionalizing the ministry. Analogous issues surfaced in Quebec, as critics charged that the province had allowed construction without thought for the future, and firms found it "almost impossible to operate with a decent profit upon invested capital."[46] But neither government would concede failure and repeal prorating. Rather, the policy became subsumed in a new regulatory framework elaborated by Canada and the United States.

Official accounts during and after the war characterized economic mobilization as an orderly, largely harmonious, endeavour. This portrait bore scant resemblance to the experiences of forest products companies, which dealt with a welter of authorities that had overlapping jurisdictions and issued duplicate or contradictory actions, some with unintended consequences.[47] While a full analysis lies outside the scope of this book, it is necessary to review how this occurred. The multifarious wartime agencies and commissions encountered serious difficulties, and their efforts were subject to intense lobbying.

From the beginning, the sector held an ambiguous priority. Some goods were important (pulp for explosives or rayon, blueprint paper, paper containers). Numerous others like writing, wrapping, and book papers were deemed non-essential. Although newspapers were key for information dissemination, some officials deemed the use of paper for advertising immoral. Newsprint received low priority relative to metals like aluminum and during the war public officials tried to divert production towards other areas, curb non-essential uses, and shape manufacturing and consumption patterns. The tasks were complicated by the cross-border trade flows and inter-relationships among demand, supply and prices for alternative goods.

Canadian producers formed voluntary groups for joint action and lobbied for public sector direction but substantive controls were not extended until 1942. Under the Department of Munitions and Supply, coordination theoretically had a unified chain of command. In fact, it was fragmented through twenty-six industrial committees, various controllers, and regional authorities. Pulp and paper companies were subject to three officials: a newsprint administrator (who guided production), a power controller (responsible for prioritizing electrical supply), and later an administrator of wood pulps (who directed the quantities to be manufactured or shipped by each mill). The surviving documentation indicates the newsprint office proceeded haphazardly. Even when regulations were issued, its personnel were reluctant to instruct companies. Rather, their letters asked for self-reports on machinery and productive capacity, with a stress upon the need for assistance rather than their power to force compliance.[48] Moreover, jurisdiction over international relations resided with a Wartime Prices and Trade Board (WPTB), which had sustained disputes with American authorities but usually acquiesced to their expectations. Despite their promises of consultation, American regulators often took unilateral action or expected their Canadian counterparts to follow their lead. Thus, although Canadian regulation was important, the regime elaborated south of the border became more crucial.

President Roosevelt initially authorized the formation of the Advisory Commission to the Council on National Defence, which was tasked with assisting the management of economic dislocations. Inflation in 1940 compelled the Commission to form a pulp and paper group. After meetings with corporate representatives and a consultant's report that deemed regulation inappropriate, the Commission declared the supply adequate and sanctioned continued market direction of prices. This stance characterized American policy for over a year, given isolationist opposition to anything that resembled wartime authority. While professing a willingness to cooperate, the American industry lobbied against rationing or quotas, policies that represented serious threats for integrated mills.[49] Nonetheless, controls were incrementally extended. The Commission's pulp and paper group was restructured as a branch within the Office of Production Management (OPM, later known as the War Production Board or WPB) that handled civilian supply activities. Official authority over prices was allocated to the Office of Price Administration (OPA), but other agencies frequently attempted to intervene. Autonomous WPB branches regulated printing, publishing, and the production of paperboard or paper containers. The coordination of transportation was divided among the Office of Defence Transportation, the U.S. Maritime Commission, and the Interstate Commerce Commission. The personnel of these agencies mushroomed, along with an array of subcommittees, liaison groups, and advisory committees.[50]

Proposing coordination was one thing, implementation another. Although public officials attempted to elaborate coherent plans and gave verbal acknowledgment to the continental character of the industry, many initiatives unfolded ad hoc, in response to immediate problems, with administrators focused more upon priorities within their own nations than the broader context. Approximately 40 per cent of the labour force in Canada and the United States was diverted into the armed forces, munitions, and other military-related industries. To secure labour, industries engaged in war work offered higher wages for a full year (versus seasonal employment in woods operations), and the occupations had deferral rights on military service. Shortages of loggers became acute, which cut output by a quarter by the summer of 1942 and nearly another third a year later. The American government attempted remedial action by designating logging as an essential activity but failed to list it as an essential *occupation* (with draft deferment), an oversight that perpetuated the labour shortage until the end of the war. A similar problem unfolded in Canada where federal officials placed low priority upon pulpwood logging, whereas timber used in aircraft manufacture received the highest rating. Moreover, thousands of workers had crossed the border during the Great Depression for seasonal employment. To minimize shortfalls in domestic production, Canada imposed a system of labour permits to check the movement, but the policy exacerbated the difficulties experienced by American producers. Both countries then encumbered forest companies with cutbacks of chlorine and copper or other metals and gave them low priority for equipment allocations, which raised expenses and weakened productive capabilities.[51]

The unwillingness to institute quotas or rationing allowed newsprint consumption to soar. Many firms began to operate near full capacity for the first time in fifteen years. With the higher output, some earned record profits and reduced their debt loads or arrears for preferred dividends, actions that publishers smeared as "war profiteering." Mutterings from public officials about the likelihood of regulation contributed to several waves of overstocking and buying hysteria. The upsurge in demand also worked against government efforts to prioritize transport movements. For example, freight car space was at a premium by early 1941, but the volume accounted for by pulp and paper shipments increased significantly. This issue was compounded when the U.S. Maritime Commission unilaterally banned coastal traffic of commercial goods, which forced producers in Quebec and the Maritimes to use railways.[52]

Attempting to control pulpwood supply, regulators generated a bottleneck that restricted continental output. The WPB received jurisdiction over deliveries in the United States. Although the agency lacked official authority over Canadian shipments, it declared them "American" the moment they crossed the border. As resource supplies dwindled, firms bought logs wherever possible, including from settlers and private operators at rates well above the stipulated ceiling prices. The Canadian government, insisting upon the need to protect domestic manufacturers, countered by restricting exports derived from Crown lands, thereby cutting off numerous American firms and prompting renewed allegations about how Canadians machinated to dominate the industry. Over several years producers lobbied for measures that might ease the shortages, including the use of prisoners of war in woods operations.[53] The WPB attempted to regulate cutting for certain types of timber but loggers, who pursued their own revenue goals, just shifted their activities to exempt species or moved to other states, which forced the agency to play catch-up. Pacific pulpwood had been shipped as far as New England and the Atlantic coast, whereas northeastern wood was sold to mills in the Lake states. Determined to restrict this crosshauling, west coast firms were permitted to supply Lake states but the northeast was reserved for local or eastern Canadian mills. Companies were given the right to transfer orders voluntarily without risk of antitrust action. Additional regulations, aimed at heading off speculative markets or temporary suspensions of production, let the WPB sanction crosshauling even if it violated contracts with publishers, while the agency could also rationalize allocations and divert pulp from "long" to "short" mills in a manner akin to the Canadian prorating scheme.[54] When permissible ceiling prices for pulpwood were lowered to minimize inflation or price gouging, the action contributed to a further decline that decreased woodcutting to three-quarters of the amount deemed necessary for a war economy. The muddle was compounded by the Canadian government's failure until 1943 to appoint an official who coordinated pulpwood shipments.[55] Not until 1944 did Canada and the United States allow higher prices that could stimulate logging. Both, instead, masked the importunate shortfall by authorizing reductions of inventories or reserves held by publishers and producers. The head of the WPB later conceded they reached "a dangerous level." The end of the European war came "in the nick of time," and prompted lower demand that shrank the gap with the available supply.[56]

Regulation of newsprint proved especially difficult because the cooperation of manufacturers and many types of consumers was required. Following the Pearl Harbor raid, American officials moved to curtail consumption. The first manoeuvres entailed conservation measures, modification of manufacturing techniques, and a classification of consumers according to their importance. Power supply facilities of American mills were designated as standby sources for other industries. Through cooperation with Canadian authorities, newsprint production in Quebec was reduced and electricity was diverted for war-related plants. Redirecting pulp that was used for making "cultural" papers (books, magazines, writing paper, or commercial printing) was relatively straightforward because much came from American mills. Although newspapers also represented "cultural" items, the reliance upon Canadian supply generated several problems. Decreased imports could damage Canada's economy and the foreign exchange earnings were integral for the war effort. Moreover, while American officials wanted lower newsprint use, they also sought more imports of pulpwood and pulp. Canadian manufacturers believed this orientation represented an attempt to rebuild the pre-1913 trade framework; American firms, in turn, feared a conversion of mills to war-related goods might facilitate a Canadian expansion into their markets.[57]

The WPB somewhat naively presumed that public acceptance would occur, but from the beginning newsprint regulation was widely opposed as an unreasonable infringement of civil liberty that amounted to "the first step in setting up a dictatorship," "an invidious movement by long-haired theorists to destroy the press," and "a collective state in this government so that people will read and hear only what they want them to read and hear."[58] Advisors to the WPB recommended as a long-term goal the reduction of output for civilian uses to a ceiling at 80 per cent of the 1940 level or to a floor at 40 per cent. Although a supply deficiency was believed inevitable, moving towards this objective took nearly a year because there was little public data about the volumes and kinds of pulp and paper. Regulators also learned from the initiatives dealing with pulpwood that intervention aimed at one forest resource invariably affected others. To accommodate the vertically-integrated companies, the WPB considered a concentration of manufacturing for some types of paper at specific mills. This strategy was abandoned in favour of policies that imposed production ceilings and stipulated companies had to withhold a fifth of their output for reserves that might be applied to wartime use. The proposal was opposed by other agencies, which derided the "unwarranted efforts" to "push through a programme before all of the facts are in."[59]

Donald Nelson, the chair of the WPB, believed curtailment required full understanding by producers and their customers, but this was never accomplished. There was no consensus about how far manufacturing should be shrunk. Producers and publishers attacked proposals for a 35 per cent reduction as catastrophic, whereas some government agencies believed that level of diversion was insufficient and would achieve virtually nothing beyond what would happen if the industry was left alone. Military officials wanted newsprint production slashed in half, accompanied by quotas for other products based upon their "different essentiality." The Division of Civilian Supply, in contrast, insisted that newspapers were indispensable and denounced the uncertainty associated with any freeze. Interagency debates over several months generated two alternative plans. One entailed a series of cuts for different forms of paper, with the severest occurring for newsprint, while the other suggested quotas for various goods.

Canada's War Prices and Trade Board had declared a willingness to cooperate on "a broad North American conception." As the pulpwood shortages intensified, the WPB decided, a priori, to cut output by 10 per cent. The Canadian regulators adopted a similar stance, "against their better judgment," because American officials were "adamant on the necessity for this step." Nonetheless, the head of the WPTB, Walter Gordon, deprecated the move as unilateral, wasteful, and without any controls over consumption: "In this particular case we were confronted with a decision of your officials." Nelson countered that his government was determined to end the speculative market in newsprint that still mushroomed.[60] A joint conference after this contretemps agreed that output might be cut from the 1941 level by one-third. Canadian representatives argued that the Americans did not understand the implications. A cutback by a quarter or more meant insufficient pulpwood for newsprint. They held out for a reduction by stages (each requiring mutual agreement), based upon an assumption the U.S. would "proceed promptly with the establishment of direct consumer control for the use or consumption of newsprint."[61]

The plan was meant to preserve the ratio of Canadian to American manufacturing but implementation unfolded in a confused manner. Producer allocations within the United States were based upon the patterns that had occurred during a narrow "base" period. The WPB consequently froze output at numerous mills with low capacity use, requiring them to operate at levels where profitability was impossible, whereas others ran at full capacity.[62] While preaching the need for curtailment, an expansion of production was permitted for alternative paper goods and after the initial 10 per cent cutback of newsprint further reductions were deferred until the autumn of 1943. The plan to concentrate production at specific mills stalled. Expectations that pulp originally manufactured by converted plants might be replaced with the output from other factories proved impossible because most lacked the necessary drying facilities and the diversion of electricity from Quebec mills reduced the supply. Meanwhile, Canadian firms, which earned a foreign exchange premium on exports, proved willing to favour American customers over their domestic clients, abetting greater consumption south of the border. This behaviour forced the Canadian government to extend its controls over shipments, an action that generated bitter recriminations from American firms.[63]

Virtually all interests opposed the efforts to limit consumption. The net paid circulation of newspapers in 1941 was treated as a base reference for regulatory orders, but this measure ignored mobilization and population movements that altered and increased circulation. The WPB's Clearance Committee objected about how prospective orders developed "in a perfunctory manner without first having an opportunity to review the facts." The number of customers imposed "almost unbearable administrative difficulties." Most small papers received exemptions from quotas. Large metropolitan papers thus bore the brunt of the restrictions. Staff for the WPB thought any appeals could be easily handled but hundreds were filed. With fewer consumer goods available during the war, WPB personnel also believed decreased advertising would cut paper use, but the proportion of newspaper content and tonnage devoted to advertising actually grew. The notion that consumption quotas would generate savings thus "turned out to be a bad guess." The cutback achieved just half of the intended goal. Moreover, regulations indicated how much newspapers could consume but not how much they could *order*, which stimulated a quasi-legal market of transfers and sales. One official noted publishing became akin to "a man whose income is dwindling and whose wife is spending her head off."[64] Nelson and the WPB backtracked as the opposition mounted. The scheme for phased cuts was deferred, with claims that there was ample supply, but as shortages intensified in 1943 another reduction was authorized. What might be done became a topic of endless news reports: small reductions were coming, "a honey of a cut" was imminent, no cuts were planned, no one really knew. The problems were compounded by bureaucratic wrangles as the controllers for printing and magazines would not curtail output unless matching levels were imposed upon newspapers.[65]

It took until early 1944 for the efforts to gain some coherence but even then it was "a pretty confused situation," a Congressional committee was told. "The printers are confused; the customers are confused; and apparently the authorities are confused ... the kinks have not been thoroughly ironed out, if they ever will be." In Canada "it seems a little bit worse up there than it does down here."[66] The WPB's organization was restructured and cross-border liaison committees facilitated greater cooperation. With difficulty, Canadian officials persuaded their American counterparts that unilateral initiatives could not work and there was legitimacy behind the fears that "the enormously greater buying power of the U.S." might "bleed Canada white of most of her supply items."[67] Newsprint usage declined from the 1941 level, but the trend was due to the regulation of production, not consumption. Both countries finally accepted the notion of an "equal" sharing of pulpwood sold in competitive markets, but it was subordinate to an understanding that Canadian firms would supply pulpwood according to designated priorities. The net result was a decline in the amount of newsprint available to levels well below the designated quotas for publishers, which forced conservation practices.[68]

Price controls added a final layer of complication. Market rates remained in force until 1942, though government authorities cautioned about the possible use of a "big stick." Whereas in Canada the WPTB held jurisdiction over both production and pricing, in the United States the latter was then allocated to a separate agency, the Office of Price Administration (OPA). American authorities still emphasized the regulation of output as the means for guiding consumption and supply – the use of price as a stimulant or a deterrent was not even studied until late 1943. The prices for pulp and other forms of paper began to rise. However, for newsprint manufacturers, although production costs inflated by nearly half from 1939 to 1941, the overhang of surplus capacity kept the list rate at $50 per ton. In late 1941 producers signalled their intention to raise it by $3 per ton, a move that was expected to receive summary approval. Instead, the OPA, having consulted only a select group of publishers, froze the maximum price "temporarily," then extended the decision "indefinitely," and added a rider that American publishers could not pay more than the 1941 level.[69] Only after the fact did OPA query the manufacturers about their costs. Paper executives expressed outrage about the agency's inconsistency since two weeks earlier it had approved a huge increase in pulpwood prices. Publishers exploited the ruling, in a partial replication of 1937, by accumulating large inventories. The decision, Canadian observers argued, created "a very black murk." The OPA had to reverse its pulpwood ruling several months later, citing how newsprint producers were "squeezed" and unexpected consequences had resulted, such as loggers cutting other forms of wood to secure better compensation.[70]

The impact was a sudden drop in profitability that pushed many producers back to breakeven status or lower. Not only were the returns on newsprint insufficient to permit greater output, American mills (when their owners could work around regulatory constraints) were also diverted to goods that offered better returns, further decreasing the supply. But producers did secure one major gain, the geographic system developed during the NRA experiment was adopted by OPA as the framework for pricing, thereby giving it full legitimacy.[71] As Canada's WTPB introduced quotas that further raised manufacturing costs, the demands from papermakers for a price increase mounted. Government representatives concerned about export earnings joined them. Despite efforts to secure an additional $10 per ton, OPA granted only a $4 increase in early 1943, insufficient to compensate for wartime inflation. Further negotiations led to an additional $4 increase, along with an acknowledgment that further adjustments were necessary. By early 1945 the list rate reached $62 per ton. Publishers denounced each increase as an unreasonable exaction by the "Canadian newsprint trust," but investigators saw this as rank hypocrisy. Increased circulation and greater advertising allowed newspapers to achieve record profits.[72]

3. Pith and substance

Wartime conditions thus generated complex issues. Clarkson was initially uncertain about how hostilities would affect his company. Despite the risk he authorized a wood cut sufficient to keep the mills at full capacity, correctly adducing that costs were likely to rise. The War Measures Act blocked the right to lockout or strike, and labour disputes were few even though many workers believed inflation eroded their financial status. Salaries for those employed in the mills and head office had not changed since 1935 and Clarkson began raising them to retain the personnel. The receiver, who anticipated the likelihood of diminished bush operations, authorized new rounds of excess cutting, but the company soon experienced a labour shortfall as workers were diverted into war industries or road construction.[73] The firm retained sufficient inventories until 1943 but the difficulties escalated. Mechanization of operations had mixed success because tractors and trucks rarely lasted longer than three years. Securing equipment became hard unless authorized by government orders but newsprint was deemed a low priority. As wartime requirements reduced power supply for mills in Quebec, some newsprint contracts were passed to Abitibi. This propelled a faster than normal conversion of pulpwood, which Clarkson feared might denude Abitibi's concessions of the most merchantable timber. But the key problem became the labour shortage. The receiver complained that once personnel were lost they could not be recovered. The woods operations generated a 1943 cut at three-fifths of the 1942 level, and by 1944 at less than two-fifths. Some, but not all, of the costs associated with a mill shutdown due to the weak supply might be covered from a fund operated by the WPTB, but this was not a scenario the receiver was willing to contemplate.[74]

The shortfall was solved through the use of German war prisoners. Defence department officials approached Clarkson about Espanola as a site for the internment of enemy aliens and soldiers. They planned to use the ghost town for camp services but then agreed to use the company's properties. The prisoners were housed in the old mill buildings and local guards moved into abandoned structures nearby. Additional camps were later situated near other operations, particularly Monteith, just south of Iroquois Falls, which became one of Canada's largest prisoner facilities. Federal officials soon encountered serious problems handling the interned because morale was poor in the isolated locations. Convinced idle prisoners would cause mischief or damage, it was deemed important to keep them occupied. Having detainees work could also show taxpayers that the expenses associated with incarceration were being offset. As the number of prisoners increased, there was consequently a movement from internment to adjacent work camps administered by companies.[75]

Through contracts encouraged by the federal government, Abitibi used prisoners in forest operations near Nipigon, Smooth Rock Falls, and Sault Ste. Marie. It was an arrangement of mutual convenience for all parties. The firm assured minimum employment for three months and offered guarantees that the prisoners would not engage in sabotage or cause other problems. Abitibi paid the Department of Labour $2.50 per day for each man, after deducting per diem food and board. To persuade Clarkson about the cost advantages, federal officials stressed: "No Workmen's Insurance or Compensation is necessary on behalf of prisoners." Housed in separate premises with civilian guards, the internees received credits for their labour equal to 50 cents per day, which allowed purchases of cigarettes and small goods in camp stores. The firm's seasonal employment expanded from 500 prisoners in 1942 to 2,320 (a third of the forest workforce) by 1945.[76] Clarkson later admitted that without this labour the company would have fallen far short of its quotas. Government officials insisted it was of "utmost importance" that prisoners work until the last possible moment so they could highlight to taxpayers how expenses were minimized. In 1946, following their repatriation, the company encountered severe shortages because veterans and others were reluctant to work in woods operations.[77]

Clarkson found it almost impossible to secure insurance against risks such as the possibility of sabotage to the electrical plants, even though most were in remote locations. Reflecting popular hysteria during the Battle of the Atlantic, he worried about a military assault. If "an Enemy submarine, or other vessel, with aeroplanes on board, could succeed in passing through the Hudson Straights into the Hudson Bay, it might be able to attack and damage the Twin Falls dam almost without effective opposition." The firm eventually insured most holdings for high premiums but never secured policies for the properties used by federal authorities. Abitibi had to agree not to sue the Crown for damages and it was liable if prisoners of war were injured, but insurance companies also refused to cover those issues.[78]

The regulatory regime impacted operations in several ways. Before the war, the company kept substantial reserves to ensure continuous operations, but after the institution of controls in 1942, all reserves were converted into pulp or newsprint and then shipped. Canadian firms were instructed to supply customers in Britain, Canada, and the United States according to assigned priorities. The regulations had an unintended consequence: they lowered the volume of wood and bush labour available to the manufacturers. When combined with production and pricing regulations, newsprint production decreased sharply and stayed well below the levels customers were authorized to buy. The office of Canada's Newsprint Controller regulated the proportion, or "position level," of orders each firm was allowed to fill. The system, analogous to prorating, emphasized how "long" companies would supposedly transfer production to "short" companies. But this almost never happened, nor was there anything to prevent a long company from increasing its volume if it gained prior approval for taking over a contract or received supply obligations from American firms. Compensation for any "excess" output would be paid into a stabilization fund, and, in theory, a short mill's deficits would allow it to make a withdrawal from the fund. Abitibi's head office, perhaps inevitably, became enmeshed in disputes and petty wrangles over the allocations associated with individual mills.[79]

When contracts were transferred to Abitibi from other mills, the firm was allowed to retain only "increment" costs or prices, which invariably were below the real manufacturing costs. In addition, because Canada placed a high priority on pulpwood shipments, Abitibi was ordered to continue shipments of that commodity even though they were much less profitable than processed paper. Government estimates were typically based upon annual costs of producers and rarely segmented out components or allowed for seasonal variations that had cost implications. The Director of National Selective Service, who controlled labour allocations, and the Power Controller, affected Abitibi's operations in unexpected ways. Shifting electricity supply for war production compelled a reduction of the Ste. Anne mill from two machines to one. Two of the seven machines at Iroquois Falls were shut down to grant "full" employment at the site. Clarkson's frustrations about the conflicting obligations were expressed in opaque corporate-speak whenever he issued reports. "Such conditions largely increased the efforts necessary to be provided by Abitibi and its subsidiaries in order to do business, while information required of the companies in respect of their operations, and the many returns which had to be provided by them in connection therewith, imposed heavy additional burdens and undue strain upon their Officers and other employees."[80]

Like other producers, Abitibi partially recovered as the demand for newsprint soared. After 1940 it hovered near breakeven, and during the final two years of the war, the financial status significantly improved in response to higher prices and demand. Clarkson had stated during the struggles over the judicial sale that he could work with a minimum working capital of $9 million. Anything over that level might be distributed to the bondholders as an instalment on the accumulated obligations. In June of 1941, eight months after the application by Noranda Mines, Montreal Trust asked for similar action. Judicial approval was sought for a distribution of $6.4 million, but against the bond principal, not the interest arrears, because they were subject to wartime taxes. But two issues blocked the planned dispersal. First, the tax status of any payments was quite unclear. Payments of interest or dividends were usually permitted but only after wartime taxes were withheld. Second, Americans and others living outside Canada could not transfer Canadian funds under foreign exchange and "trading with the enemy" regulations. "To arrive at a solution," one newspaper remarked, "would probably require two Solomons rolled into one." Although Clarkson advised the court that the outlays could be initiated within a month, it took much of the summer to secure rulings that they were not subject to income tax and did not constitute forbidden movements of capital, particularly to the still neutral United States. A $130 payment for each $1,000 in principal was made in October, the first distribution in nine years. Thereafter, determination of the monies owed became complicated because calculations had to consider the extant amount of principal, interest arrears, and compound interest.[81]

Clarkson also used the available earnings for liquidating loans or certificates (some dating back to the early receivership) and carrying out capital expenditures, which gained court approval because equipment or facilities had reached obsolescence. Promissory notes, along with unpaid interest obligations that dated from the pre-receivership era for Abitibi's electrical utilities and Manitoba Paper, were eliminated and surpluses were posted for the first time on the books of the parent firm. Clarkson also built up liquid capital by subscribing to Victory Bonds, converting cash to interest-bearing securities. These practices cumulatively began to make Abitibi look like a normal firm.[82] As the working capital expanded, the Supreme Court authorized additional distributions, sometimes applied against the bond principal and sometimes against the interest obligations. By the end of 1944 these aggregated $23 million, or about a third of everything owed to the bondholders.

Wartime conditions did not stop other stakeholders from pursuing their own interests, which included provincial efforts to strip off

Abitibi's assets. Municipal officials in Port Arthur had long sought the expropriation of Kaministiquia Power, which supplied the Fort William mill. During negotiations over the Ripley plan, the Hydro Commission failed to gain control, but it tried again after the outbreak of hostilities. Nominally presented as a scheme to improve supply for wartime industry, the real goal was an amalgamation of systems that could achieve a higher generation of electricity than was available from independent operations. But Hydro refused to pay anywhere near the actual worth. Unlike a decade earlier, Clarkson could no longer make distress sales. His decisions now received intensive scrutiny from security holders and a presiding judge, which meant assets must be liquidated near their real value.[83] Acquisition, the head of the provincial utility observed, could likely only be accomplished by force because Clarkson would not sell save under risk of expropriation. Hydro unsuccessfully lobbied the government for order-in-council that sanctioned a seizure. Clarkson then received judicial approval to seek a negotiated solution "by private treaty." He turned over the subsidiary's financial statements but was prohibited from releasing confidential appraisals of the assets. Clarkson and the court made clear that monies from a takeover had to be applied against Abitibi's outstanding bonds and interest.[84] Nothing emerged from the negotiations because Hydro officials minimized their bid, which Clarkson rejected as nonsense, and then decided to defer everything until after the war when Abitibi would be in "a much less favourable position." The facility was finally sold in 1949 – at twice Hydro's original offer price.[85]

With ebbing popularity, the Liberal administration pushed for a sale of the Espanola mill before the 1943 election. Closed for nearly fifteen years, Clarkson wanted to demolish the factory and eliminate the carrying costs but the government repeatedly denied permission. Most buildings in the town were in severe disrepair and little prospect of redevelopment seemed likely unless a new operator was found for the plant, which contained six machines installed between 1909 and 1919 that Clarkson characterized as "cannibalized." A market for various papermaking activities existed for what was left, although Abitibi's managers insisted that a sale must ban any production of newsprint. Accordingly, negotiations were undertaken with various firms, New York interests who claimed affiliation with paper manufacturers, the Swedish consul general, and Canadians working for undisclosed principals.[86]

Only the Kalamazoo Vegetable Parchment Company (KVP) of Michigan made a proposal. It was prepared to acquire the factory and timber concessions, subject to approval by regulators, for a conversion to sulphate pulp manufacturing. Federal officials were not prepared to authorize the transaction, however, and Hydro was not willing to take over a nearby electrical generation site if KVP purchased the factory. Clarkson was convinced that if the utility acquired the plant the rest of the operation could be sold gradually, which would revive Espanola "from a dead community." However, KVP soon determined that it could not convert the mill until wartime rationing ended, which exposed it to carrying charges for an operation with little return. The firm would only pay $1 million cash with just $100,000 as a deposit – subject to Abitibi's acceptance and a government waiver on timber taxes until alterations were completed. Montreal Trust, Clarkson, and McPherson privately agreed with a sale on those poor terms because it freed Abitibi from the carrying costs.[87]

When he sought approval, Clarkson secretly advised the court about "certain factors which it would not be in the interest of Abitibi to lay before the Province." There was little or no prospect that a buyer could be found that might offer a reasonable price. Conversion to sulphate production required a minimum investment of $2.5 million with no assured payback and an additional outlay was needed for the supply of sufficient electricity. Espanola might be used as a groundwood pulp factory but Clarkson doubted there was adequate demand. He claimed internal documents showed that aspect of the Espanola operation had not been profitable for more than twenty years. He could sell the paper-making machines, but that would leave the mill permanently non-functional, "definitely reduce the status of Espanola to that of a moribund community, and prejudicially affect the value of other assets there, unless sold prior to the wrecking of such a mill." It got worse. One of the timber concessions had expired in 1930, the other in 1937, and, despite assurances from the government, renewal was dubious even if Abitibi returned to solvency. The Hepburn administration had been inconsistent on cutting rights and retained the prerogative to "recapture" lands it deemed unnecessary for firms. Located on the farthest edges of the limits, the high extraction costs for the timber made any rehabilitation of the mill problematic. Clarkson accordingly doubted KVP's ability to sustain a sulphate operation. The timber concessions had become more of a liability than an asset, but could not be surrendered before a disposition of the mill since a change in provincial policies might resuscitate their worth. The sale thus was in the firm's interest even though it entailed a wipe out of $8.4 million in book value. Abitibi also had incurred other expenses for Espanola for more than a decade. Unemployed and indigent people had taken over many buildings but could not pay for rent, water, or light. Clarkson opposed

eviction on moral grounds. He lobbied the court about how the premises would be kept in better condition by the occupants than if left
vacant even though the firm was stuck with worthless accounts that
had little prospect of collection.[88]

The Liberals trumped the sale as a gain even though it soon became
clear that rehabilitation must wait until after the war. Clarkson's insis-
tence upon absolute secrecy meant that local representatives knew
nothing when questioned about the negotiations or the sale. "The irony
of it is," one legislator moaned, "that while I went through many tough
years looking after these people, now, when their hour of triumph
comes, I can claim no part, nor expect to receive any credit for the rehabilitation of their town." He needed to be seen having some role and "it
behooves us to capitalize on unusual events ... the political ball has
been "muffed" as far as I am concerned, with this deal."[89]

If Espanola had prospects, albeit in the future, Sturgeon Falls
remained derelict. The mill had one machine that remained functional
and several others that had deteriorated badly. The property was not
demolished largely because the province believed that it would just
increase local relief costs. Various interests expressed curiosity about
the mill, but a proposal was never received from individuals or firms
with sufficient resources. As a mandatory condition of sale, Clarkson
excluded its use for making newsprint. With the outbreak of war, a del-
egation from the town asked Heenan about having the factory produce
munitions. Federal inspectors examined the site but deemed the buildings unsafe and renovation costs too high. Local officials then unsuccessfully lobbied to have the mill turned over to the town. Meanwhile,
not expecting the plant to ever reopen, Clarkson sold off the oldest
machines, two to Spruce Falls as parts for pulp drying units and a third
to a Florida mill that made sulphate pulp. Abitibi nonetheless remained
the largest taxpayer for the municipality. In 1939, the Department of
Municipal Affairs took over the town's finances, and by 1941 Abitibi's
taxes were slashed by three-quarters. Sturgeon Falls remained a "dead"
town, one of the worst relief situations in Ontario with 90 per cent of
the population on support. For the citizens, the war years progressed
without any grounds for hope.[90]

Major decisions remained in abeyance while everyone waited for a
ruling on the appeal. Things had taken so long the staff within governmental agencies often were no longer familiar with earlier decisions.
For example, Hydro undertook another survey of the company's
licences because its senior executives no longer knew how resource
rights had been allocated in the past. They did not even understand the
logic behind the 1937 agreement, which stipulated reorganization

within a year or after an extension: "Just what constitutes sanctioning an extension of time is difficult to say. This might have been done indirectly or impliedly by the Government."[91]

Despite the concurrence of Ontario's political leaders on the need for a moratorium, Attorney General Gordon Conant expected a rejection of the appeal. He believed only federal authorities could then legislate a solution. Background materials were assembled for Prime Minister Mackenzie King, but his government made no efforts to review the two main options: authorize another moratorium or undertake an initiative that might force a reorganization.[92] The decision of the Judicial Committee of the Privy Council in June 1943 thus came as a surprise to almost everyone because it decisively upheld Ontario's position. Speaking for the panel, Lord Aiken declared that, when filed in 1932, the case was that of a mortgagee proceeding in Ontario courts with respect to the property and civil rights specified by the bond trust deed. It was undertaken with respect to provincial laws and subject to the exclusive authority of the provincial courts or parliament. Although a later filing had occurred under the Winding-up Act, the bondholders had not exerted a claim. They "deliberately remained outside and proceeded what may be called their provincial rights against the provincial property."

In what became an important constitutional ruling for the next forty years, the panel declared:

Once granted, the provincial law regulating the action proceeded as a provincial action, subject to the provincial law regulating the rights in such an action and subject to the sovereign power of the legislature to alter those rights ... If the rules of procedure were subsequently altered before the action came to an end, it must proceed thereafter subject to the rules as amended. The province, therefore, could enact rules in the course of the action imposing a further grant of stay, and, if it can thus impose what may be a general moratorium, there is no reason why its sovereign power should be so limited as not to enable it to impose, if it so desired, a moratorium limited to a special class of action or suitor. There appears to be no authority, and no reason, for the opinion, that legislation in respect of property and civil rights must be general in character and not aimed at a particular right. Such restriction would appear to eliminate the possibility of special legislation aimed at transferring a particular right or property from private hands to a public authority for public purposes. The legislature is supreme in these matters and its actions must be assumed to be taken with due regard for justice and good conscience. They are not, in any case, subject to control by the courts.

The panel acknowledged how Ontario's legislation tried to coerce the bondholders. It also recognized how the implementation of the McTague commission's proposals fell within federal authority. "So they are, but this Board must have cogent grounds before it arising from the nature of the impugned legislation before it can impute to a province legislation some object other than what is to be seen on the face of the enactment itself." Neither the Moratorium Act nor the royal commission specified anything other than an opportunity to consider the report's recommendations. The province also had full jurisdiction over the management and sale of public lands. "The pith and substance of this Act is to regulate property and civil rights within the province." Put simply, Ontario could change the rules of the game. The bondholders should pray it did not change them further.[93]

With the main issues settled and the province's interference with the judicial sale found valid, two routes for gaining a reorganization, the OJAA and mortgage foreclosure, were closed. The only other avenue was the one the bondholders had deemed impossible: a negotiated settlement under the CCAA. The province and most observers anticipated a quick reorganization. Those expectations were confounded, yet again, by a process that stretched out for another thirty-four months.

14

The Path towards Dawn

Cordelia obtaining the government of the Kingdom buried her father in a certain vault which she ordered to be made for him under the river Sore in Leicester and which had been built originally under the ground in honour of the god Janus. And here all the workmen of the city, upon the anniversary solemnity of that festival, used to begin their yearly labours.

– Geoffrey of Monmouth

We shall come back, no doubt, to walk down the Row and watch young people on the tennis courts by the clump of mimosas and walk down the beach by the bay ... But that will be a long time from now, and soon we shall go out of the house and go into the convulsion of the world, out of history and the awful responsibility of Time.

– Robert Penn Warren, *All the King's Men*

"SOME NORMAL FORM OF MANAGEMENT" was long past due, Ontario's premier stated in September 1943, and his government was determined to end the last newsprint receivership.[1] Abitibi had been a headline story for more than a decade but press references to the company's situation rarely appeared after the appeal decision, although the coverage of pulp and paper remained extensive, a phenomenon that reflected various issues. The never-ending Abitibi story had been one of false leads, convoluted dealings, and failed outcomes. Editors would have found the allocation of reporters or space to the topic difficult in the context of a world war ascending towards a climax. They, like many social leaders, preferred to talk about the possibility of a peacetime era characterized by robust growth and benefits for consumers. A bankrupt company associated with the hardships of the Great Depression seemed to be part of the ignominious past.

Moreover, during the receivership's final years developments unfolded as a slow-motion dance behind closed doors. Most participants kept the negotiations secret, although their views (and plots) occasionally surfaced for public view. The issues remained, to the end, who got the money, who made sacrifices, and whether Abitibi had the ability to stand on its own when solvent. While it was obvious by 1943 that a resolution would happen, the endgame appeared to outsiders as tedious, laborious, and petty. Thus, the receivership closed not in a blaze of triumph but as a whimper of exhaustion, an afterthought, a clean-up of unfinished business. This chapter examines how this occurred. The first section examines how a new government tried to bring matters under control and how the hopes for a prompt conclusion evaporated. The second part summarizes the convoluted dealings that led to a final settlement. The concluding section then reviews the efforts to restore the firm to normal operations.

1. Clean up the Abitibi mess

The cycle repeated yet again. In the wake of the Privy Council decision the price of Abitibi bonds declined, those for the stock issues rose, and ever more schemes circulated. The different equity committees met after the ruling and agreed to cooperate. The preferred stockholders proclaimed how the Privy Council had cleared the way for a sound reorganization that respected the rights of shareholders because Abitibi now had the highest working capital in its history and some of the debt had been repaid. Although the bondholders refused to make a public statement, various ideas were circulated to establish a foundation for later discussions. Many stakeholders assumed the need for lower debt, along with a simplification of the equity to just one class each of preferred and common stock, but there was little agreement about details, especially about how to compromise the claims.[2] Press reports exaggerated the degree of consensus and pulled out the old chestnut that a solution would be reached if all groups approached the negotiations in a spirit of harmony. One editor, more critically, speculated that even under the best conditions "it might take decades for the common stock to become of real value from an income-producing point of view."[3]

Less than a month after the Privy Council decision a provincial election was called, one that became a mirror image of the poll a decade earlier. Hepburn had resigned as premier the previous year (although not as Liberal leader) and then attempted to impose Attorney General Conant as his successor. Instead the party split into factions, which led to the selection of Harry Nixon (long deemed the true "heir apparent"). Conant was shuffled off with an appointment as Master of the provincial Supreme Court, a move the opposition parties derided as corrupt politics by a tired administration. Defensive and unwilling to advance new policies, Nixon tied the Liberals' re-election to the support of Prime Minister King. Hepburn, in turn, attacked his own party, calling it a "Quisling administration" that was just a tool of the federal government and too willing to suppress civil liberties during the war. While the Liberals descended into a civil war amongst themselves, Conservative George Drew campaigned as a progressive reformer who offered a "22 point" manifesto about how to ensure Ontario's postwar readjustment through social security, tax reform, labour legislation, and economic development. The policy gaps between the parties were not wide but Drew offered a change from Hepburn's Depression populism that critics had long dismissed as a mix of mercurial histrionics, pie-in-the-sky promises, and cynical manipulation of the political process. The result was a humiliating defeat, with the election of a minority Conservative government. The Liberals dropped to third place behind the Cooperative Commonwealth Federation.[4]

George Drew was the first Ontario premier who was both experienced and comfortable dealing with corporate enterprise. A key element of his platform was a depoliticization of Hydro and natural resources. Hepburn and his supporters in the early 1930s attacked how the Tories handled those activities but Drew believed that once in office the Liberals were even more corrupt and thoroughly inept to boot. He promised an end to the lush days of "timber pirates" and their "legalized robbery" of Ontario's "green gold," its public resources. Forests and minerals would be developed "for the sole benefit of the public, and not the political friends of this or any other Government."[5] The pulp mills the Liberals commissioned before the 1937 election were considered "baits" that might provide the party to secure money surreptitiously from bidders. The properties and incomplete mill of the biggest enterprise, Lake Sulphite Pulp which had fallen into bankruptcy, were sold to Brompton Pulp and Paper in 1942, but the venture remained stalled for another two years due to shortages of equipment and materials. Four other firms had done nothing, and it appeared they only sought access to the forest tracts. Drew believed the Liberals had planned a secret deal that could be sprung as an election "surprise," rather than declare the companies in formal default. Accordingly, during his first week in office, the contracts were cancelled for non-performance and the province repossessed fourteen million acres of concessions. Pressure was applied to accelerate two ventures that had a possibility of success, while restrictions were placed on sawmills as a first move for bringing small producers under control.[6]

The next logical issue entailed a resolution of the Abitibi receivership. A month after taking power, Drew appointed a three-member committee to mediate a voluntary settlement. The best interests of investors, workers, and local communities, he declared, could be served if the company was "restored to some normal form of management" because it was nearly profitable. A workable solution was only blocked by legal technicalities. The receivership represented a drag on the industry since the firm could not respond adequately to new situations.[7] The chair of the committee, Frank J. Hughes, was a director of National Trust, a former Crown attorney, and the senior partner of a Toronto law partnership. William Zimmerman was the head of another Toronto legal firm and a director of McColl-Frontenac. Gilbert Jackson was an economist who had taught at McGill University and the University of Toronto, served as an economist for the Bank of Nova Scotia, and advised the Bank of England. At the time of his appointment, Jackson chaired the Canadian Committee on Industrial Reconstruction. None of the three had substantive expertise with corporate finance, but the "Conciliation Committee" was well received because the members had not been involved with the Abitibi disputes. It was established with minimal formality, which seemed to augur flexibility. The committee's public legitimacy improved over time because few leaks of information reached speculators and other interests.[8]

One adviser told Drew the action was "long overdue" because "certain powerful interests at Ottawa, notably Herbert Symington (and I regret to say that the group included my good friend Arthur Meighen) rigidly insisted on the letter of the bond contract." Despite the efforts to mediate a solution, Sun Life, Canada Life, and the other major bondholders "insisted upon their individual rights" for honouring the bond deed to the last word. "There just wasn't any co-operation in them." If the Hughes committee failed, then a royal commission should be formed. "The finding of this Commission would undoubtedly reflect a co-operative effort to clean up the Abitibi mess and that is just the kind of plan that would pass Ontario['s] Parliament and meet all sections of public opinion as now constituted." Drew adopted this counsel and threatened that if another failure occurred a new commission would aid his government in preparing legislation to force an end."[9] The premier may have expected prompt action, but even assembling basic information took months because many participants were focused on wartime assignments that took priority. The committee also found that despite the Privy Council decision the protective committees still would not compromise.

The premier unexpectedly announced just four months later that the committee had developed "a tentative plan for the consideration of the security holders" predicated "on the belief that the debtor company should recognize and in time pay the whole of its obligations." Although he withheld disclosure of the terms, Drew proclaimed the scheme to be "fair," an assertion that led many (including some of the protective committees) to believe that the province would implement the committee's recommendations without further consultation. The premier again cautioned how "the Government is considering legislation to bring this unsatisfactory situation to an end, should the Committee fail to secure an early agreement on a voluntary basis."[10] But the statement was premature and quite misleading. The supposed "plan" was little more than a set of half-baked notions. The committee estimated Abitibi's financial obligations and then assessed the legitimacy associated with the various claims. On this basis, it suggested an immediate payment to the bondholders that reduced the amount of past-due interest owed for each $1,000 bond to $450. Projecting Abitibi's likely earnings during the postwar era, the committee thought the arrears might be reduced by $30 per year until the balance reached $165 per bond. By 1953 the debt load might amount to $36 million, which the committee deemed a reasonable amount for the firm to refinance. It also suggested warrants for common stock should be attached to the bonds, with at least 80 per cent of Abitibi's profits dedicated to a sinking fund for retiring the warrants. The failure to pay either the warrants or the sinking fund obligations would constitute grounds for a new default.[11]

Drew did not know that two months earlier the bondholders' representatives rejected this scheme as impossible to implement. They noted it was simpler to bring the firm out of receivership without a plan that had complicated terms like stock warrants. Schemes entailing warrants had been proposed back in 1937 but were deemed unworkable. In any event, they demanded the full repayment of the bond interest and principal. This stance, when announced publicly, triggered criticism from most media outlets. The *Globe and Mail*'s financial editor derided it as unwise, as little more than greed. He could not resist chortling about how the bondholders had offered $30 million back in 1939 but now could get nearly $60 million. The *Financial Post* lampooned the expectations of the different stakeholders and then remarked that even with the new scheme the preferred shareholders were unlikely to get any money for years. There was nothing in the premier's statement, it complained, that could make investors optimistic.[12] Speculation and false rumours about the plan soon circulated. The chair of the common shareholders' committee noted how the proposal was "kept in close secret" and not revealed to his group, hence "any comments thereon must be based on pure guess work." Due to a campaign by "propagandist financial writers," he complained, the scheme catered to the bond and common equity investors. The preferred shareholders apparently were offered only common stock. "It is a matter of great concern to my associates and myself to hear about the 'sacrifices' that the preferred shareholders are ready to make in accepting, in lieu of their present preferred status, the lion's share in the new common shares." The plan "reminds us of the bondholders' 'altruistic' attitude, when they endeavoured to buy all of the assets of the company, for the sum of $30,000,000.00 purely as a 'salvage' proposition." Ownership of Abitibi should be vested with the common shareholders only after the debt obligations were discharged, along with "adequately correcting the temporary hardship of the preferred shareholders, as to unearned and, consequently, unpaid dividends." Otherwise, the new set-up deprived them of any chance of recouping at least part of their investments.[13]

Negotiations resumed but remained stalled. Impatience mounted among investors from all classes, with some calling for leadership from the financial institutions that held large blocs of bonds. Concern also was expressed about rumours that the federal government might not exempt distributions to the bondholders from income or wartime taxes, especially if the payments were for interest arrears rather than principal. Therefore, Abitibi bonds continued to sell on the open market for about three-fifths of the value of the funds still owing. One investor complained about how he had bought the securities following the lead of the insurance companies because he "expected they would look after their interests promptly. I would like to see them move in this case." Others wanted to reopen old wounds as a way of forcing action. The premier should authorize an investigation of the original preferred shareholders' committee, one writer argued, because the members had secured insider information and dumped their stock after the failure of the Ripley plan.[14]

Drew reissued further statements about the government's expectations, including a commitment to protect workers and local communities once an agreement was reached. But by April, frustrated by the lack of movement, he chose to intervene directly. Senior officials from four life insurance companies were instructed to meet the premier, a manoeuvre that bypassed Symington's committee although two of the executives belonged to it. Drew reinforced how a speedy reorganization was necessary, but the details of his ultimatum have not survived.

Most likely, the premier cajoled them over their social responsibility, reminded them of his past support for the shareholders, and declared how the government might withhold any renewal of resource rights if a fair settlement did not occur. The last, of course, would render Abitibi and their stakes worthless. Drew suggested that his office might help mediate the negotiations but Hughes recommended against this so the premier "will be personally relieved of approaches from or for these men whose course will be clearly charted."[15]

The effort to apply pressure failed to jar movement, although the executives developed the outline of a tentative plan and presented it to the bondholders' committee. Meanwhile, Symington and his colleagues tried to gain the premier's sympathy by recounting past events. Their committee was "the only one which has put forth any comprehensive, complete, detailed plan." Most of the schemes circulated after 1938 were "newspaper plans." None had been sponsored by a committee that represented a class of investors. Other groups had engaged in conniving actions, while provincial legislation had treated the bondholders unfairly. Though there were legitimate differences of opinion, their committee had made sincere efforts to reorganize Abitibi on an equitable basis. In any event, they insisted, the premier had been misled. Big institutions held just a "minor" portion of the bonds. Three-quarters of the bondholders held securities with a principal amounting to less than $5,000. Much of this defence was nonsense and self-serving, including a declaration that "the 1939 plan was sound and made fair and reasonable provision for the several classes of Shareholders and creditors ranking after the security of the bonds." That statement was written by one of the committee's new lawyers who did not realize Drew had opposed the Plan of Procedure. The bondholders insisted "certain past experiences could not be overlooked," including their "exhaustive and costly efforts." A new plan might be better propounded by someone like Geoffrey Clarkson, "who has such a long and intimate knowledge of the whole situation and appears to command the respect and confidence of all concerned." But they left themselves a gigantic loophole: "there is, of course, no absolute assurance that his plan would be acceptable either to our Committee, to the general body of bondholders or to the other interests concerned." A proposal from the receiver, however, went beyond his responsibilities and required judicial authorization, which he never sought. Although the attempt to break the impasse died stillborn, Drew remained "hopeful we may soon have some evidence of real progress."[16]

But there always seemed to be something else. In September of 1940, Strachan Johnston advised Clarkson he believed the bondholders were

entitled to interest on the arrears of interest, although he did not deem
the matter important. Other investors and most newspapers denounced
the demand as outrageous when it was disclosed. The Conciliation
Committee also doubted that the claim was legitimate but acknowledged further delay would ensue if the bondholders insisted on payment. Lawyers, when asked, dismissed the possibility of collecting
compound interest, but by 1944 the potential sum was considerable.
The trust deed, in fact, was explicit: the bondholders should receive
"interest of all sums overdue at the rate which such bonds bear."[17] Roy
McPherson foolishly chose to force the issue. At a meeting of the committees for the equity investors, he gained permission to request court
approval of Abitibi's accounts, including that for the bond mortgage.
This was a normal task carried out by a liquidator, but despite the previous struggles it still had not been done. McPherson's real goal was
the disallowance of any claim for compound interest. Supported by the
provincial attorney general and the receiver, his filing stressed how
the total owed to the bondholders had never been specified despite the
reductions of the debt principal since 1941. "The tide has turned," Dalton McCarthy remarked. Although previous efforts to reorganize
Abitibi had failed, a new accounting might allow for renewed action.
To the surprise of McPherson and his counsel, lawyers for the bondholders (who did not want an outcome imposed by the government)
endorsed the motion.[18] After an initial review by the Master of the
Supreme Court, Justice Kellock agreed to hear arguments. McCarthy
contended that the trust deed only allowed repayment of the bond
principal and simple interest. The 1932 default "accelerated" maturity
of the entire debt and thereby eliminated any interest-on-interest or any
other obligations associated with the non-payment of interest coupons.
The lawyer for Montreal Trust countered that the trust deed not only
sanctioned compound interest but each coupon represented a promise
to pay a certain sum and thereby allowed a coupon holder to collect
additional interest if a default occurred. Acceleration of maturity, such
as the payments on the bond principal, could not destroy the rights
associated with subsequent coupons.[19]

Kellock's ruling in June 1944 accepted the need for a review of Abitibi's accounts, but he treated the case as a straightforward matter of contract law. Kellock disregarded what he deemed distractions raised by
the contending lawyers, like any tax implications and whether coupons
were forms of promissory notes. Instead, he stated, the liquidator and
his counsel had not proven that only simple interest was owed, nor had
they provided case precedents for this assertion. Specific terms in the
trust deed indicated how the bond coupons bore interest, along with

the right of the purchasers to have interest on overdue coupons. Kellock noted how in relevant cases remuneration included interest on past obligations. The interest rate specified in the deed was therefore applicable to the overdue portion. The justice also rejected an application to block payment in American funds.[20] In effect, McPherson's action backfired disastrously. The bondholders' claim grew by another $8.5 million. The liquidator's counsel announced his intention to seek an appeal, but a hearing was deferred and then the idea was quietly dropped.[21]

Meanwhile, Clarkson dealt with vexing and time-consuming issues that had to be resolved. Though his reports indicated slow but improving performance, resuscitation of the company remained difficult. Until 1944 the firm was unable to expand its share of markets and relied either upon contract transfers or allocations made by the Newsprint Administrator. Price and production controls kept supplies well below the quantities publishers were authorized to buy, a problem compounded by quotas that favoured smaller publishers. The needs of the biggest newspapers exceeded their designated shares of shipments. Regulatory controls were expected to terminate within six months of the end of hostilities, but newsprint production decreased during the war as firms emphasized the manufacture of other goods.[22] By 1944 these conditions triggered serious shortages and escalating prices, a situation compounded by the withdrawal of American companies that could no longer secure timber. Clarkson noted that the "abnormal state of affairs" provided an opportunity for Abitibi to build market share. Clarkson's first deals focused upon foreign markets, such as an arrangement with Canadian International Paper for the supply of newsprint to Britain.[23] He also gained approval for shifting to sales via multi-year contracts, which stabilized operations and improved marketing flexibility. While few customers were happy with the change, only three expressed overt opposition.[24]

Rebuilding a viable market position entailed not just new business but the resolution of old problems, some dating back the start of the receivership or earlier. The first move entailed a liquidation of the G.H. Mead agency. Any remaining worth, Clarkson commented, rested upon its contracts and lingering goodwill, which "cannot be said to be improving or increasing in value." Indeed, the agency was of little use given the wartime regulatory regime. He shut it down and wrote off what was left. Mead had operated at a loss until 1942 and then began reporting small profits. That development, along with a tax liability from the agency's earnings, was used to legitimate the closure. But the real goals were the internalization of marketing activities and the removal of any remaining influence by George Mead.[25] This action freed up Abitibi's ability to make deals with contractual terms that other firms had long employed. For example, Central Newspapers controlled several Indiana dailies and offered a ten-year deal for newsprint supply if $300,000 of its debenture notes were purchased. Clarkson did not like the arrangement but acquiesced because Abitibi held both the contract and the securities. It also removed any possibility that rivals might capture the business once wartime controls were lifted.[26]

A major problem was the continued indebtedness of the Hearst chain. A wide range of damage claims had been filed against the publisher and its status had not altered since 1938. Newsprint was supplied to the chain only on a cash or short-term credit basis. Abitibi's accounts included over $1.4 million of past-due sales and it retained stock in the chain's parent company as collateral. Clarkson deemed any promise from William Randolph Hearst "of little value," but the equity holding provided Abitibi with leverage that allowed it to keep the existing sales arrangements in force. In 1943 Hearst's debts were restructured through a set of mergers. The company offered a settlement of 50 cents on the dollar to its creditors, which Clarkson rejected. Complicated negotiations then generated a confidential deal that reallocated the publisher's liabilities. Abitibi created a marketing subsidiary to supply a seventh of Hearst's requirements, with guaranteed sales of 375,000 tons per annum. The publisher demanded an unqualified assurance of supply, as well as protection against any assignment of the contract if some of Abitibi's assets were later sold. The receiver could not accept these conditions since they might block a reorganization, weaken the company's competitive status, or drop the value of the Hearst securities that Abitibi held as collateral. Instead, Clarkson's and Hearst's representatives inserted a secret clause into the agreement: none of Abitibi's newsprint mills could be sold in whole or in part. This condition constrained Clarkson's actions during the final years of the receivership, but it became the means by which he could deflect attempts to force the divestiture of various subsidiaries.[27]

Abitibi's insolvency had entangled other business matters that needed resolution. Some had gone on for years and the disputes with the Sifton newspaper group are illustrative. Manitoba Paper's output relied upon contracts with newspapers in the Prairie provinces but in 1931 the Sifton chain acquired several publishers along with the terms outlined in their agreements. The contracts specified a minimum rate for sales and gave the publishers unqualified options for five-year renewals. The transition to geographic pricing in the industry created major problems because the zone rate for Manitoba exceeded that for central Canada due to freight charges, whereas the contracts stipulated that sales would occur well below that price level. A tentative agreement fell through when Abitibi's representative died before he transferred the documents to the firm. The Sifton group then reneged and demanded adherence to the original terms. Rather than lose the business, a new package, supposedly temporary, allowed the Sifton group to buy newsprint for $6 per ton below the zone price and nearly $2 below the Toronto rate. Low freight rates from Pine Falls kept the deal profitable for Abitibi. The Sifton group claimed it was still being overcharged but repetitious negotiations failed to resolve the impasse. Clarkson built up a large and undisclosed contingency fund after 1936. Nearly a third of it was designated to cover the costs if Abitibi was sued over the matter because neither side was certain how a court case might end. Late in 1944, no longer willing to delay, Clarkson declared that there must be a settlement. The receiver's position was difficult because he needed to terminate the old contract, eliminate any personal liability from the convoluted dealings, and stabilize Manitoba Paper's sales while keeping its major customer. When representatives for the Sifton group declared that they would take legal action, Clarkson treated the move as a bluff and stated that Manitoba Paper would discontinue sales at anything other than the normal Manitoba rates. This threat forced new negotiations that led to a settlement neither party liked but could live with. All prices charged before the end of 1944 were accepted as legitimate. Abitibi bought out the Sifton rights for 1945 and granted the chain a rebate that cut the realized price by $6 from the zone rate. The producer was required to pay biannually an adjusted amount that brought the price towards market levels. The Sifton group, in exchange, guaranteed a ten-year contract based upon the lowest rates Abitibi charged in Toronto and Montreal. Abitibi settled because, despite the rebate and other charges, it earned a higher net profit on sales by Manitoba Paper than was secured from other mills. But the deal also demonstrated how Clarkson and the managers made secret concessions or side deals even though they criticized the practice if done by others.[28]

During the receivership, the receiver also coped with tedious enquiries, audits, and re-audits by federal officials over Abitibi's taxable income. The company had not paid income tax since 1929 when its properties were valued at $95 million. As part of his conservation efforts, Clarkson employed every legitimate form of tax avoidance, but with the recovery of the industry after 1938 a string of disputes arose over Abitibi's "profit," the supposed worth of its assets, and the right to depreciate their value. Wartime revenue demands from the government accelerated the quarrels, but for six years no one could agree about Abitibi's tax liabilities because these depended on whether it earned "standard profits" in a "depressed industry" or it made "excess profits." A board of referees within the Department of National Revenue refused to provide guidance until all newsprint and pulp companies were investigated and a full hearing did not occur until May 1945.[29] Assuming tax levels would drop after the end of hostilities, the receiver deferred items that might exacerbate the dispute, and he stressed how Abitibi's records were (at best) inconsistent, which left considerable room for "misinterpretations." Earlier published statements had inaccurately reflected trends and the company's status, problems then exacerbated by wartime inflation. Federal officials would not discount Sturgeon Falls and Espanola even though the plants had been closed for years. They wanted higher values assigned to timber lands, most of which were in default. Clarkson considered those assessments to be "largely in opinion." Although he considered the claims unsound, Abitibi had "no option but to accept." Successive re-audits overturned earlier approvals and imposed additional assessments on prior years as federal authorities sought to extract monies from even marginal activities.[30] Clarkson's investments in Victory bonds and other securities helped build a reserve that could be applied against the final tax obligation. Ironically, the move helped foster an accumulation of liquid assets, which by 1945 raised Abitibi's working capital to a record level that was not achieved again until a decade later.[31]

2. The dirty end of the stick

Early in the summer of 1944 Clarkson reported how Abitibi's output and shipments had declined due to wartime constraints, but he also disclosed that net earnings had doubled as higher prices offset wartime inflation. The value of Abitibi securities appreciated after the publication of this portent, though sceptics remained convinced the creation of a solvent enterprise was likely only if all interests endorsed it, including the premier. "The whole Canadian investment world," one commented, "will send forth a rapturous cry when they are quite, quite sure the long, long receivership is over. There have been so many premature enthusiasms that it is well to wait for assurance this time."[32] But by the autumn the three biggest investor groups reached a series of understandings on the basis of a scheme advanced by the committee for the 6 per cent preferred holders. The need for a solution was propelled by mounting pressure from the Department of National Revenue and Abitibi's escalating working capital, which was expected to reach $34 million by the end of the year. Professing "amicable relations," the bondholders agreed to compromise the compound interest and not take an equity stake in a reorganized firm. In exchange, they could select a majority of the directors until the debt was reduced to an, as yet, unspecified level. At the close of October, the major classes announced a tentative agreement with "considerable satisfaction." Unsubstantiated tales circulated about the terms, including what equity holders might recoup. However, the negotiators ignored the small group of 7 per cent preferred stockholders. They offered those investors just an exchange of common stock even though, as a class, they ranked ahead of all others except the bondholders.[33]

The report of the Hughes Committee, submitted in November, recommended an outline of the scheme. "All parties have made certain concessions but the proposed Plan recognizes the present priorities as between classes," but it then acknowledged that the 7 per cent preferred committee sought "slightly more favourable treatment." The plan gave the bondholders the full value of their claim in new bonds. In exchange, they dropped a demand for a premium on principal payments and settled for 60 per cent of the interest-on-interest. This arrangement recalibrated the outstanding indebtedness to $53 million. Each new $1,100 bond had two components: $525 principal and $575 interest. The unsecured creditors were offered cash, although a cap was placed on the total settlement. For the 6 per cent holders, the plan cancelled all dividend arrears and divided each share into four (each with a par value of $20) and two common shares of no par value. Dividends on the new preferred shares would not be paid until 1947 or whenever the debt decreased to $35 million. Analogous terms were set for the 7 per cent holders, who were offered four new preferred shares worth $25 each for each share. Common shareholders would receive two new shares per share. An eleven-member board, comprising seven directors nominated by the bondholders and four by the common shareholders, was expected to "ensure continuity of management." The provision for bondholder representation terminated once the outstanding debt principal reached $25 million.[34]

Drew proclaimed the fundamental issues resolved after more than twelve years of legal proceedings. It now seemed only necessary to secure court approval and "while this will take time there seems to be little doubt that before long this company will be completely out of receivership and able to follow the usual procedure in every detail of its business activities." After praising the work of the different groups, he declared, "I am satisfied that the plan now produced and receiving the full agreement of all but a very small group of security holders is eminently fair to all concerned."[35] His enthusiasm was hasty. The premier failed to disclose that the Conciliation Committee had not unanimously endorsed the proposal. Jackson was convinced there still was no equity for the junior classes but was outvoted. Moreover, unacknowledged by the premier or the committee, the non-acquiescence of the 7 per cent preferred holders, which consisted of 186 investors, represented a serious obstacle. Over 60 per cent of the shares were owned or represented by: Henry Goldman Jr., a minor New York stock dealer who lacked the capabilities of his famous father, the former head of Goldman Sachs; Douglas Huycke, the manager of J.S. Bache & Company's Toronto office; and Ernest Lloyd, who headed another Toronto brokerage company, Frank S. Leslie & Co.[36] None were original investors. Rather they had picked up shares sold on the New York exchange, particularly the stock dumped by Sun Life after the failure of the Ripley plan. They knew the CCAA required approval by three-quarters of each security class, which created an opportunity for them to occupy the catbird seat. Constituting themselves as a protective committee and holding proxies from the other holders, once the plan was announced they chose to greenmail everyone else, akin to what Sun Life had done in 1927.[37]

Lloyd insisted that Abitibi was not bankrupt but had ample assets to pay off all claims. Frank Hughes alone had decided the allocation for the 7 per cent holders, he asserted. "We do not know why a split-up of our stock became part of the plan as this committee never suggested [a] change of capital structure." Noting how his committee had "decades of experience," Lloyd told Drew "splitting up of shares is created for the purpose of stock marketing. Individuals or groups of individuals with large holdings find it a most convenient method of disposing of holdings, irrespective of merit." Instead, his group wanted interest-bearing certificates in exchange for their principal and dividend arrears. "At various meetings, we were referred to as a 'nuisance stock' – evidently it was not realized that funds raised from the sale of these shares in 1915 was the nucleus of the present company. This position together with the security behind the issue, entitles the shareholder to receive its full claim of 'interest' as the certificate calls it … it remains a non-callable prior preferred share."[38]

A stream of orchestrated letters flowed into the premier's office and the press. One lawyer claimed to represent a wife who had bought the stock in 1917 and, while acknowledging Drew sought to bring "order out of chaos," he hoped the premier would "find it possible to devote just a bit more energy to protect the rights of the holders of this 'orphan stock.'" "In spite of its undoubted priority" under the Commission's plan, "this appears to be the only class of security to get 'the dirty end of the stick.'" A woman from Chicago decried, "Who is there that cannot say that the present oak tree, the Abitibi Power and Paper Company, Limited, was not the result of that acorn, the 7% preferred stock whose money started the company." Her banker thought the terms were prejudicial. Therefore Drew should use his "axe to split open the whole reason for such a scheme." Dissidents among the common shareholders also expressed unhappiness. The chair of their committee declared it had acquiesced to the proposal because, given the acceptance by other groups, the possibility of government action loomed. The dissidents tried to block the publication of the plan and then claimed the terms amounted to an "unconditional surrender." The package was "financially, economically and equitably unsound" because the debt and fixed charges remained too heavy.[39]

One opponent focused upon how the shareholders were scheduled to lose 55 per cent of their stakes, whereas those who owned bonds or preferred stock did not incur comparable sacrifices. The status of the equity holders was "highly hypothetical" and "in a most precarious position."[40] Meanwhile, the same person tried to finagle an underhanded deal from Clarkson. He claimed to represent investors with experience in the industry who wanted to buy Ste. Anne Paper. As reorganization neared, "it may be found in order to discuss such possibility. The group I am referring to is provided with ample financial resources and, due to some particular circumstances, is in a position to act promptly upon some reasonable terms." The receiver dismissed this ploy, which the investor had not realized was subject to a full judicial vetting.[41]

Acrimonious meetings were held as the Hughes committee tried to appease the opponents. The sessions generated a supplementary report submitted on Christmas Eve, which recommended a set of amendments, this time with the concurrence of all parties. Officially termed "a compromise and arrangement," it authorized reorganization under the CCAA. In crucial ways the terms resembled the recommendations from the McTague Commission, with each investor class retaining its status in the distribution. The key change entailed a decision to buy off the 7 per cent preferred shareholders. They were offered five $20 preferred shares for each $100 share, securities that also earned cumulative dividends from the beginning of 1945.[42]

In one sense, the outcome represented a victory for McPherson and those who insisted federal statutes were the only means for restructuring. But was the settlement realistic? A "pro forma" balance sheet, based upon "generally accepted accounting practice," accompanied the plan. As in 1937, this document was intended to legitimate the capital structure, but it bore no resemblance to anything generated before.

Instead, the statement concocted an alternate reality to legitimate the settlement and demonstrate that Abitibi was already solvent. Whereas the documents prepared for the Ripley plan were based upon a mix of assessments from different sources (net book value, a "net sound physical value" by the receiver, or "fair market value" by consulting engineers), this statement was composed of fantasy figures extrapolated from a supposed calculation of the "consolidated net income." The assets were estimated at $105 million versus $77.2 million in the Ripley plan or $127 million by Clarkson in his 1944 report. The position of the equity holders was valued at $43.8 million compared to $3 million in the Ripley plan. This meant there had to be sufficient assets to back the stock, a goal that was achieved by grotesque conjecture. The timber concessions (all in default) were given twice the value posted by the receiver and *twelve* times that in the Ripley plan. However, negotiations to confirm the resource rights had not even begun and there were no guarantees the properties would be restored. The mills and equipment were valued at twice that estimated by Clarkson in 1937 but then were creatively depreciated to generate a closer figure.[43]

Once again Abitibi was to be loaded with debt and other securities bearing fixed payments. Despite a liquidation of a portion of the bond principal since 1941, the fixed charges were nearly 40 per cent higher than envisaged by the Ripley plan, and they exceeded those incurred in the pre-receivership era. The funded debt alone amounted to half of the market value of Abitibi securities in 1946. Given tight markets and high prices for newsprint, it was assumed the bond principal could be reduced to $35 million within two years, but this was, as yet, only a hope. The committee and its staff refused to gauge future earnings, nor did they consider the impact of corporate taxes, which were going to be permanently higher than before the war.[44] The proposal ignored the physical state of the properties and the costs of restoration. Minimal outlays for maintenance had occurred, given Clarkson's role as a conservator of assets. Capital expenditures were insignificant before 1940 but had increased as equipment failed or wore out. Even the Ripley plan assumed a minimum of $8 million was necessary for rehabilitation. Not only had this task been postponed by another eight years, inflation after 1938 rendered replacement costs at least double the original estimates. Indeed, in the seven years after the receivership Abitibi's capital expenditures amounted to $47.8 million, and the firm depreciated obsolete assets by $64.6 million.[45] Critical opportunity costs thus were imposed by the failure of the Ripley plan. The necessary outlays would have been less and lower, while Abitibi could have better exploited wartime conditions.

Premier Drew characterized the settlement as a fair outcome, but was it really?[46] The bondholders regained their principal, interest, and 60 per cent of the interest on interest. Financial interests still were going to dominate the board of directors. As we saw earlier with Canada Power and Price Brothers, this was a normal practice where indebtedness remained high. The treatment of the unsecured creditors adhered to the Ripley plan and designated funds that exceeded the claims. The true beneficiaries of the settlement, however, were the 7 per cent preferred stockholders thanks to the greenmail by Henry Goldman and his associates. The 10,000 shares (each with a par value of $100) were converted into 50,000 "prior preferred" shares (with a par value of $20). Abitibi held the right to redeem them at a rate of $37.50 per share, but (unlike the other equity groups) the 7 per cent holders gained the right to dividends from January 1945, which also had a cumulative feature that ensured full payment. The market price of the shares soared towards $190 as investors realized their worth had almost doubled. The holders waived the right to any past dividends but the terms represented a Yuletide gift that gave them the equivalent of the principal and all unpaid dividends, securities with new dividends, as well as the right for payment in U.S. dollars (an additional premium of 11 per cent). Abitibi, to no one's surprise, redeemed the shares in 1947, one of its first initiatives after the return to solvency.

In contrast, the 6 per cent shareholders, who were owed $63.7 million, received securities with an aggregate value of $39.1 million. The new preferred stock redeemed their principal but they had to waive dividend arrears and could not earn dividends until the debt decreased below $35 million or 1947 at the earliest. The company had the right to redeem the shares, but the investors only received a compensation rate of $25 each plus any accrued dividends. In recompense, they received 60 per cent of the common stock and theoretically could exercise dominant influence once bondholder representation on the board ended.[47] The common shareholders claimed they had won because they secured *something*. Whether the settlement terms offset the time and expense associated with defending their stakes was dubious. The 1,088,117 shares were converted into 496,678 shares without par value. The Hughes plan presumed that after the other security groups were accommodated the residual book value amounted to about $13 per old common share, but this rested upon the gross asset inflation that was discussed earlier. Whether common stockholders actually got an actual return was a function of when they bought the shares. The market value of Abitibi securities appreciated after the summer of 1944, rising from $68 million to $106 million by April 1946. The price for a common share usually was less than $3.50 until the middle of 1945 but reached $8.87 by the following April. Even then, the price had not recovered to the levels experienced during the months preceding the release of the Ripley plan, and it remained well below those that prevailed before 1931. Investors who had bought in those periods incurred heavy losses. Those who bought when prices were lowest had the potential to recover their money or, perhaps, come out ahead.[48] Once again the issue was one of lost opportunities: nine years without capital improvements, nine years of conservation versus entrepreneurial initiative.

3. The longest receivership

Those who expected a speedy resolution were to be disappointed. The bondholders' council would not schedule a meeting until the other groups accepted the scheme. Meetings could not be scheduled until October 1945. Moreover, Henry Goldman was a businessman who believed a deal was a deal unless a better one came along. To the end, hoping to garner further revenues or influence, he inveigled against the arrangements for the Abitibi "problem child." The bondholders, he warned Drew, would replace the executives with men who would do their bidding. Under the Hughes plan, even with full production and high prices, the company could not earn enough to meet the fixed charges "and there is no need to mention what advantage will be taken of such events as par for exchange and competitive prices later. With money going begging for investment at 3% and 3½% the bond directors will block any plan that will mean a cut in interest rate and the 5% rate will put the company into a foreclosure and sale." He wanted the government to force a change in the board's composition, balancing it between the equity and debt holders with one government representative who would vote if a deadlock occurred. "We have a cold blooded lot of gentry to deal with." "Neither your government nor the shareholders need expect such a thing as consideration from such individuals." With splenetic fury, he declaimed:

> If some such protection is not given the shareholders now, I cannot see where they will be better off out of receivership than in the receivership. To be frank, I believe that they are far better off at present and will have a fair chance if some plan can be arranged though a smaller bond issue and lower rate of interest, while the receiver still operates and turn the company over to a new board, clean and to stay clean. I would expect strong opposition from those concerned but such selfish individuals who were able to withdraw so many millions from the company under the

classification of principal while clamouring to take over the assets under the guise of unpaid interest, to clean out the holders of all equity, and avoid income tax on receipt of the money paid them, is a class that deserves no more consideration than they have shown to others. Let yours be a gove[r]nment of and for the people, they won't forget.[49]

With an agreement accepted in principle, the premier acknowledged this whining but refused to intervene. When the 7 per cent preferred holders assembled to review the settlement, Hughes was no longer prepared to put up with continued opposition. He warned them that any amendment or effort to change the arrangement meant the process had to start over again. This killed any lingering resistance. The plan was accepted unanimously. Even Goldman seemed content. "We have come to a successful conclusion of one of the biggest things ever accomplished in Canada in company annals." He thanked Drew for "all good work and efforts in protecting shareholders of this company" and described the committee as "a valuable precedent in this country." Unbeknownst to most observers, he left to inflict the same greenmail game on other companies. The 6 per cent holders also voted unanimous approval. Their chair, D.H. Gibson, declared the "dark and stormy" troubles over due to "kindly guidance from a Government sympathetic to private enterprise and personal endeavour." Token meetings of the common equity and unsecured creditors ensued. The chair of the common shareholders' committee could not resist noting how it had been formed "against the imminent threat of virtual confiscation" and the only goal had been to ensure that they received "a fair and proper share." He commended the "constant support and encouragement" of Roy McPherson. Few others felt the liquidator had played a positive role.[50]

Negotiations over the timber concessions did not begin until the autumn of 1945 and they stretched out for six months. The approach "might appear slow to those in Abitibi desiring a fast wind-up of the receivership," the deputy minister of the lands and forests department stated, but both sides deemed it essential to reconcile the authorized wood supply for each mill with productive capabilities. The department wanted scattered lands that did not affect Abitibi's operations to revert to Crown ownership and it sought control over the Sturgeon Falls concession as a first step in rehabilitating the town. Abitibi refused to accept the latter although the wood was insufficient for a newsprint operation. As economic conditions improved, it began exploring other uses for the mill.[51] The negotiations dragged out because Abitibi's executives wanted to maintain traditional practices and include a clause "which would, in effect, let the company, and not the Government decide how the forests in the area would be managed."[52]

From the government's perspective, the final agreement represented a breakthrough and a model for leases with other companies. All of Abitibi's timberlands were made subject to a series of statutes introduced or amended during the receivership. Most dated from the Hepburn administration and strengthened the province's rights to control grants of cutting rights on Crown lands; review or exclude timber cuts, require information about company financing, inventories, and conservation practices; regulate water powers and navigation; and investigate wages and working conditions. The Tories believed the legislation, even when well-intentioned, had been ignored, poorly enforced, or overruled by political expediency. Entrenchment of the terms within the contracts was considered a step towards more professional management and a means of clarifying the relationships between the province and licensees. Clarkson acknowledged the change gave sweeping powers to the province but believed a government was likely to "be deterred by an unwillingness, on its part, to do anything which will serve to so increase the costs of pulpwood to Pulp and Paper Companies in Ontario as to leave them unable to operate unprofitably and/or to adequately compete."[53] A new management clause required the firm to inventory each property within five years, submit relevant documentation, periodically update plans, and gain prior approval for any cuts. The provisions were later incorporated in legislation the government characterized as placing all firms "on an equal footing in their management obligations." Some "detailed requirements" were not welcomed by Abitibi's forest managers, who criticized "objectionable features," such as a need to include a tentative plan of action. They complained that "the crown is asking for information which could conceivably be used 'against the Company' at some future date."[54]

Symington's committee would not schedule a meeting until the key issues were settled, but late in January it announced a ratification session. The 1939 Plan of Procedure was withdrawn and the Hughes plan endorsed. Two months later, seeming like an afterthought, the bondholders unanimously accepted the proposal. The finalized directorial set-up was analogous to the Ripley plan with seven "Class A" bondholder representatives, each of whom received two special class shares. The new common equity holders then selected the other four "Class B" directors. The bondholders appointed Douglas Ambridge as a director and the new president. He had started out as a junior engineer at Iroquois Falls and then moved to other assignments, including the head of the shipbuilding branch of the Department of Munitions and Supply and vice-president of Polymer. William Smith, who handled much of the company's general management during the receivership, was one of the few senior officers who stayed on. He was appointed as an executive vice-president and became one of the four equity directors. Everyone else on the board was new. The representatives for the bondholders included George Cottrelle, Robert Reid, Joseph Ripley, and two of their committee's lawyers, but not Herbert Symington. Harry Gundy was selected as an equity director. Industrialists comprised a third of the new board, financiers another third.[55]

A stream of legal matters occupied the following weeks: reports on the earlier distributions to bondholders, surrender of documents, submission and court approval of the agreements with the province, adjustments of the letters patent, and advertisement of final meetings. The longest receivership in Canadian history technically ended on 15 April 1946 when the federal government issued supplementary letters patent under the CCAA, but nothing was official until two weeks later when McPherson was discharged and the court sanctioned the new capital structure. Clarkson was authorized to surrender the properties and records and receive his own discharge.[56] For the receiver, things were hardly over. He spent another three months supervising the preparation of the accounts for court approval. His last report was neutral, workmanlike, but it contained several nuggets. The firm's operations remained subject to wartime regulations and Clarkson could not resist noting how federal authorities still had not decided the tax liability. The assets were lower than seven years earlier due to write-offs, but the company had healthy bank balances, significant deposits of government bonds, and strong working capital. Sales had increased only by 5 per cent and operating income by 9 per cent in 1945, but the net profit soared by 76 per cent. Abitibi could handle its interest and preferred stock obligations. To the end, following the pattern of earlier reports, Clarkson commended the assistance provided by the bondholders' council, particularly Joseph Ripley, Walter Somerville, and Robert Reid. The reorganization expenses in 1945 and 1946 were officially estimated at $2.4 million, a serious understatement of the actual costs. Most of the legal, underwriting, and consulting fees were hidden in various accounts and cannot be reconstructed. Never disclosed publicly, but buried within the auditor's notes, was a recognition that Abitibi reimbursed the bondholders' committee $3.5 million for certain expenses and compensation (or about $65 million in 2020 dollars). The other investor groups were reimbursed for their legal costs, with one exception – payment was denied to Henry Goldman's committee. Clarkson's personal remuneration across the receivership was at least $672,000 (about $13 million in 2020 dollars). The disbursements for his company's services were extensive, never disclosed, and cannot be reconstructed.[57] The payments revealed to the court were huge for the time, but it should be noted that the relevant charges since have vastly inflated. When equated into current dollars, any notion that a comparable firm now could secure executive compensation or relevant services at analogous rates (when adjusted for inflation) would be silly. Finally, at some point during the spring Clarkson supervised one essential task at the head office – a massive destruction of papers. Any secrets from the past were consigned to the flames, no ghosts were to haunt the resurrected Abitibi.

Most of these concluding events went unreported. The *Globe and Mail* and the *Financial Post* were among the few outlets that acknowledged the bondholders' meeting and the selection of new managers. In May, the *New York Times* briefly reviewed how "the sprawling papermaking empire" achieved "its newly won independence." The *Wall Street Journal* failed to do even that. The media had moved on to more interesting events: labour disruptions, the reintegration of veterans into society, postwar shortages, and an emergent cold war. But by the summer and autumn of 1946 it was apparent that things were back to business as usual. Financial analysts chose Abitibi as one of the best speculations among North American companies. Lumber operators decried their loss of influence due to the revisions of provincial forest policy, along with new regulations geared to match the demands of a corporate economy. They contended a "monopoly" use of forest concessions was associated with new leases issued to pulp and paper producers. The government should restore their ability to cut timber on the tracts because "these great natural resources belong to the people of the province," not the manufacturers.[58] The federal transport minister proclaimed Quebec's Abitibi's district had great potential and endorsed a major colonization program. Ontario's agriculture minister eulogized the untapped wealth of the north. There were twenty pulp and paper mills, "yet they have scratched only the fringe of the millions of acres of standing timber." In October George Drew announced his government had arranged for the reopening of the Sturgeon Falls mill. Employing new technology, it would manufacture corrugated board used in lining and packaging. The decision, the premier boasted, "constitutes an important advance in the full use of Ontario's forest resources."[59] The long night was indeed over.

15

Epilogue

Think now: where would your good be if there were no evil and what would the world look like without shadow? Shadows are thrown by people and things. There's the shadow of my sword, for instance. But shadows are also cast by trees and living things. Do you want to strip the whole globe by removing every tree and every creature to satisfy your fantasy of a bare world?

– Mikhail Bulgakov, *The Master and Margarita*

Deep in the human unconscious is a pervasive need for a logical universe that makes sense. But the real universe is always one step beyond logic.

– Frank Herbert, *Dune*

"CANADA HAS A MISSING GENERATION," Douglas Ambridge declared as he opened a training facility for Abitibi's engineers, most of whom were veterans. Men aged between thirty and forty, who lived through the Depression and the war, he remarked, often had not acquired the skills necessary for them to rise to their rightful places in Canadian industry. It represented a loss, not always acknowledged, but the future lay in the hands of their generation.[1] Across Northern Ontario during the years that followed the war resource companies prospered and residents anticipated a good future. Camps for bush operations quickly expanded. Many "boomers" or "floaters" looking for work were turned away because firms could not construct facilities to accommodate them fast enough. Newspapers, once again, prophesized a glorious future. "Everything from single horse 'skidders' to sleigh trains, tractors, streams, lakes and specially laid railroad links comprise the many faceted 'conveyer belt' system which dumps the woodland wealth of Northern Ontario into the lap of civilization." A mill had "a voracious appetite" and to "feed that monster takes a lot of a planning and a lot of good, honest, everyday hard work."[2] This chapter brings the study to a close. The first section summarizes Abitibi's later development, and it then answers several "whatever happened to" questions about the participants. The second section provides an opportunity to draw some summary observations.

1. Destinies

Clarkson and many others feared a slump in newsprint sales once hostilities ended and thus were cautious about new undertakings. Those beliefs proved wildly incorrect. Wartime restrictions compelled a decline in American consumption from 3.7 million tons to 3.4 million tons between 1941 and 1945. But as quotas were phased out, demand took off and reached 5.7 million tons five years later. Newsprint consumption relative to personal disposable income rose by more than 50 per cent. Whereas the United States accounted for 44 per cent of world consumption before the war, during the late 1940s it accounted for 62 per cent. World demand amounted to 9.9 million tons by 1948 versus a supply of 8.2 million tons. This trend reflected a broader dynamic, a growth of demand for all forms of paper. Despite the fluctuations from year to year and the Depression era, American consumption of newsprint had grown by more than ten times since the turn of the century.[3] Market demand immediately after the war became so severe that regulatory controls were reinstituted in a vain attempt to ensure the distribution of adequate supplies. A continued withdrawal of American firms from newsprint production contributed to the shortage and imports from Canada rose to four-fifths of the available supply. Prices escalated to $107 per ton by 1949. Canadian capacity increased by 600,000 tons between 1945 and 1950. This was accomplished mostly by speed and efficiency gains on existing equipment. The experiences of the 1920s were not repeated; a stampede into new construction failed to occur despite efforts by publishers to encourage new operations. Not only were the major firms still too weak to enlarge capacity, basic economics made it a non-viable strategy. Whereas capital costs during the 1930s ranged from $30,000 to $50,000 per ton of capacity, in the late 1940s new paper factories entailed investments that varied from $80,000 to $130,000 per ton. An International Paper executive noted his firm's mills cost one-third of new operations. "Newsprint production is profitable at $100 a ton when the mills built at pre-war prices are operating at capacity." The president of a west coast firm was blunter. "If you own an old mill which is depreciated … at the present price you can make a good return, a very fair return on your investment. We are satisfied with it." Things had changed, the U.S. Department of Commerce remarked. Pulp and paper was "by no means the place for the small-business man with his few thousand dollars of capital." For a customer determined to ensure adequate supply, it was simply cheaper to go out a buy an existing mill.[4]

The supply shortage and price inflation turned newsprint again into a political football, with congressional hearings and related investigations that went on for fifteen years. The "old price feud," as the *Wall Street Journal* remarked, was conducted solely on the American side of the border, where with newsprint "super-scarce" the publishers insisted Canadians had turned "thumbs down on making more than picayune increases in their productive capacity." The *New York Times* claimed that the papermakers made huge profits disproportionate to their manufacturing costs. "In brief, the policy seems to be to get the maximum the traffic will bear." The *Financial Post* characterized the lobbying by the American Newspaper Publishers' Association as one of the most vicious and distorted smear campaigns ever.[5] Most producers were unsympathetic. An executive for an American firm told a congressional hearing that "the newspaper publishers are reaping a harvest that they sowed themselves." The "foolish tactics" associated with their buying practices had forced prices down to uneconomic levels and inevitably bankrupted firms or compelled others to convert to alternative products.[6] Some thought they knew better. The cycle supposedly would turn once more because "never has the paper industry been in a position where it was not overbuilt for any long period of time. The enthusiasm of people who make paper is beyond all understanding. When the demand goes up. They build twice as many mills as necessary to supply, and then everybody knows it will happen again." But the *Wall Street Journal* captured, albeit pretentiously, the true character of postwar developments. "The American mania for keeping up with the news and Dick Tracy has bred cyclonic activity in the great wild woods of Canada ... To meet this pace the paper potentates are bustling as they've never bustled before. From the capital of their kingdom here in Montreal they've pulled open production throttles" to raise output, whereas the American manufacturers had abandoned newsprint "helter-skelter."[7]

When American investigators subpoenaed documents that might substantiate the publishers' allegations, George Drew's government passed legislation forbidding any removal of business records. The Americans, he declared, had hypocritically invaded Canada's territorial integrity, without applying to the federal or provincial governments, the courts, or any tribunals related to international business. Their "fishing expeditions" sought to put Canadian matters under American judicial proceedings.[8] American politicians complained loudly about this manoeuvre and suggested retaliation was appropriate, but for all the sound and fury little substantive action followed. A prominent report admitted congressional committees might, at best, keep "a continuing and wary eye," but it then descended into a tirade against earlier initiatives on the American side of the border. "One of the greatest abettors of monopoly practices has at times been the Government of the United States," which was illustrated by the NRA's and OPA's legitimation of zone pricing. Policies advocated by trade associations or industry members aimed at controlling production "should not be promulgated under the guise of Government sponsorship." Rather, public officials should maintain competition and demand firms make "a fresh and independent start in determining their independent pricing policies."[9]

Within this context, Douglas Ambridge and his new team of managers expanded production as quickly as possible. The company accelerated the use of multi-year contracts as a means of stabilizing cash flow and capacity use, but the agreements also allowed the firm to adjust prices to reflect changing market conditions. The biggest problem encountered during the initial months was securing personnel, given the loss of many employees to wartime activities and delays in demobilization. Nonetheless, Abitibi's newsprint manufacturing increased by more than a third from the 1945 level, which, when combined with the trend towards higher prices, ensured strong returns. Accordingly, less than eight months after the reorganization, the board announced a redemption of the outstanding debt. Cash was used to liquidate $8 million of the old bonds and the balance was retired by a new $45 million issue, which carried a lower interest rate. The new package cut the annual charges by two-fifths and amounted to just $2 per ton if the mills operated at full capacity, "a very moderate first charge on the gross earnings" the company noted in a significant understatement. The special issue of preferred shares issued to board members under the Hughes plan were redeemed, which brought a sudden end to bondholder control. "It is a milestone for this company," one press account declared, "because the last shackle of the receivership and bankruptcy period is struck from its limbs and for the industry as a whole because the world demand for its products is still keen and expanding." Despite the changeover, the shareholders chose two members of the old bondholder committee, Ripley and Reid, as directors, while Harry Gundy (whose firm handled the sales of securities) joined a new executive council. The process of restructuring was completed two years later when both classes of the preferred equity were liquidated. For the first time in two decades, Abitibi resumed paying dividends on the common stock.[10]

Despite the signs of financial health, Ambridge remained cautious. "Without progressive thinking and resolute action backed by adequate expenditures," there could be no guarantee Abitibi "will continue to play its present outstanding part in the economy of the nation." The tax liability remained a problem for several years. Wartime taxes were kept in a separate account until a settlement was finally reached. But reflecting the company's return to a profit-seeking management, the annual reports now decried how postwar taxes represented nearly half of the labour costs. "It is enough to pay an army of over 4,500 men a wage of more $40 per week for a whole year."[11] Ambridge's management differed from Smith's in a crucial way: significant disclosure about financial affairs, which continued the practices instituted by Clarkson. The firm was lauded as one of the few that provided not just detailed annual reports but also issued quarterly statements. This later became standard policy for most companies.[12]

The management group focused upon a redevelopment of the existing operations. As a first step, consulting engineers reappraised the properties and equipment. The exercise resulted in a revaluation of those assets from $46 million to $66.5 million, which allowed an elimination of the official consolidated deficit and the posting of a nominal surplus for the first time in fourteen years. The company consigned all previous appraisals and accounting practices to the ignominious past. Abitibi then began a massive program of deferred maintenance, plant renewal, and construction. The "catch-up" efforts impacted every element of the company's operations, but the changes at one site were illustrative of the investments. The Sturgeon Falls mill underwent a "complete rehabilitation" that included modernization of the equipment, along with the addition of a new groundwood pulp factory and a chemical plant. In response, the town's population grew from 4,000 to 7,000, with "new coats of paint on the houses," the stores doing fair business, and nearby farmers benefiting. "You can see enterprise budding everywhere," noted a taxi driver. "Some did get too old to work" during the receivership, "but as a rule all the others are far happier working. There is no percentage in being idle. People get far more out of life when they are working." While Sturgeon Falls remained a one-industry town, related businesses like sawmills contributed to the redevelopment. Press stories stressed how the factory now made synthetic goods from formerly discarded materials: waste, chips, and sawdust.

Prewar mills relied upon standard species like spruce to make news-print and fine paper. "That has ceased to be true, especially here," a worker proudly declared. These changes stimulated hopes of "great accomplishments." The plant, despite its chequered history, "translated to new uses, may have a splendid future."[13]

And so it would be for two generations as the company prospered during the mid-century boom. By 1954 newsprint accounted for four-fifths of Abitibi's production, a share that decreased over the following fifteen years with diversification into fine papers and building prod-ucts. After the burst of postwar expansion further capital outlays remained limited despite a continued growth of consumption. Instead, the firm milked the fixed and aging investments. By the early 1970s, the cost structure was higher than the industry norm, while the capacity utilization rate stayed well below major competitors. Unwilling to undertake investments in new facilities, Abitibi's executives acquired Price Brothers in a hostile amalgamation.[14] The move made Abitibi-Price the world's largest newsprint manufacturer but American con-sumption eased just after the takeover. Packaging and fine paper operations were divested in several stages. The company carried out a new wave of capital expenditures during the early 1980s that ranged from $40 to $80 per ton of capacity. In comparison, the new investment outlays by firms in the southern American states averaged between $407 and $451 per ton. Abitibi's capacity rates increasingly also fell behind those of aggressive foreign producers.[15]

By the 1990s the company's reports pushed a mix of clichés and hack-neyed phrases: "On Course," "Capitalizing on Market Leadership," "Maintaining the Vision," "Doing More with Less," and "Becoming the Finest." These attempted to mask the dependence upon a commodity with low added value and a less-than-capable management group obsessed with pursuing the established strategic recipe. Abitibi's per-formance appeared reasonable but was propped up by a devalued Canadian dollar that made its foreign earnings appear more significant. Competitive conditions and newsprint earnings eroded in an accelerat-ing pattern. Between 1980 and 2010 the industry again was reconfig-ured, this time from a continental to a global definition. Within this context, Abitibi's operations became high cost and obsolete relative to its international rivals. Demand weakened as electronic media sup-planted print publications. The managers attempted to preserve the firm's status within a declining North American industry by acquiring Stone-Consolidated and Donohue. Most of the senior managers and skilled personnel departed from those firms soon after the takeovers. With escalating costs and mounting losses, in 2007 Abitibi merged with

Bowater, now the largest American firm. "New Company, New Day," the leaders proclaimed. "Facing the challenges of our time head on, AbitibiBowater is defining itself with decisive action and a collaborative spirit. We are better able to address today's market and economic realities with actions designed to outpace the competition ... Our straightforward, no-nonsense approach is results-driven and best positions the Company to be the industry's great turnaround story." The logic behind the amalgamation, which gave the firm control over half of North American newsprint production, was analogous to the mergers of the 1920s. It proved to be an equivalent disaster – the debt-laden albatross crashed less than two years later and filed for bankruptcy protection. "Anson's Folly" gained its final title – "Bowater's Blunder."[16]

These developments occurred long after the passing of the participants in the Abitibi receivership. Geoffrey Clarkson outlived it by just three years. His firm became Clarkson Gordon, a powerhouse in the Canadian accounting profession for more than two generations. Clarkson Gordon was merged with Ernst and Young in 1989, a global service enterprise now rebranded as EY. Herbert Symington resumed executive leadership at Price Brothers after the war, along with his responsibilities to Killam's other companies, until he retired in 1957. Howard Ferguson never saw the end of the receivership. Separated by a Depression and war when death came in February of 1946, to many it seemed a universe, not just a generation, from his time in office. Even hostile newspapers eulogized about "a happy closing voyage for the old warrior," "Fergie," a political leader "who never suffered a personal defeat at the polls" had a "brilliant career" and "outstanding personality." Nary a word was raised about "Boss" Ferguson and his dubious dealings. Most of the other politicians who were involved with the receivership received warm eulogies when their time came, with two conspicuous exceptions. Mitch Hepburn was just fifty-six when he was felled by a heart attack in 1953. Because memories were still fresh about his political demise, the obituaries mixed terms like turbulent, energetic, controversial, colourful, stormy, fearless, reckless, and a great vote-getter. Peter Heenan had died five years earlier and the obituaries almost universally ignored his tenure in Hepburn's government, by then considered an embarrassment. Instead, they fondly remembered his activities as a federal Liberal and a minister of labour during the 1920s.

George Drew served as Ontario's premier for five years and is credited with encouraging a shift towards a more neutral civil service. While his party narrowly won the 1948 election, Drew lost his seat to a Cooperative Commonwealth Federation candidate, which the press attributed to a controversy about the introduction of cocktail bars in the riding. He was chosen to head the federal Progressive Conservatives but suffered crushing electoral defeats in 1949 and 1953. Although illness forced his resignation in 1956, he bequeathed a growing popularity for the party that helped his successor, John Diefenbaker, gain power a year later. Like Howard Ferguson, Drew served as High Commissioner to London, and after a short retirement he died from pneumonia in 1973. Arthur Roebuck's prejudicial conduct as Ontario's attorney general was long forgotten when he passed at the age of ninety-three. Appointed a senator in 1945, he remained a fierce partisan, mercurial and eccentric, but gained wide respect as a proponent of traditional liberalism. Sometimes characterized as "freedom's champion," he became a proponent of a Canadian Bill of Rights and divorce law reforms, opposed arbitrary power, and sought to ban compulsory retirement (especially his own).

Few things reflected how Fortune's wheel can turn as the destinies of five of the principals in this history. Charles Mitchell was arrested in March of 1933 for tax evasion based upon the disclosures during the Pecora hearings. Press stories claimed his lawyer demanded $100,000 for a retainer. Mitchell lacked the funds and solicited contributions from associates and former colleagues. He was defended during the six-week trial as a patriot, a blameless optimist who acted in good faith but became a scapegoat for the Great Depression. Mitchell was found not guilty but faced other civil charges. He was ordered by the U.S. Supreme Court to pay $1.1 million in back taxes and penalties. Rather than declare personal bankruptcy, a settlement was reached with the government, and he later repaid large loans to J.P. Morgan and Company. Mitchell, as the chair of another investment bank, then rebuilt his fortune and regained considerable respect among his Wall Street colleagues by the time of his death in December 1955.[17]

George Houk Mead went from success to success. Mead Corporation acquired companies in Indiana, Wisconsin, Tennessee, and Massachusetts and became a major force in the forest products industries. Anticipating future trends, he played a significant role in the development of operations in the Southern United States. Across Mead's career the assets of his American firms grew from $438,909 to $315 million, sales from $460,520 to $435 million, and the number of employees from 75 to 17,383. Mead's corporate realm eventually held forty-one manufacturing facilities in seventeen American states that produced a range of containers, boxes, corrugated products, technical papers, wood pulp, paperboard, and paper. In 1933 he was one of the founders of the Business Advisory Council, which worked in cooperation with the

Department of Commerce. Mead served on numerous governmental authorities during the Roosevelt and Truman administrations. These included the Hoover Commission (which dealt with the organization of the executive branch of government) and the public advisory board of the Economic Cooperation Administration, the agency responsible for managing the Marshall Plan. When Mead died in 1963 after a long illness, obituaries on both sides of the border never mentioned his experiences in Canada. Most focused upon his accomplishments after the founding of Mead Corporation in 1930, which was facilitated by some of the monies he gained from the Abitibi merger. His company sponsored a posthumous biography that laundered the executive's career.[18] Mead Corporation outlasted him by two generations but encountered variable performance that propelled a reconfiguration towards packaging and the divestiture of much of its traditional product mix. The company's identity vanished in a 2001 merger, which was followed by write-offs and liquidations amounting to two-thirds of its value and a transfer of the corporate headquarters to Richmond, Virginia. That enterprise, in turn, merged with a Tennessee producer in 2015 to form what is now Atlanta-based Westrock.[19]

After appearing before the McTague Commission, Alexander Smith disappeared from view, and in 1943 the house of Peabody Smith, defunct since 1930, was liquidated. Smith, still moderately wealthy, lived at Hyannis, Massachusetts, until he passed away in 1959 at the age of eighty-six. Terse statements buried near the bottom of the obituary pages of several American newspapers noted he had headed Abitibi and belonged to sports clubs in New York City or Montreal. In comparison, long articles appeared in the same issues about the deaths of a security guard who had succumbed to wounds and a worker who had built wagons for the Barnum and Bailey circus. Receiving the oblivion oft accorded to history's losers, Smith's passing was acknowledged neither by the Canadian press nor by the firm he had helped to construct.[20]

Archibald Graustein had reaped a fortune from his investments and set up a New York law practice after he was fired by the board of International Paper. He resurfaced once, in 1949, as a witness before a congressional committee and delivered a mix of evasive, forgetful, and false recollections about the newsprint crisis of the 1920s. International's publications have since minimized any reference to Graustein, his record wiped clean as if by the wrath of the gods. When he died in 1969, the *New York Times* highlighted the controversies during his management of International but said nothing about the rest of his life. Canadian papers never reported the death of the man they once characterized as a threat to industrial order and a manipulator of governments. But it should be acknowledged that Graustein bequeathed a worthy legacy. In 1946 he created a foundation to support the kinds of institutions that allowed his immigrant family to prosper in the United States. Named after his brother, the Graustein Memorial Fund still remains a valued organization, one dedicated to fostering "equity in education by working with those affected and inspiring all to end racism and poverty."[21]

Joseph Pierce Ripley served for eighteen years as an Abitibi director until another representative from his firm assumed the position after he suffered a mild coronary. Widely acknowledged as "the dean of Wall Street," he played an important role in financing the aviation and aeronautics sectors across the postwar era. For his contributions to international business, Ripley was named a Commander of the White Rose of Finland and a Commander of the Royal Norwegian Order of St. Olaf. His investment company became the eighth-largest in the United States and in 1966 was merged into Drexel, Harriman and Ripley. The financier served as an honorary director until death came peacefully at his Park Avenue home in New York City in November 1974, when he was eighty-five years old. He received the ultimate accolade for the successful man of affairs – a two-column obituary in the news section of the *New York Times* – with a photograph taken during his prime and his services for business, the American government, Cornell University, and charities lauded. Attention was given to his many endeavours, like funding International Zeppelin Transportation or chairing a protective committee for Imperial Russian bondholders. His thirty-four-year involvement with Abitibi went unmentioned.[22]

Drexel Burnham Lambert progressed to fortune and later infamy. The company weakened in the decade after Ripley's death but a stockbroker, Michael R. Milken, developed a new instrument for mergers and takeovers – junk bonds. The securities enabled those who facilitated business deals to reap staggering fees, but many firms that used them subsequently failed. The investment house was forced into bankruptcy when the Department of Justice prosecuted Milken for securities fraud.[23] Given the National City debacle, Ripley would have understood Drexel's plunge into questionable practices. He would have been disgusted to see how destiny came full circle.

2. Concluding perspectives

As I stressed in the Praecipe, observers in the 1930s advanced simple explanations for the collapse of the newsprint sector. They sought to identify likely culprits such as, in the vernacular of the times, "the financiers done dood it." It is a perspective that still surfaces in recent scholarship. Though issues like investment banking practices contributed to the disaster, it is facile to attribute the failures of Abitibi or other enterprises to any single factor. It is nonetheless possible to step back, to reflect upon the receivership and the wave of economic disaster as phenomena within an emergent corporate economy.

The American historian Alfred D. Chandler stressed how managerial capitalism offered great promise. Small firms carried out most economic activities until the late nineteenth century. As atomistic enterprises, the companies relied upon market mechanisms and were at the mercy of economic forces. The development of new energy sources and innovative technology, however, rendered this form of economic organization less viable. Large corporations became a dynamic for change and ultimately those types of enterprises dominated all developed economies. The industries where big manufacturing concerns arose showed the greatest growth. Across the first half of the twentieth century they generated more employment opportunities than either agriculture or services.[24] The firms supplied goods with uniform quality in high volume for much lower costs. Personal disposable income was enhanced as the prices for products dropped and as goods once deemed luxuries became more accessible. The standard of living improved with the gains in employment and wages.

Nonetheless, much of the research dealing with the rise of modern business understates the strategic problems associated with this transformation. Big corporate organizations relied upon mass manufacturing and marketing. Their properties consisted of factories and equipment, rather than the modest inventories firms retained in a pre-industrial era. Financing required capital that imposed significant fixed charges and that was secured by collateral in the form of mills and other assets. The productive technology raised not just the ratio of capital to output, but also the proportion of fixed costs. While the capacity to produce in volume was enhanced, the changes reduced the ability to adjust supply to demand. Companies could no longer cut financial losses just by dumping excess inventories. Costs could often only be avoided by going out of business or by converting to other products. This risked the sale of assets for a fraction of their value. Moreover, barriers to entry and exit rose. As a practical matter, established firms thus remained in business as long as possible and tried to increase sales that allowed their fixed costs to be spread over larger volumes. These conditions sometimes propelled expansion at the highest possible rate, whether measured by cash flow or other indices. The most successful enterprises developed administrative systems that coordinated multiple plants, each with a set of technological imperatives for achieving the lowest cost operations. In sectors like steel, chemicals, food products, and transport equipment, mergers or other forms of rationalization then converted the industries into oligopolies that reduced or eliminated price-based competition and made product differentiation a crucial element of strategic rivalry. Under the best conditions, the profits accelerated capital formation, allowed the companies to sustain growth, and ensured the ability to make investments that further reinforced competitive positions.[25]

Pulp and paper represented a sector where the transition was not successfully completed before 1945 and the rites of passage were excruciating. Technological changes allowed firms to reap greater economies and propelled the expansion of both mill and firm size. However, the capital required for establishing new plants with minimum efficient scale remained modest relative to other industries. Not only were the barriers to entry easily surmounted but many older or smaller firms persisted. In the 1920s the sector became more concentrated, but there was never a sufficient focus of market power to guarantee *effective* price leadership or collusive behaviour. The formation of corporate groups *intensified rather than diminished* price-based warfare. None had sufficient time to undertake a meaningful rationalization of productive activities before the descent into the economic singularity. The price wars and the Great Depression accomplished that task, brutally. The high fixed costs meant firms tended to earn profits only as operations approached full capacity, but since newsprint was not subject to product differentiation, demand remained beyond the ability of producers to influence or shape. The combination of these issues propelled them towards maximum output levels and the use of the sharpest, the most dangerous, weapon in the strategic arsenal – price. The formation of newspaper chains with their market power compounded this development. Shifts in bargaining positions drove a movement from a buyer's to a seller's market during the first two decades of the twentieth century. Another cycle back and forth then occurred across the next forty years.

Despite the escalation of prices that followed the Second World War, competitors drew several lessons from those experiences. Surviving producers grasped the need to alter capacity slowly, not in response to short-term demand or price fluctuations. They concentrated upon configuring operations to reap efficiency gains and raise barriers to entry, while simultaneously resisting efforts by publishers to alter the bargaining power relationship again. Especially south of the border, new entrants were inclined to focus upon higher-value products, unless there were secure niches or unexploited opportunities for commodities like newsprint. Canadian firms had fewer options. With tariff barriers still in place for other forest products, they emphasized newsprint, pulp, lumber, and low-value goods. Moreover, the United States tried to protect domestic companies with non-tariff modes of protection for numerous wood-based products. Repetitious trade disputes ensued that have continued to the present day. These developments left the Canadian industry ill-positioned for the competitive shifts that unfolded after 1980.

Historical research has also emphasized how the organizational dimensions of economic transactions were altered. The modern industrial enterprise, Chandler observed, "is a collection of operating units, each with its own specific facilities and personnel, whose combined resources and activities are coordinated, monitored, and allocated by a hierarchy of middle and top managers. It is the existence of this hierarchy that makes the activities and operations of the whole enterprise more than the sum of its operating units." Managerial capitalism was characterized by a new type of economic man, the salaried executive who guided the allocation of resources, employment, and output. In this way, the "visible hand" of professional management constrained but did not replace the invisible hand of competitive market forces, and administrative coordination became the central engine of market power.[26] It is difficult to reconcile this image with the newsprint sector, and the gap again contributes to understanding the failures and turnover that characterized the industry.

Most companies were single-product, single-location operations that did not need complex regimes. The corporate groups were little more than federations of quasi-autonomous units. International Paper and Canada Power and Paper were holding companies; Abitibi's organization was effectively the same. Following the amalgamations or mergers, operational personnel either stayed in place or were encouraged to do so. The firms were managed like corporations during the earliest stages of managerial capitalism: small head offices delegated authority to local officials who supervised mill and woods operations.[27] Missing were the layers of middle-level executives that already typified large American corporations or did so in major forestry companies after mid-century. Chandler stressed how complex technologies and product diversification propelled management by skilled professionals. The newsprint companies, however, emphasized "parallel competition," the duplication of goods already on the market. New firms were created around the notion of "market holes," that is, they appeared in response to perceptions about how the existing firms did not sufficiently meet demand and they just replicated established activities. The modest entry barriers facilitated this strategic orientation. But many firms had a critical vulnerability. The sales function was often delegated to separate or quasi-independent organizations, which meant the comprehension of market developments was, at best, filtered by the information the agents were prepared to supply. Agents, as economists have observed, do not necessarily pursue the same goals as principals.[28] While these arrangements seemed reasonable in prosperous times, they made the ability to respond to turbulent change difficult. International's ability to accumulate orders from 1927 to 1931 can be linked to its internalization of the marketing function, whereas Abitibi and other firms experienced severe problems. Clarkson recognized the issue but it took fifteen years to internalize the sales function.

Entrepreneur-promoters tended to lead the Canadian paper corporations during the period covered by this book. There certainly were prominent salaried executives, but a shift towards the dominance of professionals as top officers dates from the 1930s or later – marked by the appointment of people like LaMonte Belnap at Consolidated Paper, Richard Cullen at International, or Douglas Ambridge. Edith Penrose, in her classic study, stressed how entrepreneurs define the "production opportunity" of a firm: the potentialities that are perceived and exploited, or not. Thus, it can be "that failure is more common than success, that over the long, long period firms ... follow each other in succeeding waves into the sea and drown, or even that 'death and decay' are 'inherent in the structure of organization.'"[29] Neither of Abitibi's first two presidents can be characterized as professional managers, both were entrepreneur-promoters. These types of businessmen are crucial to "the spirit of enterprise," to use Penrose's phrase, the decisions that propel the founding of a company and the ambitious exploration of growth possibilities. The entrepreneurial roles may encompass the ability to grasp and construct production or marketing capabilities (as Anson did) and capital-raising ingenuity (Alexander Smith's expertise). A careless observer might denigrate Smith as just a "financier," but this underestimates his role. It was Smith who grasped the need to expand into newsprint production. It was Smith who was ambitious for the successive expansions. It was Smith who personally profited the most from the firm's rise. But while they carry out valuable roles, promoter-entrepreneurs have a serious flaw. Without sufficient checks their ambition may lead to grandiose visions or forceful empire-building. Smith, Edward Backus, Archibald Graustein, and Harry Gundy succumbed to similar manias. All four rose as success followed success, but this precipitated disastrous over-reach, their removal, and a transition towards management of what was left of the empires by salaried executives. Gundy alone managed to persist, a consequence of his connections in the financial sector. George Mead was one of the few papermakers who completed the transition from founder to respected administrator of a giant corporation.

The academic literature dealing with entrepreneurship has lacked the rigour associated with research into other aspects of business administration but it offers significant insights. Traditional approaches, such as those advanced by Joseph Schumpeter and David Landes, linked social contexts to the emergence of entrepreneurial capabilities, but sweeping generalizations have limited value for the appraisal of specific cases.[30] Contemporary researchers have focused upon issues like the career paths and personal histories that shaped entrepreneurs, the significance of team-building, and the role of external relationships. Successful entrepreneurs, contrary to popular stereotypes, usually do not conform to the image of risk-takers who enjoy the struggles of competitive turbulence. While achievement-oriented, they tend to be focused individuals, personally invested in a product and perceiving its development as a service to humanity. They often gauge "success" as the retention of tight personal control and the construction of a stable, effective enterprise, not necessarily a preoccupation with its profitability. Their accomplishments originate not only from the ability to recognize short-lived windows of strategic opportunity but also from the construction of coherent teams of employees and the elaboration of supportive relationships, especially with venture capitalists. Frank Anson particularly fit this perspective. Smith, in contrast, was driven by monetary and status concerns, which partially account for his ultimate failure. As success followed success, he uncritically adopted the "go-getter" behaviour that characterized investment banking throughout the 1920s.[31] Nonetheless, we should recognize that the instances of founding entrepreneurs who went on to head big enterprises always have been very few. Most either were displaced during crises or removed themselves voluntarily, their personal attributes ill-suited to handling large complex operations.

Much of the published research about the rise of managerial capitalism, like analogous work by neo-institutional economists, attributes the process of economic transformation to alterations in authority relationships and the topics stressed in business analysis.[32] The new corporate organizations, by this logic, supplanted market mechanisms because their managers emphasized productivity and efficiency. Success was demonstrated by survival and growth, whereas economically wasteful or inept enterprises failed. This perspective assumes congruence between social context and the transfigurations of company operations that unfold over time. There is some truth in the viewpoint, but as a technocratic interpretation of economic development it unreasonably oversimplifies the nature of strategic choice. All complex organizations are comprised of internal and external coalitions. The emergence and evolution of large business enterprises are not shaped only by executives, but by interactions amongst stakeholders with different goals, motives, and resources. The distribution of benefits and costs from economic change has always been uneven. Put simply, capital formation inherently has a social dimension, not just an economic one.

This book has charted how that broader context impacted the pulp and paper enterprises. For better or ill, specific types of social institutions conditioned their development. It is legitimate to stress how the firms were influenced by governmental policies, particularly the ways in which the provinces exerted social control. There is no such thing as a "non-interventionist" state because governments mould economic activities even when they are not actively involved. The rise of large corporations introduced new politico-economic tensions. As mass producers requiring extensive resource inputs, the paper companies depended upon stable assets (particularly properties, which also served as collateral for loans). They treated contracts for what they legally were: agreements that allocated property rights, defined responsibilities, and could be used as a form of protection against intrusion by external interests. While the firms assumed the risks of economic development (with their associated roles as social agents acknowledged by allocations of resource privileges), the executives also expected governments not to put up obstacles that hindered success. However, provincial administrations behaved as if they were in a pre-industrial era and treated economic investment as just another tool to be exploited for personal or electoral gain. Resource agreements were considered levers from which concessions might be extracted and benefits distributed. Of course, there was considerable legitimacy in those perspectives. Natural resources were public property and the state had the right to control their use. The contracts with the paper companies supposedly ensured production and employment levels, as well as steady revenues for the governments.

Finding a balance between these alternative perspectives proved elusive. In Atlantic Canada and Newfoundland, there were well-founded concerns about how big corporations dominated governments. In Ontario, public policy was mercurial and shaped by the obsession about northern colonization. The treatment of individual firms shifted from administration to administration, with apparent concords or understandings delayed, amended, or abrogated. Those issues contributed to Ontario's lacklustre performance after 1924 relative to the expansion that occurred elsewhere. But the descent into economic crisis made the lack of effective social control even more apparent. While, in theory, provinces might impose fines or even withdraw resource rights if firms did not fulfil their contracts, this form of action was rarely considered, let alone pursued. George Henry realized the available instruments (licence suspensions or higher taxes and fees) were cumbersome and unlikely to work, a perspective others, albeit reluctantly, realized over time. As the crisis worsened, firms were not going to maintain non-economic operations, regardless of the consequences. The unwillingness of provincial officials to undertake substantive action characterized the first crisis of 1927–9. Throughout the following decade their initiatives proved confused and half-hearted. The governments were only prepared to endorse industrial self-government, which was never likely to succeed. Similar American initiatives, like the National Recovery Administration, failed and were abandoned with few regrets.

In the best of all possible worlds, after problems occur enquiries are made, remedies are sought, and solutions are implemented. When companies have failed, both press and official enquiries (seeking scapegoats) stress the likelihood of deviant or unethical behaviour. But in the Abitibi case, as with most other instances of corporate collapse, the financial and accounting practices that masked the descent (while creative, if not feral) complied with the established rules. In practice, unravelling dubious conduct after the fact usually has proven impossible, with little public disclosure and few sanctions imposed against the responsible individuals. The issues associated with consolidation accounting, for example, remained unaltered even though they often violated common sense. Across the following century, after successive waves of failures involving mega-mergers or gross cases of managerial recklessness, there were efforts to elaborate new rules, such as the 2010 Dodd-Frank Wall Street Reform and Consumer Protection Act in the United States. The measures provided temporary, if any, amelioration of dubious conduct. Usually within a few years firms continued with their traditional practices. Their leaders called for removing the constraints, which they now derided, mythically, as impediments to growth or the generators of "unreasonable" costs.[33]

Though the McTague commission and different court rulings highlighted how Canadian corporate law was inadequate for handling large-scale failures, the experience of Abitibi and other enterprises during the Great Depression did not lead to corrective action. Whereas

American practitioners and legal scholars gave extensive attention to the topics, in Canada they received scant consideration. Despite an extensive nexus of cross-border business by the interwar era, no attempt was undertaken to negotiate accords with the United States or other countries that might regulate the bankruptcy of corporations with international operations. A few proponents acknowledged the need for a Canadian-American bankruptcy convention to smooth inconsistencies and inequities between the national systems. Canadian law did not provide for an assumption of bankruptcy jurisdiction for non-residents just because assets were located in Canada, nor did it axiomatically accept judgments from foreign jurisdictions as legitimate for Canadian developments. In the absence of statutory guidelines, judge-made rulings prevailed. In some cases, domestic law was applied to situations arising from another country. In other cases, they applied the law of the other country to situations arising, at least, in part from domestic origins. Canadian law remained fixated upon small creditors and treated bankruptcy as a matter of liquidation, not resuscitation.[34]

Procedural amendments to the Bankruptcy Act in 1949 were intended to provide "a more orderly arrangement of subjects," a simplification of terminology, and "a code for the administration of small estates in an economical and inexpensive manner."[35] The changes were later criticized as inefficient and archaic. Public officials retained insufficient investigatory powers, and the statute proved incapable of dealing with fraudulent bankruptcies, especially those associated with the postwar expansion of consumer credit. Despite subsequent amendments to ameliorate these difficulties, a major overhaul of the Bankruptcy Act was long delayed. Several attempts to pass legislation during the 1970s and 1980s ended in failure. Reforms instituted in 1992 were geared to enhancing creditor value through reorganization and rehabilitation, but it took until 2009 for the federal government to link what is now known as the Bankruptcy and Insolvency Act with the restructuring of viable, but financially troubled, enterprises. Nonetheless, the piecemeal character of Canadian legislation remains in place, despite numerous calls for further rationalization. The bankruptcy statute falls under the jurisdiction of one federal ministry; the Winding-Up and Restructuring Act is handled by two; others administer legislation related to farm debt mediation; and there are entirely different arrangements for financial or transport companies.[36]

A 1970 report claimed the Companies' Creditors Arrangement Act "worked well and gave general satisfaction to investors and companies with secured indebtedness who wished to make arrangements with their unsecured creditors."[37] The description bore scant resemblance to reality because the statute had fallen into disuse. Liquidation, not resuscitation, characterized the few cases where it was employed. Efforts to institute new legislation that might cover corporate reorganization were opposed by groups like the Dominion Mortgage and Investments Association. They stressed how secured creditors, as the primary beneficiaries, should still control the administration of insolvent enterprises. As a result, major cases proceeded under provincial "rules of court" that allowed the appointment of a receiver and/or receiver and manager when it was deemed "just or convenient" to do so. Use of the CCAA became more extensive after 1992 and reform legislation in 2009 designated it as a vehicle for large-scale corporate restructuring. Nonetheless, the existence of two federal statutes related to company reorganization was not resolved and further policy reviews inevitably have followed.[38]

These institutional issues matter because the attrition from the process of strategic rivalry is dramatic. About one-fifth of the one hundred largest non-financial enterprises in Canada in 1930 survived to 1988. Less than 5 per cent of those companies remained among the biggest firms by 2013. Even if a more contemporary framework is used, the scale of turnover remains staggering. Less than a fifth of the top one hundred non-financial companies of 1988 were still among that group a quarter-century later. The turnover was especially severe among the biggest seventy-five Canadian-controlled industrials – as most were taken over, went out of business, or were liquidated. Economic failure was particularly noticeable in the pulp and paper industry, which began a decline in the 1980s from which it never recovered. Just as a change in fashion from beaver hats wiped out the industry that led to the discovery of the middle waters, the rise of the Internet and electronic media decreased the demand for newsprint. In a series of waves, forest company operations were merged, sold, divested, and liquidated. Some provinces like Ontario moved on to new forms of resource exploitation that promised green for promoters or investors.

Thus, it is not surprising that most of the landmarks of the era discussed in this book have changed or disappeared, although there are a few exceptions. Abitibi sold Thunder Bay Paper to Cascades and it later closed the plant. The Sturgeon Falls mill was demolished in 2004; Fort William was sold for scrap in 2010; and Pine Falls was torn down in 2012. The properties in the Iroquois Falls plant closed three years later with plans that they might have new uses after restoration. The Sault Ste. Marie site was redesigned to create a cultural and tourism hub for the city. Ironically, although it was derided in the past as non-economic, Spanish River's Espanola factory continues in operation as a Domtar facility. Frank Anson's residence in Montreal's Westmount district remains a well-kept private home. Herbert Molson's Montreal mansion serves as a consulate for the Russian Federation, while Charles Mitchell's residence in New York City is a French consulate. Alexander Smith's apartment building at 999 Lakeshore Drive in Chicago remains a much-sought-after location. A branch of the Harris Bank, which is controlled by the Bank of Montreal, is situated where Peabody Houghteling first did business. The bottom floors of another building in Chicago, where the firm relocated about the time of Abitibi's creation, have survived and are mounted by a skyscraper. The towers at 63 and 67 Wall Street where Smith and Graustein had their business offices are now luxury residences. Osgoode Hall, of course, remains as both a heritage building and a venue for Ontario's Court of Appeal and Supreme Court. In contrast, Abitibi's head office across the street was demolished in 1968, the site used as a parking lot for several decades after the company relocated to more modern facilities. A tower with government offices now is situated at 408 University Avenue. Some ruins from Alexander Smith's headquarters can be found, like remnants from an ancient civilization, scattered through Scarborough's Guildwood Park and Gardens – a poignant reminder that all things, including corporate empires, are mortal. *Sic transit gloria mundi*.[39]

APPENDICES

Appendix 1 Newsprint Annual Supply and Demand, 1899–1946

Year	Total Production 000 tons U.S.	Canada	U.S. Demand 000s tons	Annual Capacity (310 days) U.S.	Canada	North American Prod. as % of Total Capacity	U.S. Supply as % of U.S. Demand	Canada Exports as % of U.S. Demand
1899	569	n.a.	478	968	82	- -	100	- -
1904	913	n.a.	743	1,093	132	- -	100	- -
1909	1,168	159	1,153	1,466	185	80	98	2
1914	1,313	470	1,567	1,541	462	89	80	20
1915	1,239	549	1,501	1,511	634	83	76	24
1916	1,315	662	1,690	1,464	684	92	72	28
1917	1,359	722	1,824	1,541	704	93	69	31
1918	1,260	770	1,759	1,450	760	92	66	34
1919	1,323	849	1,875	1,336	828	100	67	33
1920	1,512	938	2,193	1,548	939	99	60	31
1921	1,237	852	1,975	1,668	1,074	76	58	33
1922	1,447	1,143	2,451	1,639	1,200	91	53	37
1923	1,521	1,330	2,750	1,578	1,388	96	52	41
1924	1,481	1,418	2,737	1,632	1,561	91	51	43
1925	1,563	1,619	2,943	1,774	1,715	91	47	43
1926	1,686	2,068	3,307	1,763	1,931	102	47	47
1927	1,517	2,290	3,445	1,968	2,475	86	43	51
1928	1,415	2,612	3,515	1,891	2,993	82	40	54
1929	1,409	2,984	3,780	1,695	3,225	89	36	57
1930	1,226	2,791	3,563	1,712	3,600	76	37	57
1931	1,203	2,516	3,245	1,636	3,825	68	36	54
1932	1,047	2,186	2,840	1,650	3,840	59	34	54
1933	928	2,282	2,692	1,703	3,847	58	30	57
1934	990	2,911	3,107	1,238	3,861	77	27	62
1935	947	3,176	3,345	1,081	3,914	83	25	62
1936	938	3,675	3,692	1,008	3,869	95	22	66
1937	976	3,998	3,825	1,000	3,883	102	24	73
1938	832	2,893	3,422	960	4,204	72	24	58
1939	954	3,175	3,520	988	4,293	78	27	62
1940	1,056	3,770	3,731	1,075	4,368	89	28	69

(*Continued*)

Appendix 1 (Continued)

Year	Total Production 000 tons U.S.	Canada	U.S. Demand 000s tons	Annual Capacity (310 days) U.S.	Canada	North American Prod. as % of Total Capacity	U.S. Supply as % of U.S. Demand	Canada Exports as % of U.S. Demand
1941	1,044	3,771	3,930	1,085	4,341	89	27	70
1942	967	3,455	3,816	1,126	4,400	80	26	72
1943	811	3,219	3,627	1,100	4,315	74	23	74
1944	721	3,265	3,243	1,033	4,358	74	24	75
1945	726	3,592	3,481	981	4,301	82	24	75
1946	775	4,506	4,296	849	4,265	103	22	77

Sources: U.S., Department of Agriculture, Forest Service and Timber Conservation Board; Department of Commerce, Bureau of Foreign and Domestic Commerce; Bureau of the Census.

Note: This appendix is a reconciliation of data from numerous reports published annually or periodically. Information about production, consumption, and imports was revised almost constantly. Individual reports often had gaps or missing entries. Statistics published close to a sample year varied from later adjustments. Government estimates of capacity levels normally were based upon annual lists printed in *Editor and Publisher*; for selective years, these were cross-verified via industry directories.

Appendix 2 Traits of the North American Newsprint Industry, 1890–1940

2.1 Newsprint Firms and Mills

	1890	1900	1910	1920	1930	1940
U.S. firms	129	65	56	34	38	16
Canada firms	13	12	12	16	26	23
Newfoundland firms	--	--	1	1	2	2
Total North America firms	142	77	69	51	66	41
U.S. newsprint mills	134	81	71	46	39	20
Canada newsprint mills	14	12	12	19	36	38
Newfoundland newsprint mills	--	--	1	1	2	2
Total North America newsprint mills	148	93	84	66	77	60
U.S. daily capacity tons	1,243	3,355	4,746	4,341	5,646	4,450
Canada daily capacity tons	87	265	540	2,850	11,549	14,747
Newfoundland daily capacity tons	--	--	200	215	839	1,265
Total North America daily capacity tons	1,330	3,620	5,486	7,406	18,034	20,462

2.2 Entry and Exit of U.S. Newsprint Mills

	Beginning of Decade		Entering mills		Exiting Mills	
	No. of Mills	Average Daily Capacity Tons	No. of Mills	Average Daily Capacity tons	No. of Mills	Average Daily Capacity tons
1890–1900	134	8.8	58	46.8	111	9.1
1900–1910	81	38.5	36	62.0	46	20.7
1910–1920	71	66.0	14	94.1	40	52.5
1920–1930	46	94.4	9	123.8	17	47.6
1930–1940	39	144.8	2	215.0	22	119.6

2.3 Entry and Exit of Canadian Newsprint Mills

	Beginning of Decade		Entering mills		Exiting Mills	
	No. of Firms	Average Daily Capacity Tons	No. of Mills	Average Daily Capacity tons	No. of Mills	Average Daily Capacity Tons
1890–1900	14	6.2	7	24.1	9	4.7
1900–1910	12	22.1	5	51.8	6	8.1
1910–1920	12	45.0	13	166.1	4	14.3
1920–1930	19	150.0	20	334.1	3	48.2
1930–1940	36	320.8	3	131.6	1	38.0

2.4 American Mill Size, Daily Ton Capacity

	1890	1900	1910	1920	1930	1940
0–10	99	20	4	--	--	--
11–20	26	19	10	1	--	--
21–50	8	24	27	22	5	1
51–100	1	12	15	9	12	4
101–200	--	6	12	9	14	9
201–300	--	--	3	2	5	3
301–400	--	--	--	2	2	4
401–500	--	--	--	1	--	--
>500	--	--	--	--	1	1
Total	134	81	71	46	39	22

2.5 Canadian Newsprint Mill Size, Daily Ton Capacity

	1890	1900	1910	1920	1930	1940
0–10	12	6	4	1	--	--
11–20	2	2	2	0	--	--
21–50	--	2	2	1	1	--
51–100	--	2	3	4	1	3
101–200	--	--	1	5	7	6
201–300	--	--	--	7	11	7
301–400	--	--	--	1	6	7
401–500	--	--	--	--	4	2
>500	--	--	--	--	6	13
Total	14	12	12	19	36	38

2.6 Firm Percentage Share of North American Newsprint Capacity

	1890	1900	1910	1920	1930	1940
All American firms	93.5	92.7	86.5	57.0	30.0	21.7
All Canadian firms	6.5	7.3	11.4	37.4	65.2	72.1
Largest 4 firms	12.3	51.5	41.8	37.4	47.2	40.8
Largest 4 U.S. firms	12.3	51.5	53.3	33.4	16.7	13.4
Largest 4 Canadian firms	3.7	5.9	8.6	17.7	37.8	40.5
International Paper	--	42.8	33.6	16.6	17.5	12.3
Abitibi	--	--	--	3.2	13.8	11.9

2.7 American Mill Size Share of North American Newsprint Capacity

	1890	1900	1910	1920	1930	1940
Under 0.1%	4	3	1	--	--	--
0.1 to 0.2	10	7	3	--	2	--
0.2 to 0.3	17	11	5	2	4	--
0.3 to 0.4	16	8	5	8	4	1
0.4 to 0.5	18	4	5	4	5	3
0.5 to 0.75	23	12	14	11	8	4
0.76 to 1.0	14	10	9	4	6	4
1.0 to 1.5	20	9	10	5	5	4
1.5 to 2.5	10	8	7	7	4	3
2.5 to 5.0	3	8	12	5	1	1
>5.0	--	1	--	1	--	--
Total mills	135	81	71	47	39	20

2.8 Canadian Mill Size Share of North American Newsprint Capacity

	1890	1900	1910	1920	1930	1940
Under 0.1%	--	1	--	1	--	--
0.1 to 0.2	2	3	4	--	--	--
0.2 to 0.3	5	2	1	--	1	--
0.3 to 0.4	--	1	--	1	--	3
0.4 to 0.5	3	--	1	--	1	--
0.5 to 0.75	1	2	1	1	1	3
0.75 to 1.0	2	--	--	3	4	5
1.0 to 1.5	--	1	2	2	12	5
1.5 to 2.5	1	2	2	3	7	9
2.5 to 5.0	--	--	1	8	10	13
> 5.0	--	--	--	--	--	--
Total mills	14	12	12	19	36	38

Sources: Rated capacity from *Lockwood's Directory of the Paper and Allied Trades* (New York: Lockwood Trade Journal, 1891, 1911, 1920, 1931, 1941); *Post's Paper Mill Directory* (New York: L.D. Post, 1920, 1921, 1941); *National Directory of the Canadian Pulp and Paper Mills and Allied Trades* (Gardenvale, PQ: National Business Publications, 1929, 1930).

Notes: Most producers did not segment rated capacity by type of paper. The data are based upon firm reports and potentially overstate the capacity devoted to newsprint. Investigations by the FTC misrecorded capacity or firm activities and included companies or mills that supposedly had newsprint among their capabilities but did not produce significant amounts.

Appendix 3 Capitalization of Paper Companies, 1920 and 1930 ($ Millions)

	Total Debt	Preferred Stock	Common Stock	Aggregate Capital	Percentage Debt & Preferred
1920					
Pulp & Newsprint Producers					
Abitibi Power & Paper	$10.2	$1.0	$5.0	$16.2	69.1
Brompton Pulp & Paper	2.2	2.0	7.0	11.2	37.5
Canada Paper	0.2	0.3	0.6	1.1	45.5
Fraser	2.3	0.0	10.0	12.3	18.7
Lake St. John Pulp & Paper	0.0	2.0	2.0	4.0	50.0
Kaministiquia Pulp & Paper (rec. 1921)	0.5	0.0	0.7	1.2	41.7
Laurentide Pulp & Paper	5.0	0.0	28.0	30.8	16.2
Mattagami Pulp & Paper (rec. 1921)	5.1	1.5	2.0	8.6	76.7
Minnesota & Ontario Paper	3.5	2.0	5.0	10.5	52.4
Price Brothers	6.3	0.0	42.7	49.0	12.9
Riordan Company (rec. 1921)	19.6	40.0	40.0	99.6	49.8
St. Regis Paper of Canada	0.0	1.5	0.1	1.6	93.8
St. Maurice Paper	1.4	0.0	7.9	9.3	15.1
Saguenay Paper (bankrupt 1924)	14.3	3.5	4.4	22.2	80.2
Spanish River Pulp & Paper	14.2	8.6	8.0	30.8	74.0
Whalen Pulp & Paper (rec. 1923)	7.8	2.1	8.0	17.9	55.3
Other Paper Producers					
Dryden Pulp & Paper	1.5	0.0	3.5	4.5	33.3
Howard Smith	2.7	1.5	2.5	6.7	62.7
Provincial Paper	0.6	1.7	3.5	5.8	39.7
Wayagamack Pulp & Paper	3.9	0.0	5.0	8.9	43.8
Total	$101.3	$67.7	$185.9	$352.2	
Percentage of Aggregate Capital	29.6%	19.8%	54.3%	100.0%	

	Total Debt	Preferred Stock	Common Stock	Aggregate Capital	Percentage Debt & Preferred
1930					
Large Integrated Producers					
Abitibi Power & Paper (rec. 1932)	$59.8	$35.4	$19.0	$114.2	83.4
Canada Power & Paper (rec. 1931)	109.9	32.0	41.8	186.6	77.3
Fraser (reorganized, 1932)	30.0	0.0	14.0	44.0	68.2
Great Lakes Paper (rec. 1931)	12.2	10.0	19.0	41.2	53.9
International Power & Paper (US)*	357.6	267.6	67.4	692.6	90.3
IPP Canada & Newfoundland subsidiaries	132.2	45.4	12.4	190.1	93.5
Minnesota & Ontario Paper (US rec. 1931)	29.9	4.0	10.1	44.0	77.0
Price Brothers (rec. 1933)	11.5	6.6	42.7	60.8	29.8
Other Newsprint Producers					
Anglo-Canadian (divested 1931)	3.0	8.0	0.0	11.0	100.0
Anticosti Corporation	5.2	3.0	0.0	8.2	100.0
Bathurst Power & Paper	0.0	0.0	24.2	24.2	0.0
British Columbia Pulp & Paper	5.0	0.6	3.0	8.6	65.1
Brompton Pulp & Paper	0.0	0.9	15.0	15.9	5.6
Donnacona Paper	11.5	0.0	3.0	14.5	79.3
Dryden Paper	1.5	0.0	5.4	6.9	21.7
Lake St. John Paper	9.2	3.6	1.0	13.8	92.7
Mersey Paper	6.4	5.0	0.8	12.2	93.4
Ontario Paper	0.0	2.0	0.0	2.0	100.0
St. Lawrence Paper	3.1	14.5	5.6	23.2	75.8
Spruce Falls Power & Paper	15.1	13.9	0.2	29.2	99.3
Thunder Bay Paper (to Abitibi 1931)	0.0	0.0	2.0	2.0	0.0
Other Paper Producers					
Hinde & Dauche	1.7	0.0	1.1	2.8	60.7
Howard Smith	12.7	4.5	2.9	20.1	85.6
Provincial Paper	5.0	3.5	0.1	8.6	98.8
Rolland Paper	2.5	1.5	1.3	5.3	75.5
Canadian Total	**$467.5**	**$194.4**	**$224.6**	**$886.5**	
Percentage of Aggregate Capital	53.4%	21.7%	25.3%	100.0%	

Sources: Compiled from data published in *Financial Post Survey of Industrial Securities*, *Annual Financial Review*, *Moody's Survey of Industrials*, *Poor's Survey of Industrials*.

Notes: rec. indicates firm later went bankrupt.

* The aggregate capital of International Paper includes minority stakes unspecified in company reports. Data published by the firm understated the investments because some were obscured through holding companies or electrical utilities. Annual surveys by other sources normally misstated the capitalization of the Newfoundland and New Brunswick subsidiaries.

Appendix 4 Reorganizations among Canadian Newsprint Companies

Receivership:	Abitibi 1932–1946	Canada Power 1930–1931	Great Lakes 1931–1936	Price Brothers 1932–1937
Divestitures	Murray Bay Paper, OPS, Espanola, Kaministiquia Power	Anglo-Canadian, Thunder Bay Paper	Great Lakes separated from parent Minnesota & Ontario	Donnacona Paper
Write-downs	Book assets reduced from $181.0M to $87.3M	Book assets reduced from $213.0M to $84.2M	Book assets reduced from $43.1M to $17.4M	Book assets reduced from $75.8M to $59.3M
Disposition of Firm	Attempted judicial sale, remained independent	Remained Independent, but Weak	Meighen group forced sale to consortium	Takeover wars Killam gained Control
Loss in Market Value	> 90% by 1933	> 75% by 1931	100% by 1932	> 95% by 1933
Settlement:				
Bondholders	100% of principal & 90% of interest in bonds & cash	100–125% of principal, interest deferral in exchange for common stock	60% of principal and equity stakes via voting trust	140% in cash for bond principal, accrued interest, and premium
Preferred Equity	160–180% by class	Varying amounts of n.p.v. common stock		100% of principal & n.p.v. common stock
Common Equity	14%	10%	0%	1% and option to buy convertible debentures
Unsecured Creditors	14%	10%	0%	0%

	1932 Structure at Insolvency	1937 Ripley Plan	1939 Plan of Procedure	1941 McTague Plan	1946 Reorganized Structure
Asset Value	$191,696,000 [book assessment]	$77,187,000 [appraised value]	$30,000,000 [descriptive value]	Denied any possibility of setting value	$124,869,000 [declared value]
Board of Directors	Board dissolved, bondholders seized control	Nominal change of management, bondholders get board majority	Management not specified, bondholders control board	Management not specified, 4 bondholder & 3 shareholder directors	New managers, bondholders get board majority until 1947
First Mortgage Bonds	$54,055,000 original principal 5% first mortgage bonds [$48,267,000 outstanding on 1 June 1932]	$48,267,000 principal & $15,189,022 interest; to new (a) 5% $24,133,500, (b) 5% $33,796,000, (c) 241,335 common shares; also (d) 4.5% $14,000,000 new bonds	$48,267,000 principal & $19,910,318 interest; to 1,610,680 common shares held in escrow for warrants @ $36 per share	$48,267,000 principal & interest to 1 December 1940; no compound interest; bond maturity extended from 1953 to 1965; sinking fund eliminated	$53,094,000 remaining principal & interest; bondholders do not get equity stake; allowed $1,100 bond for each $1,000 [$525 for outstanding balance of principal, $575 in interest]
7% Preferred Shares	10,000 shares @ $100 p.v. [$1,000,000 valuation]	To 50,000 common shares & 50,000 warrants [14.0% of total]	To 6% of common share warrants	Reduce dividend to 3.5% and make non-cumulative	To 5 preferred shares $20 p.v. & dividends January1945 [$2,083,000 valuation]
6% Preferred Shares	348,818 shares @ $100 p.v. [$39,382,000 valuation]	To 1,220,863 common shares & 1,395,272 warrants for [75.5% of total]	To 72% of common shares & warrants	Reduce dividend to 3%, make non- cumulative	To 4 preferred shares @ $20 p.v. and 2 common shares; no dividend before 1947 [$39,060,000 valuation]
Common Shares	1,088,116 shares n.p.v. [$57,784,000 valuation]	To 108,812 common shares & 544,059 warrants [6.7% of total]	To 6% of common warrants	Get nothing	2 common get 1 common n.p.v. [$3,264,000 valuation]
General Creditors	$749,000 claim	Full & immediate settlement in cash	To 16% of common warrants	50% of total claim paid over 4 years	100% with cap of $900,000 but no interest
Annual Funding Obligations	$6,076,258 excluding OPS and sinking fund	$4,026,020 excluding sinking fund	Not specified	Not specified	$4,873,000 excluding sinking fund

Appendix 6 Battle of the Plans, 1937

Capital Structure:

	1932 Structure & Accrued Charges	2nd McPherson June 1937	Ripley July 1937	Drayton October 1937
Debt	5% mortgage bonds, $48,267,700; accrued interest, $15,189.022	1st mortgage serial bonds, $37,960,200; 2nd mortgage income bonds, $35,717,580	1st mortgage bonds, $14,000,000; general mortgage & convertible bonds, $24,133,500; convertible debentures, $33,786,900	1st mortgage bonds, $36,200,250; 2nd mortgage income & convertible bonds, $22,926,825
Total	$63,456,032	$73,677,780	$71,920,400	$59,127,075
Preferred Equity	7% preferred 10,000 shares, $1,000,000 & accrued divid. of $402,500 6% preferred 348,818 shares, $34,881,800 & accrued divid. $13,080,675	– –	– –	– –
Common Equity n.p.v.	1,088,117 shares	3,500,000 shares (1,837,305 for issue & warrants for 1,576,550)	3,500,000 shares (1,837,305 for issue & warrants or bond conversion for 1,576,550)	3,516,530 shares (2,093,640 for issue & warrants for 1,422,890)

Rates of Exchange:

Bonds per $1,000	$600 1st mortgage bonds; $700 2nd mortgage bonds; $40 principal of fractional warrants each; can exchange 2nd mortgage bonds with 10 warrants per $100, $1.25 cash	$500 convertible bonds; $700 convertible debentures; 5 common shares n.p.v.	$750 1st mortgage bonds; $475 2nd mortgage bonds; 5 common shares n.p.v. (but declared value of $116.59)
7% Preferred for Each Share	5 common shares n.p.v.	5 common shares n.p.v. and warrant rights	6 common shares n.p.v. and warrant rights
6% Preferred for Each Share	4.5 common shares n.p.v.	3.5 common shares n.p.v. and warrant rights	4.5 common shares n.p.v. and warrant rights
Common for Each Share	1 for 5 old shares & warrant rights	1 for 10 old shares & warrant rights	1 for 5 old shares & warrant rights
Creditors 7	100% cash	New firm will handle	100% cash
Annual Charges:			
Fixed	$1,850,510	$1,836,375	$1,910,013
Sinking Fund	1,000,000	500,000	500,000
Preferred Stock or Income Bonds	1,785,8789	1,689,345	1,146,341
Total	$4,616,389	$4,026,020	$3,556,354

Creditors
$2,413,350
1,500,000
2,162,908
$6,076,258

Participants

Abitibi Power and Paper (Pre-Receivership)

Frank H. Anson, President, 1912–23 [d. 1923]

W.A. Black, Vice-President, 1923–32, Board of Directors 1923–32; Vice-President and Managing Director, and then President, Ogilvie Flour Mills

John Homer Black, Vice-President and Manager of Abitibi Canyon project, 1930–1; President, Dominion Construction Limited, 1931–4 [d. 1934]

Joseph G. Gibson, Secretary and Counsel, Spanish River Pulp and Paper, 1914–27

George F. Hardy, Consulting Engineer

D. Lorne McGibbon, Board of Directors, 1912–14

George Houk Mead, Chair and Board of Directors, 1928–32; President, Spanish River Pulp and Paper, 1915–27

Victor Mitchell, Board of Directors, 1913–32 [d. 1932]

Shirley Ogilvie, Vice-President, 1912–23

Edson Pease, Board of Directors, 1923–30; Royal Bank of Canada [d. 1930]

Alexander Smith, Board of Directors, 1914–32; President, 1923–32; Peabody Houghteling and Peabody Smith, Chicago and New York

Thomas Tait, Board of Directors, 1912–32

Abitibi Power and Paper (Receivership)

Geoffrey Teignmouth Clarkson, Receiver and Manager, 1932–46; Clarkson, Gordon, Dilworth and Nash; E.R.C. Clarkson and Sons [d. 1948]

Frederick Curzon Clarkson, Liquidator, 1932–5; E.R.C. Clarkson and Sons

G.W. Holder, Manager, Sturgeon Falls

Roy Sharvell McPherson, Liquidator, 1935–46; Thorne, Mulholland, Howland and McPherson

L.R. Wilson, Vice-President and Managing Director, 1928–46

T.E. Silver, Mills manager

W.H. Smith, Assistant managing director

H. Young, Treasurer

Bondholders' Representative Committee, 1932–1939

Joseph Pierce Ripley, 1932–9, Chair; Vice-President, National City Company of New York; Harriman Ripley, New York

W.A. Arbuckle, 1935–9, Secretary-Treasurer, Great Britain and Canada Investment Corporation

Charles M. Bowman, 1932; Chair, Mutual Life Assurance of Canada [d. 1932]

Milton Cross, 1935–9, Vice-President, National City Company of New York; Brown Harriman and Company of New York

Andrew Fleming, 1935–9, President, Hartt & Adair Coal Company of Montreal, Representative for Sun Life Assurance

Stanton Griffis, 1932–5, Hemphill Noyen & Company of New York

Harold P. Janisch, 1932–5, Vice-President, National Bank of Boston

John Leslie, 1932–5, Vice-President, Canadian Pacific Railway, Montreal

George W. Pearson, 1932–5, Vice-President, Continental Illinois Company of Chicago

Edward E. Reid, 1932–9, Managing Director, London Life

Walter Harold Somerville, 1932–9, General Manager, Mutual Life of Canada

Bondholders' Defensive Committee, 1937–1941

Sir Henry Lumley Drayton, Chair, former Minister of Finance

A.D. Cobban, Vice-President, Wood Gundy and Company

Hon. R.B. Hanson, M.P. and Interim Leader of the Opposition; director, Fraser Companies

J.A. Kilpatrick, Chair, Canada Iron Foundries

H. McKay, 1939–41, W.C. Pitfield and Co.

Ward C. Pitfield, 1937–9, W.C. Pitfield and Company [d. 1939]

P.J. Walters, Director, Crown Trust

Bondholders' Protective Committee, 1939–1946

Herbert J. Symington, Chair; Royal Securities; President, Trans-Canada Airlines; Wartime Power Controller of Canada

W.A. Arbuckle, Investment Committee of the British Insurance
Association, the Association of Investment Trusts, Alliance
Investment Corp. of Canada, Canadian Stockholders Investment
Corporation of Montreal, Great Britain and Canada
Stanton Griffis, Trustee of estate of W.E. Griffis
Rt. Hon. Senator Arthur Meighen, Canadian General Investment Trust
Edward E. Reid, London Life [d. 1941]
Robert H. Reid, London Life
Joseph Pierce Ripley, Harriman, Ripley of New York
W.H. Somerville, Mutual Life of Canada
Allan R. Graydon, Secretary

Common Shareholders' Committee, 1937–1938

Collin Brooks, Chair, Representative of Lord Rothermere
Robert Crombie, Royal Trust
Roy Stephenson, Crown Life
James Henry Gundy

Common Shareholders' Committee, 1939–1946

R.G. Meech, Chair; Loblaws Groceterias
C.A. Cushing, lawyer, Montreal
Clair C. Holland, Fleming and Co.
Harry B. Housser, H.B. Housser and Co.
Col. K.R. Marshall, President Standard Fuel of Canada
Léopold-A. Renaud, Managing Director, Comptoir Nationale de
Placement
William A. Sands, lawyer, New York
L.M. Wood, Wood, Fleming and Co.

General Creditors' Protective Committee, 1939–1946

Clement Tremblay, Chair; Ayers Limited
B.V. Atkinson, Brandram-Henderson
G. Harold Fisk, Montreal
A.L. Sanderson, Vice-Chair, Marine Trust, Buffalo

Preferred Stockholders' Committee, 1932–1938

Lt.-Col. Herbert Molson, Chair; President, Molson's Brewery; Board of
Directors for National City Bank of New York [d. 1939]
Armitage Ewing, Ewing and McFadden Barristers, Montreal

William Hastie, Assistant to the President, Canada Life Assurance
  [d. 1940]
Allen G. Hoyt, Vice-President, City Bank Farmers Trust Company of
  New York
J. Colin Kemp, consulting engineer and former executive of The
  National City Company

6% Preferred Shareholders' Protective Committee, 1939–1943

David H. Gibson, Chair; President, Board of Trade of the City of Toronto
H. Brooke Bell, K.C., Toronto
F.H. Deacon, President, Conger Lehigh Coal Company
C.M. Keys, investment counsellor, New York
W.H. Moore, Chair of Monterey Railway, Light and Power; Director,
  Massey-Harris
Arthur G. Slaght, K.C., Toronto
Stanley Stanger, President, Guardian Trust, Montreal
Howard Webster, Director, Imperial Trust

7% Preferred Shareholders' Protective Committee, 1944–1946

Henry Goldman, Jr., Gale, Bishop & Co., New York
Ernest Lloyd, Frank S. Leslie & Co., Toronto
Douglas Huycke, J. S. Bache & Co., Toronto

The Independent Committee, 1939–1940

Thomas Bradshaw, Chair; President, North American Life [d. 1939]
Hon. G. Howard Ferguson, former premier of Ontario [d. 1946]
Hon. Gordon W. Scott, Montreal [d. 1940]
J.Y. Murdoch, President, Noranda Mines

The Conciliation Committee, 1944–1946

Frank J. Hughes, Chair, lawyer, Toronto
Gilbert Jackson, economist
William Zimmerman, lawyer, Toronto

Financiers, Underwriters, and Schemers

E.A. Charlton, Montreal; former vice-president of Canadian
  International Paper
Arthur D. Cobban, Vice-President, Wood Gundy

H. Collette, Crédit Anglo-Français
L.M. Collins, Collins, King
James Henry "Harry" Gundy, Wood Gundy; former president of
    Canada Power and Paper
Edward Benson Kernaghan, International Service Company of
    Toronto
C.M. Keys, New York
Izaak Walton Killam, President, Royal Securities
Rt. Hon. Senator Arthur Meighen, Canadian General Investment Trusts
Charles E. Mitchell, Chair, National City Bank and National City
    Company of New York
A.J. Nesbitt, President, Nesbitt, Thomson, Montreal
Robert Oliver Sweezey, Montreal
Gordon Taylor, A.E. Osler and Company

Government of Ontario

Gordon D. Conant, Attorney-General 1933–43; Premier 1943
George A. Drew, Ontario Securities Commissioner, 1932–4; Leader of
    the Opposition, 1938–43; Premier, 1943–8
G. Howard Ferguson, Minister of Lands and Forests, 1914–19; Premier,
    1923–30 [d. 1946]
William Finlayson, Minister of Lands and Forests, 1926–34 [d. 1943]
George S. Henry, Premier, 1930–4; Leader of the Opposition, 1934–7
Mitchell F. Hepburn, Leader of the Opposition, 1932–4; Premier, 1934–42
Peter Heenan, Minister of Lands and Forests, 1934–41
N. O. Hippel, Minister of Lands and Forests, 1942–3
Arthur W. Roebuck, Attorney-General, 1934–7

Judiciary and Commissioners

James R. Aitken, Lord of Appeal in Ordinary, Judicial Committee of
    the Privy Council
F.H. Barlow, Master, Supreme Court of Ontario
Lyman Duff, Supreme Court of Canada
Sir James H. Dunn, Abitibi Royal Commission; President, Algoma Steel
Albert E. Dyment, Abitibi Royal Commission; Chair of Canadian
    General Electric [d. 1944]
John G. Gillanders, Ontario Court of Appeal
James McNairn Hall, Supreme Court of Ontario; Chair, Sturgeon Falls
    Relief Enquiry [d. 1935]
William T. Henderson, Supreme Court of Ontario
Roy Lindsay Kellock, Supreme Court of Ontario

Arthur Kingstone, Supreme Court of Ontario [d. 1938]
Francis R. Latchford, Supreme Court of Ontario; OPS Royal
 Commission [d. 1939]
Arthur Masten, Supreme Court of Ontario [d. 1942]
William Edward Middleton, Supreme Court of Ontario
Charles Patrick McTague, Chair of Abitibi Royal Commission;
 Supreme Court of Ontario
William Renwick Riddell, Supreme Court of Ontario [d. 1945]
William Roach, Justice, Supreme Court of Ontario
Robert Spelman Robertson, Supreme Court of Ontario
George H. Sedgewick, Supreme Court of Ontario [d. 1940]
Robert Smith, Supreme Court of Ontario; OPS Royal Commission
 [d. 1942]

Lawyers

N.T. Berry, for the second Liquidator, R.S. McPherson
R.C.H. Cassels, for individual defendants
R.O. Daly, for the Common Shareholders' Protective Committee,
 1939–43
Lewis Duncan, for Ontario Hydro, 1935
R.M. Fowler, for the Abitibi Royal Commission
W. Kaspar Fraser, for the General Creditors' Protective Committee
Allan R. Graydon, for the individual defendants and the Bondholders'
 Protective Committee, 1942–46
W. George Hanna, for Ontario Hydro
William H. Hearst, former Premier of Ontario, for Abitibi Power and
 Paper
C.G. Heward, for the Preferred Stockholders' Committee
John Strachan Johnston, for Montreal Trust and the Receiver, 1932–41
 [d. 1941]
W. Judson, for the Common Shareholders' Protective Committee, 1939–43
George Kilmer, for Abitibi Power and Paper [d. 1928]
E.G. Long, for the Preferred Shareholders' Committee
D.L. McCarthy, for the Bondholders' Defensive Committee
Frederick R. MacKelcan, National Trust Company
E. Gordon McMillan, for the second Liquidator, R.S. MacPherson
C.R. Magone, for the Government of Ontario
H.E. Manning, for the Common Shareholders' Protective Committee
G.W. Mason, for the Abitibi Royal Commission
James C. McRuer, for the Hydro Commision of Ontario, OPS Royal
 Commission

Glyn T. Osler, for the personal defendants and the Bondholders'
   Protective Committee
James Layton Ralston, for the Bondholders' Defensive Committee, 1937–40
Robert S. Robertson, for the Hydro Commision of Ontario, 1935–7,
   and for the Liquidator, 1937–8
Arthur W. Roebuck, for the common shareholders, 1937–9
Newton W. Rowell, for Preferred Shareholders' Committee and
   unsecured creditors [d. 1941]
Gerald Ruel, for Noranda Mines
Harold Wilson Shapley, for the first Liquidator, Frederick Clarkson
Arthur G. Slaght for the Province of Ontario, 1934–7; for Wood
   Gundy, 1937–8; the Preferred Shareholders' Protective Committee,
   1938–43
Bethune Smith, for Abitibi and the Bondholders' Representative
   Committee
A.M. Stewart, for the Government of Ontario
J.L. Stewart, for the General Creditors' Protective Committee
Gordon Taylor
W. Norman Tilley, for Abitibi, the Bondholders' Representative
   Committee, and individual defendants, 1932–42 [d. 1942]
J. Donald S. Tory, for Montreal Trust and the Receiver, 1941–6
Ward Wright, for the second liquidator, R.S. McPherson

Hydro-Electric Power Commission of Ontario
[HEPCO or Ontario Hydro]

John R. Cooke, Chair 1931–4 [d. 1934]
Fred A. Gaby, Chief Engineer, 1912–34
T.H. Hogg, Chair and Chief Engineer, 1937–47
R.T. Jeffrey, Municipal Engineer
I.B. Lucas, General Counsel, 1928–34
T. Stewart Lyon, Chair, 1934–7; former editor of *The Globe*
Charles A. Magrath, Chair, 1925–31
Rt. Hon. Senator Arthur Meighen, Commissioner, 1931–4
Walter W. Pope, Secretary
T.B. McQuesten, Commissioner, 1934–7
Arthur W. Roebuck, Commissioner, 1934–7

Third Parties

Edward Wellington Backus, President, Backus-Brooks [d. 1934]
John Bracken, Premier of Manitoba

William Hugh Coverdale, Coverdale and Colpitts Consulting Engineers
Maurice Duplessis, Premier of Quebec, 1936–9
Sir Joseph Flavelle, Chair, Bank of Commerce and National Trust
Robert Hayes, Eastern Manitoba Development Bureau
Zotique Mageau, Mayor, Sturgeon Falls
George W. Mead, President, Consolidated Water Power and Paper of
  Wisconsin
Lord Rothermere, Chair, *Daily Mail* Group [d. 1940]
H.H. Stevens, Minister of Industry, 1930–5
Louis-Alexandre Taschereau, Premier of Quebec, 1920–36
Noah A. Timmins, President, Hollinger Consolidated Gold Mines
Charles Wadge, Assistant Secretary, Canada Packers

Notes

Praecipe

1 Scholarly studies include P. Tufano, "Business Failure, Judicial Intervention, and Financial Innovation: Restructuring U.S. Railroad in the Nineteenth Century," *Business History Review*, 71:1 (1997), 1–40; F.L. Clarke, G.W. Dean, and K.G. Oliver, *Corporate Collapse: Regulatory, Accounting and Ethical Failure* (Melbourne: Cambridge University Press, 1997); S. Hamilton and A. Micklethwait, *Greed and Corporate Failure: The Lessons from Recent Disasters* (London: Palgrave Macmillan, 2006). Useful popular accounts include D. Miller, *The Icarus Paradox: How Exceptional Companies Bring About Their Own Downfall* (New York: Harper Business, 1990); E. Malmsten, E. Portanger, and C. Drazin, *Boo Hoo: $135 Million, 18 Months ... A Dot.Com Story from Concept to Catastrophe* (New York: Arrow, 2001); B. McLean and P. Elkind, *The Smartest Guys in the Room: The Amazing Rise and Scandalous Fall of Enron* (New York: Portfolio Trade, 2004).
2 M. Kuhlberg, "'In the Power of the Government': The Rise and Fall of Newsprint in Ontario, 1894–1932" (PhD diss., York University, 2002), 373.
3 AO, RG-22-5089, MS 2615, S.C.O., Index to Civil and City Suits, 4A.
4 B.E.C. Boothman, "High Finance and Low Strategy: Corporate Collapse in the Canadian Pulp and Paper Industry, 1919 to 1932," *Business History Review*, 74:4 (2000), 614.
5 H.V. Nelles, *The Politics of Development: Forests, Mines, and Hydro-Electric Power in Ontario, 1849–1941* (Toronto: Macmillan, 1974). J. Mochoruk, *Formidable Heritage: Manitoba's North and the Cost of Development, 1870 to 1930* (Winnipeg: University of Manitoba Press, 2004), 377. R.P. Gillis and T.R. Roach, *Lost Initiatives: Canada's Forest Industries, Forest Policy, and Forest Conservation* (Westport, CT: Greenwood, 1986), 259. M. Kuhlberg, *In the Power of the Government: The Rise and Fall of Newsprint in Ontario, 1894–1932* (Toronto: University of Toronto Press, 2015).

6 S. Gray, "The Government's Timber Business: Forest Policy and Administration in British Columbia, 1912–1928," *BC Studies*, 81 (1989), 24–49. J.K. Hiller, "The Origins of the Pulp and Paper Industry in Newfoundland," *Acadiensis*, 11:2 (1982), 42–68; J.K. Hiller, "The Politics of Newsprint: The Newfoundland Pulp and Paper Industry, 1915–1939," *Acadiensis*, 19:2 (1990), 3–39. W. Parenteau, "The Woods Transformed: The Emergence of the Pulp and Paper Industry in New Brunswick, 1918–1931," *Acadiensis*, 22:1 (1992), 5–43. J.-P. Charland, *Les pâtes et papiers au Québec, 1880–1980: technologies, travail et travailleurs* (Quebec City: Institut québécois de reserche sur la culture, 1990).

7 S. Côté, "Les voies de la monopolization: le cas de l'usine de papier du travail au XXe siècle" (PhD diss., Université de Montréal, 1978). B. Brideau, "Entre profit et paternalism: la papetière de Bathurst et ses ouviers de 1907 à 1945" (MA thesis, Université de Moncton, 1999). N. Lang, "La compagnie Fraser Limited, 1918–1974: étude de l'évolution des strategies économiques, des structures administratives et de l'organisation du travail à l'usine d'Edmundston au Nouveau-Brunswick" (PhD diss., Université de Montréal, 1994). J. Bellau, "L'industrialization à Trois-Rivières" (MA thesis, L'université du Québec à Trois-Rivières, 1979). A. Dion, "L'industrie des pâtes et papiers en Mauricie, 1887–1929" (MA thesis, L'université du Québec à Trois-Rivières, 1981).

8 K.M. Abel, *Changing Places: History, Community, and Identity in Northeastern Ontario* (Montreal: McGill-Queen's University Press, 2006). R. Hardy and N. Séguin, *Forêt et société en Mauricie. La formation d'une région* (Quebec City: Septentrion, 2011). W.R. Wightman and N.M. Wightman, *The Land Between: Northwestern Ontario Resource Development, 1800 to the 1990s* (Toronto: University of Toronto Press, 1997). J.L. Manore, *Cross-Currents: Hydroelectricity and the Engineering of Northern Ontario* (Waterloo, ON: Wilfrid Laurier University Press, 1999).

9 J.A. Guthrie, *The Newsprint Paper Industry: An Economic Analysis* (Cambridge, MA: Harvard University Press, 1941); J.A. Guthrie, *The Economics of Pulp and Paper* (Pullman: State College of Washington Press, 1950). N.K. Ohanian, *The American Pulp and Paper Industry, 1900–1940: Mill Survival, Firm Structure, and Industry Relocation* (Westport, CT: Greenwood, 1993). T.J.O. Dick, "Canadian Newsprint, 1913–1930: National Policies and the North American Economy," *Journal of Economic History*, 42:3 (1982), 659–87.

10 J.-A. Lamberg, J. Näsi, J. Ojala, and P. Sajasalo, eds., *The Evolution of Competitive Strategies in Global Forestry Industries* (New York: Springer, 2006). J.-A. Lamberg, J. Ojala, M. Peltoniemi, and T. Särkkä, eds., *The Evolution of Global Paper Industry 1800–2050: A Comparative Analysis* (New York: Springer, 2012).

11 See P. Fridenson, "Business Failure and the Agenda of Business History," *Enterprise and Society*, 5:4 (2004), 562–82.
12 Many accounts deal with the evolution of manufacturing techniques, but see especially R.H. Clapperton, *The Paper-Making Machine: Its Invention, Evolution, and Development* (London: Pergamon Press, 1967).
13 A.D. Chandler, *Scale and Scope: The Dynamics of Managerial Capitalism* (Cambridge, MA: Harvard University Press, 1990), 113.
14 A.D. Chandler, *The Visible Hand: The Managerial Revolution in American Business* (Cambridge, MA: Harvard University Press, 1977), 8.
15 C. Armstrong, *Blue Skies and Boiler Rooms: Buying and Selling Securities in Canada 1870–1940* (Toronto: University of Toronto Press, 1997); C. Armstrong, *Moose Pastures and Mergers: The Ontario Securities Commission and the Regulation of Share Markets in Canada, 1940–1980* (Toronto: University of Toronto Press, 2001).
16 V. Carosso, *Investment Banking in America: A History* (Cambridge, MA: Harvard University Press, 1970); J. Seligman, *The Transformation of Wall Street: A History of the Securities and Exchange Commission and Modern Corporate Finance* (Boston: Houghton Mifflin, 1982); L.E. Davis and R.E. Gallman, *Evolving Financial Markets and International Capital Flows: Britain, the Americas, and Australia, 1865–1914* (London: Cambridge University Press, 2001); A.D. Morrison and W.J. Wilhelm, *Investment Banking: Institutions, Politics and Law* (London: Oxford University Press, 2007).
17 C. Royster, *The Fabulous History of the Dismal Swamp Company: A Story of George Washington's Time* (New York: Knopf, 1999).
18 An ancient Roman saying: "If you listen very closely, you can hear the gods laughing."

1. Empire Ontario

 1 E.E. Rich, *The Fur Trade and the Northwest to 1857* (Toronto: McClelland and Stewart, 1967), 24–68. An English translation of De Troyes's journal, along with other accounts, can be found in W.A. Kenyon and J.R. Turnball, eds., *The Battle for James Bay, 1686* (Toronto: Macmillan, 1971). The appellation "Abitibi" can be found in a map prepared in 1685 by Hubert Jallot, which is retained in the LAC collections. See also R. Blanchard, *L'Abitibi-Témiscamingue*, Vol. 4, Troisième Série, Études Canadiennes (Grenoble: Imprimerier Allier, 1949), 19–20.
 2 E.A. Mitchell, *Fort Timiskaming and the Fur Trade* (Toronto: University of Toronto Press, 1977), 10–22.
 3 The perspective applied here draws upon the research of Fernand Braudel and D.W. Meinig. The application of the metropolitan thesis to Canadian history is exemplified by the works of J.M.S. Careless, including

"Frontierism, Metropolitanism, and Canadian History," *Canadian Historical Review* 35:1 (1954): 1–21; *Frontier and Metropolis in Canada: Regions, Cities, and Identities to 1914* (Toronto: University of Toronto Press, 1989); and *Careless at Work: Selected Canadian Historical Studies* (Toronto: Dundurn Press, 1990).

4 For the sense of mission in Upper Canada, S.F. Wise and R.C. Brown, *Canada Views the United States: Nineteenth-Century Political Attitudes* (Toronto: Macmillan, 1967); and J. Errington, *The Lion, the Eagle, and Upper Canada: A Developing Colonial Ideology* (Montreal: McGill-Queen's University Press, 1987). The term "western kingdom" was initially raised in MTL, John Beverley Robinson, *A Letter to the Right Hon. Earl Bathurst, K. G. on the Policy of Uniting the British North American Colonies* (London: William Clowes, 1825), 56–7.

5 Imperial dreams and Canadian character are well surveyed by C. Berger, *The Sense of Power: Studies in the Ideas of Canadian Imperialism, 1867–1914* (Toronto: University of Toronto Press, 1970), 128–76.

6 M. Zaslow, *The Opening of the Canadian North: 1870–1914* (Toronto: McClelland and Stewart, 1971), 147–72.

7 *Globe*, 22 October 1864. LOSP, No. 72 (1895), T. Gibson, "The Hinterland of Ontario," *Bureau of Mines, 1894 Annual Report,* 135.

8 AO, PC, 1894, No. 20, A.S. Hardy, *Our Northern Districts: Eastern Algoma, North Nipissing, Rainy River and the Temiscaming Settlement* (Toronto: Warwick Bros. and Rutter, 1894), 28. AO, F248, B272852, Memorial to the Ontario Government on Timber Licenses, 6 April 1905.

9 The boundary question was appraised by C. Armstrong, *The Politics of Federalism: Ontario's Relations with the Federal Government, 1867–1942* (Toronto: University of Toronto Press, 1981), 14–22; and Zaslow, *The Opening of the Canadian North,* 147–57. Zaslow surveyed the difficulties in "Edward Barnes Borron, 1820–1915: Northern Pioneer and Public Servant Extraordinary," in F.H. Armstrong, H.A. Stevenson, and J.D. Wilson, eds., *Aspects of Nineteenth-Century Ontario* (Toronto: University of Toronto Press, 1974), 297–311.

10 AO, PC, 1878, No. 23, A. Kirkwood and J.J. Murphy, *The Undeveloped Lands in Northern and Western Ontario* (Toronto: Hunter Rose and Co., 1878), 7–8. Dominion surveys of Northeastern Ontario were *Report of the Geological Survey of Canada*: (1872–73), 112–35; (1875–76), 294–342; 1877–78, Part C, 1–37; (1887–88, J6–J80). All are at available at https://geoscan.nrcan.gc.ca. A useful review is in CIHM, 6163, *Report on the Basin of Moose River and the Adjacent Country Belonging to the Province of Ontario* (Toronto: Warrick, 1890), also published as LOSP, No. 87 (1890).

11 *Our Northern Districts,* 6, 11, 3. Gibson, "The Hinterland of Ontario," 103, 113.

12 Surveys were published in reports of the Bureau of Mines: LOSP, No. 38 – Part II (1898–9), "The Nipissing-Algoma Boundary," 175–96; No. 5 – Part I (1904), "The Abitibi Region," 104–21; No. 5 – Part I (1905), "Explorations in Abitibi," 184–247.

13 B.-B. Gourd, "La Colonization des Clay Belts du Nord-Ouest Québécois et Du Nord-est Ontarien," *Revue D'Histoire L'Amérique Française*, 27:2 (1973), 235–76. A good survey is G.L. McDermott, "Advancing and Retracting Frontiers of Agricultural Settlement in the Great Clay Belt of Ontario and Quebec" (PhD diss., University of Wisconsin, 1959).

14 LOSP, No. 33 – Part I (1901), *Report of the Commissioner of Crown Lands for 1900*, vi.

15 AO, PC, L & F Misc., Box 6, No. 1, Department of Crown Lands, *Land Settlement in New Ontario: A Short Account of the Advantages Offered Land Seekers in Ontario* (Toronto: L.K. Cameron, 1903), 13, 17.

16 AO, PC, A Misc., Box 2, No. 10, *Northern Ontario, A New Land Nearby: Climate, Soil, Bush Life as Viewed by Settlers* (Toronto: King's Printer, 1915), 6.

17 LAC, Temiskaming and Northern Ontario Railway Commission, Temiskaming and Northern Ontario Railway: *Northern New Ontario's Colonization and Tourist Railway Line* (Toronto: TNORR, 1906), 1. AO, ONOR, No. 7, *Temiskaming and Northern Ontario Railway Commission, Fortunes for Farmers in New Ontario* (Toronto: TNORR, 1911), 6. AO, PC, N-Box, No. 7, *Temiskaming and Northern Ontario Railway Commission, Facts About New Ontario's Great Clay Belt* (Toronto: TNORR, n.d.), 3, 5.

18 AO, PC, N-box, No. 8, R.A. Burriss, *New Ontario: Numerous Questions Asked and Answered* (Toronto, n.d.), 3, 6. F.A. Wightman, *Our Canadian Heritage: Its Resources and Possibilities* (Toronto: William Briggs, 1905), 107.

19 PC, 1913, No. 26, B.E. Fernow, *Conditions in the Clay Belt of New Ontario* (Ottawa: Commission of Conservation, 1913), 7. *Canadian Annual Review*, 1914, 359.

20 *Globe*, 21 February 1900. Slightly more than 800,000 people inhabited Northern Ontario 110 years later.

21 H.N. Smith, *Virgin Land: The American West as Symbol and Myth* (Cambridge, MA: Harvard University Press, 1950), chaps. 11–12, 15, 20. L. Marx, *The Machine in the Garden: Technology and the Pastoral Ideal in America* (New York: Oxford University Press, 1964), 122–33. E. Foner, *Free Soil, Free Labour, Free Men: The Ideology of the Republican Party Before the Civil War* (New York: Oxford University Press, 1995), esp. the introductory essay, viii–xxxix.

22 AO, PC, Govt Doc, A Misc., Box 2, No. 10, *Northern Ontario, A New Land Nearby: Climate, Soil, Bush Life as Viewed by Settlers* (Toronto: King's Printer, 1915), 3–6. Govt Doc A Misc., Box 2, No. 4, Department of Agriculture, *Ontario the Premier Province of Canada: Settlers' Opinions* (Toronto: King's Printer, 1911), 18. PC, 1910, No. 46, Department of Agriculture, *New*

Ontario, Canada: Situation, Size, Climate, Products, Resources, Progress and Advantages (Toronto: King's Printer, 1910), 10.

23 AO, PC, Govt Doc, L&F Misc., Box 6, No. 2, *Land Settlement in New Ontario* (Toronto: n.p., 1903), 18. AO, E.J. Ashton, "Ontario's Own Northland," *United Empire: The Royal Colonial Institute Journal*, 20 (July, 1929), 374.

24 T.R. Roach, "The Pulpwood Trade and the Settlers of New Ontario," *Journal of Canadian Studies*, 22:3 (1987), 78–88. D.E. Pugh, "Ontario's Great Clay Belt Hoax," *Canadian Geographical Journal*, 90:1 (1975), 19–25.

25 *Globe*, 12 March 1920.

26 AO, RG18-66, Report of the Commission of Enquiry, Kapuskasing Colony (1920), 6, 8. AO, RG3, 04-0-142, Kapuskasing file.

27 K.M. Abel, *Changing Places: History, Community, and Identity in Northeastern Ontario* (Montreal: McGill-Queen's University Press, 2006), 15–66. R.S. Lambert and P. Pross, *Renewing Nature's Wealth: A Centennial History of the Public Management of Land, Forests, and Wildlife in Ontario, 1763–1967* (Toronto: Queen's Printer, 1967), 300–12.

28 *Globe*, 14 April 1920. *Toronto World*, 13 April 1920. RG3, 4-0-206, Soldiers' Settlement – Kapuskasing, Evidence of Hon. G.H. Ferguson.

29 AO, RG18-118, Proceedings, 11 December 1940, 1272–6.

30 *PPMC*, 22 March 1928, 397.

31 *Sudbury Star*, 14 January 1931.

32 RG18-118, Proceedings, 11 December 1940, 1275.

33 RG18-118, Proceedings, 11 December 1940, 1277b.

34 J.E. Hodgetts, *From Arm's Length to Hands On: The Formative Years of Ontario's Public Service, 1867–1940* (Toronto: University of Toronto Press, 1995), chaps. 5–7. For a useful cross-comparison, see S. Skrownek, *Building a New American State: The Expansion of National Administrative Capacities, 1877–1920* (New York: Cambridge University Press, 1982), esp. Part II.

35 L.A. Sandberg, "Forest Policy in Nova Scotia: The Big Lease, Cape Breton Island, 1899–1960," *Acadiensis*, 20:2 (1991), 105–28. J.K. Hiller, "The Origins of the Pulp and Paper Industry in Newfoundland," *Acadiensis*, 11:2 (1982), 42–68. C.S. Beach, "Pulpwood Province and Paper State: Corporate Reconstruction, Underdevelopment and Law in New Brunswick and Maine, 1890–1930" (PhD diss., University of Maine, 1991), 38–106, 160–206. S. Gray, "The Government's Timber Business: Forest Policy and Administration in British Columbia, 1912–1928," *BC Studies*, 81 (1989), 24–49.

36 See C. Armstrong, *Blue Skies and Boiler Rooms: Buying and Selling Securities in Canada, 1870–1940* (Toronto: University of Toronto Press, 1997).

37 AO, RG18-125, Box 1, *Report of the Ontario Royal Commission on Forestry* (Toronto: King's Printer, 1947), 9–10.

38 Lambert and Pross, *Renewing Nature's Wealth*, 250–76, 335–53. W.R. Wightman and N.M. Wightman, *The Land Between, Northwestern Ontario Resource Development, 1800 to the 1990s* (Toronto: University of Toronto Press, 1997), 177–82. H.V. Nelles, *The Politics of Development: Forests, Mines, and Hydro-Electric Power in Ontario, 1849–1941* (Toronto: Macmillan of Canada, 1974), 377–81.

39 AO, RG18-79, Proceedings, II, Testimony of C.C. Hele. *Globe*, 28 May 1920. There is no doubt Ferguson repeated the practice when he resigned as Premier in 1931. Mitch Hepburn and Peter Heenan also removed or destroyed many files

40 Nelles, *The Politics of Development*, 64–87. R.P. Gillis and T.R. Roach, *Lost Initiatives: Canada's Forest Industries, Forest Policy, and Forest Conservation* (Westport, CT: Greenwood, 1986), 84–7.

41 *Globe*, 17 February 1899. *MT*, 10 March 1899. LOSP, No. 3 (1901), *Report of the Commissioner of Crown Lands for the Year 1900*, vi.

42 LOSP, No. 3 (1902), *Report of the Commissioner of Crown Lands for the Year 1901*, xiii.

43 LAC, MG30-D29, XXXVIII, A.S. Hardy to J.S. Willison, 4 November 1897, marked "private and confidential." Nelles, *Politics of Development*, 45–7. Wightman and Wightman, *The Land Between*, 125.

44 RG3, 04-0-146, F.J. Niven to E.C. Drury, 28 May 1920; C.C. Robinson to Drury, 16 November 1920.

45 SO, [1914] 4 Geo V, c.12, Export of Pulpwood. The amendments were buried in omnibus Statute Law Amendment Acts.

46 RG3, 04-0-189, J.E. Boyle to Drury, 11 May 1920; 04-0-186, H.J. Wheeler to Drury, 21 January 1920; R.J. McLaughlin to Drury and Executive Council, 8 January 1920. SO, [1920], 10–11 Geo V, c.14, Exportation of Pulpwood.

47 Author's estimates from U.S. Census and Department of Commerce data in *Statistical Abstract of the United States* (annual, issues 1908 to 1939) and from data in annual reports of Ontario's Department of Lands, Forests and Mines. Export and import shares were measured by cords, not value or cost. American and Canadian data closely match. This likely indicates the governments recorded most of the international trade, notwithstanding the surreptitious practices.

48 Canada, Department of the Interior, *Forest Products of Canada, 1910: Pulpwood*, Bulletin 26 (Ottawa: Government Printing Bureau, 1911), 14.

49 S. Kuznets, *Modern Economic Growth: Rate, Structure and Spread* (New Haven, CT: Yale University Press, 1966), 63–72. A. Maddison, *Monitoring the World Economy, 1820–1992* (Paris: OECD, 1995), 62–3. A. Maddison, *Dynamic Forces in Capitalist Development: A Long-Run Comparative View* (New York: Oxford University Press, 1991), 49–51.

50 I. Drummond, ed., *Progress Without Planning: The Economic History of Ontario from Confederation to the Second World War* (Toronto: University of Toronto Press, 1987), 364.

51 B.E.C. Boothman, "The Foundations of Canadian Big Business" (paper presented at the Fifth Canadian Business History Conference, McMaster University, Hamilton, ON, 16 September 1998).

52 Statistics Canada, *Historical Statistics of Canada*, 2nd ed. (Ottawa, 1983), Series F334-4, F342-8, G188-202.

53 Statistical data to 1920 are from E. Bloomfield, "Lawyers as Members of Urban Business Élites in Southern Ontario, 1860 to 1920," in C. Wilton, ed., *Beyond the Law: Lawyers and Business in Canada, 1830 to 1930*, vol. 4 of *Essays in the History of Canadian Law* (Toronto: Butterworths, 1990), 112–47. Data for 1932 and 1940 and for the size of the partnerships are the author's estimates based upon the annual directories by H. Cartwright, ed., *The Canadian Law Lists* (Toronto: Canada Law List Publishing).

54 A.J. Richardson, "Canada's Accounting Elite: 1880–1930," *Accounting Historians Journal*, 16:1 (1989), 1–21.

55 This paragraph uses data collated from *The Financial Post Directory of Canadian Directors and Officials* (Toronto: Maclean Publishing) for 1931, 1934, and 1937.

56 *Canadian Law Times*, 27 (1907), 788, 792. After a long period of perceived overcrowding in the profession and weak revenues, the new environment was welcomed by others. See R.D. Gidney and W.P.J. Millar, *Professional Gentlemen: The Profession in Nineteenth-Century Ontario* (Toronto: Univesity of Toronto Press, 1994), 262–7, 346–8.

57 "Presidential Address of 1919," *Canadian Law Times* 39 (1919), 541. The angst within the profession is summarized in J.F. Newman, "Reaction and Change: A Study of the Ontario Bar, 1880 to 1920," *University of Toronto Faculty of Law Review* 32:1 (1974), 51–74.

58 "Combinations in Canada," *Canadian Law Times*, 40 (1920), 440–1.

59 M.J. Horwitz, *The Transformation of American Law, 1780–1860* (Cambridge, MA: Harvard University Press, 1977), esp. chaps. 1, 2, 6, and 7. See also W. Nelson, *The Americanization of the Common Law: The Impact of Legal Change on Massachusetts Society* (Cambridge, MA: Harvard University Press, 1975); W.J. Hurst, *The Legitimacy of the Business Corporation in the United States* (Charlottesville: University Press of Virginia, 1970).

60 M.J. Horwitz, *The Transformation of American Law, 1870–1960: The Crisis of Legal Orthodoxy* (New York: Oxford University Press, 1992), 33–64, 145–92. See also P.L. Rosen, *The Supreme Court and Social Science* (Urbana: University of Illinois Press, 1972); H. Hovenkamp, *Enterprise and American Law, 1836–1937* (Cambridge, MA: Harvard University Press, 1991), Parts IV and VI.

61 The literature relating to law and business in Canada remains focused on the pre-industrial era. See the following by R.C.B. Risk: "The Nineteenth-Century Foundations of the Business Corporation in Ontario," *University of Toronto Law Journal*, 23:3 (1973), 270–306; "The Golden Age: The Law About the Market in Nineteenth-Century Ontario," *University of Toronto Law Journal*, 26:3 (1976), 307–46; and "The Last Golden Age: Property and the Allocation of Losses in Ontario During the Nineteenth Century," *University of Toronto Law Journal*, 27:2 (1977) 199–239. Also P.J. George and P.J. Sworden, "John Beverley Robinson and the Commercial Empire of the St. Lawrence," *Research in Economic History*, 11 (1988), 217–42.

62 "Observations on the Use and Value of American Reports in reference to Canadian Jurisprudence," *Upper Canada Law Journal*, 3 (1857), 3.

63 *North British and Mercantile Insurance Co. v. London Liverpool and Globe Insurance Co.*, 44 L.J. Ch. 537, 538. *Bank of Toronto v. Lambe*, [1887] 12 App. Cas., 587, [1889] 42 Ch.D. 330.

64 J.M. MacIntyre, "The Use of American Cases in Canadian Courts," *University of British Columbia Law Review* 2 (1966), 478–90. For more recent patterns, see C.P. Manfredi, "The Use of United States Decisions by the Supreme Court of Canada Under the Charter of Rights and Freedom," *Canadian Journal of Political Science*, 23:3 (1990), 499–518; and G. Gentili, "Canada: Protecting Rights in a 'Worldwide Rights Culture': An Empirical Study of the Use of Foreign Precedents by the Supreme Court of Canada, 1982–2010," in T. Groppi and M.-C. Ponthoreau, eds., *The Use of Foreign Precedents by Constitutional Judges* (London: Hart, 2013), 39–68.

65 W.R.P. Parker, *Frauds on Creditors and Assignments for the Benefit of Creditors* (Toronto: Canada Law Book, 1903). L. Duncan, *The Law and Practice of Bankruptcy in Canada* (Toronto: Carswell, 1922). V. Mitchell's *A Treatise on the Law Relating to Canadian Commercial Corporations* (Montreal: Southam Press, 1916) served as a reference tool for more than thirty years and contained most of the precedents for corporate operations, including almost all of those used in proceedings of the Abitibi case.

66 M. Keller, *Affairs of State: Public Life in Late Nineteenth-Century America* (Cambridge, MA: Harvard University Press, 1977), 173–4, 431–4. E.M. Dodd, "Statutory Developments in Business Corporation Law, 1886–1936," *Harvard Law Review*, 50:1 (1936), 33–6. H.M. Bowman, "The States' Power over Foreign Corporations," *Michigan Law Review*, 9:7 (1911), 549–75. See *Doyle v. Continental Insurance Company*, [1876] 94 U.S. 535; *Barron v. Burnside*, [1887] 121 U.S. 186; *Allgeyer v. Louisiana*, [1897] 165 U.S. 578.

67 UKS, [1867] 30 & 31 Victoria, c. 3, British North America Act, s. 91:2, 92:10, 92:11, 92:13. See also A. Lajoie, *Le pouvoir déclaratoire du Parlement: augmentation discrétionnaire de la compétence fédérale au Canada* (Montreal: Presses de l'Université de Montréal, 1969).

68 Armstrong, *The Politics of Federalism*, 14–113.
69 [1894] 189 A.C. 199.
70 M.J. Horwitz, "*Santa Clara* Revisited: The Development of Corporate
   Theory," *West Virginia Law Review*, 88 (1985), 173–224. M.J. Sklar, *The
   Corporate Reconstruction of American Capitalism, 1890–1916: The Market, The
   Law, and Politics* (New York: Cambridge University Press, 1988), 43–57.
   See *Santa Clara County v. Southern Pacific Railroad*, [1886] 118 U.S. 394;
   Chicago, Milwaukee and St. Paul Railway Co. v. Minnesota, [1890] 134 U.S. 418;
   *Interstate Commerce Commission v. Cincinnati, New Orleans, and Texas Railway
   Co.*, [1897] 167 U.S. 479.
71 F.W. Wegenast, *The Law of Canadian Companies* (Toronto: Carswell, 1931),
   20–3, 59–64. *Ashbury Railway v. Riche*, [1875] L.R. 7 H.L. 753, 44 L.J. Ex. 185.
   Bonanza Creek Gold Mining v. the King, [1916] 1 AC 566, 26 DLR 273.
72 Mitchell, *Canadian Commercial Corporations*, 47–8, citing *Hattersley v.
   Shelbourne*, 10 W.R. 881; L.J. Ch. 873; *Ernest v. Nichols*, 6 H.L. Cas. 40; *Great
   Northern Railway Co. v Eastern Counties Railway Co.*, 9 Hare, 306. SO, [1914]
   4 Geo V, c. 178, s. 10, Ontario Companies Act removed the impediment.
73 Quebec Civil Code, Art. 2022. SQ, [1914] 4 Geo, V, c. 51, Loi sur les
   Pouvoirs Spéciaux des Corporations. Wegenast, *Law of Canadian Companies*,
   452–61.

2. Anson's Folly

1 H.E. Aldrich and C.M. Fiol, "Fools Rush In? The Institutional Context of
   Industry Creation," *Academy of Management Review*, 19:4 (1994), 645–70.
   M.T. Hannan and J.H. Freeman, *Organizational Ecology* (Cambridge, MA:
   Harvard University Press, 1989). The available studies suggest the average
   time for an industry to establish cognitive legitimacy is twenty-nine years,
   although there are examples where the period can be as low as fifteen
   years.
2 United States, Department of Agriculture, *How the United States Can Meet
   Its Present and Future Pulpwood Requirements*, Bulletin 1241 (Washington:
   Department of Agriculture, 1924), 55.
3 *PPMC*, 4 January 1917, 1; 15 March 1916, 121.
4 *PPMC*, 11 January 1917, 42
5 *PPMC*, December 1912, 370.
6 J.L. Bishop, *A History of American Manufactures*, vol. 1 (Philadelphia:
   Edward Young, 1866), 207–11.
7 D.C. Smith, "Wood Pulp and Newspapers, 1867–1900," *Business
   History Review*, 38 (1964), 328–45. J.A. McGaw, *Most Wonderful Machine:
   Mechanization and Social Change in Berkshire Paper Making, 1801–1885*
   (Princeton: Princeton University Press, 1987), chap. 7. G.B. Magee,

Productivity and Performance in the Paper Industry: Labour, Capital, and Technology in Britain and America, 1860–1914 (New York: Cambridge University Press, 1997), 26–87.

8 G.J. Baldasty, *The Commercialization of News in the Nineteenth Century* (Madison: University of Wisconsin Press, 1992), 81–101. R.L. Kaplan, *Politics and the American Press: The Rise of Objectivity, 1865–1920* (New York: Cambridge University Press, 2002), 104–39.

9 U.S., Bureau of Census, *Manufactures* (Washington: GPO, 1920), Tables 1, 16. U.S., Department of Agriculture, *American Forests and Forest Products*, Statistical Bulletin 21 (Washington: GPO, 1928), Table 154.

10 A.J. Cohen, "Technological Change as Historical Process: The Case of the U.S. Pulp and Paper Industry, 1915–1940," *Journal of Economic History*, 44 (1989), 779. N.R. Lamoreaux, *The Great Merger Movement in American Business, 1895–1904* (New York: Cambridge University Press, 1985), 43–5, 139–41. R.E. Caves, M. Fortunato, and P. Ghemawat, "The Decline of Dominant Firms, 1905–1929," *Quarterly Journal of Economics*, 99 (1984), 523–7.

11 N.K. Ohanian, *The American Pulp and Paper Industry, 1900–1940: Mill Survival, Firm Structure, and Industry Relocation* (Westport, CT: Greenwood, 1993), 44–57, 77. The firm and mill statistics in Appendix 2 vary from Ohanian's tables due to issues of whether smaller producers actually made newsprint in the sample years.

12 *Globe*, 11 April and 22 November 1899.

13 U.S., Forest Service, *Wood Used in Pulp, in 1905* (Washington: GPO, 1906), 8–9; *Timber Supply of the United States*, Circular 97 (Washington: GPO, 1907). American Forestry Association, *Proceedings of the American Forest Congress* (Washington: H.M. Sutter, 1906), 13–21, 103–23. *WP*, 29 December 1899; *NYT*, 21 December 1899.

14 J. Niosi, "La Laurentide (1887–1928): pionnière du papier journal au Canada," *Revue d'Histoire de l'Amérique Française*, 29 (1975), 375–415. J.-P. Charland, *Pâtes et papiers au Québec, 1880–1980: technologies, travail et travailleurs* (Quebec: Institut québécois de recherche sur la culture, 1990), 95–140. H.V. Nelles, *The Politics of Development: Forests, Mines, and Hydro-Electric Power in Ontario, 1849–1941* (Toronto: Macmillan, 1974), 48–107. R.S. Kellogg, *Pulpwood and Woodpulp in North America* (New York: McGraw-Hill, 1923), 224–32.

15 LOSP, No. 3 (1902), *Report of the Crown Lands Department*, xii.

16 LOSP, No. 3 (1900), *Report of the Crown Lands Department*, xiv; No. 3 (1901), *Report of the Crown Lands Department*, x; No. 3 (1902), *Report of the Crown Lands Department*, xii.

17 *PPMC*, January 1905, 27.

18 M. Kuhlberg, "'In the Power of the Government': The Rise and Fall of Newsprint in Ontario, 1894–1930" (PhD diss. York University, 2002), 57–101.

19 *PPMC*, February 1906; 28 January 1905, 26.
20 *Globe*, 2 May 1902, 28 April 1902.
21 *Globe*, 27 April 1900, 28 April 1902. *Paper Mill and Wood Pulp News*, 22 March 1902, 4.
22 *PPMC*, January 1905, 25.
23 LOSP, No. 49 (1900), Agreement between the Commissioner of Crown Lands and the Blanche River Pulp and Paper Company Limited; No. 3 (1905), *Report of the Crown Lands Department*, viii. *Globe*, 31 May 1901, 14 January 1903. *PPMC*, January 1905, 26–7.
24 LOSP, No. 71 (1902), Agreement between the Commissioner of Crown Lands and the Montreal River Pulp Company; No. 3 (1905), *Report of the Crown Lands Department*, viii. *Globe*, 6 March 1902. *PPMC*, May 1903; 22 June 1903, 61.
25 *Paper Mill and Wood Pulp News*, 28 September 1899, 10; 29 March 1902, 5. LOSP, No. 76 (1903), Agreement between His Majesty ... and the Keewatin Power Company, Limited, 4 April 1901. *Globe*, 10, 11 April 1901. AO, RG4-32, MS 7591, Proposed Application for Extension of Pulpwood Concessions Granted to Keewatin Power Co., 1902; B505409, General File, Backus and Kenora Development, 1921. AO, RG3, 05-0-009, Outline of Attempts to Develop Industry in Kenora Area prior to November 1919. *PPMC*, June 1903, 61; November 1904, 316–17; April 1906, 95.
26 *PPMC*, January 1905; 21 January 1906, 4; October 1907, 225. The Tories returned the deposits of cancelled concessionaries after several threatened legal action. This move was just an effort to cut the contracts clear without further encumbrances and did not demonstrate whether the government considered the licensees as speculators or businessmen who had failed to complete their obligations within the specified periods. See AO RG75-57, OC59/394, OC62/401, and OC63/19.
27 *PPMC*, January 1906, 5.
28 *Globe*, 6 April 1906. *PPMC*, February 1906, 45–7; April 1906, 94–5.
29 R.P. Gillis and T.R. Roach, *Lost Initiatives: Canada's Forest Industries, Forest Policy, and Forest Conservation* (Westport, CT: Greenwood, 1986), 98–103. For contrast, see S.P. Hayes, *Conservation and the Gospel of Efficiency: The Progressive Conservation Movement, 1890–1920* (Cambridge, MA: Harvard University Press, 1959); and R. Nash, *Wilderness and the American Mind* (New Haven, CT: Yale University Press, 1967).
30 AO, RG18-79, B249424, Proceedings, II, Testimony of C.C. Hele. *Globe*, 28 May 1920.
31 *Globe*, 11 April and 28 May 1902, AO, PC, 1905, No. 18, *A pure ballot and an honest count: Mr. J.P. Whitney, LL.D., K.C., M.P.P., for premier, 25 January 1905* (Toronto: n.p., 1905), 5, 60–1.

32 RG18-79, B249439, 346, *General Conditions with Respect to Pulpwood Areas Offered for Lease by Tender* (Toronto: L.K. Cameron, 1906), 4–6, 9–11. *PPMC*, January 1905, 4–5; June 1906, 146; January 1907, 19.

33 *PPMC*, October 1907, 225. RG18-79, B249437, 283 Timber Dues and Revenue. *PPMC*, April 1906, 92. The estimate of annual expenditures on colonization roads as a proportion of revenues from Northern Ontario was calculated from data in annual budget submissions.

34 *Globe*, 6 April and 26 May 1906; 3 January 1903.

35 RG18-70, B249439, 346, *General Conditions*.

36 *Globe*, 7, 25, 28 October 1898. AO, RG18-79, B249439, 346, Agreement between Her Majesty … and The Sturgeon Falls Pulp Company (Limited), 6 October 1898 (Toronto: Warwick Bros., 1899), 6.

37 LOSP, No. 3 (1900), *Report of the Crown Lands Department*, xiv. *Globe*, 23 February and 14 July 1899, 22 February and 2 April 1900. Lloyd initially planned to set up operations in the Ottawa River valley.

38 *Globe*, 28 March and 29 August 1901, 21 May 1902.

39 RG18-79, B249439, 348 and 349, Order-in-Council and Indenture Re Sturgeon Falls Pulp Company and Imperial Paper Mills. *PPMC*, September 1904, 278; March 1905, 111–12; April 1905, 140; November 1905, 301–2; September 1906, 214. *Globe*, 8 July 1904. When the firm became insolvent, it owned $2.25 million in bonds, had unsecured claims of $400,000, and owed $750,000 to the Sovereign and Quebec Banks. The mill was not brought into compliance with the provincial lease, with a daily output of 72 tons, until after the acquisition by Spanish River.

40 *Diehl v. Carritt*, [1907] OJ No. 45, 15 OLR 202. *Imperial Paper Mills of Canada Limited v. Quebec Bank*, [1912] OJ No. 162, 26 OLR 637, 6 DLR 475, 22 OWN 703. *Diehl v. Carritt*, [1915] OJ No. 265, 9 OWN 109. Re *Imperial Paper Mills of Canada Limited, Diehl v. Carritt*, [1915] OJ No. 630, 7 OWN 630. *PPMC* (1907), 159, 190, 202, 234; (1908), 163 164, 190. *Globe*, 30 May 1907, 10 May 1901.

41 *PPMC* (1909), 139, 159, 184; (1911), 228, 303, 415; (1912), 137. *Globe*, 5 May 1909.

42 The biographical sketch has been derived from the following sources: D.W. Ambridge, *Frank Harris Anson (1959–1923): Pioneer in the North* (Montreal: Newcomen Society in North America, 1952); Railway Age, *The Biographical Directory of the Railway Officials of America for 1887* (Chicago: Railway Age, 1887), 19; H.J. Morgan, ed., *The Canadian Men and Women of the Time* (Toronto: William Briggs, 1912), 30; and obituaries in periodicals and newspapers during November of 1923. Anson's birth date is not certain. Publications prior to his involvement with Abitibi list it as 24 October 1861; after 1914 it is usually cited as 24 October 1859. Anson's involvement with the Texas Sugar Refinery can be found in *Galveston Daily News*, 15 and 16 September, 1 October 1924.

43 RG3, 1-0-1, Abitibi and Iroquois Falls.

44 LOSP, 1904, No. 5, "The Abitibi Region," 104–21; 1905, No. 5, "Explorations in Abitibi" and "Agricultural Resources of Abitibi," 184–247; 1909, No. 4, "Lake Abitibi Area," 263–83.

45 U.S., House of Representatives, Select Committee under Resolution 344, *Pulp and Paper Investigation Hearings*, V, CSS 5546 (Washington: GPO, 1909), 2396–7.

46 *Globe*, 11 January 1911. *PPMC*, January 1911, 55; May 1911, 212; July 1911, 213; 22 March 1928, 397. For the *Chicago Tribune's* interest, see C. Wiegman, *Trees to News: A Chronicle of the Ontario Paper Company's Origin and Development* (Toronto: McClelland and Stewart, 1953), 11.

47 RG18-79, B249441, 428, Map of Abitibi concession; 429, General Conditions with respect to the Abitibi Pulp Limit, 15 August 1912. LOSP, No. 3 (1912), *Annual Report of the Department of Lands, Forests and Mines*, vi.

48 *PPMC*, June 1912, 181–2.

49 Timmins *Daily Press*, 26 November 1914, cited in Abel, *Changing Places*, 62.

50 AO, F150-8, B273507, Murray, Mather & Co., Circular for Abitibi Power and Paper Ltd., 1914. *PPMC*, 15 April 1913, 269–74. See AO, RG1-E-4-B, III, 8–9, 15 August 1912, F.H. Anson and S. Ogilvie, to W.H. Hearst, series of assignments for transfer of original pulpwood agreement to firm.

51 Congress, *Pulp and Paper Hearings*, I, 25 April 1908, 38.

52 L.E. Ellis, *Print Paper Pendulum: Group Pressures and the Price of Newsprint* (New Brunswick, NJ: Rutgers University Press, 1948), 39–68

53 For Norris, *WP*, 29 April 1910; *WSJ*, 10 June 1910. U.S., Tariff Board, *Report on the Pulp and News-print Paper Industry* (Washington: GPO, 1911), 24–41, 52–6. U.S., Tariff Commission, *Reciprocity with Canada: A Study of the Arrangement of 1911* (Washington: GPO, 1920), 47–9.

54 LOSP, 1913, No. 3, Appendix 33, The Abitibi Pulp Limit Agreement, 77–83. AO, MU1311, *Northern Ontario – Its Progress and Development under the Whitney Government* (ca. 1914).

55 AO, RG55-1, 147/135, Letters Patent of Abitibi Pulp and Paper Mills; 117/89, Letters Patent of Abitibi Pulp and Paper Ltd. F6-3, B253639, Env. 1, Memorandum for Mr. Gibson re. Abitibi Pulp Limit, 23 October 1913. LAC, RG95, Series 1, 2493, Abitibi incorporation papers. *PPMC*, 1 February 1913, 114; 1 May 1913, 294; 1 August 1913, 523. *Toronto World*, 27 June 1913. J. Moody, "Preferred Stocks as Investments, *Annuals of the American Academy of Political and Sciences*, 35:3 (May 1910), 63–71.

56 Biographies are derived from *Canadian Who's Who*, 1910.

57 *Journal of Commerce*, 2 June 1928.

58 F.C. James, *The Growth of Chicago Banks* (New York: Harper, 1938), II, 673–99, 789. Bureau of Business Research, College of Commerce and

Business Administration, "Investment Banking in Chicago," *University of Illinois Business Research Bulletin*, 29:13 (1931), 7–12, 40–1. F.C. Jaher, *The Urban Establishment: Upper Strata in Boston New York, Charleston, Chicago and Los Angeles* (Urbana: University of Illinois Press, 1982), 543–5.

59 F.M. Huston, *Financing an Empire: A History of Banking in Illinois* (Chicago: S.J. Clarke, 1926), II, 536–7; IV, 132–6. G.R. Horne. "The Receivership and Reorganization of the Abitibi Power and Paper Company, Limited" (PhD diss., University of Michigan, 1954), 35–6.

60 *FP*, 14 February 1914. *PPMC*, 15 February 1914, 110; 1 April 1914, 218. F150, B273507, 8-0-23, Murray, Mather and Co., Circular, 7% Cumulative Preferred Stock, Abitibi Power and Paper Ltd., 1914.

61 *PPMC*, 15 July 1914, 421.

62 *Globe*, 10 February 1914. *CFC*, 14 February 1914.

63 *Journal of Commerce* reprinted in *PPMC*, 15 February 1914, 111.

64 F150, B273507, 8-0-23, D. Dobie to J.S. Gillies, 16 October 1914. Gillies turned down the offer citing the risk of forest fire in the region.

65 CIHM, 84744, *Record and Policy of the Whitney Government, Ontario Elections, 1914* (Toronto: n.p., 1914), 46–7, 50.

66 AO, F6, MU1309, Env. 1, J.A. McAndrews to W. Hearst, 11 October 1913. *Globe*, 6 September 1913.

67 *PPMC*, 15 February 1913, 142; 15 April 1913, 269–71; 15 February 1914, 110–11. *WSJ*, 4 July 1913.

68 *WSJ*, 31 March 1913. *PPMC*, 15 October 1913, 601; 1 January 1914, 26.

69 *FP*, 29 March 1913, 14 June 1913. *PPMC*, 15 November 1913, 761; 15 December 1913, 821.

70 *FP*, 7 January 1914. *PPMC*, 15 April 1914, 215; 15 May 1914, 315; 15 August 1914, 501; 1 August 1915, 404; 1 November 1915, 639. *Globe*, 13 October 1914, 10 July 1915.

71 LAC, RG33-53, Brief submitted to the Paper Control Tribunal by the counsel for the paper manufacturers, September 1917.

72 *Globe*, 6 September 1913. *PPMC*, 15 July 1915, 399; 15 May 1914, 316.

73 *MG*, 22 June 1914. *PPMC*, 1 July 1914, 399; 15 March 1915, 186.

74 RG3, 04-0-260, Copies, Lease 1860 to Shirley Ogilvie and Frank Harris Anson, 17 September 1912; Lease 1898 (amendment), 9 January 1914. AO, F5-1, B273279, J.L. Englehart to J.P. Whitney, 23 March 1912; B273281, A. Beck to Whitney, 2 May 1913 and reply. OHA, ORR401.1, Box 124, Beck to Hearst, 10 May 1912; H.G. Acres to Beck, 4 February and 14 March 1913. *FP*, 11 April 1914.

75 LAC, RG10, Microfilm reel C-8017, Timiskaming Agency, Abitibi Reserve, Compensation for Lands Flooded by Abitibi, 1915–19. *PPMC*, 1 January 1916, 16.

76 RG3, 04-0-260, Licence of Occupation 513 to Abitibi Pulp and Paper, 20 January 1913. *FP*, 16 November 1912, 29 March 1913. *PPMC*, 15 February 1915, 112; January 1916, 16. Kuhlberg, *In the Power of the Government*, 138, portrays the conditions as unreasonable but the company usually ignored them. The firm objected to the power reservation but was prepared to accept a reservation of electricity if it was for municipal supply, not the railroad. RG3, 04-0-260, Beck to Drury, 8 December 1920. After Abitibi's takeover of Twin Falls, the firm considered the railroad's rights surrendered. *CSI*, E1.

77 *PPMC*, 1 August 1916, 346; 1 September 1916, 289; 1 October 1916, 340. *Globe*, 2, 14 August, 12 September 1916.

78 RG18-79, B249441, 434, Anson to Ferguson, 23 May 1916; Anson to Smith, 25 May 1916.

79 RG18-79, B249441, 434, Anson to Smith, 2 June 1916.

80 RG3, 04-0-186, Anson to Drury, 29 September 1920. 04-0-189, Anson to Drury, 17 September 1920.

81 *PPMC*, 15 July 1916, 322; 1 September 1916, 291. RG3, 05-0-009, Anson and Smith to Ferguson, 3 May 1917. C.C. Hele to A. Grigg, 9 May and 16 May 1917.

82 RG3, 05-0-009, Anson to Drury, 29 September 1920; Outline of Attempts to Develop Industry in Kenora Area prior to November 1919.

83 RG3, 05-0-009, Report on Western English River, 8 February 1919; Report on English River Valley South of Transcontinental, 27 June 1919. Anson to Drury, 29 and 28 September 1920.

84 RG18-79, B249441, Anson to G.H. Kilmer, 23 April 1917; Kilmer to Anson, 25 October 1916, "Private."

85 RG18-79, B249441, 432, Anson to Ferguson, 28 June 1918; Anson to Kilmer, 20 August 1918; Smith to Anson, 11 December 1918

86 RG18-79, B249441, 431, Ferguson to Anson, 14 April 1919; 434, Anson to Smith, 2 June 1916.

87 RG18-79, B249441, 434, Anson to Royal Securities, 27 April 1919. W.C. Pitfield to Anson, 28 April 1919. B249442, 435 Peabody Houghteling, Circular 1026, Abitibi $1,500,000 First Mortgage 6% Gold Bonds, June 1919.

88 RG18-79, Proceedings, 10435. *ME, Globe*, 11 October 1921.

89 RG3, 04-0-260, Drury to A. Beck, 29 November 1920; A. Grigg to W.W. Pope, 4 August 1920.

90 Lambert and Pross, *Renewing Nature's Wealth*, 263–7, acknowledge but understate the chaos and lack of controls within the ministry. RG18-79, B249423, Report of the Timber Commission, 26 June 1922, 14, 33, 39–42, 64. B249424, Proceedings, 1500–08, 1798, 1818.

91   W.L. Chamberlain and G.W. Edwards, *The Principles of Bond Investment* (New York: Henry Holt, 1927), 490–4. See also T.S. McGrath, *Timber Bonds* (Chicago: Craig-Wayne, 1911); A.F. Jones, "The Accountant's Relation to Timber Bond Issues," *Annals of the American Academy of Political and Social Science*, 41 (1912), 51–8. Company sponsored booklets include Clarke L. Poole, *Timber Land Bonds Analyzed as Investments for Banks and Trust Companies* (Chicago: Clarke L. Poole, 1913); C. Fentress and M. Corr, *Timbers: An Analysis of Timber-Secured Bonds as Investments for Individual, Bank, Trust, and Insurance Funds* (Chicago: Mercantile Press, 1927).

92   *Globe*, 7 April 1919.

93   *Editor and Publisher*, 3 February 1917, 10, 30.

94   *FP*, 12 April 1919.

95   *PPMC*, 15 February 1917, 180. *Moody's Public Utilities and Industrials*, 1916, 114; *Moody's Survey of Industrials*, 1921, 1665.

96   RG18-79, B249441, 400, Anson to Ferguson, 7 May 1919. *Moody's Survey of Industrials*, 858. Kuhlberg, *In the Power*, 143, contended the firm was "completely dumbfounded" by the decision. Anson, in fact, sought what he could get away with. The outcome may have been a disappointment but could not have been a surprise. There was no financial stringency in forest products from 1915 to 1920, rather it was a period of record profits. See RG18-79, B249435, 141–3, Shevlin-Clarke financial statements.

97   *PPMC*, 13 June 1918, 20; 3 October 1918, 887; 13 November 1919, 972; 1 September 1921, 906.

98   *FP*, 8 November 1919. *PPMC*, 21 June 1917, 614; 15 January 1920, 66.

99   RG18-79, B249442, 435, Peabody Houghteling, Circular 1026, Abitibi $1,500,000 First Mortgage 6% Gold Bonds, June 1919; 437, Circular 1096, 1 March 1921, Abitibi $4,000,000 8% consolidated mortgage sinking fund gold bonds. *FP*, 27 September 1919.

100 *PPMC*, 16 December 1920, 1280.

101 *PPMC*, 17 February 1921, 181–2.

102 *Globe*, 14 April 1920.

3. An Industry in Transformation

1   *PPMC*, 12 January 1920, 154; 15 January 1920, 55. *FP*, 31 January 1920.

2   U.S., Department of Agriculture, *Pulpwood Consumption and Wood-Pulp Consumption, 1920* (Washington: GPO, 1922), 12, 23, 28–9; Timber Depletion, Lumber Prices, *Lumber Exports, and Concentration of Timber Ownership* (Washington: GPO, 1920), 27–8. A.B. Recknagel, *The Forests of New York State* (New York: Macmillan, 1923), 35–42. For a detailed survey, see G.P. Ahern, *Forest Bankruptcy in America: Each State's Own Story*, 2nd ed. (Washington: Shenandoah Publishing, 1934).

3 R.S. Kellogg, *Pulpwood and Wood Pulp in North America* (New York: McGraw-Hill, 1923), 137–72. U.S., Congress, Senate, *Pulpwood Supply in Alaska*, CSS 9209 (Washington: GPO, 1930); *National Pulp and Paper Requirements in Relation to Forest Conservation*, CSS 9909 (Washington: GPO, 1935), 9–10. Department of Agriculture, *A National Plan for American Forestry*, I, CSS 9740 (Washington: GPO, 1933), 258–70.

4 U.S., Congress, Senate, *Survey of Pulp Woods on the Public Domain*, CSS 7671 (Washington: GP0, 1920), 5. U.S. Department of Agriculture, *Pulpwood Consumption*, 12.

5 U.S., Department of Agriculture, *American Forests and Forest Products*, Bulletin 21 (Washington: GPO, 1928), Tables 143, 149, 155.

6 U.S., War Industries Board, *Prices of Paper* (Washington: GPO, 1919), 11–12. Congress, Senate, *Report of the Federal Trade Commission on the News-Print Paper Industry*, CSS 7246 (Washington: GPO, 1917), 23–4, 32–3. Most studies estimated the average cost of newsprint production prior to 1916 in the range of $31 to $34. That left an average profit of $5 per ton, a very weak return on the invested capital, which explained why many American companies failed to conduct reforestation, build reserves, or make proper allowances for depletion.

7 U.S., Department of Agriculture, *Pulpwood Consumption and Wood-Pulp Consumption, 1917* (Washington: GPO, 1919), 2–3, 7–8. *Survey of Pulp Woods*, CSS 7671, 7. *PPMC*, 9 January 1919, 9. It appears that about half of the loss of American capacity between 1913 and 1918 entailed the conversion of mills owned by International Paper, which then was slow to exploit the advances in newsprint prices.

8 *Editor and Publisher*, 31 March 1917, 11; 27 November 1919, 18. *News-Print Industry*, CSS 7246, 58–60. Much of the "evidence" in the FTC 1917 report was reprinted word for word from articles in *Editor and Publisher*, a pattern repeated in the 1930 study.

9 *News-Print Paper Industry*, 15, 55–7. *Editor and Publisher*, 3 January 1917, 10.

10 *FP*, 7 January and 28 January 1921.

11 *FP*, 5 November 1920, 7 October 1921, 29 September 1922.

12 *FP*, 10 December 1923. *Globe*, 21 June 1921.

13 *FP*, 7 October 1921, 29 September 1922.

14 *WSJ*, 1 December 1920; 1 and 14 March 1921. R.S. Kellogg, *Newsprint Paper in North America* (New York: Newsprint Service Bureau, 1948), 24–5. *PPMC*, 1 April 1920, 351; August 1936, 502.

15 *WSJ*, 11 October 1922, 29 March 1923, 23 June 1924.

16 *Globe*, 23 May 1924, 1 October 1924.

17 *FP*, 1 January 1923, 11 April 1924.

18 *Maclean's*, 15 April 1921, 14.

19 *PPMC*, 3 May 1923, 450.

20 N.K. Ohanian, *The American Pulp and Paper Industry, 1900–1940: Mill Survival, Firm Structure, and Industry Relocation* (Westport, CT: Greenwood, 1993), 15, 22.

21 NARA, RG151.10.2, 87338, Statements Presented at Hearings of the U.S. Timber Conservation Board, 10 June 1931. For American production, capacity and import patterns see, U.S., Department of Agriculture, *American Forests and Forest Products*, Statistical Bulletin 21 (Washington: GPO, 1928), 266–89.

22 Ohanian, *American Pulp and Paper Industry*, 28, 46–7. A.R. Markusen, *Profit Cycles, Oligopoly and Regional Development* (Cambridge, MA: MIT Press, 1985), 245–6. J.A. Guthrie, *The Economics of Pulp and Paper* (Pullman: State College of Washington Press, 1950), 136–8, 144–8.

23 *Survey of Pulp* Woods, CSS 7671, 7–8. U.S., Bureau of the Census, Fifteenth Census of the United States, *Manufactures*, II (Washington: GPO, 1930), 572. See also Recknagle, *The Forests of New York*, 35–8; NYSL, State of New York, *The Paper and Pulp Industries of New York State* (Albany: Division of Commerce, 1942), 30–3.

24 U.S., Department of Agriculture, *Timber Depletion*, 28. U.S., Department of Commerce, *United States Pulp and Paper Industry* (Washington: GPO, 1938), 67–9. H. Hunter, "Innovation, Competition, and Locational Changes in the Pulp and Paper Industry: 1880–1950" *Land Economics*, 31:4 (1955), 320–4.

25 U.S., Department of Agriculture, *American Forests and Forest Products* (Washington, GPO, 1928), Tables 140 and 146; *Forest Products: 1930* (Washington: GPO, 1931), 8. For Ontario, estimates from U.S. Census and Department of Commerce data and from data in annual reports of Ontario's Department of Lands, Forests and Mines. Export and import shares were measured by cords, not value or cost. American and Canadian data closely match. This indicates the governments recorded most of the international trade, notwithstanding some of the surreptitious practices that unfolded in forest operations. Any claims that the trade was much larger in volume than indicated by official records appears unwarranted.

26 AO, RG49-115, B248795, Proceedings of the Conference called by the Minister of Lands and Forests, 12 March 1940, 45. RG3, 06-0-697, L.R. Wilson to Ferguson, 23 February 1925; L.R. Wilson to Lyons, 23 February 1925.

27 See T.R. Roach and R. Judd, "A Man for All Seasons: Frank John Dixie Barnjum, Conservationist, Pulpwood Embargoist and Speculator!" *Acadiensis*, 20:2 (1991), 129–44; W. Parenteau and L.A. Sandberg, "Conservation and the Gospel of Economic Nationalism: The Canadian Pulpwood Question in Nova Scotia and New Brunswick, 1918–1925," *Environmental History Review*, 19:2 (1995), 55–83. Canada, Parliament,

Sessional Paper 310, *Report of the Royal Commission on Pulpwood* (Ottawa: King's Printer, 1924), 257.

28 LAC, RG39-13, Royal Commission on Pulpwood, Evidence, V, 470. J.W. Shipley, *Pulp and Paper-Making in Canada* (Toronto: Longmans, Green, 1929), 118–19. RG3, 04-0-186, H.J. Wheeler to Drury, 21 January 1920; R.J. McLaughlin to Drury, Bowman and Executive Council, 8 January 1920.

29 RG3, 06-0-698, K.S. Maclachlan to Ferguson, 10 February 1925; 06-0-1250, Ferguson to W.G. Mitchell, 23 February 1926.

30 K.R. Harrigan, *Strategies for Vertical Integration* (Toronto: D.C. Heath, 1983), 1–14. R.E. Caves and R.M. Bradburd, "The Empirical Determinants of Vertical Integration," *Journal of Economic Behavior and Organization*, 9:3 (1988), 265–9.

31 H. Hovenkamp, "The Law of Vertical Integration and the Business Firm: 1880–1960," *Iowa Law Review*, 95:3 (2010), 863–918. M.A. Adelman, "Integration and Antitrust Policy," *Harvard Law Review*, 63:1 (1949), 27–77. G.E. Hale, "Vertical Integration: Impact of the Antitrust Laws upon Combinations of Successive Stages of Production and Distribution," *Columbia Law Review*, 49:7 (1949), 921–54. R. Bork, "Vertical Integration and the Sherman Act: The Legal History of an Economic Misconception," *University of Chicago Law Review*, 22:1 (1954), 157–201. J.S. McGee and L.R. Bassett, "Vertical Integration Revisited," *Journal of Law and Economics*, 19:1 (1976), 167–238.

32 A.B. Laffer, "Vertical Integration by Corporations, 1929–1964," *Review of Economics and Statistics*, 51 (1969), 91–3. D.J. Richards and D. Carlton, "Vertical Integration in Competitive Markets Under Uncertainty," *Journal of Industrial Economics*, 27:3 (1979), 189–209. M.A. Salinger, "Vertical Mergers and Market Foreclosure," *Quarterly Journal of Economics*, 103:2 (1988), 345–56. M. Perry, "Vertical Integration: Determinants and Effects," in R. Schmalaensee and R.D. Willig, eds., *Handbook of Industrial Organization* (New York: North Holland, 1989), 183–255. M. Riordan, "Competitive Effects of Vertical Integration," in P. Buccirossi, ed., *Handbook of Antitrust Economics* (Cambridge, MA: MIT Press, 2008), 145–82.

33 AO, RG18-118, Proceedings, VIII, 15 November 1940, 812–13.

34 U.S., Tariff Commission, *Report to the United States Senate on Wood Pulp and Pulpwood*, Report No. 126, Second Series (Washington: GPO, 1938), 94–5. U.S., Congress, House of Representatives, "Power in the Cellulose Industries," in *Columbia River and Minor Tributaries: Letter from the Secretary of War*, I, CSS 9756 (Washington: GPO, 1933), 356.

35 *PPMC*, 21 April 1921, 429; 8 April 1920, 370; 3 June 1920, 595, 601.

36 *PPMC*, 12 May 1921, 497; 16 May 1921, 5622; 3 June 1921, 672; 4 August 1921, 816; 9 November 1922, 967; 13 September 1923, 907. Discussions of the Riordan failure and the implications were extensive in newspapers from 1921 to 1925.

37 Author's estimate from *National Directory of Canadian Pulp and Paper Mills and Allied Trades*. Ohanian, *American Pulp and Paper Industry*, 114.

38 A.M. Lee, *The Daily Newspaper in America* (New York: Macmillan, 1937), 215–17, 718–19, 728–9. This study is the only one that compares alternative measures including census, marketing surveys, and industry tabulations. The annual data published in *Editor and Publisher* usually understated the number of papers and circulation.

39 Lee, *The Daily Newspaper*, 218–20. J.C. Busterna, "Trends in Daily News Paper Ownership," *Journalism and Mass Communication Quarterly*, 65:4 (1988), 831–8. U.S., Senate, *Report of the Federal Trade Commission on the Newsprint Paper Industry*, CSS 8360 (Washington: GPO, 1930), 62, 72.

40 *WP*, 18 June 1920. *Editor and Publisher*, 6 August 1932, 25.

41 U.S., Congress, Senate, *Tariff Hearings: H.R. 7456, Free List*, Testimony of William J. Pape, Publishers' Buying Corporation, CSS 7969 (Washington: GPO, 1921), 4889.

42 L.E. Ellis, *Print Paper Pendulum: Group Pressures and the Price of Newsprint* (New Brunswick, NJ: Rutgers University Press, 1948) deals with this issue but relies upon legislative debates and several publisher periodicals.

43 International Paper, *Why Newsprint is High* (New York: International Paper, 1918). LAC, RG33-53, Inquiry into the Manufacture, Sale, Price, and Supply of Newsprint in Canada, Interim Report, 18 January 1918, 12, and Exhibit 10.

44 U.S., Federal Trade Commission, *Report on the News-print Paper Industry, 13 June 1917* (Washington: GPO, 1917), 18, 57, 13. As indicated in the narrative, the report must be read with caution because it mixed factual information on issues like production techniques and machinery with rationalizations, speculations, and innuendo about producer conduct. I was able to match much of the evidence in the report page by page with different issues of *Editor and Publisher*. Criticism of the biases of the FTC report can be found in *PPMC*, *Paper*, and *Paper Trade Journal* across the period of 1917 to 1921.

45 U.S., Federal Trade Commission, *Report*, 130. E.O. Merchant, "The Government and the News-Print Paper Manufacturers," *Quarterly Journal of Economics*, 32:3 (1918), 238–56; 34:2 (1920), 313–28. Ellis, *Print Paper Pendulum*, 106–24. Merchant was a University of Chicago economist who advised the FTC and later conceded the intervention from 1917 to 1919 was a conspicuous failure.

46 *PPMC*, 12 January 1920, 153–4. *NYT*, 29 December 1921.

47 J.P. Hagenauer, "Labour Cost of Production in the Pulp and Paper Industry," *Paper Trade Journal*, 50 (25 April 1935), 29–39. C.W. Boyce, "The Pulp and Paper Industry," in J.G. Glover and R.L. Lagai, eds., *The Development of American Industries: Their Economic Significance* (New York:

Prentice-Hall, 1941), 148–50. D.C. Smith, *History of Papermaking in the United States, 1691–1969* (New York: Lockwood Trade Journal, 1971), 619.

48 J.A. Guthrie, *The Newsprint Paper Industry: An Economic Analysis* (Cambridge, MA: Harvard University Press, 1941), 93–126. L.T. Stevenson, *The Background and Economics of American Papermaking* (New York: Harper and Brothers, 1940), 71–129. A. Cohen, "Technological Change as Historical Process: The Case of the U.S. Pulp and Paper Industry, 1915–1940," *Journal of Economic History*, 44:3 (1984), 775–99.

49 M.W. Watkins, *Industrial Combinations and Public Policy: A Study of Combination Competition and the Public Welfare* (Boston: Houghton Mifflin, 1927), 176.

50 Canadian accounts often have cited V.W. Bladen, *An Introduction to Political Economy* (Toronto: University of Toronto Press, 1958), chap. 6. His discussion of newsprint was drawn from newspaper articles and is superficial even by the scholarly standards of the time.

51 See U.S., Federal Trade Commission, *The News-print Paper Industry* (Washington: GPO, 1917); *Newsprint Paper Industry*, CSS 9320 (Washington: GPO, 1930).

52 U.S., Congress, Senate, *National Pulp and Paper Requirements in Relation to Forest Conservation*, CSS 9878 (Washington: GPO, 1935), 67.

53 See P. Temin, *Iron and Steel in Nineteenth-Century America: An Economic Enquiry* (Cambridge, MA: MIT Press, 1964); D. Hounshell, *From the American System to Mass Production, 1800–1932: The Development of Manufacturing Technology in the United States* (Baltimore: John Hopkins University Press, 1984).

54 Congress, Senate, *Newsprint Paper Industry*, 111–13. LAC, RG33-53, R1133-0-6-E, Interim Report, Inquiry into the Manufacture, Sale, Price, and Supply of Newsprint in Canada, 18 January 1918, 24–6. American Pulp and Paper Association, *A Capital and Income Survey of the United States Pulp and Paper Industry, 1934–43* (New York: APPA, 1944), 15.

55 *PPMC*, 27 April 1922, 338.

56 G.J. Stigler, *Capital and Rates of Return in Manufacturing Industries* (Princeton: Princeton University Press, 1963), 212–13.

57 Ohanian, *American Pulp and Paper*, 64–6, 83–5. Kellogg, *Newsprint Paper*, 15–25.

58 *NYT*, 13 April 1901.

59 N. Lamoreaux, *The Great Merger Movement in American Business, 1895–1904* (New York: Cambridge University Press, 1985), 126–32. U.S. Congress, House of Representatives, *Pulp and Paper Investigation Hearings*, CSS 5542 (Washington: GPO, 1909), 25 April 1908, 24–5; 12 May 1908, 730–3, 744–9; 16 May 1908, 1078–9, 1211–12.

60 *WSJ*, 24 August 1927. Watkins, *Industrial Combinations and Public Policy*, 189. S. Livermore, "The Success of Industrial Mergers," *Quarterly Journal of Economics*, 50:1 (1935), 77–80, 95.

61 *WSJ*, 15 February 1911. HUBL, International Paper, *AR* (1918), 7–8; (1915), 6–7.

62 *WSJ*, 6 October 1913. HUBL, International Paper, *AR* (1919), 12–13. *WSJ*, 15 July 1916, *PPMC*, 4 July 1918, 599. *Globe*, 21 April and 23 December 1920.

63 Canada, *Census of Canada* (1901), III, xxix, lxiii; (1910), III, 6, 168–9. *Spanish River Pulp & Paper Mills, Limited v. Ahnapee & Western Railway Company*, [1926] 113 ICC 343–52 and [1927] 120 ICC 251. Mill capacity was reverified using annual issues of *Post's Paper Mill Directory* and *Lockwood's Paper Mill Directory*.

64 The issues were well covered in the trade press. For how contemporaries viewed them, see S.C. Phillips, "The Use of Wood Pulp for Paper-making," *Journal of the Society of Arts*, 53 (19 May 1905), 1–34; G. Clapperton, *Practical Paper-Making* (London: Crosby Lockwood, 1907); C.F. Cross, E.J. Bevan, and R.W. Sindall, *Wood Pulp and Its Uses* (New York: Van Nostrant, 1911); U.S., Department of Agriculture, Forest Service, *The Grinding of Spruce for Pulpwood* (Washington: GPO, 1915); G.S. Witham, *Modern Pulp and Paper Making: A Practical Treatise* (New York: Chemical Catalogue, 1920).

65 *PPMC*, February 1927, 79–80, 185–92; March 1933, 215–18. Canadian Pulp and Paper Association, *Reference Tables*, November 1947. Canada, Department of Trade and Commerce, *The Pulp and Paper Industry in Canada* (Ottawa, 1947, 1952). Hunter, "Innovation, Competition, and Locational Changes," 319–20.

66 *Newsprint Paper Investigation*, [1933] 197 ICC 748.

67 Senate, *News-Print Paper Industry*, 88–9, 91–107.

68 Kellogg, *Newsprint Paper in North America*, 24. Boyce, "The Paper and Pulp Industry," 145–7.

69 *FP*, 25 February 1921; 13 August 1920. *PPMC*, 25 May 1922, 424.

70 *PPMC*, 17 August 1922, 687.

71 *PPMC*, 6 December 1923, 1203.

72 The assets and liabilities of life insurance companies were summarized in the annual reports issued by the Superintendent of Insurance. The statements documented all bond and stock holdings by each firm, how the composition of assets changed by year, and relevant regulatory policies. The summaries of life insurance holdings are drawn from spreadsheets compiled for the period of 1909 to 1940.

73 The exception was London Life, which decreased its bond holdings and expanded into mortgages for urban real estate, a strategy that also created serious problems for the company during the Great Depression. LLA, James Campbell et al., "A History of London Life Insurance" (unpublished typescript), 388–447.

74 From his 1926 address to Sun Life sales agents, quoted in G.H. Harris, *The President's Book: The Story of the Sun Life Assurance Company of Canada* (Montreal: Sun Life Assurance, 1928), 194.

75 Harris, *The President's Book*, 193, 196. J. Schull, *The Century of the Sun: The First Hundred Years of the Sun Life Assurance Company of Canada* (Toronto: Macmillan, 1971), 58.

76 MLCA, 81.22.152, Bond Department, A History of the Investments of Mutual Life Assurance of Canada in Pulp and Paper Company Securities, 23 May 1933. The company's official history minimized the selection of poor investment vehicles, noting merely "it appears that this type of investment was given too much emphasis for many of these corporation bonds, especially those of pulp and paper companies, fell into default in the thirties." See, Mutual Life Assurance of Canada, *A Century of Mutuality* (Waterloo, ON: Mutual Life of Canada, 1970), 65.

77 *FT* quoted in *PPMC*, 13 December 1928, 1785. *Maclean's*, 15 October 1928.

78 Canadian practices with respect to the treatment of common stock paralleled those in the United States where the use of arbitrarily low par values emerged after 1918. B. Graham and D.L. Dodd, *Security Analysis*, 2nd ed. (New York: McGraw-Hill, 1940), 379.

79 Guthrie, *The Newsprint Paper Industry*, chap. 5.

80 *CSI*, A1.

81 Canada, Dominion Bureau of Statistics, *Consolidations in Canadian Industry and Commerce, January 1, 1900, to December 31, 1933* (Ottawa: DBS, 1934), 8–9.

82 R. Sobel, *The Great Bull Market: Wall Street in the 1920s* (New York: W.W. Norton, 1968), 88–95.

83 M.T. Leary and M.R. Roberts, "Do Peer Firms Affect Corporate Financial Policy?" *Journal of Finance*, 69:1 (2014), 139–78. J.R. Graham and C. Harvey, "The Practice of Corporate Finance: Evidence from the Field," *Journal of Financial Economics*, 60:2 (2001), 186–243. I. Welch, "Capital Structure and Stock Returns," *Journal of Political Economy*, 112:1 (2004), 106–31. M.Z. Frank and V.K. Goyal, "Capital Structure Decisions: Which Factors are Reliably Important?" *Financial Management*, 38:1 (2009), 1–37.

84 L. Larwood and W. Whittaker, "Managerial Myopia: Self-Serving Biases in Organizational Planning," *Journal of Applied Psychology*, 62:2 (1977), 194–8. J.B. Brown, "Understanding the Better than Average Effect: Motives (Still) Matter," *Personality and Social Psychology Bulletin*, 38:2 (2012), 209–19.

85 J.B. Heaton, "Managerial Optimism and Corporate Finance," *Financial Management*, 31:2 (2002), 33–45. U. Malmendier and G.A. Tate, "CEO Overconfidence and Corporate Investment," *Journal of Finance*, 60:6 (2005), 661–700. I. Ben-David, J.R. Graham, and C.R. Harvey, "Managerial Miscalibration," *Quarterly Journal of Economics*, 128:4 (2013), 1547–84.

86 Quoted in J.T. Saywell, "F.H. Deacon and Co., Investment Dealers: A Case Study of the Securities Industry, 1897–1945," *Ontario History*, 85:2 (1993), 175.

87 *Re London and General Bank*, [1912] 106 Law Times 285.

88 *Spackman v. Evans*, [1868] L.R., 3 H.L. 171, 193; 37 L.J. Ch. 752.

89 *Re Kingston Cotton Mills Co.*, [1896] 2 Ch. 279 at 688, 65 L.J. Ch. 673.

90 *Re London and General Bank*, [1895] 2 Ch., 682. 64 L.J. Ch. 866. See also *Henry Squire (Cash Chemist) Ltd v. Ball, Baker & Co.*, [1911] 27 T.L.R. 269 aff'd 28 T.L.R. 81, 106 Law Times 197.

91 *Re London and General Bank*, [1895] 2 Ch., 685. 64 LJ Ch. 866.

92 *Re Owen Sound Lumber Co.*, OLR, [1917] 28, 424 and DLR [1917] 33, 486. Weganast, *The Law of Canadian Companies*, 812–13. V. Mitchell, *A Treatise on the Law Relating to Canadian Commercial Corporations* (Montreal: Southam Press, 1916), 1139–45.

93 The best presentation of the proprietary theory can be found in C.B. Couchman, *The Balance-Sheet: Its Preparation, Content and Interpretation* (New York: Journal of Accountancy 1924). The entity theory was summarized by W.A. Paton, *Accounting Theory* (New York: Ronald Press, 1922). Useful reviews can be found in M. Chatfield, *A History of Accounting Thought* (Hinsdale: Dryden Press, 1974), 220–5. G.J. Previts and B.D. Merino, *A History of Accounting in America: A Historical Interpretation of the Cultural Significance of Accounting* (Columbus: Ohio University Press, 1979), 169–80, 220–3.

94 See H.A. Finney, *Consolidated Statements for Holding Companies* (New York: Prentice-Hall, 1923), and W.H. Childs, *Consolidated Statements: Principles and Procedures* (Ithaca, NY: Cornell University Press, 1949).

95 R.G. Walker, *Consolidated Statements: A History and Analysis* (New York: Arno Press, 1978), 77, 353.

96 *Kierskowski v. Grand Trunk Railway*, [1859] 10 LCR, 47. Mitchell, *Canadian Commercial Corporations*, 1377.

97 See Finney, *Consolidated Statements*, chaps. 2–3.

98 R.G.H. Smails, *Accounting Principles* (Toronto: Ryerson Press, 1948), 343.

99 An address by the Security and Exchange Commission's chief accountant well explored how these were not esoteric or petty concerns but had very serious implications. United States, Securities and Exchange Commission, "Accounting Aspects of Business Combinations: Address of Andrew Barr, 27 August 1958," https://www.sec.gov/news/speech/1958/082758barr .pdf.

4. Building the Corporate Realm

1 *PPMC*, 12 July 1923, 692; 19 November 1925, 1335.

2 C. Eis, "The 1919–1930 Merger Movement in American Industry," *Journal of Law & Economics*, 12:2 (1969), 267–96.

3 Reprinted in *PPMC*, 18 October 1923, 1034.

4 W. Thorp, "The Changing Structure of Industry," in President's
Conference on Unemployment, *Recent Economic Changes in the United
States*, I (New York: McGraw-Hill, 1929), 167–218. U.S., Congress, Senate
Temporary National Economic Committee, *The Structure of Industry*, XXVII
(Washington: GPO, 1941), Parts II–V.

5 *Maclean's*, 1 February 1920, 74–5. There is no way to verify the shareholders
and their stakes. The reporter was referring to Alexander Smith and
possibly Frank Anson.

6 *FP*, 29 December 1919, 29 September 1922. *WSJ*, 5 January 1920. *Globe*, 24
March 1920, 12 and 27 April 1920. *PPMC*, 1 January 1920, 15; 13 May 1920,
518.

7 *FP*, 3 January 1920. *PPMC*, 13 May 1920, 548. *Globe*, 7 May 1920, 17
November 1920.

8 *FP*, 1 April 1921; 1 July 1921; 22 and 29 September 1922. *Globe*, 25 June
1921. *Maclean's*, August 1921, 6. *WSJ*, 23 August 1922.

9 *PPMC*, 19 May 1921, 537–8.

10 *PPMC*, December 1921, 198.

11 *MG*, *Globe*, 2 November 1923. *PPMC*, 8 November 1923, 1091, 1107; 13
March 1924, 299.

12 *MG*, 12 November 1923. L.R. Wilson, "A Few High Spots in the Life of L.R.
Wilson" (Toronto, unpublished manuscript, 1945), 35.

13 The transition from senior executives based in manufacturing or
marketing to those who stressed finance was linked by neo-institutional
sociologists to post-1950 economic conditions. In fact, the shift
occurred earlier and more as an ebb and flow within specific industries.
For examples of the neo-institutional perspective, see N. Fligstein,
The Transformation of Corporate Control (Cambridge, MA: Harvard
University Press, 1990); G.F. Davis, K.A. Diekmann, and C.H. Tinsley,
"The Decline and Fall of the Conglomerate Firm in the 1980s: The
Deinstitutionalization of an Organizational Form," *American Sociological
Review*, 59:4 (1994), 547–70.

14 *FP*, 1 April 1933.

15 L.S. Evans, *A Standard History of Ross County, Ohio*, II (Chicago: Lewis
Publishing, 1917), 500–1. The quasi-aristocratic status of the Meads was
most evident in the *Dayton Daily News*, which, for decades, fawned over
the family in a manner akin to how the media in our time have treated
the British "Royals." George Mead rarely missed a chance to exploit
his connections. When Sir William Hearst (who later became Premier
Whitney's successor) left Sault Ste. Marie in 1912 for Toronto, Mead
bought his home, "Eastbourne," and flipped it to the Lake Superior Paper
Company for use as an executive residence. Abitibi after 1928 used the
home to accommodate visitors.

16 J.H. Ingham, ed., *Biographical Dictionary of American Business Leaders* (Westport, CT: Greenwood, 1983), 912–13. Mead Corporation, *In Quiet Ways: George H. Mead, the Man and the Company* (Dayton, OH: Mead Corporation, 1970), 21–75. This romanticized biography is partially accurate for events prior to 1909 but misleading about his activities north of the border, which were dismissed as the "Canadian venture." Contrary to what was probably the intent, Mead's wealth and patronizing attitudes dominate the narrative. The book hints at, but does not elaborate upon, the business and social hostility he engendered.

17 D. McDowall, *Steel at the Sault: Francis H. Clergue, Sir James Dunn, and the Algoma Steel Corporation, 1901–1956* (Toronto: University of Toronto Press, 1984), 23–49. Mead Corporation, *In Quiet Ways*, 56–7.

18 *Paper Mill and Wood Pulp News*, 6 April 1899, 16; 11 August 1900, 4; 25 July 1903, 3. *Globe*, 17 January and 10 November 1900. A quarter of the output was sold to Japan. Clergue had to chase sales in other geographically distant markets like France and Mexico though he described American demand as unlimited. For shining beacon, Kuhlberg, *In the Power of the Government*, 64. His account relies upon G. Carruthers, *Paper-Making* (Toronto: Garden City Press Co-operative, 1947), 663–88, a partially ghost-written account that contained many errors.

19 *OS*, 58 Vict. [1895], ch. 118, An Act to Incorporate the Sault Ste. Marie Pulp and Paper Company. *Globe*, 17 and 24 June 1899. *WP*, 24 September 1903. Sault Ste. Marie *News*, 23 January 1897, 20 October 1900. *PPMC*, May 1903, 10–14, 20; July 1903, 87.

20 SMPL, 996.9.23, 10076, A-3, General Returns of the Operations of the Lake Superior Paper Company for 1902–4. *PPMC*, September 1903, 140–1; April 1904, 11; May 1907, 113; May 1908 126. *Globe*, 18 and 30 May 1908.

21 McDowall, *Steel at the Sault*, 54–9. *WSJ*, 4 January and 8 February 1909; 25 February 1911. *Globe*, 26 October 1910. SMPL, 996.9.23, Hist-Misc Box 4, 20689, Contacts and Agreements in regards to property purchases and titles related to Lake Superior Paper Company, 1911.

22 SMPL, 996.9.23, Hist-Mortgage, Box 1, 16683, First Mortgage, Lake Superior Paper Company to Royal Trust Company, 1 March 1911. *WSJ*, 2 March and 3 April 1911. *PPMC*, January 1912, 25. Sault *Star*, 11 May and 28 August 1912.

23 Mead Corporation, *In Quiet Ways*, 98.

24 *MT*, 2 October 1909, 1422; 29 January 1910, 543; 19 March 1910, 1254; 18 June 1910, p. 2514.

25 The following draws upon my unpublished essay, "'Runs Up and Down, and Mostly Down, Forever': Spanish River and the Emergence of the Canadian Newsprint Industry."

26 *Canadian Men and Women of the Time*, 1017. *Globe*, 18 February 1901, 2 May 1902, 3 January 1903. *PPMC*, June 1903, 48–9; July 1904, 217; September 1905, 262; August 1906, 207–8.

27 *PPMC*, June 1907, 137; July 1907, 156; October 1908; 257; 15 February 1913, 141; 15 April 1913, 282. *Globe*, 29 February 1908, 5 April 1913.

28 *Globe*, 6 June and 13 July 1907, 2 December 1910. *PPMC*, December 1910, 294.

29 *MG*, 23 November 1910. *PPMC*, January 1911, 55; March 1911, 125. SMPL, 992.10, Hist-Mortgage, Box 1, 16678, Deed of Trust and Mortgage, Spanish River Pulp & Paper Mills and Montreal Trust, 1 December 1910; 16687 and 16702, Supplemental Deed, 2 October 1911; 16693, Indenture, 1 November 1911.

30 SMPL, 992.10, Hist-Mortgage, Box 1, 16689, Deed of Trust and Mortgage, Ontario Pulp & Paper Company to Royal Trust, 1 January 1912. *FP*, 13 September 1913.

31 *Globe*, 8 April and June 1912. *WSJ*, 22 March 1912.

32 *MT*, 28 June 1913, 1166, 19 July 1913, 177. *Globe*, 16 June, 17 and 30 July 1913. "Merger genius" in *PPMC*, November 1911, 389.

33 *MT*, January 1913 (Annual), 76–7.

34 *MT*, 23 August 1913, 305; 18 October 1913, 635, 650. *FP*, 15 November 1913. SMPL, Hist.-Mortgage, Box 1, 16686, Mortgage Deed of Trust Between Lake Superior Paper and Montreal Trust, 1 September 1913. This document, which completed the requirements for the merger, was not signed until a week after Grant's "'resignation.'"

35 *PPMC*, 15 February 1917, 180. *Globe*, 30 April 1920. *MT*, 27 September 1913, 532.

36 Quoted in Mead Corporation, *In Quiet Ways*, 100.

37 SMPL, 992.10, Hist-Mortgage Box 1, 16700, Memorandum of Agreement between Spanish River and Canadian Paper Sales, 1 October 1915.

38 SMPL, 992.10, 16698, W.E. Stavert to Bondholders, 20 November 1914. *Globe*, 8, 10 December 1914. *WSJ*, 12 December 1914. *MT*, 18 December 1914, 14.

39 *Globe*, 13 September and 4 October 1917; 9 September 1918; 3 September 1920.

40 *PPMC*, 9 September 1920, 954; 17 February 1921, 191. *MT*, 23 April 1920, 50; 19 March 1920, 32; 7 May 1920, 48; 14 January 1921, 32, 50; 8 September 1922, 26.

41 *PPMC*, 7 October 1920, 1053.

42 AO, RG18-79, B249439, 353, Ferguson to Spanish River Pulp and Paper, 25 September 1919; 358, Ferguson to Mead, 30 October 1919.

43 RG18-79, Proceedings, 7821–89, 14 February 1921; 7890–8534, 25–8 April 1921; Report of the Timber Commission, 26 June 1922, 65. See also *Globe* 2 and 25 February, 13 May 1921.

44 LOSP, No. 3 – Appendix 44 (1924), "Agreement Between His Majesty the King and the Spanish River Pulp and Paper Mills, 15 May 1923," 219–23. Kuhlberg, *In the Power of the Government*, 270–1, stated the Tories imposed the conditions. After the election, they did alter the pricing terms but not the substance of the agreement. AO, RG75-57, OC 131/332, 13 September 1923.

45 AO, RG18-118, Proceedings, XI, 11 December 1940, 1277b. *Globe*, 21 June 1923.

46 SMPL, 992.10, A-3, Box 1, 9752, Spanish River Pulp and Paper to Ferguson, Application for Timber, 19 September 1919. A-1, Box 1, 10409, Report on Spanish River Pulp and Paper Mills Ltd., 1921. MC-8, Box 1, Sec V T-39, 8692, Data for Estimation of Theoretical Annual Cut – Spanish Concession, 1930. A-2, Box 2, 1238, R.O. Sweezey to Mead, Investigation of Spanish River and Sturgeon Falls Limits, 5 December 1917. Hist-Mortgage, Box 2, 16708, Map or Plan Referred to in Approved Recommendation to Council and Signed by Minister, Hon. G.H. Ferguson, 19 July 1926. K-5, Map Ledgers, 66 and 69, Concessions of the Spanish River Pulp and Paper Mills Ltd., 1928.

47 SMPL, 996.9.23, Hist-Mortgage, Box 1, 16696, Algoma Central and Hudson Bay Railway and Lake Superior Paper, Right to Cut Pulpwood on Certain Lands 1 March 1911. AO, RG 1-122, W-8-128 and W-8-550, B271810 and B271815, Algoma Central & Hudson Bay Railway & Spanish River Pulp & Paper Company; transferred to Lake Superior Paper.

48 SMPL, 996.9.15, Hist-Mortgage, Box 6, 20789, Crown and Algoma Central Railway Timber Agreements, 1925; 996.9.23, Box 2, 16705, Agreement between the Algoma Central and Hudson Bay Railway Company and Lake Superior Paper Company, 1 September 1925. AO, RG1-246-3, 42245, R.H. Smith to Ferguson, 23 June 1926.

49 RG1-246-3, 5937, Mead to Ferguson, 17 September 1919; Application of G.H. Mead and J.O. Heyworth, 24 November 1919; Mead to Ferguson, 13 August 1926. OHA, 90.003.30, C. Magrath to Ferguson, 29 August 1928; 90.003.29, F. Gaby to Commission, 23 October 1928.

50 *PPMC*, 19 August 1920, 870.

51 SMPL, 992.10, Hist.-Mortgage, Box 1, 16679, Mortgage Trust Deed, Spanish River Pulp and Paper Mills to Montreal Trust, 1 September 1919; 16697, Option to Purchase, Spanish River Pulp and Paper Mills and Peabody Houghteling, 15 October 1919; 16681, Deed of Trust And Mortgage From the Spanish River Pulp and Paper Mills in Favor of Montreal Trust, 1 March 1921.

52 RG18-79, B249439, 353, Smith to Mead, 9 October 1919; B249441, 397 Circular, Peabody Houghteling, Spanish River $3.5 million 6% mortgage lien gold bonds, October 1919. Kuhlberg, *In the Power of the Government*,

116, declared Mead wrote the copy, which is possible but there is no evidence. The content of the circular was standard for similar offerings by Peabody Houghteling.

53 *WSJ*, 4 and 5 February 1924; 20 March 1924; 6 May 24. *FP*, 11 April 1924. *Globe*, 8 April and 14 May 1924.

54 *Globe*, 26 September 1924. *MG*, 13 January 1925. *FP*, 16 January 1925. *Globe*, 21 August 1924, 10 and 13 January 1925; 4 and 5 April 1925. *WSJ*, 10 January 1925. *MG*, 30 May 1925.

55 *FP*, 29 May 1925; 23 June 1926.

56 *WT*, 9 July 1925.

57 *Northern Canada Power v. Hollinger Consolidated Gold Mines*, OR, 54 (1923), 511–13. RG3, 04-0-354, J.B. Holden to E.W. Drury, 16 February 1923; Holden to N.W. Rowell, 19 February 1923. Correspondence related to northern water powers is scattered across numerous files, including "Long Sault Power," "Hollinger," "Hydro-Electric Power Commission of Ontario," or those related to specific manufacturers and lawyers.

58 RG3, 04-0-354, Anson to Drury, 1 March 1923.

59 RG3, 04-0-354, Drury to Anson, 1, March and 2 March 1923; Rowell to Drury, 2 March 1923.

60 RG3, 04-0-354, G.H. Kilmer to Drury, 10 March 1923; Rowell to Raney, 28 March 1923; Drury to Kilmer, 9 April 1923.

61 RG3, 04-0-354, Kilmer to Drury, 12 April 1923; Drury to Rowell, 14 April 1923.

62 RG3, 06-0-601, S. Lyons to Hollinger Consolidated Gold Mines, 18 March 1924; Holden to Lyons, 28 March 1924; A. Smith to Ferguson, 14 August 1924.

63 RG3, 06-0-500, Hollinger Development: Island Falls, and 06-0-601, Long Sault Rapids.

64 Kuhlberg, *In the Power of the Government*, 251–2. His assertion is based on RG3, 06-0-601, Holden to Lyons, 28 March 1924, written at the inception of the project, which noted the firm already had made an initial $1 million investment and "financial obligations amounting in the aggregate to a much larger sum." No company anywhere was capable of building a generation station at the scale of the Island Falls facility for a mere $1.5 million during the 1920s. Hollinger's costs were never disclosed because the company paid cash and floated $2.3 million in short-term loans. In *Globe*, 28 April 1924, it declared the minimum budget was $4 million, with another $750,000 for the transmission lines. Smith offered $5 million. Abitibi's engineer estimated the construction costs at $5.3 million. Hollinger's personnel thought at least $6 million (RG3, 06-0-500, Timmins to Ferguson, 16 January 1925). Timmins sought $6.5 million, they settled at $5.5 million. Timmins told shareholders this recouped the investment costs but he did not reveal the delayed form of payment. His refusal to release

contractual materials related to Island Falls further suggests the loss was deemed significant. HUBL, Hollinger Consolidated Gold Mines, *AR* (1925), 2–3, and *Globe*, 19 May 1925.

65 RG3, 06-0-500, Agreement of Sale between Hollinger Consolidated Gold Mines and Abitibi Power and Paper, 13 May 1925. *WSJ*, 6 May 1925. *FP*, 15 and 22 May 1925. The bonds, nominally $100, were assessed at a worth of $90 due to the serial feature. This made the net present value of the deal to Hollinger no more than $4.95 million. Abitibi expended another $1.6 million to bring the station and transmission network into conformity with its own requirements. Abitibi's final valuation of the property was moderately close to the capital outlays. I was unable to find evidence that the terms of the lease for Island Falls had any material impact.

66 *NYT*, 1 December 1917, 14 November 1922. *MG*, 22 June 1928. *PPMC*, 28 June 1928, 884

67 *Globe*, 8 May, 10 and 20 September 1926. *PPMC*, 28 June 1928, 887.

68 *OS*, 9 Edw. VII [1909], ch. 69, Act Respecting Aid to Certain Railroads, 4d and 4e. RG3, 05-0-070, Bowman to Lieutenant-Governor-in-Council, 25 June 1920; T. Gibson to H. Mills, 12 July 1920.

69 RG3, 05-0-070, Press Statement by Drury, 27 July 1920; Statement, Minister of Railways and Canals, n.d. LAC, RG43-A-I-2, 616, 19489, Grand Trunk Pacific Railway Co. – Mead Investment Co. *Globe*, 27 and 29 July 1920.

70 *PPMC*, 29 July 1920, 811, 816; 16 September 1920, 966, 982. *CSI*, G15. RG1-246-3, 32405, Application of Fort William Paper, 10 June 1922.

71 RG3, 04-0-384, Bowman to Drury, 6 March 1923; Fort William Pulpwood, February–April 1923. *PPMC*, 10 August 1922, 682; 5 October 1922, 862; 22 March 1923, 319.

72 RG3, 04-0-408, F.N. Youngman to Bowman, 17 March 1923. RG1-264-3, 32405, Agreement between the Crown and Fort William Paper, 22 March 1923.

73 *Globe*, 26 September and 3 October 1923. LOSP, No. 3 (1926), *Report of the Minister of Lands and Forests for 1925*, 11. *PPMC*, 8 November 1923, 1105.

74 RG3, 06-0-469, Memorandum of Conference re. Fort William Power matters with Adam Beck, 13 January 1925; C.C. Hele to Ferguson, 5 March 1925.

75 RG3, 06-0-469, C.C. Hele to Ferguson, 5 March 1925; Supply of Power to Kaministiquia Power Co., 12 March 1925; G. McCrea to Ferguson, 14 October 1925; G.R. Gray to Ferguson, 25 November 1925; Magrath to Ferguson, 19 December 1925. LOSP, No. 46 (1925), Hydro Electric Commission of Ontario, *AR* for 1924, 31–3; No. 26 (1926), *AR* for 1925, 31–3; No 26 (1927), *AR* for 1926, x–xi, 38–40.

76 RG3, 06-0-674, E.E. Johnson to Ferguson, 25 February 1925; 06-0-1319, Lyons to Ferguson, 3 May 1926.

77 LOSP, No. 3 (1926), *Report of the Minister of Lands and Forests for 1925*, 11.
RG1-246-3, 39865, Tenders on West Side of Lake Nipigon, September 1925.
LOSP, No. 3 – Appendix 30 (1927), Agreement Between His Majesty … and
Provincial Paper Mills, 27 February 1926, 84, 86. At the time of the tender,
300,000 cords of pulpwood were estimated in Provincial's concession. In
CSI, G25, this was recalibrated to 3 million cords, and Provincial Paper
held another 1.5 million in a separate concession. The correspondence
related to the political shenanigans is copious but located in less accessible
fonds. TBHSA, A83/1, Files 3 and 4, were part of a cache buried in a tin
box under a house in Thunder Bay. See also AO, RG1-246-3, land files
19284 (I), 61304 (I), 66423 (I).

78 *CSI*, G16. TBHSA, A83/2/3, Draft of Fort William Pulp and Paper
Agreement, n.d. LOSP, No. 3 (1927), Agreement between His Majesty the
King and Fort William Paper Company, 21 September 1926.

79 *MG*, 4 June 1926. *Moody's Manual of Industrials* (1927), 1868. 81.20.150,
Report to the Bondholders' Protective Committee, 18 August 1932, 4. *CSI*,
G16-17. *Globe*, 13 April 1956.

80 *WT*, 17 June 1925, 18 November 1924. For a fine analysis, J. Mochoruk,
*Formidable Heritage: Manitoba's North and the Cost of Development, 1870 to
1930* (Winnipeg: University of Manitoba Press, 2004), 270–89, 302–1. The
following account summarizes the most crucial developments and the
interpretation varies from Mochoruk's at different points.

81 AM, NR 0225, GR7721, Department of Interior File 1325 and 12655. CCA
0059, GR6427, Manitoba Pulp and Paper Company Limited. LAC, RG15-
D-V-1, 1284, 604012, W.W. Cory to B.L. York, 10 January 1921; P. Locke to
York, 12 January 1921.

82 604012, Tender Pulpwood Berth No. 1. *Canada Gazette*, 54:35 (26 February
1921), 3534–7. 604012, York to J.D. McArthur, 20 March 1922.

83 604012, McArthur to J. Lougheed, 23 November 1921; Locke to York, 24
February 1922; McArthur to Stewart, 22 September 1922.

84 G.H. Seaman to Stewart, 11 June 1923, and A.T. Thompson to Cory, 12 June
1923, reprinted in *WT*, 12 June 1925.

85 604012, Part 2, McArthur to Stewart, 1 August 1924, and Stewart to
McArthur, 9 September 1924. RG15, 1286, 616290, Part 1, Stewart to
McArthur, 4 September 1924.

86 *Winnipeg Free Press*, 20 November 1924. AM, MG13, 12, 4–44, D.A. Keizer
to J. Bracken, 25 November 1924. See Mochoruck, Formidable Heritage,
279–87, for a detailed analysis.

87 616290, Part 1, Bracken to Stewart, 21 November 1924; Cory to York, 6
December 1924. *WT*, 24 and 27 November, 24 December 1924.

88 *WT*, 18 December 1924, 9 April 1925, 23 March 1925.

89 *WT*, 4 and 5, 29 May 1925.

90 *WT*, 9 and 19 June 1925. 604012, Part 4, His Majesty George V and the Manitoba Pulp and Paper Company Ltd. re. Manitoba Pulpwood Sale, 12 June 1925. Schedule C, which contained the key provisions, was authorized as an order-in-council, PC 885, 5 June 1925.

91 *WT*, 8 and 22 June 1925.

92 *Globe*, 12 August 1925. LAC, RG95-1, 1645. 095/33426, Manitoba Paper Company Limited. *NYT*, 1 April 1926. 604012, W.N. Hurlburt to Peabody Houghteling, 24 March 1926.

93 *WT*, 16 July 1925.

94 *WT*, 9 and 30 July 1925. LAC, RG15-D-V-1, 1286, 616290 Agreement between His Majesty … and Manitoba Paper Company, 12 February 1927. RG13-A-2. v.1968, 1927–237, Department of the Interior – Agreement with Manitoba Paper Co., Ltd. re price of pulpwood. 1927/02; 309, 1926–1850, Department of the Interior – Agreement with Manitoba Paper Co. for additional wood supplies. *WT*, 6 April 1929, 2 February 1927.

95 AO, F8, MU1032, Folder 4, General Conditions with Respect to the Metagami Pulp Limit, offered for lease by tenure, 31 December 1913. *PPMC*, 4 January 1917, 1.

96 AO, RG22-5800, 1339/21, *National Trust v. Mattagami Pulp and Paper*, Mortgage Deed of Trust, 1 May 1916. *PPMC*, 1 March 1916, 114.

97 *PPMC*, 3 April 1919, 338; 22 May 1919, 486; 5 June 1919, 532; 12 June 1919, 562–4; 27 November 1919, 1030. 1339/21, Statements of claim, 27 July and 4 September 1925.

98 D. MacKenzie, *The Clarkson Gordon Story* (Toronto: University of Toronto Press, 1989), 23–6, 32–3. *Globe*, 7 December 1923.

99 1339/21, Statement of claim, 27 July 1925; Affidavit of G.T. Clarkson, 28 July 1925; Memorandum on Mattagami, 10 February 1927.

100 RG3, 06-0-1173, Circular letters of I.W. Killam, 20 June 1925, 23 February 1926; D. Chisholm to Ferguson, 15 April 1926.

101 RG3, 06-0-615, Ferguson to C. Dix, 1 April 1925. *Porcupine Advance*, 31 October 1923, 11 June 1924, 7 October and 2 December 1926.

102 RG3, 04-0-359, W.J. Boland to Drury, 7 May 1923; 06-0-615, Boland to Ferguson, 25 April 1925. Drury's instructions are written on the 1923 letter.

103 RG3, 06-0-615, C. McCrea to Ferguson, 23 February 1925.

104 1339/21, Order, 17 May 1926.

105 *CSI*, L-1.

106 *Globe*, 14 and 25 February 1927, 7 and 14 March 1927. *NYT*, 11 March 1927. *FP*, 18 March 1927.

107 *FP*, 15 April and 14 October 1927. *Globe*, 10 and 22 October 1927. *Barron's*, 10 October 1927. *WSJ*, 22 October 1927.

108 *FT*, 9 December 1927.

109 The terms of exchange for Spanish River became three options (or combinations of any two of the three). These ranged from 1.33 shares of Abitibi 6 per cent preferred to 1 share of Abitibi 6 per cent preferred and 0.5 shares of Abitibi common for each 7 per cent Spanish River preferred share. Widespread confidence about the merger led most of the Spanish River preferred shareholders to receive Abitibi common stock.

110 *WSJ*, 22 and 28 October 1927. *NYT*, 27 October 1927. *FP*, 28 October 1927. *Globe*, 25 and 26 October 1926.

111 V. Morawetz, "Shares without Nominal or Par Value," Harvard Law Review, 26: 8 (1913), 729–31. C. Wickersham, "The Progress of the Law on No Par Value Common Stock," *Harvard Law Review*, 37:4 (1924), 464–77. For a full analysis of the theoretical and practical issues for business, along with a review of state laws, see J.R. Wildman and W. Powell, *Capital Stock Without Par Value* (Chicago: A.W. Shaw, 1928). This book was lauded as one of the premier contributions to the accounting literature during the 1920s.

112 Scudder, Stevens, and Clark, *Investment Counsel* (Boston: Scudder, Stevens, and Clark, 1922), 9–20. D. Langmuir, *The Fixed Trust: A Statement of Underlying Principles* (New York: Distributors Group, 1931), 8. E.L. Smith, *Common Stocks as Long Term Investments* (New York: Macmillan, 1925), 4–5. Smith's monograph was a thoughtful monograph that argued the returns on common stocks were superior to bonds and other securities. Brokers and other investment dealers lured clients with very selective quotes from the study.

113 *FP*, 28 October 1927, 18 November 1927. *Globe*, 15 November and 14 December 1927.

114 *MG, NYT*, 14 November 1927. *FP*, 18 November and 9 December 1927, 20 January 1928.

115 *FT*, 28 October 1927. *MT*, 27 January 1928. *NYT*, 25 October 1927. *FP*, 28 October 1927. *Globe*, 25 October, 15 and 16 November, 14 December 1927.

116 *Globe*, 19 January 1928, 18 May 1928, 18 June 1928. *PPMC*, 29 June 1928, 888.

117 YUL, Ndy79 C1+Ab5h, A plan for the acquisition by Abitibi Power & Paper Company, Limited, of the common capital stock of the Spanish River Pulp and Paper Mills, Limited, Fort William Power Company, Limited, Manitoba Paper Company, Limited, Ste. Anne Paper Company, Ltd., Murray Bay Paper Company, Ltd. (New York: s.n., 1927), 2.

118 81.20.151, Block Piles, Advances to Ste. Anne, 27 March 1933, noted much of the wood in piles at Espanola and Sturgeon Falls were at least five to six years old, predating the onset of the industry's crisis.

119 2994/32, Condensed and approximate statement of affairs as of 10 September 1932, from standpoint of bondholders, Schedule A. HUBL,

Price Waterhouse, Report on Abitibi Power and Paper Company Financial Statements, 2 March 1933.

120 SMPL, B-2, Box 1, File 6, 16825–9, E.R.C. Clarkson and Sons, Spanish River Pulp and Paper Company in Liquidation, 1928. This set of records includes balance sheets, tables of assets and liabilities, trial balances, and general ledgers.

121 *CSI*, J2-J16. This appendix recorded known construction costs, purchases associated with the different operations, and the declared book values in 1927. In at least one case, Fort William Paper, George Mead was caught in blatant asset inflation. Before Abitibi bought its investment stake, the company hired an independent engineer for an appraisal and his report forced a reduction of the book value by a quarter. But the firm was still overvalued in the share exchange.

122 *FP*, 9 March 1928. *WSJ*, 27 January 1928. *Globe*, 2 March and 13 April 1928.

123 Quoted in Mead Corporation, *In Quiet Ways*, 111.

124 Kuhlberg, *In the Power of the Government*, 306. He declared that National City conducted the estimates, and orchestrated the overvaluation, of the licenses and properties. In fact, Abitibi's management carried out those activities and they were largely complete before the underwriting.

125 Estimates of the Canadian securities business during the 1920s have not been developed, but see R.C. Michie, "The Canadian Securities Market, 1850–1914," *Business History Review*, 62:1 (1988), 35–73.

126 V. Carosso, *Investment Banking in America* (Cambridge, MA: Harvard University Press, 1970), 84–98, 271–81. W.N. Peach, *The Security Affiliates of National Banks* (Baltimore: Johns Hopkins University Press, 1941), Table 1, 83.

127 W.H. Kniffin, *American Banking Practice – A Treatise on the Practical Operation of a Bank* (New York: McGraw-Hill, 1921), 149. T.J. Kavanaugh, *Bank Credit Methods and Practice* (New York: Bankers Publishing 1921), 17–32. For textbooks, M.B. Foster, *Banking* (New York: Alexander Hamilton Institute, 1917); C.A. Phillips, *Bank Credit: A Study of the Principles and Factors Underlying Advances Made by Banks to Borrowers* (New York: Macmillan 1920). For banking manuals, see the New York National City Bank of New York, *The Banking Apprenticeship Plan* (New York: National City Bank of New York, 1917) and *The Work of Number Eight* (New York: National City Bank of New York, 1919).

128 Most would be familiar today to business students. M.D. Miller, *Bank Loans on Statement and Character* (New York: Ronald Press, 1927), 135–249. R.F. Prudden, *The Bank Credit Investigator* (New York: Bankers Publishing, 1922), 52–129. G.G. Munn, *Bank Credit: Principles and Operating Procedure* (New York: McGraw-Hill, 1925).

129 G.G.P. Knapp, *How Banks Increase Their Business* (Chicago: Rand McNally, 1926), 4. *NYT*, 15 July 1927.

130 Most accounts of National City's activities were written after the Wall Street crash or the Pecora hearings and are sensationalist and prejudicial. More objective interpretations include T.F. Huertas and J.L. Silverman, "Charles E. Mitchell: Scapegoat of the Crash?" *Business History Review*, 60:1 (1986), 81–103; G.J. Benson, *The Separation of Commercial and Investment Banking* (New York: Macmillan, 1990), 20–134.

131 Peach, *The Security Affiliates*, 20.

132 F.L. Allen, *The Lords of Creation* (New York: Harper and Brothers, 1935), 311–15. J. Seligman, *The Transformation of Wall Street: A History of the Securities and Exchange Commission and Modern Corporate Finance* (Boston: Houghton Mifflin, 1982), 24–5. Y Amihud, T.S.Y. Ho, and R.A. Schwartz, *Market Making and the Changing Structure of the Securities Industry* (Lexington: Lexington Books, 1985), 151–76.

133 E. Wilson, "Sunshine Charley," *New Republic*, 59 (28 June 1933), 177–8. B. Barton, "Is There Anything Here that Other Men Couldn't Do?" *American Magazine*, 95 (February 1923), 128–35.

134 National City Company, *Putting Your Dollars to Work* (New York: National City, 1928). A. Dawley, *Struggles for Justice: Social Responsibility and the Liberal State* (Cambridge, MA: Harvard University Press, 1991), 327–30.

135 National City Bank of New York, *If We Divided All the Money: How Much Do You Think You Would Get?* (New York: National City Bank of New York, 1920), 3, 15.

136 USEEP, 22 February 1933, 1828–39; 27 February 1933, 2051–117; 28 February 1933, 2122–69, 2170–2.

137 *Globe*, 16 May 1928. YUL, Ndy79 C1+Ab5h, $16,000,000, Abitibi Power & Paper Company, Limited, 6% cumulative preferred stock, par value $100 per share (New York: s.n., 1928); $10,000,000, Abitibi Power & Paper Company, Limited (6% cumulative preferred stock, par value $100 per share) (New York: s.n., 1928).

138 *NYT*, 27 April and 28 May 1928. *WSJ*, 28 April 1928. *Globe*, 16 and 28 May 1928. *FP*, 1 June 1928. Press accounts were confused about the specific terms for exchanges of securities and how various bonds were liquidated and then refinanced. The additional $13 million in preferred stock raised the fixed charges by $1.46 per ton at 80 per cent of capacity.

139 AO, RG4-32, B247998, F.H. Kilmer, Re. Registration of Mortgage, Abitibi Power and Paper Co. and the Montreal Trust Co., 1928. YUL, Ndy79 C1+Ab5h, McGibbon, Mitchell and Stairs, "Indenture and Mortgage from Abitibi Power and Paper Co. Ltd. in favour of Montreal Trust Company (Canadian Trustee) and the National City Bank of New York (Authenticating Trustee), Securing an Issue of First Mortgage Gold Bonds, 1 June 1928."

140 YUL, Ndy79 C1+Ab5h, $50,000,000, Abitibi Power & Paper Company, Limited (organized under the Companies Act of the Dominion of Canada): first mortgage gold bonds, series A, 5%, due 1953: to be dated June 1, 1928, to mature June 1, 1953 (New York: s.n., 1928). *WSJ*, 28 June and 2 July 1928.

141 Calculated from *CSI*, L1-L2.

142 The scholarly literature on mergers is massive but contains few efforts to gauge later performance or the realization of prophesized gains. Useful appraisals include G. Meeks, *Disappointing Marriage: A Study of the Gains from Mergers* (New York: Cambridge University Press, 1977); D.J. Ravenscraft and F.M. Scherer, *Mergers, Sell-Offs and Economic Efficiency* (Washington: Brookings Institution, 1987); R.E. Caves, "Mergers, Takeovers and Economic Efficiency: Foresight vs. Hindsight," *International Journal of Industrial Organization* 7:1 (1989), 151–74; F.R. Lichtenberg, *Corporate Takeovers and Productivity* (Cambridge, MA: MIT Press, 1992). I benefited from the analysis in L.-H. Röller, J. Stennek, and F. Verboven, "Efficiency Gains from Mergers," in F. Ilzkovitz and R. Meiklejohn, eds., *European Merger Control: Do We Need an Efficiency Defence?* (London: Edward Elgar, 2006), 84–201.

143 *WSJ*, 7 March 1929.

144 A marvellous description by Charles Vining. JLAO, 75 (1941), Appendix 1, 24 April 1940, 170.

5. From Prosperity to Crisis

1 *NYT*, 15 March 1926, 23 January 1928. On both dates his yacht was disabled off Lookout Lightship and was towed to Charleston by the Coast Guard.

2 *Galveston Daily News*, 1 October 1924. *Parker v. New England Oil Corporation*, 8 F. 2d 392 [D. Mass. 1925] and 13 F. 2d 158 [D. Mass. 1926]. The case dealt with their maladministration of the corporate estate. The court decided the alleged market conspiracy was not germane and dismissed it.

3 *NYT*, 3 April 1929, 8 April 1929, 4 May 1929, 29 August 1929.

4 Author's translation and adaptation from Book III, chap. 8, in P. Villey and V.-L. Saulnier, eds., *Les essais de Michel de Montaigne* (Paris: Presses Universitaires de France, 1965), 410.

5 U.S., Department of Agriculture, *American Forests and Forest Products*, Statistical Bulletin 21 (Washington: GPO, 1928), Table 155. U.S., Congress, Senate, *National Pulp and Paper Requirements in Relation to Forest Conservation*, CSS 9878 (Washington: GPO, 1935), 71. U.S., Bureau of the Census, *Census of Manufactures: Newspapers, Periodicals, et al.* (Washington: GPO, 1947), Tables 6A and 6F.

6 U.S., Congress, Senate, *Survey of Pulp Woods on the Public Domain*, CSS 7671 (Washington: GP0, 1920), 5–6. Department of Agriculture, *How the United States Can Meet Its Present and Future Pulpwood Requirements*, Bulletin 1241 (Washington: Department of Agriculture, 1924), 32. R.S. Kellogg, *Pulpwood and Wood Pulp in North America* (New York: McGraw-Hill, 1923), 219.

7 See U.S., Department of Agriculture, *Regional Development of the Tongass National Forest, Alaska*, Bulletin 950 (Washington: GPO, 1921); U.S. Congress, Senate, *Pulpwood Supply in Alaska*, CSS 9204 (Washington: GPO, 1930). U.S., Department of Agriculture, *Timber Depletion and the Answer*, Circular 112 (Washington: GPO, 1927); *America and the World's Woodpile*, Circular 21 (Washington: GPO, 1928).

8 A.N. Pack, *Our Vanishing Forests* (New York: Macmillan, 1923), 90. G.P. Ahern, *Deforested America* (Washington: n.p., 1928), 5.

9 J. Cameron, *The Development of Governmental Forest Control in the United States* (Baltimore: Johns Hopkins University Press, 1928), 102. Although an academic work, this is a delightful swashbuckling polemic that reflects social concerns about American forest practices.

10 O.E. McGillicuddy, "The Paper and Paper Production Situation," *North American Review*, 1 January 1924, 616–20. *Globe*, 25 June and 5 December 1925. *FP*, 8 July and 31 August 1923, 28 April 1924.

11 *Maclean's*, 1 January 1924. *Globe*, 3 June 1924, 2 January 1925, 23 and 28 March 1925.

12 *WSJ*, 26 March 1925. *Barron's*, 26 April 1926. *FP*, 30 July and 27 August 1926, 5 June 1925. *Globe*, 23 April 1925.

13 *Maclean's*, 1 January 1925; 15 October 1928.

14 *Maclean's*, 15 April 1927.

15 *FP*, 2 and 30 July 1926, 10 August 1923, 1 October 1924. *PPMC*, January 1925 (annual issue), 96–8. *FP*, 20 August 1926.

16 *FP*, 6 February 1925, 27 May 1927. U.S., Department of Agriculture, *American Forests and Forest Products*, Tables 151 and 152.

17 *NYT*, 29 June 1924. *WSJ*, 10 October 1923. *NYT*, 14 November 1923. *WSJ*, 9 April 1924. *Globe*, 29 April 1924.

18 *Globe*, 23 May 1924. *WSJ*, 31 October 1924. *Globe*, 20 June 1925.

19 *FP*, 5 and 26 June, 17 July, 4 September 1925.

20 W. Hamilton and Associates, *Price and Price Policies* (New York: McGraw-Hill, 1938), 531. I. Till, "The Fiction of the Quoted Price," *Law and Contemporary Problems*, 4:3 (1937), 363–74.

21 N.K. Ohanian, *The American Pulp and Paper Industry, 1900–1940: Mill Survival, Firm Structure, and Industry Relocation* (Westport: Greenwood, 1993). L.T. Stevenson, *The Background and Economics of American Papermaking* (New York: Harper and Brothers, 1940), 218–19.

22 J.R. Withrow, "Basing-Point and Freight-Rate Price Systems Under the Anti-Trust Laws," *University of Pennsylvania Law Review*, 85:7 (1937), 690–715. M.J. Beckmann, "Spatial Price Policies Revisited," *Bell Journal of Economics*, 7:2 (1976), 619–30. M.P. Espinosa, "Delivered Pricing, FOB Pricing, and Collusion in Spatial Markets," *RAND Journal of Economics*, 23:1 (1992), 64–85. M. Zhang and R.J. Sexton, "FOB or Uniform Delivered Prices: Strategic Choices and Welfare Effects," *Journal of Industrial Economics*, 49:2 (2001), 197–220.

23 Congress, Senate, *Newsprint Paper Industry*, CSS 9320 (Washington: GPO, 1930), 49–51.

24 Most arguments that International Paper acted as a price leader during this period are derived from two studies by the FTC. However, the surviving records in NARA RG122.4 suggest the analysis drew upon *NYT* stories. The alternative pattern emerges if the *Globe*, *FP*, *MG*, *PPMC*, and *WSJ* are also used for tracking.

25 *PPMC*, 27 April 1922, 338.

26 JLAO, 75 (1941), Appendix 1, 24 April 1940, 173–4.

27 *Globe*, 27 June 1925.

28 *PPMC*, 5 November 1925, 1265.

29 *FP*, 30 October 1925.

30 Canada, House of Commons, Proceedings of the Standing Committee on Banking and Commerce, Exhibits 48 and 65, 1052. 1058–9. E.H. Bowman, "Strategy and the Weather," *Sloan Management Review*, 17:2 (1976), 49–62. This pioneering essay documented how corporate reports attribute positive performance to executive leadership and poor results to external conditions, the "weather."

31 ANQ, P350, Discours, XXI, Speech to Club St. Denis, 14 avril 1923. For a full analysis, see B.L. Vigod, *Quebec Before Duplessis: The Political Career of Louis-Alexandre Taschereau* (Montreal: McGill-Queen's University Press, 1986), 108–43; and Y. Roby, *Les Québécois et les investissements américains (1918–1929)* (Quebec City: Les Presses de l'Université Laval, 1976), 119–206.

32 *MG*, 9 December 1927. *Industrial Canada*, 27:10 (1927), 66.

33 *Globe*, 30 June 1925. 30 July 1925. *WSJ* and *Globe*, 5 April 1926. *Globe*, 2 June 1925. *NYT*, 11 February 1925.

34 *Globe*, 4 December 1925, 10 September 1926.

35 Author's translation from V. Gratton, "Actions et répercussions," *Actualité économique*, 3:9 (1927), 180.

36 *MG*, 5 November 1928. *Globe*, 30 July 1925.

37 Quebec, *Rapport du ministre des terres et forêts du Québec*, 1925–6, 28–30; and for 1926–7, 27.

38 Author's translation from *Débats de l'Assemblée législative (débats reconstitués)*, 16e législature, 4e session, 11 janvier 1927, retrieved from

http://www.assnat.qc.ca/en/travaux-parlementaires/assemblee
-nationale/16-4/journal-debats/19270111/92085.html. *PPMC*, 13 January
1927, 62; 20 January 1927, 20. *Globe*, 12 January 1927. *NYT*, 16 January
1927. Many newspapers mangled the conversion to English. The *New York
Times* presented the statement as a muse: "Is it not time to ask whether this
extraordinary expansion should not have some limit ... [and] be better to
slow up a little and not lend too much encouragement to the establishment
of new mills?"

39 *NYT*, 18 December 1927. *MG*, 8 June and 5 November 1928. *Globe*, 8 and 9
June 1928.

40 *Saturday Night*, 24 November 1928. The timing of the article and several
others that followed within two weeks was hardly coincidental – it
matched the Montreal meetings on industry stabilization.

41 *Globe*, 2 February 1926. *PPMC*, 4 February 1926, 136.

42 *Globe*, 16 June 1925. LOSP, No. 3 (1926), *Annual Report of the Department of
Lands and Forests for 1925*, 12.

43 LOSP, No. 3 (1926), 7–8.

44 RG3, 06-0-893, H.E. McGill to Ferguson, 20 November 1926; Ferguson to
Finlayson, 11 November 1926; C.C. Hele to McGill, 29 November 1926.
Sudbury Star, 19 January 1927.

45 LOSP, No. 3 – Appendix 45 (1924), Abitibi Power and Paper Company
Ltd., Additional Area, 12 July 1923, 225. *CSI*, G2. RG3, 6-0-467, Ferguson
to Lyons, 4 November 1925; 6-0-893, Ferguson to Wilson, 22 April
1926. The terms of the agreement, including the preamble (which was
hardly offensive with its discussion of Abitibi's capital structure since
everything was already public knowledge), were written by the Farmers'
administration, *not* the Conservatives. Abitibi personnel estimated the
extraction costs at $9.50 per cord, more than twice the costs of normal
operations.

46 RG22-5800, 1339/21, Memorandum on Mattagami valuation, 1 October
1926. RG1-246-3, 3267, I, Kilmer to Finlayson, 26 February 1927; Finlayson
to Cain, 4 March 1927. W. Cain to Finlayson, Finlayson to Cain, 28
February 1927. LOSP, No. 3 (1928), *Report of the Department of Lands and
Forests for 1927*, 14. RG3, 6-0-467, Ferguson to Lyons, 4 November 1925; 6-0-
893, Ferguson to Wilson, 22 April 1926.

47 RG3, 04-0-142, Kapuskasing file, which contains the contract of October
1920; 05-0-66, Spruce Falls Pulp and Paper Limited. P.J. Butcher, "The
Establishment of a Pulp and Paper Industry at Kapuskasing" (master's
thesis, University of Western Ontario, 1978), 88–92. E.C. Drury, *Farmer
Premier: The Memoirs of E.C. Drury* (Toronto: McClelland and Stewart,
1966), 132.

48 Butcher, "Kapuskasing," 112–25. LOSP, No. 3 – Appendix 31 (1927), Agreement between His Majesty the King ... and the Spruce Falls Company, 5 January 1926. F9-1-0-11, B253672, J.H. Black to Ferguson, 19 February 1929.

49 *FP*, 4 September 1925.

50 International Paper, *The International Paper Company, 1898–1924: Its Origin and Growth in a Quarter of a Century* (New York: International Paper, 1924). T. Heinrich, "Product Diversification in the U.S. Pulp and Paper Industry: The Case of International Paper, 1899–1941," *Business History Review*, 75:3 (2001), 475–82.

51 *WSJ*, 28 and 30 May 1924. *NYT*, 30 May 1924. *FP*, 6 June 1924. The firm's official position was that Dodge (who was seventy-three years old) resigned voluntarily but there was little doubt the Chace Boston interests (who pushed for Graustein's appointment and in 1936 for his removal) precipitated the coup. Dodge was promoted to the figurehead position of chairman and left that position the next year, bitter about how the board had treated him.

52 *WSJ*, 12 June 1924; *Barron's*, September 1924, 3 May 1926, 30 July 1928. By 1929 Graustein owned 70,000 common shares, about 7 per cent of the stock.

53 *WSJ*, 28 June, 8 July, and 10 September 1924. *FP*, 24 June and 4 July 1925. *Globe*, 1 October 1925. Graustein was still on the bondholders' protective committee during the judicial sale. The bondholders received approximately twice the amount of the principal and arrears on their securities.

54 YUL, Ndy79 U2 +In8h, Map showing timber lands of International Paper Co. (in Quebec) and the Riordon and Gatineau Cos. (New York: International Paper, 1925); *Properties of International Paper Company and Affiliated Companies* (New York: International Paper, 1928); Ndy54 U2 +In7m, *Gatineau River Properties of International Paper and Power Company* (New York: International Paper, 1928).

55 *WSJ*, 20 March and 5 May 1925. *FP*, 15 May 1925.

56 YUL, Ndy79 C1 +C16h, International Paper, *Gatineau Newsprint Paper Mill* (New York: International Paper, 1926); *Three Rivers Mill of Canadian International Paper Company* (New York: International Paper, 1926). *NYT*, 17 October 1925.

57 *Barron's*, 20 March 1925; *WSJ*, 17 October and 10 November 1925, 1 January 1927. YUL, Ndy79 U2 +In8h, *Survey of Expansion of International Paper Company During 1927* (New York: International Paper Co., 1928), 4–12; *Survey of Expansion of Canadian Hydro-Electric Corporation, Limited, Gatineau Power Company, Canadian International Paper Company and Affiliated*

Companies During 1928 (New York: International Paper and Power Company, 1929), 1–6.

58 W. Parenteau, "The Woods Transformed: The Emergence of the Pulp and Paper Industry in New Brunswick, 1918–1931," *Acadiensis*, 22:1 (1992), 14–16, 2–23.

59 New Brunswick, *Synoptic Reports of the New Brunswick Legislative Assembly* (1920), Appendix, 11.

60 New Brunswick, *Annual Report of the Department of Lands and Mines* (1929), 10–11; (1930), 8–9.

61 BEA, SMT, 8/26, Confidential Memorandum as to the Newfoundland Power and Paper Co., 24 January 1927; 8/27, Memorandum of Principal Terms of Proposed Option, 13 May 1927. *WSJ*, 5 August 1927, 26 January and 14 May 1928.

62 New Brunswick, *Synoptic Reports* (1926), 18.

63 Heinrich, "Product Diversification," 484–7. HUBL, International Power and Paper, *AR* (1930), 20–1.

64 *Globe*, 9 October 1919. *NYT*, 3 October 1925, 22 July 1927, 14 April and 2 October 1928. *WSJ*, 7 April 1926; 7 August 1928.

65 F8-8, B299684, Quebec Power Contract and Gatineau Contract files. LOSP, No. 26 (1927), *Annual Report of the Hydro-Electric Power Commission of Ontario for 1926*, viii.

66 *Barron's*, 3 May and 16 April 1926. *FP*, 24 June 1927.

67 *FP*, 7 September 1928. For the reaction to International Paper's licenses, see Parenteau, "The Woods Transformed," 29–34, 40–1; J.K. Hiller, "The Politics of Newsprint: The Newfoundland Pulp and Paper Industry, 1915–1939," *Acadiensis*, 19:2 (1990), 25–7.

68 *Barron's*, 16 October 1927. *WSJ*, 28 April 1926, 11 April 1928.

69 *NYT*, 4 June 1923. *WSJ*, 23 July 1923; 12, 22, and 24 January 1924. *PPMC*, 29 March 1923, 342. Holt's and Gundy's backgrounds are available in many sources but useful insights are C. Armstrong and H.V. Nelles, *Monopoly's Moment: The Organization and Regulation of Canadian Utilities* (Toronto: University of Toronto Press, 1988), 101–6, 297–9; D. McDowall, *Quick to the Frontier: Canada's Royal Bank* (Toronto: McClelland and Stewart, 1993), 82, 239–43.

70 *WSJ*, 1 November 1923, 16 and 19 July 1924. *FP*, 30 March 1923, 4 January 1924, 23 April and 7 May 1926. *Moody's Manual of Investments: American and Foreign, 1927* (New York: John Moody, 1928), 2688. Port Alfred was a fine illustration of how the press misread a company's status. The firm was presumed to be doing well because it had a low capitalization per ton, the mills were located near timber, and Holt was in charge.

71 BANQ, P149, Minute Books of Directors' Meetings, M–8-6, 25 November 1925, 43–6; M-9-7, 9 December 1925, 51. Gilles Piédalue, "Les groupes

financiers et la guerre du papier au Canada, 1920–1930," *Revue d'Histoire de l'Amérique Française*, 30:2 (1976), 240.

72 Canada, House of Commons, Proceedings of the Standing Committee, 771, 787.

73 M.D. Shutter, ed., *History of Minneapolis, Gateway to the Northwest*, Vol. 3 (Chicago: S.J. Clarke, 1923), 298–306. Backus-Brooks has not been researched in any depth. A sympathetic treatment (but non-critical about Backus himself) is M. Kuhlberg, "'eyes wide open'": E.W. Backus and the Pitfalls of Investing in Ontario's Pulp and Paper Industry, 1902–1932," *Journal of the Canadian Historical Association*, 16:1 (2005), 201–33. More balanced is the account in J. Mochoruk, *Formidable Heritage: Manitoba's North and the Cost of Development, 1870 to 1930* (Winnipeg: University of Manitoba Press, 2004), 271–88. Even with the jump to a large size in the 1920s, three or four persons apparently held most of the common stock of Minnesota and Ontario, with Backus retaining the majority.

74 *Fort Frances Times and Rainy Lake Herald*, 15 April 1913. F8, B2996894, Ontario Research Foundation, J.W. Flavelle to G. Grant, 5 February 1929. Even newspapers hostile to the Tories viewed Backus as "a lordly personage," a dishonest manipulator who evaded or ignored obligations. See *Globe*, 18 August, 30 September, 9 and 23 December 1920.

75 RG3, 05-0-009, Kenora Development and English River file packages, and RG49-19, 1922, No.76, "English River/Backus Correspondence" contain much of the documentation. See also C.M. Johnston, *E.C. Drury: Agrarian Idealist* (Toronto: University of Toronto Press, 1986), 175–80. The Tories were hypocritical but some allegations had substance, given the rather slimy support Backus received from Peter Heenan.

76 AO, RG49-19, 1925, No. 65, "Great Lakes Paper correspondence"; RG1-E-3-B, Box 3, A-16, The Ontario and Minnesota Pulp and Paper Company – Early History. LOSP, No 53 (1929), Return on E.W. Backus timber cutting rights. *Fort Frances Times and Rainy Lake Herald*, 28 July 1927. PPMC, 19 January 1928, 75.

77 Congress, Senate, Temporary National Economic Committee, *Price Behavior and Business Policy*, I (Washington: GPO, 1941), 271–2. United States, Interstate Commerce Commission, Bureau of Statistics, *Freight Revenue and Value of Commodities Transported on Class I Steam Railways in the United States*, annuals for 1928, 1930, 1933 and 1936 (Statements 2911, 3242, 3552, 3747).

78 *Import Newsprint Paper from Thorold, Ontario, to Chicago Ill.*, [1931] 176 ICC 243. *Newsprint Paper to Chicago*, [1933] 194 ICC 148.

79 For American practices: M.S. Heath, "The Rate Structure," *Law and Contemporary Problems*, 12:3 (1947), 405–15; J. Langdon, "Criteria in the Establishment of Freight Rate Divisions," *Cornell Law Review*, 39:2

(1954), 213–36. For Canadian policy, K. Cruickshank, *Close Ties: Railways, Government, and the Board of Railway Commissioners, 1851–1933* (Montreal: McGill-Queen's University Press, 1991), chaps. 6 and 7. Actual rates (versus published tariffs) could only be ascertained by waybill studies. See *Class Rate Investigation, 1939, and Consolidated Freight Classification*, [1945] 262 ICC 447: 467, 601–4.

80 *New England Investigation*, [1913] 27 ICC 560: 575. *Official Classification Rates on Paper*, [1916] 38 ICC 120: 121–9. Competition within the U.S. also tended to suppress long-haul rates for newsprint.

81 *Newsprint Paper Investigation*, [1933] 197 ICC 738: 754–6. *Minnesota and Ontario Paper Co. v. Northern Pacific Railway*, [1922] 73 ICC 133 and [1923] 66 ICC 571. *Lake Superior Paper Company v. Director General, Ahnapee and Western Railway*, [1921] 61 ICC 709, 64 ICC 34. Lakehead companies were more successful in gaining access to Tennessee and other southern points. See *Knoxville Traffic Bureau v. Canadian Pacific Railway*, [1925] 101 ICC 605.

82 Across the 1920s the geographic definition of this group of manufacturers broadened from those in the immediate vicinity of Grand-Mère to include most firms in the southern areas of the province, sometimes also Ottawa-Hull or the Gatineau.

83 *Proposed Increases on Woodpulp to United States Points*, 7 JORR 282. *Eastern Rates Case*, [1916] 6 JORR 133: 219–20. The Millinocket rate to Chicago applied to imports from Québec, which allowed an additional 1,550 kilometres at a rate of just 3.1 cents per cwt.

84 *Lake Superior Paper and Spanish River Pulp and Paper Mills v. Canadian Pacific Railway*, [1918] JORR 123, 165. *Spanish River Pulp and Paper Mills v. Ahnapee and Western Railway*, [1926] 113 ICC 343, 120 ICC 251. The latter case placed Espanola at a significant disadvantage on transport costs relative to Sault Ste. Marie, which partially explains the early decisions for closing the mill.

85 AO, F208, B289479, Newsprint Statistics, W. Cain to W. Finlayson, 4 March 1931.

86 *FP*, 7 May 1926. *WSJ*, 25 October 1924. *Globe*, 13 May 1926. *FP*, 14 May 1926. *Globe*, 3 July 1926.

87 *WSJ*, 14 May 1926, 1 January 1927. *Globe*, 9 November 1926.

88 *FP*, 14 January 1927.

89 *PPMC*, 22 April 1926, 463; 29 April 1926, 478; 20 May 1926, 585.

90 *Globe*, 10 May 1927. *WSJ*, 11 May 1927. *NYT*, 24 June 1927. *PPMC*, 12 May 1927, 598, 602–3.

91 *FP*, 22 April 1927.

92 LAC, RG95, Series 1, 534. Canadian Newsprint Co., incorporation papers. *NYT*, 24 June 1927. *PPMC*, 30 June 1927, 828. *CSI*, A-9. MLCA, 81.22.150, Report to the Bondholders' Protective Committee by the Chairman of the Committee, 18 August 1932, 11.

93 *Globe*, 10 May 1927. *WSJ*, 11 May 1927. *FP*, 11 March 1927.
94 *FP*, 22 April and 13 May 1927. *NYT*, 11 May 1927.
95 *FP* 1 July 1927. *WSJ*, 20 December 1927. BANQ, P149, 1983-03-011/6 and 7, contains the minute books of the Canadian Newsprint Company and Canadian Paper Sales but the documents do not provide information about the logic behind decisions of the governing board.
96 *FP*, 16 September 1927, 17 October 1927. *PPMC*, 18 August 1927, 1027–8; 29 September 1927, 1212; 6 October 1927, 1255.
97 *PPMC*, 28 July 1928, 1026.
98 *NYT*, 30 May and 17 June 1928. *Globe*, 18 June 1928. The former president of the Canadian Newsprint Company, William Hurlbut, misrepresented the pricing arrangement. His testimony during the 1929 FTC investigation and subsequent enquires proved untrustworthy. Senate, *Newsprint Paper Industry*, 36.
99 *FP*, 11 May 1928. *JOC*, 9 June 1928.
100 *FP*, 18 May 1928. *Pittsburgh Press*, 12 June 1928. *WT*, 18 June 1928. *Globe*, 31 October 1928. Many of the details were first disclosed in small papers like *Gouverneur Free Press* and *Canadian Jewish Chronicle*.
101 *FP*, 11 May 1928. *JOC*, 23 June 1928.
102 *JOC*, 5 May 1928. *NYT*, 5 May, 8 August 1928. *PPMC*, 26 July 1928, 1031.
103 Kuhlberg, *In the Power of the Government*, 277–9, offers no documentary evidence for an innuendo that Hurlbut was a "Benedict Arnold" who engineered the crisis for International Paper. He resigned from Spanish River during the spring of 1927, where he had been employed in sales for eight years. With the elimination of redundant positions after the merger, there was no likelihood of a return. He was hired later in the spring by International Paper. I was unable to substantiate that it occurred "practically the same day." Kuhlberg's reference is to the press announcement in *PPMC*, 19 July 1928, 998, which repeats *NYT*, *WSJ*, 11 July 1928. Contrary to his claim, International did not get the Hearst contract with the collapse of the deal. The other firms that abandoned the sales organization secured the business. As recounted below, the deal with International occurred six months later.
104 AO, F1188, B228307, 1.12, Ker to H. Anderston, 20 November 1929; Ker to V. Massey, 16 December 1929.
105 Producers regularly destroyed records of pricing practices but for Abitibi see SMPL, 992.10, 26358, 1933 Newsprint Freight Rates – Abitibi Mills, which contains breakouts of prices and zone policies for U.S. customers.
106 J.A. Guthrie, *The Newsprint Paper Industry: An Economic Analysis* (Cambridge, MA: Harvard University Press, 1941), 84–9, 94–7, 108–9, 181–9.
107 *In the Matter of United States Steel, et al.*, [1924] 8 FTC 1: 28–30, 50. B.G. Herbert, "Delivered Pricing as Conspiracy and as Discrimination: The

Legal Status," *Law and Contemporary Problems*, 15:2 (1950), 181–226. *Pacific States Paper Trade Association v. Federal Trade Commission*, [1925] 4 F (2d) 457 [1927] 273 U.S. 52.

108 *FP*, 13 May 1928, 2 November 1928. *Newsprint Paper Industry*, 85.

109 *Globe*, 30, 31 May 1928. *NYT*, 31 May 1928. *FP*, 25 May 1928.

110 *JOC*, 5 May 1928. *FP*, 25 May 1928.

111 *FP*, 6 and 29 June 1928. *PPMC*, 7 June 1928, 763; 14 June 1928, 809; 21 June 1928, 847–8.

112 *WT*, 9 and 28 June 1928.

113 *FP*, 22 June, 15 June 1928. T.B. Macaulay, "The Battle of the Lake Regillus," verse VIII, *Lays of Ancient Rome*.

114 *Journal of Commerce*, 23 and 30 June 1928. *MG*, *NYT*, 31 May 1928. *Globe*, 9, 28 June 1928. *PPMC*, 12 July 1928, 948.

115 *Globe*, 12 and 15 June, 26 August 1928.

116 *FP*, 6, 13, 27 July 1928.

117 *PPMC*, 12 July 1928; 19 July 1928, 9; 6 September 1928, 1245–6. *Globe*, 15 and 16, 8 October 1928.

118 AO, F8, B299692, Finlayson to Ferguson, 19 July, 3 August 1928; Ferguson to Taschereau, 28 August 1928; Taschereau to Ferguson, 20 August 1928.

119 J. Eddy, *The New Competition* (New York: Stevens Press, 1912), 5. *Dr. Miles Medical Co. v. John D. Park and Sons Co.*, [1911] 220 U.S. 412.

120 H.D. Tosdal, "Open Price Associations," *American Economic Review*, 7:2 (1917), 331–52. G.H. Montague, "Recent Developments in Trade Association Law," *Annals of the American Academy of Political and Social Science*, 139:9 (1928), 38–43.

121 A. Dawley, *Struggles for Justice: Social Responsibility and the Liberal State* (Cambridge, MA: Harvard University Press, 1991), 319–27. P.D. Reagan, *Designing a New America: The Origins of New Deal Planning, 1890–1943* (Amherst: University of Massachusetts Press, 1999), 111–39. H. Hoover. *American Individualism* (New York: Doubleday Page, 1922), 18–19, 42–4. See also W.J. Donovan, "The Legality of Trade Associations," *Proceedings of the Annals of the Academy of Political Science*, 11:4 (1926), 19–26.

122 The best account is R.F. Himmelberg, *The Origins of the National Recovery Association: Business, Government, and the Trade Association Issue, 1921–1933* (New York: Fordham University Press), especially chaps. 4 and 7.

123 *WSJ*, 30 June 1928. Montreal *Star*, 30 October 1928. *MG*, 30, 31 October 1928. *Globe*, *NYT*, 31 October 1928. *PPMC*, 1 November 1928, 1558. Price based the options on estimated per ton mill costs of $42.50 and overhead of $13.50. The latter did not include depreciation or taxes, which made the offer very good for buyers.

124 Montreal *Star*, 30 October 1928. *MG*, 31 October 1928. *WSJ*, 1 November 1928. *Barron's*, 5 November 1928.

125 *NYT*, 5 November and 31 October 1928. *Globe*, 31 October 1928.
126 *Globe*, 30 October 1928. *MG*, 31 October 1928.
127 *Barron's*, 19 November 1928. *WSJ*, 15 November 1928. *Globe*, 31 October 1928.
128 *FP*, 2, 23 November 1928.
129 *NYT*, 5 November 1928, and *MG*, 6 November 1928 for admissions by Taschereau that they did not know the producers were already meeting. In *MG*, 7 November, the premiers back-tracked and emphasized their support for a formal conference. *WSJ*, 15 November 1928. *Barron's*, 19 November 1928, for leaks of the decisions prior to the release of the Ferguson letter.
130 AO, F8-3, B299692, Ferguson to CEOs of Abitibi Fibre, Abitibi Pulp and Paper, Beaver Wood Fibre, Dryden Paper, Fort Frances Pulp and Paper, Fort William Paper, Great Lakes Paper, Kenora Paper Mills, Lake Superior Paper, Nipigon, Provincial Paper, Spanish River Pulp and Paper Mills, Spruce Falls Power and Paper, 19 November 1928.
131 *Globe*, 20 November 1928. P. Oliver, *G. Howard Ferguson: Ontario Tory* (Toronto: University of Toronto Press, 1977), 347. AO RG3 or F8 contain a few letters acknowledging receipt or asserting the statement did not apply. It appears most companies did not even bother to answer.
132 *Globe*, 21 November 1928. *MG* and *NYT*, 21 November 1928. *PPMC*, 22 November 1928, 1667; 29 November 1928, 1710–14, 1730–2. *NYT*, 24 November 1928.
133 *Globe*, *MG*, *NYT*, 24 November 1928. *PPMC*, 6 December 1928, 1763.
134 *Editor and Publisher*, 15 December 1928.
135 *NYT*, 12 December 1928. *Globe*, 8 January 1929. *FP*, 30 November 1928. *PPMC*, 7 February 1929.
136 *PPMC*, 13 December 1928, 1773–4.
137 *Globe*, 24 November 1928. *NYT*, 3 January 1929. *MG*, 22 January 1929.
138 F8-3, B299692, Graustein to Ferguson, 11 December 1928; Ferguson to Graustein, 11 December 1928.
139 *The Nation*, 17 April 1929, 447.
140 *PPMC*, 24 January 1929. WSJ, 11 January 1929. *MG*, 22 January 1929. *FP*, January 1929.
141 *Ottawa Citizen*, 2 October 1930. *CFC*, 128 (9 March 1929): 1470–1. *PPMC*, 3 January and 7 March 1929.
142 *PPMC*, 28 February 1929. Author's translation from *Débats de l'Assemblée législative (débats reconstitués)*, 17e législature, 2e session, 7 mars 1929, at: http://www.assnat.qc.ca/fr/travaux-parlementaires/assemblee -nationale/17-2/journal-debats/19290307/92271.html.
143 F1198, B228307, 1.12, Ker to J.P. Kenney, 3 April 1929; Ker to L.B. Palmer, 3 April 1929; Ker to H.W. Cressy, 1 April 1929.
144 F8-3, B299692, Ferguson to Taschereau, 11 January 1930.

145 OS, 19 Geo. V [1930], ch.13, The Pulpwood Conservation Act. Lands and
    Forests Department, *AR*, 1927, 14–15. *PPMC*, 14 February 1929. *MG*, 7
    February 1929. *Globe*, 1, 7, 12 February 1929. Finlayson never said the
    province intended to "control the pulp and paper industry." The quote
    was: "The House is familiar with the provisions made, years ago, for
    the furtherance of the industry. It is now proposed to control the cutting
    and production to avoid the mistakes of the previous century and with
    the hope of could be placed on a permanent basis within five years on a
    sustained yield basis and with assured supply."

146 *Globe*, 26 February 1929. R.S. Lambert and P. Pross, *Renewing Nature's
    Wealth: A Centennial History of the Public Management of Lands, Forests, and
    Wildlife in Ontario, 1763–1967* (Toronto: Queen's Printer, 1967), 199–201.
    PPMC, 21 February 1929, 267–8.

147 For the type of data collected and its use, see SMPL, 992.10, 9868, Data for
    the Pulpwood Conservation Act, 1929; 17464, Annual Report, Wood Cut
    & Acquired Wood Cut, 1934–5 Season, 22 April 1936.

148 AO, F9-1-0-8, B253663, J.H. Black to Ferguson, 19 February 1929. F8-3,
    B299692, Ferguson to Black, 6 May 1929.

149 F9-1-0-09, B253666, F.J. Sensenbrenner to Ferguson, 4 April 1930, F9-1-0-
    11, B253672, Sensenbrenner to Ferguson, 13 January 1931.

150 Senate, *Newsprint Paper Industry*, 18–22.

151 *Saturday Night*, quoted in *PPMC*, 16 May 1929, 723.

152 F8-3, B299692, T.W. McGarry to Ferguson, 17 July 1929; enclosed unsigned
    (probably Backus to McGarry), 22 July 1929; enclosed unsigned 2 (probably
    Backus to McGarry), 22 July 1929.

153 *Globe*, 4 October 1929. *Maclean's*, 1 October 1929, 88–9.

6. From Crisis to Catastrophe

1 AO, F8, B291811, J. Flavelle to D. Carnegie, 3 December 1926.

2 *Globe*, 3 January 1931.

3 U.S., Congress, Senate, *Control of White-Paper Business, Hearing before the
  Committee on Agriculture and Forestry* (Washington: GPO, 1929), 30 January
  1929, 18.

4 Canada, House of Commons, *Debates*, 11 March 1929, 829.

5 *PPMC*, 8 July 1920, 724; 19 August, 880; 26 August 1920, 904. *Canadian
  Lumberman and Woodworker*, 1 August 1920, 17. Local interests never
  organized or developed the firm. A municipal councillor invited
  proposals and the town later provided land and tax concessions but, from
  the beginning, the venture was launched by investment bankers and
  industrialists based in Toronto or New York. The head of the firm was the
  president of a small Wisconsin pulp manufacturer.

6 *PPMC*, 23 February 1922, 146; 13 April 1922, 313. *Globe*, 3 August 1923.

7 LOSP, No. 3 – Appendix 33 (1927), Agreement of 30 January 1926 between His Majesty the King ... and Thunder Bay Paper Company, Limited, 104–11.

8 MLCA, 81.20.151, Report to the Bondholders' Protective Committee by the Chairman of the Committee, 18 August 1932, 20–2. BPC meeting minutes, 15 February 1933.

9 81.20.151, Report to the Bondholders' Protective Committee, 26.

10 S. Coté, "Les Voies de la monopolisation: Le cas de l'usine de papier de Bathurst" (PhD diss., Université de Montréal, 1978), 252–312. *CSI*, 24–30.

11 *PPMC*, 1 June 1913, 383–6; 15 December 1916, 436–7; 11 January 1917, 55; 8 February 1917, 164, 177; 21 February 1918, 177; 28 February 1918, 216.

12 AO, RG3, 04-0-186, A.O. Gagnier to Drury, 18 September 1920. AO, RG1, 533-0-6, Conditions with Respect to the Nipigon Pulp and Paper Limit, 21 October 1920. LOSP, No. 3 – Appendix 21 (1922), Agreement between His Majesty ... and the Provincial Paper Mills, 15 July 1921, 276–81.

13 LOSP, No. 3 – Appendix 30 (1926), Agreement between His Majesty ... and the Provincial Paper Mills, 27 February 1926, 81–9. MLCA, 81.20.150, Report to the Bondholders' Protective Committee by the Chairman of the Committee, 18 August 1932, 17. *CSI*, G25-7.

14 *FP*, 9 January 1930. *Globe*, 26 March 1927, 7 January 1930. *WSJ*, 11 April 1927. Equity holders in the 1927 deal received a staggering $135 per common share and $107 for preferred. Exchange trading transactions indicate Dominion probably unloaded the stock in stages from April to October 1930 and therefore garnered about $2.5 million versus the $3 million assumed during the January sale.

15 *WSJ*, 14 January 1930. *PPMC*, 16 January 1930, 63–4. *Globe*, 10 January and 20 November 1930.

16 OHA, 90.003.28, Kilmer to S. Lyons, 26 June 1925, 22 January 1926. ORR 633.01, 91.029, Canadian Northern Power, Kilmer to L.R. Wilson, 7 September 1926.

17 RG3, 06-0-893, Smith to Ferguson, 27 October 1926; Ferguson to Finlayson, 11 November 1926. OHA, 90.003.28, Water Lease 26, 11 November 1926. Critics later alleged the involvement of Sir William Hearst for Abitibi constituted a conflict of interest. The surviving correspondence and testimony at the Latchford-Smith Royal Commission indicate that Hearst handled the discussions to minimize that possibility. Even the Liberal counsel appointed for the enquiry conceded that his conduct was beyond reproach. Hearst charged nominal expenses and all key issues were handled by Abitibi's counsel, George Kilmer.

18 *Cobalt Northern Miner*, 29 January 1927.

19 *Sudbury Star*, 2 February 1927, 18 May 1927, 17 May 1930. F8-8, B299683, Kirkland Lake Power Situation, Autumn 1927, contains some of the complaints from mining companies.

20 RG3, 06-0-1250, J. Drinkwater to Ferguson, 6 May 1926 and 15 May 1926. *Cochrane Northland Post*, quote from 25 February 1927. Other developments are from the issues of 23 April 1926, 7 January 1927, 11 March 1927.

21 *Sudbury Star*, 24 September 1927, 16 November 1927, 3 December 1927.

22 Magrath's administration has been surveyed in M. Denison, *The People's Power: A History of Ontario Hydro* (Toronto: McClelland and Stewart, 1960), 180–8, and in K.R. Fleming, *Power at Cost: Ontario Hydro and Rural Electrification, 1911–1956* (Montreal: McGill-Queen's University Press, 1992), 112–30. *Sudbury Star*, 16 February 1927. OHA, 90.003.31, F.R. Gaby to Hydro-Electric Power Commission of Ontario, 9 March 1927.

23 F8-8, B299684, Magrath to Ferguson, 12 April 1927; B299683, Magrath to Ferguson, 7 September 1928.

24 *Sudbury Star*, 16 February 1927, 30 November 1928, 7 January 1928.

25 F8-8, B299683, C.D.H. MacAlpine to Ferguson, September 1928. *Sudbury Star*, 27 February 1929, 13 March 1929.

26 F8-8, B299683, Magrath to Ferguson, 29 October 1928; Gaby to Magrath, 23 October 1928.

27 *Sudbury Star*, 20 March 1929, 23 March 1929.

28 *Sudbury Star*, 29 June 1929.

29 OHA, 90.002.31, Smith to Gaby, 10 December 1928; Smith to Magrath, 25 May 1929.

30 90.003.31, Magrath to Smith, 7 October 1929. OHA, ORR 530, Box 188, contains the estimates from Hydro's engineers and a memo from Gaby to Jeffrey, 7 October 1929, which was used word-for-word by Magrath. The estimates were prepared by the spring of 1929 and the delay behind Magrath's response resulted from the failure to gain total ownership over Wanapitae Power, which would allow development in adjacent areas of New Ontario.

31 OHA, 90.003, Proceedings, 22 August 1934, 2273–4. Lower production costs were a benefit advertised to legitimate the OPS bonds but the gains were not substantive. Abitibi's staff refused to give estimates to the firms selling the securities and the correspondence emphasized an ability to meet the interest obligations, not the savings. ORR 633.01, 91.029, Abitibi-OPS, G.F. Hardy to Dominion Securities, 3 July 1930; John McDougall to L.R. Wilson, 29 June 1931; L.R. Wilson to John McDougall, 30 June 1931.

32 90.003.28, Gaby to Commission, 15 January 1930, 21 January 1930. 90.003.20, Hydraulic Department of the Hydro-Electric Power Commission of Ontario, Mississagi River Proposed Power Development Reports and Estimates, 13 March 1930.

33 OHQ, Minutes of Commission, 15 January 1930, 21 January 1930. OHA, ORR 530, Memo of conversation with Alexander Smith, 17 January 1930. 90.003.31, Magrath to Ferguson, 27 February 1930.

34 *Globe*, 12 April 1930.

35 OHA, 90.003.27, Minutes of Meeting of Directors, Abitibi Power and Paper Company, 9 April 1930. 90.003.28, Jeffrey to Gaby, 9 April 1930; Minute of Hydro-Electric Power Commission, 11 April 1930. 90.003.29, Gaby to Commission, 10 April 1930. 90.003.22, Indentures between the Abitibi Power and Paper Company Limited and the Hydro Electric Commission of Ontario, 4 June and 5 July 1930.

36 Sudbury *Star*, 2 August and 9 September 1930.

37 Toronto *Telegram*, 30 May 1930. *Globe*, 12 April 1930.

38 90.003.31, Magrath to Ferguson, 8 July 1930.

39 OHQ, Minute of Commission, 3 December 1930, 14 January 1931. 90.003.20, Jeffrey to Gaby, 5 January 1932, W. G. Hanna to Lucas, 7 March 1932.

40 MLCA, 81.20.150, Report to the Bondholders' Protective Committee, 33.

41 90.003.28, L.R. Wilson to A.R. Fullerton and C.W. Fleming, 19 July 1930. RG18-118, Proceedings, IX, 9 December 1940, 1035.

42 90.003.28, J.H. Gundy to Smith, 26 July 1930.

43 *PPMC*, 10 July 1930, 39.

44 AO, F8-3, B299692, T.W. McGarry to Ferguson, 1 August 1929. Production data for March to May 1930 in file. Copy, unsigned but likely E.W. Backus, Minneapolis, 6 August 1929. *MG*, 14 October 1929.

45 *Globe* 14 October 1929. *Editor and Publisher*, 12 October 1929. *PPMC*, 14 February 1929, 238; 14 March 1929, 376; 18 April 1929, 566; 16 May 1929, 709–12; 27 June 1929, 947–54; 5 December 1929, 873–4; 26 December 1929, 959–61.

46 *Ottawa Journal*, 14 October 1929. AO, F9-1-0-09, B253666, Sensenbrenner to Ferguson, 4 April 1930.

47 *FP*, 23 April 1931.

48 F9-1-0-11, B253672, Ferguson to Sensenbrenner, 10 January 1931; Sensenbrenner to Ferguson, 13 January 1931.

49 *Globe*, 14 October. *NYT*, 14, 19, 27 November 1929.

50 *NYT*, 28 November 1929. *Globe*, 22 and 30 November 1929. *PPMC*, 28 November 1929, 859–60.

51 AO, F1198, B228307, 1.12, Ker to F.N. Southam, 20 November and 26 November 1929; Ker to Canadian Press, 27 November 1929.

52 F1198, B228307, 1.12, Ker to T.R. Ker, 3 December 1929; Ker to Harry Anderston, 20 November 1929.

53 F1198, B228307, 1.12, A. Partridge to Ker, 4 December 1929. 1.13, W.G. Chandler to Ker, 3 January 1930.

54 *Montreal Star*, 26 November 1929. *NYT*, 29 November 1929. AO, F1188, B228307, 1.13, Ker to L.B. Palmer, 17 January 1930; 1.12, Graustein to Taschereau, 22 November 1929.

55 *PPMC*, 12 December 1929, 893–4. *WSJ*, 10 December 1929. *NYT*, 9 December 1929. *St. Louis Star*, 6 December 1929. *Washington Post*, 11 December 1929. *Globe*, 10 December 1929.

56 *Montreal Star*, 16 October 1929. Y. Roby, *Les Québécois et les investissements américains (1918–1929)* (Quebec City: Les Presses de l'Université Laval, 1976), 203–5.

57 *Globe*, 11 December 1929. *NYT*, 17, 11 December 1929.

58 *NYT*, 13, 22, 31 December 1929. *WSJ*, 6 January 1930.

59 F1198, B228307, 1.13, Ker to Chandler, 9 January 1930; Ker to J.H. Price, 9 May 1930; Chandler to Ker, 3 January 1930.

60 BANQ, *Après 32 ans de régime libéral: (texte complet du discours à l'Assemblée législative, le 5 février 1930, par M. Camillien Houde, chef de l'opposition provinciale, lors du débat sur le budget)* (S.I.: s.n. 1930), 14. *MG*, 10 and 15 January 1930. *Le Devoir*, 24 March 1930. Author's translation. In Jean de la Fontaine's poem, Perette dreams of all the money she will gain from the sale of the milk in her bucket, but then she slips and loses everything.

61 *PPMC*, 23 January 1930, 131–2. AO, F8-3, B299692, Taschereau to Ferguson, 16 January 1930; Ferguson to Taschereau, 11 January 1930.

62 HUBL, IP, *AR* (1927), 25. International Power and Paper, *AR* (1928), 8–9, 14. *Globe*, 10 April 1929.

63 BEA, SMT 4/40, International Power and Paper of Newfoundland, Report of J.L. Fearing, 2 March 1932. J.A. Guthrie, *The Newsprint Paper Industry: An Economic Analysis* (Cambridge, MA: Harvard University Press, 1941), Table 7, 239.

64 HUBL, A.D. Watts and Co., *Analysis of the International Power and Paper Company: History and Prospects* (Montreal: A.D. Watts, 1929), 18, 22.

65 YUL, Ndy79 U2 +In8h, Memorandum regarding plan dated June 28, 1928, for formation of new holding company, 15 August 1928; Ndy79 C1 +C16h, *International Paper Group* (New York: International Paper, 1929). T. Heinrich, "Product Diversification in the U.S. Pulp and Paper Industry: The Case of International Paper, 1898–1941," *Business History Review*; 75:3 (2001), 489–91.

66 U.S., Congress, Senate, *Newspaper Holdings of the International Paper and Power Co.*, CSS 9125 (Washington: GPO, 1929), Documents 11 and 12.

67 Congress, Senate, *Utility Corporations*, CSS 8858-7 (Washington: GPO, 1929), Document 92, Part 14, 82–3. *NYT*, 12 April, 30 April 1929. Quotes are from the hearings before a Massachusetts legislature committee and the Federal Trade Commission.

68 *Boston Post*, 16 May 1929. *Daily Capital Journal* [Salem, Oregon], 23 April 1929. *NYT*, 29 May 1929.

69 *Reading Times*, 18 April 1929. *NYT*, 30 April 1929. *WP*, 30 April 1929. CSS 8858-7, 51–2, 82–3, 84. Graustein's testimony before congressional committees always contained selective statements, professed memory lapses, and falsehoods mixed with factual statements, the last often occurring when there were written documents in the possession of the committees.

70 CSS 8858-7, 177. See also, *WP*, 16 May 1929. *NYT*, 5, 16, 19 May 1929. In the most bizarre twist during the hearings, Graustein attempted to minimize IPP's electrical holdings, suggesting at points that the book worth of US$300 million vastly exaggerated their strategic value relative to the pulp and paper operations.

71 RG3, 03-08-0-125, H. Turmaine to Henry, 18 March 1931. The business likely would have violated the contract with G.H. Mead, which was responsible for all American sales.

72 HUBL, IPP, *AR* (1930), 16–18. *Moody's Manual of Industrial Corporations* (1935), 2430–3; (1936), 1338–9. IPP refused to publish the Canadian data for 1930 and 1931 until after Graustein's removal from office. The income statements appear consistent but variations in the balance sheets from 1927 to 1933 were never explained.

73 *PPMC*, 26 September 1929, 507. BEA, SMT 4/39, Lord Norman to Hopkins, 9 April 1930; G. Barnes to Bramford, 8 April 1930. SMT 8/30, J.F. Taylor to E.N. Travers, 26 February 1930; Taylor to Norman, 29 March 1930. SMT 2/19, Graustein to Taylor, 10 April 1930; Taylor to Graustein, 25 April 1930.

74 J.K. Hiller, "The Politics of Newsprint: The Newfoundland Pulp and Paper Industry, 1915–1939," *Acadiensis*, 19:2 (1990), 27. *FP*, 6 March 1930. *WSJ*, 8 March, 20 May, 10 June 1930. *Attorney General and Minister of Agriculture and Mines v. Jardine and Martin*, [1930] Decisions of the Supreme Court of Newfoundland, 446, 522.

75 *MG, NYT*, 19 September 1930. *PPMC*, 25 September 1930, 354. With its passage into receivership in 1931, Canada Power gave up development plans in Newfoundland and the Hearst ownership stake became worthless.

76 A.M. Lee, *The Daily Newspaper in America* (New York: Macmillan, 1937), 727–8, 745. U.S., Senate, *Preliminary Report and Supplements: Newsprint Production and Supply* (Washington: GPO, 1956.), 13–16. U.S., Department of Commerce, *Newspapers, Periodicals, Books and Miscellaneous Publishing* (Washington: GPO, 1949), Table 6-A.

77 81.20.150, Report to the Bondholders' Protective Committee by the Chairman, 18 August 1932, 11. AO, F8-3, B299692, J.H. Black to Ferguson,

series of memos from 4 March to 22 May 1930 containing tabular data on capacity levels and output for 1929 and 1930.

78 *MG, NYT*, 26 September 1930. *WSJ*, 27 September 1930. *FP*, 25 September 1930. *Globe*, 2 April 1931. *PPMC*, 2 October 1930, 379–81, 408.

79 *Globe*, 27 September 1930. *NYT*, 27 September 1930. *Globe*, 29 September 1930.

80 BANQ, P137, Sous-série 10, D138 and D139, *Price Brothers v. Abitibi Power and Paper et al.* See also *MG, NYT*, 5 April 1933. Kuhlberg, *In the Power of the Government*, 292, cites data about the equalization payments from the filing of 17 February 1931 as fact and not what it was – an argument used to support the claim.

81 81.20.150, Report, 18 August 1932, 38.

82 *Financial Times of Montreal*, 14 April 1931. *MS*, 14 April 1931.

83 *NYT*, 21 April 1931. JLAO, 25 (1941), 24 April 1941, 172.

84 *Globe, NYT*, 22 April 1931. *Barron's*, 27 April 1931. *PPMC*, 23 July 1931, 858. *FP*, 6 February 1932.

85 AO, RG18-118, Proceedings, 15 November 1940, 896–7.

86 *FP*, 18, 25 December 1930. *WSJ*, 6 October 1930; 20 December 1930. *NYT*, 24 October 1930; 2, 13, 20 December 1930; 28 January 1931.

87 *NYT*, 3 May 1931. The inspection, in practical business terms, meant little. International never stated why it did not acquire the firms but likely the decision reflected their non-economic status.

88 *Globe*, 14 November 1930. *NYT*, 15 November, 21 December 1931. *WSJ*, 22 December 1931. *FP*, 26 December 1931.

89 *PPMC*, 18 February 1932, 3. *FP*, 14 May 1932.

90 HUBL, Abitibi Power and Paper, *AR* (1930), 1; (1929), 1.

91 HUBL, Abitibi Power and Paper, *AR* (1930), 2–3. *FP*, 12 March 1931.

92 G.R. Horne, "The Receivership and Reorganization of the Abitibi Power and Paper Company, Limited" (PhD diss., University of Michigan, 1954), 78, 80. MLCA, 81.20.150, Report to the Bondholders' Protective Committee by the Chairman of the Committee, 18 August 1932, 46.

93 HUBL, *RR* (1933), 21. *FP*, 1 April 1933.

94 AO, RG22-5800, B126995, 2994/32, *Montreal Trust v. Abitibi Power and Paper*, G.H. Mead, 25 February 1933.

95 AO, RG18-188, 15 November 1940, 891. MLCA, 81.20.151, G.H. Mead to G.T. Clarkson, 2 March 1933. E.E. Reid to Clarkson, 19 May 1933.

96 *Sudbury Star*, 26 August, 4 and 25 October, 1 November 1930.

97 *MG*, 31 January 1930. RG3, 06-0-1541, J.R. Pattison to Ferguson, 18 April 1930; N.B. Darrell to Ferguson, 16 May 1930; Ferguson to Darrell, 19 May 1930.

98 RG3, 08-0-092, J.J. Milne to Henry, 30 January 1931. RG3, 08-0-125, H. Turmaine to Henry, 18 March 1931.

99 AO, RG3, 08-0-125, A. McNaughton to Henry, 6 April 1931; T.F. Milne to Henry, 14 April 1931; A.E. Blagdon to Henry, 17 April 1931.
100 D. Spanner, "'The Straight Furrow': The Life of George S. Henry, Ontario's Unknown Premier" (PhD diss., University of Western Ontario, 1994), 12. *TS*, 6 December 1930. *Globe*, 15 March 1933. Henry was one of the major investors in Toronto's City Dairy and his connections to insurance companies were well known.
101 AO, F9-1-0-14, B253678, Henry to Ferguson, 24 February 1933. RG3, 08-0-125, Henry to Turmaine, 13 April 1931; Henry to McNaughton, 11 April 1931. *Globe, MG*, 6 March 1931.
102 *Globe*, 9 May 1931. *NYT*, 15, 16, 22 April 1931; 7 May 1931. Coverage of the discussions in the American papers was more thorough and objective than in Canadian journals.
103 *Globe*, 11 July 1931. *PPMC*, 16 July 1931.
104 RG3, 08-0-092, Finlayson to Henry, 30 July 1931; Smith to Finlayson, 30 July 1931. *PPMC*, 17 December 1931, 1380.
105 2994/32, 25 February 1933, Memorandum, Ste. Anne Paper. *NYT*, 22 March and 3 April 1931. BANQ, P350, XV, dossier d, Taschereau to A. Smith, 1 avril 1931; J.B. White to Taschereau, 9 juin 1931; J.-V. Boucher to Taschereau, 16 octobre 1931.
106 RG3, 08-0-125, Crabtree to Henry, 20 October 1931. F9-1-0-14, B253678, Clarkson to Henry, 21 February 1933.
107 F9-1-0-13, B253678, Ferguson to Henry, 24 December 1932; F9-1-0-14, B253678, Henry to Ferguson, 9 January 1933.
108 F9-1-0-12, B253675, Ferguson to Henry, 10 December 1931.
109 MLCA, 81.20.150, Report to the BPC, 18 August 1932, 19–26; Clarkson to Somerville, 22 February 1933; 81.20.151, BPC meeting minutes, 15 February 1933. *CSI*, 16–19, F-4. The acquisition was not disclosed until the first report by the receiver in 1933 and full details were not revealed until the *Compilation* was published in 1937.
110 *CSI*, K-1. SMPL, 922.10, 16747, Soo Division Private Correspondence Re: Shutdown, 31 July 1931; 16741–5, Espanola Division, Private Correspondence Re.: Shutdown, 30 June 1931.
111 *WSJ*, 30 June 1931. *Globe*, 27 June 1931. *Barron's*, 6 July 1931.
112 F.W. Weganast, *The Law of Canadian Companies* (Toronto: Carswell, 1931), 672–3, contains detailed case citations. See also F.B. Gore-Browne, *Handbook on the Formation, Management and Winding Up of Joint Stock Companies*, 34th edition (London: Jordan and Sons, 1919), 433.
113 HUBL, Abitibi Power and Paper, *AR* (1931), 1.
114 *NYT*, 7 March 1932. *Globe*, 7 March. *WSJ*, 8, 15 March 1932. *FP*, 12 March 1932.
115 HUBL, Abitibi, *AR* (1931), 2–3; *RR* (1933), 2–3. Horne. "Receivership and Reorganization," 72, 77, 84–6.

116 OHA, ORR 104, 90.004, Proceedings, 3: 222–6; ORR 104, 90.003.29, I.B. Lucas self-memos, 27 and 29 February 1932, 2 March 1932. Henry later denied involvement until April and claimed Hydro started the deliberations for a bailout. Smith approached the premier in mid-February and, on 2 March, a conference of the consultants and Hydro officers, with Henry briefly attending, was held in the chambers of the Speaker of the Legislative Assembly.

117 OHA, ORR 104, 90.003, Clarkson, Gordon, Dilworth, Guilfoyle and Nash, Memorandum on Abitibi Power and Paper Company Limited and Abitibi Canyon Development, 18 March 1932, 7–15, 17.

118 ORR 104, 90.003, Memorandum on Abitibi, 25–30. ORR 633.01, 91.029, Abitibi-OPS, April 1932. The Abitibi-OPS bonds had a nominal value of $6.6 million and a market value of approximately $1 million in March 1932.

119 90.003, I.B. Lucas, self-memo, 23 April 1932; 90.004, Proceedings, 3: 242; 16: 2290–4, 2323, 2329–30.

120 *Montreal Star*, 30 May 1932.

7. The Vale of Receivership

1 *FT*, 17 June 1932.

2 *Globe*, 15 October 1930.

3 A.U. Romasco, *The Poverty of Abundance: Hoover, the Nation, the Depression* (New York: Oxford University Press, 1965), 85.

4 A. Smith, *The Wealth of Nations* (London: Penguin, 1982), 325. This section of the chapter is derived from my essay "A State of Confusion and Incompleteness: The Treatment of Commercial Failure in Canada, 1840–1933," *ASAC Conference Proceedings*, 18:24 (St. John's, NF: Memorial University, 1997), 11–20.

5 W. Blackstone, *Commentaries on the Laws of England*, 4 vols. (London: Oxford Clarendon Press, 1766), 430.

6 R. Efrat, "The Evolution of Bankruptcy Stigma," *Theoretical Inquiries in Law*, 7:2 (2006), 364–93.

7 I. Ramsay, "Models of Consumer Bankruptcy: Implications for Research and Policy," *Journal of Consumer Policy* 20:2 (1997), 269–87. T.W. Zywicki, "Bankruptcy Law as Social Legislation," *Texas Review of Law and Politics*, 5:2 (2001), 408–19. M. Quilter, "Bankruptcy and Order," *Monash University Law Review*, 39:1 (2013), 189–212.

8 R. Tassé, J.D. Honsberger, and P. Carignan, *Bankruptcy and Insolvency: Report of the Study Committee on Bankruptcy and Insolvency Legislation* (Ottawa: Information Canada, 1970), 86.

9 There is a massive literature on the topic of discharge. Particularly useful are T.H. Jackson, "The Fresh-Start Policy in Bankruptcy Law," *Harvard*

Law Review, 98:7 (1985), 1393–1448; M. Howard, "A Theory of Discharge in Consumer Bankruptcy," *Ohio State Law Journal*, 48:4 (1987), 1047–88; C.J. Tabb, "The Historical Evolution of the Bankruptcy Discharge," *American Bankruptcy Law Journal*, 65:3 (1991), 325–72. For more theoretical appraisals, see D. Boshkoff, "The Bankrupt's' Moral Obligation to Pay His Discharged Debts: A Conflict Between Contract Theory and Bankruptcy Policy," *Indiana Law Journal*, 47:1 (1971), 36–69; H.M. Hurd and R. Brubaker, *Debts and the Demands of Conscience: The Virtue of Bankruptcy* (London: Oxford University Press, 2016).

10 R.J. Rosenberg, "Intercorporate Guaranties and the Law of Fraudulent Conveyances: Lender Beware," *University of Pennsylvania Law Review*, 125:2 (1976), 235–63. R. Squire, "Strategic Liability in the Corporate Group," *University of Chicago Law Review*, 78:2 (2011), 602–21. A.J. Casey, "The New Corporate Web: Tailored Entity Partitions and Creditors' Selective Enforcement," *Yale Law Journal*, 124:8 (2015), 2680–744.

11 UKS, [1542] 34 and 35 Henry VIII, c.4, State of Bankrupts Act. The issues of early legislation are summarized by W. Jones, "The Foundations of English Bankruptcy," *Transactions of the American Philosophical Society*, 69 (1979), Part 3, 1–63; and I.P.H. Duffy, "English Bankrupts, 1571–1861," *American Journal of Legal History*, 24:4 (1980), 283–305. For the implications, see I. Treiman, "Acts of Bankruptcy: A Medieval Concept in Modern Bankruptcy Law," *Harvard Law Review*, 52 (1938), 189–215.

12 L.E. Levinthal, "The Early History of English Bankruptcy," *University of Pennsylvania Law Review*, 67:1 (1919), 1–20; G. Glenn, "Essentials of Bankruptcy: Prevention of Fraud, and Control of the Debtor," *Virginia Law Review*, 23:4 (1937), 373–88. J.M. Olmstead, "Bankruptcy a Commercial Regulation," *Harvard Law Review*, 15:10 (1902), 829, 833.

13 The best history of relevant American law is D.A. Skeel, *Debt's Dominion: A History of Bankruptcy Law in America* (Princeton: Princeton University Press, 2001). For early practices, see also T.A. Freyer, *Producers versus Capitalists: Constitutional Conflict in Antebellum America* (Charlottesville: University of Virginia Press, 1994).

14 C.B.R. Dunlop, *Creditor and Debtor Law in Canada* (Toronto: Carswell, 1981), chap. 5. G. Craig, *Upper Canada: The Formative Years 1784–1841* (Toronto: McClelland and Stewart, 1963), 30–1.

15 CIHM, 53131, Practical Hints to the Retail Merchant on How to Make Business Successful (Toronto: E.T. Bromfield, 1869), 11, 31.

16 CIHM, 53355, P. Adamson, *Open Letter to Municipalities in Canada West* (Huron: n.p., 1864).

17 Canada, *House of Common Debates*, 1869, 252–8, 264–5.

18 See the fine analysis in T.G.W. Telfer, *Ruin and Redemption: The Struggle for a Canadian Bankruptcy Law, 1867–1919* (Toronto: University of Toronto Press, 2014), chaps. 2 and 3.

19 CIHM, 4168, E.R.C. Clarkson, *Bankruptcy Legislation* (Toronto: n.p., 1883), 4–5.

20 CIHM, 25173, Address on Bankruptcy Legislation in Canada before the Canadian Manufacturers' Association (Toronto: Dudley and Burns, 1900), 12–13.

21 CIHM, 12490, Fallacy of Insolvency Laws and Their Baneful Effects (Belleville: n.p., 1885), 9–10.

22 *Attorney-General of Ontario v. Attorney-General for the Dominion* (Voluntary Assignments Case), [1894] A.C. 189. The right to pass voluntary assignment codes was confirmed in *Tooke Brothers Ltd. v. Brock and Latterson Ltd.*, [1907] ELR 270–2.

23 SC, [1882], 43 Vic., c. 23, An Act Respecting Insolvent Banks, Insurance Companies, Buiding Societies, and Trading corporations. [1886] 47 Vic., c. 129, retitled as the Winding-Up Act. For cases lacking proof of insolvency, *Re. Cramp Steel Company (Limited)*, [1908] OJ No. 113, 6 OLR 230.

24 *Re Canadian Shipbuilding Co.*, [1912], 26 OLB 564; 3 OWN. 1476; 4 OWN 157. *Harrison v. Nepisiquit Lumber Co., Ltd.*, [1912] 11 ELR 314. For the status of receivers relative to liquidators, *In Re. Joshua Stubbs Ltd.* [1891] 1 Ch. 475; *Riordon Co. v. John W. Danforth Co.*, [1923] SCR 319. The numerous problems associated with the Winding-Up Act were reviewed in V. Mitchell, *A Treatise on the Law Relating to Canadian Commercial Corporations* (Montreal: Southam Press, 1916), 1453–1517.

25 T.G.W. Telfer, "The Canadian Bankruptcy Act of 1919: Public Legislation or Private Interest?" *Canadian Business Law Journal*, 24 (1994–5), 357–403. Telfer, *Ruin or Redemption*, chaps. 8 and 9. For the tenor of discussions, Canada, House of Commons, *Debates* (1919), 1981–2014.

26 RSC, 9–10 Geo. V [1919], c. 36, An Act Respecting Bankruptcy. J. Honsberger, "Bankruptcy Administration in the United States and Canada," California Law Review, 63:6 (1975), 1531.

27 The terminology and confused presentation of the Bankruptcy Act, as it appeared to contemporaries, is summarized in L. Duncan, *Law and Practice of Bankruptcy in Canada* (Toronto: Carswell, 1922). Duncan, at thirty-eight, argued the administration of American bankruptcy law was lax, where the statutes "have too often been administered they were a clearing house for the liquidation of debts, a sort of constant Jubilee."

28 F.W. Weganast, *The Law of Canadian Companies* (Toronto: Burroughs, 1931) 99–107. In *Re. Warren Brothers & Co. Ltd.*, [1922] OLR 214, the judge indicated the Bankruptcy Act supplanted the Winding-Up Act except where there were special grounds.

29 In *Re. Pound, Son, and Hutchins*, [1889] 42 Ch.D. 402.

30 In *Re. Canadian Western Steel Co. Ltd.* [1922] 2 C.B.R. 494. RSC, 12–13 Geo. V. [1922], c. 8, The Bankruptcy Act Amendment Act.

31 Honsberger, "Bankruptcy Legislation," 1532–6, provides a good review of the deficiencies. Data released by the Superintendent of Bankruptcies listed 11,867 failures between 1921 and 1924 with declared assets of $215 million and liabilities of $281.7 million. For 1930 to 1933, there were 10,586 failures with $144.7 million in declared assets and $119.8 million in liabilities.

32 W.J. Donovan, *Report submitted to the Hon. Thomas D. Thatcher, Judge of the United States District Court for the Southern District of New York, on March 22, 1930* (New York: Court Press, 1931), 237.

33 Canada, House of Commons, *Debates* (1952–3), 1269. See the fine discussion in V.E. Torrie, "Protagonists of Company Reorganisation: A History of the Companies' Creditors Arrangement Act (Canada) and the Role of Large Secured Creditors" (PhD diss., University of Kent at Canterbury, 2015), 84–102. Public access to the thesis was granted after this book was completed and revised.

34 Canada, *Canada Year Book* (Ottawa: Dominion Bureau of Statistics, 1930), 951–4; (1935), 1033–5.

35 See, for example, P. Ollerenshaw, "Innovation and Corporate Failure: Cyril Lord in UK Textiles, 1945–68," *Enterprise and Society*, 7:4 (2006), 777–811.

36 *Panama, New Zealand and Australian Royal Mail Co.*, [1870] L.R. 5 Ch. 318; *Strong v. Carlyle Press*, [1893] 1 Ch. 268; *Government Stock Co. v. Manila Rail Co.*, [1897] A.C. 86; *Evans v. Rival Granite Quarries Ltd.*, [1910] 2 K. B. 979, 999; *Gordon Mackay & Co., Ltd. v. Larocque*, [1927] 2 DLR 1150. Mitchell, *Canadian Commercial Corporations*, 1279–90.

37 *M. J. O'Brien Ltd. v. British America Nickel Corporation Ltd.*, [1927] A.C. 369. Mitchell, *Canadian Commercial Corporations*, 1341–7. W.K. Fraser, "Reorganization of Companies in Canada," *Columbia Law Review*, 27:8 (1927), 932–57.

38 Mitchell, *Canadian Commercial Corporations*, 1583–93. Weganast, *The Law of Canadian Companies*, 681–9. For court attitudes towards secured and unsecured creditors, *Riordan Co. v. John W. Danforth Co.*, [1923] SCR 319. Receivership as a standard action dates from *David Lloyd & Co.*, [1877] 6 Ch. D. 339. Also *Re Brampton Gas Co.*, [1902] 4 OLR 509: 518, "it is the right of a debenture holder or mortgagee of the company to bring his action against the company to realize his security ... and the leave is granted almost as a matter of course."

39 The American literature is extensive but useful contemporary analyses include T.A. Thacher, "Some Tendencies of Modern Receiverships," *California Law Review*, 4:1 (1915), 32–49; C.T. Payne, "The General Administration of Equity Receiverships of Corporations," *Yale Law Journal*, 31:7 (1922), 685–701; R.K. Hill, "Consent Receiverships in Federal Equity Practice," *Chicago-Kent Law Review*, 11:4 (1933), 267–77; W.O. Douglas,

"Protective Committees in Railroad Reorganization," *Harvard Law Review*, 47:4 (1934), 565–89.

40 U.S. Congress, Senate, Hearings Before a Special Committee of Investigation of Bankruptcy and Receivership Proceedings in United States Courts, 23 February 1934 (Washington: GPO, 1934), 1275. E.H. Levi and J.W. Moore, "Bankruptcy and Reorganization: A Survey of Changes," *University of Chicago Law Review*, 5:1 (1937), 1–40, cross-compared American, British, and Canadian practices.

41 T. Arnold, *The Folklore of Capitalism* (Princeton: Princeton University Press, 1936), 231–46. See also Securities and Exchange Commission, *Report on the Study and Investigation of the Work Activities, Personnel and Functions of Protective and Reorganization Committees*, Part I (Washington: GPO, 1935).

42 *FP*, 11, 18 June 1932.

43 C. Rohrlich, "Protective Committees," *University of Pennsylvania Law Review*, 80:5 (1932), 674–81. "Protective Committees and Reorganization Reform," *Yale Law Journal*, 47:2 (1937), 229–33. Security and Exchange Commission, "Protective and Reorganization Committees," Part I, Section IV, in Report on the Study and Investigation of the Work Activities, Personnel and Functions of Protective and Reorganization Committees, provides a detailed review.

44 *FP*, 18 June 1932.

45 *WSJ*, 6 June 1932. *Globe*, 3, 7 June 1932. *PPMC*, June 1932, 187. *FP*, 25 June 1932. For the inability to acknowledge the failure, *WSJ*, 30 July and 2 August 1932; *Globe* and *NYT*, 1 August 1932.

46 MLCA, 81.20.150, Minutes, First Bondholders' Protective Committee meeting, 10 June 1932. *WSJ*, 17 June 1932. *Globe*, 16 June 1932. The meeting was held at 360 St. James Street, the headquarters of the Royal Bank of Canada, an ironic choice given the disputes that soon unfolded.

47 U.S. Congress, Temporary National Economic Committee, *Investigation of Concentration of Economic Power: Investment Banking*, Part 22, 12–14 December 1939 (Washington: GPO, 1940), 11417.

48 *NYT*, 3 March and 15 July 1931, 12 June 1929.

49 MLCA, 81.22.150, Ripley to E. Bowman, 15 June 1932.

50 MLCA, 81.22.154, Ripley to Clarkson, 15 March 1935. *FP*, 25 June 1932.

51 *Globe*, *NYT*, 1 August 1932. *FP*, 6 August 1932.

52 *FP*, 25 June 1932. *Mail and Empire*, 21 June 1932.

53 *Saturday Night*, 13 August 1932.

54 MLCA, 81.22.150, *Report to the Bondholders' Protective Committee by the Chairman of the Committee*, 18 August 1932, 54. This is the only surviving copy and is marked "Strictly Confidential, for use of the members of the Committee."

55 81.22.150, *Report to the BPC*, 8.

56 81.22.150, *Report to the BPC*, 11–12.

57 81.22.150, *Report to the BPC*, 48–53.

58 81.22.150, *Report to the BPC*, 55. The scale of the losses was so staggering that Ripley refused to give a copy of his confidential report to Edward Beatty, the head of the Bankers' Committee.

59 Estimated by recasting the accounting statements supplied in the Ripley report and AO, RG 52-5800, 2996/32, Statement of Affairs as of 15 September 1932.

60 81.20.150, Minutes, Second BPC meeting, Royal York, 23 August 1932.

61 Legally bound to supervise or control, creditors had right to expect reasonable degree of attention from a receiver or that officer could be held accountable and penalized. *Plisson v. Duncan* [1905], 36 S.C.R., 647.

62 Weganast, *The Law of Canadian Companies*, 674–84.

63 AO, RG22-5800, B126995, 2996/32, *Montreal Trust v. Abitibi Power and Paper Ltd.*, Affidavits of J.F. Hobkirk and G.T. Clarkson, 8 and 9 September 1932; Order, 12 September 1932; Bond, 13 September 1932.

64 RG22-5800, 616/32, petition of 15 September 1932, affidavits of Wadge and Shapley, 22 September 1932; orders and consents of 28 September and 15 November 1932. 2996/32, Consent Decree, 27 September 1932; Order, 7 December 1932 authorizing Montreal Trust to proceed notwithstanding the winding-up order. A formalist who believed in the sanctity of property rights, Sedgewick routinely accepted requests from creditors friendly to bondholders for extensions of the Winding-Up Act rather than the Bankruptcy Act, despite the *Canadian Western Steel* ruling, cited in note 28 above.

65 MLCA, 81.22.150, "Confidential," Ripley to Bowman, 30 September 1932.

66 AO, F45, B294852, Deposition of Harold Wilson Shapley, 17 June 1935, 8–14; L. Duncan to Roebuck, 27 June 1935. 2996/32, Order, 7 December 1932.

67 2996/32, Order, 7 December 1932.

68 JLAO, 75 (1941), Appendix 1, 25 April 1940, 242.

69 MLCA, 81.22.150, Reid to Somerville, 20 March 1933. 2994:32, 1179, Memorandum, Salaries and Allowances, 25 February 1933.

70 MLCA, 81.22.151, Reid to Somerville, 19 May 1933.

71 MLCA, 81.22.150, D.G. Calvert to Reid, 13 March 1933; 81.20.155, Reid to Osler, 14 November 1935. Calvert had worked for G.H. Mead Co. and was general manager of Fort William Paper for more than a decade. Married into a well-known family in London, Ontario, he was secretly used by Reid as an information source, thereby providing the bondholders' council with appraisals that sometimes disproved assertions from Clarkson or the firm's executives.

72 MLCA, 81.20.150, D.G. Calvert Report on Abitibi, 13 March 1933.

73 HUBL, Abitibi Power and Paper, *RR* (1933), 1.
74 2994/32, Condensed and approximate statement of affairs as of 10
   September 1932, from standpoint of bondholders, Schedule A. HUBL,
   Price Waterhouse, Report on Abitibi Power and Paper Company Financial
   Statements, 2 March 1933. 81.20.156, Surveys and valuations of Abitibi
   assets, 10 March 1936. 81.20.159, Colpitts and Coverdale report on
   valuation of properties, 15 April 1937.
75 Estimates derived from *CSI*, L1-3. The realized price for newsprint is
   after deductions for transportation, agency costs, and any concessions to
   purchasers. It does not include Thunder Bay Paper or Provincial Paper.
   81.20.151, Minutes, Bondholders' Representative Committee meeting, 15
   February 1933, for Clarkson's expectations. 2996/32, Statement of Affairs
   as of 10 September 1932, Schedule 1, for cash situation.
76 2996/32, Statement of Affairs, Estimated operating results.
77 2996/32, Schedule 2, Royal Bank advances. 2996/32, Royal Bank claim and
   securities, 25 February and 9 June 1933; Order, 9 June 1933.
78 81.22.151, Osler to Ripley, 18 April 1933, 28 April 1933; Conference
   minutes, 24 April 1933.
79 2996/32, Royal Bank claim, 25 November 1933. 82.20.153, Royal Bank
   claim, 30 November 1934.
80 *FP*, 21 January 1933.
81 *FP*, 25 March 1933, 1 April 1933.

8. A Time for Investigations

1 P.F. Drucker, *The End of Economic Man: A Study of the New Totalitarianism*
   (New York: John Day, 1939), 60–1.
2 AO, RG 52-5800, B126995, 2994/32, estimated operating results for one
   year at $45 per ton; Statement of Affairs, 10 September 1932, Schedule
   4; Memorandum, Pulpwood purchases, 23 February 1933. MLCA,
   81.20.150, Calvert to Reid, 13 March 1933. The bondholder's council
   never understood how Clarkson and Abitibi's executives arrived at
   the estimates. The costs of production at Iroquois Falls were lowered
   by a write-off of wood inventories, while those for moderate cost mills
   appear to have been raised. Regardless of the calculation technique or
   the level of production, the Espanola and Sturgeon Falls plants were
   non-economic by any mode of calculation, given the prices prevailing
   between 1932 and 1942.
3 AO, RG3, 08-0-192, J.J. Milne to G.H. Henry, 30 January 1931; 09-0-125, A.
   McNaughton to Henry, 9 March 1931, 6 April 1931; 08-0-125, T.F. Milne to
   Henry, 14 April 1931. *Sudbury Star*, 28 March 1931, 8 April 1931.
4 RG3, 08-0-125, Henry to H. Turmain, 13 April 1931.

5 2994/32, Anson Pension, 25 February 1933.
6 81.22.151, BRC Minutes, 15 February 1933; 2994/32, Memoranda, Manitoba Paper, 25 February 1933.
7 *WT*, 7 January, 23 February, 18 April, and 24 May 1933. 2994/32, 1179, Memoranda, Manitoba Paper, 9 June 1933. MLCA, 81.22.151, Clarkson to Osler 13 May 1933; Clarkson to Ripley, 23 May 1933; 81.20.152, Osler to Reid, 28 September 1933. An order for another 50,000 cords was placed in 1934 and was legitimated as a buffer against labour difficulties. 81.22.153, Osler to Ripley, 8 May 1934, and Memorandum, Manitoba Paper, 7 May 1934; 81.20.154, Clarkson to Ripley, 18 March 1935.
8 J. Struthers, *No Fault of Their Own: Unemployment and the Canadian Welfare State, 1914–1941* (Toronto: University of Toronto Press, 1983), 25–43. *Globe*, 12 January 1933.
9 AO, F9-1-0-12, B253675, G.D. Robertson to Henry, 27 September 1930; Order-in-Council, 14 October 1930. RG3, 08-0-417, J.D. Monteith to Henry, 24 February 1933. J. Struthers, *The Limits of Affluence: Welfare in Ontario, 1920–1970* (Toronto: University of Toronto Press, 1994), 77–9.
10 AO, RG 18-97, Report of the Inquiry as to the Handling of Unemployment and Direct Relief at Sturgeon Falls, Ontario, 1933, 4–6.
11 RG 18-97, Report of the Inquiry, 6–8.
12 RG3 08-0-125, A.E. Blagdon to Henry, 17 April 1931. *Sudbury Star*, 15 April 1931, 9 May 1931.
13 *Sudbury Star*, 9 December and 23 December 1931.
14 RG3, 03-08-0-211, W. Gow to Henry, 29 September 1931.
15 *Globe*, 12 January 1933.
16 *Globe*, 12 January 1933. *OJ*, 20 January 1933.
17 *Globe*, 17, 18, and 23 January 1933. RG 18-97, *Sturgeon Falls Enquiry Report*, 14–15, 43–8.
18 *Globe*, 18 January 1933. *OJ*, 11 February 1933.
19 *OJ*, 1 February 1933. RG18-97, Sturgeon Falls Enquiry Report, 14–15, 48.
20 *Globe*, 12, 14, and 26 January 1933.
21 *Globe*, 7 February 1933.
22 *Globe*, 18 January 1933, 27 January 1933.
23 AO, RG18-118, Proceedings, Royal Commission on Abitibi Power and Paper, 1213–20. RG3, 302, Statement of Facts on Behalf of Sturgeon Falls Board of Trade, Re: Abitibi Royal Inquiry, 10 December 1940. E. Goltz, "Espanola: The History of a Pulp and Paper Town," *Laurentian University Review*, 6:3 (1974), 75–104.
24 *Globe*, 30 September 1930, 28 October 1930.
25 *FT*, 8 January 1932.
26 *FP*, 8 April 1933.

27 C.W. Gilbert, *The Mirrors of Wall Street* (New York: G.P. Putnam's Sons, 1933), 9, 161. E. Wilson, *Travels in Two Democracies* (New York: Harcourt Brace and Co., 1936), 59.

28 F.A. Allen, *The Lords of Creation* (New York: Harper and Row, 1935). M. Lowenthal, *The Investor Pays* (New York: Alfred A. Knopf, 1933).

29 F8-2, B299694, Bennett to Ferguson, 18 January 1932.

30 Canada, House of Commons, Proceedings of the Select Standing Committee on Banking and Commerce, 22 May 1934, 764–816; 23 May 1934, 893–926.

31 *PPMC*, June 1934, 347–8.

32 U.S., Congress, Senate, Committee on the Judiciary. *Uniform System of Bankruptcy*, 2 vols. (Washington: GPO, 1932–3).

33 Congress, House of Representatives, Committee on the Judiciary. *Equity Receiverships* (Washington: GPO, 1930). United States. Congress. House of Representatives. Committee on Banking and Currency, *Receiverships of Joint-Stock Land Banks under the Federal Farm Loan Act*, 2 volumes (Washington: GPO, 1930). Senate, Special committee to investigate the administration of bankruptcy and receivership proceedings in United States courts, *Investigation of Bankruptcy and Receivership Proceedings in United States Courts*, 9 volumes (Washington: GPO, 1934–6).

34 Congress, House of Representatives, Select committee to investigate real estate bondholders' reorganizations, *Investigation of Real Estate Bondholders' Reorganizations*, 21 volumes (Washington: GPO, 1934–8).

35 Congress, Senate, Committee on the Judiciary, *Amendment of Bankruptcy Laws–Bankruptcy of Municipalities* (Washington: GPO, 1934). House, Committee on the Judiciary, Special Subcommittee on Bankruptcy and Reorganization, *Municipal Bankruptcy Compositions* (Washington: GPO, 1940).

36 Congress, House, Committee on the Judiciary, *Reorganization of Railroads Under the Bankruptcy Act: Report* (Washington: GPO, 1935). Senate, Committee on Interstate Commerce, *Investigation of Railroad Financing* (Washington: GPO, 1935). Senate, Committee on Interstate Commerce, *Investigation of Railroads, Holding Companies And Affiliated Companies*, 26 volumes (Washington: GPO, 1939–40).

37 USSSEP, 11–21 April, 10–287, for Whitney's testimony. M. Perino, *The Hellhound of Wall Street: How Ferdinand Pecora's Investigation of the Great Crash Forever Changed American Finance* (New York: Penguin, 2010), provides an entertaining history.

38 *NYT*, 25 January 1933. Columbia University, "The Reminiscences of Ferdinand Pecora," III (New York: Oral History Research Office, 1962), 655.

39 F. Pecora, *Wall Street Under Oath: The Story of Our Modern Money Changers* (New York: Simon and Schuster, 1939), 3–4. The critics were numerous,

including Roosevelt adviser R. Moley, *After Seven Years* (New York: Harper and Brothers, 1939), 177. See also S.E. Kennedy, *The Banking Crisis of 1933* (Lexington: University Press of Kentucky, 1973), 104–26.

40 USSSEP, 3 June 1932, 767–90.

41 USSSEP, 21 February 1933, 1762–9, 1780–3; 24 February 1933, 2030–42.

42 USSSEP, 22 February 1933, 1841–63, 1889–1919. Washington *Daily News*, 1 March 1933.

43 USSSEP, 21 February 1933, 1785–8, 1778–9, 1811–14.

44 USSSEP, 21 February 1933, 1764–7, 1874–7.

45 USSSEP, 21 February 1933, 1812–14. "Reminiscences," 685–7.

46 *NYT*, 28 February 1933; *Nation*, 137 (8 March 1933), 248–9; *Commonweal*, 17 (14 March 1933), 535; *Colliers*, 91 (April 1933), 50.

47 MLCA, 81.22.151, Reid to Somerville, 7 March 1933.

48 J.A. Kouwenhoven, *Partners in Banking: A Historical Portrait of a Great Private Bank, Brown Brothers Harriman & Co.* (New York: Doubleday, 1968), 198.

49 MLCA, 81.20.154, Clarkson to M.G. Angus, 11 March 1935; Ripley to Clarkson, 15 March 1935; Somerville to Angus, 26 March 1935.

50 OHA, 90.003, Proceedings, 7: 919–25, 947–9; 8: 1094–1125. *ME*, 1 and 5 April 1933. Contrary to subsequent allegations, the meeting and Gundy's role were street knowledge.

51 LAC, MG-26-I, C-3582, 129762–4, D.M. Hogarth to Henry, 23 June 1932, "Private and Confidential."

52 OHA, ORR 633.01, 91.029, L.R. Wilson to W.B. Crombie, 11 July 1932; Hardy to L.R. Wilson, 21 July 1932.

53 OHA, ORR 127.2, Notes on the Graph of Power Resources and Demands of Southern Ontario, 17 August 1932.

54 Cochrane *Northland Post*, 28 June, 10 July 1932. Kapuskasing *Northern Tribune*, 10 July 1932. *Globe*, 27 June, 8 and 12 July 1932.

55 OHA, 90.003, Proceedings, 3: 301–3; 5: 553; 1175–6. *Globe*, 25 June 1932. *FP*, 9 July 1932.

56 90.003, Proceedings, 3: 231–7, 242–3, 265–80, 283, 286; 4: 315; 5: 539, 585.

57 90.003, Proceedings, 5: 558; 7: 993–4; 8: 1086–9, 1177–86, 1201–2. AO, F9-1-0-13, B253677, Henry to Cooke, 28 July 1932. The new financial structure lowered annual interest costs by $750,000 or 18.5 per cent from the original OPS scheme.

58 *FP*, 16 July 1932. *Sudbury Star*, 13 and 27 July 1932.

59 *TS*, 26 June 1932. *Globe*, 26 July, 1 August 1932.

60 OHA, ORR 633.01, 91.029, J.R. Cooke to Montreal Trust, 13 October 1932; L.R. Wilson to W.B. Crombie, 17 October 1932; W.W. Pope to Strachan Johnston, 1 November 1932. RG 22-5800, 3554/32, *Montreal Trust v. Ontario Power Service*, Affidavit of F.A. Gaby, 15 November 1932; Statement of Claim, 28 November 1932.

61 3555/32, Agreement between Ontario Hydro and Montreal Trust, 26 April 1933; Order, 29 April 1933.

62 Leopold Macaulay, Interview, 1 December 1965, cited in N. McKenty, *Mitch Hepburn* (Toronto: McClelland and Stewart, 1967), 69.

63 AO, PC, 1933, No. 16, *The Abitibi Canyon Power Development, 5 April 1933*. *ME*, 6 April 1933.

64 F9-1-0-14, B253679, Henry to J.F. Fotheringham, 12 April 1933; Henry to Ferguson, 28 April 1933.

65 F9-1-0-14, B253679, Henry to Flavelle, 18 April 1933. Western University, ARCC Archives, B4919-28, Edmund Carty Diary, 20 January 1934.

66 AO, RG4, 4-02, Box 4, "Former Cabinet Ministers who were also Directors of Companies," 16 March 1933. OHA, 90.003, Box 19-18, Latchford-Smith Proceedings, IV, 19 July 1934, 375–7. York University Archives, F34, George S. Henry Appointment Books, 1930–4 record his meetings and sessions at North American Life but do not provide specifics on topics under discussion.

67 F9-1-0-14, B253679, Meighen to Henry, 6 March, 27 March 1933. Henry to Meighen, 27 March 1933. LAC, MG26-I, C-3582, 130130-1, Meighen to Henry, 1 April 1934. Meighen was disingenuous when asked later. He told one editor that when the trust bought OPS bonds in May 1932 that "there was no talk whatever that ever I heard of the Government acquiring the property." He claimed to have been in Ottawa through the summer. "I had nothing in the world to do directly or indirectly or however remotely with the negotiations." C-3583, 130461-3, Meighen to F.D. Ross, 25 January 1934.

68 *TS*, 6 April 1933. *Globe*, 6 April 1933. *Toronto Telegram*, 6 April 1933.

69 *ME*, 20 June 1934.

70 *Globe*, 31 May 1933. *Saturday Night*, 11 November 1933.

71 AO, F45, B294813, Hepburn to Roebuck, 3 November 1932. *Globe*, 12 March 1934.

72 Spikes used to guide logs down rivers.

73 *Globe*, 16 April 1934. F45, B294822, W.A. Taylor to Roebuck, 29 March 1933; Roebuck to Hepburn, 27 September 1933.

74 F45, B294822, Briefing memos for Roebuck, n.d., late 1933; Roebuck to Harry Johnson, 28 December 1933.

75 LAC, MG27-III-G8, VIII, Correspondence 1937.

76 *Globe*, 7 April, 8 and 15 July 1933.

77 F45, B294813, Roebuck to H. Johnston, 9 August 1933; Roebuck to Hepburn, 27 September 1933. For Hepburn's use of the claims, see *Globe*, 7, 21 April 1933; 6, 28 May 1933; 30 October 1933; 28 May 1934.

78 F9-1-0-15, B253681, Ferguson to Henry 24 October 1933; Henry to Ferguson, 10 November 1933.

79 F9-1-0-14, B253679, Meighen to Henry, 6 March 1933, 27 March 1933. F9-1-0-15, B253681, 30 October 1933; Henry to Meighen, 10 November 1933.

80 RG3, Box 219, F. Denton to Slaght, 16 July 1934. Queen's University Archives, F01985, Dominion Construction Ltd., Abitibi Canyon film, 1933.

81 *Globe*, 6, 8, 9 June 1934. For the use of private investigators, see Saywell, *Just Call Me Mitch*, 147. For the efforts to buy off opposition candidates, see AO, F9-1-0-16, B253683, H. Smith to Henry, 26 April 1934, 14 May 1934; Henry to Smith, 27 April 1934. B253684, W. Clysdale to Henry, 1 June 1934.

82 *Globe*, 16 June 1934. *ME*, 19 June 1934. LAC, MG26K, M3178-603713, H. Smith to Bennett, n.d. (late June 1934).

83 *Globe*, 5 January 1934; 1 May 1934. LAC, MG26-I, C-3583, Meighen to Bennett, 1 May, 26 June 1934; P.C. 1462, Bennett to Governor-General, 26 June 1934.

84 OHA, ORR 633.01, 91.029, T.S. Lyons to Roebuck, 22 February 1936.

85 AO, F45, B294820, G.N. Gordon to Roebuck, 16 July 1934. F10, MU4935, King to Hepburn, 12 July 1934.

86 AO, RG3, Box 227, A.M. Latchford to Slaght, 10 July 1934.

87 W.R. Graham, *Arthur Meighen, a Biography: No Surrender*, Vol. 3 (Toronto: Clarke Irwin, 1965), 55.

88 C. Backhouse and N.L. Backhouse, *The Heiress vs. the Establishment: Mrs. Campbell's Campaign for Legal Justice* (Vancouver: UBC Press, 2004), 263–4. *Globe*, 8, 9 June 1934. P. Boyer, *A Passion for Justice: The Legacy of James Chalmers McRuer* (Toronto: UTP, 1994), 98–9. Saywell's biography of Hepburn minimizes the ugly side of the relationship or how rumours about Slaght's conduct compelled W.L.M. King to reject his appointment to a junior cabinet position in 1935.

89 OHA, 90.003, Proceedings, II, 17 July 1934, 19–27.

90 90.003, Proceedings, XV, 21 August 1934, 2064–6.

91 90.003, Proceedings, IX, 2 August 1934, 1246–8, 1312. Latchford went after Strachan Johnston over his role as the titular president of Electric Power Company (controlled by Sun Life of Canada), which supplied central Ontario. During 1916 a buyout by HEPCO was arranged with generous terms that still rankled the justice. See W.R. Plewman, *Adam Beck and the Ontario Hydro* (Toronto: Ryerson Press, 1947), 193–4.

92 90.003, Proceedings, XIV, 17 August 1934, 1884, 1931–5, 1962.

93 90.003, Proceedings, VIII, 31 July 1934, 1130–9; v.9, 2 August, 1286–1310; XVI, 22 August 1934, 2260–6.

94 RG18-105, Report of the Latchford-Smith Royal Commission, 16, 6–7, 18, 26. Original copies of the report are also located in AO, RG 49-19, No. 49 (1934), and OHA file 90.003. Unrecognized by most people at the time, the report was reprinted in the *Annual Report of the Hydro-Electric Power Commission, 1934*, Appendix IV, 448–74.

95 RG18-105, Report, 19, 21–4.

96 RG18-105, Report, 19, 21–4.

97 RG18-105, Report, 19, 43.
98 LAC, MG26-K, 419319, Meighen to Bennett, 1 August 1934; 419316, Meighen to A.W. Merriam, 23 July 1934.
99 LAC, MG26-I, 214, Meighen to Bennett, 4 January 1935; Bennett to Meighen, 7 January 1935. Canada, Senate, *Debates*, 22 January 1935, 3–5.
100 *Toronto Telegram*, 4 December 1936. *Globe*, 3, 4 December 1936; 24 February 1937; 4, 23 March 1937. LAC, MG26-I, 173, Meighen to John Morrison, 2 March 1937.
101 LAC, MG30-E82, 16, C.A. Magrath to A.V. White, 31 March 1939, "private"; White to Magrath, 13 January 1940. For Henry's accusations, which were made several times, *Globe*, *Mail and Empire*, and *Toronto Telegram* for 22 February, 27 March 1935. The *Globe* trivialized the charge and pushed a load of baloney about how the Liberals' "young leader" handled the former premier.
102 RG3, 306, T.H. Hogg to Hepburn, 31 October 1940. OHA, ORR 633.01, 91.029, Abitibi-OPS, Gundy to H.C. Nixon, 25 July 1942.

9. The Search for Stability

1 AO, RG3, 10-0-95, Sir Charles Fitzpatrick to M.F. Hepburn, 21 September 1934.
2 RG3, 10-0-1, R.O. Sweezey to Hepburn, Sweezey to Peter Heenan, 24 July 1934. Sweezey's grand boondoggle and its fruits are deliciously narrated in T.D. Regehr, *The Beauharnois Scandal: A Story of Canadian Entrepreneurship and Politics* (Toronto: University of Toronto Press, 1990).
3 C.W. Hofer, "Turnaround Strategies," *Journal of Business Strategy*, 1:1 (1980), 19–31.
4 AO, RG22-5800, B126995, 2994/32, *Montreal Trust v. Abitibi Power and Paper*, G.H. Mead, 25 February 1933.
5 MLCA, 81.20.151 G.H. Mead to Clarkson, 2 March 1933. 81.22.155, Ripley to BRC, 13 September 1935.
6 MLCA, 81.22.150, Calvert to Reid, 7 March 1933. 81.20.151, Reid to Clarkson, 19 May 1933.
7 T. Heinrich, "Product Diversification in the U.S. Pulp and Paper Industry: The Case of International Paper, 1898–1941," *Business History Review*, 75:3 (2001), 493. MLCA, 81.20.152, Motion, Acquire G.H. Mead, 9 June 1933.
8 81.22.150, Osler to Ripley, 14 March 1933. 81.20.152, Minutes, BRC meeting, 8 September 1933. 2994/32, Sales contracts and policies, 25 February 1933; G.H. Mead and Co., 9 June 1933.
9 2994/32, G.H. Mead, 30 October. MLCA, 81.20.152, Indebtedness to G.H. Mead, revolving credit, 4 December 1933.

10 HUBL, Abitibi Power and Paper, *RR* (1936), 4. 2994/32, G.H. Mead, 2 April
1942. *FP*, 30 May 1936. Mead's official biography misrepresented what
occurred. "Several years later, he sold the sales company to the Abitibi
receiver – the price had by then dropped to $750,000 – to help the company
get back on its feet, and for the remainder of his life he remained in Abitibi
employ as a consultant. But, while he by no means closed the door on
the experience he had gained in Canada, he closed it tight on the Abitibi
merger and collapse." Mead Corporation, *In Quiet Ways: George H. Mead,
the Man and the Company* (Dayton, OH: Mead Corporation, 1970), 111.

11 2994/32, Murray Bay Paper, 25 February 1933.

12 81.22.151, Calvert to Reid, 13 March 1933; A.P. Thornhill to J.E. Fortier, 16
January 1933.

13 2994/32, Murray Bay Paper, 25 February 1933, 9 June 1933. MLCA,
81.20.150, A.P. Thornhill to J.E. Fortier, 16 January 1933; 81.20.151, BRC
Meeting Minutes, 15 February 1933.

14 2994/32, Murray Bay Paper, 9 June 1933. MLCA, 81.20.151, Glyn Osler to
Reid, 7 April 1933. 81.20.152, Minutes, BRC meeting, 8 September 1933.

15 2994/32, Ste. Anne Paper, 25 February and 27 March 1933. MLCA,
81.22.155, St. Anne Paper, 16 October 1935.

16 MLCA, 81.22.155, Ripley to BRC, 13 September 1935; Ripley to Clarkson,
31 October 1935.

17 MLCA, 81.22.156, Ripley to BRC, 30 January, 10 February 1936. C.
Wiegman, *Trees to News: A Chronicle of the Ontario Paper Company's Origin
and Development* (Toronto: McClelland and Stewart, 1953), 27–88, 113–70.

18 81.20.150, A.P. Thornhill to J.E. Fortier, 16 January 1933; Clarkson to
Somerville, 22 February 1933.

19 81.20.151, BPC meeting minutes, 15 February 1933. 2994/32, Thunder Bay
Paper, 25 February, 27 March, 9 June 1933.

20 81.20.155 Ripley to BRC, 15 September 1935, 13 March 1936; Stock
Purchase of Thunder Bay Paper, 3 April 1936. 81.20,156, Thunder Bay
Paper, 25 March 1936. AO, 2994/32, Thunder Bay Paper, final compromise
of claim, 12 June 1936.

21 LAC, RG15, 1287, 625079, H.R. Rowatt to Clarkson, 14 February 1934.
MLCA, 81.22.154, Clarkson to Ripley, 18 March 1935. 81.20.155, Minutes,
BRC meeting, 10 October 1935; Motion, Compromise of Claim of Manitoba
Paper v. Peabody Securities, 16 October 1935.

22 I. Radforth, *Bush Workers and Bosses: Logging in Northern Ontario, 1900–1980*
(Toronto: University of Toronto Press, 1987), 25–106.

23 *Globe*, 23, 27, and 28 November 1933.

24 81.20.153, Clarkson to Ripley, 4 January 1934.

25 81.20.153, Clarkson to Ripley, 18 April 1934; Osler to Ripley, 30 April 1934.

26 *Globe*, 15 September; 2, 9, and 12 October 1934.

27 *Globe*, 16, 18, 22, 23, and 24 October; 3 and 5 November 1934. Radforth,
    Bush Workers and Bosses, 131–3.
28 *FP*, 11 May 1935. See also, *FP*, 25 April, 4 June 1932.
29 81.20.154, F.G. Fleming to Somerville, 14 June 1935; B.B. Osler to
    Somerville, 26 June 1935. 2994/32, Order by Middleton, 13 September
    1935, Order by the Master; 7 October 1935.
30 81.22.155, Ripley to BRC, 13 September 1935.
31 *Barron's*, 2 December 1935.
32 D. McDowall, *Steel at the Sault: Francis H. Clergue, Sir James Dunn, and the
    Algoma Steel Corporation, 1910–1956* (Toronto: University of Toronto Press,
    1984), 124–45. McDowall argued Hepburn did not know about Dunn's
    involvement but that assumes complete naiveté by the premier. Hepburn
    was briefed on any significant corporate reorganization during his term
    of office. Dunn's role was headlined in American papers well before
    introduction of the Algoma bill. See *NYT*, 4, January 1935, *WSJ*, 8 January
    1935.
33 Re. Empire Mining Company, [1891] 1 Ch. 215. The practice was
    sanctioned under UKS, 8 Edw VII [1908], ch. 69, s.120, British Companies
    (Consolidation) Act. See also Palmer, Company Precedents (10th ed.), 430–
    2. The main precedent in American jurisprudence was Canada Southern
    Railway v. Gebhard, [1883] 109 U. S. 527, 3 Sup. Ct. 363.
34 OS, 25 Geo. V [1935], ch. 76, An Act Respecting Algoma Steel Corporation,
    Limited. McDowall, Steel at the Sault, 146–51.
35 *Globe*, 8 April 1935.
36 *OS*, 25 Geo. V [1935], ch. 32, An Act to Amend the Judicature Act. *TS*, 8
    March 1935. *Globe*, 10 April 1935.
37 *Globe*, 8, 12, 28 January 1935.
38 MLCA, 81.22.155, R.O. Sweezey and Co., Abitibi Power and Paper, 29
    January 1935. *Globe*, 7 March, 13 April, 7 June 1935. Sweezey assumed
    his company would underwrite the bonds and preferred shares, another
    unlikely proposition.
39 *Globe*, 8 June 1935. MLCA, 81.201.54, Ripley to Somerville, 6, 13 February
    1935; Hugh Griffith to Ripley, 11 February 1935.
40 MLCA, 81.20.157, Osler to Ripley, 1 April 1936; Ripley to Osler, 3 April
    1936.
41 OHA, ORR104.1-1, The Hydro Enquiry, Address by the Attorney-General
    Hon. Mr. Roebuck, 27 February–1 March 1935.
42 OHA, ORR 530, Hogg to Lyon, 21 December 1936. AO, RG49-113,
    Proceedings of the Select Committee investigating Hydro Power Contracts
    and Hydro Administration, 1135–44. OHA, ORR 127.2, F.A. Gaby, Trends
    of Electrical Demands in Relation to Power Supplies (Toronto: Hydro-
    Electric Power Commission of Ontario, 1933), 13–31, which documented

how Hydro normally underestimated demand and therefore "always
endeavoured to move in advance of actual requirements."

43 *MG*, 25 March 1935. J.T. Saywell, *"Just Call Me Mitch": The Life of Mitchell F. Hepburn* (Toronto: University of Toronto Press, 1991), 200–5.

44 AO, F45, B294852, Report on Claims of Hydro-Electric Power Commission of Ontario Against Abitibi Power and Paper Company Limited and its Subsidiaries, 30 April 1935, 2–7, 35. AO, F45, MU2490, L. Duncan to T.S. Lyon, 5 April 1935.

45 OHQ, Minute of Commission, 14 May 1935. Copy also in AO, F45, MU2490.

46 F45, B294852, Application by Lewis Duncan and Affidavit of W.W. Pope, 17 May 1935. *TT*, 18 May 1935. *Globe*, 20 May 1935.

47 F45, B294852, Deposition of F.C. Clarkson, 17 June 1935.

48 F45, B294852, Deposition of Harold Wilson Shapley, 17 June 1935, 24–5.

49 F45, B294852, Deposition of Harold Wilson Shapley, 47–9.

50 F45, B294852, Duncan to Roebuck, 19 June 1935; R.S. Robertson to Lyon, 18 December 1935. OHQ, Minute of Commission, 18 October 1935.

51 OHA, ORR 633.01, 91.029, Abitibi-OPS, T.S. Lyon to Roebuck, 22 February 1936.

52 ORR 530, I.B. Lucas to Gaby and Jeffrey, 22 February 1934; Hydro purchase of Espanola power, April 1934–February 1936. RG3, 232, Lyon to Hepburn, 20 August 1935; 238, Lyon to Hepburn, 23 August 1935.

53 RG3, 9-0-245, Lyon to Hepburn, 17 December 1936; 9-0-143.1, Lyon to Hepburn, 20 August 1935.

54 *Globe*, 27 January 1933; *PPMC*, February 1933, 91–4, 162; May 1933, 315. LAC, MG2-III-B9, Stevens Papers, XXVII, draft notes of speech, 25 January 1933.

55 D.R. Richberg, *Tents of the Mighty* (New York: Willett, Clark & Colby, 1930), 196–203. A.M. Schlesinger, *The Coming of the New Deal* (Boston: Houghton Mifflin, 1958), 93–4. A. Dawley, *Struggles for Justice: Social Responsibility and the Liberal State* (Cambridge, MA: Harvard University Press, 1991), 362–4.

56 E. Hawley, *The New Deal and the Problem of Monopoly* (Princeton: Princeton University Press, 1966), 53–71.

57 NARA, RG9, National Recovery Administration Records, Johnson to Richberg, 26 December 1933; Address of Hugh Johnson to National Association of Manufacturers, 7 December 1933, NRA Release 2126. See also, Schlesinger, *The Coming of the New Deal*, 107–10. H. Johnson, *The Blue Eagle: From Egg to Earth* (New York: Doubleday, Doran, 1935), 196–204.

58 Schlesinger, *The Coming of the New Deal*, 121. Johnson, *The Blue Eagle*, 177–81. D.R. Richberg, *The Rainbow* (New York: Doubleday Doran, 1936), 159–63.

59 *PPMC*, August 1933, 493–5, 501, 528.

60 *NYT*, 24, 25 October 1933. *WSJ*, 26, 28, and 30 October, 4 November 1933. *Globe*, 3 November 1933.
61 NRA, *Codes of Fair Competition, No. 111–150*, III (Washington: GPO, 1934), 103–13. *NYT*, 14, 17 December 1933. See also L.E. Ellis, *Print Paper Pendulum: Group Pressures and the Price of Newsprint* (New Brunswick, NJ: Rutgers University Press, 1947), 154–61, which provides an overview of the NRA conflicts between producers and publishers.
62 Publishers' Association arguments from *NYT*, 19 January 1934, 2 and 3 February 1934, 7 April 1934, 20 July 1934, 1 and 4 August 1934. NARA, RG9, NRA, Newsprint Recommendations, Volume A contains an objective assessment, "Industrial Advisor's Report on Recommendations of Newsprint Code Authority."
63 *NYT*, 2 February 1934. *WP*, 2 February 1934. Detailed statements are in NARA, RG9.4.8, 652787, Hearings on Proposed Recommendations in Respect of the Stabilization of the Newsprint Industry and Elimination of Unfair Practices and Destructive Prices, 1 February 1934.
64 *WP*, 29 April 1934. *NYT*, 3, 4 August 1934. *WSJ*, 4, 8, 14 August 1934.
65 *Schechter Poultry Corp. v. United States*, [1934] 295 U.S. 495. Justice Brandeis later claimed the decision meant, "This is the end of this business of centralization, and I want you to go back and tell the president that we're not going to let this government centralize everything." FDR Library, 49–162, Statement of Thomas Corcoran, 3 April 1939. Much of the ruling was reversed in *National Labor Relations Board v. Jones & Laughlin Steel Corporation*, [1937] 301 U.S. 1.
66 NARA, RG9.4.8, Newsprint Recommendations, Volume B-1. E. Jones, Paper Industry Study, Department of Commerce Office of National Recovery Administration (Washington: unpublished, 1936), 401–3, 425–7.
67 BANQ, P350, XIX, dossier a, Procès-Verbal, 19 December 1934.
68 AO, RG3, 10-0-320, ANPA Bulletin 210, 27 February 1935 [bold typeface in original]. See also H.V. Nelles, *The Politics of Development: Forests, Mines, and Hydro-Electric Power in Ontario, 1849–1941* (Toronto: Macmillan of Canada, 1974), 452–3.
69 BANQ, P350, XIX, Taschereau to Hepburn, 12 March 1935.
70 RG3, 9-0-29, Hepburn to Bennett, 10 November 1934; Bennett to Hepburn, 10 November 1934; 9-0-67, Hepburn to J.-F. Pouliot, 28 February 1935.
71 RG3, 9-0-67, Hepburn to Taschereau, 18 March 1935; 229, Press statement on newsprint, 24 October 1934.
72 RG3, 9-0-67, Heenan to Hepburn, 22 February 1935. 2994/32, Department of Justice Investigation, 29 September 1939.
73 RG3, 9-0-150, Hepburn to Taschereau, 18 March 1935.
74 R.S. Lambert and P. Pross, *Renewing Nature's Wealth* (Toronto: Queen's Printer, 1967), 328–30, 335–9. Nelles, *Politics of Development*, 454. RG1,

E-10, Department of Lands and Forests, Woods and Forests, Order-in-Council Book 4, 144RG3, 9-0-44, F. Noad to Heenan, 29 August 1934; 3-10-45, Noad to Heenan, 21 October 1935; 10-0-48, Heenan to Hepburn, 22 February 1935. *PPMC*, February 1935, 109; March 1935, 188. Frederick Noad was deputy minister until he was fired in May 1935, less than a year after his appointment. The removal has been attributed to an order from Hepburn but it is more likely the acid-tongued civil servant was fired for questioning the government's motives. Noad was a scribbler who repetitiously approached newspapers, politicians, and congressional committees with claims that he had "secret" information.

75 RG49-115, B248795, Proceedings, 23 January 1940, 215–16.
76 RG3, 9-0-67, A.W. Leslie to Hepburn, 1 February 1935; F.R. McKelcan to Hepburn, 4 February 1935.
77 RG3, 10-0-320, G.M. Cottrelle to Hepburn, 15 April 1935.
78 RG3, 9-0-200, Sweezey to Hepburn, 21 February 1935. Sweezey to Taschereau, 16 February 1935; RG 3, 245, Sweezey to Hepburn, 1 May 1935.
79 9-0-150, C. Vining to Hepburn, Some Conclusions Regarding Newsprint, 18 February 1935.
80 9-0-150, Vining to Hepburn, 24 June 1935; Vining to Hepburn, 23 October 1935.
81 9-0-150, The Newsprint Bulletin, No. 8, November 1935; C.K. Blandin to Hepburn, 15 October 1935.
82 RG3, 260, Heenan to Vining, 4 March 1936; Taschereau to Heenan, 11 March 1936; Heenan to Taschereau, 24 March 1936.
83 *Quebec Statutes*, 25–6 Geo. V [1935], ch 22, Forest Resources Protection Act. *OS*, 1 Ed. VIII [1936], ch. 22, An Act to Regulate the Forest Resources of the Province of Ontario.
84 RG3, 260, Vining to Hepburn 1 and 8 June 1936.
85 RG3, 260, Hepburn to Vining, 8 June 1936.
86 BANQ, P350, XIX, Taschereau to Vining, 1 June 1936. RG3, 260, A. Godbout to Vining, 25 June 1936.
87 *NYT*, 19 February and 27 March 1936. *WSJ*, 3 March and 16 June 1936.
88 *FP*, 1 and 8 August 1936.
89 RG3, 10-0-517, Unsigned, Vining to Heenan, 9 August 1936.
90 *FP*, 7 March 1936.
91 MLCA, 81.20.157, Newsprint Contracts, 16 June 1936. AO, 2994/32, Order, Pro-rating, 10 July 1936; Memo, Department of Justice Investigation, 29 September 1939.
92 *Globe*, 19 October, 10 November, and 19 December 1936.
93 AO, RG3, 10-0-320, R.O. Sweezey and Company, The Future of the Canadian Newsprint Industry, undated but circa autumn 1935.

10. Reorganization Plots

1 *Lincoln Printing Co. vs. Middle West Utilities Co.*, [1934] 6 F. Supp. 682–3 (N.D. Ill).

2 *FP*, 12 and 26 February, 9 April 1931.

3 *FP*, 28 May and 4 June 1931. As with Abitibi, many of the largest holders of Canada Power bonds were life insurance companies. *NYT*, 14 July 1931.

4 *Annual Financial Review* (1932), 296–307. *FP*, 4 and 11 June 1931. *Globe*, 4 June 1931. The transactions associated with the formation and reorganization of Canada Power and Paper are documented in House of Commons, Proceedings of the Select Committee on Banking and Commerce, 22 and 23 May 1934, 762–926.

5 The precedents typically cited included *Re. Alabama, New Orleans, Texas and Pacific Junction Railway Co.* [1891] Ch. 213–248; *Re. English, Scottish and Australian Chartered Bank* [1893] 3 Ch. 385 (C.A.). For an account of British rulings relevant to Canada, see J. Gold, "Preference Shareholders in the Reconstruction of English Companies," *University of Toronto Law Review*, 5 (1943–4), 282–323. Contemporary American practices are summarized in E.M. Dodd, "Fair and Equitable Recapitalizations," *Harvard Law Review*, 55 (1939), 780–818.

6 *FP*, 18 and 25 June, 14 November 1931.

7 *PPMC*, June 1932, 187, 189, 210. *FP*, 25 June 1932.

8 *WSJ* and *NYT*, 28 May and 3 June 1932. *FP*, 4 and 11 June 1932. The investment trust was the first casualty of the failure and was forced into liquidation during the summer.

9 *Globe* and *NYT*, 5 and 6 June 1932. *FP*, 11 June 1932.

10 *Globe*, 29 July 1932. *FP*, 25 June 1932. *NYT*, 29 and 30 July, 2 August 1932.

11 *Globe*, 31 August and 20 September 1932. *NYT*, 24 August 1932. *PPMC*, July 1932, 241; August 1932, 269, 296.

12 *MG*, *NYT*, 24 June 1933.

13 *Globe*, 22 June 1933. *NYT*, 8 July 1933.

14 *NYT*, 1 October 1933. *PPMC*, October 1933, 589.

15 *Globe*, 1 and 25 November 1933. *PPMC*, November 1933, 673. *NYT*, 31 October 1933.

16 *Globe* and *NYT*, 19 December 1933, 17 January 1934. *Globe*, 19 January and 13 February 1934.

17 *PPMC*, January 1934, 41–2; February 1934, 59; March 1934, 227–8.

18 *NYT*, 22 May and 20 June 1934. *PPMC*, June 1934, 381–2; July 1934, 440.

19 *Globe* and *NYT*, 11 April 1936.

20 *Globe* and *NYT*, 24 February, 26 March, 30 April 1936.

21 *NYT*, *WSJ*, *Globe*, 18 and 19 November 1936.

22 *NYT*, 29 November 1936.

23 *FP*, 21 November 1936. *Globe*, 30 November 1936.

24 *Globe*, 31 December 1936, 10 January 1937. *FP*, 9 January 1937.

25 *FP*, 14 July 1934, 2 May 1936, 6 March 1937. *Barron's*, 31 May 1937.

26 *Shawinigan Standard*, 1 June 1949. Jones served with the firm (along with Mersey Paper) until his death and was succeeded as president by A.C. Price. Jones raised and commanded the 227nd Battalion of the Canadian Expeditionary Force between 1914 and 1919. Killam claimed to have found him among the "cross-section of better people" in Montreal men's clubs.

27 AO, RG22-5800, 2194/31, *National Trust v. Great Lakes Paper*, Statement of claim and affidavit of F.R. MacKelcan, 13 July 1931. *WSJ*, 1 May 1928. *PPMC*, 26 September 1929, 473–7, 496.

28 *WSJ*, 3 March 1931. *Globe*, 2 March and 10 and 17 July 1931.

29 2194/31, First and interim report of receiver, 30 July 1931, 11 August 1931. Cross-examination of F.R. MacKelcan, 19 December 1935, 1–5. *NYT*, 30 August 1933. Backus himself concurrently was the plaintiff in an unsuccessful effort to place the Tennessee Publishing Company in receivership and recoup bond obligations. The officers of that firm later were convicted for fraud and conspiring to destroy any apparent liability for their actions.

30 AO, F9-1-0-16, B253682, Env. 1, Circular, E.W. Backus to Minnesota and Ontario Bondholders, 5 January 1934, sketched a creative version of the collapse that almost no one accepted. For the claims of a "plot," USSSEP, 3 April 1934, 7645–99. *WSJ*, 12 and 13 January 1934. *WT* and *Minneapolis Journal*, 13 July 1934.

31 *PPMC*, February 1934, 177–8. *NYT*, 10 January, 5 and 6 February, 8 April, and 3 October 1934. *WP*, 15 February and 10 June 1934. *WT*, 7 April 1934.

32 For death, *Globe*, *MG*, *NYT*, 30 October 1934. For the Minnesota and Ontario reorganization, *WT*, 11 January and 1 March 1941.

33 2194/31, Cross-examination of F.R. MacKelcan, 19 December 1935, 6–8.

34 2194/31, Cross-examination of F.R. MacKelcan, 14.

35 2194/31, Cross-examination of F.R. MacKelcan, 33. Affidavits of F.R. MacKelcan, 11 August 1931, 2 and 13 June 1932. Affidavit of Louis L. Lang, 19 December 1935.

36 *FT*, 18 May 1935. *Globe*, 23 July, 13 August, 11 and 21 September 1935. Rumours of bids by Abitibi, Hearst, and other publishers circulated across the summer. The press called the final option the "Gefaell-Aldrich" proposal in all accounts. This was based upon a stenographer's error. The bid came from the newspaper publisher, the agent was just a co-signer.

37 2194/31, Cross-examination of F.R. MacKelcan, 21–50; Affidavit of F.R. MacKelcan and Order, 25 June 1936. MLCA, 81.20.155, Minutes, Meeting of 10 October 1935. RG3, 245, L. M. Collins to Holders of Great Lakes Paper Co. Bonds, 1 November 1935.

38 AO, RG3, 245, Sweezey to Hepburn, 1 May 1935; Resolution unanimously approved at a meeting of Canadian newsprint manufacturers in Montreal, 16 October 1935; Vining to Hepburn, 23 October 1935.

39 *FP*, 2 and 9 November 1935. RG3, 245, A.R. Graustein to Hepburn, 4 November 1935.

40 RG3, 245, C. Vining, "Great Lakes Paper Company and the Gefaell Proposals," 25 October 1935. MLCA, 81.20.155, To National Trust Co. Ltd., Re: Great Lakes, Offer of Black Sturgeon Newsprint, Ltd. The complex deal would have split the equity into three classes with only one group having voting rights. Canadian producers agreed to take a specified amount of production annually in exchange for representation on the board of directors. Meighen's objections appear valid. Policy changes required two-thirds approval from the board and disputes were subject to a sustained arbitration process, which could have left the debt holders literally holding the bag.

41 RG3, 245, H. Badanai to Hepburn, 4 November 1935; Heenan to Hepburn, 29 October 1935.

42 *FP*, 2 November 1935. *Globe*, 5 November 1935.

43 *Globe*, 11 November 1935. *NYT*, 12 November 1935.

44 A.J. Thomson to Heenan, 24 March 1936; Heenan to Thomson, 26 March 1936, in JLAO, 75 (1941), Appendix 1, 6 May 1940, 641–3. *ME*, 25 March 1936.

45 RG3, 9-0-252, Mimeo, Great Lakes Paper Company, Cost of production, July 1936. C.H. Carlisle to GLP Bondholders, 28 September 1936. Carlisle to Hepburn, 5 August 1936.

46 JLAO, 75 (1941), Appendix 1, 6 May 1940, 644–5. AO, RG3, 9-0-252, Carlisle to Hepburn, 28 September 1936. RG3, 11-0-13, Carlisle to Great Lakes Paper security holders, 9 February 1937. For failure to earn interest fully, *GM*, 9 February 1937.

47 RG3, 260, Vining to Ralston, 9 August 1937; 278, Carlisle to Vining, 15 February 1937.

48 RG3, 278, Heenan to Carlisle, 12 March 1937; RG3, 279, Carlisle to Duplessis, 4 May 1937; Carlisle to Hepburn, 5 May 1937.

49 RG3, 278, Hepburn to Vining, 20 July 1937.

50 81.22.156, Ripley to BRC, 30 January; BRC to Abitibi bondholders, 27 March 1936. 81.20.158, Ripley to Somerville, 1 October 1936.

51 81.23.157, Memorandum, 31 January 1936; Circular letter, BRC to Abitibi Bondholders, 27 March 1936.

52 81.20.158, Ripley to Somerville, 1 October 1936.

53 81.22.156, Ripley to BRC, 30 January, 10 and 21 February 1936.

54 81.22.156, Osler to Ripley, 1 April 1936; Ripley to Osler, 3 April 1936. 81.20.158, Ripley to Somerville, 1 October 1936. AO, RG 22-5089, 2994/32, 1177, Ripley affidavit, 26 January 1937.

55 *CSI*, 40–6, 83–4, Exhibit Q. HUBL, Abitibi Power and Paper, *RR* (1937), 14–15, 16–19. The calculations did not include anything for working capital, took no account contributions from the common stock of Provincial Paper, or monies that might be received if defunct properties were liquidated. The engineers recommended an annual depreciation charge of $1.48 million. In contrast, during 1928, based upon a production basis for depreciation and operations at 94.7 per cent, Abitibi had charged $1.7 million. Clarkson's estimates of working capital needs were quite judgmental and rested upon an arbitrary rule of $12.50 to $15 per ton of production.

56 F10, MU 4936, Reasons of Public Policy why Abitibi Reorganization should proceed immediately, n.d. Marked "private and strictly confidential."

57 81.20.157, Newsprint Contracts, 16 June 1936. RG3, 10-0-562, Bethune Smith to Hepburn, 20 May 1937.

58 OHA, ORR530, Box 188, T.H. Hogg to T.S. Lyon, 19 and 21 December 1936. RG49-19, SP 46 (1939), A.M. McCrimmon to H.C. Nixon, 21 January 1937.

59 RG49-19, SP 46 (1939), Memorandum of Conference between HEPCO, Clarkson and Ripley by T.H. Hogg and R.T. Jeffrey, 26 January 1937; Nixon to McCrimmon, 28 January 1937.

60 RG49-19, SP 46, Lyon to Nixon, 28 January 1937; G. Hanna to A.E. Semple, 12 February 1937.

61 RG49-19, SP 46, Lyon to Nixon, 28 January 1937.

62 RG 49-19, SP 46, H.C. Draper to Nixon, 22 January 1937.

63 RG 49-19, SP 46, G. Osler to W. Cain, 2 March 1937. F45, MU 2490, Counter claims, n.d.; A. Humphries to Roebuck, 20 March 1937; Note by Roebuck, 21 March 1937.

64 ORR530, Box 188, W.G. Hannah to Roebuck, 16 March 1937. F45, MU 2490, Speech on Crystal Falls acquisition, 22 March 1936. *Globe, NYT*, 23 March 1937.

65 RG 49-19, SP 46, Hepburn to Lieutenant Governor in Council, 5 May 1937; Order-in-Council, 2 June 1937.

66 81.23.158, Ripley to BRC, 18 December 1936; Somerville to Ripley, 22 December 1936.

67 81.20.158, Ripley to Somerville, 1 October 1936.

68 81.20.157, Field Glore and Company, Report Re. Proposed Merger of the Following Canadian Companies, 3–4, 8. J.C. Kemp to BRC, 27 March 1936, noted Charlton "believes International Paper is approaching a serious crisis in its financial position but, he is obviously very bitter about this company for who he worked so long and I am not sure that his judgment is altogether unprejudiced."

69 81.20.157, 7–10, 14; Exhibits D, E.

70 81.20.157, Charlton Plan, as Affecting Abitibi, 1 April 1936.

71 81.20.157, Ripley to BRC, 3 April 1936; Kemp to Ripley, 39 March 1936.

72 81.20.158, F.T. Webb to Somerville, 26 November 1936.

73 *FP*, 5 June 1937. *Barrons*, 31 May 1937, 17.

74 81.23.158, Rothermere to Clarkson, 31 October, 3 and 26 November 1936. Rothermere was a supporter of fascist regimes and appeasement. See I. Kershaw, *Making Friends with Hitler: Lord Londonderry, the Nazis, and the Road to War* (New York: Penguin, 2005).

11. The Battle of the Plans

1 T. Arnold, *The Folklore of Capitalism* (New Haven, CT: Yale University Press, 1936), 230.

2 F. Fukuyama, *Trust: The Social Virtues and the Creation of Prosperity* (London: Penguin, 1995), chaps. 1–5.

3 MLCA, 81.23.162, H.J. Symington to J.P. Ripley, 31 May 1937.

4 AO, RG22-5800, 2994/32, *Montreal Trust v. Abitibi Power and Paper*, Affidavit, J.P. Ripley, 26 January 1937. Statement of Claim, 15 February 1937; Statement of Defence, 16 February 1937.

5 AO, RG3, 10-0-562, S. Johnston to B. Smith 8 March 1937. Johnston and Wright submitted the final documents to the government after they were drafted by Glyn Osler and even though all the parties knew who had done the work.

6 AO, RG3, 10-0-562, Smith to M.F. Hepburn, 20 May 1937. V. Mitchell, *A Treatise on the Law Relating to Canadian Commercial Corporations* (Montreal: Southam Press, 1916), 1482–98.

7 2994/32, Notice of Motion and P. Wright affidavit; 19 February 1937; Order, 25 February 1937. Notice of Motion and R.S. McPherson affidavit, 16 February 1937; Appeal motions, 1 and 12 March 1937. MLCA, 81.23.162, Ripley to Bondholders' Representative Committee, 27 May 1937.

8 81.20.159, W.H. Somerville to Ripley, 19 April 1937.

9 *WSJ*, 4 and 14 August, 22 September 1936. *NYT*, 18 October 1936, *Barrons's*, 15 February 1937.

10 81.20.159, Somerville to J.G. Singer, 3 March 1937.

11 *NYT*, November 1936, 25 March 1937.

12 81.20.159, Address of Charles Vining to the Canadian Club of Montreal, 1 February 1937.

13 *NYT*, *WSJ*, 20 March 1937. *GM*, 27 March 1937.

14 *FP*, 27 March 1937. 81.20.159, Clarkson to Somerville, 9 April 1937.

15 AO, RG 49-19, SP 49, Bondholders' Representative Committee Report, 17 March 1937.

16 Press stories, along with Arthur Slaght who was a solicitor for Wood Gundy, claimed that the firm owned $3 million in Abitibi preferred shares. The company later declared it held 11,604 shares in 1937 but almost all

were in trust for clients. AO, RG-18, Proceedings, 16 November 1940, 696; 9 December 1940, 1114.

17 81.20.160, Ripley to BRC, 17 May 1937. 81.20.163, Memorandum of Comment on Various Plans for Reorganization of Abitibi, 17 June 1937. *FP*, 15, 22, 29 May 1937. *Globe*, 3 and 27 May 1937.

18 RG3, 10-0-562, Criticism of the Liquidator of Abitibi Power and Paper Company Limited in regard to a plan of reorganization submitted by Glyn Osler on 1 February 1937, 27 February 1937.

19 81.20.162, Plan of Compromise or Arrangement Proposed by Roy Sharvell McPherson, Preliminary Proof, No. 1, 15 May 1937. Marked "Absolutely Confidential for members of the Bondholders' Representative Committee only." 81.23.160, Ripley to BRC, 21 and 24 May 1937. 81.20.150, Ripley to Somerville, 18 May 1937.

20 81.20.163 Memorandum of Comment on Various Plans for Reorganization of Abitibi, Confidential for BRC and PSC, 17 June 1937. 81.20.159, Ripley to Arbuckle, Cross, Fleming, Griffis, and Somerville, 27 May 1937. HUBL, *RR*, 7 October 1937, 13–16, made detailed estimates at alternative pulp prices and demonstrated how McPherson's calculations were fictitious.

21 *FP*, 22 May 1937.

22 *GM*, 15 and 19 May, 5 July, 8 September 1937. *WSJ*, 29 May 1937.

23 *GM*, 15 and 19 May 1937. *FP*, 24 July 1937.

24 *FP*, 31 July 1937. It was a measure of Brooks's diplomatic skills that he remained on good terms with both Hepburn and Roebuck. Following the attorney general's resignation in April 1937 the relationship between the politicians descended into one of mutual loathing, often characterized by vitriolic critiques of each other in the legislature and the press.

25 RG3, 10-0-562, Harrison and Company, Plan of Reorganization for Abitibi Power and Paper Co. Ltd. *FP*, 29 May 1937. *WSJ*, 27 May 1937. *GM*, 28 May 1937. In 81.20.163, Memorandum of Comment, Ripley dismissed the new bonds as insufficient capital and without value. He could not figure out how the firm derived the "hypothetical earnings."

26 F45, MU 2542, Brooks to Roebuck, 17 November 1937. F45, MU 2542, Affidavit of J.C. Kemp, 1 June 1937; Motion under the Winding-Up Act, Affidavit of R.S. McPherson, 25 June 1937; Order, 2 July 1937.

27 F45, MU 2542, Memoranda re. Abitibi Common and Preferred Shareholders, 29 June 1937. *GM*, 7 July 1937.

28 *GM*, 26 June 1937.

29 81.20.159, Ripley to Somerville, 17 April 1937.

30 81.20.159, Ripley to Bondholders' Representative Committee, 30 April 1937. *FP*, 22 May 1937.

31 *GM*, 14 May 1937. RG 49-19, SP 46, Cain to Blake 22 March 1937.

32 2994/32, HEPCO Agreement, 5 and 15 June 1937 [both sealed and marked confidential]. 81.20.162, Ripley to BRC, 4 June 1937. RG 49-19, SP 46, Cain to Heenan, 22 June 1937.

33 81.20.159, Ripley to Bondholders' Representative Committee, 30 April 1937; Ripley to W. Hastie, 21 April 1937.

34 81.20.159, Summary of Modified Plan Considered by the Preferred Shareholders' Committee, 29 April 1937; Ripley to Representative Committee, 30 April 1937.

35 81.20.160, Ripley to Somerville, 13 May 1937; Somerville to Ripley, 4 May 1937. *WSJ*, 15 May 1937.

36 81.20.150, Ripley to Somerville, 18 May 1937. 81.20.162, Ripley to BRC, 27 May and 1 June 1937; Minutes, Telephone conference, 31 May 1937. *FP*, 5 June 1937.

37 81.20.162, Ripley to BRC, 4 and 16 June 1937; H. Molson to BRC, 10 June 1937.

38 81.20.162, 16 and 18 June 1937.

39 RG49-10, SP 46, R.S. McPherson, Plan of Compromise or Arrangement, 9 June 1937, 4–6.

40 RG 49-19, SP 46, E.G. McMillan to Hepburn, 16 June 1937.

41 *GM*, 16 June and 29 July 1937. *FP*, 7 August 1937. 81.20.163, Memorandum of Comment on Various Plans for Reorganization of Abitibi, 17 June 1937.

42 81.20.163, M. Cross, Comparative Analysis of Liquidator's and Bondholders' Plans for Reorganization of Abitibi, 17 June 1937. Several UNB students majoring in finance independently reached similar results using the data in McPherson's proposal and copies of Abitibi's statements.

43 *CSI*, 47. HUBL, *RR*, 7 October 1937, 15–6. Clarkson published the letter related to the second study in his annual report, probably with malicious glee, since it showed how unreliable McPherson's assertions were.

44 81.20.162, Ripley to Somerville, 21 July 1937. *GM*, 22 and 24 July 1937.

45 81.20.163, Plan of Sale of Assets and Reorganization, 21 July 1937.

46 81.20.162, Ripley to BRC, 4 June 1937. 81.20.162, Drafts, Preliminary Plan, 22 April and 16 May 1937. 19. *GM*, 16 October 1937.

47 81.20.163, J.P. Ripley, A Discussion of the Plan of Sale of Assets and Reorganization, 21 July 1937.

48 *Barron's*, 10 May 1937.

49 *WSJ*, 26 April, 18 May, and 26 July 1937, *GM*, 20 May 1937.

50 *GM*, 26 July 1937. *WSJ*, 28 August and 20 October 1937.

51 HUBL, *RR*, 1 October 1937, 11. *GM*, 13 and 19 May, 11 and 12 August 1937.

52 *CSI*, A8, L1-2. HUBL, *RR* (1937), 4–6.

53 *NYT*, 15 December 1937.

54 U.S., Securities and Exchange Commission, *Report on the Study and Investigation of the Work, Activities, Personnel, and Functions of Protective and Reorganization Committees*, 8 vols. (Washington: GPO, 1937–40).

55 *WSJ*, 25 March, 28 September, 31 July 1937.
56 E. McCaffery, "Corporate Reorganization under the Chandler Bankruptcy Act," *California Law Review*, 26:6 (1938), 643–63. C. Wilde, "The Chandler Act," *Indiana Law Review*, 14:2 (1938), 93–148. V.L. Leibell, "The Chandler Act – Its Effect Upon the Law of Bankruptcy," *Fordham Law Review*, 9:3 (1940), 380–409.
57 *WSJ*, 3 June 1937. *GM*, 27 July 1937. *Financial Times*, 28 July 1937.
58 *GM*, 28, 30 July and 3 August 1937. *FP*, 24 July and 7 August 1937.
59 AO, RG3, 277, R. Rankin to Hepburn, 23 February 1937. Rankin was a Liberal patronage beneficiary who got the heating contracts for Toronto hospitals.
60 RG 3, 273, G.A. Lewis to Hepburn, 17 May 1937; J.O. Quenneville to Hepburn, 25 June 1937; Hepburn to Quenneville, 28 July 1937.
61 81.20.164 Ripley to Somerville, 4 August 1937. 2994/32, Affidavit, J.F. Hopkirk, 13 July 1937. 81.20.163, Preferred Shareholders Protective Committee to 7% and 6% holders, 31 August 1937. *GM*, 2 September 1937.
62 81.20.159 G.R.G. Baker to Somerville, 24 February 1937.
63 81.20.164, Minutes of Dominion Mortgage and Investment Association Meeting, 23 August 1937; Reid to Somerville, 13 September 1937. *FP*, 7 August and 18 September 1937.
64 81.20.159, Ripley to Bondholders' Representative Committee, 30 April and 1 June 1937; 81.20.162 Symington to Ripley, 31 May 1937; Ripley to Symington, 3 June 1937.
65 81.20.158, Ripley to Bondholders' Representative Committee, 12 December 1936; Ripley to Rothermere, 28 November 1936. 81.20.162, Symington to Ripley, 31 May 1937.
66 *GM*, 23 and 24 September 1937.
67 81.20.164, Rothermere to McPherson, 23 September 1937.
68 81.20.164, Ripley to Rothermere, 27 September 1937; Circular letter, Bondholders Representative Committee to Bondholders, 27 September 1937.
69 *GM*, 29 September 1937. *NYT*, 27 and September 1937.
70 *FP*, 2 October 1937. *GM*, 8 October 1937. RG18-118, Circular Letter from the Bondholders' Defensive Committee, 7 October 1937, in Proceedings, III, 6 November 1940, 382–5.
71 *GM*, 30 September 1937.
72 G.R. Horne, "The Receivership and Reorganization of the Abitibi Power and Paper Company, Limited" (PhD diss., University of Michigan, 1954), 210. *GM*, 8 October 1937; *FP*, 16 October 1937. RG18-118, Proceedings, IX, 9 December 1940, 1144–5.
73 *FP*, 9 and 16 October 1937. *GM*, 12 October 1937.
74 81.20.164, Proposed Amendments to Plan of Sale of Assets and Reorganization, as approved at meeting of bondholders held 15 October 1937.

75 *GM, MG, TS, WT,* 16 November 1937. *FP,* 23 October 1937. Press reports were selective in the coverage of the meeting and most did not convey the full range of the debate.

76 *FP,* 16 October 1937.

77 2994/32, 1178, Affidavit by R.S. McPherson, 3 September 1937; Statement of Defence for Abitibi by the Liquidator, 16 September 1937.

78 2994/32, 1177, Examination of R.S. McPherson, 1 October 1937; Notice of Motion, 2 October 1937; Order by Kingstone, 7 October 1937. Justice McTague on 21 July had issued an order authorizing a special examiner to depose McPherson.

79 2994/32, Affidavits on production, 15 and 22 October 1937.

80 2994/32, Admissions at trial, 26 October 1937. *Montreal Trust Co. v. Abitibi Power and Paper* [1937] OJ No. 327, OR 939, 4 DLR. 369, OWN 617, CarswellOnt 62. *OJ,* 7 October 1937.

81 *GM,* 4 and 10 November 1938. *NYT,* 11 November 1937.

82 *OJ,* 10 November 1938. *GM,* 11 November 1937. *FP,* 20 November 1937.

83 *GM, OJ,* 12 November 1937.

84 F45, B294901, Appeal Notes. This file contains Roebuck's transcription of the pleadings, which were made objectively, without commentary or asides.

85 *WT,* 12 November 1937.

86 *GM, NYT,* 11 November 1937. *CFC,* 20 November 1937.

87 *GM,* 14 and 22 November 1937. *OJ,* 19 November 1937. 81.20.164, Ripley to Osler, 29 November 1937.

88 81.23.164, Ripley to Osler, 29 November 1937; Johnston to Osler, 16 and 18 December 1937; Osler to Johnston, 18 December 1937; Ripley to Bondholders' Representative Committee, 23 December 1937.

89 *Montreal Trust Company v. Abitibi Power and Paper Company Ltd. et al.,* [1938] OR 81.

90 F45, 294901, Roebuck to Brooks, 5 and 18 January 1938.

12. Darkest Hours

1 See F.L. Stetson, "Preparation of Corporate Bonds, Mortgages, Collateral Trusts, and Debenture Instruments," in F.L. Stetson and Associates, *Some Legal Phases of Corporate Financing, Reorganization and Regulation* (New York: Macmillan, 1917), 34–48; W. Lilly, *Individual and Corporation Mortgages: A Statement for Laymen of the Legal Principles* (New York: Doubleday Page, 1921), 36–130.

2 L.S. Posner, "Liability of the Trustee Under the Corporate Mortgage Indenture," *Harvard Law Review,* 42:2 (1928), 198–248. P.M. Payne, "Exculpatory Clauses in Corporate Mortgages and Other Instruments," *Cornell Law Quarterly,* 20:2 (1934), 171–96.

3 F45, B294901, Roebuck to Brooks, 18 and 31 January, 3 February 1938.

4 *GM*, 18 and 19 January 1938. *NYT*, 18 January 1938. *FP*, 22 January 1938.

5 MLCA, 81.20.164, J.P. Ripley to W. Somerville, 20 January 1937; Bondholders' Representative Committee to Holders of Abitibi First Mortgage Bonds, 1 February 1938. *GM*, 3 February 1938.

6 AO, F45, B294901, *Montreal Trust v. Abitibi Power & Paper*, Notice of Appeal, 31 January 1938. *GM*, 21 February 1938.

7 F45, B294901, Summary of appeal book index and case background, 15 March 1938.

8 F45, B294901, Appeal Notes. F45, B294901, Memorandum of Facts and Law submitted on behalf of the defendant, Abitibi Power & Paper Company, Limited, by its Liquidator, March 1938. *GM*, 18 March 1939.

9 AO, F45, B294901, Memorandum of Facts and Law submitted on behalf of Wood Gundy, 14 March 1938.

10 AO, F45, B294901, Memorandum of Facts and Law submitted on behalf of Lord Rothermere and the Common Shareholders' Protective Committee, 15 March 1938. While other aspects of Roebuck's submission were reported, the crucial comments about the vote were never recognized in press stories. *GM*, 30 March 1938.

11 *GM*, 16, 17 March 1938. F45, B294901, Appeal Notes.

12 F45, B294901, Appeal Notes. *GM*, 31 March 1938.

13 *Montreal Trust Company v. Abitibi Power & Paper Co. Ltd. et al.* [1938] OJ No. 448, [1938] OR. 589, [1938] 4 DLR 529, 20 CBR 32

14 The majority ruling was based upon *Attorney-General of Ontario v. Attorney-General for Canada*, [1894] A.C. 189; *La Compagnie Hydraulique de St. Francois v. Continental Heat and Light Co.*, [1909] A.C. 194 and *Royal Bank v. LaRue et al.*, [1928] A.C. 187, 8 C.B.R. 579.

15 MLCA, 81.20.164, Ripley to Somerville, 20 January 1938. *Globe*, 22 March 1939.

16 The expenses were considered high by the standards of the time but were very small relative to those incurred for similar reorganizations during the early twenty-first century.

17 *FP*, 20 May 1939.

18 C. Cox, *Canadian Strength* (Toronto: Ryerson Press, 1946), 178.

19 *CFC*, 17 December 1938. For Molson, *GM*, 22, 24 March 1938.

20 Data collated from annual statements of insurance company bond and stock holdings in *Report of the Superintendent of Insurance of the Dominion of Canada*, 1934 to 1939. *GM*, 11 March 1939.

21 D.A. Irwin, "Gold Sterilization and the Recession of 1937–1938," *Financial History Review*, 19:3 (2012), 24967. C.D. Romer, "What Ended the Great Depression?" *Journal of Economic History*, 52:4 (1992), 757–84. K.D. Roose, *The Economics of Recession and Revival: An Interpretation of 1937–38* (New Haven, CT: Yale University Press, 1954).

22 *WSJ*, 20 March, 18 June, 31 August 1937. *Barron's*, 21 June 1937.
23 *WSJ*, 13, 19, and 30 October; 28 December 1937. *FP*, 29 January and 19 March 1938. *GM*, 23 August 1938.
24 *FP*, 15 January, 2 April, 18 June 1938.
25 T. Heinrich, "Product Diversification in the U.S. Pulp and Paper Industry: The Case of International Paper, 1898–1941," *Business History Review*, 75:3 (2001), 493–9. HUBL, International Power and Paper, *AR* (1934), 7–8; (1938), 12; (1940), 12–13.
26 *WP*, 2 September 1937. *NYT*, 21 March and 26 October 1938; 30 December 1940.
27 2994/32, News and Magazine Paper Corporation contracts, 22 March 1938; Indebtedness of Hearst Corp. to Mead and Abitibi, 15 February 1939; Contingency reserve, 17 March 1939; Hearst indebtedness, 1 December 1943.
28 RG3, 292, Heenan to Hepburn, 26 February 1938; H.C. Draper to Hepburn, 26 May 1938.
29 H.V. Nelles, *The Politics of Development: Forests, Mines and Hydro-Electric Power in Ontario 1849–1941* (Toronto: Macmillan of Canada, 1974), 458.
30 JLAO (1941), Appendix 1, 23 April 1940, 156, 159.
31 JLAO (1941), 23 April 1940, 182, 184–5.
32 RG3, 292, Memorandum on Conferences of Premiers in Montreal, original draft, 20 January 1938; Hepburn to Duplessis, 14 February 1938.
33 JLAO (1941), Appendix 1, 24 April 1940, 164, 182, 186.
34 JLAO (1941), 24 April 1940, 207.
35 *FP*, 8 June 1940. JLAO (1941), 24 April 1940, 187, 192. *Editor and Publisher*, 19 November 1938.
36 JLAO, 24 April 1940, 218. *GM*, 6, 11 and 12 January 1938. *FP*, 15 January 1938.
37 *Saturday Night*, 12 June 1937. *GM*, 7, 11, 14, 28 January 1938. *NYT*, 20 January 1938.
38 *NYT*, 14 February 1939. NARA, RG122.4, "Newsprint Paper Decree Investigation," January 1939, 13, 52, 85. The report was not released at the time, which represented a gauge of the failed expectations, but was published by Congress eight years later.
39 *NYT*, 24 May 1939. Congress, Senate, Special Committee to Study Problems of American Small Business, Survival of a Free Competitive Press (Washington: GPO, 1947), iv.
40 JLAO, 75 (1941), Appendix 1, 24 April 1940, 218, 201, 195; 23 April 1940, 157.
41 2994/32, Department of Justice Investigation, 29 September 1939. JLAO, 75 (1941), 19 January 1940, 132; 23 April 1940, 152–4, 159.
42 RG3, 316, Vining to Hepburn, 14 May 1941. JLAO (1941), Appendix 1, 23 April 1940, 154.

43 RG3, 278, Hepburn to Vining, 29 July 1937.

44 *GM*, 14, 15, 16 and 28 November, 6 December 1938. *FP*, 19 November 1938. *WSJ*, 19 November 1938.

45 *GM*, 23 December 1938. JLAO (1941), Appendix 1, 6 May 1940, 639, 641. See also Vining, Newspaper Prorating, 47–52.

46 RG3, 300, Kellogg to Hepburn, 21 March 1939.

47 RG3, 299, Heenan to Hepburn, 24 March 1939. RG3, 300, P. Kellogg to Hepburn, 12 April and 9 May 1939; Heenan to Hepburn, 13 May 1939.

48 RG3, 300, Heenan to Hepburn, 13 May 1939.

49 RG3, 297, W.E. Rowe to Hepburn, 6 June 1939.

50 *GM*, 8 June 1939. *WSJ*, 4 October 1939. JLAO, 75 (1941), Appendix 1, 23 April 1940, 129–30. The orders-in-council were reprinted in Vining, Newsprint Prorating, 84–5.

51 JLAO, 75 (1941), Appendix 1, 23 April 1940, 155.

52 AO, RG3, 306, Petition Against Exemptions from Government Requirements in Newsprint Prorating, 8 April 1940. JLAO, 75 (1941), 1 May 1940, 512–19. *GM*, 28 May 1940. *NYT*, 28 June 1939. *GM*, 29 June 1939 and 13 March 1940.

53 The most prominent misinterpretation of prorating was by the 1941 McTague commission which claimed: "From the evidence adduced it is clear that Abitibi cannot hope to improve its financial position should the policy of proration not be continued … and we think that the Government should do all it legitimately can to keep it in force." RG18-118, *Report of the Royal Commission Inquiring into the Affairs of Abitibi Power and Paper Co. Ltd.*, 13–14.

54 2994/32, Department of Justice Investigation, 29 September 1939; Future newsprint supply, 15 October 1945.

55 2994/32, Memoranda, Wood Cut of 1939/40, 28 July and 11 September 1939; Department of Justice investigation, 29 September 1939. HUBL, *RR* (1939–42 inclusive). As long as pro-rating remained in effect, the annual output of each mill was posted on the first page in the report.

56 RG3, 302, S. Johnston to Hepburn, 13 September 1940; Clarkson to Hepburn, 17 October 1940. *Fort William Times Journal*, 17 October 1940.

57 RG3, 302, S. Johnston to Hepburn, 13 September 1940. *GM*, 24 September 1940.

58 HUBL, *RR* (1938), 3; (1939), 2, Exhibits 1-A and 1-B. Similar conclusions based upon an exhaustive appraisal of the financial statements are provided in G. Horne, "The Receivership and Reorganization of the Abitibi Power and Paper Company Ltd." (PhD diss., University of Michigan, 1954), 181–207.

59 R.B. Willis, "Corporate Reorganization in Canada," *Quarterly Review of Commerce*, 8:3 (1941), 193–6. *FP*, 21 December 1940.

60 *GM*, 4 and 28 November 1938. *WSJ*, 29 November 1938.
61 RG49-19, SP46, Gordon McMillan to W.C. Cain, 6 October 1938. RG3, 10-0-889, Memorandum Re: Bondholders' Position, 11 March 1939; Memorandum Re: Abitibi, 10 March 1939.
62 RG3, 10-0-889, H.H. Black to Hepburn, 15 March 1939.
63 RG3, 10-0-889, Bondholders' Defensive Committee to Holders of Abitibi First Mortgage Bonds and Certificates, February 1939. *GM*, 24 February 1939. RG3, 10-0-889, A.G. Slaght to Hepburn, 27 February 1939.
64 RG49-19, SP 46, Order-in-Council, 9 March 1939; Heenan to G.S. Paul, 14 March 1939. Hepburn's speech from transcriptions in *TS*, 9 March 1939; *GM*, 11 March 1939; *FP*, 18 March 1939. Hepburn claimed to have received the bondholders' proposal a day before his speech but it was vetted through the cabinet and HEPCO over the preceding two weeks.
65 *GM*, 13, 14, 15, 16, 17, 28 March 1939. *WSJ*, 15 March 1939. *FP*, 18 March and 8 April 1939.
66 For the Conservative concern about preferred shareholders, see *FP*, 5 October 1939. Monthly summaries of sales of Abitibi securities on Canadian exchanges were published in *Annual Financial Review* until 1941 and the estimates are derived from that data.
67 F45, B294901, Notes for speech in Legislative Assembly, March 1939. *OJ*, 16 March 1939.
68 RG49-19, SP46 (1939), Plan of Procedure on Behalf of Bondholders for the Purchase of Assets of Abitibi Power and Paper Company, Limited, by a New Company, 15 March 1939.
69 *MT*, 102 (1939), 493–4. *GM*, 11 March 1939. *FP*, 1 April 1939. *PPMC*, March 1939.
70 *FP*, 15 April 1939. *GM*, 7 April 1939.
71 RG49-19, SP46, Calvin Snyder to Heenan, 21 March 1939; A.G. Alexander to Heenan, 20 March 1939; J.J. Panneton to Hepburn, 24 March 1939.
72 F45, B294901 Stanley Stanger, Abitibi Power & Paper Company, Limited: Foreclosure or Compromise, to Preferred Shareholders' Committee, 8 April 1939. *Lincoln Printing Co. v. Middle West Utilities Co.*, OJ, 74 F.2d 779.
73 F45, B294901 Stanley Stanger, Abitibi Power & Paper Company. The pamphlet was copied extensively in newspapers. See *GM*, 25 April 1939.
74 F45, B294901, Roebuck to Brooks, 14 March 1939; Memoranda, Protective Committee for Abitibi Power and Paper Company, General Creditors, to General Creditors, 10 April, 17 April 1939. *GM*, 2 April, 12 April 1939.
75 F45, B294901, Protective Committee for Abitibi Power and Paper Company Preferred Shareholders, Notice, 18 March 1939. RG 49-19, SP46 (1939), D.H. Gibson to Hepburn, 20 March 1939.
76 RG49-19, SP46 (1939), D.H. Gibson to Hepburn, 20 March 1939.
77 *FP*, 25 March, 8 April 1939.

78 *GM*, 18 March, 6 and 25 April 1939.
79 RG49-19, SP46 (1939), Symington to Heenan, 29 March 1939. *CFC*, 13 and 27 May 1939.
80 *CFC*, 10 May 1939. *GM*, 13 May 1939. *FP*, 20 May 1939.
81 *FP*, 3 June 1939. *GM*, 13 July 1939.
82 RG3, 10-0-889, G.H. Ferguson, T. Bradshaw and G.W. Scott to committee heads, 23 August 1939. Bradshaw to Symington, 25 August 1939, 2 September 1939.
83 *MT*, 102 (1939), 440, 444. *GM*, 25 August, 25 September, and 3 October 1939. *WSJ*, 3 October 1939. *NYT*, 4 October 1939.
84 RG3, 10-0-889, H.J. Symington to Bradshaw, 11 and 30 August, 11 September 1939.
85 *GM*, 1 and 5 September, 6 November 1940.
86 RG3, 10-0-889, Hepburn to Symington, 18 September 1939; Symington to Hepburn, 20 September 1939.
87 RG3, 10-0-889, G.T. Clarkson to Hepburn, 20 October 1939.
88 RG18-118, Proceedings, XI, 11 December 1940, 1268–9, 1270–1; XIV, 8 January 1941, 1555. Officials of Sun Life, contrary to Ferguson's testimony, never disagreed with the bondholders' executive and likely were trying to fob off the committee by saying a compromise solution was possible.
89 *GM*, 3 January 1940.
90 *GM*, 13 and 29 February, 6 March 1940. *FP*, 17 February 1940.
91 *GM*, 11 April 1940.
92 *FP*, 4 May 1940.
93 RG3, 10-0-967, Symington to Hepburn, 13 May 1940; Hepburn to Symington, 22 May 1940; G. McMillan to Hepburn, 22 May 1940; Heenan to Hepburn, 21 May 1940.
94 *GM*, 15 June and 28 May 1940.
95 2994/32, Notice of Motion, 20 May 1940; Affidavit, John Hobkirk, 20 May 1940. *GM*, 20 May and 10 June 1940.
96 *Montreal Trust v. Abitibi Power and Paper*, [1940] O.J. No. 161, [1940] OWN 307, 1940 CarswellOnt 174. 2994/32, Order by Middleton, 10 June 1940.
97 2994/32, Dismissal of appeal motion, 20 June 1940; Master's meeting on sale, 20 July 1940; Advertisement and conditions of sale, 26 July 1940. *MG*, 21 June 1940. *GM*, 8 and 28 August 1940.
98 *GM*, 17 and 27 July, 8 and 10 August, 4 September 1940.
99 RG 3, 302, Symington to G. Taylor, 1 October 1940.
100 RG3, 10-0-967, P.L. Rockfort to Hepburn, 13 October 1940; M. Kennedy to Hepburn, n.d.
101 *GM*, 17 and 27 July, 8 and 10 August, 4 September 1940.
102 RG 3, 302, G. Gaudry to Hepburn, 21 August 1940. N.E. Wainwright to Hepburn, 4 September 1940. Like Ferguson, Mitch Hepburn culled his

papers before leaving office and many letters (often reproduced in the press) are missing. Most of the surviving correspondence in the premier's files opposed the sale and any statements in support likely were removed.

103 *GM*, 15 and 28 August, 30 September 1940.
104 *GM*, 3 and 4 October 1940.
105 *FP*, 14 September 1940.
106 RG3, 10-0-967, R.B. Hanson to Hepburn, 16 August 1940.
107 RG3, 10-0-967, D. L. McCarthy to Hepburn, 9 September 1940.
108 2994/32, Affidavit of R.G. Gordon, 4 October 1940; Notice of Motion by Noranda Mines, 5 October 1940. *GM*, 11, 12, 15 October 1940. *Montreal Trust v. Abitibi Power and Paper Co. Ltd. et al.*, [1940] O.J. No. 251. The informal offer was for $40.3 million but below the reserve price.
109 2994/32, Report of Judicial Sale, 24 October 1940. *GM*, 15 October 1940.

13. A Constitutional War

 1 AO, RG18-118, Proceedings, VIII, 15 November 1940, 891–2, 920–4, 1014.
 2 *GM*, 17 October, 18 October, 24 October 1940.
 3 AO, RG3, 10-0-967, G.R. Magone to G.D. Conant, 18 October 1940.
 4 RG3, 10-0-967, Press release re Abitibi, October 1940. *GM*, 18 October 1940. *CFC*, 26 October 1940, 2482. The bulk of Drew-related documents for Abitibi pre-1943 in LAC, MG-32-C-3 (I, 4; LX, 535; LXIX, 614, 615; XCII, 879) repeat other sources or are printed materials and newspaper clippings.
 5 RG3, 10-0-967., Copy, Order-in-Council, 1 November 1940. *GM*, 25 and 26 October, 2 November 1940.
 6 RG3, 10-0-967, G.D. Conant to Hepburn, 29 November 1940. *WSJ*, 30 November 1940.
 7 RG18-118, Proceedings, X, 10 December 1940, 1250.
 8 RG18-118, XIV, 8 January 1941, 1535, 1543; VI, 13 November 1940, 787.
 9 RG18-118, XI, 11 December 1940, 1274–5; X, 10 December 1940, 1220–9. RG3, 10–0-967, Statement of Facts presented by Z. Mageau on Behalf of the Sturgeon Falls board of Trade Re: Abitibi Royal Inquiry, 10 December 1940.
10 RG18-118, VIII, 15 November 1940, 940, 942.
11 RG18-118, VIII, 15 November 1940, 940, 961, 947. Symington was disingenuous. Evidence presented to the commission indicated numerous investors held on to their stakes, but he was correct about how shares placed on exchange turned over many times.
12 RG18-118, VIII, 15 November 1940, 970–1, 973–4.
13 RG18-118, Report of Royal Commission Inquiring into the Affairs of Abitibi Power and Paper Co. Ltd., 17 April 1941, 5–6.

14 RG18-118, Report, 12–13.

15 RG18-118, Report, 18.

16 RG18-118, Report, 19–20.

17 G.R. Horne, "The Receivership and Reorganization of the Abitibi Power and Paper Company, Limited" (PhD diss., University of Michigan, 1954), 278.

18 RG3, 214, C.P. McTague to Hepburn, 18 March 1941. RG3, 416, C. Parent to Conant, 1 April 1943.

19 RG 3, 10-0-967, G. Gaudry to Hepburn, 21 August 1940; D.L. McCarthy to Hepburn, 9 September 1940.

20 See E.V. Murphy, *Economic Analysis of a Mortgage Foreclosure Moratorium* (Washington, DC: Congressional Research Service, 2008); A.J. Jaffe and J.M. Sharp, "Contract Theory and Mortgage Foreclosure Moratoria," *Journal of Real Estate Finance and Economics*, 12:1 (1996), 77–96; K.M. Pence, "Foreclosing on Opportunity: State Laws and Mortgage Credit," *Review of Economics and Statistics*, 88:1 (2006), 177–82.

21 D.C. Wheelock, "Changing the Rules: State Mortgage Foreclosure Moratoria During the Great Depression," *Federal Reserve Bank of St. Louis Review*, 90:6 (2008), 569–83. U. Sommer and Q. Li, "Judicial Decision Making in Times of Financial Crises," *Judicature*, 95:2 (2011), 68–77. For law and the 2007–12 crisis, see G. Walsh, "The Finger in the Dike: State and Local Laws Combat the Foreclosure Tide," *Suffolk University Law Review*, 44 (2011), 149–91; A.P. Williams, "Foreclosing Foreclosure: Escaping the Yawning Abyss of the Deep Mortgage and Housing Crisis," *Northwestern Journal of Law & Social Policy*, 7:2 (2012), 454–509.

22 See V.E. Torrie, "Federalism and Farm Debt during the Great Depression: Political Impetuses for the Farmers' Creditors Arrangement Act, 1934," *Saskatchewan Law Review*, 82 (2019), 203–57. House of Commons, *Debates*, 4 June 1934, 3639.

23 RG3, 8-0-106, Henry to J.B. Laidlaw, 28 November 1931; Laidlaw to Henry, 27 November 1931; T.B. German to Henry, 26 August 1931.

24 SO, [1932] 22 Geo. V, Ch. 49, An Act to give further Power to Courts with respect to the Recovery of Money Secured by Mortgage and Similar Matters.

25 RG3, 8-0-310 and 8-0-311 contain the correspondence about the legislation. *ME*, 25 February 1933, and *FP*, 1 April 1933, for the intra-caucus disagreement. SO, [1933] 23 Geo. V, Ch. 35, Mortgagors' and Purchasers' Relief Act.

26 SO, [1941] Geo. VI, Ch. 1, An Act Respecting a certain Bond Mortgage made by the Abitibi Power and Paper Company Limited to the Montreal Trust Company. RG3, 214, Conant to Hepburn, 9 October 1941.

27 For the removal of the commission's counsel, see *GM*, 9 and 10 January 1941. Hepburn and Attorney General Conant denied wrong-doing and claimed the lawyer had "been put up" by Ottawa.

28 *CFC*, 27 July 1940, 538.

29 *CFC*, 28 June 1941, 4114. *FP*, 5 July 1941.

30 RG22-5800, 2994/32, Notice of Motion and Affidavit, 9 October 1941; Notices of Motion, 17 October 1941, 25 November 1940.

31 *Montreal Trust v. Abitibi Power and Paper Co. Ltd. et al.*, [1941] OWN, 425. 2994/32, Order by Middleton, 4 December 1941; Notice of Settlement, 13 December 1941.

32 *Montreal Trust v. Abitibi Power and Paper Co.* Ltd. et al., [1942] O.J. No. 26. *GM*, 6, 10 January 1942.

33 *GM*, 6, 7 February 1942.

34 *Montreal Trust v. Abitibi Power and Paper Co. Ltd. et al.*, [1942] 2 DLR, 354–5, 358–9, 361–2, 369–70, 376. *Dominion Law Review* noted the case "undoubtedly presents a constitutional issue of great difficulty which largely arises from the application of that none too certain yardstick for determining where legislative jurisdiction resides under our constitutional scheme, namely the pith and substance rule."

35 SO, [1942] 6 Geo. VI, Ch. 2, The Abitibi Moratorium Constitutional Act; 6 Geo. VI, Ch. 3, The Abitibi Power & Paper Company Limited Moratorium Act, 1942. *GM*, 24 March 1942.

36 *GM*, 27 March 1942.

37 *GM*, 11, 14, 17 April 1942. OS, [1937] 1 Geo. VI, Ch. 98, The Privy Council Appeals Act.

38 *Montreal Trust v. Abitibi Power and Paper Co. Ltd. et al.*, [1942] OR, 334, 338–9.

39 *Montreal Trust v. Abitibi Power and Paper*, 344–5.

40 *GM*, 11 June 1942, for Tilley's death and commentaries. Johnston received a favourable obituary in *GM*, 15 September 1940, whereas the controversies from Latchford's lengthy career and partisan conduct were circumvented by a summary "public service" eulogy in *GM*, 15 August 1938.

41 *GM*, 9 January, 2 February, 17 May 1940. *OC*, 20 January 1941. The likely impact of war on pulp and newsprint was surveyed in U.S., Tariff Commission, *The European War and United States Imports* (Washington: Tariff Commission, 1939), B-150-62. It forecast the shortfall of wood pulp but erroneously believed no significant issues would occur with newsprint.

42 JLAO, 75 (1941), Appendix 1, 23 April 1940, 189.

43 *GM*, 28 May 1940. *NYT*, 25 January, 4 February 1941. *GM* 10 May 1940; 27 January 1941 JLAO, 75 (1941), Appendix 1, 23 April 1940, 200, 207.

44 JLAO, 75 (1941), Appendix 1, 23 April 1940, 208, 196.

45 *FP*, 18 January 1941. AO, RG3, 316, Vining to Hepburn, 14 May 1941. See also RG49-115, Exhibit 42, Vining's review of prorating for Cote.

46 *GM*, 7 March 1940.

47 Economic mobilization in Canada and the United States during the Second
World War remains an unexplored subject. J. de N. Kennedy, *History of the
Department of Munitions and Supply: Canada in the Second World War*, 2 vols.
(Ottawa: King's Printer, 1950) was a flawed account. Industrial committees
were largely ignored and the paper industry was not considered. The
only substantive analysis of American practices is L.E. Ellis, *Newsprint:
Producers, Publishers, Political Pressures* (New Brunswick, NJ: Rutgers
University Press, 1960). Relying upon sources like the *ANPA Bulletin* and
Editor and Publisher, his account is misleading or outright wrong.

48 LAC, RG64-A-18, R200-243-2-E, Pulp and Paper Administration, 1942–5.
MG26-J1, 324, C-6806, 276262–5; 325, C-6807, 276861–72. Controller
letters are in RG28, Records relating to the Department of Munitions and
Supplies, "Central Registry Files," LXVII. Some difficulties were due to
turnover in the controller's office. It was initially headed by Charles Vining
but he was transferred to handle information services and was succeeded
by I. Weldon.

49 NARA, 179.2.2, T.B. McCabe, Supply of and Demand for Woodpulp, 27
August 1940; Minutes, Advisory Commission to Council of National
Defense, 24 July 1940; L. Henderson to F.D. Roosevelt, 26 July 1940. *NYT*,
31 July 1940. The detailed report was submitted a month after the public
announcement of adequate supply.

50 179.2.3, OPM Administrative Order 11, 24 June 1941. 179.2.2, C.W. Boyce,
Organization and Personnel of the Pulp and Paper Branch, War Production
Board, 1 July 1942. 179.2.1, Policy Analysis and Records Branch, Policies
and Procedures on Dollar-a-year and without compensation employees
of the War Production Board and Predecessor Agencies, 26 May 1944,
Appendix A. This account outlines the results of bureaucratic struggles
among the agencies that claimed jurisdiction. 179.2.2, J.L Weiner to A.
Richard (undated, likely December 1942) was blunt about the perceived
chaos. "We have suffered in the past from the multiplicity of channels
through which comments and recommendations are made."

51 179.2.4, Pulp and Paper Group, Advisory Commission, Progress Report for
the period ending 31 December 1940. 179.2.3, Orders, M-19 (chlorine), 28
July 1941; L-11 (chlorine), 1 November 1941; M-9c (copper), 15 July 1941;
P-79 (denial of priority for repair work), 14 November 1941. For Canada,
Department of Mines and Resources, *Canada's Forests and the War* (Ottawa:
King's Printer, 1947), 31–3; *GM*, 9 December 1941 and 19 October 1942.
Also NARA, 179.2.2, War Production Board, Minutes 17 November 1942.
Under Conservation Order M-241, the annual consumption of iron and
steel by American paper firms decreased from 386,000 tons to 51,500 tons;
under L-11 the industry's use decreased from 30 per cent to 12 per cent of
chlorine output.

52 Combined Committee on Nonfood Consumption Levels, *The Impact of the War on Civilian Consumption in the United Kingdom, the United States, and Canada* (Washington: GPO, 1945), 9–13, 17–19, 53–4. Congress, Senate, Select Committee on Small Business, *Newsprint for Tomorrow* (Washington: GPO, 1952), 28–9.

53 NARA, 179.2.3, Order M-93, Restrictions on Pulp Allocations 14 March 1942; L-120, Manufacture of certain fine papers, 4 July 1942. *Foreign Commerce Weekly*, 6:5, 21 January 1942. *NYT*, 19 January 1942.

54 NARA, 179.2.3, Orders, M-93; ODT 18-A-1. M-244 Order M-241.

55 NARA, 179.2.2, R.W. Buckley to Materials Coordinating Committee, United States and Canada, February 1942. Civilian Production Administration, *Pulp and Paper Policies of the War Production Board and Predecessor Agencies, May 1940 to January 1944* (Washington: GPO, 1944), 55–8. Wartime Prices and Trade Board, *Canadian War Orders and Regulations*, III, Order 331 (Respecting Pulpwood), 5 November 1943, 128–9.

56 Congress, House of Representatives, *Brand Names and Newsprint* (Washington: GPO, 1945), 25 January 1944, 1345; 28 January 1944, 1391. War Production Board, *Wartime Production Achievements and the Reconversion Outlook, Report of the Chairman, 9 October 1945* (Washington: GPO, 1945), 83, 85.

57 NARA, 179.2.1, D. Winton to A.I. Henderson, 18 August 1942.

58 179.2.1, D.M. Nelson to R.P. Patterson and J.V, Forrestal, 28 October 1942. 179.2.2, War Production Board, Minutes, 17 November 1942, 16 February 1943. *NYT*, 9 February 1943.

59 179.2.3, M-93, Woodpulp Allocation, 12 March 1942. E.W. Reid to F. Eberstadt, 24 November 1942.

60 179.2.1, W. Gordon to Nelson, 7 October 1942; Nelson to W. Gordon, 10 October 1942.

61 179.2.1, E.R. Gay to J.L. Weiner, Comments on Programme for the Curtailment of the Pulp and Paper and Related Industries, 28 September 1941.

62 NARA, 179.2.2, WPB, Minutes, 17 November 1942, 16 February 1943. 179.2.3, Order M-241, 31 October 1942. *Pulp and Paper Policies of the War Production Board*, 80–3. The relevant order was amended five times during 1943 as the WPB tried, unsuccessfully, to resolve the problems.

63 179.2.2, Minutes, Meeting between WPB Officials and the Canadian Government, 2 and 3 March 1943. Woodpulp Allocation Industry Advisory Committee, 21–4 April 1943.

64 Congress, *Brand Names and Newsprint*, 15 October 1943, 1147–8. Senate, Committee on Banking and Currency, *Preliminary Report and Supplements: Newsprint Production and Supply* (Washington: GPO, 1956), 9, 11.

65 179.2.1, G. Olmstead to D.S. Leslie, 26 March 1943. W.G. Chandler to Nelson, 15 February 1943. 179.2.2, WPB, Minutes, 16 February 1943.

66 *Brand Names and Newsprint*, 28 January 1944, 1398.

67 179.2.1, Nelson to C.D. Howe, 15 July 1943; Howe to Nelson, 26 July 1943; H. Borden to all Canadian Controllers, 20 July 1943; Nelson to C. Hull, 8 September 1943.

68 179.2.2, Minutes, Joint WPB-WPTB meeting, 20 October 1943. *Preliminary Report and Supplements*, 7.

69 *NYT*, 9 January, 20 and 24 March, 30 April 1942.

70 *FP*, 4 and 25 April 1942. *GM*, 30 April 1942. *NYT*, 22 July 1942. 179.2.2, WPB, Minutes, 20 July 1943.

71 *GM*, 15 December 1942. *FP*, 11 December 1943. *Brand Names and Newsprint*, 26 July 1945, 235, 245; 31 July 1945, 328.

72 *NYT*, 10 July 1943. Congress, Senate, Hearings of the Special Subcommittee to Study the Problems of Small Business, 4 March 1947, 2–21, 36–41; 6 March 1947, 175–90.

73 2994/32, Pulpwood, 29 June 1940; 1940/41 Wood Cut, 19 July 1940; Labour Rates, 18 April 1940; Employee Salaries, 7 August 1940; Mill Labour, 15 April 1941.

74 2994/32, Wood operations, 7 April 1942; 1943/1944 Wood Cut, 18 March 1943. Wartime Prices and Trade Board, *Canadian War Orders and Regulations*, Order 222 (Respecting Compensation for Allotted Newsprint), I (Ottawa: King's Printer, 1943–5), 206–7.

75 2994/32, Espanola and Sturgeon Falls, 29 June 1940; Prisoners of War, 23 February 1944. LAC, RG24, C1, 7236-34-3, Files 32, 43, 48, 49, Department of Labour work projects, Abitibi Power and Paper Ltd. SMPL, 992.10, 9621, P.O.W. Labour Camp Instructions, Operating Procedures, 1944, "strictly confidential."

76 SMPL, 992.10, WM 40–46, Box 1, 9655, Agreement between Abitibi Power and Paper Co. Ltd. and His Majesty the King, 4 January 1944. 2994/32, Agreement between Abitibi and His Majesty the King in right of the Dominion of Canada, 1 December 1943. LAC, RG27, 951, Files 1–10, Salaries and Compensation for POWs, Abitibi Power and Paper Ltd., 1943–6.

77 2994/32 Memoranda, Prisoners of War, 4 February 1946; 1945/1946 Wood Cut, 4 February 1946. SMPL, 992.10, WM 40–46, Box 2, 13525, Prisoners of War, Circular Letter 1/46, January 1946. 40–46, Box 1, 9699, Att. Mr. Kishbaugh, 10 June 1946.

78 2994/32, Wartime Risk Insurance, 29 September 1942; Sault Ste. Marie, 3 August 1943.

79 2994/32, Future newsprint supply, 15 October 1945; Commodity Prices Stabilization Corporation, 26 July 1944. HUBL, *RR* (1943), 3.

80 LAC, RG19, 383, 101-102-16, WPTB – Newsprint Industry, 1943–7.
   RG64-A-18, R200-243-2-E, Pulp and Paper Administration, 1942–5. HUBL,
   RR (1943), 4.
81 2994/32, Affidavits, J. Hobkirk and G.T. Clarkson, 6 June 1941; Order, 7
   June 1941. *FP*, 14 June 1941. *GM*, 7 June, 12 July 1941.
82 2994/32, AED, 1 April 1941; Set-off of subsidiary obligations, 18 April 1941;
   Victory Bonds, 13 February and 1 October 1942, 12 October 1943.
83 2994/32, Kaministiquia Power, 27 March 1933, 17 March 1939; Set-off of
   subsidiary obligations, 18 April 1941, 17 October 1942.
84 RG3, 324, T.H. Hogg to Hepburn, 25 September 1942; Conant to Hepburn,
   30 September 1942; Hepburn to Hogg, 2 October 1942. ORR633.01, 91.029,
   Clarkson to Hogg, 4 and 13 December 1943.
85 2994/32, Memorandum, Kaministiquia Power, 10 May 1944. ORR633.01,
   91.029, Proposed Purchase of Kam Power Company, 23 March 1944; R.T.
   Jeffrey to R.L. Hearn, 2 February 1949.
86 2994/32, Clarkson to N.O. Hippel, 16 October 1942; Memorandum,
   Espanola and Sturgeon Falls, 15 November 1938.
87 2994/32, Espanola (A), 19 October 1942; Espanola (C), 14 December 1942,
   which includes the contract between Abitibi and KVP, 7 December 1942.
88 2994/32, Espanola (B), 19 October 1942. This was marked "Confidential.
   Only to be revealed to the Court, the members of the executive committee
   of the BPC, the Liquidator and their Counsel." Memorandum, Espanola
   Receivables, 18 March 1943. HUBL, *RR* (1943), 7. *CFC*, 25 January 1943, 340.
89 RG3, 428, 2-G, Conant and C.F. Bulmer to A. Matthews, Report of
   Committee of Executive Council, 5 January 1943. RG3, 416, W.L. Miller to
   Hippel, 14 January 1943.
90 2994/32, Sturgeon Falls Newsprint Property, 12 October 1939; Sale of
   Sturgeon Falls machines, 5 November 1940, 2 June 1941; Sturgeon Falls
   taxes, 4 December 1941, 2 February 1942.
91 OHA, ORR 530, M. Holden to J. Dibblee, 20 April 1942.
92 RG3, 416, Conant to Charles Parent, 5 April 1943. LAC, MG26, J2, 287,
   P-305, XIV, Ontario – Action of the Bondholders Protective Committee of
   the Abitibi Power and Paper Co.
93 *Montreal Trust v. Abitibi Power and Paper Co. Ltd. et al.,* [1943] A.C., 546–8.
   The decision was often called within law schools the "Darth Vader ruling,"
   after the Sith's statement in *The Empire Strikes Back*.

14. The Path towards Dawn

1 *NYT*, 21 September 1943.
2 *FP*, 17 July and 14 August 1943. *Globe*, 16 July, 5 August, 1 and 10
  September 1943.

3 *GM*, 10 September 1943.

4 N. McKenty, *Mitch Hepburn* (Toronto: McClelland and Stewart, 1967), 259–69. J. Saywell, *"Just Call Me Mitch": The Life of Mitchell F. Hepburn* (Toronto: University of Toronto Press, 1991), 494–511.

5 *GM*, 19 and 17 July 1943.

6 *GM*, 25 August and 11 September 1943. RG3, 10-0-1218, Lake Sulphite Paper.

7 *GM*, 20 September 1943.

8 *FP*, 25 September 1943. *GM*, 21 September 1943. *Barron's*, 15 November 1943.

9 AO, RG3-17, B396753, 2-G, A. Ross to Drew, 20 August 1943. *FP*, 25 September 1943. *CFC*, 27 September 1943, 1237. *NYT*, 21 September 1943.

10 *GM*, *NYT*, 29 January 1944.

11 B396753, 2-G, Memorandum by Hughes Committee re Abitibi Power and Paper Company Limited, undated (circa January 1944).

12 *GM*, 31 January 1944. *FP*, 5 February 1944.

13 B396753, 2-G, L.-A. Renaud to F.J. Hughes, G. Jackson, and W. Zimmerman, 8 February 1944.

14 *GM*, 17 April and 1 May 1944.

15 B396753, 2-G, Drew to A.N. Mitchell, A.B. Wood, R.H. Reid, and W.H. Somerville, 28 April 1944; Hughes to Drew, 28 April 1944.

16 B396753, 2-G, G. Graydon to Drew, 18 May 1944; R.H. Reid to Drew, 23 May 1944; Drew to Reid, 31 May 1944.

17 AO, RG22-5800, 2994/32, *"Montreal Trust v. Abitibi Power and Paper,"* Johnston to Clarkson, 4 September 1940. OHA, 90.003.16, McGibbon, Mitchell and Stairs, Indenture and Mortgage from Abitibi Power and Paper Co. Ltd. in favour of Montreal Trust Company and the National City Bank of New York, 1 June 1928, Paragraph 19.

18 2994/32, Notice of Motion and Affidavit of R.S. McPherson, 13 March 1944. *GM*, 2 February, 15 March, and 20 April 1944.

19 *GM*, 4 May 1944. AO, 2994/32, Order by Kellock, 10 June 1944.

20 *Montreal Trust Company v. Abitibi Power & Paper Company Ltd. et al.*, [1944] OJ No. 467, OR 515, 3 DLR 505.

21 2994/32, Notice of Motion, 15 June 1944. *GM*, 22 June and 31 October 1944.

22 2994/32, Future Newsprint Supply, 15 October 1945; Sale of Newsprint to Newsprint Supply Co., 16 October 1945.

23 2994/32, Future Newsprint Supply, 15 October 1945. Contractual memoranda, 3 July and 8 August 1945, 25 February 1946. The memoranda were marked "high confidential" or "only to be revealed to the Court" and were sealed.

24 U.S. Congress, House of Representatives, *Hearings before the Subcommittee on Study of Monopoly Power*, 14, Part 6B, N-252, G.H. Mead Co.,

Memorandum re. Telephone Conversation with Mr. W.H. Smith, 5 January 1945. N-247, G. H. Mead Co. to W.H. Smith, 5 April 1945.

25 2994/32, G.H. Mead, 2 April 1942; Balance Sheet Format, 8 May 1943; Asset Write-offs, 15 April 1944.

26 2994/32, Central Newspapers, 28 May and 15 June 1944; Order, 22 June 1944.

27 2994/32, Hearst Indebtedness, 1 December 1943, 11 January 1944, 24 July 1945; Hearst Supply Contract, 24 March 1944; Hearst, 10 May 1944.

28 2994/32, Sifton Contracts, 30 April 1945, 29 November 1945.

29 HUBL, *RR* (1942), 2; (1943), 3; (1944), 4; (1945), 3.

30 2994/32, Johnston to Clarkson, 4 September 1940. Charges Against Earnings, 31 March 1941; Determination of Standard Profits, 21 January 1942; Excess Profits Taxes, 6 April 1945; Taxable Income, 14 May 1945.

31 2994/32, Third Victory bond subscription, 19 October 1942; Victory Bond Subscription, 15 April 1944. HUBL, Abitibi Power and Paper, *AR* (1947), 7; (1955), 12.

32 HUBL, *RR* (1944), 203. *GM*, 27 July 1944.

33 *GM*, 27 July, 2 and 16 August, 31 October 1944. *FP*, 15 July 1944.

34 B396753, 2-G, Report of the Hughes Committee to the Prime Minister of Ontario (re. Abitibi Power and Paper Company, Limited), 23 November 1944; W. Zimmerman to Drew, 30 November 1944.

35 LAC, MG32-C-3, 306, 197, Settlement of Abitibi and Power Co., 23 November 1944.

36 No one ever confused Henry Jr. with his illustrious father. Unlike other members of the family, he never worked for Goldman Sachs. Relegated to a minor firm, he became known for petty attempts to bilk other investors and died in 1955, just fifty-eight years old.

37 The press never caught on to what happened with the 7 per cent preferred stock. G.R. Horne, "The Receivership and Reorganization of the Abitibi Power and Paper Company, Limited" (PhD diss., University of Michigan, 1954), 302, acknowledged they "managed to force considerable concessions" but did not realize the greenmail for what it was. In *GM*, 9 November 1945, Goldman admitted he pulled the same manoeuvre during the reorganization of Canadian Vickers. He also attempted to control the reorganization of Harding Carpets during 1946.

38 B396753, 2-G, E.A. Lloyd to Drew, 27 November 1944.

39 B396753, 2-G, M.C. Purvis to Drew, 1 December 1944; B. Kaplan to Drew, 7 December 1944. *FP*, 2 December 1944.

40 B396753, 2-G, L.-A. Renaud to R.G. Meech, 22 November 1944; Renaud to Zimmerman, 23 November 1944. *FP*, 2 December 1944.

41 B396753, 2-G, Renaud to Clarkson, 9 December 1944. Various parties attempted to finagle or compel sales of different properties until March 1946. Clarkson advised the court about the attempts, usually to end them.

42 *FP*, 2 December 1944. B396753, 2-G, Supplementary Report of Hughes Committee, 27 December 1944; F.J. Hughes to Drew, 7 June 1946.

43 *CSI*, Exhibit R. HUBL, *RR* (1945), Exhibit I. 2994/32, Price Waterhouse, Pro-Forma Financial Statements as at December 31, 1944, Prepared in Connection with the Plan of Reorganization, 10 May 1945. Abitibi never used any of the materials prepared for the Hughes plan. Instead, the consulting engineers employed in 1937 reassessed the properties and the results (which were analogous to those published by Clarkson) formed the basis of the financial statements published in the 1946 annual report.

44 Draper, Dobie and Company, Abitibi Power and Paper Co. Ltd., 1 December 1944.

45 HUBL, Abitibi Power and Paper, *AR* (1952), 9.

46 MG32-C-3, 306, 205, Statement, Abitibi Power and Paper Co., 4 January 1945.

47 B396753, 2-G, Plan of Reorganization of Abitibi Power and Paper Company, February 1945, Proof No. 2, Appendices A and B.

48 Abitibi's declared book value in the 1946 annual report, unlike that by the Hughes committee, came close to market estimates. It would have been equivalent to $9.53 per old common share.

49 B396753, 2-G, H. Goldman to Drew, 10 September 1945. Drew to Goldman, 15 September 1945.

50 *TS*, 9 October 1945. *GM*, 5, 6, 10, and 11 October 1945. 2994/32, Affidavit, D. Guest of Blake, Anglin, Osler and Cassels, 12 November 1945.

51 B396753, 2-G, F.A. MacDougall to G.G. Blackstock 15 October 1945. 2994/32, Sturgeon Falls, 12 March 1946.

52 RG1-481-1, B733539, F.A. MacDougall memo, 14 January 1946. Tentative negotiations, in fact, had started during 1941 in anticipation of the report from the Abitibi Royal Commission. The tedious discussions and government demands are in AO, RG1-134, B271999, Abitibi Pulp and Paper, Co. Correspondence, I.

53 2994/32, Reorganization, 26 March 1946, Section 5.

54 JLAO, 30 (1947), Speech from the Throne, 9. *OS*, [1947], 11 Geo. VI, ch. 37, An Act to provide for Forest Management. The agreements were reprinted in LOSP, No. 3 (1947), *Report of Department of Lands and Forests for 1946*, 163–212. SMPL, 992.10, H-2, Box 2, 16020, Outline of Government Requirements Covering the Management of Ontario's Pulpwood Concessions, June 1949.

55 *GM*, 25 January, 16 March, and 1 May 1946. *FP*, 23 March 1946. *NYT*, 17 May 1946.

56 2994/32, Affidavits, G.F. Harkness, T.R. Wilcox, 29 April 1946; Notice of Motion, 30 April 1946.

57 HUBL, Abitibi Power and Paper, *RR* (1946), 4–11; *AR* (1948), 7. 2994/32, Accounts of the Receiver and Manager for the Period of 1 January to 30

April 1946, 3 July 1946, Exhibit 3; Memo, Price Waterhouse, 3 July 1946. The expenses for services rendered by Clarkson's company were buried in numerous accounts and cannot be reconstructed. The receiver was paid $48,000 per year (the same rate as Alexander Smith) but would have reaped additional income from services for the province, Hydro, or other parties.

58 *Barron's*, 5 August 1946. AO, F4624, 2-0-50, B848099, Brief of the Ontario Forest Industries Association to the Royal Commission on Forestry, December 1946.

59 *GM*, 6 and 10 August, 2 October 1946.

15. Epilogue

1 *GM*, 27 January 1947.

2 *GM*, 4 February 1947.

3 U.S., Congress, Senate, Special Committee to Study Problems of Small Business, *Newsprint Supply and Distribution*, CSS 11114 (Washington: GPO, 1947), 3–8. House of Representatives, *Hearings before the Subcommittee on Study of Monopoly Power*, 14, Part 6B, Exhibits N-15 and N-62. C.H. Friedman, *The Newsprint Problem: Ten Questions and Answers* (New York: American Newspaper Guild, 1948), 9, 13, 20.

4 Congress, House of Representatives, *Monopoly Power Hearings*, 6B, Exhibit N-7. 6A, Hearings, 29 June 1950, 678; 18 July 1950, 945, 980; 23 June 1950, 394–5. *FP*, 16 December 1950.

5 *WSJ*, 27 May 1950. *NYT*, 3 April 1947. *FP*, 27 May 1950.

6 Congress, Senate, Special Committee to Study the Problems of Small Business, *Hearings*, 6 March 1947, 157; 11 March 1947, 236.

7 Congress, Problems of Small Business, *Hearings*, 6 March 1947, 187. *WSJ*, 4 November 1947.

8 *OS*, 11 Geo. VI (1947), ch. 10, An Act to Prevent the Improper Removal of Business Records from Ontario. JLAO, 30 (1947), 27 October 1947, 945–7.

9 Congress, House of Representatives, *Report of the Subcommittee on Monopoly Power: Part I, Newsprint*, CSS 11496 (Washington: GPO, 1951), 129.

10 HUBL, Abitibi Power and Paper, *AR* (1946), 6; (1949), 5–6. *GM*, 24 January 1947.

11 HUBL, Abitibi Power and Paper, *AR* (1947), 8.

12 *FP*, 30 April 1949.

13 SMPL, 992.10, H-2, Box 2, Notes on Discussion of the Sturgeon Falls Working Plan, 12 October 1954. HUBL, Abitibi Power and Paper, AR (1946), 7, 16, 22. *GM*, 27 January 1947, 18 September 1948, 20 September 1951. The Sturgeon Falls mill was sold to Macmillan-Bloedel in 1979. Weyerhauser, which later acquired the British Columbia company, walked

away from the mill, claiming it was not a "core business," rather than meet environmental regulations imposed by the Conservative government.

14 P. Mathias, *Takeover: The 22 Days of Risk and Decision that Created the World's Largest Newsprint Empire, Abitibi-Price* (Toronto: Maclean-Hunter, 1976), 4–6, 180–4. T.R. Roach, *Newsprint: Canadian Supply and American Demand* (Durham, NC: Forest History Society, 1994), 48.

15 J. Ojala, J.-A. Lamberg, A. Ahola, and A. Melander, "The Ephemera of Success: Strategy, Structure and Performance in the Forestry Industries," in J.-A. Lamberg, J. Näsi, J. Ojala, and P. Sajasalo, eds., *The Evolution of Competitive Strategies in Global Forestry Industries* (New York: Springer, 2006), 259–71. P. Clancy, *Micropolitics and Canadian Business: Paper, Steel and the Airlines* (Peterborough, ON: Broadview Press, 2004), 127. M.E. Porter, *Canada at the Crossroads: The Reality of a New Competitive Environment* (Ottawa: Business Council on National Issues, 1991), 10–12.

16 U.S., Securities and Exchange Commission, 001-33776, 10-K, AbitibiBowater Inc. (2008), 1–13; (2010), 1–24, 10-Q (2009), 1–60. AbitibiBowater, *AR* (2007), 1. Canada, Superior Court, District of Montreal, 500-11-036133-0984, *In the Matter of the Plan of Compromise or Arrangement of AbitibiBowater Inc., and Abitibi-Consolidated Inc., and Bowater Canadian Holdings*, Information Circular, 2 August 2010, 12–17, 55–63; Order, 17 April 2009.

17 *NYT*, 15 December 1955. M.I. Perino, *The Hellhound of Wall Street: How Ferdinand Pecora's Investigation of the Great Crash Forever Changed American Finance* (New York: Penguin, 2010), 297–8.

18 J.N. Ingham, ed., *Biographical Dictionary of American Business Leaders*, vol. 2 (Westport, CT: Greenwood, 1983), 912–15. J.P. Jack P. Oden, "Development of the Southern Pulp and Paper Industry, 1900–1970" (PhD diss., Mississippi State University, 1973). *NYT*, *WP*, *Globe*, 2 January 1963. Mead's daughter, Elsie Louise, in 1939 married Arlen Specter, later a long-serving Republican senator for Pennsylvania. Mead Corporation disappeared in a merger with other packaging companies and that company was amalgamated during 2015 into what is now Atlanta-based Westrock. Some press outlets characterized the 2015 takeover as a "fire sale."

19 *WSJ*, 30 August 2001, 26 January 2015. *NYT*, 7 September 2001, 29 January 2002, 6 August 2004, 19 January 2005, 26 January 2015. HUBL, Westrock Company, Form 10-K for Fiscal Year 2015, items 1–3.

20 *NYT* and *Chicago Tribune*, 15 January 1959. *GM*, 15 January 1959, copied the four line AP release but buried it on page 36 beneath a story about a scholastic basketball game.

21 *NYT*, 2 February and 19 May 1936; 18 September 1969. For the foundation named for his brother, see http://www.wcgmf.org/.

22 *NYT*, 19 November 1974.

23 D.G. Stone, *April Fools: An Insider's Account of the Rise and Collapse of Drexel Burnham* (New York: D.I. Fine, 1990).

24 S. Kuznets, *Modern Economic Growth: Rate Structure and Spread* (New Haven, CT: Yale University Press, 1966), 86–159; W.W. Rostow, *The World Economy: History & Prospect* (Austin: University of Texas Press, 1978), 47–54, 448–55. A.D. Chandler, *Scale and Scope: The Dynamics of Industrial Capitalism* (Cambridge, MA: Harvard University Press, 1990), 3–9.

25 A.S. Eichner, "Business and the Market Mechanism," in I. Berg, ed., *The Business of America* (New York: Harcourt, Brace and World, 1968), 167–200. A.S. Eichner, "The Micro Foundations of the Corporate Economy," *Managerial and Decision Economics*, 4:3 (1983), 136–52.

26 Chandler, *Scale and Scope*, 15. A.D. Chandler, *The Visible Hand: The Managerial Revolution in American Business* (Cambridge, MA: Harvard University Press, 1977), 10–11.

27 O. Zunz, *Making America Corporate, 1870–1920* (Chicago: University of Chicago Press, 1990), 37–55.

28 See. J.W. Pratt and R.J. Zeckhauser, eds., *Principals and Agents: The Structure of Business* (Cambridge, MA: Harvard Business School Press, 1985), 37–54, 151–212. The essays by K.J. Arrow, R.G. Eccles, and H.C. White provide useful introductions to the vast literature in economics and law.

29 E.T. Penrose, *The Theory of the Growth of the Firm* (Oxford: Basil Blackwell, 1959), 32.

30 J. Schumpeter, *The Theory of Economic Development: An Inquiry into Profits, Capital, Credit, Interest, and the Business Cycle* (Livingston: Transaction Publishers, 1934); D.S. Landes, *The Unbound Prometheus: Technological Change and Industrial Development in Western Europe from 1750 to the Present* (New York: Cambridge University Press, 1969); D.S. Landes, *The Wealth and Poverty of Nations: Why Some Are so Rich and Some so Poor* (New York: W.W. Norton, 1998).

31 B.J. Bird, *Entrepreneurial Behavior* (Glenview: Scott, Foresman, 1989), chaps. 7–10; A. Cuervo, D. Ribeiro, and S. Roig, eds., *Entrepreneurship, Theory and Perspective* (New York: Springer, 2007), chaps. 7–10; S.C. Santos, A. Caetano, C. Mitchell, H. Landström, and A. Fayolle, eds., *The Emergence of Entrepreneurial Behaviour: Intention, Education and Orientation* (Northhampton: Edward Elgar, 2017), chaps. 2–4, 9, 11.

32 O.E. Williamson, *Markets and Hierarchies: Analysis and Antitrust Implications* (New York: Free Press, 1975), chap. 2; O.E. Williamson, *The Economic Institutions of Capitalism: Firms, Markets, Relational Contracting* (New York: Free Press, 1985), chaps. 3–4.

33 F.L. Clarke, G.W. Dean, and K.G. Oliver, *Corporate Collapse: Regulatory, Accounting and Ethical Failure* (Melbourne: Cambridge University Press, 1997), 232–40. J.W. Markham, *A Financial History of Modern U.S.*

Corporate Scandals: From Enron to Reform (New York: Routledge, 2006), Parts III and IV. M.N. Baily, A. Klein, and J. Schardin, "The Impact of the Dodd-Frank Act on Financial Stability and Economic Growth," *Russell Sage Foundation Journal of the Social Sciences*, 3:1 (2017), 20–47.

34 J.D. Honsberger, "The Need for a Rapprochement of the Bankruptcy Systems of Canada and the United States," *McGill Law Journal*, 18:2 (1972), 151–6; J.D. Honsberger, "Bankruptcy Administration in the United States and Canada," *California Law Review*, 63:6 (1975), 1515–45.

35 Canada, Senate, *Debates*, 6 October 1949, 97–8.

36 Canada, Advisory Committee on Bankruptcy and Insolvency, *Proposed Bankruptcy Act Amendments: Report* (Ottawa: Consumer and Corporate Affairs Canada, 1986), 18. Senate, Standing Committee on Banking, Trade and Commerce, *Debtors and Creditors Sharing the Burden* (Ottawa: Senate, 2003), 9–17, 205–13. Industry Canada, *Fresh Start: A Review of Canada's Insolvency Laws* (Ottawa: Industry Canada, 2014), 17–18.

37 R. Tassé, J.D. Honsberger, and P. Carignan, *Bankruptcy and Insolvency: Report of the Study Committee on Bankruptcy and Insolvency Legislation* (Ottawa: Information Canada, 1970), 20.

38 J.P. Sarra, *Creditor Rights and the Public Interest: Restructuring Insolvent Corporations* (Toronto: University of Toronto Press, 2003), 16. A solid analysis is V.E. Torrie, "Protagonists of Company Reorganisation: A History of the Companies' Creditors Arrangement Act (Canada) and the Role of Large Secured Creditors" (PhD diss., University of Kent at Canterbury, 2015).

39 "Thus passes the glory of the world."

Bibliography

I. Archival and Document Collections

Archives of Ontario
    RG1 Crown Lands/Natural Resources
    RG3 Premiers' Papers
    RG4 Attorney General's Papers
    RG6-44 Treasury Policy Planning Division subject files
    RG18 Commissions and Enquiries
        18–34 Forestry Protection, 1897–1898
        18–66 Kapuskasing Colony Enquiry, 1920
        18–79 Timber Commission, 1922
        18–96 HEPCO, 1932
        18–97 Sturgeon Falls Royal Commission, 1933
        18–105 Latchford-Smith Royal Commission, 1934
        18–118 Abitibi Royal Commission, 1940
        18–125 Forestry Royal Commission, 1947
    RG22-5800 Supreme Court of Ontario
        712/20 New Ontario v. Mattagami (1)
        885/20 New Ontario v. Mattagami (2)
        1327/20 New Ontario v. Mattagami (3)
        1487/20 National Trust v. Great Lakes Paper
        1339/21 National Trust v. Mattagami
        614/22 Northern Canada Power v. Hollinger
        615/22 Northern Canada Power v. Canadian Mining
        1841/22 National Trust v. Carrick
        2194/31 National Trust v. Great Lakes Paper
        2994/32 Montreal Trust v. Abitibi Power & Paper
        3554/32 Montreal Trust v. Ontario Power Service
        240, 1932 Abitibi v. Royal Bank

RG 35 Hydro-Electric Commission of Ontario
RG49 Sessional Papers
RG53 Corporate Records
   53–18 Company charters, letters of patent of incorporation, 1880–1923
   53–40 Supplementary letters patent, 1887–1923
RG75 Cabinet Office and Executive Council Records
F6 W.H. Hearst fonds
F7 E.C. Drury fonds
F8 G.H. Ferguson fonds
F9 G.H. Henry fonds
F10 M.F. Hepburn fonds
F12 G.D. Conant fonds
F30 P. Heenan fonds
F45 A.W. Roebuck fonds
F150 Gillies Lumber Company fonds
F208 E.E. Johnson fonds
F248 Lumbermans' Association of Ontario fonds
F1014 F.A. MacDougall fonds
F1055 F.A. Gaby fonds
F1056 R.L. Hearn fonds
F1198 F.I. Ker fonds
F1482 C. Hyson fonds
F4624 Ontario Forest Industries Association fonds
PC Pamphlet Collection
Archives of Manitoba
   CCA0059 Companies Office, corporation documents
   MG15 John Bracken fonds
   NR0225 Land Branch files
Bibliothèque et Archives Nationales du Québec
   P6 Fonds Consolidated Paper Corporation Limited
   P51 Fonds Julien-Edouard-Alfred Dubuc
   P137 Fonds Famille Foran
   P149 Fonds Consolidated Bathurst Incorporated
   P350 Fonds Louis-Alexandre Taschereau
   P666 Fonds de la Compagnie Price Brothers
Bank of England Archives
   SMT 2 International Power and Paper of Newfoundland
   SMT 3 Charles Bruce-Gardner papers
   SMT 4 Hugh Crompton Bischoff papers
   SMT 7 James Frater Taylor papers
   SMT 8 Branch Bank Office Files – Newfoundland Power and Paper Co. Ltd.

Canadian Institute for Historical Microreproductions
Corporate Document Collections
    Harvard University, Baker Library
    McGill University
    University of Michigan
    University of New Brunswick
    Yale University
Columbia University, Centre for Oral History
    Sp. Coll. Reminiscences of Ferdinand Pecora, 1962
FDR Library
    49–162 H.L. Hopkins fonds
Hoover Institution Archives
    68008 R.L. Moley papers
Library and Archives Canada
    MG26-I A. Meighen fonds
    MG26-J W.L.M. King fonds
    MG26-K R.B. Bennett fonds
    MG26-L L. St. Laurent fonds
    MG27-II-D3 N.W. Rowell fonds
    MG27-III-B22 R.B. Hanson fonds
    MG27-III-B9 H.H. Stevens fonds
    MG27-III-G8 L. Zolf fonds
    MG30-A51 Sir J. Dunn fonds
    MG30-D29 J.S. Willison fonds
    MG30-E82 C. Magrath fonds
    MG32-B4 M. Sauvé fonds
    MG32-C3 G.A. Drew fonds
    RG13-A2 Department of Justice
    RG15 Department of the Interior
    RG24 Department of National Defence
    RG27 Labour Canada
    RG28 Department of Reconstruction and Supply
    RG33-13 Royal Commission on Pulpwood
    RG33-53 Royal Commission on the Manufacture, Sale, Price, and Supply of
      Newsprint
    RG39 Royal Commission on Pulpwood, Freight Rates
    RG64 Wartime Prices and Trade Board fonds
    RG95 Incorporation papers
Great-West Life Assurance records
London Life Insurance records
National Archives and Records Administration

RG9 National Recovery Administration
RG122 Federal Trade Commission, Economic Investigations
RG151 Records of the Bureau of Foreign and Domestic Commerce
RG179 Records of the War Production Board
RG188 Records of the Office of Price Administration
Ontario Hydro Archives (now Ontario Power Generation)
ORR 104 Government Control
90.003 Latchford-Smith Commission, proceedings and exhibits
ORR 127 Load Forecasting
ORR 401 Water Powers
ORR 402 Bulk Electricity Systems
ORR 503 Public Criticism and Participation
ORR 530 Direct Customers
ORR 600 Law and Legal Affairs
ORR 633 Acquired Companies
Ontario Hydro Headquarters (now Ontario Power Generation)
Minutes of the Hydro-Electric Power Commission of Ontario
Provincial Archives of New Brunswick
MC1246 R.B. Hanson fonds
Queen's University Archives
F01985 Abitibi Canyon
Sault Ste. Marie Public Library
992.10 Abitibi Power & Paper Ltd. fonds
996.9.15 Consolidated Lake Superior Company fonds
996.9.23 Lake Superior Paper Company fonds
Sun Life Financial Corporate Archives
Sun Life historical files (Montreal)
Mutual Life Assurance of Canada records (Waterloo)
81.20 Abitibi Power & Paper Protective Committee
Thunder Bay Museum
A83 James A. Little/Donald M. Hogarth fonds
A55 G.R. Duncan fonds
Western University, Archives and Research Collection Centre
B4919-28 Arthur and Edmund Carty papers
York University Archives
F34 George S. Henry papers

II. Legal Materials

Statutes

Statutes of Canada
Statutes of Ontario

Statutes of Quebec
United Kingdom Statutes

Legal Cases and Rulings

Allgeyer v. Louisiana, [1897] 165 U.S. 578.
Ashbury Railway v. Riche, [1875] L.R. 7 H.L. 753, 44 L.J. Ex. 185.
Attorney General and Minister of Agriculture and Mines v. Jardine and Martin,
  [1930] Decisions of the Supreme Court of Newfoundland, 446, 522.
Attorney-General of Ontario v. Attorney-General for the Dominion, "Voluntary
  Assignments Case," [1894] AC 189.
Bank of Toronto v. Lambe, [1887] 12 AC 587, [1889] 42 Ch.D. 330.
Barron v. Burnside, [1887] 121 U.S. 186.
Bonanza Creek Gold Mining v. the King, [1916] 1 AC 566, 26 DLR 273.
Re Brampton Gas Co., [1902] 4 OLR 509.
Canada Southern Railway v. Gebhard, [1883] 109 U.S. 527, 3 Sup. Ct. 363.
Re Canadian Shipbuilding Co., [1912], 26 OLB 564, 3 OWN 1476, 4 OWN 157.
Re. Canadian Western Steel Co., [1922] 2 CBR 494.
Chicago, Milwaukee and St. Paul Railway v. Minnesota, [1890] 134 U.S. 418.
Class Rate Investigation, 1939, [1945] 262 ICC 447, 467.
Re. Cramp Steel, [1908] OJ No. 113, 6 OLR 230.
David Lloyd & Co., [1877] 6 Ch.D. 339.
Diehl v. Carritt, [1907] OJ No. 45, 15 OLR 202.
Diehl v. Carritt, [1915] OJ No. 265, 9 OWN 109.
Doyle v. Continental Insurance, [1876] 94 U.S. 535.
Dr. Miles Medical Co. v. John D. Park and Sons Co., [1911] 220 U.S. 412.
Eastern Rates Case, [1916] JORR, File 25547.
Re. Empire Mining Company, [1891] 1 Ch. 215.
Ernest v. Nichols, 6 H.L. Cas. 40.
Evans v. Rival Granite Quarries Ltd., [1910] 2 K.B. 979.
Gordon Mackay & Co., Ltd. v. Larocque, [1927] 2 DLR 1150.
Government Stock Co. v. Manila Rail, [1897] A.C. 86.
Great Northern Railway v. Eastern Counties Railway, [1851] 9 Hare, 306.
Harrison v. Nepisiquit Lumber, [1912] 11 ELR 314.
Hattersley v. Earl of Shelbourne, [1862] L.J. Ch. 873.
Henry Squire (Cash Chemist) Ltd v. Ball, Baker & Co., [1911] 27 TLR 269 aff'd 28
  TLR 81, 106 Law Times 197.
Imperial Paper Mills of Canada v. Quebec Bank, [1912] OJ No. 162, 26 OLR 637, 6
  DLR 475, 22 OWN 703.
Re. Imperial Paper Mills of Canada, Diehl v. Carritt, [1915] OJ No. 630, 7 OWN 630.
Import Newsprint Paper from Thorold, Ontario, to Chicago, Ill., [1931] 176 ICC 243.
Interstate Commerce Commission v. Cincinnati, New Orleans, and Texas Railway,
  [1897] 167 U.S. 479.

Re. Joshua Stubbs Ltd., [1891] 1 Ch. 475.

Re Kingston Cotton Mills, [1896] 2 Ch. 279, 65 L.J. Ch. 673.

Kierskowski v. Grand Trunk Railway, [1859] 10 LCR, 47.

Knoxville Traffic Bureau v. Canadian Pacific. Railway, "'Knoxville Case,'" [1925] 101 ICC 605.

Northern Canada Power versus Hollinger Consolidated Gold Mines, [1923] 54 OR 511.

La Compagnie Hydraulique de St. Francois v. Continental Heat and Light, [1909] A.C. 194.

Lake Superior Paper Company v. Director General, Ahnapee and Western Railway, [1921] 61 ICC 709, 64 ICC 34.

Lincoln Printing v. Middle West Utilities, [1934] N.D. Ill. 6 F. Supp. 682.

Re London and General Bank, [1895] 2 Ch., 682. 64 L.J. Ch. 866.

Re London and General Bank, [1912] 106 Law Times, 285.

Minnesota and Ontario Paper v. Northern Pacific Railway, [1922] 73 ICC 133 and [1923] 66 ICC 571.

Montreal Trust v. Abitibi Power and Paper, [1937] OWN 612, OR 939.

Montreal Trust v. Abitibi Power and Paper, [1938] OJ No. 448, OR 589, 4 DLR 529, 20 CBR 32.

Montreal Trust v. Abitibi Power and Paper, [1941] OWN 425.

Montreal Trust v. Abitibi Power and Paper, [1942] OJ No. 26.

Montreal Trust v. Abitibi Power and Paper, [1942] 2 DLR 354.

Montreal Trust v. Abitibi Power and Paper, [1943] AC 546.

Montreal Trust Company v. Abitibi Power & Paper, [1944] OJ No. 467, OR 515, 3 DLR 505.

National Labor Relations Board v. Jones & Laughlin Steel, [1937] 301 U.S. 1.

New England Investigation, [1913] 27 ICC 560.

Newsprint Paper Investigation, [1933] 197 ICC 748.

Newsprint Paper to Chicago [1933] 194 ICC 148.

North British and Mercantile Insurance v. London Liverpool and Globe Insurance, [1877] 44 L.J. Ch. 537.

M.J. O'Brien v. British America Nickel Corporation, [1927] AC 369.

Official Classification Rates on Paper, [1916] 38 ICC 120.

Re Owen Sound Lumber, [1917] 28 OLR 424, 33 DLR 486.

Panama, New Zealand and Australian Royal Mail, [1870] L.R. 5 Ch. 318;

Paper and Paper Articles from Canada and New England, "'Nashville Case,'" [1923] 78 ICC 258.

Re. Pound, Son, and Hutchins, [1889] 42 Ch.D. 402.

Rates to and from Nashville, [1921] 61 ICC 308.

Rates to, from, and between Points South of Ohio River, [1921] 64 ICC 107.

Riordon v. John W. Danforth, [1923] SCR 319.

Royal Bank v. LaRue, [1928] A.C. 187, 8 C.B.R. 579.

Santa Clara County v. Southern Pacific Railroad, [1886] 118 U.S. 394.

Schechter Poultry Corp. v. United States, [1934] 295 U.S. 495.

Spackman v. Evans, [1868] L.R., 3 H.L. 171, 193; 37 L.J. Ch. 752.

Spanish River Pulp and Paper Mills v. Ahnapee and Western Railway, [1926] 113 ICC 343, 120 ICC 251.

Strong v. Carlyle Press, [1893] 1 Ch. 268.

Tooke Brothers v. Brock and Latterson, [1907] ELR 270.

Re. Warren Brothers & Co. Ltd., [1922] OLR 214.

III. Newspapers, Periodicals, and Trade Papers

Actualité économique

American Magazine

A.N.P.A. Bulletin

Barron's

Boston Post

Canadian Law Times

Canadian Lumberman and Woodworker

Chicago Tribune

Cobalt Northern Miner

Cochrane Northland Post

Collier's

Commercial and Financial Chronicle

Commonweal

Daily Capital Journal

Dayton Daily News

Editor and Publisher

Financial Post

Financial Times

Foreign Commerce Weekly

Fort Frances Times and Rainy Lake Herald

Fort William Times Journal

Galveston Daily News

Industrial Canada

Le Devoir

Maclean's

Manitoba Free Press

Minneapolis Journal

Monetary Times

Montreal Gazette

Montreal Daily Jewish Chronicle

Montreal Journal of Commerce

Montreal Star

Le Devoir
Nation
New Republic
New York Times
North American Review
Ottawa Citizen
Ottawa Journal
Paper
Paper Trade Journal
Pittsburgh Press
Porcupine Advance
Pulp and Paper Magazine of Canada
Reading Times
St. Louis Star
Saturday Night
Shawinigan Standard
Sudbury Star
Toronto Star
Toronto Globe
Toronto Globe and Mail
Toronto Mail and Empire
Toronto World
Wall Street Journal
Washington Daily News
Washington Post
Winnipeg Free Press
Winnipeg Tribune

IV. Government Documents

Canada

Advisory Committee on Bankruptcy and Insolvency. *Proposed Bankruptcy Act Amendments: Report.* Ottawa: Consumer and Corporate Affairs Canada, 1986.

Canada Gazette

Department of Mines and Resources. *Canada's Forests and the War.* Ottawa: King's Printer, 1947.
Department of the Interior. *Forest Products of Canada, 1910: Pulpwood.* Bulletin 26. Ottawa: Government Printing Bureau, 1911.

Dominion Bureau of Statistics. *Canada Year Book*. Annual.

Dominion Bureau of Statistics. *Historical Summaries of Consolidations in Canadian Industries*. Ottawa: King's Printer, 1934.

Fernow, B.E. *Conditions in the Clay Belt of New Ontario*. Ottawa: Commission of Conservation, 1913.

House of Commons. *Debates*.

House of Commons. *Proceedings of the Standing Committee on Banking and Commerce*. Ottawa: King's Printer, 1934.

Industry Canada. *Fresh Start: A Review of Canada's Insolvency Laws*. Ottawa: Industry Canada, 2014.

Kennedy, J. de N. *History of the Department of Munitions and Supply: Canada in the Second World War*. 2 volumes. Ottawa: King's Printer, 1950.

Office of the Superintendent of Insurance, *Annual Reports*, 1905–40.

Senate, Debates

Senate, Standing Committee on Banking, Trade and Commerce. *Debtors and Creditors Sharing the Burden*. Ottawa: Senate, 2003.

Statistics Canada. *Historical Statistics of Canada*. 2nd ed. Ottawa: Information Canada, 1983.

Tassé, R., J.D. Honsberger, and P. Carignan. *Bankruptcy and Insolvency: Report of the Study Committee on Bankruptcy and Insolvency Legislation*. Ottawa: Information Canada, 1970.

Wartime Prices and Trade Board. *Canadian War Orders and Regulations*. 7 volumes. Ottawa: King's Printer, 1943–5.

New Brunswick

Department of Lands and Mines. Annual Reports.
Synoptic Reports of the New Brunswick Legislative Assembly.

Ontario

Journals of the Legislative Assembly of Ontario
Sessional Papers

Quebec

Rapport du ministre des terres et forêts du Québec, annuel.
Débats de l'Assemblée législative (débats reconstitués).

United States

Bureau of Census. *Manufactures*. Washington: GPO, 1920, 1930.

Bureau of Census. *Census of Manufactures: Newspapers, Periodicals, et al.* Washington: GPO, 1947.

Civilian Production Administration. *Pulp and Paper Policies of the War Production Board and Predecessor Agencies, May 1940 to January 1944.* Washington: War Production Board, 1946.

Combined Committee on Nonfood Consumption Levels. *The Impact of the War on Civilian Consumption in the United Kingdom, the United States, and Canada.* Washington: GPO, 1945.

Congress, House of Representatives. *Pulp and Paper Investigation Hearings.* 6 vols. CSS 5542-6. Washington: GPO, 1909.

– *Columbia River and Minor Tributaries: Letter from the Secretary of War.* Vol. 1. CSS 9756. Washington: GPO, 1933.

– *Pulpwood Investigation: Hearings.* Washington: GPO, 1941.

– *Brand Names and Newsprint.* Washington: GPO, 1943–5.

– *Report of the Subcommittee on Monopoly Power: Part I, Newsprint.* CSS 11496. Washington: GPO, 1951.

Congress, National Economic Committee. *Investigation of Concentration of Economic Power: Investment Banking.* Washington: GPO, 1940.

Congress, Senate. *Report of the Federal Trade Commission on the News-print Paper Industry, 13 June 1917.* CSS 7246. Washington: GPO, 1917.

– *Survey of Pulp Woods on the Public Domain.* CSS 7671. Washington: GP0, 1920.

– *Tariff Hearings: H.R. 7456, Free List.* CSS 7969. Washington: GPO, 1921.

– *Hearings, Control of White-Paper Business.* Washington: GPO, 1929.

– *Newspaper Holdings of the International Paper and Power Co.* CSS 9125. Washington: GPO, 1929.

– *Utility Corporations.* CSS 8858-7. Washington: GPO, 1929.

– *Newsprint Paper Industry.* CSS 9320. Washington: GPO, 1930.

– *Report of the Federal Trade Commission on the Newsprint Paper Industry.* CSS 8360. Washington: GPO, 1930.

– *Pulpwood Supply in Alaska.* CSS 9204. Washington: GPO, 1930.

– *National Pulp and Paper Requirements in Relation to Forest Conservation.* CSS 9878. Washington: GPO, 1935.

– *Publications of the Temporary National Economic Committee.* 43 vols. Washington: GPO, 1941.

– *Economic Concentration and World War II.* Washington: GPO, 1946.

– *Newsprint Supply and Distribution.* CSS 11114. Washington: GPO, 1947.

– *Survival of a Free Competitive Press.* Washington: GPO, 1947.

– *Newsprint for Tomorrow.* CSS 11572. Washington: GPO, 1952.

– *Preliminary Report and Supplements: Newsprint Production and Supply*. Washington: GPO, 1956.

Department of Agriculture. *The Grinding of Spruce for Pulpwood*. Washington: GPO, 1915.

– *Timber Depletion, Lumber Prices, Lumber Exports, and Concentration of Timber Ownership*. Washington: GPO, 1920.

– *Lumber Exports, and Concentration of Timber Ownership*. Washington: GPO, 1920.

– *Regional Development of the Tongass National Forest, Alaska*. Bulletin 950. Washington: GPO, 1921.

– *How the United States Can Meet Its Present and Future Pulpwood Requirements*. Bulletin 1241. Washington: GPO, 1924.

– *Timber Depletion and the Answer*. Circular 112. Washington: GPO, 1927.

– *American Forests and Forest Products*. Statistical Bulletin 21. Washington: GPO, 1928.

– *America and the World's Woodpile*. Circular 21. Washington: GPO, 1928.

– *Forest Products: 1930*. Washington: GPO, 1931.

– *Pulpwood Consumption and Wood-Pulp Consumption, 1917*. Washington: GPO, 1919.

– *Pulpwood Consumption and Wood-Pulp Consumption, 1920*. Washington: GPO, 1922.

– *A National Plan for American Forestry*. 2 vols. Washington: GPO, 1933.

Department of Commerce. *Statistical Abstract of the United States*. Washington: GPO, annual 1908–49.

– *United States Pulp and Paper Industry*. Washington: GPO, 1938.

– *Newspapers, Periodicals, Books and Miscellaneous Publishing*. Washington: GPO, 1949.

Federal Trade Commission. *Newsprint Paper Decree Investigation*. Washington: GPO, 1939.

Forest Service. *Wood Used in Pulp, in 1905*. Washington: GPO, 1906.

– *Timber Supply of the United States*. Circular 97. Washington: GPO, 1907.

Interstate Commerce Commission, Bureau of Statistics. *Freight Revenue and Value of Commodities Transported on Class I Steam Railways in the United States*. Washington: GPO, annual.

Murphy, E.V. *Economic Analysis of a Mortgage Foreclosure Moratorium*. Washington, DC: Congressional Research Service, 2008.

Securities and Exchange Commission. *Report on the Study and Investigation of the Work Activities, Personnel and Functions of Protective and Reorganization Committees*. 8 vols. Washington: GPO, 1937–40.

– "Accounting Aspects of Business Combinations: Address of Andrew Barr, 27 August 1958." https://www.sec.gov/news/speech/1958/082758barr.pdf.

State of New York. *The Paper and Pulp Industries of New York State.* Albany: Division of Commerce, 1942.

Tariff Commission. *Pulp and News-Print Industry.* Washington: GPO, 1911.

– *Reciprocity with Canada: A Study of the Arrangement of 1911.* Washington: GPO, 1920.

– *Report to the United States Senate on Wood Pulp and Pulpwood.* Report No. 126, Second Series. Washington: GPO, 1938.

– *The European War and United States Imports.* Washington: Tariff Commission, 1939.

War Industries Board. *Prices of Paper.* Washington: GPO, 1919.

War Production Board. *Wartime Production Achievements and the Reconversion Outlook, Report of the Chairman, 9 October 1945.* Washington: GPO, 1945.

V. Corporate and Business Association Publications

Abitibi Power and Paper. *Compilation of Statements and Information obtained by the Bondholders' Representative Committee, 21 July. 1937.* Toronto: n.p. 1937.

American Pulp and Paper Association. *A Capital and Income Survey of the United States Pulp and Paper Industry, 1934–43.* New York: APPA, 1944.

Canadian Pulp and Paper Association. *Reference Tables.* Annual.

Clarke L. Poole. *Timber Land Bonds Analyzed as Investments for Banks and Trust Companies.* Chicago: Clarke L. Poole, 1913.

Fentress, C., and M. Corr. *Timbers: An Analysis of Timber-Secured Bonds as Investments for Individual, Bank, Trust, and Insurance Funds.* Chicago: Mercantile Press, 1927.

Friedman, C.H. *The Newsprint Problem: Ten Questions and Answers.* New York: American Newspaper Guild, 1948.

International Paper. *Why Newsprint Is High.* New York: International Paper, 1918.

International Paper. *The International Paper Company, 1898–1924: Its Origin and Growth in a Quarter of a Century.* New York: International Paper, 1924.

Mead Corporation. *In Quiet Ways: George H. Mead, the Man and the Company.* Dayton, OH: Mead Corporation, Private printing, 1970.

National City Bank of New York. *The Banking Apprenticeship Plan.* New York: National City Bank of New York, 1917.

– *The Work of Number Eight.* New York: National City Bank of New York, 1919.

– *If We Divided All the Money: How Much Do You Think You Would Get?* New York: National City Bank of New York, 1920.

National City Company. *Putting Your Dollars to Work.* New York: National City, 1928.

Scudder, Stevens, and Clark. *Investment Counsel.* Boston: Scudder, Stevens, and Clark, 1922.

Watts, A.D., and Co. *Analysis of the International Power and Paper Company: History and Prospects.* Montreal: A.D. Watts, 1929.

VI. Directories and Surveys

Annual Financial Review
Canadian Annual Review
Canadian Law Lists
Canadian Who's Who
Financial Post Directory of Canadian Directors and Officials
Financial Post Survey of Industrials
Lockwood's Directory of Paper and Allied Trades
Moody's Manual of Investments: American and Foreign
Moody's Manual of Industrial Holdings
Moody's Public Utilities and Industrials
Moody's Survey of Industrials
National Directory of the Canadian Pulp and Paper Mills and Allied Trades
Poor's Survey of Industrials
Poor's Survey of Financial Securities
Post's Paper Mill Directory

VII. Secondary Sources

Abel, K.M. *Changing Places: History, Community, and Identity in Northeastern Ontario*. Montreal: McGill-Queen's University Press, 2006.

Adelman, M.A. "Integration and Antitrust Policy." *Harvard Law Review*, 63:1 (1949), 27–77.

Ahern, G.P. *Deforested America*. Washington: n.p., 1928.

– *Forest Bankruptcy in America: Each State's Own Story*. 2nd ed. Washington: Shenandoah Publishing, 1934.

Aldrich, H.E., and C.M. Fiol. "Fools Rush In? The Institutional Context of Industry Creation." *Academy of Management Review*, 19:4 (1994), 645–70.

Allen, F.L. *The Lords of Creation*. New York: Harper and Row, 1936.

Ambridge, D.W. *Frank Harris Anson (1959–1923): Pioneer in the North*. Montreal: Newcomen Society in North America, 1952.

Amihud, Y, T.S.Y. Ho, and R.A. Schwartz. *Market Making and the Changing Structure of the Securities Industry*. Lexington: Lexington, 1985.

American Forestry Association. *Proceedings of the American Forest Congress*. Washington: H.M. Sutter, 1906.

Armstrong, C. *The Politics of Federalism: Ontario's Relations with the Federal Government, 1867–1942*. Toronto: University of Toronto Press, 1981.

Armstrong, C. *Blue Skies and Boiler Rooms: Buying and Selling Securities in Canada, 1870–1940*. Toronto: University of Toronto Press, 1997.

Armstrong, C. *Moose Pastures and Mergers: The Ontario Securities Commission and the Regulation of Share Markets in Canada, 1940–1980*. Toronto: University of Toronto Press, 2001.

Armstrong, C., and H.V. Nelles. *Monopoly's Moment: The Organization and Regulation of Canadian Utilities*. Toronto: University of Toronto Press, 1988.

Arnold, T. *The Folklore of Capitalism*. Princeton: Princeton University Press, 1936.

Backhouse, C., and N.L. Backhouse. *The Heiress vs. the Establishment: Mrs. Campbell's Campaign for Legal Justice*. Vancouver: UBC Press, 2004.

Baily, M.N., A. Klein, and J. Schardin. "The Impact of the Dodd-Frank Act on Financial Stability and Economic Growth." *Russell Sage Foundation Journal of the Social Sciences*, 3:1 (2017), 20–47.

Baldasty, G.J. *The Commercialization of News in the Nineteenth Century*. Madison: University of Wisconsin Press, 1992.

Barton, B. "Is There Anything Here that Other Men Couldn't Do?" *American Magazine*, 95 (February 1923), 128–35.

Beach, C.S. "Pulpwood Province and Paper State: Corporate Reconstruction, Underdevelopment and Law in New Brunswick and Maine, 1890–1930." PhD diss. University of Maine, 1991.

Beckmann, M.J. "Spatial Price Policies Revisited." *Bell Journal of Economics*, 7:2 (1976), 619–30.

Bellau, J. "L'industrialization à Trois-Rivières." MA thesis, L'université du Québec à Trois-Rivières, 1979.

Ben-David, I., J.R. Graham, and C.R. Harvey. "Managerial Miscalibration." *Quarterly Journal of Economics*, 128:4 (2013), 1547–84.

Benson, G.J. *The Separation of Commercial and Investment Banking*. New York: Macmillan, 1990.

Berger, C. *The Sense of Power: Studies in the Ideas of Canadian Imperialism, 1867–1914*. Toronto: University of Toronto Press, 1970.

Bird, B.J. *Entrepreneurial Behavior*. Glenview: Scott, Foresman, 1989.

Bishop, J.L. *A History of American Manufactures*. Vol. 1. Philadelphia: Edward Young, 1866.

Blackstone, W. *Commentaries on the Laws of England*. 4 vols. London: Oxford Clarendon Press, 1766.

Bladen, V.W. *An Introduction to Political Economy*. Toronto: University of Toronto Press, 1958.

Blanchard, R. *L'Abitibi-Témiscamingue*. Vol. 4. Troisième Série, Études Canadienne. Grenoble: Imprimerier Allier, 1949.

Bloomfield, E. "Lawyers as Members of Urban Business Elites in Southern Ontario, 1860 to 1920." In C. Wilton, ed., *Beyond the Law: Lawyers and Business in Canada, 1830 to 1930*, 112–47. Vol. 4 of *Essays in the History of Canadian Law*. Toronto: Butterworths, 1990.

Boothman, B.E.C. "A State of Confusion and Incompleteness: The Treatment of Commercial Failure in Canada, 1840–1933." *ASAC Conference Proceedings*, 18:24, 11–20. St. John's, NF: Memorial University, 1997.

- "The Foundations of Canadian Big Business." Paper presented at McMaster University, Fifth Canadian Business History Conference, McMaster University, Hamilton, ON, 1998.
- "High Finance and Low Strategy: Corporate Collapse in the Canadian Pulp and Paper Industry, 1919 to 1932." *Business History Review*, 74:4 (2000), 611–56.
Bork, R. "Vertical Integration and the Sherman Act: The Legal History of an Economic Misconception." *University of Chicago Law Review*, 22:1 (1954), 157–201.
Boshkoff, D. "The Bankrupt's' Moral Obligation to Pay His Discharged Debts: A Conflict Between Contract Theory and Bankruptcy Policy." *Indiana Law Journal*, 47:1 (1971), 36–69.
Bowman, E.H. "Strategy and the Weather." *Sloan Management Review*, 17:2 (1976), 49–62.
Bowman, H.M. "The States' Power over Foreign Corporations." *Michigan Law Review*, 9:7 (1911), 549–75.
Boyce, C.W. "The Pulp and Paper Industry." In J.G. Glover and R.L. Lagai, eds., *The Development of American Industries: Their Economic Significance*, 125–58. New York: Prentice-Hall, 1941.
Boyer, B. *A Passion for Justice: The Legacy of James Chalmers McRuer*. Toronto: University of Toronto Press, 1994.
Brideau, B. "Entre profit et paternalism: la papetière de Bathurst et ses ouviers de 1907 à 1945." MA thesis, Université de Moncton, 1999.
Brown, J.B. "Understanding the Better than Average Effect: Motives (Still) Matter." *Personality and Social Psychology Bulletin*, 38:2 (2012), 209–19.
Bureau of Business Research, College of Commerce and Business Administration. "Investment Banking in Chicago." *University of Illinois Business Research Bulletin*, 29:13 (1931), 1–41.
Busterna, J.C. "Trends in Daily News Paper Ownership." *Journalism and Mass Communication Quarterly*, 65:4 (1988), 831–8.
Butcher, P.J. "The Establishment of a Pulp and Paper Industry at Kapuskasing." Master's thesis, University of Western Ontario, 1978.
Cameron, J. *The Development of Governmental Forest Control in the United States*. Baltimore: Johns Hopkins University Press, 1928.
Careless, J.M.S. "Frontierism, Metropolitanism, and Canadian History." *Canadian Historical Review*, 35:1 (1954), 1–21.
- *Frontier and Metropolis in Canada: Regions, Cities, and Identities to 1914*. Toronto: University of Toronto Press, 1989.
- *Careless at Work: Selected Canadian Historical Studies*. Toronto: Dundurn Press, 1990.
Carosso, V. *Investment Banking in America: A History*. Cambridge, MA: Harvard University Press, 1970.

Carruthers, G. *Paper-Making*. Toronto: Garden City Press Co-operative, 1947.

Casey, A.J. "The New Corporate Web: Tailored Entity Partitions and Creditors' Selective Enforcement." *Yale Law Journal*, 124:8 (2015), 2680–744.

Caves, R.E. "Mergers, Takeovers and Economic Efficiency: Foresight vs. Hindsight." *International Journal of Industrial Organization*, 7:1 (1989), 151–74.

Caves, R.E., and R.M. Bradburd. "The Empirical Determinants of Vertical Integration." *Journal of Economic Behavior and Organization*, 9:3 (1988), 265–79.

Caves, R.E., M. Fortunato, and P. Ghemawat. "The Decline of Dominant Firms, 1905–1929." *Quarterly Journal of Economics*, 99 (1984), 523–46.

Chamberlain, W.L., and G.W. Edwards. *The Principles of Bond Investment*. New York: Henry Holt, 1927.

Chandler, A.D. *The Visible Hand: The Managerial Revolution in American Business*. Cambridge, MA: Harvard University Press, 1977.

– *Scale and Scope: The Dynamics of Managerial Capitalism*. Cambridge, MA: Harvard University Press, 1990.

Charland, J.-P. *Pâtes et papiers au Québec, 1880–1980: technologies, travail et travailleurs*. Quebec City: Institut québécois de recherche sur la culture, 1990.

Chatfield, M. *A History of Accounting Thought*. Hinsdale, IL: Dryden Press, 1974.

Childs, W.H. *Consolidated Statements: Principles and Procedures*. Ithaca, NY: Cornell University Press, 1949.

Clancy, P. *Micropolitics and Canadian Business: Paper, Steel and the Airlines*. Peterborough, ON: Broadview Press, 2004.

Clapperton, G. *Practical Paper-Making*. London: Crosby Lockwood, 1907.

Clapperton, R.H. *The Paper-Making Machine: Its Invention, Evolution, and Development*. London: Pergamon Press, 1967.

Clarke, F.L., G.W. Dean, and K.G. Oliver. *Corporate Collapse: Regulatory, Accounting and Ethical Failure*. Melbourne: Cambridge University Press, 1997.

Cohen, A.J. "Technological Change as Historical Process: The Case of the U.S. Pulp and Paper Industry, 1915–1940." *Journal of Economic History*, 44:3 (1984), 775–99.

Côté, S. "Les voies de la monopolization: le cas de l'usine de papier du travail au XXe siècle." PhD diss., Université de Montréal, 1978.

Couchman, C.B. *The Balance-Sheet: Its Preparation, Content and Interpretation*. New York: Journal of Accountancy, 1924.

Cox, C. *Canadian Strength*. Toronto: Ryerson Press, 1946.

Craig, G. *Upper Canada: The Formative Years 1784–1841*. Toronto: McClelland and Stewart, 1963.

Cross, C.F., E.J. Bevan, and R.W. Sindall. *Wood Pulp and Its Uses*. New York: Van Nostrant, 1911.

Cuervo, A., D. Ribeiro, and S. Roig, eds. *Entrepreneurship, Theory and Perspective.* New York: Springer, 2007.

Cruickshank, K. *Close Ties: Railways, Government, and the Board of Railway Commissioners, 1851–1933.* Montreal: McGill-Queen's University Press, 1991.

Davis, G.F., K.A. Diekmann, and C.H. Tinsley, "The Decline and Fall of the Conglomerate Firm in the 1980s: The Deinstitutionalization of an Organizational Form." *American Sociological Review,* 59:4 (1994), 547–70.

Davis, L.E., and R.E. Gallman. *Evolving Financial Markets and International Capital Flows: Britain, the Americas, and Australia, 1865–1914.* London: Cambridge University Press, 2001.

Dawley, A. *Struggles for Justice: Social Responsibility and the Liberal State.* Cambridge, MA: Harvard University Press, 1991.

Denison, M. *The People's Power: A History of Ontario Hydro.* Toronto: McClelland and Stewart, 1960.

Dick, T.J.O. "Canadian Newsprint, 1913–1930: National Policies and the North American Economy." *Journal of Economic History,* 42:3 (1982), 659–87.

Dion, A. "L'industrie des pâtes et papiers en Mauricie, 1887–1929." MA thesis, L'université du Québec à Trois-Rivières, 1981.

Dodd, E.M. "Statutory Developments in Business Corporation Law, 1886–1936." *Harvard Law Review,* 50:1 (1936), 33–6.

– "Fair and Equitable Recapitalizations." *Harvard Law Review,* 55 (1939), 780–818.

Donovan, W. J. "The Legality of Trade Associations." *Proceedings of the Annals of the Academy of Political Science,* 11:4 (1926), 19–26.

– *Report submitted to the Hon. Thomas D. Thatcher, Judge of the United States District Court for the Southern District of New York, on March 22, 1930.* New York: Court Press, 1931.

Douglas, W.O. "Protective Committees in Railroad Reorganization." *Harvard Law Review,* 47:4 (1934), 565–89.

Drucker, P.F. *The End of Economic Man: A Study of the New Totalitarianism.* New York: John Day, 1939.

Drummond, I., ed. *Progress Without Planning: The Economic History of Ontario from Confederation to the Second World War.* Toronto: University of Toronto Press, 1987.

Drury, E.C. *Farmer Premier: The Memoirs of E.C. Drury.* Toronto: McClelland and Stewart, 1966.

Duffy, P.H. "English Bankrupts, 1571–1861." *American Journal of Legal History,* 24:4 (1980), 283–305.

Duncan, L. *Law and Practice of Bankruptcy in Canada.* Toronto: Carswell, 1922.

Dunlop, C.B.R. *Creditor and Debtor Law in Canada.* Toronto: Carswell, 1981.

Eddy, J. *The New Competition.* New York: Stevens Press, 1912.

Efrat, R. "The Evolution of Bankruptcy Stigma." *Theoretical Inquiries in Law*, 7:2 (2006), 364–93.

Eichner, A.S. "Business and the Market Mechanism." In I. Berg, ed., *The Business of America*, 167–200. New York: Harcourt, Brace and World, 1968.

– "The Micro Foundations of the Corporate Economy." *Managerial and Decision Economics*, 4:3 (1983), 136–52.

Eis, C. "The 1919–1930 Merger Movement in American Industry." *Journal of Law & Economics*, 12:2 (1969), 267–96.

Ellis, L.E. *Print Paper Pendulum: Group Pressures and the Price of Newsprint*. New Brunswick, NJ: Rutgers University Press, 1947.

– *Newsprint: Producers, Publishers, Political Pressures*. New Brunswick, NJ: Rutgers University Press, 1960.

Errington, J. *The Lion, the Eagle, and Upper Canada: A Developing Colonial Ideology*. Montreal: McGill-Queen's University Press, 1987.

Espinosa, M.P. "Delivered Pricing, FOB Pricing, and Collusion in Spatial Markets." *RAND Journal of Economics*, 23:1 (1992), 64–85.

Evans, L.S. *A Standard History of Ross County, Ohio*. Vol. 2. Chicago: Lewis Publishing, 1917.

Finney, H.A. *Consolidated Statements for Holding Companies*. New York Prentice-Hall, 1923.

Fligstein, N. *The Transformation of Corporate Control*. Cambridge, MA: Harvard University Press, 1990.

Fleming, K.R. *Power at Cost: Ontario Hydro and Rural Electrification, 1911–1956*. Montreal: McGill-Queen's University Press, 1992.

Foner, E. *Free Soil, Free Labor, Free Men: The Ideology of the Republican Party Before the Civil War*. New York: Oxford University Press, 1995.

Foster, M.B. *Banking*. New York: Alexander Hamilton Institute, 1917.

Frank, M.Z., and V.K. Goyal. "Capital Structure Decisions: Which Factors are Reliably Important?" *Financial Management*, 38:1 (2009), 1–37.

Fraser, W.K. "Reorganization of Companies in Canada." *Columbia Law Review*, 27:8 (1927), 932–57.

Freyer, T.A. *Producers versus Capitalists: Constitutional Conflict in Antebellum America*. Charlottesville: University of Virginia Press, 1994.

Fridenson, P. "Business Failure and the Agenda of Business History." *Enterprise and Society*, 5:4 (2004), 562–82.

Fukuyama, F. *Trust: The Social Virtues and the Creation of Prosperity*. London: Penguin, 1995.

Gentili, G. "Canada: Protecting Rights in a Worldwide Rights Culture': An Empirical Study of the Use of Foreign Precedents by the Supreme Court of Canada, 1982–2010." In T. Groppi and M.-C. Ponthoreau, eds., *The Use of Foreign Precedents by Constitutional Judges*, 39–68. London: Hart, 2013.

George, P.J., and P.J. Sworden. "John Beverley Robinson and the Commercial Empire of the St. Lawrence." *Research in Economic History*, 11 (1988), 217–42.

Gidney, R.D., and W.P.J. Millar. *Professional Gentlemen: The Profession in Nineteenth-Century Ontario*. Toronto: University of Toronto Press, 1994.

Gilbert, C.W. *The Mirrors of Wall Street*. New York: G.P. Putnam's Sons, 1933.

Gillis, R.P., and T.R. Roach. *Lost Initiatives: Canada's Forest Industries, Forest Policy, and Forest Conservation*. Westport, CT: Greenwood, 1986.

Glenn, G. "Essentials of Bankruptcy: Prevention of Fraud, and Control of the Debtor." *Virginia Law Review*, 23:4 (1937), 373–88.

Gold, J. "Preference Shareholders in the Reconstruction of English Companies." *University of Toronto Law Review*, 5:2 (1943–4), 282–323.

Goltz, E. "Espanola: The History of a Pulp and Paper Town." *Laurentian University Review*, 6:3 (1974), 75–104.

Gore-Browne, F.B. *Handbook on the Formation, Management and Winding Up of Joint Stock Companies*. 34th ed. London: Jordan and Sons, 1919.

Gourd, B.-B. "La Colonization des Clay Belts du Nord-Ouest Québécois et Du Nord-est Ontarien." *Revue D'Histoire L'Amérique Française*, 27:2 (1973), 235–76.

Graham, B., and D.L. Dodd. *Security Analysis*. 2nd ed. New York: McGraw-Hill, 1940.

Graham, J.R., and C. Harvey. "The Practice of Corporate Finance: Evidence from the Field." *Journal of Financial Economics*, 60:2 (2001), 186–243.

Graham, W.R. *Arthur Meighen, a Biography: No Surrender*. Vol. 3. Toronto: Clarke Irwin, 1965.

Gratton, V. "Actions et repercussions." *Actualité économique*, 3:9 (1927), 176–80.

Gray, S. "The Government's Timber Business: Forest Policy and Administration in British Columbia, 1912–1928." *BC Studies*, 81 (1989), 24–49.

Guthrie, J.A. *The Newsprint Paper Industry: An Economic Analysis*. Cambridge, MA: Harvard University Press, 1941.

– *The Economics of Pulp and Paper*. Pullman: State College of Washington Press, 1950.

Hagenauer, J.P. "Labour Cost of Production in the Pulp and Paper Industry." *Paper Trade Journal*, 50 (25 April 1935), 29–39.

Hale, G.E. "Vertical Integration: Impact of the Antitrust Laws upon Combinations of Successive Stages of Production and Distribution." *Columbia Law Review*, 49:7 (1949), 921–54.

Hamilton, S., and A. Micklethwait. *Greed and Corporate Failure: The Lessons from Recent Disasters*. London: Palgrave Macmillan, 2006.

Hamilton, W., and Associates. *Price and Price Policies*. New York: McGraw-Hill, 1938.

Hannan, M.T., and J.H. Freeman. *Organizational Ecology*. Cambridge. MA: Harvard University Press, 1989.

Hardy, R., and N. Séguin. *Forêt et société en Mauricie. La formation d'une région.* Quebec City: Septentrion, 2011.

Harrigan, K.R. *Strategies for Vertical Integration.* Toronto: D.C. Heath, 1983.

Harris, G.H. *The President's Book: The Story of the Sun Life Assurance Company of Canada.* Montreal: Sun Life Assurance, 1928.

Hawley, E. *The New Deal and the Problem of Monopoly.* Princeton: Princeton University Press, 1966.

Hayes, S.P. *Conservation and the Gospel of Efficiency: The Progressive Conservation Movement, 1890–1920.* Cambridge, MA: Harvard University Press, 1959.

Heath, M.S. "The Rate Structure." *Law and Contemporary Problems,* 12:3 (1947), 405–15.

Heaton, J.B. "Managerial Optimism and Corporate Finance." *Financial Management,* 31:2 (2002), 33–45.

Heinrich, T. "Product Diversification in the U.S. Pulp and Paper Industry: The Case of International Paper, 1898–1941." *Business History Review,* 75:3 (2001), 467–505.

Herbert, B.G. "Delivered Pricing as Conspiracy and as Discrimination: The Legal Status." *Law and Contemporary Problems,* 15:2 (1950), 181–226.

Hill, R.K. "Consent Receiverships in Federal Equity Practice." *Chicago-Kent Law Review,* 11:4 (1933), 267–77.

Hiller, J.K. "The Origins of the Pulp and Paper Industry in Newfoundland." *Acadiensis,* 11:2 (1982), 42–68.

– "The Politics of Newsprint: The Newfoundland Pulp and Paper Industry, 1915–1939." *Acadiensis,* 19:2 (1990), 3–39.

Himmelberg, R.F. *The Origins of the National Recovery Association: Business, Government, and the Trade Association Issue, 1921–1933.* New York: Fordham University Press, 1976.

Hodgetts, J.E. *From Arm's Length to Hands On: The Formative Years of Ontario's Public Service, 1867–1940.* Toronto: University of Toronto Press, 1995.

Hofer, C.W. "Turnaround Strategies." *Journal of Business Strategy,* 1:1 (1980), 19–31.

Honsberger, J.D. "The Need for a Rapprochement of the Bankruptcy Systems of Canada and the United States." *McGill Law Journal,* 18:2 (1972), 147–69.

– "Bankruptcy Administration in the United States and Canada." *California Law Review,* 63:6 (1975), 1515–45.

Hoover, H. *American Individualism.* New York: Doubleday Page, 1922.

Horne, G.R. "The Receivership and Reorganization of the Abitibi Power and Paper Company, Limited." PhD diss., University of Michigan, 1954.

Horwitz, M.J. *The Transformation of American Law, 1780–1860.* Cambridge, MA: Harvard University Press, 1977.

– "*Santa Clara* Revisited: The Development of Corporate Theory." *West Virginia Law Review,* 88 (1985), 173–224.

– *The Transformation of American Law, 1870–1960: The Crisis of Legal Orthodoxy.* New York: Oxford University Press, 1992.

Hounshell, D. *From the American System to Mass Production, 1800–1932: The Development of Manufacturing Technology in the United States.* Baltimore: John Hopkins University Press, 1984.

Hovenkamp, H. *Enterprise and American Law, 1836–1937.* Cambridge, MA: Harvard University Press, 1991.

– "The Law of Vertical Integration and the Business Firm: 1880–1960." *Iowa Law Review*, 95:3 (2010), 863–918.

Howard, M. "A Theory of Discharge in Consumer Bankruptcy." *Ohio State Law Journal*, 48:4 (1987), 1047–88.

Huertas, T.F., and J.L. Silverman. "Charles E. Mitchell: Scapegoat of the Crash?" *Business History Review*, 60:1 (1986), 81–103.

Hunter, H. "Innovation, Competition, and Locational Changes in the Pulp and Paper Industry: 1880–1950." *Land Economics*, 31:4 (1955), 313–27.

Hurd, H.M., and R. Brubaker. *Debts and the Demands of Conscience: The Virtue of Bankruptcy.* London: Oxford University Press, 2016.

Hurst, W.J. *The Legitimacy of the Business Corporation in the United States.* Charlottesville: University Press of Virginia, 1970.

Huston, M. *Financing an Empire: A History of Banking in Illinois.* Chicago: S.J. Clarke, 1926.

Ingham, J.N., ed. *Biographical Dictionary of American Business Leaders.* Vol. 2. Westport, CT: Greenwood, 1983.

Irwin, D.A. "Gold Sterilization and the Recession of 1937–1938." *Financial History Review*, 19:3 (2012), 249–67.

Jackson, T.H. "The Fresh-Start Policy in Bankruptcy Law." *Harvard Law Review*, 98:7 (1985), 1393–1448.

Jaffe, A.J., and J.M. Sharp. "Contract Theory and Mortgage Foreclosure Moratoria." *Journal of Real Estate Finance and Economics*, 12:1 (1996), 77–96.

Jaher, F.C. *The Urban Establishment: Upper Strata in Boston New York, Charleston, Chicago and Los Angeles.* Urbana: University of Illinois Press, 1982.

James, F.C. *The Growth of Chicago Banks.* New York: Harper, 1938.

Johnson, H. *The Blue Eagle: From Egg to Earth.* New York: Doubleday, Doran, 1935.

Johnston, C.M. *E.C. Drury: Agrarian Idealist.* Toronto: University of Toronto Press, 1986.

Jones, A.F. "The Accountant's Relation to Timber Bond Issues." *Annals of the American Academy of Political and Social Science*, 41:5 (1912), 51–8.

Jones, W. "The Foundations of English Bankruptcy." *Transactions of the American Philosophical Society*, 69 (1979), Part 3, 1–63.

Kaplan, R.L. *Politics and the American Press: The Rise of Objectivity, 1865–1920.* New York: Cambridge University Press, 2002.

Kavanaugh, T.J. *Bank Credit Methods and Practice*. New York: Bankers Publishing, 1921.

Keller, M. *Affairs of State: Public Life in Late Nineteenth-Century America*. Cambridge, MA: Harvard University Press, 1977.

Kellogg, R.S. *Pulpwood and Wood Pulp in North America*. New York: McGraw-Hill, 1923.

– *Newsprint Paper in North America*. New York: Newsprint Service Bureau, 1948.

Kennedy, S.E. *The Banking Crisis of 1933*. Lexington: University Press of Kentucky, 1973.

Kenyon, W.A., and J.R. Turnball, eds. *The Battle for James Bay, 1686*. Toronto: Macmillan, 1971.

Kershaw, I. *Making Friends with Hitler: Lord Londonderry, the Nazis, and the Road to War*. New York: Penguin, 2005.

Kouwenhoven, John A. *Partners in Banking: A Historical Portrait of a Great Private Bank, Brown Brothers Harriman & Co*. New York: Doubleday, 1968.

Knapp, G.G.P. *How Banks Increase Their Business*. Chicago: Rand McNally, 1926.

Kniffin, W.H. *American Banking Practice – A Treatise on the Practical Operation of a Bank*. New York: McGraw-Hill, 1921.

Kuhlberg, M. "'In the Power of the Government': The Rise and Fall of Newsprint in Ontario, 1894–1932." PhD diss., York University, 2002.

– "'eyes wide open': E.W. Backus and the Pitfalls of Investing in Ontario's Pulp and Paper Industry, 1902–1932." *Journal of the Canadian Historical Association*, 16:1 (2005), 201–33.

– *In the Power of the Government: The Rise and Fall of Newsprint in Ontario, 1894–1932*. Toronto: University of Toronto Press, 2015.

Kuznets, S. *Modern Economic Growth: Rate, Structure and Spread*. New Haven, CT: Yale University Press, 1966.

Laffer, A.B. "Vertical Integration by Corporations, 1929–1964." *Review of Economics and Statistics*, 51 (1969), 91–3.

Lajoie, A. *Le pouvoir déclaratoire du Parlement: augmentation discrétionnaire de la compétence fédérale au Canada*. Montreal: Presses de l'Université de Montréal, 1969.

Lamberg, J.-A., Näsi, J. Ojala, and P. Sajasalo, eds. *The Evolution of Competitive Strategies in Global Forestry Industries*. New York: Springer, 2006.

Lamberg, J.-A., J. Ojala, M. Peltoniemi, and T. Särkkä, eds. *The Evolution of Global Paper Industry 1800–2050: A Comparative Analysis*. New York: Springer, 2012.

Lambert, R.S., and P. Pross. *Renewing Nature's Wealth: A Centennial History of the Public Management of Lands, Forests and Wildlife in Ontario, 1763–1967*. Toronto: Queen's Printer, 1967.

Lamoreaux, N.R. *The Great Merger Movement in American Business, 1895–1904*. New York: Cambridge University Press, 1985.

Landes, D.S. *The Unbound Prometheus: Technological Change and Industrial Development in Western Europe from 1750 to the Present*. New York: Cambridge University Press, 1969.
– *The Wealth and Poverty of Nations: Why Some Are so Rich and Some so Poor*. New York: W.W. Norton, 1998.
Lang, N. "La compagnie Fraser Limited, 1918–1974: étude de l'évolution des strategies économiques, des structures administratives et de l'organisation du travail à l'usine d'Edmundston au Nouveau-Brunswick." PhD diss., Université de Montréal, 1994.
Langdon, J. "Criteria in the Establishment of Freight Rate Divisions." *Cornell Law Review*, 39:2 (1954), 213–36.
Langmuir, D. *The Fixed Trust: A Statement of Underlying Principles*. New York: Distributors Group, 1931.
Larwood, L., and W. Whittaker. "Managerial Myopia: Self-Serving Biases in Organizational Planning." *Journal of Applied Psychology*, 62:2 (1977), 194–8.
Leary, M.T., and M.R. Roberts. "Do Peer Firms Affect Corporate Financial Policy?" *Journal of Finance*, 69:1 (2014), 139–78.
Lee, A.M. *The Daily Newspaper in America*. New York: Macmillan, 1937.
Leibell, V.L. "The Chandler Act – Its Effect Upon the Law of Bankruptcy." *Fordham Law Review*, 9:3 (1940), 380–409.
Levi, E.H., and J.W. Moore. "Bankruptcy and Reorganization: A Survey of Changes." *University of Chicago Law Review*, 5:1 (1937), 1–40.
Levinthal, L.E. "The Early History of English Bankruptcy." *University of Pennsylvania Law Review*, 67:1 (1919), 1–20.
Lichtenberg, F.R. *Corporate Takeovers and Productivity*. Cambridge, MA: MIT Press, 1992.
Lilly, W. *Individual and Corporation Mortgages: A Statement for Laymen of the Legal Principles*. New York: Doubleday Page, 1921.
Livermore, S. "The Success of Industrial Mergers." *Quarterly Journal of Economics*, 50:1 (1935), 68–96.
Lowenthal, L. *The Investor Pays*. New York: Alfred A. Knopf, 1933.
MacIntyre, J.M. "The Use of American Cases in Canadian Courts." *University of British Columbia Law Review*, 2 (1966), 478–90.
MacKenzie, D. *The Clarkson Gordon Story*. Toronto: University of Toronto Press, 1989.
Maddison, A. *Dynamic Forces in Capitalist Development: A Long-Run Comparative View*. New York: Oxford University Press, 1991.
– *Monitoring the World Economy, 1820–1992*. Paris: OECD, 1995.
Magee, G.B. *Productivity and Performance in the Paper Industry: Labour, Capital, and Technology in Britain and America, 1860–1914*. New York: Cambridge University Press, 1997.

Malmendier, U., and G.A. Tate. "CEO Overconfidence and Corporate Investment." *Journal of Finance*, 60:6 (2005), 661–700.

Malmsten, E., E. Portanger, and C. Drazin, *Boo Hoo: $135 Million, 18 Months … A Dot.Com Story from Concept to Catastrophe*. New York: Arrow, 2001.

Manfredi, C.P. "The Use of United States Decisions by the Supreme Court of Canada Under the Charter of Rights and Freedom." *Canadian Journal of Political Science*, 23:3 (1990), 499–518.

Manore, J.L. *Cross-Currents: Hydroelectricity and the Engineering of Northern Ontario*. Waterloo, ON: Wilfrid Laurier University Press, 1999.

Markham, J.W. *A Financial History of Modern U.S. Corporate Scandals: From Enron to Reform*. New York: Routledge, 2006.

Markusen, A.R. *Profit Cycles, Oligopoly and Regional Development*. Cambridge, MA: MIT Press, 1985.

Marx, L. *The Machine in the Garden: Technology and the Pastoral Ideal in America*. New York: Oxford University Press, 1964.

Mathias, P. *Takeover: The 22 Days of Risk and Decision that Created the World's Largest Newsprint Empire, Abitibi-Price*. Toronto: Maclean-Hunter, 1976.

McCaffery, E. "Corporate Reorganization under the Chandler Bankruptcy Act." *California Law Review*, 26:6 (1938), 643–63.

McDermott, G.L. "Advancing and Retracting Frontiers of Agricultural Settlement in the Great Clay Belt of Ontario and Quebec." PhD diss., University of Wisconsin, 1959.

McDowall, D. *Steel at the Sault: Francis H. Clergue, Sir James Dunn, and the Algoma Steel Corporation, 1910–1956*. Toronto: University of Toronto Press, 1984.

– *Quick to the Frontier: Canada's Royal Bank*. Toronto: McClelland and Stewart, 1993.

McGaw, J.A. *Most Wonderful Machine: Mechanization and Social Change in Berkshire Paper Making, 1801–1885*. Princeton: Princeton University Press, 1987.

McGee, J.S., and L.R. Bassett, "Vertical Integration Revisited." *Journal of Law and Economics*, 19:1 (1976), 167–238.

McGillicuddy, O.E. "The Paper and Paper Production Situation." *North American Review*, 1 January 1924, 616–20.

McGrath, T.S. *Timber Bonds*. Chicago: Craig-Wayne, 1911.

McKenty, N. *Mitch Hepburn*. Toronto: McClelland and Stewart, 1967.

McLean, B., and P. Elkind. *The Smartest Guys in the Room: The Amazing Rise and Scandalous Fall of Enron*. New York: Portfolio Trade, 2004.

Meeks, G. *Disappointing Marriage: A Study of the Gains from Merger*. London: Cambridge University Press, 1977.

Merchant, E.O. "The Government and the News-Print Paper Manufacturers." *Quarterly Journal of Economics*, 32:3 (1918), 238–56; and 34:2 (1920), 313–28.

Michie, R.C. "The Canadian Securities Market, 1850–1914." *Business History Review*, 62:1 (1988), 35–73.

Miller, D. *The Icarus Paradox: How Exceptional Companies Bring About Their Own Downfall*. New York: Harper Business, 1990.

Miller, M.D. *Bank Loans on Statement and Character*. New York: Ronald Press, 1927.

Mitchell, E.A. *Fort Timiskaming and the Fur Trade*. Toronto: University of Toronto Press, 1977.

Mitchell, V. *A Treatise on the Law Relating to Canadian Commercial Corporations*. Montreal: Southam Press, 1916.

Mochoruk, J. *Formidable Heritage: Manitoba's North and the Cost of Development, 1870 to 1930*. Winnipeg: University of Manitoba Press, 2004.

Moley, R. *After Seven Years*. New York: Harper and Brothers, 1939.

Montague, G.H. "Recent Developments in Trade Association Law." *Annals of the American Academy of Political and Social Science*, 139:9 (1928), 38–43.

Moody, J. "Preferred Stocks as Investments." *Annuals of the American Academy of Political and Sciences*, 35:3 (1910), 63–71.

Morawetz, V. "Shares without Nominal or Par Value." *Harvard Law Review*, 26:8 (1913), 729–31.

Morgan, H.J., ed. *The Canadian Men and Women of the Time*. Toronto: William Briggs, 1912.

Morrison, A.D., and W.J. Wilhelm. *Investment Banking: Institutions, Politics and Law*. London: Oxford University Press, 2007.

Munn, G.G. *Bank Credit: Principles and Operating Procedure*. New York: McGraw-Hill, 1925.

Mutual Life Assurance of Canada. *A Century of Mutuality*. Waterloo, ON: Mutual Life of Canada, 1970.

Nash, R. *Wilderness and the American Mind*. New Haven, CT: Yale University Press, 1967.

Nelles, H.V. *The Politics of Development: Forests, Mines, and Hydro-Electric Power in Ontario, 1849–1941*. Toronto: Macmillan of Canada, 1974.

Nelson, W. *The Americanization of the Common Law: The Impact of Legal Change on Massachusetts Society*. Cambridge, MA: Harvard University Press, 1975.

Newman, J.F. "Reaction and Change: A Study of the Ontario Bar, 1880 to 1920." *University of Toronto Law Review*, 32:1 (1974), 51–74.

Niosi, J. "La Laurentide (1887–1928): pionnière du papier journal au Canada." *Revue d'Histoire de l'Amérique Française*, 29:3 (1975), 375–415.

Oden, J.P. "Development of the Southern Pulp and Paper Industry, 1900–1970." PhD diss., Mississippi State University, 1973.

Ohanian, N.K. *The American Pulp and Paper Industry, 1900–1940: Mill Survival, Firm Structure, and Industry Relocation*. Westport, CT: Greenwood, 1993.

Ojala, J., J.-A. Lamberg, A. Ahola, and A. Melander. "The Ephemera of Success: Strategy, Structure and Performance in the Forestry Industries." In J.-A. Lamberg, J. Näsi, J. Ojala, and P. Sajasalo, eds., *The Evolution of Competitive Strategies in Global Forestry Industries*, 259–71. New York: Springer, 2006.

Oliver, P. *G. Howard Ferguson: Ontario Tory*. Toronto: University of Toronto Press, 1977.

Ollerenshaw, P. "Innovation and Corporate Failure: Cyril Lord in UK Textiles, 1945–68." *Enterprise and Society*, 7:4 (2006), 777–811.

Olmstead, J.M. "Bankruptcy a Commercial Regulation." *Harvard Law Review*, 15:10 (1902), 829–43.

Pack, A.N. *Our Vanishing Forests*. New York: Macmillan, 1923.

Parenteau, W. "The Woods Transformed: The Emergence of the Pulp and Paper Industry in New Brunswick, 1918–1931." *Acadiensis*, 22:1 (1992), 5–43.

Parenteau, W., and L.A. Sandberg. "Conservation and the Gospel of Economic Nationalism: The Canadian Pulpwood Question in Nova Scotia and New Brunswick, 1918–1925." *Environmental History Review*, 19:2 (1995), 55–83.

Parker, W.R.P. *Frauds on Creditors and Assignments for the Benefit of Creditors*. Toronto: Canada Law Book, 1903.

Paton, W.A. *Accounting Theory*. New York, 1922.

Payne, C.T. "The General Administration of Equity Receiverships of Corporations." *Yale Law Journal*, 31:7 (1922), 685–701.

Payne, P.M. "Exculpatory Clauses in Corporate Mortgages and Other Instruments." *Cornell Law Quarterly*, 20:2 (1934), 171–96.

Peach, W.N. *The Security Affiliates of National Banks*. Baltimore: Johns Hopkins University Press, 1941.

Pecora, F. *Wall Street Under Oath: The Story of Our Modern Money Changers*. New York: Simon and Schuster, 1939.

Pence, K.M. "Foreclosing on Opportunity: State Laws and Mortgage Credit." *Review of Economics and Statistics*, 88:1 (2006), 177–82.

Penrose, E.T. *The Theory of the Growth of the Firm*. Oxford: Basil Blackwell, 1959.

Perino, P. *The Hellhound of Wall Street: How Ferdinand Pecora's Investigation of the Great Crash Forever Changed American Finance*. New York: Penguin, 2010.

Perry, M. "Vertical Integration: Determinants and Effects." In R. Schmalaensee and R.D. Willig, eds., *Handbook of Industrial Organization*, 183–255. New York: North Holland, 1989.

Phillips, C.A. *Bank Credit: A Study of the Principles and Factors Underlying Advances Made by Banks to Borrowers*. New York: Macmillan 1920.

Phillips, S.C. "The Use of Wood Pulp for Paper-Making." *Journal of the Society of Arts*, 53 (19 May 1905), 1–34.

Piédalue, G. "Les groupes financiers et la guerre du papier au Canada, 1920–1930." *Revue d'Histoire de l'Amérique Française*, 30:2 (1976), 233–58.

Plewman, W.R. *Adam Beck and the Ontario Hydro*. Toronto: Ryerson Press, 1947.

Porter, M.E. *Canada at the Crossroads: The Reality of a New Competitive Environment*. Ottawa: Business Council on National Issues, 1991.

Posner, L.S. "Liability of the Trustee Under the Corporate Mortgage Indenture." *Harvard Law Review*, 42:2 (1928), 198–248.

Pratt, J.W., and R.J. Zeckhauser, eds. *Principals and Agents: The Structure of Business*. Cambridge, MA: Harvard Business School Press, 1985.

Previts, G.J., and B.D. Merino. *A History of Accounting in America: An Historical Interpretation of the Cultural Significance of Accounting*. Columbus: Ohio University Press, 1979.

"Protective Committees and Reorganization Reform." *Yale Law Journal*, 47:2 (1937), 229–33.

Prudden, R.F. *The Bank Credit Investigator*. New York: Bankers Publishing, 1922.

Pugh, D.E. "Ontario's Great Clay Belt Hoax." *Canadian Geographical Journal*, 90:1 (1975), 19–25.

Quilter, M. "Bankruptcy and Order." *Monash University Law Review*, 39:1 (2013), 189–212.

Radforth, I. *Bush Workers and Bosses: Logging in Northern Ontario, 1900–1980*. Toronto: University of Toronto Press, 1987.

Railway Age. *The Biographical Directory of the Railway Officials of America for 1887*. Chicago: Railway Age, 1887.

Ramsay, I. "Models of Consumer Bankruptcy: Implications for Research and Policy." *Journal of Consumer Policy* 20:2 (1997), 269–87.

Ravenscraft, D.J., and F.M. Scherer. *Mergers, Sell-Offs and Economic Efficiency*. Washington: Brookings Institution, 1987.

Reagan, P.D. *Designing a New America: The Origins of New Deal Planning, 1890–1943*. Amherst: University of Massachusetts Press, 1999.

Recknagel, A.B. *The Forests of New York State*. New York: Macmillan, 1923.

Regehr, T.D. *The Beauharnois Scandal: A Story of Canadian Entrepreneurship and Politics*. Toronto: University of Toronto Press, 1990.

Rich, E.E. *The Fur Trade and the Northwest to 1857* Toronto: McClelland and Stewart, 1967.

Richards, D.J., and D. Carlton. "Vertical Integration in Competitive Markets under Uncertainty." *Journal of Industrial Economics*, 27:3 (1979), 189–209.

Richardson, A.J. "Canada's Accounting Elite: 1880–1930." *Accounting Historians Journal*, 16:1 (1989), 1–21.

Richberg, D.R. *Tents of the Mighty*. New York: Willett, Clark & Colby, 1930.

– *The Rainbow*. New York: Doubleday Doran, 1936.

Riordan, M. "Competitive Effects of Vertical Integration." In P. Buccirossi, ed., *Handbook of Antitrust Economics*, 145–82. Cambridge, MA: MIT Press, 2008.

Risk, R.C.B. "The Nineteenth-Century Foundations of the Business Corporation in Ontario." *University of Toronto Law Journal*, 23:3 (1973), 199–239.

– "The Golden Age: The Law About the Market in Nineteenth-Century Ontario." *University of Toronto Law Journal*, 26:3 (1976), 307–46.

– "The Last Golden Age: Property and the Allocation of Losses in Ontario During the Nineteenth Century." *University of Toronto Law Journal*, 27:2 (1977), 199–239.

Roach, T.R. "The Pulpwood Trade and the Settlers of New Ontario." *Journal of Canadian Studies*, 22:3 (1987), 78–88.
– *Newsprint: Canadian Supply and American Demand*. Durham, NC: Forest History Society, 1994.
Roach, T.R., and R. Judd. "A Man for All Seasons: Frank John Dixie Barnjum, Conservationist, Pulpwood Embargoist and Speculator!" *Acadiensis*, 20:2 (1991), 129–44.
Roby, Y. *Les Québécois et les investissements américains (1918–1929)*. Quebec City: Les Presses de l'Université Laval, 1976.
Rohrlich, C. "Protective Committees." *University of Pennsylvania Law Review*, 80:5 (1932), 674–81.
Röller, L.-H., J. Stennek, and F. Verboven. "Efficiency Gains from Mergers." In F. Ilzkovitz and R. Meiklejohn, eds., *European Merger Control: Do We Need an Efficiency Defence?* 84–201. London: Edward Elgar, 2006.
Romasco, A.U. *The Poverty of Abundance: Hoover, the Nation, the Depression*. New York: Oxford University Press, 1965.
Romer, C.D. "What Ended the Great Depression?" *Journal of Economic History*, 52:4 (1992), 757–84.
Roose, K.D. *The Economics of Recession and Revival: An Interpretation of 1937–38*. New Haven, CT: Yale University Press, 1954.
Rosen, P.L. *The Supreme Court and Social Science*. Urbana: University of Illinois Press, 1972.
Rosenberg, R.J. "Intercorporate Guaranties and the Law of Fraudulent Conveyances: Lender Beware." *University of Pennsylvania Law Review*, 125:2 (1976), 235–63.
Rostow, W.W. *The World Economy: History & Prospect* Austin: University of Texas Press, 1978.
Royster, C. *The Fabulous History of the Dismal Swamp Company: A Story of George Washington's Time*. New York: Knopf, 1999.
Salinger, M.A. "Vertical Mergers and Market Foreclosure." *Quarterly Journal of Economics*, 103:2 (1988), 345–56.
Sandberg, L.A. "Forest Policy in Nova Scotia: The Big Lease, Cape Breton Island, 1899–1960." *Acadiensis*, 20:2 (1991), 105–28.
Santos, S.C., A. Caetano, C. Mitchell, H. Landström, and A. Fayolle, eds. *The Emergence of Entrepreneurial Behaviour: Intention, Education and Orientation*. Northhampton: Edward Elgar, 2017.
Sarra, J.P. *Creditor Rights and the Public Interest: Restructuring Insolvent Corporations*. Toronto: University of Toronto Press, 2003.
Saywell, J.T. *"Just Call Me Mitch": The Life of Mitchell F. Hepburn*. Toronto: University of Toronto Press, 1991.
– "F.H. Deacon and Co., Investment Dealers: A Case Study of the Securities Industry, 1897–1945." *Ontario History*, 85:2 (1993), 167–92.

Schlesinger, A.M. *The Coming of the New Deal*. Boston: Houghton Mifflin, 1958.

Schull, J. *The Century of the Sun: The First Hundred Years of the Sun Life Assurance Company of Canada*. Toronto: Macmillan, 1971.

Schumpeter, J. *The Theory of Economic Development: An Inquiry into Profits, Capital, Credit, Interest, and the Business Cycle*. Livingston: Transaction Publishers, 1934.

Seligman, J. *The Transformation of Wall Street: A History of the Securities and Exchange Commission and Modern Corporate Finance*. Boston: Houghton Mifflin, 1982.

Shipley, J.W. *Pulp and Paper-Making in Canada*. Toronto: Longmans, Green, 1929.

Shutter, M.D., ed. *History of Minneapolis, Gateway to the Northwest*. Chicago: S.J. Clarke, 1923.

Skeel, D.A. *Debt's Dominion: A History of Bankruptcy Law in America*. Princeton: Princeton University Press, 2001.

Sklar, M.J. *The Corporate Reconstruction of American Capitalism, 1890–1916: The Market, The Law, and Politics*. New York: Cambridge University Press, 1988.

Skrownek, S. *Building a New American State: The Expansion of National Administrative Capacities, 1877–1920*. New York: Cambridge University Press, 1982.

Smails, R.G.H. *Accounting Principles*. Toronto: Ryerson Press, 1948.

Smith, A. *The Wealth of Nations*. London: Penguin, 1982.

Smith, D.C. "Wood Pulp and Newspapers, 1867–1900." *Business History Review*, 38 (1964), 328–45.

– *History of Papermaking in the United States, 1691–1969*. New York: Lockwood Trade Journal, 1971.

Smith, E.L. *Common Stocks as Long Term Investments*. New York: Macmillan, 1925.

Smith, H.N. *Virgin Land: The American West as Symbol and Myth*. Cambridge, MA: Harvard University Press, 1950.

Sobel, R. *The Great Bull Market: Wall Street in the 1920s*. New York: W.W. Norton, 1968.

Sommer, U., and Q. Li. "Judicial Decision Making in Times of Financial Crises." *Judicature*, 95:2 (2011), 68–77.

Spanner, D. "'The Straight Furrow': The Life of George S. Henry, Ontario's Unknown Premier." PhD diss., University of Western Ontario, 1994.

Squire, R. "Strategic Liability in the Corporate Group." *University of Chicago Law Review*, 78:2 (2011), 602–21.

Stetson, F.L. "Preparation of Corporate Bonds, Mortgages, Collateral Trusts, and Debenture Instruments." In F.L. Stetson and Associates, *Some Legal Phases of Corporate Financing, Reorganization and Regulation*, 1–77. New York: Macmillan, 1917.

Stevenson, L.T. *The Background and Economics of American Papermaking*. New York: Harper and Brothers, 1940.

Stigler, G.J. *Capital and Rates of Return in Manufacturing Industries*. Princeton: Princeton University Press, 1963.

Stone, D.G. *April Fools: An Insider's Account of the Rise and Collapse of Drexel Burnham*. New York: D.I. Fine, 1990.

Struthers, J. *No Fault of Their Own: Unemployment and the Canadian Welfare State, 1914–1941*. Toronto: University of Toronto Press, 1983.

– *The Limits of Affluence: Welfare in Ontario, 1920–1970*. Toronto: University of Toronto Press, 1994.

Tabb, C.H.J. "The Historical Evolution of the Bankruptcy Discharge." *American Bankruptcy Law Journal*, 65:3 (1991), 325–72.

Telfer, T.G.W. "The Canadian Bankruptcy Act of 1919: Public Legislation or Private Interest?" *Canadian Business Law Journal*, 24 (1994–5), 357–403.

– *Ruin and Redemption: The Struggle for a Canadian Bankruptcy Law, 1867–1919*. Toronto: University of Toronto Press, 2014.

Temin, P. *Iron and Steel in Nineteenth-Century America: An Economic Enquiry*. Cambridge, MA: MIT Press, 1964.

Thacher, T.A. "Some Tendencies of Modern Receiverships." *California Law Review*, 4:1 (1915), 32–49.

Thorp, W. "The Changing Structure of Industry." In President's Conference on Unemployment, *Recent Economic Changes in the United States*. Vol. 1, 167–218. New York: McGraw-Hill, 1929.

Till, I. "The Fiction of the Quoted Price." *Law and Contemporary Problems*, 4:3 (1937), 363–74.

Torrie, V.E. "Protagonists of Company Reorganisation: A History of the Companies' Creditors Arrangement Act (Canada) and the Role of Large Secured Creditors." PhD diss., University of Kent at Canterbury, 2015.

– "Federalism and Farm Debt during the Great Depression: Political Impetuses for The Farmers' Creditors Arrangement Act, 1934," *Saskatchewan Law Review*, 82 (2019), 203–57.

Tosdal, H.D. "Open Price Associations." *American Economic Review*, 7:2 (1917), 331–52.

Treiman, I. "Acts of Bankruptcy: A Medieval Concept in Modern Bankruptcy Law." *Harvard Law Review*, 52 (1938), 189–215.

Tufano, P. "Business Failure, Judicial Intervention, and Financial Innovation: Restructuring U.S. Railroads in the Nineteenth Century." *Business History Review*, 71:1 (1997), 1–40.

Vigod, B.L. *Quebec Before Duplessis: The Political Career of Louis-Alexandre Taschereau*. Montreal: McGill-Queen's University Press, 1980.

Villey, P., and V.-L. Saulnier, eds. *Les essais de Michel de Montaigne*. Paris: Presses Universitaires de France, 1965.

Walker, R.G. *Consolidated Statements: A History and Analysis*. New York: Arno Press, 1978.

Walsh, G. "The Finger in the Dike: State and Local Laws Combat the Foreclosure Tide." *Suffolk University Law Review*, 44 (2011), 149–91.

Watkins, M.W. *Industrial Combinations and Public Policy: A Study of Combination Competition and the Public Welfare*. Boston: Houghton Mifflin, 1927.

Wegenast, F.W. *The Law of Canadian Companies*. Toronto: Carswell, 1931.

Welch, I. "Capital Structure and Stock Returns." *Journal of Political Economy*, 112:1 (2004), 106–31.

Wheelock, D.C. "Changing the Rules: State Mortgage Foreclosure Moratoria During the Great Depression." *Federal Reserve Bank of St. Louis Review*, 90:6 (2008), 569–83.

Wickerham, C. "The Progress of the Law on No Par Value Common Stock." *Harvard Law Review*, 37:4 (1924), 464–77.

Wiegman, C. *Trees to News: A Chronicle of the Ontario Paper Company's Origin and Development*. Toronto: McClelland and Stewart, 1953.

Wightman, F.A. *Our Canadian Heritage: Its Resources and Possibilities*. Toronto: William Briggs, 1905.

Wightman, W.R., and N.M. Wightman. *The Land Between: Northwestern Ontario Resource Development, 1800 to the 1990s*. Toronto: University of Toronto Press, 1997.

Wilde, C. "The Chandler Act." *Indiana Law Review*, 14:2 (1938), 93–148.

Wildman, J.R., and W. Powell, *Capital Stock Without Par Value*. Chicago: A.W. Shaw, 1928.

Williams, A.P. "Foreclosing Foreclosure: Escaping the Yawning Abyss of the Deep Mortgage and Housing Crisis." *Northwestern Journal of Law & Social Policy*, 7:2 (2012), 454–509.

Williamson, O.E. *Markets and Hierarchies: Analysis and Antitrust Implications*. New York: Free Press, 1975.

– *The Economic Institutions of Capitalism: Firms, Markets, Relational Contracting*. New York: Free Press, 1985.

Willis, R.B. "Corporate Reorganization in Canada." *Quarterly Review of Commerce*, 8:3 (1941), 192–206.

Wilson, E. "Sunshine Charley." *New Republic*, 59 (28 June 1933), 177–8.

– *Travels in Two Democracies*. New York: Harcourt Brace, 1936.

Wilson, L.R. "A Few High Spots in the Life of L.R. Wilson." Toronto: n.p., 1945.

Wise, S.F., and R.C. Brown. *Canada Views the United States: Nineteenth-Century Political Attitudes*. Toronto: Macmillan, 1967.

Witham, G.S. *Modern Pulp and Paper Making: A Practical Treatise*. New York: Chemical Catalogue, 1920.

Withrow, J.R. "Basing-Point and Freight-Rate Price Systems Under the Anti-Trust Laws." *University of Pennsylvania Law Review*, 85:7 (1937), 690–715.

Zaslow, M. *The Opening of the Canadian North: 1870–1914*. Toronto: McClelland and Stewart, 1971.

– "Edward Barnes Borron, 1820–1915: Northern Pioneer and Public Servant Extraordinary." In F.H. Armstrong, H.A. Stevenson, and J.D. Wilson, eds.,

Aspects of Nineteenth-Century Ontario, 297–311. Toronto: University of Toronto Press, 1974.

Zhang, M., and R.J. Sexton. "FOB or Uniform Delivered Prices: Strategic Choices and Welfare Effects." *Journal of Industrial Economics*, 49:2 (2001), 197–220.

Zunz, O. *Making America Corporate, 1870–1920*. Chicago: University of Chicago Press, 1990.

Zywicki, T.W. "Bankruptcy Law as Social Legislation." *Texas Review of Law and Politics*, 5:2 (2001), 394–431.

Index